New Rider's Reference Guide to AutoCAD Release 13

Randall A. Maxey
Erik W. Olson

New Riders Publishing, Indianapolis, Indiana

New Riders' Reference Guide to AutoCAD Release 13

By Randall A. Maxey and Erik W. Olson

Published by:
New Riders Publishing
201 West 103rd Street
Indianapolis, IN 46290 USA

All rights reserved. No part of this book may be reproduced or transmitted in any form or by any means, electronic or mechanical, including photocopying, recording, or by any information storage and retrieval system, without written permission from the publisher, except for the inclusion of brief quotations in a review.

Copyright © 1995 by New Riders Publishing

Printed in the United States of America   2 3 4 5 6 7 8 9 0

```
Maxey, Randall A., 1960-
   New Riders' Reference Guide to AutoCAD 13 / Randall A. Maxey, Erik
 W. Olson
       p.     cm.
    Includes index.
    ISBN 1-56205-237-3 : $24.00
    1. AutoCAD (Computer file)  2. Engineering design—Data
 processing.  3. Computer-aided design.   I. Olson, Erik W., 1963-
 . II. Title.
 TA174.M383    1995
 620'.0042'02855369—dc20                                       94-48225
                                                                   CIP
```

Warning and Disclaimer

This book is designed to provide information about the AutoCAD computer program. Every effort has been made to make this book as complete and as accurate as possible, but no warranty or fitness is implied.

The information is provided on an "as is" basis. The author and New Riders Publishing shall have neither liability nor responsibility to any person or entity with respect to any loss or damages arising from the information contained in this book or from the use of the disks or programs that may accompany it.

Publisher	*Don Fowley*
Associate Publisher	*Tim Huddleston*
Product Development Manager	*Rob Tidrow*
Marketing Manager	*Ray Robinson*
Director of Special Projects	*Cheri Robinson*
Managing Editor	*Tad Ringo*

About the Author

Randall A. Maxey is the founding owner of R.A. Maxey and Associates, a consulting firm located in Westerville, Ohio. Born and raised in central Ohio, Maxey shares his household with his wife, Sheryl, and their four sons: Andrew, Jason, Joshua, and Jared. Maxey graduated from high school in 1978 and has attended The Ohio State University, Franklin University, and Marion Technical College. His consulting firm, started in 1989, provides technical knowledge and expertise to firms seeking to improve the proficiency of their engineering and design efforts. He has contributed to the New Riders books *Inside AutoCAD LT for Windows* and *Hands-On AutoCAD Release 12*. Readers are invited to contact Maxey through CompuServe. His CIS number is 73207,3343.

Erik W. Olson graduated cum laude from UCLA with a degree in Materials Engineering. He has customized AutoCAD for use in electrical, mechanical, and civil engineering, surveying, and architectural fields since 1987. Olson has been an AutoCAD and AutoLISP programming instructor since 1989. As a computer applications programmer and consultant, Olson has experience programming in AutoLISP, C/C++, and Assembler. In 1992, Olson won the *CADENCE* magazine AutoCAD Top Gun California regional competition and was ranked in the top 5 finalists of this nationwide competition.

Acknowledgments

Randall Maxey would like to thank the following for their part in contributing to this book:

Thanks and love to his wife Sheryl and his boys Andrew, Jason, Joshua, and Jared for their undying support and confidence in him. Thanks to them for understanding why daddy was locked up in his office for days on end playing with his computer. He thanks God for His blessings.

Thanks to the New Riders crew out west. Thanks to Rusty Gesner for instilling that desire to produce the perfect AutoCAD books. Thanks to Kevin Coleman for putting up with my hundreds of questions on how to produce the perfect screen shots. And thanks to Margaret Berson for trying to beat into my head how to recognize what "passive voice" is.

Many, many thanks to Alicia Buckley at New Riders for lending a listening ear. Thanks for putting up with all my gripes and complaints and making this project a fairly smooth one. Alicia, you're the greatest.

Thanks to John Kane, Dennis Hill, Amy Bezek, and the rest of the New Riders staff for tying all this conglomeration together into one heck of a book.

Thanks to Art Cooney at Autodesk for his timely information and unending patience with all of us folks.

Many thanks to all those folks who contribute to the AutoCAD forum on CompuServe. Without their insights, experiences, and inspiration this book would not have been possible.

Erik Olson wishes to thank:

Alicia Krakavitz for her cooperation in setting an appropriate completion schedule.

Dennis C. Hill for his careful and thoughtful editing of the content.

Randall A. Maxey for procedural and content advice.

And finally, his wife Jennifer for understanding the requirements of late-night authoring.

Trademark Acknowledgments

All terms mentioned in this book that are known to be trademarks or service marks have been appropriately capitalized. New Riders Publishing cannot attest to the accuracy of this information. Use of a term in this book should not be regarded as affecting the validity of any trademark or service mark. AutoCAD is a registered trademark of Autodesk, Inc.

Product Director
Dennis C. Hill

Acquisitions Editor
Alicia Buckley

Production Editors
Amy Bezek, John Kane

Copy Editors
Geneil Breeze, Laura Frey,
Sarah Kearns, Stacia Mellinger,
Cliff Shubs, Phil Worthington,
Lillian Yates

Technical Editors
Tom Bledsaw, David Laiewski

Marketing Copywriter
Tamara Apple

Acquisitions Coordinator
Tracey Turgeson

Publisher's Assistant
Karen Opal

Cover Designer
Dan Armstrong

Book Designer
Kim Scott

Production Team Supervisor
Katy Bodenmiller

Graphics Image Specialists
Dennis Sheehan, Clint Lahnen

Production Analyst
Dennis Clay Hager, Angela D. Bannan

Production Team
Carol Bowers, Micheal Brumitt,
Jama Carter, Charlotte Clapp,
Mary Ann Cosby, Rich Evers,
Donna Harbin, Mike Henry,
Aleata Howard, Louisa Klucznik,
Kevin Laseau, Shawn MacDonald,
Donna Martin, Kim Mitchell,
Cheryl Moore, Casey Price,
Linda Quigley, Erich J. Richter,
SA Springer, Jill Tompkins,
Mark Walchle, Mary Beth Wakefield,
Jeff Weissenberger

Table of Contents

Introduction 1

How This Book is Different from Most AutoCAD Books 2
Who Should Read This Book? 2
Conventions Used in This Book 2
How This Book is Organized 5
Common Command Features 9
New Riders Publishing 18

Command Reference 21

3D 21
A 47
B 91
C 117
D 153
DIM 225
E 291
F-G 315
H-I 345
L 369
M 401
N-O 463
P 475
Q-R 529
S 583
T 653
U 695
V 709
W-Z 729

Introduction

IT SEEMS that with any software package in use today, there is a need for a comprehensive single source for command descriptions involving each function of the software. As the complexity and functionality of AutoCAD increases with each new release, this need is even greater. The advent of AutoCAD Release 13 has created a totally rewritten graphical user interface in the

Windows version, and an abundance of new and changed command functionality in all versions, to warrant further exploration. The addition of a new 3D engine and drawing objects—such as NURBS splines, true ellipses, rays, infinite lines, and others—begs for in-depth explanation of their usage.

In *New Riders' Reference Guide to AutoCAD Release 13*, the authors have attempted to thoroughly document each command, along with every prompt and dialog box feature associated with that command. This guide was designed to complement other New Riders books such as *Inside AutoCAD Release 13 for Windows* and your *AutoCAD User's Guide* and *AutoCAD Command Reference* shipped with your AutoCAD package.

How This Book is Different from Most AutoCAD Books

New Riders' Reference Guide to AutoCAD Release 13 has been designed and written to accommodate the way you work. The authors and editors at New Riders Publishing know that you probably do not have a great deal of time to page through the documentation that came with your AutoCAD software, and that you need to quickly learn how the AutoCAD commands work.

This book, therefore, does not lead you through endless exercises for every AutoCAD command. Each command summary has complete descriptions of each command option, as well as relevant pointers to commands that perform similar or complementary functions. The examples focus on the ways in which the commands are most often used.

Who Should Read This Book?

New Riders' Reference Guide to AutoCAD Release 13 is written for two types of readers: experienced AutoCAD users who are interested in coming up to speed as quickly as possible with the new features of Release 13, and new AutoCAD users who are looking for a quick reference to AutoCAD's abundance of commands.

Conventions Used in This Book

It is our hope that this book will become a part of your desktop as much as your keyboard is. *New Riders' Reference Guide to AutoCAD Release 13* is an indispensable tool for finding complete explanations of AutoCAD commands. With this in mind, you should become familiar with the conventions used in this book.

Notational Conventions

The conventions used for showing various types of text throughout this book are, insofar as possible, the same as those used in the hard-copy documentation supplied with AutoCAD or the *Microsoft Windows User's Guide*.

- Key combinations appear in the following format:

  Key1+Key2: When you see a plus sign (+) between key names, you should hold down the first key while pressing the second key. Then release both keys. In most commands, for example, Ctrl+C is the shortcut key for the Cancel option.

  Key1, Key2: When a comma (,) appears between key names, you should press and release the first key, and then press and release the second key.

- On-screen, AutoCAD underlines the letters of some buttons in the dialog boxes that can be used as hot keys. For example, the Size button in the Plot Configuration dialog box is displayed on-screen as **S**ize. The underlined letter is the letter you can type to choose that option. (In this book, however, such letters are displayed in bold, underlined type: **S**ize.)
- Text that is displayed by the AutoCAD program often appears in a special typeface.
- Information you type is in **boldface**. This applies to individual letters and numbers, as well as text strings. This convention, however, does not apply to special keys, such as Enter, Esc, or Ctrl.
- New terms appear in *italics*.
- In the examples, the (Enter) symbol represents the Enter key.

Notes, Tips, and Warnings

New Riders' Reference Guide to AutoCAD Release 13 includes many special "sidebars" that are set apart from the normal text by icons. This book includes three distinct types of sidebars: "Notes," "Tips," and "Warnings." These passages have been given special treatment so that you can instantly recognize their significance and easily find them for future reference.

A *note* includes "extra" information you should find useful, but which complements the discussion at hand instead of being a direct part of it. A note might describe special situations that can arise when you use AutoCAD under certain circumstances, and might tell you what steps to take when such situations arise. Notes also might tell you how to avoid problems with your software and hardware.

A *tip* provides you with quick instructions for getting the most from your AutoCAD system as you follow the discussion. A tip might show you how to conserve memory in some setups, how to speed up a procedure, or how to perform one of many time-saving and system-enhancing techniques.

A *warning* tells you when a procedure might be dangerous—that is, when you run the risk of losing data, locking your system, or even damaging your hardware. Warnings generally tell you how to avoid such losses, or they describe the steps you can take to remedy these situations.

Illustrations and Your Graphics Display

The illustrations for this book were created by capturing screen displays. All Windows screen displays were captured from systems using Super VGA display controllers set for 800×600-pixel resolution, 256-color mode under Windows. All DOS screen displays were captured at 800×600-pixel resolution utilizing the Vibrant display driver supplied with AutoCAD Release 13. White backgrounds and monochrome vectors were used for reproduction clarity. When the command being discussed behaves the same for either version (DOS or Windows) and the user interface is not an issue, the image was cropped to show only the drawing area. Figures referencing dialog boxes have been cropped to show the dialog box only. Your display may not appear exactly as shown, depending on the display driver you are using and any color settings you have configured.

How This Book is Organized

New Riders' Reference Guide to AutoCAD Release 13 is organized alphabetically by command. The thumb tabs and command headings at the top of each page make it easy for you to find a command quickly. For this reason, unlike most books, this book does not have a table of contents or index. Each command description is further organized into components, described in the following.

Command Access

AutoCAD Release 13 offers a number of choices for accessing commands—command line, pull-down menu, screen menu, and tablet menu. These methods are common to both the Windows and DOS platforms. The Windows version adds additional command access options through toolbars and their tool buttons and flyouts, and the status line (see fig. I.1).

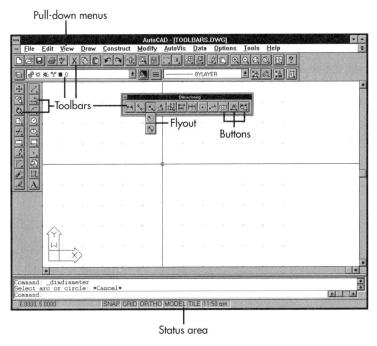

Figure I.1. *The AutoCAD Release 13 for Windows screen.*

In this book, the various ways a command may be accessed are listed, with the exception of the tablet menu. The tablet menu supplied with AutoCAD is logically arranged with the command names and icons shown. The tablet icons correlate to the tool buttons on the Windows version of AutoCAD where appropriate.

Command Line Access

All commands can be typed in at the keyboard as shown in the command heading. Do this by typing the name of the command and pressing Enter. Some AutoCAD commands are *transparent* commands, meaning that they can be accessed while in another command. They can also be used as the primary command. Transparent commands are shown with an apostrophe (') preceding their name in the command heading. To use the command transparently, you must type the apostrophe preceding the command name. To avoid confusion when discussing transparent commands, the apostrophe is not used when showing the command name. It is only shown in the command heading.

Some commands in AutoCAD Release 13 are dialog-based commands that also have command-line counterparts. These commands are denoted with a dash (-) preceding the command name in the heading. To use the command-line version of the command, you must precede the command name with a dash when typing the command.

Tool Buttons

On the Microsoft™ Windows version of AutoCAD Release 13, toolbars are utilized as one method of accessing commands (refer to fig. I.1). Most toolbars consist of tool buttons. Some toolbars may also contain pull-down list boxes or other features.

Some tools on the toolbars also access a *flyout*. These are like sub-menus or command options related to the main tool. Flyouts are designated with a small triangular arrow in the lower right corner of the tool button. A flyout menu is shown in figure I.1.

If a command has an associated tool button, this is shown in the command access section just under the command name heading. You will see the name of the tool, the name of the main toolbar, and then the name of the flyout if there is one. The format is as follows:

    Toolbar: *(Main Toolbar, Flyout Name)*

Some toolbars and flyouts have multiple tools for accessing options of a command. In these cases, there is no one tool specified, only the main toolbar and flyout name. With tool access, you will see the associated toolbar with the specific tool(s) identified to make it easier for you to find.

Pull-Down Menu Access

For pull-down menu access of commands, you are shown the main menu label, and then any sub-menu items. These are in the following form:

    Pull down: File, Exit

The hot keys used to access the menus are shown for you. You can access these by holding down the Alt key and pressing the letter designating the hot key.

There are two menus available for the Windows version of AutoCAD Release 13—the standard Windows ACAD menu and the ACADFULL menu. Since the ACADFULL menu offers nearly the same pull-down options as the DOS ACAD menu, references made to pull-down selections available in the DOS ACAD menu can also be accessed in Windows from the ACADFULL menu, unless noted as (DOS only). Pull-down menu options that are not available in the standard Windows ACAD menu are shown as *italicized*.

Screen Menu Access

For those who use the screen menu on the DOS version or opt for the screen menu in the Windows version, the sequence of menu selections to access the command is shown. Though some commands have several methods of access through the screen menu, only the most direct methods have been listed. The screen menu selections shown follow the format found in the Windows ACADFULL menu.

Command Description

After the command access section, there will be a command summary. This gives you a quick, general idea of the functionality and purpose of the command. It is not meant to be comprehensive—that comes later. Use this command description to get an overview of the command.

Prompts and Options

If the command is a command-line command or can be used as such, this section details all of the prompts and options that are displayed while using the command. The main command prompt and its options is usually shown first. Following that, each option is shown in bold print and is discussed in detail in outline form. This is useful if you are trying to use a command, get stuck, and need to find out what the prompt is expecting for input. You can quickly glance down the left margin of the page to find the prompt.

If there are subprompts within a command, they are indented or shown under a separate heading to show the hierarchy of the prompt. For example, the PLINE command has two sets of prompts—one each for line segments and arc segments. These are treated separately under the main PLINE prompt.

Some options are not offered when you use icons or pull-downs because you specify those options on the basis of which icon or pull-down option you select.

The system variable EXPERT controls the display of certain command prompts. The discussion of commands within this book assumes that EXPERT is set to the default of 0, displaying all prompts normally.

Dialog Box Items

If the command is a dialog-based command or at some point displays a dialog box, those features are discussed in this section. Each button, list box, pull-down list box, check box, image box, or other feature is shown in bold and discussed in detail in outline form. A quick glance down the left margin will help you find the feature about which you are inquiring.

Duplicate dialog box and command line commands, such as DDUNITS and UNITS, may appear to be needless redundancy. Often the command-line version is retained to provide backward compatibility for earlier versions of AutoCAD that did not support a dialog box user interface. These command-line commands provide a programming interface for AutoCAD scripts and user-defined AutoLISP functions. From a user's point of view, it is almost always preferable to use the dialog box version of these commands.

Examples

The examples shown in this book are simple exercises meant to show you one possible use for the command. They are not complex or involved to confuse you. Some commands do not have examples. Some commands simply need no further explanation or example. Others did not lend themselves well to an example.

Each example exercise is in a two-column format. User instructions and actual command-line output (prompts and options) are shown in the left column. Explanations are shown in the right column. You can follow the examples step-by-step and expect to see the same results you are given in the text. All prompts shown in the text and examples are the standard default values. As you use AutoCAD, it reflects the commands and options you have used and the values you have specified through the system variables that are affected. This adaptive process allows AutoCAD to mold itself to the way you work, but it can make the prompts and options you see differ slightly from those you find in the text.

Some example exercises utilize sample drawings that are installed with AutoCAD Release 13. When this is the case, the authors try to mention the drawing's location to make it easier for you to find. Typically, they are located in the \ACADR13\COMMON\SAMPLE directory if you installed both the DOS and Windows version, or in the \ACADR13\DOS\SAMPLE or \ACADR13\WIN\SAMPLE directory for a single installation.

Related Commands

At the end of every unit, you are given a list of any commands that may be related to the command just discussed. Use this list to clarify certain points or topics discussed in the text and to gain a more generalized understanding of the commands involved. Many commands are similar or have similar prompts and options. This list serves to assist you in broadening your understanding.

All drawing and constructing commands are affected by the current layer, color, line type, and so on. Blocks, Dimensions, and External References involve almost all other types of objects and are not therefore cross-referenced. For the same reason, the commands DDMODIFY, DDCHPROP, CHPROP, and CHANGE, used to control these settings within objects, do not go into extensive command cross-references.

Related System Variables

System variables are used by AutoCAD for a variety of purposes. Some control dimensioning features and appearance. Some control your drawing setup in terms of units and scaling. Some system variables are used to assist your drawing productivity. There are dozens of AutoCAD system variables. If the command being discussed affects or is affected by any system variables, they will be listed for you.

For a complete discussion of system variables and their function, see your AutoCAD documentation or the *Inside AutoCAD* series of books by New Riders Publishing.

Common Command Features

Many commands share common features or can accept similar types of input. Those items include file selection dialog boxes, point specification, wild-card usage, and others.

File Selection Dialog Boxes

For many of its commands, AutoCAD uses a file selection dialog box in addition to or instead of command-line parameters. When any command expects a file name, you will see one of these dialog boxes. The Open Drawing dialog box is perhaps the most elaborate. The other standard file selection dialog boxes are much simpler. The following four figures illustrate the types of file selection dialog boxes you will see in AutoCAD (see figs. I.2 through I.5). The only command-specific variations you see in these dialog boxes are the title and the default file type (extension) of the file the command is expecting. For instance, for the LOAD command, the dialog box is titled Select Shape File and defaults to the file extension SHX. The LINETYPE command, on the other hand, uses the same dialog box features, but is titled Select Linetype File and looks for files with an LIN file extension.

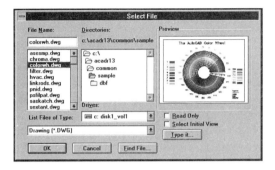

Figure I.2. *The Windows Open Drawing dialog box.*

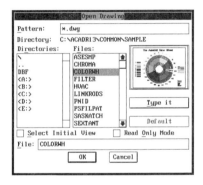

Figure I.3. *The DOS Open Drawing dialog box.*

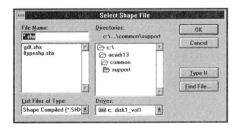

Figure I.4. *A standard Windows file selection dialog box.*

Common Command Features

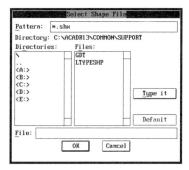

Figure I.5. *A standard DOS file selection dialog box.*

This entire discussion of file selection dialog boxes is predicated on the default value of the FILEDIA (FILE DIAlogs) system variable being set to 1. If FILEDIA is set to 0, command-line prompts are issued instead of the dialog boxes being displayed. Also, for those commands that do not normally issue file selection dialog boxes, but accept file names for input (BLOCK and INSERT, for example), you may enter a tilde [~] when prompted for a file name. This will display a file selection dialog box pertinent to the command.

Drawing Selection Dialog Box Items

The dialog box for selecting a drawing file is discussed in the following. Differences between the Windows and DOS platforms are noted.

Preview. The Preview image box displays a bitmap of the selected file. If the Preview box is blank after selecting a file, the file is either a drawing created with AutoCAD Release 12 or earlier, or is not a valid drawing file. A drawing must be saved with Release 13, or you must use the MAKEPREVIEW command to create a preview image.

Pattern. (DOS) This edit box contains the pattern specification for files to appear in the Files list box below. The wild cards ? and * can be used to refine the list to desired file names.

Directories. (DOS)
Directories. (Windows) This list box contains a listing of the subdirectories available from the current directory, which is displayed following the Directories label above it. Use the scroll bar to display more file names and drive letters. Double-click on a directory name or drive letter to change the current directory.

Drives. (Windows) This pull-down list box displays available drives.

List Files of Type. (Windows) Use this pull-down list box to select the type of files by their three-letter extension to list in the Files list box.

File. (DOS) Displays the name of the selected file in an edit box. You may type the name of a desired file here or edit an existing name.

Files. (DOS)
File Name. (Windows) This list box contains a listing of the files available in the current directory. Use the scroll bar to display more file names. Double-click on a file name, or click on it once and click on the OK button to proceed. The Windows Select File dialog box contains an additional edit box for entering or displaying the desired file name.

Read Only Mode. (DOS)
Read Only. (Windows) When this box is checked, AutoCAD does not allow any modifications to the selected drawing to be saved in the drawing file. You can, however, use SAVEAS to save the changes to another file name. This check box only appears for the OPEN command and is omitted from similar Select File dialog boxes.

Select Initial View. Checking this box permits you to select a view defined in the selected drawing to be displayed when the drawing loads. A simple dialog box appears when you enter the drawing editor for you to make your selection. This check box only appears for the OPEN command and is omitted from similar Select File dialog boxes.

Type it. Use the Type it button to close the dialog and enter the name of the drawing file at the command line prompt, Enter drawing name.

Network. (Network installations only) Use this button to connect to network drives.

Find File. (Windows only) Use the Find File button to display the Browse/Search dialog box, shown in figures I.6 and I.7.

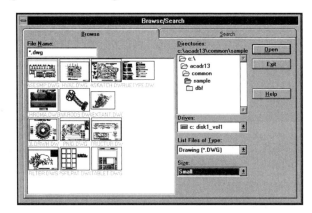

Figure I.6. *The Browse/Search dialog box Browse area.*

Common Command Features 13

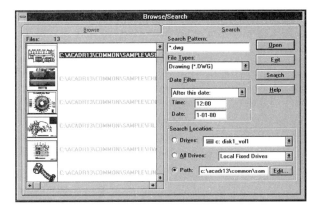

Figure I.7. *The Browse/Search dialog box Search area.*

The Browse Dialog Box (Windows Only)

The following section discusses the Browse area of the Browse/Search dialog box. The Browse dialog box is used to quickly locate and preview drawing files and their names. There is a large image tile that displays thumbnail sketches (preview images) of all the drawings in the specified directory. If there are more images than can fit within the preview box, scroll bars appear on the right or bottom of the box. Double-click on a preview image or select an image and choose Open to open the drawing file.

Some common dialog box features such as **D**irectories, Dri**v**es, and List Files of **T**ype function as described earlier.

File Name. Use this edit box to specify the file name or pattern of names to show in the preview box. The default is all drawing files (*.DWG). You may use wild-card patterns to narrow the list of drawings. For example, you could specify S*.DWG to preview all drawings with names beginning with the letter S. The specified files are shown in the preview box with their associated names. If no preview exists for the drawing, an empty box with an "X" is shown instead of the preview image. See the MAKEPREVIEW and PREFERENCES command for making preview image files for drawings that are not saved in Release 13 format.

Size. This pull-down list box determines the size of the preview image for each drawing shown in the image box. The choices are Small, Medium, and Large. The larger sizes show more detail, but decrease the number of images that can be seen at one time.

The Search Dialog Box (Windows Only)

The Search dialog box is used for searching the local or network disk drives for drawings. You specify a search pattern for the file names to search for. You can also specify files with dates before or after a certain date. You can search user-defined drive and subdirectories, a specific drive, or all drives (local or network). When you begin a search by choosing the Sea**r**ch button, the search status is shown in the upper left corner of the dialog box. The number of files found matching the search criteria is shown in addition to the current path being searched. When the search is complete, an image area appears and any found files are shown with their preview image (if any) and associated file name. If no files are found, this image area remains blank.

Search Pattern. Use this edit box to specify a search pattern of files to locate. The default is all drawings (*.DWG).

File Types. This pull-down list box only offers the choice of drawing files.

Date Filter. This pull-down list box offers the two choices of finding a file dated Before this date or After this date. You specify the date in the Time and Date edit boxes, as follows:

- **Time.** Use this edit box to specify a time criteria for searching for files before or after this time.
- **Date.** Use this edit box to specify a date criteria for searching for files before or after this date.

Search Location. This area of the Search dialog box contains three options for specifying where on the local or network drives to search. These are discussed in the following:

- **Drives.** The radio button sets this option, and the pull-down list box lists all drives available on your system or the network, depending on the setting of All Drives. Use this option to search one drive only.
- **All Drives.** The radio button sets this option. The value in the pull-down list box determines whether the local fixed drives, network drives, or all drives (including floppy drives and compact disc drives) will be searched.
- **Path.** Use this radio button to specify the search to a specific path named in the edit box.

Edit. Use the Edit button to display the Edit Path dialog box, shown in figure I.8. With this dialog box, you can type in or select drives and path names and add them to a search list using the Add button. Provisions are also made for removing path names from the list using the Delete and Delete All buttons.

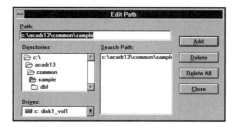

Figure I.8. *The Edit Path dialog box.*

Standard File Selection Dialog Boxes

Most other dialog boxes that request a file name are not as elaborate as those used for the OPEN command (refer to figs. I.4 and I.5). They do not require a preview area and are much simpler in design. There are some common features, however—these are listed in the following. See the previous section concerning their function.

- **P**attern (DOS)
- **D**irectories (Windows)
  Di**r**ectories (DOS)
- Dri**v**es (Windows)
- **L**ist Files of Type (Windows)
- **F**ile (DOS)
- F**i**les (DOS)
  File **N**ame (Windows)
- **T**ype it
- Network
- **F**ind File (Windows only)

Wild-Card Characters

Many commands accept the use of wild-card characters for filtering lists of data. For example, many commands have a ? option for listing data. You can use wild-card characters at this option to narrow the list. The following table lists valid wild-card characters and their function.

Table I.1
Available Wild Cards

Wild Card	Meaning
@	Matches any alphanumeric character.
#	Matches any number.
*(asterisk)	Matches any character or characters including an empty character string. You can use the asterisk anywhere in the string.
.(period)	Matches any nonalphanumeric character.
?	Matches any single character.
~(tilde)	Matches any pattern except the one following the tilde.
-(hyphen)	Matches a range of characters when used within brackets, such as [5-9] to match 5, 6, 7, 8, or 9.
'(apostrophe)	Matches the special character that follows, such as '?. Matches a ? instead of using the ? as a wild card.
,(comma)	Separates wild cards, such as red,blue.
[...]	Matches any one of the enclosed characters.
[~...]	Matches any character not enclosed.

Other Things You Should Know

There are a host of other items concerning the content and layout of this book you should know. These are discussed in the following paragraphs.

Accelerator Keys. In order for AutoCAD to be more compliant with the standard Microsoft™ Windows user interface, AutoCAD for Windows provides Windows accelerator keys that perform many Windows-related functions. For example, pressing Ctrl+C is a Windows Copy command that copies data to the Windows Clipboard. Ctrl+C is not, by default, used to cancel a command. In Windows, use the Esc key to cancel a command. See the PREFERENCES command to change this. The following table lists the accelerator keystroke combinations used in the standard AutoCAD menu file.

Table I.2
Accelerator Keystrokes for Windows

Function	Keystrokes
Ctrl+O (Ortho mode)	[Ctrl+L]
Ctrl+V (switch viewports)	[Ctrl+R]
Undo	[Ctrl+Z]
Cut	[Ctrl+X]
Copy	[Ctrl+C]
Paste	[Ctrl+V]
Open	[Ctrl+O]
Print	[Ctrl+P]
New	[Ctrl+N]
Save	[Ctrl+S]

Object Snaps. The terms "object snap" and "osnap" are used interchangeably throughout the book. See the DDOSNAP command for details on valid object snap points.

Object Selection. Frequently throughout this book, when you are asked to select objects within an AutoCAD drawing, the authors ask you to use any "valid object selection method." These selection methods are described in detail under the SELECTION command.

Noun-Verb Selection. In conjunction with Object Selection, some commands will accept a predefined selection set. For example, if grips are enabled, you can select objects, and then choose the command you want to act on those objects. This can effectively reduce the number of keystrokes necessary. For example, if you have an active selection set and then choose the ERASE command, the ERASE command accepts the predefined selection set and does not stop to prompt again for a selection set. Some commands will not accept predefined selection sets.

Point Specification. You will frequently find the term *specify* used in conjunction with identifying a point location. This indicates that you can pick the point or enter it at the command prompt as a rectangular, relative, polar, cylindrical, or spherical coordinate. Any points selected or coordinates input at the command line are referenced to the current UCS.

TIP When you want to use the last point specified, simply enter an @ without any distance or angle. AutoCAD interprets the @ symbol as specifying the last point.

Use Ortho mode, Snap mode, and object snap settings to simplify the point selection process. Ortho mode locks subsequent locations to the nearest horizontal or vertical location. Snap mode enables you to copy at precise user-specified increments. Object snap overrides enable you to select points in relation to other existing entities.

AutoCAD SQL Environment (ASE) Commands. Since the advanced topic of ASE does not apply to the general use of AutoCAD, commands specific to ASE are not included. See your AutoCAD documentation for a discussion of these commands.

New Riders Publishing

The staff of New Riders Publishing is committed to bringing you the very best in computer reference material. Each New Riders book is the result of months of work by authors and staff who research and refine the information contained within its covers.

As part of this commitment to you, the NRP reader, New Riders invites your input. Please let us know if you enjoy this book, if you have trouble with the information and examples presented, or if you have a suggestion for the next edition.

Please note, though: New Riders staff cannot serve as a technical resource for AutoCAD Release 13 or for questions about software- or hardware-related problems. Please refer to the documentation that accompanies AutoCAD Release 13 or to the applications' Help systems.

If you have a question or comment about any New Riders book, there are several ways to contact New Riders Publishing. We will respond to as many readers as we can. Your name, address, or phone number will never become part of a mailing list or be used for any purpose other than to help us continue to bring you the best books possible. You can write us at the following address:

>New Riders Publishing
>Attn: Associate Publisher
>201 W. 103rd Street
>Indianapolis, IN 46290

If you prefer, you can fax New Riders Publishing at (317) 581-4670.

You can send electronic mail to New Riders from a variety of sources. NRP maintains several mailboxes organized by topic area. Mail in these mailboxes will be forwarded to the staff member who is best able to address your concerns. Substitute the appropriate mailbox name from the list below when addressing your e-mail. The mailboxes are as follows:

ADMIN	Comments and complaints for NRP's Publisher
APPS	Word, Excel, WordPerfect, and other office applications
ACQ	Book proposal inquiries by potential authors
CAD	AutoCAD, 3D Studio, AutoSketch, and CAD products
DATABASE	Access, dBASE, Paradox, and other database products
GRAPHICS	CorelDRAW!, Photoshop, and other graphics products
INTERNET	Internet
NETWORK	NetWare, LANtastic, and other network-related topics
OS	MS-DOS, OS/2, and all other operating systems except UNIX and Windows
UNIX	Unix
WINDOWS	Microsoft Windows (all versions)
OTHER	Anything that doesn't fit in to the preceding categories

If you use an MHS e-mail system that routes through CompuServe, send your messages to the following:

mailbox @ NEWRIDER

To send NRP mail from CompuServe, use the following address:

MHS: *mailbox* @ NEWRIDER

To send mail from the Internet, use the following address format:

mailbox@newrider.mhs.compuserve.com

NRP is an imprint of Macmillan Computer Publishing. To obtain a catalog or information, or to purchase any Macmillan Computer Publishing book, call (800)428-5331.

Thank you for selecting *New Riders' Reference Guide to AutoCAD Release 13*!

3D

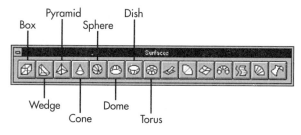

Pull-down: *D**raw*, *Su**rfaces*, 3D *O**bjects*
Screen: DRAW2, SURFACES

The 3D command is an AutoLISP program that enables you to create three-dimensional surface objects, including boxes, spheres, domes, dishes, meshes, pyramids, cones, and wedges. Each object is constructed as a polygon mesh.

> Don't confuse the 3D command with the ACIS solid object commands BOX, CONE, SPHERE, TORUS, and WEDGE. These create 3DSOLID objects, while the 3D command only creates 3D polygon mesh surfaces.

The 3D command prompts you to specify which type of object you want to draw. The 3D.LSP file also defines individual commands that you can execute at the `Command:` prompt to draw specific objects. These individual object commands are AI_BOX, AI_CONE, AI_DISH, AI_DOME, AI_MESH, AI_PYRAMID, AI_SPHERE, AI_TORUS, and AI_WEDGE. You can enter values or pick points relative to the current UCS to show distances and angles at the prompts.

> All running object snaps are turned off at the beginning of the 3D command and are turned back on at the end of the command. You will have to select individual object snaps while using the 3D command.

> When prompted to enter a number of segments, don't enter a number too large. You can create surfaces with up to 32,766 segments, but it takes a long time. Specify the least number of segments that will generate a surface smooth enough to suit your application. Also, choose at least five segments. Surfaces with four or fewer segments are very difficult to visualize.

Prompts and Options

Box/Cone/DIsh/DOme/Mesh/Pyramid/Sphere/Torus/Wedge   This is the initial prompt for the 3D command. The sections that follow list the prompts and options for each object type.

Box

Corner of box   Specify the first corner of the box by entering a coordinate or by picking a point in the graphics window.

Length   Enter the length of the box along the X axis or pick a point. Ortho mode turns on automatically.

Cube/<Width>   Enter the width of the box along the Y axis or specify the cube option by entering **C**. If you choose the cube option, the distance that you entered for the length also is used for both the width and the height of the box. If you pick a point or enter a different value for the width, the box will be rectangular.

Height   Specify the height of the box along the Z axis. Ortho mode turns off automatically. Be careful when picking a point on the screen because the true 3D distance (measured from the corner of the box) to the point picked is used as the height of the box.

Rotation angle about Z axis   Specify the angle to rotate the box around its starting corner. There is no default. You must enter a number or pick a point. If you press Enter, AutoCAD responds with the following:

```
Requires valid numeric angle, second point, or option keyword.
<Rotation angle>/Reference:
```

Do not try to choose the Reference option—doing so cancels the command.

Cone

Base center point   Specify the center point of the base of the cone.

Diameter/<radius> of base   Specify a value or pick a point to show a distance for the radius of the cone, or enter **D** if you prefer to specify a value for the cone's diameter.

Diameter of base   Enter a value or pick a point to show a distance for the diameter of the cone's base.

Diameter/<radius> of top <0>   Create a pointed cone by accepting the default of 0. Create a truncated cone by specifying a different radius for the top, or enter **D** to specify the diameter at the top of the cone. The radius of the top is permitted to be larger than the base.

To create an open cylinder, set the top and bottom radius values for a cone to the same number.

Diameter of top <0>   Enter a value or pick a point to specify the diameter of the cone top. Create a pointed cone by entering a value of zero. The diameter of the top is permitted to be larger than the base.

Height   Specify the height along the Z axis from the base point to the top of the cone.

Number of segments <16> The outer surface of the cone is created from a series of 3D mesh faces. This prompt enables you to specify the number of faces that should be used. The cone has no top or bottom surface.

Dish, Dome, and Sphere

Both the dome and dish are 90-degree hemispheres. The dome is the upper half of a sphere, and the dish is the lower half.

Center of dish, Center of dome, or Center of sphere Pick a point or enter the coordinates of the center of the dish, dome, or sphere.

Diameter/<Radius> Enter a value or pick a point to show a distance for the dish, dome, or sphere's radius, or enter **D** for the Diameter option.

Diameter If you selected the Diameter option at the previous prompt, enter the diameter or pick a point to show the diameter distance.

Number of longitudinal segments <16> Enter the number of facets that are to be used to approximate the shape of the dish, dome, or sphere.

Number of latitudinal segments <8> Enter the number of facets that will be used to approximate the shape of the dish, dome, or sphere. The default number of latitudinal segments for a sphere is 16.

Mesh

A mesh is a four-sided surface, defined by four arbitrary 3D points at the corners, and divided by vertices in two directions, M and N. After you locate each corner of the mesh area, the surface is created within the four sides defined by the corners. Since the four corner points need not be coplanar, a mesh can be created with a twist in it.

`First corner:`, `Second corner:`, `Third corner:`, and `Fourth corner:`

At these prompts, specify the four corner points of the mesh.

Mesh M size Specify the number of vertices in the M direction (from the first to the fourth corner points). When requesting this number, AutoCAD highlights the side representing the M direction.

Mesh N size Specify the number of vertices in the N direction (from the first to the second corner points). When requesting this number, AutoCAD highlights the side representing the N direction.

The Pyramid option creates pyramids with three- or four-sided bases that can meet at a top point or be truncated with a three- or four-sided top. A pyramid with a four-sided base also can terminate in a top ridge, specified by two points.

First base point:, Second base point:, and Third base point:

At these prompts, specify the corner points of the pyramid base.

Tetrahedron/<Fourth base point>:

A pyramid's base can be three- or four-sided. Specify a point to create a four-sided base pyramid, or enter a **T** for the Tetrahedron option to close the current triangle and draw the pyramid with a three-sided base.

The next prompt you see is determined by the number of sides you specified for the base of the pyramid. If you are creating a tetrahedron, you will receive the following prompt:

Top/<Apex point>:

As you locate each point of the top or ridge of a pyramid, AutoCAD creates a rubber-band line to its associated base corner. When specifying these points, or a single apex point, you should supply points with a Z coordinate different than the base; otherwise, the top of the pyramid will lie within the same plane as the base.

You control the shape for the top of the tetrahedron at this prompt. If you specify an apex point, the sides of your pyramid will meet at that single point. If you enter a **T** for the Top option, you are prompted for three points to define the corners of the top, as follows:

First top point:, Second top point:, and Third top point:

At these prompts, specify the corner points of the top of the pyramid.

For a four-sided pyramid base, your top options are as follows:

Ridge/Top/<Apex point>:

This prompt appears after you specify a fourth point for the base of the pyramid. Specify an apex point to create a pyramid in which the sides meet at a single point.

The Top option enables you to specify the four corner points to create a faceted top for the pyramid, as follows:

First corner:, Second corner:, Third corner:, and Fourth point:

You specify the corner points of the top of the pyramid at these prompts.

The Ridge option enables you to specify two endpoints of the top edge line. The pyramid's four sides will slope to meet this line.

First ridge point You specify the first endpoint of the ridge edge. The side defined by the first and fourth base points meet at this point. The sides defined by the first and second base points, and by the third and fourth base points, meet along the ridge edge.

Second ridge point You specify the second endpoint to the ridge edge. The side defined by the second and third base points meets at this point.

> When you specify the points used to create the pyramid's ridge or top, always locate the points in the same order and direction as the first two base points. Locating these points out of order results in a twisted pyramid.

Torus

Center of torus Specify the center point of the torus.

Diameter/<radius> of torus This is the outside radius for the torus. Enter a value or pick a point to show a distance for the radius. You also can enter a **D** for the Diameter option.

Diameter If you specified the Diameter option at the previous prompt, enter the diameter value here or pick a point to show a distance for the outside diameter of the torus.

Diameter/<radius> of tube You size the torus by entering a value or picking a point to show a distance for the radius of the tube. You also can enter a **D** for the Diameter option.

Diameter If you specified the Diameter option at the previous prompt, enter the diameter value here or pick a point to show the distance for the diameter of the tube.

Segments around tube circumference <16> Enter the number of segments to use to approximate the cross section of the torus tube.

Segments around torus circumference <16> Enter the number of segments used to approximate the diameter of the torus.

Wedge

Corner of wedge You can enter a value or pick a point for the first corner of the wedge. A wedge is created in a manner similar to the 3D box. The only difference is that the top of the wedge slopes down along its width to meet its base.

Length Specify the length along the X axis of the wedge's base. Ortho mode is turned on automatically.

Width Specify the width along the Y axis of the wedge's base.

Height Specify the height of the wedge in the Z axis. Ortho mode is turned off automatically. Be careful if picking a point on the screen because the true 3D distance (measured from the corner of the wedge) to the point picked is used as the height of the wedge.

Rotation angle about Z axis Specify the rotation angle by which to rotate the wedge about its first corner point. There is no default. You must enter a number or pick a point. If you press Enter, AutoCAD responds with the following:

```
Requires valid numeric angle, second point, or option keyword.
<Rotation angle>/Reference:
```

If you get this prompt, do not try to choose the Reference option; doing so cancels the command.

Examples

The following examples show you how to create the 3D objects discussed previously. The examples assume that the 3D.LSP file has been loaded into AutoCAD. The examples show the creation of objects in three viewports, one with a plan view, one with a front view, and one with a 3D view taken from a viewpoint of 3,-3,1 looking toward the origin 0,0,0.

Command: **3D** (Enter)	Starts 3D command
Box/Cone/DIsh/DOme/Mesh/Pyramid/ Sphere/Torus/Wedge: **B** (Enter)	Chooses Box option
Corner of box: **2,2** (Enter)	Positions corner of box (see fig. 3D.1)

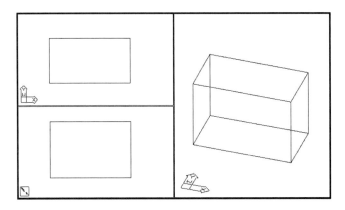

Figure 3D.1. *The 3D box.*

Length: **15** (Enter)	Box length is 15 units along X axis
Cube/<Width>: **8** (Enter)	Width is 8 units along Y axis
Height: **10** (Enter)	Height is 10 units along Z axis
Rotation angle about Z axis: **0** (Enter)	Box is not rotated about Z axis
Command: **AI_CONE** (Enter)	Starts AI_CONE command
Base center point: **10,6.5** (Enter)	Specifies center of cone base (see fig. 3D.2)

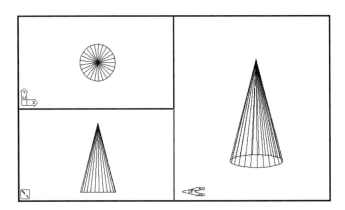

Figure 3D.2. *The 3D cone.*

Diameter/<radius> of base: **4.0** (Enter)	Sets base radius to 4.0 units
Diameter/<radius> of top <0>: (Enter)	Makes a pointed cone

Height: **15** (Enter)	Sets cone height to 15 units along Z axis
Number of segments <16>: **24** (Enter)	Makes the cone a bit smoother than the default
Command: **3D** (Enter)	Starts the 3D command
Box/Cone/DIsh/DOme/Mesh/Pyramid/ Sphere/Torus/Wedge: **DO** (Enter)	Specifies the Dome option
Center of dome: **10,6.5,5** (Enter)	Locates the center of the dome (see fig. 3D.3)

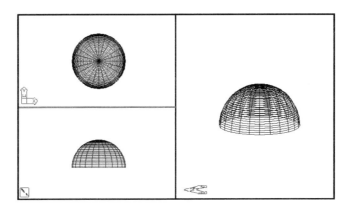

Figure 3D.3. *The 3D dome.*

Diameter/<radius>: **6.0** (Enter)	Specifies the radius of the dome
Number of longitudinal segments <16>: **24** (Enter)	Makes the dome smoother around the circumference in the X,Y plane
Number of latitudinal segments <8>: **30** (Enter)	Makes the dome smoother around the circumference in the X,Z plane
Command: **3D** (Enter)	Invokes 3D command
Box/Cone/DIsh/DOme/Mesh/Pyramid/ Sphere/Torus/Wedge: **M** (Enter)	Specifies Mesh option
First corner: **4,4** (Enter)	Sets first corner point of mesh (see fig. 3D.4)

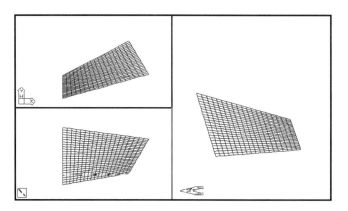

Figure 3D.4. *The 3D mesh with 25 M vertices and 20 N vertices.*

Second corner: **16,10,2** (Enter)	Sets second 3D corner point of mesh
Third corner: **19.5,4.25,8** (Enter)	Sets third corner point of mesh
Fourth corner: **4,0,10** (Enter)	Sets final corner point of mesh
Mesh M size: **25** (Enter)	Sets number of mesh vertices along side between first and fourth corners to 25
Mesh N size: **20** (Enter)	Sets number of mesh vertices along side between first and second corners to 20
Command: **3D** (Enter)	Begins 3D command
Box/Cone/DIsh/DOme/Mesh/Pyramid/Sphere/Torus/Wedge: **P** (Enter)	Specifies Pyramid option
First base point: **6,3** (Enter)	Sets first corner point of base (see fig. 3D.5)
Second base point: **@8<0** (Enter)	Sets second base corner point
Third base point: **@10<105** (Enter)	Sets third corner point
Tetrahedron/<Fourth base point>: **@2<180** (Enter)	Sets fourth corner point of base (makes a pyramid with a 4-sided base)
Ridge/Top/<Apex point>: **T** (Enter)	To make a truncated top
First top point: **9,5,7** (Enter)	Sets first top corner point

3D

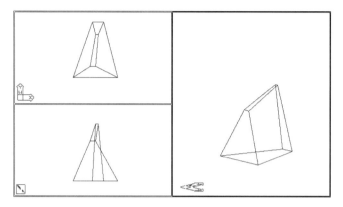

Figure 3D.5. *The 3D four-sided pyramid.*

Second top point: **10,5,7** (Enter)	Sets second point of top
Third top point: **10.5,10.5,10** (Enter)	Sets third top point
Fourth top point: **10,10.5,10** (Enter)	Sets last top point of a truncated, 4-sided pyramid
Command: **3D** (Enter)	Starts the 3D command
Box/Cone/DIsh/DOme/Mesh/Pyramid/Sphere/Torus/Wedge: **S** (Enter)	Specifies the Sphere option
Center of sphere: **10,7,4** (Enter)	Locates 3D center point of sphere (see fig. 3D.6)

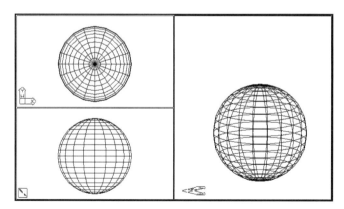

Figure 3D.6. *The 3D sphere.*

`Diameter/<radius>: 7` (Enter)	Specifies radius distance
`Number of longitudinal segments <16>: 20` (Enter)	Makes the sphere slightly smoother around the circumference in the X,Y plane
`Number of latitudinal segments <16>: 20` (Enter)	Makes the sphere slightly smoother around the circumference in the X,Z plane
`Command: 3D` (Enter)	Initiates 3D command
`Box/Cone/DIsh/DOme/Mesh/Pyramid/Sphere/Torus/Wedge: T` (Enter)	Specifies Torus option
`Center of torus: 10,7,2` (Enter)	Specifies 3D center of torus (see fig. 3D.7)

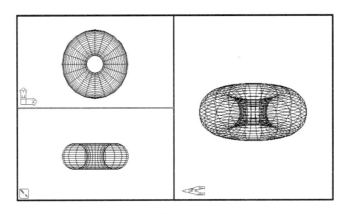

Figure 3D.7. *The 3D torus.*

`Diameter/<radius> of torus: 8` (Enter)	Sets major diameter of torus
`Diameter/<radius> of tube: 3` (Enter)	Sets minor diameter of torus
`Segments around tube circumference <16>: 20` (Enter)	Makes the torus slightly smoother around the minor diameter
`Segments around torus circumference <16>: 40` (Enter)	Makes the torus much smoother around the major diameter
`Command: 3D` (Enter)	Starts the 3D command

```
Box/Cone/DIsh/DOme/Mesh/Pyramid/          Specifies the Wedge option
Sphere/Torus/Wedge: W Enter

Corner of wedge: 4,4 Enter               Locates corner of base of wedge
                                         (see fig. 3D.8)
```

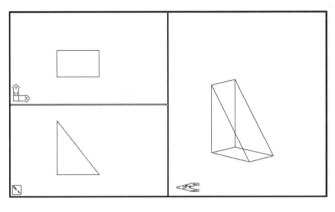

Figure 3D.8. *The 3D wedge.*

```
Length: 8 Enter                          Specifies length along X axis
Width: 5 Enter                           Indicates width along Y axis
Height: 10 Enter                         Specifies height along Z axis
Rotation angle about Z axis: 0 Enter     Specifies no rotation from X axis
```

Related Commands

DVIEW	EDGESURF	HIDE	PEDIT
PLAN	RENDER	REVSURF	RULESURF
SHADE	TABSURF	VPOINTUCS	

Related System Variables

SURFTAB1	SURFTAB2	SURFU	SURFV

3DARRAY

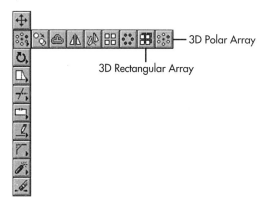

Toolbar: *3D Rectangular/Polar Array (Copy)*
Pull-down: *Construct, 3D Array* (DOS Only)
Screen: CONSTRUCT, 3Darray

The 3DARRAY command is an AutoLISP program that enables you to create 3D rectangular and polar arrays in model space. An array repeats the selected objects in a regularly spaced circular (polar) or rectangular pattern.

Rectangular arrays created with this command have rows, columns, and levels in the X, Y, and Z axes, respectively, of the current UCS. If you try to create a row with only one row and one column and one level, AutoCAD responds with the following:

```
One-element array, nothing to do.    Please try again
```

Polar arrays created by 3DARRAY are similar to polar arrays created by the ARRAY command. The difference is that the axis of rotation can be at any orientation in space, rather than being restricted to rotating about a base point in the current construction plane, perpendicular to the Z axis of the current UCS.

Prompts and Options

Select objects   Use any of the normal AutoCAD selection methods to select the objects that you want arrayed.

Rectangular or Polar Array (R/P)   Specify whether you are creating a rectangular, polar, or circular array. The prompts for circular are identical to those for polar.

If you specify a rectangular array, you will receive the following prompts:

Number of rows (---)<1>   Enter the number of rows you want to create. Rows are groups of objects parallel to the X direction.

Number of columns (¦¦¦)<1>   Enter the number of columns (parallel to the Y direction) you want to create.

Number of levels (...)<1>   Enter the number of levels you want made in the Z direction.

Distance between rows (---)   This prompt appears if you entered a number other than 1 at the `Number of rows (---)<1>:` prompt. Ortho mode is turned on, if it's not already. Enter the distance (in the Y direction) between each of the succeeding rows. A negative distance creates succeeding rows in the negative Y direction.

Distance between columns (¦¦¦)   This prompt appears if you entered a number other than 1 at the `Number of columns (¦¦¦)<1>:` prompt. Enter the distance (in the X direction) between each of the succeeding columns. A negative distance creates succeeding rows in the negative X direction.

Distance between levels (...)   This prompt appears if you entered a number other than 1 at the `Number of levels (...)<1>:` prompt. Enter the distance (in the Z direction) between each of the succeeding levels. A negative distance creates succeeding rows in the negative Z direction.

If you specify a polar or circular array, you will see the following prompts:

Number of items   Enter the number of copies that you want to create with the polar array.

Angle to fill <360>   Enter the portion of a circle, in degrees, in which you want to place the objects. The default value of 360 degrees causes the items that you are copying to be distributed within a full circle. Entering a positive angle creates the copies in a counterclockwise direction, and a negative angle creates the copies in a clockwise direction.

Rotate objects as they are copied? <Y>   When creating polar or circular arrays, you can rotate each copy or maintain their original orientation.

Center point of array   Specify the first point of the axis about which the objects are to be arrayed.

Second point on axis of rotation   Specify the second point of the axis around which the objects are arrayed. This point is used as a point on the positive Z axis. The objects will be copied in a manner similar to a 2D polar array.

Example

The following example shows you how to use the 3DARRAY routine to create a rectangular array in model space. First create a cube, 4.0 units long on each side, using the Box option in the 3D command (see fig. 3D.9).

Command: **3DARRAY** (Enter)	Starts the 3DARRAY command
Select objects: *Pick the box*	Selects the object to array
Select objects: (Enter)	Finishes selecting objects
Rectangular or Polar Array (R/P)? **R** (Enter)	Specifies rectangular array
Number of rows (---)<1>: **4** (Enter)	Specifies 4 rows
Number of columns (¦¦¦) <1>: **4** (Enter)	Specifies 4 columns
Number of levels (...)<1>: **3** (Enter)	Specifies 3 levels
Distance between rows (---): **4.0** (Enter)	Sets 4 units between adjacent rows
Distance between columns (¦¦¦): **4.0** (Enter)	Sets 4 units between adjacent columns
Distance between levels (...): **4.0** (Enter)	Sets 4 units between adjacent levels

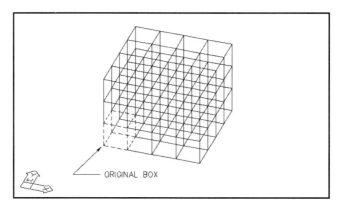

Figure 3D.9. *The arrayed 3D box.*

Related Commands

ARRAY   INSERT   MINSERT   UCS

3DFACE

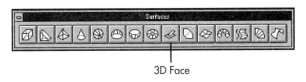

3D Face

Toolbar: *3D Face (Surfaces)*
Pull-down: *D*raw, *Su*rfaces, 3D *F*ace
Screen: DRAW2, SURFACES, 3Dface:

The 3DFACE command creates flat faces that are made of three or four sides. The corners for these faces are entered in either clockwise or counterclockwise direction. 3D faces are not filled with color. Three-dimensional faces can be created at any orientation; the selected corners can have different Z coordinates.

Three-dimensional faces are given a graduated shade with the RENDER command. They are given a uniform shading with the SHADE command and treated as opaque by the HIDE command. The faces cannot be given a thickness. The edges can be made invisible as the faces are created or changed to invisible with the EDGE or DDMODIFY commands.

Prompts and Options

First/Second/Third/Fourth point   Corner points are entered in a circular direction, either clockwise or counterclockwise around the face. To make a triangular face, press Enter when prompted for the fourth point. Until you press Enter or cancel, the 3DFACE command repeats the third point and fourth point prompts to create adjacent 3D faces.

You may use the following options with the 3DFACE command:

Invisibl. If the edge you are defining should be invisible, type **I**, or select the Invisibl option from the screen menu, before specifying the point that begins that edge. Enter the Invisibl option before picking the point and before entering any object snap modes or point filters.

ShowEdge. This screen menu option sets the SPLFRAME system variable to 1, which displays all invisible edges after the next screen regeneration.

HideEdge. This screen menu option sets the SPLFRAME system variable to 0, which makes any hidden edges invisible after the next screen regeneration.

The SPLFRAME system variable also can be set manually.

Example

The following example creates two 3D faces (see fig. 3D.10). The common edge between the two faces (from coordinates 0,3,3 to 6,3,3) is invisible.

Command: **3DFACE** (Enter)	Invokes 3DFACE command
First point: **6,0,0** (Enter)	Locates first corner point
Second point: **0,0,0** (Enter)	Specifies second corner point
Third point: **I** (Enter)	Selects invisible option
0,3,3 (Enter)	Identifies third corner point
This corner point also will be used as the first corner point for the next 3DFACE object drawn with this command. The edge from this point will be invisible.	
Fourth point: **6,3,3** (Enter)	Specifies last corner of first 3DFACE, second corner point of second 3DFACE
Third point: **6,6,0** (Enter)	Locates third corner point
Fourth point: **0,6,0** (Enter)	Identifies fourth corner point
Third point: (Enter)	Finished 3DFACE command

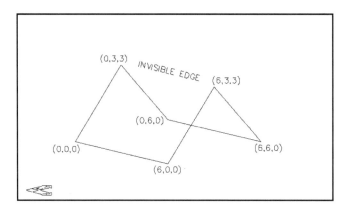

Figure 3D.10. *Three 3D faces.*

Related Commands

DDMODIFY	EDGE	EDGESURF	HIDE
PFACE	RENDER	REVSURF	RULESURF
SHADE	SOLID	TABSURF	3DMESH

Related System Variable

SPLFRAME

3DMESH

3D Mesh

Toolbar: *3D Mesh (Surfaces)*
Pull-down: *Draw, Surfaces, 3D Mesh*
Screen: DRAW2, SURFACES, 3Dmesh:

The 3DMESH command creates an M×N three-dimensional polygon mesh, defined by the locations of each of its vertices. The 3DMESH command forms a net-like surface, each face of which is defined by four vertices. You must specify the coordinates for the corners of the faces.

Begin by specifying the number of vertices in the two directions of the mesh, known as the M and N directions. Most of the other commands that create polygon meshes (EDGESURF and REVSURF, for example) determine the M and N mesh size from the values in the system variables SURFTAB1 and SURFTAB2. The 3DMESH command requires you to enter them.

After entering the number of vertices in the M and N directions, the 3DMESH command prompts you for the locations of all the vertices in order.

This command is best suited for use by third-party programs that automate the selection of coordinate points. For most purposes, you should use one of the other 3D surface commands. After the mesh is created, you can edit it with the PEDIT command. If the mesh is exploded, it is replaced with individual 3D faces.

> **NOTE**
>
> Another command that produces a very similar polygon mesh is the Mesh option of the 3D command. This option enables you to specify only the outer four corners of the mesh. You then enter the number of vertices in the M and N directions. The internal vertices are calculated as they fall between the four corners.

Prompts and Options

`Mesh M size:`

`Mesh N size:`

Enter the number of vertices in the M and N directions of the mesh. These values can be any positive integer between two and 256.

`Vertex (m,n)` Specify the coordinates or pick a point to show the position of the *m,n* vertex, in which *m* and *n* denote the location of the vertex in the mesh. This prompt repeats for each *m,n* location in the mesh until all the vertex locations for the mesh are specified.

Example

The following example creates a simple 3DMESH (see fig. 3D.11).

Command: **3DMESH** (Enter)	Invokes 3DMESH command
Mesh M size: **4** (Enter)	Sets number of vertices along M direction to 4
Mesh N size: **3** (Enter)	Sets number of vertices along N direction to 3
Vertex (0, 0): **0,0,0** (Enter)	Specifies vertex location
Vertex (0, 1): **0,1,1** (Enter)	Specifies vertex location
Vertex (0, 2): **0,2,1** (Enter)	Specifies vertex location
Vertex (1, 0): **2,0,1** (Enter)	Specifies vertex location
Vertex (1, 1): **2,2,0** (Enter)	Specifies vertex location
Vertex (1, 2): **2,3,1** (Enter)	Specifies vertex location
Vertex (2, 0): **4,0,2** (Enter)	Specifies vertex location

```
Vertex (2, 1): 4,1,1 Enter          Specifies vertex location
Vertex (2, 2): 4,2,0 Enter          Specifies vertex location
Vertex (3, 0): 6,0,0 Enter          Specifies vertex location
Vertex (3, 1): 6,1,0 Enter          Specifies vertex location
Vertex (3, 2): 6,2,2 Enter          Specifies vertex location
```

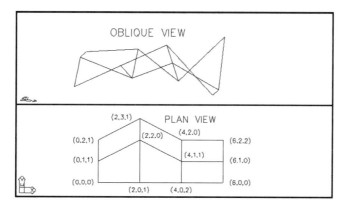

Figure 3D.11. *A 4×3 mesh created with the 3DMESH command.*

Related Commands

3D, Mesh   3DFACE   DDMODIFY   EDGESURF
PEDIT   PFACE   REVSURF   RULESURF
TABSURF

Related System Variables

SURFTYPE   SURFU   SURFV

3DPOLY

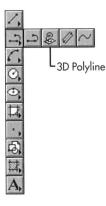
3D Polyline

Toolbar: *3D Polyline (Draw, Polyline)*
Pull-down: <u>D</u>raw, 3D <u>P</u>olyline
Screen: DRAW1, 3Dpoly:
Screen: DRAW2, SURFACES, 3Dpoly:

The 3DPOLY command creates special polylines that can have vertices located anywhere within 3D space. These polylines differ from 2D polylines in that they cannot contain arcs, tangent information, or widths. Curves can be approximated by drawing multiple short, straight segments, and then spline fitting the 3D polyline using the PEDIT command. Three-dimensional polylines are always displayed with a continuous linetype.

Prompts and Options

From point Specify the starting point of the 3D polyline.

Endpoint of line Enter or select an endpoint for the current segment. This prompt repeats until you press Enter or cancel to finish the command or specify the close option. Each endpoint you select becomes the starting point for the next segment.

Close Closes the polyline from the last endpoint to the starting point of the polyline.

Undo Removes the point selection.

Example

The following example demonstrates how to construct a simple three-dimensional polyline (see fig. 3D.12).

3DPOLY

Command: **3DPOLY** (Enter)	Invokes 3DPOLY command
From point: **0,0,0** (Enter)	Specifies starting point of 3D polyline
Close/Undo/<Endpoint of line>: **2,1,3** (Enter)	Specifies endpoint of first segment
Close/Undo/<Endpoint of line>: **4,0,-1** (Enter)	Specifies endpoint of next segment
Close/Undo/<Endpoint of line>: **5,4,3** (Enter)	Specifies endpoint of next segment
Close/Undo/<Endpoint of line>: **2,5,1** (Enter)	Specifies endpoint of next segment
Close/Undo/<Endpoint of line>: **C** (Enter)	Selects Close option. Last segment drawn to starting point of 3D polyline

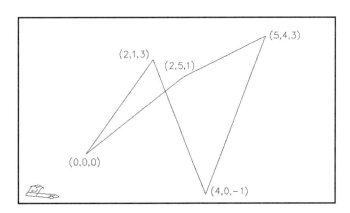

Figure 3D.12. *A 3D polyline created with the 3DPOLY command.*

Related Commands

PEDIT   PLINE   SPLINE

Related System Variables

SPLFRAME   SPLINETYPE

3DSIN

Pull-down: File, Import, 3D Studio
Screen: FILE, IMPORT, 3DSin:

The 3DSIN command is used to import files created with Autodesk's 3D Studio. The 3DSIN command reads the 3D Studio file and imports the geometry and rendering attributes such as materials, texture mapping, light, and cameras.

Issuing the 3DSIN command displays the 3D Studio File Import dialog box, shown in figure 3D.13. After you find and select the 3D Studio file you want to import, choose OK to display the 3D Studio File Import Options dialog box (see fig. 3D.14).

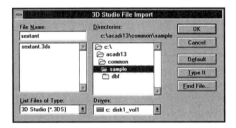

Figure 3D.13. *The 3D Studio File Import dialog box.*

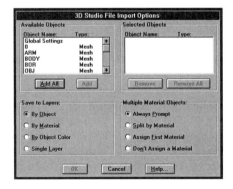

Figure 3D.14. *The 3D Studio File Import Options dialog box.*

The 3D Studio File Import Options dialog box contains the following items:

Available Objects. The Available Objects box contains a list box and **A**dd all and A**d**d buttons. The list box contains a list of 3D Studio objects within the file and their object types. Select the objects you want to import or choose the **A**dd All button to import all the objects. As you select objects, they are moved to the Selected Objects list box.

Selected Objects. As you select available objects, they are listed in the Selected Objects list box. Use the **R**emove and Remo**v**e All buttons to delete selected objects from the list.

Save to Layers. The Save to Layers box contains radio buttons that determine how the 3D Studio objects are divided into AutoCAD layers. AutoCAD can sort the 3D Studio objects according to object (By **O**bject), material (By **M**aterial), or color (**B**y Object Color), or place everything on a single layer (Single **L**ayer).

Multiple Material Objects. This area contains radio buttons for determining how 3D Studio objects that might have more than one material assigned to them are processed by AutoCAD. AutoCAD has to know how to process those objects because each AutoCAD object can have only one material property. The options are Always **P**rompt, **S**plit by Material, Assign **F**irst Material, and Do**n**'t Assign a Material.

Related Command

3DSOUT

3DSOUT

Pull-down: **F**ile, **E**xport, 3D Studio
Screen: FILE, EXPORT, 3DSout:

The 3DSOUT command creates an Autodesk 3D Studio file format (3DS). This command saves the geometry of the objects, view, lights, and materials that might be in the AutoCAD drawing. The 3DSOUT command exports circles, polygonal and polyface meshes, and objects with surface characteristics. Issuing the 3DSOUT command displays the 3D Studio Output File dialog box, shown in figure 3D.15. After you type a file name and choose OK, the 3D Studio File Export Options dialog box appears, as shown in figure 3D.16.

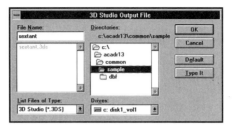

Figure 3D.15. *The 3D Studio Output File dialog box.*

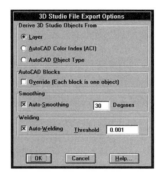

Figure 3D.16. *The 3D Studio File Export Options dialog box.*

The 3D Studio File Export Options dialog box contains the following items:

Derive 3D Studio Objects From. This dialog box area contains a series of radio buttons for determining how to divide the AutoCAD drawing into 3D Studio objects. The options are Layer, AutoCAD Color Index, and AutoCAD Object Type.

AutoCAD Blocks. This section of the dialog box contains the check box, Override (Each block is one object). By checking this box, you force AutoCAD to export each block object in the drawing separately as a 3D Studio object.

Smoothing. The Smoothing section contains an Auto-Smoothing check box and a Degrees edit box for specifying the angle of smoothing.

Welding. The Welding area of the dialog box contains an Auto-Welding check box and Threshold edit box. Welding means that vertices in close proximity to one another will be mreged into a single vertex.

Related Command

3DSIN

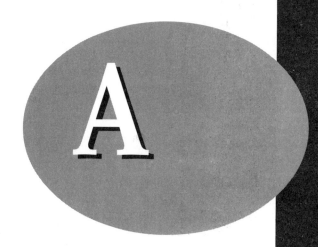

'ABOUT

Pull-down: **H**elp, **A**bout AutoCAD
Screen: HELP, About

The ABOUT command displays a dialog box containing software licensing information and the contents of the ACAD.MSG file in a list box. The licensing information is useful for technical and customer support. It lists the version and serial number of the software as well as the name and phone number of the AutoCAD dealer supplied during installation.

The ACAD.MSG file is loaded at the time of AutoCAD's installation and initially contains introductory information pertaining to AutoCAD. The ACAD.MSG file can be customized or deleted using any ASCII text editor and may differ from system to system. If the ACAD.MSG file has been deleted, the dialog box appears but the list box is empty. If this file contains more lines than the list box can display, a vertical scroll bar appears at the right of the list box.

Related Command
'HELP

ACISIN

Pull-down: File, Import, SAT... (DOS only)
Screen: FILE, IMPORT, SATin:

The ACISIN command imports a file in the Standard ACIS Text file format (in the Import File dialog box under "List Files of Type:" select ACIS(*.SAT)"). This file format directly represents the ACIS models in your drawing and often is used to import ACIS solid models created in other CAD-related packages into AutoCAD.

ACIS solids, regions, and bodies are stored in their own coordinate system and are represented in AutoCAD's WCS. If you import an ACIS solid, change your UCS, and import the same ACIS solid again, the second imported solid is placed in exactly the same location as the first.

SAT files do not contain any color, layer, or linetype information. The solids, regions, and bodies defined in the SAT file will be imported onto the current layer.

Prompts and Options

When you execute the ACISIN command, it displays the Select ACIS File dialog box listing all the files with an SAT extension in the current system directory. Select a file or enter the path and file name of an existing SAT file to import.

If FILEDIA is off, you'll be prompted at the Command: line with the following:

File name   Enter the name of an existing SAT file to import. Do not enter the SAT extension because ACISOUT automatically attaches the extension SAT to the file name you specify. You can supply a full path name.

Example

This example shows how the ACISIN command imports ACIS solids, regions, and bodies from an SAT file. Figure A.1 shows the ACIS objects after the import.

```
Command: ACISIN (Enter)                 Begins the ACISIN command
File name: ACIS_TST (Enter)             Specifies SAT file name
```

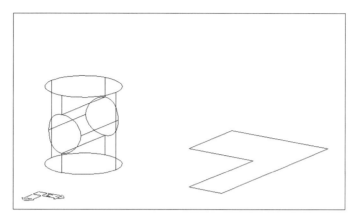

Figure A.1. *Importing ACIS objects.*

Related Commands

ACISOUT	AMECONVERT	DXBIN	DXFIN
GIFIN	IMPORT	PCSIN	PSIN
TIFFIN	WMFIN		

Related System Variable

FILEDIA

ACISOUT

Pull-down: **F**ile, **E**xport
Screen: FILE, EXPORT, ACISout:

The ACISOUT command creates a file in the Standard ACIS Text file format (in the Export Data dialog box under "List Files of Type:," select "ACIS(*.SAT)"). This file format directly represents the ACIS models in your drawing and often is used to export ACIS solid models from AutoCAD to other CAD-related packages. The ACISOUT command enables you to select ACIS solids and regions for export.

Prompts and Options

When you execute the ACISOUT command, it prompts you to select objects.

Select objects Select all of the ACIS solids, regions, or bodies to export. ACISOUT ignores any objects that are not ACIS solids, regions, or bodies.

ACISOUT then displays the Create ACIS File dialog box, listing files with the SAT extension in the current system directory. Enter the name of the SAT file to contain the exported solids information or select an existing file to overwrite. ACISOUT automatically attaches the extension SAT to the file name you specify.

If the FILEDIA system variable is off (set to 0), you'll be prompted at the Command: line with the following:

File name <C:\R13\ACIS_TST> Enter the name of the SAT file to contain the exported solids information. Do not enter the SAT extension because ACISOUT automatically attaches the extension SAT to the file name you specify. You can supply a full path name with the file name.

If you've selected some objects that are not ACIS solids, regions, or bodies, the ACISOUT command reports the following:

```
Ignored xx objects that are not regions, solids, or ACIS bodies.
```

Example

This example shows how the ACISOUT command exports existing ACIS solids, regions, and bodies to an SAT file. Figure A.2 shows the ACIS objects before the export.

Command: **ACISOUT** (Enter)	Starts the ACISOUT command
Select objects: **ALL** (Enter)	Specifies all objects
2 found	
Select objects: (Enter)	Completes the selection
File name: **ACIS_OUT** (Enter)	Specifies SAT file name
Ignored 1 object that is not a region, solid or ACIS body.	

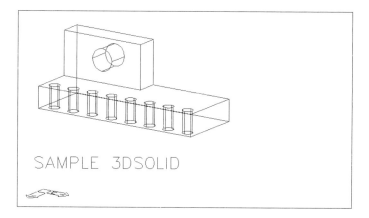

Figure A.2. *Exporting ACIS objects.*

Related Commands

ACISIN   AMECONVERT   DXBIN   DXFOUT
EXPORT   STLOUT

Related System Variable

FILEDIA

ALIGN

—Align

Pull-down: *M*odify, *A*lign
Screen: MODIFY, Align:

The ALIGN command is used to simultaneously move and reorient objects in two-dimensional or three-dimensional space. The ALIGN command is independent of the current User Coordinate System (UCS). You determine the new orientation by specifying two sets of points: source points and destination points. One pair of points will move selected objects. Two pairs of points are required for a 2D alignment. Three pairs are required for a 3D alignment, but also can be used for a 2D alignment.

ALIGN is especially useful when you need to move and rotate objects in two or three axes. Repeated uses of the ALIGN command can replace several executions of MOVE and ROTATE.

Prompts and Options

Select objects   Select the objects to align in a new location by any object selection method. You then are prompted alternatively for a source point and its corresponding destination point.

1st source point   Specify a point relative to the selected objects to align with its corresponding destination point. As each source point is specified, a rubber-band reference line is generated to assist in the specification of the associated destination point.

1st destination point   Specify the location corresponding to the 1st source point.

2nd source point   If you press Enter at this prompt, the Align command moves the selected objects relative to the points specified. To perform 2D transformations, select a second source point.

2nd destination point   Specify the location corresponding to the 2nd source point.

3rd destination point   If you press Enter at this prompt, you receive an additional prompt prior to performing a 2D alignment. To perform a 3D transformation, specify a third point outside the plane of the first two pairs of points.

3rd destination point   Specify the location corresponding to the 3rd source point. The 3D transformation is then performed and the Align command is complete.

<2d> or 3d transformation   This prompt is issued only when you press Enter at the 3rd source point prompt. If you specify a 2D transformation, any Z axis differences in the pairs of source-destination points is ignored. If you enter **3** to specify a 3D transformation, the Z components of the source-destination points you specified are included in moving and rotating the selected objects.

The source-destination point sets that you specify indicate the direction the transformation is to take. They do not have to actually align with each other after the transformation in order to work.

Example

The following example uses ALIGN to move and rotate an object in two dimensions so that it aligns with other objects (see fig. A.3). Use the END-POINT tool to pick the source and destination points.

Command: **ALIGN** (Enter)	Issues the ALIGN command
Select objects: *Pick point* ① *(see fig. A.3)*	Specifies the objects to align
Select objects: (Enter)	Terminates object selection
1st source point: *Pick point* ②	Specifies first point to move from
1st destination point: *Pick point* ③	Specifies where to move the source
2nd source point: *Pick point* ④	Specifies a second source point
2nd destination point: *Pick point* ⑤	Specifies the location for the second source point
3rd source point: (Enter)	Terminates point selection
2d or 3d transformation: (Enter)	Defaults to 2D transformation

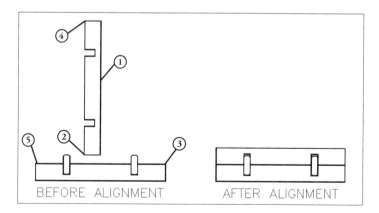

Figure A.3. *Objects moved and rotated in one step with ALIGN.*

Related Commands

MOVE   ROTATE   ROTATE3D

Related System Variable

GRIPS

AMECONVERT

AME Convert

Toolbar: *AME Convert (Solids)*
Pull-down: *Draw, Solids, AME Convert*
Screen: DRAW 2, SOLIDS, AME conv.

AMECONVERT converts 3D solid models or regions created with AutoCAD *Advanced Modeling Extension* (AME) Versions 2 and 2.1, to their ACIS equivalents. New ACIS objects are created, and the existing AME solid models or regions are retained. To ensure future compatibility and reduce the drawing file size, you should delete the old AME objects after using AMECONVERT.

Since the Release 13 solid modeler is more precise than the earlier AME 2 and 2.1 were, interpretation errors can alter the characteristics of a converted solid. Refer to the AutoCAD Command Reference manual for details.

Prompts and Options

Select objects   Use any of the normal AutoCAD selection methods to select all of the objects that you want converted. AMECONVERT ignores any objects that are not AME solid models or regions.

Example

The following example shows how the AMECONVERT command converts existing AME solid models or regions to their ACIS equivalents. Figure A.4 shows the results of the conversion.

```
Command: AMECONVERT (Enter)         Issues the AMECONVERT command
Select objects: ALL (Enter)         Specifies all objects
2 found
Select objects: (Enter)             Ends the selection process
Ignored 1 object that is neither an
AME solid nor a region.
```

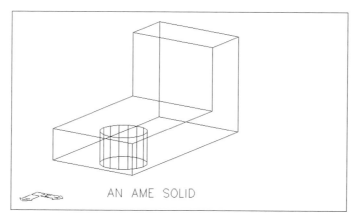

Figure A.4. *Converting AME solids and regions.*

Related Commands
ACISIN   ACISOUT   EXPLODE   RENDER
RMAT

'APERTURE

The APERTURE command sets the size of the *object snap selection target*, the box-like target that appears at the intersection of the crosshairs while you use object snap selection. The aperture's size refers to its width and height in pixels. The value must be a whole number between 1 and 50. This value is stored in the ACAD.CFG file, remaining the same for all subsequent editing sessions until you change it.

Aperture size directly affects the number of possible points AutoCAD must check to find the best qualified match for your object snap setting. A small aperture setting speeds object snap selection. A large setting is easier to see and requires less pointing accuracy, but it can make selecting a specific location in a dense drawing difficult. Experiment with various settings to find the one that works best for you.

Prompts and Options

`Object snap target height (1-50 pixels) <10>`   You can specify a new target height at this prompt to assign a new value to the APERTURE system variable. The aperture box is square, so the height controls the width. The initial default value for APERTURE is 10.

> The DDOSNAP dialog box contains a scroll bar and example graphic for dynamically adjusting the size of the APERTURE box.

Example

The following example shows how different values affect the size of the aperture box.

Command: **APERTURE** (Enter)	Issues the APERTURE command
Object snap target height (1-50 pixels) <10>: **30** (Enter)	Specifies the new aperture height
Command: **LINE** (Enter)	Issues the LINE command
From point: **NEA** (Enter)	Selects the NEAREST object snap; note the increased size of the aperture box
to *Press Esc*	Cancels the command

Related Commands

DDOSNAP   EDGE   OSNAP

Related System Variable

APERTURE

'APPLOAD

Pull-down: **T**ools, A**p**plications
Screen: TOOLS, APPLOAD:

The APPLOAD command enables you to selectively list and load AutoLISP, AutoCAD Development System (ADS), and AutoCAD Runtime eXtension (ARX) applications. You also can unload ADS and ARX applications. Issuing APPLOAD displays the Load AutoLISP, ADS, and ARX Files dialog box, shown in figure A.5. A user-defined list of applications can be saved and redisplayed each time the APPLOAD command is issued. By maintaining a list of commonly used applications, you can save time loading them. APPLOAD saves the default list in APPLOAD.DFS.

Figure A.5. *The Load AutoLISP, ADS, and ARX Files dialog box.*

Do not edit the APPLOAD.DFS file. Make your changes through the APPLOAD command.

Dialog Box Items

The Load AutoLISP, ADS, and ARX Files dialog box contains the following items:

Files to Load. This list box contains a list of the application(s) you have previously saved. Use the list to select applications to load, unload, or remove from the list. If the list of applications is longer than the list box, a vertical scroll bar appears on the right side of the list box. The MAXSORT system variable controls the order of the applications listed. If no selections have been made, AutoCAD disables the **L**oad, **U**nload, and **R**emove buttons.

File. Choosing the **F**ile button displays the Select AutoLISP, ADS, or ARX File dialog box, from which you can locate and select an application from any available drive or directory to put in the Files to Load list box. The **L**ist Files of Type selection box controls the type of applications that are displayed in the list box.

Remove. The **R**emove button deletes all selected applications from the Files to Load list box.

Load. The **L**oad button loads into memory all AutoLISP, ADS, and ARX applications selected in the Files to Load dialog box. The button is disabled if all the selected applications are already loaded.

Unload. This option unloads all selected ADS and ARX applications. It is disabled if all the selected applications are not loaded. Unloading an ADS or ARX application frees system memory.

AutoLISP applications cannot be unloaded. Therefore, in order to save memory, you should avoid loading unnecessary applications.

Save List. If this check box is checked, the APPLOAD.DFS file is updated when you select **L**oad, **U**nload, or **E**xit. To prevent updates to the APPLOAD.DFS file, be sure **S**ave List is unchecked.

Example

The following example loads one AutoLISP and ADS program and unloads the ADS program. If you are using the DOS version of AutoCAD, substitute the GEOMCAL.EXE file for one of your own.

Command: **APPLOAD** (Enter)	Starts the APPLOAD command and displays the Load AutoLISP, ADS, and ARX Files dialog box
Choose **F***ile and display the* ACADR13\COMMON\SUPPORT *directory*	Displays the Select AutoLISP, ADS, or ARX File dialog box
Double-click on 3DARRAY.LSP *in the* Files *list box*	Selects a file to add to the Files to Load list box and returns to the Load AutoLISP, ADS, and ARX Files dialog box
Choose **F***ile and display the* ACADR13\WIN *directory*	Displays the Select AutoLISP, ADS, or ARX File dialog box

Select ADS(*.EXE) *from the* List Files of Type *selection box*	Displays all the *.EXE files
Double-click on GEOMCAL.EXE *in the* Files *list box*	Selects a file to add to the list and returns to the Load AutoLISP, ADS, and ARX Files dialog box.
Click on 3DARRAY.LSP *and* GEOMCAL.EXE *in the* Files to Load *list box*	Selects the files
Choose Load	Loads the files into memory
Command: (Enter)	Reissues the APPLOAD command
Select 3DARRAY.LSP *from the* Files to Load *list box and choose* Remove	
Select GEOMCAL.EXE *from the* Files to Load *list box and choose* Unload	

Related System Variable

MAXSORT

ARC

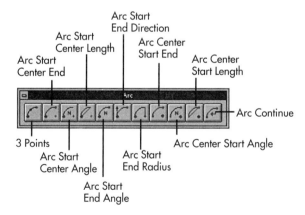

Toolbar: *(Draw, Arc)*
Pull-down: Draw, Arc
Screen: DRAW 1, Arc:

The ARC command creates arcs of any length or radius. By using this command, you can draw an arc with 1 of 11 basic options. Ten of these options for drawing arcs utilize various combinations of the arc properties. This command also includes an option for continuing an arc that is tangent to the preceding arc or line segment. These options can be accessed through the Arc toolbar. Figure A.6 illustrates the various controlling parameters for generating an arc.

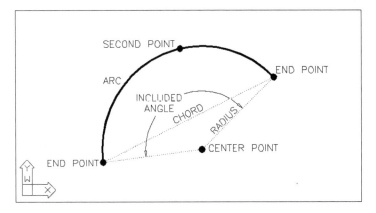

Figure A.6. *Various arc parameters.*

Prompts and Options

The following prompt appears when you issue the ARC command:

Center/<Start point>:

<Start point>   At this prompt, pick the starting point of the arc. Enter **C** to access the Center option. Press Enter to continue an arc that is tangent to the preceding arc or line segment.

Center   At this prompt, pick the center of the arc.

Subsequent prompts appear depending on the method of arc construction you chose previously.

<Second point>   When you are creating an arc by specifying three points, pick the second point at this prompt. This is a point through which the arc will pass.

End point   Prompts you to specify the endpoint of the arc.

Angle   Specifies the included angle of the arc. A negative value draws the arc clockwise; a positive value draws the arc counterclockwise.

Length of chord   Specifies a length for the arc's chord segment (the distance between the arc endpoints).

Radius Specifies the radius for the arc you want to create.

Direction Defines a direction from which the arc will be drawn tangent to the last point on the drawing.

Preset Option Sequences

The following arc construction methods are preprogrammed into the ARC toolbar buttons and selectable from the pull-down and screen menus (the screen menu selections are abbreviated).

3 Points. Specifies the starting point, included point, and endpoint.

Start, Center, End. Specifies the starting point, center of the arc's radius, and endpoint.

Start, Center, Angle. Specifies the starting point, center of the arc's radius, and included angle of the arc.

Start, Center, Length. Specifies the starting point, center of the arc's radius, and length of the arc's chord.

Start, End, Angle. Specifies the starting point, endpoint, and included angle.

Start, End, Direction. Specifies the arc starting point, endpoint, and arc direction.

Start, End, Radius. Specifies the starting point, endpoint, and arc's radius.

Center, Start, End. Specifies the center of the arc's radius, starting point, and endpoint. This option is the same as the Start, Center, End option, but the points are selected in a different order.

Center, Start, Angle. Specifies the center of the arc's radius, starting point, and arc's included angle.

Center, Start, Length. Specifies the center of the arc's radius, starting point, and length of the arc's chord.

Arc Continue. Starts an arc from the endpoint of the last arc, line, or polyline segment created.

Example

The following example illustrates how to create arcs by using different arc options.

Select the 3 Points tool	Issues the ARC command
`Command: _arc Center/<Start point>:` *Pick point ① (see fig A.7)*	Specifies one endpoint of the arc
`Center/End/<Second point>:` *Pick point ②*	Specifies a point on the arc
`End point:` *Pick point ③*	Specifies the other endpoint of the arc
Choose the Arc Center Start Angle tool	Issues the ARC command
`Command: _arc Center/<Start point>: _c Center:` *Pick point ④*	Specifies the center point of the arc
`Start point:` *Pick point ⑤*	Specifies the first endpoint of the arc
`Angle/Length of chord/<End point>: _a Included angle:` **90**	Specifies the included angle in degrees

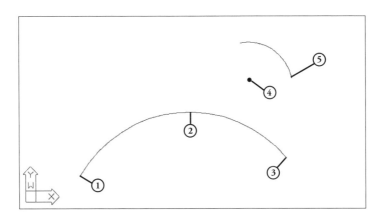

Figure A.7. *Arcs created by using the three-point and center, start, end options.*

Related Commands

ELLIPSE   FILLET   PLINE   VIEWRES

Related System Variable

LASTANGLE

AREA

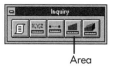

Toolbar: *Area (Object Properties, Inquiry)*
Pull-down: **E**dit, In**q**uiry, Area
Screen: ASSIST, INQUIRY, Area:

The AREA command calculates the area of an AutoCAD object (such as a 2D polyline or circle) or an area defined by a group of points. AREA also can be used for calculating the perimeter, line length, or circumference of an object. The area of an open polyline is calculated as if a straight segment existed between the start and end points. You also can use AREA to create a running total area by adding and subtracting areas.

To define a boundary for measurement, you must pick three or more nonlinear, coplanar points (same Z value). Use the same method when selecting polylines for measurement; the polyline must contain three or more nonlinear, coplanar points. Figure A.8 illustrates the correct and incorrect point selection order for defining area boundaries.

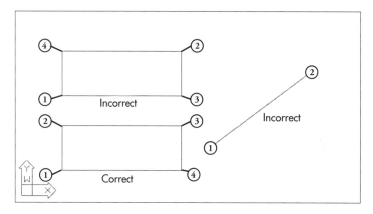

Figure A.8. *Correct and incorrect boundary selections.*

Prompts and Options

The following prompt appears when you issue the AREA command:

`<First point>/Object/Add/Subtract:`

`<First point>` Use this option to calculate the area defined by a group of points specified on the fly. At this prompt, enter or pick the first point of the group.

After you enter the first point, the `Next point:` prompt appears. This prompt is repeated so you can enter any additional points to the group. After you enter all the points, press Enter to end the area-selection process.

`Object` Use this option to select a polyline, polygon, ellipse, or circle to define the boundary of the area to be calculated.

`Add` Use this option to keep a running total area by adding successive object areas or areas defined by points to previous ones.

`Subtract` Use this option to subtract the area of the selected polyline, polygon, ellipse, circle, or defining points from the running total area.

Many third-party applications create temporary polyline boundaries to simplify area calculation and ensure accurate results. You can do the same. By using ENDpoint and INTersection object snap modes, draw a polyline around the area you want to calculate. You might also use the BPOLY command to automatically place the polyline. Use the AREA command's Entity option to select the temporary polyline. After you receive your calculations, you can erase the polyline or store it on a layer that is turned off.

Example

The following example uses the AREA command's Add option to illustrate how this option performs. The entity shown in figure A.9 is a polyline. You will use the Entity option to calculate the polyline's area first, then pick a few points to define an additional area to calculate.

Choose the AREA *tool.*

`Command: _area`	Issues the AREA command
`<First point>/Object/Add/Subtract: A`	Selects the Add option

AREA

`<First point>/Object/Subtract: O`	Selects the Object option
`(ADD mode) Select objects:` *Pick point* ① *(see fig A.9)*	Selects the polyline for area calculation and displays object area and perimeter data
`Area = 48.0557, Perimeter = 30.7317`	
`Total area = 48.0557`	
`(ADD mode) Select objects:` (Enter)	Terminates object selection

Use the ENDPOINT tool when selecting the following points.

`<First point>/Object/Subtract:` `_endp of` *Pick point* ②	Selects the first point defining the area boundary
`(ADD mode) Next point: _endp of` *Pick point* ③	Selects a second point for the area boundary
`(ADD mode) Next point: _endp of` *Pick point* ④	Selects the third point for the area boundary
`(ADD mode) Next point: _endp of` *Pick point* ⑤	Selects the fourth point for the area boundary
`(ADD mode) Next point:` (Enter)	Terminates point selection and displays area and perimeter data for the area defined and total area calculated for the two areas
`Area = 2.8287, Perimeter = 6.7622`	
`Total area = 50.8843`	
`<First point>/Object/Subtract:` (Enter)	Terminates the AREA command

NOTE: When you add or subtract areas, AutoCAD does not recognize overlapping boundaries. Make selections carefully to obtain accurate results.

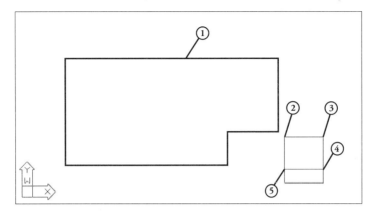

Figure A.9. *Using AREA's add option to determine the sum of two separate areas.*

Related Commands
BOUNDARY   LIST   MASSPROP

Related System Variables
PERIMETER

ARRAY

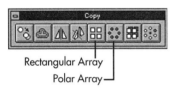

Toolbar: *Rectangular Array or Polar Array (Modify, Copy)*
Pull-down: *Construct*, *Array*
Screen: CONSTRCT, Array:

The ARRAY command creates multiple copies of objects that repeat at regularly spaced intervals. The ARRAY command can work in the X direction (columns), Y direction (rows), or both, each with its own spacing. ARRAY also can place multiple copies in a circle or arc, creating a polar array with the option of rotating the objects as they are placed.

You can array objects in a positive or negative direction in relation to the origin of the source object(s).

> If you are creating a rectangular array, you can specify the X and Y spacing with just two screen picks. The X and Y difference between the two points determines the row and column spacing. The spacing is not the distance between objects but rather the distance between corresponding points on the objects (see fig. A.10).
>
> If the array you are creating is not parallel to the current X and Y axes (if it is rotated at 60 degrees, for example), you can use the Snap Angle option in the DDRMODES command dialog box. This option rotates the crosshairs and the direction for the X and Y axes, thus enabling you to create a rotated array.
>
> ARRAY creates copies within the X and Y axes of the current User Coordinate System (UCS). If you need to create arrays within 3D space, use the 3DARRAY.LSP routine supplied in the SUPPORT directory when you installed AutoCAD Release 13. 3DARRAY can be found on the **C**onstruct pull-down menu as Arra**y** 3D.

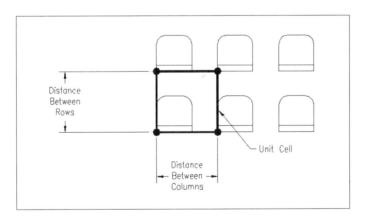

Figure A.10. *Properly determining row and column spacing.*

Prompts and Options

`Select objects` This prompt asks you to select the objects to be arrayed. You can select any type or number of AutoCAD objects, including 3D surfaces and solids. After you select an object, the prompt repeats, so you can select additional objects. Press Enter to end the selection process.

`Rectangular or Polar Array (R/P) <R>`   The default option is to create a rectangular array. If you wish to create a polar array instead, type **P**.

Rectangular Array

`Number of rows (---) <1>`   At this prompt, three hyphens remind you that rows are horizontal along the X axis of the current UCS. Enter the number of rows you want to make parallel to the X axis. You must make at least one row parallel (the default).

`Number of columns (¦¦¦) <1>`   The three vertical bars in this prompt remind you that columns are vertical along the Y axis of the current UCS. You enter the number of columns you want to make parallel to the Y axis. The default value, 1, also is the minimum value.

`Distance between rows (---)`   This prompt appears only during rectangular arrays with two or more rows. This prompt requests the vertical spacing between rows. A negative value creates an array in a negative direction from the origin of the source objects.

`Distance between columns (¦¦¦)`   This prompt appears only during rectangular arrays with two or more columns. This prompt requests the horizontal spacing between columns. Negative column spacing values are created in the same way as negative row spacing values. When creating bidirectional arrays, you can use a combination of negative and positive values for row and column spacing.

Polar Array

`Center point of array`   You see this prompt when you create polar (circular) arrays. The center point refers to the polar reference point, about which the selected objects are arrayed.

`Number of items`   This prompt refers to the number of copies of your selected objects. The original object selection is included in this count.

`Angle to fill (+=ccw, -=ccw) <360>`   The angle you supply at this prompt determines the portion of a circle to be filled during a polar array. The default value, 360, is for a full circle. You cannot enter values greater than 360. A positive value arrays the objects counterclockwise; a negative value arrays the objects clockwise.

`Rotate objects as they are copied? <Y>`   If you answer Y (the default), objects are rotated relative to the center point of the array. If you answer N, the objects maintain the orientation of the source objects.

Example

This example demonstrates both the rectangular and polar options of the ARRAY command. Figures A.11 and A.12 illustrate how the ARRAY command can be used to arrange computer desks within a room.

Choose the Rectangular Array tool	Issues the ARRAY command with the rectangular option
Command: _select	Issues the SELECT command to select objects for the ARRAY command
Select objects: *Select objects at* ① *(see fig. A.11)*	Selects the objects to array

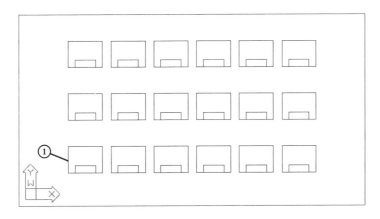

Figure A.11. *Creating a rectangular array.*

Select objects: (Enter)	Terminates the selection set
Command: _array	The ARRAY command issued automatically
Select objects: _p	The Previous object selection issued by AutoCAD
4 found	
Select objects:	Object selection terminated by AutoCAD
Rectangular or Polar array (R/P) <R>: _r	The Rectangular option issued by AutoCAD

Number of rows (---) <1>: **3** (Enter)	Specifies the number of rows of the selected objects to create
Number of columns (¦¦¦) <1>: **6** (Enter)	Specifies the number of columns to create
Distance between rows (---): **36** (Enter)	Specifies the row distance between corresponding points on the objects
Distance between columns (¦¦¦): **30** (Enter)	Specifies the column distance between corresponding points on the objects
Command: (Enter)	Reissues the ARRAY command
Select objects: *Select the objects at ① (see fig. A.12)*	Selects the objects to array

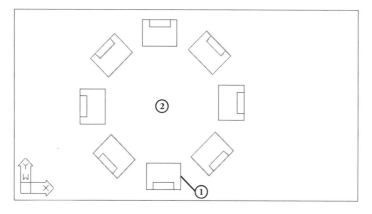

Figure A.12. *Creating a polar array.*

4 found	
Select objects: (Enter)	Terminates object selection
Rectangular or Polar array (R/P) <R>: **P** (Enter)	Specifies the Polar option
Center point of array: *Pick point ②*	Specifies the point for the center of the array
Number of items: **8** (Enter)	Specifies the number of items to array
Angle to fill (+=ccw, -=ccw) <360>: (Enter)	Accepts the default of 360 degrees
Rotate objects as they are copied? <Y> (Enter)	Accepts the default to rotate objects

Related Commands

3DARRAY   COPY   MINSERT

Related System Variable

SNAPANG

ARX

Screen: FILE, MANAGE, Arx:

The ARX command manages AutoCAD Runtime eXtension (ARX) applications. The ARX command is intended for use by AutoCAD Runtime eXtension application developers and does not offer very helpful information to the AutoCAD user. It is used to load and unload ARX applications, set the command priority, and list information about the current ARX object class hierarchy. See the *AutoCAD Customization Guide* or *AutoCAD Release 13 Developer's Guide* (available for developers from Autodesk) for more information.

Prompts and Options

Load Opens the Select Runtime Extension File dialog box. Enter or select the name of an ARX application to load it into the drawing editor. If the application is not on the AutoCAD search path, specify the full path name of the application.

You can use the ARX command to load and unload ARX applications from within menu macros.

Popcmds Enter the command directory at the `Command Directory Name:` prompt, and AutoCAD registers the commands in this directory as having first priority. AutoCAD responds with:

```
Now Top Priority
```

Different ARX applications can define commands with the same name. When searching for an ARX-defined command, AutoCAD searches the Popcmds directories one at a time, until the command is found. To ensure that the appropriate command is used, ARX application developers should pop their command directory to the top of the list immediately prior to issuing the command. This command option is commonly used from within menu macros.

Unload Enter the name of a previously loaded ARX application to unload from AutoCAD. Some ARX applications can consume large amounts of memory and hinder performance. Unloading them frees the memory used by them and improves performance.

> Do not use ARX to Load or Unload the Render utility. The RENDER.ARX utility has uncommon ties to AutoCAD and manipulating it with the ARX command could force you to exit AutoCAD with possible adverse affects on your system. If you need the memory space that RENDER takes up, use the RENDERUNLOAD command instead, and AutoCAD will recognize the RENDER command and load RENDER.ARX automatically when you need it next.

`What to List: CLasses/<Commands>/Objects/Programs/Services` Selecting the ? option from the `Load/Popcmds/Unload/?/<eXit>:` prompt displays this prompt. Enter an option to list information from the ARX object class hierarchy.

eXit Exits the ARX command and returns to the `Command:` prompt.

Related Command

APPLOAD

ATTDEF

The ATTDEF command (an abbreviation of ATTribute DEFine) is the command-line version of the DDATTDEF dialog box driven command. For more information on attributes and their creation, see the DDATTDEF command.

Prompts and Options

```
Attribute modes  --  Invisible:N  Constant:N  Verify:N  Preset:N
Enter (ICVP) to change, RETURN when done:
```

Enter I, C, V, or P to change the status of visibility, constancy, verification, or preset for this attribute. This changes the state of the specified property. Entering I, for example, changes invisibility from No to Yes, or from Yes to No. Press Enter when the attribute state is set correctly.

Invisible This option controls attribute visibility.

Constant This option sets a fixed value for the attribute that cannot be changed.

Verify This option instructs AutoCAD to reprompt for the value of the attribute.

Preset Use this option to establish a non-constant attribute with a default value.

Attribute tag Define the name of the tag used to store attribute data that the user enters.

Attribute prompt Enter the prompt that you want AutoCAD to display when inserting a block with this attribute attached, or press Enter to specify no attribute prompt.

Default attribute value Enter a default value for this attribute, if desired.

After you set the preceding options, ATTDEF prompts you for text options: justification, insertion point, height, and rotation. Like the TEXT, DTEXT, AND MTEXT commands, ATTDEF uses the current text style.

Example

This example creates three attributes next to a previously drawn hexnut (shown in side view—see fig. A.13). The first two attributes are visible, and the third will normally be invisible. After the attributes are defined, use the BLOCK command to create a block definition, select the hexnut lines, and then pick the attribute definitions one at a time in the order you want to have them presented when inserting.

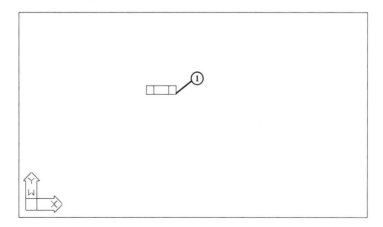

Figure A.13. *The side view of the hexnut before defining attributes with ATTDEF.*

Command: **ATTDEF** (Enter)	Starts ATTDEF command
Attribute modes -- Invisible:N Constant:N Verify:N Preset:N	
Enter (ICVP) to change, RETURN when done: (Enter)	No changes. This attribute will be normally visible
Attribute tag: **SIZE** (Enter)	Specifies the name SIZE for this attribute
Attribute prompt: **Enter size of nut** (Enter)	Specifies the prompt to display when inserting the block with this attribute
Default attribute value: (Enter)	No default value when inserting
Justify/Style/<Start point>: *Pick* ① *(See fig. A.13)*	Places the attribute near the object
Height <0.2000>: (Enter)	Accepts default text height
Rotation angle <0>: (Enter)	Accepts default rotation angle
Command: **ATTDEF** (Enter)	Repeats ATTDEF command
Attribute modes -- Invisible:N Constant:N Verify:N Preset:N	
Enter (ICVP) to change, RETURN when done: (Enter)	No changes. This next attribute will be normally visible
Attribute tag: **WEIGHT** (Enter)	Specifies the name WEIGHT for this attribute
Attribute prompt: **Enter weight of nut** (Enter)	Specifies the prompt to display when inserting the block with this attribute
Default attribute value: (Enter)	No default value when inserting
Justify/Style/<Start point>: (Enter)	Places second attribute below first
Command: **ATTDEF** (Enter)	Starts ATTDEF command for third attribute
Attribute modes -- Invisible:N Constant:N Verify:N Preset:N	
Enter (ICVP) to change, RETURN when done: **I** (Enter)	Changes visibility from N to Y
Attribute modes -- Invisible:Y Constant:N Verify:N Preset:N	

ATTDEF

```
Enter (ICVP) to change,              No additional changes. This attribute
RETURN when done: (Enter)            will be normally invisible

Attribute tag: PRICE (Enter)         Specifies the name PRICE for this
                                     attribute

Attribute prompt:                    Specifies the prompt to display when
Enter price of nut (Enter)           inserting the block with this attribute

Default attribute value: (Enter)     No default value when inserting

Justify/Style/<Start point>: (Enter) Places third attribute below second
                                     (see fig. A.14)
```

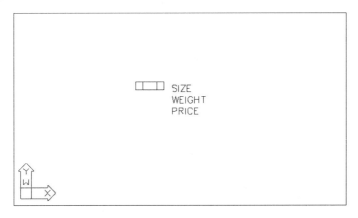

Figure A.14. *Three attributes, before creating a block definition.*

Related Commands

ATTDISP	ATTEDIT	ATTEXT	ATTREDEF
BLOCK	DDATTDEF	DDATTE	DDATTEXT
DDINSER	INSERT	TEXT	

Related System Variables

AFLAGS	ATTDIA	ATTMODE	ATTREQ

ATTDISP

Pull-down: **O**ptions, **D**isplay, **A**ttribute Display
Screen: OPTIONS, DISPLAY, AttDisp:

The ATTDISP command controls visibility of attributes attached to inserted blocks. This command can override the visibility mode assigned to the attribute when the attribute was created. ATTDISP is useful for viewing attributes that normally are invisible, and for turning off the visibility of all attributes. Use of the ATTDISP command causes the screen to regenerate if REGENAUTO is set to on.

> The ATTDISP command can be executed transparently by preceding the command name with an apostrophe ('ATTDISP). This will cause a REGEN at the conclusion of the current command.

Prompts and Options

`Normal/ON/OFF <Normal>` The default is whatever the current attribute display status is. The current display status is kept in the system variable ATTMODE.

`Normal` This option displays attributes according to the attribute's defined visibility mode (visible or invisible).

`ON` This option turns on the visibility of all attributes, regardless of defined visibility mode. The assigned visibility mode is retained, and you can restore it by using the Normal option.

`OFF` This option turns off the visibility of all attributes, regardless of assigned visibility mode. Use the Normal option to restore the assigned visibility mode.

Example

This example shows the display of all attributes using the ATTDISP command. Before changing the attribute display, only those attributes assigned the visibility mode are visible, as shown in figure A.15. ATTDISP is then used to force on the display of all attributes, exposing the normally invisible price attribute.

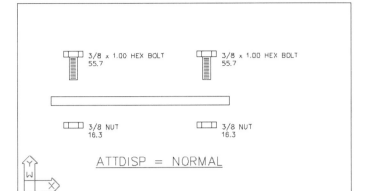

Figure A.15. *Attributes attached to blocks displayed normally.*

```
Command: ATTDISP                    Starts ATTDISP command

Normal/ON/OFF <Normal>: ON          Specifies that all attributes are to be
                                    displayed (see fig. A.16). Ignores
                                    individual settings

Regenerating drawing
```

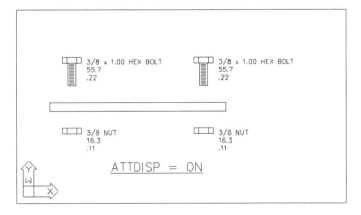

Figure A.16. *All attributes displayed using ATTDISP.*

Related Commands

ATTEDIT   ATTEXT   ATTREDEF   BLOCK
DDATTDEF   DDATTE   DDATTEXT   DDINSERT
INSERT   REGENAUTO

Related System Variables

ATTDIA   ATTMODE   ATTREQ

ATTEDIT

Edit Attribute Globally

Toolbar: *Edit Attribute Globally (Attribute)*
Pull-down: *M*odify, Attri*b*ute, Edit *G*lobally

ATTEDIT (an abbreviation for ATTribute EDIT) edits the characteristics of inserted attributes. You can edit an attribute's value, position, height, angle, style, layer, or color. You also can edit attribute values from attributes matching a specific name, from inserts matching a specific name, or globally.

AutoCAD does not highlight attributes when you select them. The attributes are highlighted during editing.

You can't change the visibility, constancy, verification, or preset properties of inserted attributes. Use the ATTREDEF command to add attributes to inserted blocks.

TIP You can edit a block's multiple attribute values more easily from the DDATTE dialog box. However, you can't edit position, height, angle, style, layer, or color with DDATTE.

Prompts and Options

`Edit attributes one at a time? <Y>`   If you answer Y, you edit each attribute individually. If you answer N, you edit the attributes globally (value only), and the following message appears:

`Global edit of attribute values.`

Answering N also generates the following additional prompt:

`Edit only attributes visible on screen? <Y>`

This prompt appears for global edits of attribute values. If you answer no, then AutoCAD will change all attributes in the drawing that match the block, tag name, and value patterns. AutoCAD will also print a message in this case:

`Drawing must be regenerated afterwards.`

`Block name specification <*>`   Press Enter to edit attributes from any inserted block. Enter a block name pattern to edit attributes from only blocks matching that name. You can use wild cards at this prompt.

`Attribute tag specification <*>`   Press Enter to edit any attributes from the matched blocks. Enter a tag name pattern to edit attributes from the matched blocks that match the pattern. You can use wild cards at this prompt.

`Attribute value specification <*>`   This prompt enables you to edit attributes with specific values only. Press Enter to edit all attributes matching the tag name pattern from the matched blocks. Enter a value pattern to edit only attributes from the matched blocks, with the matched tag name, with a value that matches the value pattern. This prompt often is used for globally updating one value to another across multiple blocks. You can use wild cards at this prompt.

`Select attributes`   Select attributes individually at this prompt by picking them from the graphics window. Attributes must be visible to be selected. If the attributes were not originally set to be visible, you must set ATTDISP to ON before selecting attributes at this prompt. Attributes are not highlighted as you pick them, but will be highlighted when editing.

At the Select attributes: prompt, AutoCAD is looking for a single selection. To select multiple objects, you must change to another selection method by entering a key letter such as 'W' to make a window selection.

Value/Position/Height/Angle/Style/Layer/Color/Next <N> This prompt, and the following options, appears if you have chosen to edit attributes one at a time. Select the option to change for this attribute. Press Enter to edit the next attribute.

> **Value** Use this option to change the value of the currently selected attribute.
>
> **Position** This option enables you to change the insertion point or text justification point of the currently selected attribute.
>
> **Height** This option enables you to change the text height of the currently selected attribute.
>
> **Angle** This option enables you to change the rotation angle of the currently selected attribute.
>
> **Style** This option enables you to change the text style assigned to the currently selected attribute.
>
> **Layer** This option enables you to change the layer assignment of the currently selected attribute.
>
> **Color** This option enables you to change the color assigned to the currently selected attribute.
>
> **Next <N>** Use this option when you are finished editing the currently selected attribute to go on to the next attribute in the selection set.

If you choose to edit attributes globally, you are only prompted for the string value to change.

String to change Enter the current attribute value, or that part of the current attribute value to change.

New string Enter the new attribute value, or the value to replace that part of the current attribute value selected with the String to change option.

Example

This example uses the attribute created and inserted with the ATTDEF command. It alters the height of the SIZE attribute to 0.375 (see fig. A.17).

```
Command: ATTEDIT (Enter)                   Starts ATTEDIT command
Edit attributes one at a time?             Selects individual attribute edit
<Y> (Enter)
Block name specification <*>: (Enter)      From all blocks
```

`Attribute tag` `specification <*>:` **`SIZE`** `(Enter)`	Specifies only editing of attributes with tag name of SIZE
`Attribute value specification` `<*>:` `(Enter)`	Edits attribute with any value
`Select Attributes:` *Pick at ① and ②* *(see fig. A.17)*	Selects the two SIZE attributes for the 3/8 hexnuts
`2 attributes selected.`	

`Value/Position/Height/Angle`
`/Style/Layer/Color/Next`
`<N>:` **`H`** `(Enter)`
	Specifies height option

`New height <0.2000>:` **`.375`** `(Enter)`	Enters new height

`Value/Position/Height/Angle`
`/Style/Layer/Color/Next`
`<N>:` `(Enter)`
	Go on to next attribute in selection set

`Value/Position/Height/Angle`
`/Style/Layer/Color/Next`
`<N>:` **`H`** `(Enter)`
	Specifies height option

`New height <0.2000>:` **`.375`** `(Enter)`	Enters new height

`Value/Position/Height/Angle`
`/Style/Layer/Color/Next`
`<N>:` `(Enter)`
	Go on to next attribute in selection set. Since only 2 attributes are selected, this ends ATTEDIT (see fig. A.18)

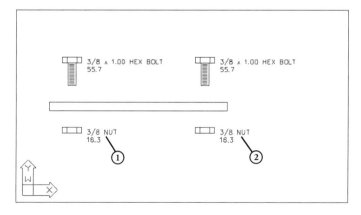

Figure A.17. *Changing the height of an inserted attribute using ATTEDIT.*

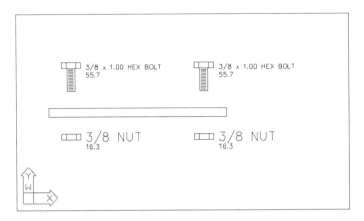

Figure A.18. *The attributes with new height after using the ATTEDIT command.*

Related Commands

ATTDISP   ATTEDIT   ATTEXT   ATTREDEF
BLOCK   DDATTDEF   DDATTE   DDATTEXT
DDINSERT INSERT

Related System Variables

ATTDIA   ATTMODE   ATTREQ   HIGHLIGHT

ATTEXT

ATTEXT (an abbreviation of ATTribute EXTraction) reads attribute information contained in the block insertions of the current drawing and writes this information to a file. You can extract this information in several standard ASCII-file formats so the data can be imported into database or spreadsheet programs for further processing and analysis.

One example of an ATTEXT application is creating component schedules. With proper planning and setup, you can extract attributes to build material lists, door schedules, and for a variety of other purposes.

> The DDATTEXT command offers a dialog box for extracting the information from the drawing, and is much easier to use. It has the same functionality as the ATTEXT command.

Template Files
Refer to the DDATTEXT command.

Prompts and Options

`CDF, SDF or DXF Attribute extract (or Objects)? <C>` Specify the type of extraction to perform.

CDF CDF, an acronym for *Comma Delimited Format*, extracts the attribute and insert information and places commas between each field in the output file. The CDF option requires a template file. This option extracts the attribute information from the entire drawing. The output format places single quotes around all character fields.

SDF SDF, an acronym for *Space Delimited Format*, extracts the attribute and insert information and places spaces between each field in the output file. The SDF option also requires a template file. This option extracts the attribute information from the entire drawing. This format can be imported into dBase III database files.

DXF DXF, which stands for *Drawing Interchange Format*, extracts the attribute information from the entire drawing. The output file has an extension of DXX, identifying it as a Drawing Interchange Extract file.

`Objects` This option enables you to select specific objects for attribute extraction using one of the preceding formats.

`Select objects` This prompt appears if you choose the Objects option. Use any of the standard AutoCAD object selection methods to select insert objects to export. Any object select that is not an insert object will be ignored.

Example

This example uses a template file to extract all of the attribute values from a drawing. Use an ASCII text editor to create a extract template file with the following lines:

```
BL:NAME     C015000
SIZE        C030000
WEIGHT      N008002
PRICE       N005002
```

Make sure there is one and only one linefeed character at the end of the last line. AutoCAD will report an error if blank lines exist in the template file. Save it under any name with a TXT extension.

```
Command: ATTEXT                          Starts the ATTEXT command

ATTEXT CDF, SDF or DXF Attribute         Specifies comma delimited output
extract (or Objects)? <C>: C             format, displays select Template File
                                         dialog box (see fig. A.19)
```

Select the template file you just created

Enter the name of an output file   The output file has a default TXT
                                          extension

```
4 records in extract file.
```

Figure A.19. *The Create extract file dialog box.*

Related Commands

ATTDEF	ATTDISP	ATTEDIT	ATTEXT
ATTREDEF	BLOCK	DDATTDEF	DDATTE
DDATTEXT	DDINSERT	EXPORT	INSERT

Related System Variables

ATTDIA   ATTMODE   ATTREQ   HIGHLIGHT

ATTREDEF

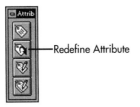

Redefine Attribute

ATTREDEF

Toolbar: *Redefine Attribute (Attribute)*
Pull-down: *M̲odify, Attri̲b̲ute, R̲edefine*

The ATTREDEF command redefines an existing block with attributes. ATTREDEF preserves attribute values if the new block definition contains an identical attribute tag. The command searches the entire drawing for all occurrences of a specific block, and replaces them with the updated definition.

Unfortunately, there are some restrictions on using ATTREDEF. ATTREDEF does not preserve the previous layer of the block—all replacement blocks are inserted on the current layer.

In addition, if you redefine an existing block and remove attributes, and then explode blocks that were created with attributes prior to redefining the block, the current block with its attributes is inserted and exploded instead.

ATTREDEF requires the block to be redefined to have attributes. If the block definition has no attributes, then ATTREDEF will report this, and not perform the redefinition. Thus, you cannot remove all attributes from blocks using ATTREDEF.

> Handles (unique references to AutoCAD objects which are always on in AutoCAD Release 13) assigned to blocks are lost. ATTREDEF deletes the existing blocks, and inserts new ones in their place. New handles are assigned to the new blocks.

Prompts and Options

Name of Block you want to redefine Enter the name of an existing block. If the block doesn't exist, ATTREDEF responds with the following:

```
Block SOMENAME is not defined. Please try again.
```

Select Objects for new Block Select the objects to be included in the new block definition, including any attributes required. If no objects are selected, ATTREDEF responds with the following:

```
No new block selected. Please try again.
```

Insertion base point of new block Pick the desired base point for the insertion point of the new block. If the base point of the new block is the same point as the base point of the existing block, when the block is redefined, the new blocks will be inserted at exactly the same position as the previous blocks.

Example

The following example uses the ATTREDEF command to redefine all the HEXNUT blocks in the drawing. Insert and explode a HEXNUT block, and add an attribute with a tag name called Material using the ATTDEF command. Then use the ATTREDEF command to add this attribute to all occurrences of the HEXNUT block in the drawing.

Command: **ATTREDEF** (Enter)	Begins the ATTREDEF command
Name of the Block you want to redefine: **HEXNUT** (Enter)	Specifies the block to redefine
Select Objects for new Block: *Select objects* ① *(see fig. A.20)*	Select the graphical objects (lines), then the attributes
Insertion base point of new block: *Pick point* ②	Picks the same insertion point as the existing HEXNUT block, redefines existing HEXNUT block (see fig. A.21)

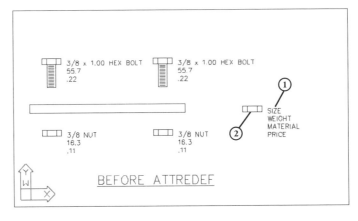

Figure A.20. *Redefining the HEXNUT block with the ATTREDEF command.*

Related Commands

ATTDEF	ATTDISP	ATTEDIT	ATTEXT
BASE	BLOCK	DDATTDEF	DDATTE
DDATTEXT	OOPS		

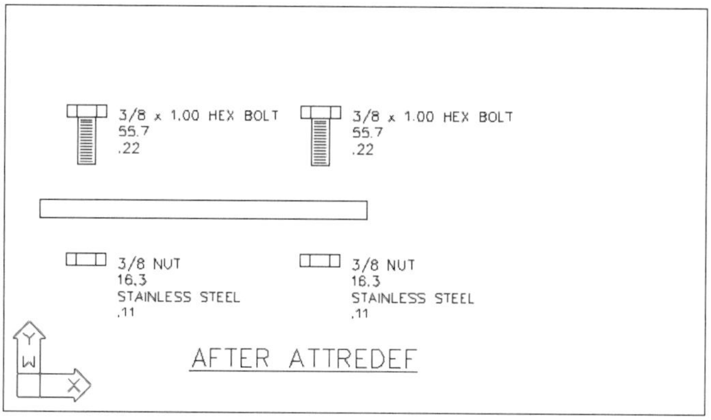

![Figure A.21 illustration]

Figure A.21. *The redefined HEXNUT block.*

Related System Variables

ATTDIA   ATTMODE   ATTREQ

AUDIT

Pull-down: **F**ile, **M**anagement, **A**udit
Screen: FILE, MANAGE, Audit:

The AUDIT command verifies the integrity of your drawings. When you invoke AUDIT from the drawing editor, AutoCAD corrects any errors in the current drawing file automatically, or it can leave all errors uncorrected (the default)—but recommend specific corrective action.

Prompts and Options

`Fix any errors detected? <N>`   If you answer No, AutoCAD creates a report that documents any errors found and recommends corrective action. If you answer Yes, AutoCAD creates a report and automatically performs the recommended corrective action. Any objects requiring corrective action are placed in the previous selection set.

> You can save the previous selection set as a group and then access the objects one at a time.

The system variable AUDITCTL controls whether an audit log file is written during the AUDIT command. To create an audit file, change the value of AUDITCTL to 1. This can be done at the Command: prompt by typing **AUDITCTL**, or from the screen menu (choose FILE, Manage, Audit, Auditctl). The audit file will be placed in the same directory and have the same name as your drawing with an extension of ADT.

AUDIT does not correct all drawing errors. In cases where AUDIT is unable to recover damaged information, try using the RECOVER command.

Example

The following shows the contents of a sample audit log file.

```
Drawing: C:\DWGS\NRP5432   Autodesk, Inc.   AutoCAD AUDIT REPORT      Page 1
  Release: R.0.75   Microsoft Windows            09/30/94 16:12:25
Auditing Header
DXF Name       Current Value      Validation     Default
GRIDUNIT       -0.00 -0.00        0.00 0.00      -0.00 -0.00
SNAPUNIT       -0.00 -0.00        0.00 0.00      -0.00 1.000000E+020
Error found in auditing header variables
VPORT 50       -7.343562E+211     0.00 - 6.28    0.00
Auditing Entities Pass 1
DXF Name       Current Value      Validation     Default
GRIDUNIT       -0.00 -0.00        0.00 0.00      -0.00 -0.00
SNAPUNIT       -0.00 -0.00        0.00 0.00      -0.00 1.000000E+020
GRIDUNIT       -0.00 -0.00        0.00 0.00      -0.00 -0.00
SNAPUNIT       -0.00 -0.00        0.00 0.00      -0.00 1.000000E+020
GRIDUNIT       -0.00 -0.00        0.00 0.00      -0.00 -0.00
SNAPUNIT       -0.00 -0.00        0.00 0.00      -0.00 1.000000E+020
GRIDUNIT       -0.00 -0.00        0.00 0.00      -0.00 -0.00
SNAPUNIT       -0.00 -0.00        0.00 0.00      -0.00 1.000000E+020
GRIDUNIT       -0.00 -0.00        0.00 0.00      -0.00 -0.00
SNAPUNIT       -0.00 -0.00        0.00 0.00      -0.00 1.000000E+020
Total errors found 13 fixed 0
```

Related Command

RECOVER

Related System Variable

AUDITCTL

AV (Windows Only)

The AV command is an alias for the DSVIEWER command. See the description for the DSVIEWER command for more information.

Related Command

DSVIEWER

Related System Variables

VIEWCTR   VIEWSIZE   VSMAX   VSMIN

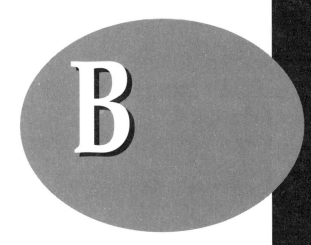

'BASE

The BASE command defines the insertion point of the current drawing. The results of this command are evident only when you insert the drawing as a block into another drawing or use the drawing as an external reference for another drawing.

Prompts and Options

Base point <current base point>   This prompt requests a new base point and offers the current base point as the default. If you supply a 2D point, AutoCAD assumes that the Z value is equal to the current elevation.

Related Commands

BLOCK   INSERT   XREF

Related System Variable

INSBASE

> **TIP** Drawings created by using the WBLOCK command often have objects and insertion base points floating in space. If you have such files in your block library you should take the time to clean them up. Move the objects to the vicinity of the origin, reset the drawing limits, relocate the insertion base point using the BASE command, and purge the drawing.

-BHATCH

Hatch

Toolbar: *Hatch (Draw, Hatch)*
Pull-down: ***D**raw, **H**atch, **H**atch*
Screen: CONSTRCT, Bhatch

BHATCH draws crosshatching (or poche) within a boundary area. You can use standard AutoCAD patterns, patterns as defined by the *International Organization of Standardizatio*n (ISO), or create user-defined patterns or custom patterns. To create hatching, you pick a point inside the region to fill. Unlike the HATCH command, BHATCH creates a temporary closed polyline boundary object automatically by tracing over existing intersecting objects surrounding the point you pick. You can elect to retain the boundary for later use or for creating additional drawing geometry.

The dialog box enables you to specify the hatch pattern name, angle, style, and scale. You can define your own simple hatch patterns, specify certain objects to consider for boundary calculations, experiment by selecting and viewing boundary selection sets, pre-explode the hatch block, and preview hatches—all before actually applying the hatch to your drawing. Figure B.1 shows the main BHATCH dialog box.

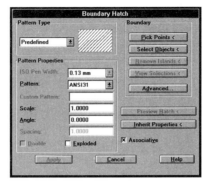

Figure B.1. *The primary BHATCH dialog box.*

Dialog Box Items

Pattern Type. This area of the dialog box contains a drop-down list box and an image button for defining the type and pattern of your hatch pattern.

The drop-down list box contains three choices for the type of pattern: Predefined, User-defined, and Custom. The Predefined type is used to select a standard AutoCAD hatch pattern. These pattern definitions are contained in a file named ACAD.PAT.

The User-defined type is used when you want to create a hatch pattern using lines. These lines will have the current linetype style assigned to them. You can optionally create a 90-degree crosshatch by checking the Double check box when you use the User-defined option. When using this option, you also can specify the spacing between hatch lines as well as their angle.

Use the Custom pattern type when you want to use a pattern that is contained in another pattern file.

The pattern image is a button that displays the type of hatch pattern that will be generated. Clicking on this button will cycle through all of the patterns defined in the pattern file.

AutoCAD features more than 65 predefined hatch patterns in the file ACAD.PAT. These patterns include brick, stone, wood, grass, and other textures. Several of the ANSI and ISO standards also are included.

Pattern Properties. This area of the dialog box contains a variety of items used to control the appearance and other properties of your hatch pattern. Each of these items is discussed in the following:

> **ISO Pen Width.** When you choose an ISO pattern from the Pattern Type drop-down list box described previously, the ISO Pen Width drop-down

list box is enabled. It contains various pen widths for determining the line spacing of your hatch pattern. Choosing a value from this list changes the value in the Sca_le edit box. This option is not available for any pattern other than an ISO pattern.

P_attern. This drop-down list box reflects the name of the hatch pattern as defined in a pattern definition file, such as ACAD.PAT. It correlates to the image shown in the Pattern Type image button. This option is not available for User-defined or Custom pattern types.

Custom Pattern. Use this edit box for inserting the name of a custom pattern. This option is only available for Custom pattern types.

Sca_le. This edit box must contain a positive real number to define the scale of the hatch pattern. The scale is reflected in the relative spacing of the lines from one another as well as the spacing between dashes and dots making up each line in the pattern. This option is not available with Custom pattern types.

A_ngle. This edit box must contain a real number used for determining the angle at which the hatch pattern will be drawn. This angle is relative to the current *User Coordinate System* (UCS). The number you enter does not necessarily correspond with the angle of the individual line segments in the pattern, but rather the relative angle of the entire pattern. The pattern shown in the Pattern Type image button is always shown at a 0-degree angle.

S_pacing. This edit box is highlighted only when you choose a User-defined pattern in the Pattern Type drop-down list. When you type a positive real number in this edit box, you are specifying the distance between parallel line segments in the hatch pattern.

D_ouble. This check box is only available for User-defined pattern types. When you check this box, AutoCAD will draw additional lines at 90-degrees to your lines specified for a User-defined pattern. These lines will have the same scale and spacing.

E_xploded. This check box determines whether or not the hatch pattern you create will remain a hatch block (one object) or consist of individual line objects.

Exploding hatch patterns will significantly add to the size of your drawing file. It is recommended that you do not explode the hatch pattern. Instead, it is best to erase the hatch and re-create it. If a hatch pattern is created with associative hatching, you loose that

> associativity when you explode it. Also, if the hatching is associative, you can use the HATCHEDIT command to modify your hatch pattern properties instead of exploding and editing the resulting objects.

Boundary. This area of the dialog box contains five buttons that determine how hatching boundaries are created. These items are discussed in the following:

> **Pick Points.** Click on this button to pick a point inside the area(s) you want to hatch. After you pick a point, AutoCAD analyzes the current object-selection set to create a hatch boundary. You can control the objects considered for boundary creation by selecting specific objects or by using the Advanced Options button.
>
> **Select Objects.** Click on this button to select the objects on-screen to be considered for the hatch boundary.
>
> **Remove Islands.** Click on this button to remove internal island boundaries so that the hatch pattern will be generated through them.
>
> **View Selections.** Click on this button to view the current boundary set after you have selected items for hatching or created a boundary.
>
> **Advanced.** Click on this button to display the Advanced Options dialog box (see fig. B.2).

Figure B.2. *The Advanced Options dialog box.*

The Advanced Options dialog box is the same as the BOUNDARY command's Boundary Creation dialog box with the following exceptions:

Style. Use this drop-down list box or image button to determine what style of hatching is to be created. The three options are Normal, Outer, and Ignore. Select the option from the list or click on the image button to cycle through the options. Hatch pattern styles are explained later in the Prompts and Options section.

Retain Boundaries. When this box is checked, it creates a new closed polyline object from the calculated boundary.

Refer to the BOUNDARY command for the other options in this dialog box.

Preview Hatch. Click on this button to see a temporary example of how the hatch would appear if created with the current settings.

Inherit Properties. Click on this button to copy the hatch properties (scale, angle, pattern, etc.) from an existing hatch pattern on the drawing. You are prompted to select a hatch pattern.

Associative. Check this box (the default) to create a hatch pattern associated with the boundary geometry. This creates an intelligent hatch pattern that retains its pattern name, properties, and boundary set. If, for instance, you later stretch the boundary to modify an enclosed text string, the hatch pattern automatically updates to fill the modified area. If you perform editing that causes the hatch's boundary to open, the hatch automatically changes to non-associative.

Sometimes a hatch pattern can be reluctant to update. When this occurs select the hatch pattern, click on the PROPERTIES icon, and press Enter or choose OK. The hatch pattern will then update. This technique also will confirm the associative status of a hatch; if the hatch is associative, the Modify Associative Hatch dialog box is opened.

Apply. Click on this button to apply the hatch pattern to the selected area with the current settings.

You can control the point where AutoCAD starts drawing a hatch pattern using the SNAPBASE system variable. For example, if you have a brick hatch pattern, you want a full brick pattern to start in the lower left of your building elevation. Set SNAPBASE to the lower corner of the building and force AutoCAD to start the hatch pattern there. SNAPBASE is normally at 0,0 of the current UCS, and can be relocated once the hatch is created.

Prompts and Options

The command-line version of the BHATCH command (-BHATCH) has many of the same options as the dialog box version discussed previously. Entering -BHATCH presents the following prompt:

```
Properties/Select/Remove islands/Advanced/<Internal point>:
```

Properties   The Properties option presents the following prompts for specifying the hatch pattern name, scale, and angle.

> **Pattern (? or name/U,style) <ANSI31>**   At this prompt, you enter a pattern name or type **?** to see a list of available patterns. The default is the current pattern. If no pattern has yet been used, you can enter its name with an optional style, or you can use the U option to create a user-defined pattern. Hatch pattern styles are explained later in this section.
>
> The specified hatch pattern must be defined in the file ACAD.PAT or stored in a file with the pattern name and a PAT extension. If you want to use a hatch pattern named GLASS, for example, it must be in the ACAD.PAT file or a file named GLASS.PAT.
>
> **Pattern(s) to list <*>**   You enter the names of patterns you want to list, using wild cards if desired. All hatch-pattern definitions stored in the ACAD.PAT file are listed. This option does not list patterns that are defined in other files.
>
> Hatching style, which you specify by placing a comma and the style letter after the pattern name, affects the manner in which hatching occurs. The hatch boundary forms the limits within which the hatch will fill. If objects are within the outermost boundary that is chosen, and those objects form another boundary, the hatching stops at that inner boundary. Hatch styles determine how AutoCAD regards these inner boundaries.
>
> The first hatch style, N (Normal), tells the HATCH command that all boundaries found are valid. AutoCAD fills every other closed region found within the selected boundary objects. This style has the same effect as using no style name at all. The second style type, O (fill Outermost), fills only the area defined by the outermost set of boundaries. The final hatch style, I (ignore Internal boundaries), completely fills the area defined by the outermost boundary, regardless of any other possible boundaries found.
>
> Finally, different objects are hatched differently by the HATCH command. Text, attributes, and shape objects have a rectangular boundary that follows the outline of the letters or the shape. AutoCAD recognizes solids and trace objects and does not perform hatching within their boundaries. Blocks are hatched according to the arrangement of objects

within the blocks. If the objects form boundaries, those boundaries are treated as normal object boundaries. Paper-space viewports are considered valid boundaries, so the HATCH command fills the viewport with the selected pattern.

Angle for crosshatch lines <0>   The U option, for defining a user-specific hatch pattern, presents this prompt. This pattern is a simple repeating line pattern with a set distance between each line. You can enter a value for the pattern angle or pick two points that describe the angle of the pattern.

Spacing between lines <1>   You enter the number of drawing units for the spacing between each line in the user-defined pattern.

Double hatch area? <N>   The user-defined hatch is a single series of repeating lines. This option adds another set of repeating lines drawn perpendicular to the first set of lines using the same spacing.

Scale for pattern <1>   This prompt is displayed after you enter a valid pattern name at the first HATCH command prompt. You enter a scale factor to be applied to the pattern definition to enlarge or reduce the hatch drawn.

Angle for pattern <0>   At this prompt, you enter an angle to rotate the pattern. Note that some hatch patterns are angled by default.

Select   This option presents the Select objects: prompt for specifying the objects to hatch.

Remove islands   After you have created a hatch boundary by selecting an internal point, use the Remove islands option to remove internal islands from the boundary set. This option presents the following prompt:

<Select island to remove>/Undo:

Advanced   The Advanced option presents the following prompt:

Boundary set/Retain polyline/Island detection/Associativity/<eXit>:

Boundary Set   See the BOUNDARY command.

Retain polyline   This option is used to retain the polyline used for the hatch boundary. This option presents the prompt Retain derived polylines? <N>.

Island detection   See the BOUNDARY command.

Associativity   This option determines whether or not the hatch pattern created is associated with its boundaries. Refer to the HATCHEDIT command.

eXit   This option exits the Advanced options.

<Internal point>   This is the default option for the -BHATCH command. You specify a point inside the desired hatch boundary.

-BHATCH

Example

The following example uses BHATCH to hatch an area bounded by various intersecting and nonintersecting objects (see fig. B.3). BHATCH performs this operation much faster than the HATCH command does.

Command: **BHATCH** (Enter)	Issues the BHATCH command
Click once on the Pattern Type image button	Sets the pattern name to ANSI32
Click on the Pick Points *button*	Prompts for the internal point for the boundary calculation
Select internal point *Pick* ①	Specifies the internal boundary point
Select internal point (Enter)	Terminates boundary calculation
Click on the Apply *button to finish hatching (see fig. B.4)*	

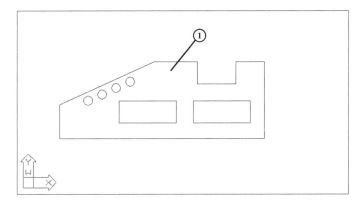

Figure B.3. *The area to hatch.*

Related Commands

BOUNDARY   EXPLODE   HATCH   HATCHEDIT

Related System Variables

HPANG   HPBOUND   HPDOUBLE   HPNAME
HPSCALE   HPSPACE   SNAPBASE

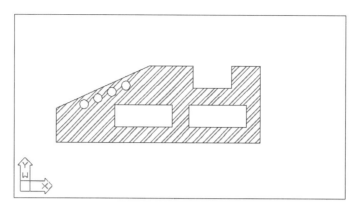

Figure B.4. *Completed hatch and boundary pick point.*

'BLIPMODE

The BLIPMODE command controls the creation of blips when you pick points on-screen.

A *blip* is a small plus sign (+) that appears at each pick point. Blips are not objects—you can clear them from the screen by using the REDRAW command. If you do not want to use blips, use BLIPMODE to turn off blip generation.

You also can control blips from the Drawing Aids dialog box (DDRMODES) command.

Prompts and Options

ON/OFF <On>   When BLIPMODE is on (the default), blips appear at pick points. When BLIPMODE is off, AutoCAD does not generate blips when you pick points.

Example

The following example shows how AutoCAD draws objects with BLIPMODE turned on and off (see fig. B.5).

'BLIPMODE

Command: **BLIPMODE** (Enter)	Issues the BLIPMODE command
ON/OFF <On>: (Enter)	Accepts the default value
Command: **LINE** (Enter)	Issues the LINE command
From point: *Pick point* ① (see fig. B.5)	Specifies line endpoints
To point: *Pick point* ②	
(Enter)	Terminates the LINE command
Command: **BLIPMODE** (Enter)	Issues the BLIPMODE command
ON/OFF <On>: **OFF** (Enter)	Turns BLIPMODE off
Command: **LINE** (Enter)	Issues the LINE command
From point: *Pick point* ③	Specifies line endpoints
To point: *Pick point* ④	
(Enter)	Terminates the LINE command

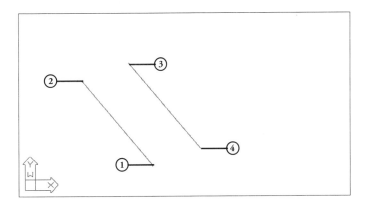

Figure B.5. *Using BLIPMODE.*

Related Command

DDRMODES

Related System Variable

BLIPMODE

BLOCK

Block
Insert Block

Pull-down: <u>C</u>onstruct, <u>B</u>lock

The BLOCK command groups AutoCAD objects together to form a single object within a drawing called a *block definition*. Blocks aid in organizing and drawing repetitive objects, reduce the size of the drawing, reduce drawing time, and enable the use of attributes.

When you create a block definition, you give it a name. You can then insert the block by its name. When you insert a block, you create a reference to the block's definition that has individual entity characteristics such as location, color, layer, or linetype. A block can be inserted as many times as needed. Inserting multiple copies of a block, rather than duplicating the individual objects, reduces the size of the drawing database. Blocks can be inserted at any X, Y, and Z scale and rotated at any angle.

> The entity property value *BYBLOCK* reflects the fact that individual insertions of a block are treated as unique objects within a drawing. You can assign a color or linetype to an inserted copy of a block using the change properties button. The objects within the block that were assigned BYBLOCK color or linetype properties will assume the values assigned the copy of the block.

To create versatile blocks, avoid assigning properties to a block's objects. If an entity within a block is assigned a specific layer, color, or linetype, you can no longer change these properties without exploding the block—it is *hard-coded*. In contrast, *soft-coded* objects within a block are defined on layer 0 with color and linetype BYLAYER or BYBLOCK. The appearance of the *soft-coded* objects in each inserted block is controlled by the layer the block is inserted on and the color and linetype the block is assigned.

Prompts and Options

Block name (or ?)   At this prompt, you specify a block name that is unique and not more than 31 characters in length. Letters, numbers, the dollar sign, the hyphen, and the underscore are valid characters for block names. The ? option displays the following prompt to list the blocks currently defined within the drawing:

`Block(s) to List <*>:`

You can press Enter at this prompt to list all the blocks currently defined within the drawing. You can use wild-card combinations to create more specific lists (the lists are presented in alphanumeric order).

Insertion base point This prompt requests the reference point, relative to the block itself, that will be used when inserting copies of the block.

Select objects Select the objects you want included in your block. You can use any standard object selection method.

When defining a block with attributes, the sequence in which you select the attributes to include establishes the sequence in which they will be displayed—such as when you insert, edit, or list the block.

After you have selected objects and the block has been created, the original objects are erased from the screen. You can use the OOPS command to restore those objects back into the drawing.

Example

This example demonstrates both the creation of a block as well as its reinsertion into the drawing using the INSERT command. The objects shown in figure B.6 are both the original objects and the block after its insertion.

Click on the BLOCK *tool*	Issues the BLOCK command
`Command: _block` `Block name (or ?):` **CAD-MAN** (Enter)	Specifies the name for the block
Use the ENDPOINT *tool to pick the following point*	
`Insertion base point: _endp of` *Pick point* ① *(see fig. B.6)*	Specifies the point that will be used to insert the block
`Select objects: Other corner: 8 found` *Pick points* ② *and* ③	Selects the objects to include in the block

```
Select objects: (Enter)                    Terminates object selection
Command: OOPS (Enter)                      Restores original objects to the
                                           screen
Command: INSERT (Enter)                    Issues the INSERT command
Block name (or ?): CAD-MAN (Enter)         Specifies the name of the block to
                                           insert
Insertion point: Pick point (4)            Specifies where to place the block
X scale factor <1> / Corner / XYZ:         Accepts default scale of 1
(Enter)
Y scale factor (default=X): (Enter)        Accepts default scale
Rotation angle <0>: (Enter)                Accepts default angle of 0
Command:
```

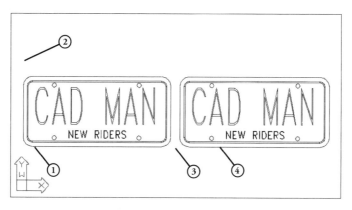

Figure B.6. *The objects that form the block.*

Related Commands

3DSOUT	ATTDEF	ATTDISP	ATTREDEF
BASE	DDATTDEF	DDINSERT	EXPLODE
GROUP	INSERT	MINSERT	OOPS
PURGE	RENAME	SHAPE	WBLOCK
XBIND	XPLODE	XREF	

Related System Variable

INSNAME

BMPOUT (Windows Only)

The BMPOUT command extracts selected objects as a Bitmap Image file. A *bitmap image* is a pixel-by-pixel definition of the screen display. Rather than describing where lines are, a bitmap image shows that a bunch of pixels all in a row are the same color. Most painting and screen layout programs use one form of bitmap image or another.

You must supply the output file name and the objects to be included in the bitmap image. These objects can be selected using any of the object selection methods.

Unfortunately, there are some drawbacks with BMPOUT. For example, the BMP file that is created cannot be read by Microsoft Paintbrush. If you attempt to open this BMP file with Paintbrush, you get an error message complaining that the format of this BMP is not supported.

BMPOUT is sensitive to screen resolution. This is due to the BMP file format. Create your BMP images in no greater than 800×600 resolution.

Prompts and Options

File name   If FILEDIA is off, you'll be prompted at the command line to enter a file name. Enter the full file name, including the .bmp extension. If FILEDIA is on, you'll see the Select BMP File dialog box appear. In this case, you don't need to include the .bmp extension in the file name edit box—AutoCAD will append the .bmp extension automatically.

If you are in Windows with multiple applications running, be sure to supply a full path with your file name. This saves the time otherwise spent searching to find where the file landed.

Select Objects   Select the objects to be included in the bitmap image output file, using any of the standard AutoCAD object selection methods.

Be aware that objects not in or perpendicular to the plane of the current UCS may cause the BMPOUT utility to fail.

Example

This example shows you how to create a BMP file consisting of objects selected in your drawing. Open an existing drawing (the sample COLORWH.DWG is shown here), or create a new drawing (see fig. B.7). Note that FILEDIA is turned off in this example, and the full file name (including the .bmp extension) is entered at the File name prompt.

```
Command: BMPOUT                        Starts BMPOUT command

File name <COLORWH>:                   Specifies output BMP file name
COLORWH.BMP

Select objects: ALL                    Selects all objects in drawing

587 found

Select objects: (Enter)                Finishes object selection
```

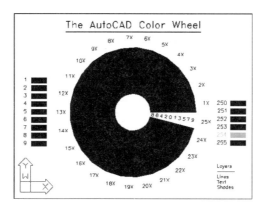

Figure B.7. *The BMPOUT file selection box.*

Related Commands

COPYCLIP	COPYHIST	COPYLINK	CUTCLIP
DXFOUT	EXPORT	MSLIDE	PCXOUT
PSOUT	SAVEIMG	TIFFIN	WMFOUT

-BOUNDARY

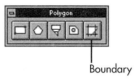

Toolbar: *Boundary, (Draw, Polygon)*
Pull-down: *Construct, Bounding Polyline*
Screen: CONSTRUCT, BOUNDAR:

The BOUNDARY command creates a new polyline object or region that outlines an area defined by existing objects. BOUNDARY performs a subset of the functions of the BHATCH command, but it does not hatch the enclosed area. Figure B.8 shows the Boundary Creation dialog box.

Figure B.8. *The Boundary Creation dialog box.*

BOUNDARY is especially useful for creating irregular closed polylines from construction lines, arcs, circles, and other objects.

Dialog Box Items

As shown in figure B.8, the Boundary Creation dialog box offers the following options:

Object Type. Use this pull-down list box to specify whether the BOUNDARY command will generate a polyline boundary or region.

Define Boundary Set. Options in this group specify the way boundary objects are calculated. Clicking on the Make New Boundary Set button enables you to pick objects on-screen. If a selection set is already active, the From E<u>x</u>isting Boundary Set radio button is enabled, and you can add or remove objects. The From E<u>v</u>erything on Screen radio button causes all visible objects to be considered.

<u>R</u>ay Casting. This option specifies the direction that AutoCAD first searches to find boundary objects. You can choose one direction from the positive and negative X and Y axes by selecting a method from the drop-down list box. This option is not available unless Island <u>D</u>etection is turned off.

Island <u>D</u>etection. This box is checked by default so that AutoCAD will determine if there are any islands (internal objects) within the boundary selection set. Clear this box to prevent boundaries from being drawn around islands.

Boolean Subtract Islands. This check box is enabled only when you select Region as the object type for the boundary. Checking it will subtract islands from the region. Clearing it will force AutoCAD to ignore islands when creating the region.

<u>P</u>ick Points. Click on this button to pick a point on-screen to define the area from which you want a polyline or region to be made.

Prompts and Options

The command-line version of the BOUNDARY command (-BOUNDARY) has many of the same options as the dialog box version discussed above. -BOUNDARY presents the following prompt:

```
Advanced options/<Internal point>
```

Advanced options   This option issues the following prompt:

```
Boundary set/Island detection/Object type/<eXit>
```

> **Boundary set**   Use this option if you want to define new boundary sets for hatching. This option displays the following prompt:
> ```
> Specify candidate set for boundary
> New/<Everything>:
> ```
> If the New option is selected, you are presented with a `Select objects:` prompt.
>
> **Island detection**   This option is used to determine whether or not AutoCAD will consider "islands" (objects within other boundaries) as a part of the hatch boundary. This option displays the following prompt:
> ```
> Do you want island detection? <Y>.
> ```

-BOUNDARY

Object type   This option determines whether the boundary object is a polyline or region. It issues the following prompt:

Region/Polyline/<Polyline>:.

<eXit>   This option exits the Advanced options.

<Internal point>   This is the default option for the -BOUNDARY command. It is asking you to pick a point for boundary calculation.

Example

The following example uses BOUNDARY to create a closed polyline boundary out of various construction objects. Figure B.9 shows the original objects and the polylines created by the BOUNDARY command.

Command: **BOUNDARY** (Enter)	Issues the BOUNDARY command
Click on the Pick Points button	Issues prompt for selecting a point
Select internal point: *Pick point* ①	Specifies point for boundary calculation
Selecting everything... Selecting everything visible... Analyzing the selected data... Analyzing internal islands...	
Select internal point: (Enter)	Terminates boundary calculation
BOUNDARY created 8 polylines	

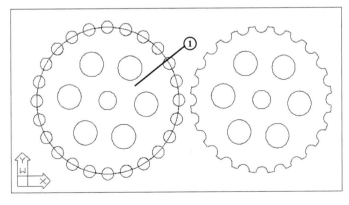

Figure B.9. *Boundary polylines created by BOUNDARY.*

Related Commands

BHATCH   HATCH   PLINE   REGION

Related System Variable

HPBOUND

BOX

Toolbar: *(Solids, Box)*
Pull-down: *Draw, Solids, Box* (DOS Only)
Screen: DRAW2, SOLIDS, Box:

The BOX command creates a three-dimensional ACIS SOLID shaped like a box. The box is placed parallel to the current UCS. The size of the box can be specified by length, width, and height, or by picking two opposite base corners and entering a height. A cube also can be created.

Don't confuse the BOX command with the 3D command's Box option. The BOX command creates an ACIS SOLID object, while the 3D command's Box option creates a polygon mesh surface object.

Prompts and Options

`Center/<Corner of box><0,0,0>` Specify the first corner of the box. You may also choose the Center option to specify the centroid position of the box. The default places the corner of the box at the origin of the current UCS.

> To create a rotated box, rotate the UCS, and then use the BOX command to create the box.

`Center of box <0,0,0>` Pick a point in the graphics window, or enter the coordinates for the center point of the box. The default places the center of the box at the origin of the current UCS.

`Cube/Length/<other corner>` Pick a point, or enter the coordinates of the other corner of the box. If the other corner lies in the same construction plane as the first corner, you'll be prompted to enter the height of the box. If the other corner lies above or below the first corner, the difference in elevation is used as the height. If the other corner lies directly above the first corner, AutoCAD responds with the following:

`Box of zero length not permitted.`

You are re-prompted to pick the other corner. You can choose the Cube option to specify a box having the same length and width and height. Choose the Length option to specify a differing length, width, and height.

`Length` Specify the length of the box along the X axis. If you choose the Cube option, this length also is used for the width and height.

`Width` Specify the width of the box along the Y axis, either by picking two points to show a distance, or entering a number.

`Height` Specify the height of the box along the Z axis.

Example

The following example shows you how to create an ACIS SOLID box object. The example shows the creation of the box with a view taken from a viewpoint of 3,-3,1 looking toward the origin, 0,0,0 (see fig. B.10).

```
Command: BOX (Enter)                    Starts BOX command
Center/<Corner of box>                  Specify first corner of box
<0,0,0>: 5,5,2 (Enter)
```

```
Cube/Length/<other corner>:        Use Length option
L Enter
Length: 6 Enter                    Specify a length of 6
Width: 2 Enter                     Specify a width of 2
Height: -3 Enter                   Specify a height of -3
```

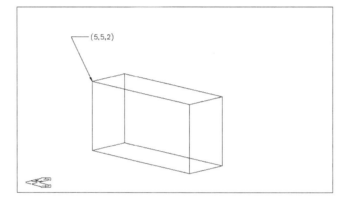

Figure B.10. *An ACIS SOLID box.*

Related Commands

EXTRUDE   INTERFERE   INTERSECTION
SUBTRACT   UNION

BPOLY

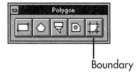

See BOUNDARY.

BREAK

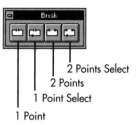

1 Point
1 Point Select
2 Points
2 Points Select

Toolbar: *(Modify, Break)*
Pull-down: *Modify, Break*
Screen: MODIFY, Break:

The BREAK command removes a portion of a line, arc, polyline, spline, xline, ray, ellipse, or circle, and prompts you to select the target object and specify the first and second points of the break. You can break only one entity at a time. If the first and second break points are identical, the entity is divided at that point. Break cannot be used with solid objects.

Prompts and Options

Select object Select the object to break. By default, the point by which you pick the object is considered the first point of the segment to remove, unless you respecify the point below. Only one entity can be selected at one time.

Enter second point (or F for first point) Select another point on the object to break between. The original object-selection point becomes the opposite end of the break, and the portion of the entity between the two points will be removed. If you enter an **F** to specify the first point of the break, the following prompts appear:

> **Enter first point** You specify a first point of the break that is different from the original object-selection point.
>
> **Enter second point** The second point determines the portion of the entity to remove.

To break a line or other object into two segments with no gap between them, use the @ symbol to specify the second break point. The @ symbol tells AutoCAD to use the last point selected.

TIP

Preset Options

The AutoCAD menu has four preprogrammed versions of the BREAK command, as follows (see the BREAK toolbar, shown previously):

1 Point. Use this to break an object into two segments without creating a gap. The point used to select the object becomes the first and second break point. It is the same as the command sequence BREAK @.

1 Point Select. Use this option to select the object and then specify the single break point. It is the same as the command sequence BREAK F @.

2 Points. This option is used to create a gap in the selected object. The point used to select the object becomes the first break point. You specify the second break point. It is the same as issuing the BREAK command without preprogrammed options.

2 Points Select. Use this option to create a gap in the selected object by specifying the two break points regardless of the point used to select the object. It is the same as the command sequence BREAK F.

The points you pick to specify the break do not have to reside on the object you are breaking. AutoCAD generates the nearest x value and y value to the current cursor location. For accurate breaks, however, use appropriate object snaps.

Example

This example demonstrates how you can use the BREAK command to remove a section of an object. Figure B.11 shows both the original object and the result of using the command.

Command: **BREAK** (Enter)	Issues the BREAK command
Select object: *Pick point* ① (*see fig. B.11*)	Selects the object to break
Enter second point (or F for first point): **F** (Enter)	Chooses the first point option
Enter first point: *Pick point* ②	Specifies the first break point
Enter second point: *Pick point* ③	Specifies the second break point

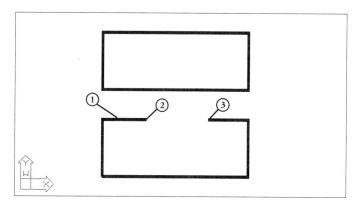

Figure B.11. *The objects before and after using BREAK.*

Related Command

TRIM

Related System Variable

LASTPOINT

'CAL

Calculator

Toolbar: *Calculator (Object Snap)*
Pull-down: **T**ools, Calc**u**lator
Screen: TOOLS, GeomCal:

The CAL command is an online geometry calculator that evaluates points, vectors, or real and integer expressions. Calculations can use object snap modes to access existing geometry, and CAL can be issued transparently within another command to provide a point or number. CAL can also be used in AutoLISP functions.

NOTE: If you use the AutoCAD object snap modes in your expressions, enter the three-character abbreviations of the object snap modes. You must pick objects—you cannot use the object selection methods.

The geometry calculator is ideally suited to solving engineering and physics problems involving linear algebra and vector calculus. CAL follows the standard mathematical order of precedence in evaluating expressions. Vectors and points are entered as a set of points or distance and angles. When you enter points in the WCS, use the * prefix, as in [*2,3,4]. Use the * for the dot product of vectors and the & for the cross products of vectors. Numbers also can be entered in scientific notation. You can include ' and " for feet and inches on distances. Angles default to degrees; however, you can use the r suffix for radians or the g suffix for gradians. All angles are converted to degrees. See the *AutoCAD Command Reference* for a complete list of the CAL functions and modes.

NOTE: The CAL command is implemented through an external *AutoCAD Development System* (ADS) file named GEOMCAL.EXE or GEOMCAL.EXP. If the CAL command does not function, you might need to load this external file. To do so, type the following at the command prompt:

```
(xload "geomcal") (Enter)
```

Examples

The following examples use CAL to solve equations and to return points and vectors to other commands (see fig. C.1).

Command: **CAL** (Enter)	Issues the CAL command
>> Expression: **A=(5.25+10.5)/1.5^2** (Enter) 7.0	Assigns the value of an expression to variable A
Command: (Enter)	Re-issues the CAL command
CAL >> Expression: **B=3*(14-7)** (Enter) 21	Assigns the value of an expression to variable B
Command: (Enter)	Re-issues the CAL command

CAL >> Expression: **B/A** (Enter) 3.0	Calculates the value of the value assigned to variable B divided by the value assigned to variable A

In the next example, you will convert a calculated distance from inches to centimeters.

Command: (Enter)	Re-issues the CAL command
CAL >> Expression: **CVUNIT(DIST(END,INT),INCH,CM)** (Enter)	Specifies the expression to evaluate
>> Select entity for END snap: *Pick point ① (see fig. C.1)*	Specifies the first point for the DIST function
>> Select entity for INT snap: *Pick point ②*	Specifies the second point for the DIST function
5.08	Calculated value

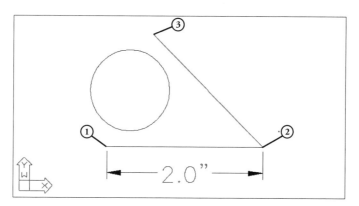

Figure C.1. *Objects and pick points for CAL.*

In the following example, you will draw a circle at the calculated midpoint between two line endpoints, with a radius one-third the distance between the two endpoints.

Click on the CIRCLE tool	
Command: _circle (Enter)	Issues the CIRCLE command
3P/2P/TTR/<Center point>: 'CAL (Enter)	Issues the CAL command transparently
>> Expression: MEE (Enter)	Executes the shortcut of the expression (end+end)/2
>> Select one endpoint for MEE: *Pick point ③ (see fig. C.1)*	Specifies one endpoint for the mee function
>> Select another endpoint for MEE: *Pick point ①*	Specifies the second endpoint
Diameter/<Radius>: 'CAL (Enter)	Re-issues the CAL command transparently
>> Expression: DIST(END,END)/3 (Enter)	Calculates one-third the distance between two endpoints
>> Select entity for END snap: *Pick point ③*	Specifies one endpoint for the distance calculation
>> Select entity for END snap: *Pick point ①*	Specifies the second endpoint

CHAMFER

Chamfer

Toolbar: *Chamfer (Modify, Feature)*
Pull-down: <u>C</u>onstruct, C<u>h</u>amfer
Screen: CONSTRCT, Chamfer:

The CHAMFER command creates a bevel, called a *chamfer*, between two nonparallel lines or on continuous segments of 2D polylines. CHAMFER extends or optionally trims lines as necessary and adds a line to create the beveled edge. With 2D polylines, it adds vertices and a new segment representing the bevel. CHAMFER can also be used to bevel the edges of solid objects.

CHAMFER

You must supply the distance for the start of the bevel from the intersection of the two segments. You can set different distances for each side of the chamfer to create custom bevels.

> If the TRIMMODE system variable is set to 0, the chamfer will be created, but the existing lines will not be trimmed.

Prompts and Options

```
(TRIM mode) Current chamfer Dist1 = 0.0000, Dist2 = 0.0000
Polyline/Distance/Angle/Trim/Method/<Select first line>
```

<Select first line>   The default choice at this prompt is to select the first of two lines for chamfering. The first chamfer distance is applied to this line. You then select a second line at the prompt `Select second line:`. Your selection completes the CHAMFER command. The second chamfer distance is applied to this line.

Polyline   With this option, you select a 2D polyline for chamfering. AutoCAD attempts to apply the chamfer at every vertex between two segments of the polyline. This option displays the prompt:

`Select 2D polyline:`

Distance   The Distance option enables you to preset the chamfer distances applied to both sides of the objects' intersection. This option displays the prompt `Enter first chamfer distance <current>:`. You can type a distance or specify a distance by picking two points on the screen. At the next prompt, `Enter second chamfer distance <current>:`, you specify a distance from the intersection where the chamfer will start on the second line selected. This value defaults to be the same distance as the value for the first chamfer distance.

> CHAMFER can be used to join lines at their point of intersection by using first and second distances of 0 (see also FILLET).

Angle   Use the angle option to specify the angle of the chamfer starting a specified distance from the objects' intersection. The following two prompts are displayed:

`Enter chamfer length on the first line <0.0000>:`

`Enter chamfer angle from the first line <0.0000>:`

Trim Use the trim option to trim the objects to the chamfer line or leave them as they are. This option presents the following prompt:

```
Trim/No trim <Trim>:
```

Method Use this option to determine how the chamfer is calculated and drawn. The two choices are Angle and Distance. This option issues the following prompt:

```
Distance/Angle <Distance>:
```

Example

This example demonstrates the differences between chamfering two lines and chamfering a single polyline with the CHAMFER command. Figure C.2 shows the results of using the CHAMFER command on both types of objects.

Click on the CHAMFER tool	Issues the CHAMFER command
`Command: _chamfer`	
`(TRIM mode) Current chamfer Length = 1.0000, Angle = 45.0000`	
`Polyline/Distance/Angle/Trim/Method/ <Select first line>:` **D** (Enter)	Selects the Distance option
`Enter first chamfer distance <0.0000>:` **.3** (Enter)	Specifies the chamfer distance along the first selected line
`Enter second chamfer distance <0.3000>:`	Specifies the distance along the second selected line
`Command:` (Enter)	Re-issues the CHAMFER command
`CHAMFER`	
`(TRIM mode) Current chamfer Dist1 = 0.3000, Dist2 = 0.0000`	
`Polyline/Distance/Angle/Trim/Method/ <Select first line>:` **P** (Enter)	Selects the Polyline option
`Select 2D polyline:` *Pick point* ① *(see fig. C.2)*	Selects the polyline to chamfer
`6 lines were chamfered`	
`Command:` (Enter)	Re-issues the CHAMFER command
`CHAMFER`	

CHAMFER

```
(TRIM mode) Current chamfer
Dist1 = 0.3000, Dist2 = 0.0000

Polyline/Distance/Angle/Trim/Method/          Selects the Angle option
<Select first line>: A (Enter)

Enter chamfer length on the first             Specifies the distance from the
line<1.0000>: .5 (Enter)                      intersection for the chamfer

Enter chamfer angle from the first            Specifies the angle of the chamfer
line <45.0000>: 45 (Enter)

Command: (Enter)                              Re-issues the CHAMFER command

CHAMFER

(TRIM mode) Current chamfer
Length = 0.5000, Angle = 45.0000

Polyline/Distance/Angle/Trim/Method/          Selects the first line to chamfer
<Select first line>: Pick point ②

Select second line: Pick point ③              Selects the second line to chamfer
```

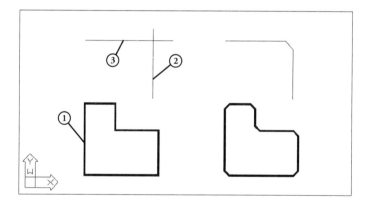

Figure C.2. *Using the CHAMFER command.*

Related Commands

FILLET   TRIM

Related System Variables

CHAMFERA   CHAMFERB   CHAMFERC   CHAMFERD
CHAMMODE   TRIMMODE

CHANGE

Pull-down: <u>M</u>odify, Poi<u>n</u>t
Screen: MODIFY, Change:

The CHANGE command changes existing objects' properties, including color, linetype, layer, and text style. You can use CHANGE whenever you want to modify the properties of selected objects, edit text, or change a point's location.

Prompts and Options

`Select objects` At this prompt, you can choose objects individually or by using one of the other object selection options. Except for lines with a zero thickness, all objects must be parallel to the current *User Coordinate System* (UCS). The prompt repeats until you press Enter to end the object-selection process. When you finish object selection, the following prompt is displayed:

`Properties/<change point>:`

Property

`Change what property (Color/Elev/LAyer/LType/ltScale/Thickness)` At this prompt, you can change various properties of the objects you have selected.

The first option, `Color`, changes the color of selected objects. Objects with an explicit color assignment do not take on the color characteristics of the layer they reside on. To force objects to assume the parent layer's color, assign the special BYLAYER color property.

The `Elev` option sets the base elevation of the objects selected.

The `LAyer` option changes the layer on which the selected objects reside. The target layer must already exist.

> If you specify a layer that does not exist, AutoCAD displays the message `Layer not found` and prompts you for another layer name. Use the transparent 'DDLMODES command, which enables you to create a new layer, and then return to the CHANGE command.

The LType option changes the linetype of selected objects. Objects with an explicit linetype assignment do not take on the linetype characteristics of the layer on which they reside. To force objects to assume the parent layer's linetype, assign the special BYLAYER linetype property.

Use the ltScale option to change the linetype scale of the selected object independently of the LTSCALE system variable setting.

The Thickness option changes the thickness, or extrusion value, of selected objects.

Don't confuse "thickness" with line "width." *Thickness* refers to how an object is extruded or "stretched" in the Z direction. Use the PEDIT command to assign a width to a line, polyline, or arc.

Change Point

This option acts in different ways, depending on object type, as shown in the following table.

Table C.1
Change Point Option Functions

Object Type	Function of Change Point Option
Lines	Enables you to move the endpoints of selected lines. If Ortho mode is turned on, the selected lines are drawn horizontally or vertically, depending on the new point selected. If Ortho mode is turned off, the selected lines converge at the new point.
Text	Edits each text object in your selection set. You can change the text style, height, rotation angle, or text string.
Circle	Resizes the circle's radius. The circle's center point remains stationary.
Block	Changes the insertion point or the rotation angle of selected blocks.
Attribute Definition	Edits attribute definitions just like text, with a few additional options. You also can change the attribute tag, prompt, and default value.

Example

The following example shows how to use CHANGE on line objects.

Command: **CHANGE** (Enter)	Issues the CHANGE command
Select objects: *Pick points ① and ② (see fig. C.3)*	Selects the object to change
2 found	
Select objects: (Enter)	Ends object selection
Properties/<Change point>: *Pick point ③*	Specifies the change point

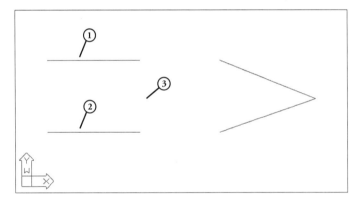

Figure C.3. *Two lines with changed endpoints before and after.*

Related Commands

CHPROP DDCHPROP DDEDIT DDMODIFY
SCALE   SPELL

CHPROP

CHPROP, which stands for *CHange PROPerties*, offers a simple, direct method for modifying the properties of existing objects instead of using the Properties option of the CHANGE command. It also modifies the properties of all the objects in a selection set at the same time. CHPROP performs a subset of the editing options available with the CHANGE command.

CHPROP

> The functionality of the CHPROP command has been replaced by the DDCHPROP and DDMODIFY commands.

Prompts and Options

See the CHANGE command options under Property.

Example

This example shows how the CHPROP options enable you to perform most of the same types of object editing as the CHANGE command. Figure C.4 shows both the original and new versions of the line objects modified with this command.

Command: **CHPROP** (Enter)	Issues the CHPROP command
Select objects: *Pick point* ① *and* ② *(see fig. C.4)*	Selects the objects to modify
2 found	
Select objects: (Enter)	Terminates object selection
Change what property (Color/LAyer/LType/Thickness) ? **LT** (Enter)	Specifies the linetype option
New linetype <BYLAYER>: **HIDDEN** (Enter)	Specifies the linetype to use
Change what property (Color/LAyer/LType/Thickness) ? (Enter)	Terminates the CHPROP command

Related Commands

CHANGE   DDCHPROP   DDEDIT   DDMODIFY

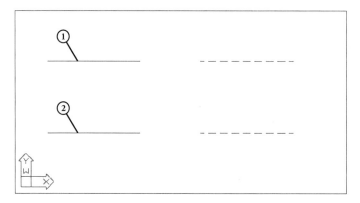

Figure C.4. *Line objects modified by the CHPROP command's LType option.*

CIRCLE

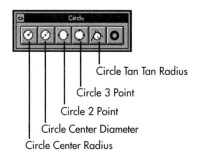

Toolbar: *(Draw, Circle)*
Pull-down: *Draw, Circle*
Screen: DRAW1, Circle:

The CIRCLE command draws circles. Circles are created at the current elevation, parallel to the current *User Coordinate System* (UCS). By setting the ELEV command's THICKNESS option to a non-zero value, you also can create 3D cylinders. These cylinders are simply extruded circles that have a top or bottom, not to be confused with cylinder 3D solids.

The VIEWRES system variable controls the display of curved surfaces such as circles. See the VIEWRES command for more information.

Prompts and Options

The CIRCLE command displays the following prompt:

```
3P/2P/TTR/<Center point>:
```

3P The 3P option enables you to define a circle by specifying three points on the circle's circumference. This option displays the following prompts in sequence for specifying the points:

```
First point:
Second point:
Third point:
```

2P The 2P option enables you to create a circle by selecting two points defining the diameter. The following prompts are displayed in sequence:

```
First point on diameter:
Second point on diameter:
```

TTR The TTR option (Tangent to/Tangent to/Radius) enables you to specify two points on existing objects that will be tangent to the new circle, and then supply the new circle's radius. If no circle can be drawn that meets the specifications you supply, AutoCAD responds with `Circle does not exist`.

AutoCAD automatically assigns the tangent object snap override to the first two points you pick. The TTR option displays the following prompts in sequence:

```
Enter Tangent spec:
Enter second Tangent spec:
Radius <current>:
```

<Center point> This default option enables you to specify the center point of the circle. This option displays the prompt shown in the first item of this list:

> **Diameter/<Radius> <current>** You specify the circle's radius (the default option) or enter D to select the diameter option. You can enter a value from the keyboard or pick two points on the screen to specify the radius distance.
>
> **Diameter** At this prompt, you enter a value for the circle's diameter. You can enter a value from the keyboard or pick two points on the screen to specify the diameter distance.

Example

This example demonstrates two methods for creating circles, as shown in figure C.5.

```
Command: CIRCLE (Enter)                                     Issues the CIRCLE command

3P/2P/TTR/<Center point>:                                   Specifies the center of the circle
Pick point ① (see fig. C.5)

Diameter/<Radius>: 1.5 (Enter)                              Specifies the radius of the circle

Command: (Enter)                                            Reissues the CIRCLE command

CIRCLE 3P/2P/TTR/<Center point>: TTR (Enter)                Specifies the Tangent to/
                                                            Tangent to/Radius option

Enter Tangent spec: Pick point ②                            Selects the first object to which
                                                            the circle must be tangent

Enter second Tangent spec: Pick                             Selects the second object to
point ③                                                      which the circle must be tangent

Radius <1.5000>: 2.25 (Enter)                               Specifies the circle radius
```

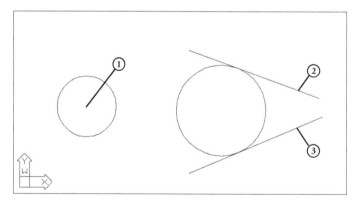

Figure C.5. *Circles created using the Center/Radius and Tangent to/Tangent to/Radius options.*

Related Commands

DONUT   ELLIPSE   VIEWRES

Related System Variables

CIRCLERAD   VIEWRES

'COLOR

Screen: DATA, Color:

The COLOR command controls the color of new objects. The DDCOLOR command has replaced the function of COLOR.

TIP

> For best results, keep the color value specified by the COLOR command set to BYLAYER. Use the LAYER command's default color to control object color, which helps to easily identify different layers in your drawing and to redefine colors.

Prompts and Options

New object color <BYLAYER> Valid entries include BYLAYER (the default), and BYBLOCK. You also can enter a color number or name at the prompt. The COLOR command accepts a number from 1 to 255 or the name of the first seven colors (see the DDCOLOR command for a list of these).

Related Command

DDCOLOR

Related System Variable

CECOLOR

COMPILE

Pull-down: <u>T</u>ools, Compi<u>l</u>e
Screen: TOOLS, Compile:

The COMPILE command transforms font and shape definition files (SHP files) into their vector equivalent SHX files. AutoCAD requires font and shape definitions be in vector format, as found in SHX files, in order to display them. In addition to AutoCAD's native shape source file format, SHP, COMPILE also transforms Adobe Type1 font files (PFB files) into SHX files.

The STYLE command references these compiled font files that contain text-character definitions to create styles for use by the dimensioning, TEXT,

DTEXT, and MTEXT commands. A compiled shape file contains either a text-character definition, or definitions of symbols for use by the LOAD and SHAPE commands.

When you issue the COMPILE command, AutoCAD displays the Select Shape or Font File dialog box listing SHP files. Select the desired source file name; AutoCAD compiles it into a SHP file. If successful, COMPILE displays a command-line message noting the size and name of the file produced. COMPILE responds with an error message if it encounters errors in the source file, such as the following:

```
Bad shape definition at line 34 of TXT.shp:
No end-of-shape marker
```

Example

The following example shows you how to transform the standard italic text definition file, ITALIC.SHP, into its vector equivalent, ITALIC.SHX, using the COMPILE command.

Command: **COMPILE**   Starts COMPILE command

Select ITALIC.SHP *from the* COMMON/FONTS/SOURCE
directory (see fig. C.6)

```
Compiling shape/font description file

Compilation successful. Output file

ITALIC.shx contains 27162 bytes.
```

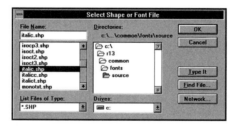

Figure C.6. *The Select Shape or Font File dialog box.*

Related Commands

LOAD   SHAPE   STYLE

CONE

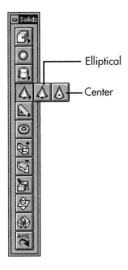

Toolbar: *(Solids, Cone)*
Pull-down: *D̲raw, CONE Su̲rfaces*
Screen: DRAW2, SOLIDS, Cone:

The CONE command creates a three-dimensional ACIS SOLID shaped like a cone. The cone can be placed parallel to the current UCS, or oriented by specifying the center point of the base and the apex point. The size of the cone can be specified by the radius or diameter of the base, and the height. The shape of the base of the cone can either be round or elliptical.

Don't confuse the CONE command with the 3D command's Cone option. The CONE command creates an ACIS SOLID object, while the 3D command's Cone option creates a polygon mesh surface object.

TIP

> To create a truncated ACIS SOLID cone, create a pointed ACIS SOLID cone first. Then create an ACIS SOLID box at the position to truncate the cone, making sure the box encloses the portion of the cone that you want to remove. Use the SUBTRACT command to subtract the box from the cone to create a truncated cone.

Prompts and Options

Elliptical/<center point> <0,0,0> Specify the center point of the base of the cone. You may also choose the Elliptical option to create a cone with an ellipsoidal base.

Diameter/<Radius> Specify a value or pick a point to show a distance for the radius of the cone, or enter **D** if you prefer to specify a value for the diameter of the cone's base.

Diameter Enter a value or pick a point to show a distance for the diameter of the cone's base.

Apex/<Height> Enter a value or pick a point to show a distance for the height of the cone. You may also enter **A** to choose the Apex option, and specify the apex point of the cone.

Apex Pick a point in the graphics window, or enter the coordinates of the desired apex point of the cone. The cone will then be oriented such that the height of the cone is measured from the center point of the base to this apex point.

Center/<Axis endpoint> This prompt appears if you choose the Elliptical option to create a cone with a base shaped like an ellipse. Pick a point in the graphics window, or enter the coordinates of the first endpoint for one of the axes of the ellipse. You may also choose the Center option to pick the center point of the ellipse.

Center of ellipse <0,0,0> This prompt appears after choosing the Center option if you also chose the Elliptical option to create a cone with an ellipse shaped base. Pick a point in the graphics window, or enter the coordinates of the center of the ellipse.

Axis endpoint This prompt appears after you have specified the center of the ellipse. Pick a point in the graphics window, or enter coordinates to locate the edge of the ellipse as measured from the ellipse's center.

Axis endpoint 2 This prompt appears after picking the first axis endpoint. Pick the second axis endpoint for the ellipse of the cone base.

Other axis distance Enter the distance for the ellipse's other axis, as measured from the center point of the ellipse. You can also show a distance by picking a point in the graphics window.

Example

This example shows how to create an ACIS SOLID Cone object. The viewpoint is taken from the point 3,-3,1 looking toward the origin, 0,0,0 (see fig. C.7).

```
Command: CONE (Enter)                    Starts CONE command
Elliptical/<center point>                Specify center of cone base
  <0,0,0>: 8,4,-2 (Enter)
Diameter/<Radius>: 3 (Enter)             Enter a base radius of 3 units
Apex/<Height>: 6 (Enter)                 Enter a height of 6 units
```

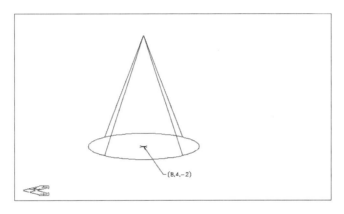

Figure C.7. *An ACIS SOLID Cone object.*

Related Commands

INTERFERE   INTERSECTION   SUBTRACT   UNION

CONFIG

Pull-down: **O**ptions, **C**onfigure
Screen: OPTIONS, Config:

The CONFIG command enables you to configure the devices that AutoCAD uses and the various parameters that control the way AutoCAD works. You can configure AutoCAD any time the program is active, even with a drawing loaded. See your *AutoCAD Interface, Installation, and Performance Guide* for details on choices available on your particular computer platform.

The current AutoCAD configuration is stored in the ACAD.CFG file. Each section in the ACAD.CFG file lists configuration options for a specific device.

While it's possible to edit the ACAD.CFG file directly, remember that any incorrect instructions will result in AutoCAD not operating properly. It is possible to edit the ACAD.CFG file incorrectly, and cause AutoCAD to fail to run. If this happens, delete or rename the ACAD.CFG file, and restart AutoCAD. AutoCAD will build a new ACAD.CFG file.

Prompts and Options

When you first execute the CONFIG command, it displays your current hardware configuration. A configuration menu is then displayed. It offers the following choices:

Exit to drawing editor   This option returns to the drawing when you are finished making additions or changes. You are always prompted to save any changes, even if no changes were made.

Show current configuration   This option displays a list of the current hardware configuration. The currently selected and configured video display, digitizer, and plotter(s) are displayed.

Allow detailed configuration   This option enables prompting for advanced configuration information by the other configuration options. Additional questions will be asked when configuring individual devices.

Configure video display   This option enables selection of a different video display, or changes to the current one.

Configure digitizer   This option enables selection of a different pointing device, or changes to the current one.

Configure plotter   This option enables selection and configuration of hard-copy output devices. Up to 29 different hard-copy devices can be specified and configured.

Configure system console   This option enables selection of platform-specific console options. Not all platforms have system console options that may be changed.

Configure operating parameters   This option enables configuration of various directories, files, data integrity, and networking features. This option presents a menu with the following options:

```
Exit to configuration menu
Alarm on error
Initial drawing setup
Default plot file name
Plot spooler directory
Placement of temporary files
Network node name
Automatic-save feature
Speller dialect
Full-time CRC validation
Automatic Audit after DXFIN, or DXBIN
Login name
File locking
Authorization
```

Enter selection <0> Enter the number corresponding to your choice and follow the prompts displayed.

Example

The following example shows how to change the current login name using the CONFIG command. This change forces AutoCAD to exit. It is a good idea to save your current drawing before running the CONFIG command. You can verify your current login name from the system variable LOGINNAME.

Command: **CONFIG** (Enter)   Begins the CONFIG command

AutoCAD will display your header banner, then the current configuration, then configuration menu options.

```
Current AutoCAD configuration
  Video display:
    Accelerated Display Driver by Rasterex (International) a.s for
    Autodesk, Inc
      Version: 13
  Digitizer:
    Current System Pointing Device
  Plotter:
    System Printer ADI 4.2 - by Autodesk, Inc
      Model:
      Version: R.0.90-1
  Speller Dialect:
    American English
Press RETURN to continue:

Configuration menu
  0.  Exit to drawing editor
  1.  Show current configuration
```

```
    2.  Allow detailed configuration
    3.  Configure video display
    4.  Configure digitizer
    5.  Configure plotter
    6.  Configure system console
    7.  Configure operating parameters
Enter selection <0>: 7 (Enter)
```
Configure operating parameters

```
Configure operating parameters

    0.  Exit to configuration menu
    1.  Alarm on error
    2.  Initial drawing setup
    3.  Default plot file name
    4.  Plot spooler directory
    5.  Placement of temporary files
    6.  Network node name
    7.  Automatic-save feature
    8.  Speller Dialect
    9.  Full-time CRC validation
    10. Automatic Audit after DXFIN, or DXBIN
    11. Login name
    12. File locking
    13. Authorization

Enter selection <0>: 11 (Enter)
```
Change login name

```
Enter default login
name or . for none <>:
Gottfried Stutz (Enter)
```
Enter desired login name

```
Configure operating parameters

    0.  Exit to configuration menu

    1.  Alarm on error
    2.  Initial drawing setup
    3.  Default plot file name
    4.  Plot spooler directory
    5.  Placement of temporary files
    6.  Network node name
    7.  Automatic-save feature
    8.  Full-time CRC validation
    9.  Automatic Audit after DXFIN, or DXBIN
    10. Login name
    11. File locking

Enter selection <0>: (Enter)
```
Exit to configuration menu

The header information displays, and you are returned to the first menu.

```
Configuration menu

    0.  Exit to drawing editor
    1.  Show current configuration
    2.  Allow detailed configuration
    3.  Configure video display
    4.  Configure digitizer
    5.  Configure plotter
    6.  Configure system console
    7.  Configure operating parameters

Enter selection <0>: (Enter)         Exit to drawing editor
```

If you answer N to the following question, all configuration changes you have just made will be discarded.

```
Keep configuration                   Keep change to login name
changes? <Y> (Enter)
```

Related Commands

| PLOT | PREFERENCES | RCONFIG | REINIT |
| TABLET | TBCONFIG | | |

Related System Variables

| LOGINNAME | PLOTID | PLOTTER | POPUPS |
| SCREENBOXES | SCREENMODE | TABMODE | |

COPY

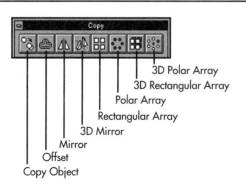

Copy Object
Offset
Mirror
3D Mirror
Rectangular Array
Polar Array
3D Rectangular Array
3D Polar Array

Toolbar: *Copy Object (Modify, Copy)*
Pull-down: <u>C</u>onstruct, <u>C</u>opy
Screen: CONSTRUCT, Copy:

The COPY command makes single or multiple copies of as many existing objects as you want. The original selection set remains unchanged after the copy is made.

Prompts and Options

`Select objects`   At this prompt, you can choose objects by any valid object-selection method. The prompt repeats until you press Enter to end the object-selection process.

`<Base point or displacement>/Multiple`   The default `Base point or displacement` option specifies the point from which you are copying the objects. You can specify a 2D or 3D point. If you use a 2D point, the COPY command uses the current elevation setting for the Z value. After picking the base point or typing the displacement, you are prompted with `Second point of displacement`. You specify the point to which you are copying the objects. (You can specify a 2D or 3D point.) If you use a 2D point, the COPY command uses the current elevation setting for the Z value.

> *Basepoint* means, "Which point do I want to use as a reference point for the objects?"
>
> *Displacement* simply means, "How far from the base point in the x, y, and z directions do I want to copy the object?"

The `Multiple` option enables you to make multiple copies of the selection set, repeating the `Second point of displacement` prompt until you press Enter or Ctrl+C.

Example

The objects shown in figure C.8 represent a window, which you can duplicate by using the COPY command.

```
Command: COPY (Enter)                    Issues the COPY command

Select objects: Pick point ①             Specifies one corner of the object
(see fig. C.8)                           selection window
```

```
Other corner: Pick point ②              Specifies the opposite corner
5 found
Select objects: (Enter)                 Terminates object selection
<Base point or displacement>/Multiple:  Specifies the base point
Pick any point
Second point of displacement: @48<0 (Enter)  Copies the objects 48" in the
                                             zero-degree direction
```

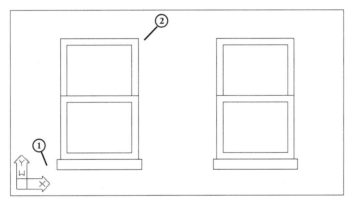

Figure C.8. *Using the COPY command to duplicate a group of objects.*

Related Commands

ARRAY   INSERT   MIRROR   OFFSET

COPYCLIP (Windows Only)

Copy

    Toolbar: *Copy (Standard Toolbar)*
    Pull-down: <u>E</u>dit, <u>C</u>opy

The COPYCLIP command copies selected objects from the graphics window to the Windows Clipboard. The selected objects are retained in the drawing.

When copying objects to the Clipboard, a view of the entire drawing window is created, and the selected objects are placed in that view. Some applications change the scale factor of the objects when resizing the pasted view.

To control the size and shape of the pasted view, resize the AutoCAD graphics window to be just slightly larger than the objects to be copied to the Clipboard.

Prompts and Options

Select objects This prompt appears if you have not pre-selected objects. At this prompt, you can choose objects individually or by using one of the other object-selection options. The prompt repeats until you press Enter to end the object-selection process.

Example

This example shows you how to use the COPYCLIP command to copy AutoCAD objects to the Windows Clipboard. The color indicators from the left side of the sample drawing COLORWH.DWG are first copied to the Clipboard, then pasted into Paintbrush (see fig. C.9).

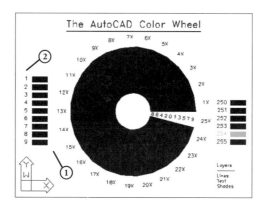

Figure C.9. *Using the COPYCLIP command to copy objects to the Clipboard.*

COPYCLIP (Windows Only)

Open the sample drawing COLORWH.DWG

Command: **COPYCLIP** (Enter)	Starts COPYCLIP command
Select objects: **C** (Enter)	Use Crossing option to select objects
First corner: ① *(see fig. C.9)*	First corner of crossing
Other corner: ②	Opposite corner of crossing
18 found	
Select objects: (Enter)	Finish selecting objects

Launch Microsoft Paintbrush

Maximize the Paintbrush window.

Choose **E**dit, **P**aste	Copies the objects from the Clipboard into Paintbrush (see fig. C.10)

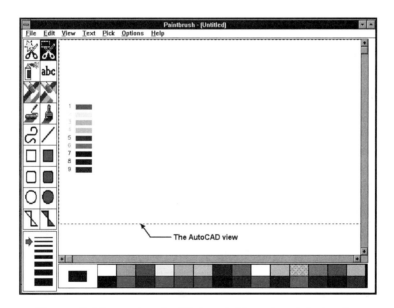

Figure C.10. *Pasting the Clipboard objects into Paintbrush.*

Related Commands

BMPOUT   COPYHIST   COPYLINK   CUTCLIP   OLELINK

COPYEMBED (Windows Only)

COPYEMBED is the undocumented equivalent to COPYCLIP. See the COPYCLIP command for information.

Related Commands

COPYCLIP   OLELINK

COPYHIST (Windows Only)

Keyboard: Shift+right mouse button (When the text window is active)

The COPYHIST command copies the AutoCAD command history to the Windows Clipboard. Up to the last 1,024 lines of command history from the AutoCAD text window are copied. If some of the command prompts or your responses are too long to fit onto one line, AutoCAD wraps these long lines into two or more lines in the command history window.

You can insert the command history into a text editor (such as Notepad or Windows Write) after you've copied it to the Clipboard.

Example

This example shows you how to copy the command history from the AutoCAD text window to the Windows Clipboard, then insert it into Notepad.

Command: **COPYHIST** (Enter)	Copies command history to Windows Clipboard (see fig. C.11)
Launch Notepad	
Maximize the Notepad window	
Choose **E**dit, **P**aste	Copies the command history into Notepad (see fig. C.12)

COPYHIST (Windows Only)

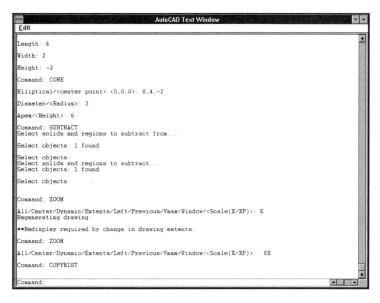

Figure C.11. *Saving the command history using the COPYHIST command.*

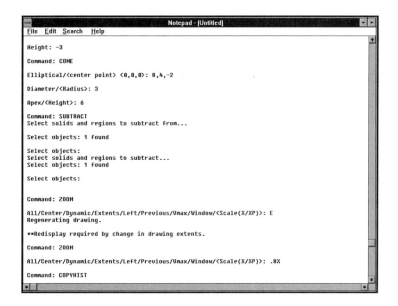

Figure C.12. *Inserting the Clipboard contents into Notepad.*

Related Commands

BMPOUT   COPYCLIP   COPYLINK   CUTCLIP

COPYLINK (Windows Only)

Pull-down: **E**dit, Copy **V**iew

The COPYLINK command copies a link to the current view in the drawing to the Windows Clipboard. Anything visible in the current view will be visible in the destination document when the link is pasted. If the current view does not have a name, AutoCAD saves the current view with the name OLE followed by a number.

When copying the view to the Clipboard, the size of the view also is copied. Prepare the desired size and shape of the view by resizing the graphics window before copying the view to the Windows Clipboard with COPYLINK.

When inserted into another Windows application, the link represents the current view of the drawing. Any changes made to the drawing will be reflected in the associated document. Some applications require manually updating the links in order for changes to be displayed.

Example

This example demonstrates copying a link to the current view of the AutoCAD drawing to the Windows Clipboard using the COPYLINK command.

Create a section view, as shown in figure C.13.	
Command: **COPYLINK** (Enter)	Executes COPYLINK command, copies the current view to Windows Clipboard
Launch Windows Write	
Maximize the Windows Write window	
Add a description for the section view	
Choose **E**dit, Paste **S**pecial, Paste **L**ink	Copies the link from the AutoCAD view into Windows Write (see fig. C.14)

COPYLINK (Windows Only)

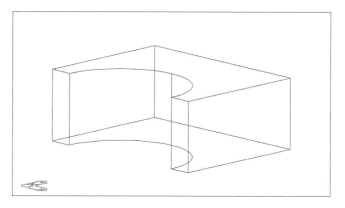

Figure C.13. *Using the COPYLINK command to copy the current view to the Clipboard.*

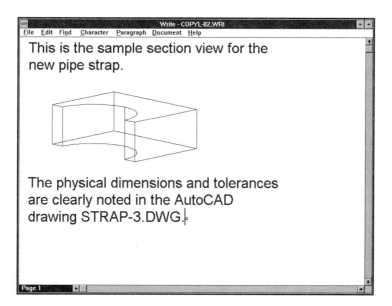

Figure C.14. *Pasting the drawing link into Windows Write.*

Related Commands

BMPOUT   COPYCLIP   COPYHIST   COPYLINK
CUTCLIP DDVIEW   OLELINK

CUT

CUT is not a valid AutoCAD command. It appears on the Edit menu and runs the CUTCLIP command. See the CUTCLIP command for more information.

CUTCLIP

Cut

Toolbar: *Cut(Standard Toolbar)*
Pull-down: Edit, Cut

The CUTCLIP command copies selected objects from the graphics window to the Windows Clipboard. If the objects have been pre-selected, the CUTCLIP command deletes the objects. If no objects are pre-selected, you will be prompted to select the objects to copy to the Windows Clipboard and then prompted again for the objects to be deleted.

Prompts and Options

`Select objects` This prompt appears if you have not pre-selected objects. At this prompt, you can choose objects individually or by using one of the other object-selection options. Press Enter to end the object-selection process and export the image. You again are prompted to select objects. If you reselect the objects after exporting the image (use the previous selection option), they will be deleted when you press Enter.

You must press Enter twice to finish selecting objects.

Example

This example demonstrates copying AutoCAD objects to the Windows Clipboard using the CUTCLIP command. Sketch the baseplate, as shown in figure C.15.

CUTCLIP

`Command: CUTCLIP `[Enter]	Starts the CUTCLIP command
`Select objects: C `[Enter]	Use Crossing option to select objects
`First corner:` ① *(see fig. C.15)*	First corner of crossing
`Other corner:` ②	Opposite corner of crossing
`16 found`	
`Select objects: `[Enter]	Finish selecting objects
`Select objects: `[Enter]	Second response required to finish when objects are not preselected
Launch Windows Write	
Maximize the Windows Write window	
Add a description for the baseplate	
Choose **E**dit, **P**aste	Pastes the baseplate object into the current Windows Write document (see fig. C.16)

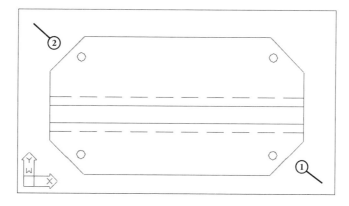

Figure C.15. *Using the CUTCLIP command to copy the baseplate to the Clipboard.*

Related Commands

BMPOUT   COPYCLIP   COPYEMBED   COPYHIST
COPYLINK   CUTCLIP

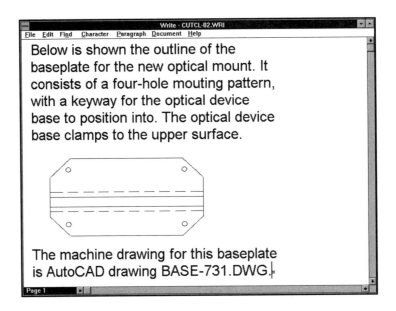

Figure C.16. *Pasting the baseplate into Windows Write.*

CYLINDER

Toolbar: *(Solids, Cylinder)*

Pull-down: *D*raw, S*o*lids, C*y*linder
Screen: DRAW2, SOLIDS, Cylindr:

The CYLINDER command creates a 3D ACIS SOLID shaped like a cylinder. The CYLINDER can be placed parallel to the current UCS, or oriented by specifying the center point of the base and the center point of the other end. The size of the CYLINDER can be specified by the radius or diameter of the base, and the height. The shape of the CYLINDER can either be round or elliptical.

CYLINDER

> To create an ACIS SOLID shaped like a tapered cylinder, see the CONE command.
> **TIP**

Prompts and Options

Elliptical/<center point> <0,0,0>   Specify the center point of the base of the cylinder. You also can choose the Elliptical option, to create a cylinder with an ellipsoidal cross section.

Diameter/<Radius>   Specify a value or pick a point to show a distance for the radius of the cylinder, or enter D if you prefer to specify a value for the diameter of the cylinder.

Diameter   Enter a value or pick a point to show a distance for the diameter of the cylinder.

Center of other end/<Height>   Enter a value or pick a point to show a distance for the height of the cylinder. You also can enter C to choose the Center of other end option, and specify the center point of the opposing end of the cylinder.

Center of other end   Pick a point in the graphics window, or enter the coordinates of the desired center point of the opposing end of the cylinder. The cylinder then will be oriented such that the height of the cylinder is measured from the center point of the base to this Center of other end point.

<Axis endpoint>/Center   This prompt appears if you choose the Elliptical option to create a cylinder with a cross section shaped like an ellipse. Pick a point in the graphics window, or enter the coordinates of the first endpoint for one of the axes of the ellipse. You also can choose the Center option to pick the center point of the ellipse.

Center of ellipse <0,0,0>   This prompt appears after choosing the Center option if you also chose the Elliptical option to create a cylinder with an ellipse-shaped cross section. Pick a point in the graphics window, or enter the coordinates of the center of the ellipse.

Axis endpoint   This prompt appears after you have specified the center of the ellipse. Pick a point in the graphics window, or enter coordinates to locate the edge of the ellipse as measured from the ellipse's center.

Axis endpoint 2   This prompt appears after picking the first axis endpoint. Pick the second axis endpoint for the ellipse of the cylinder base.

Other axis distance   Enter the distance for the ellipse's other axis, as measured from the center point of the ellipse. You also can show a distance by picking a point in the graphics window.

Example

This example shows how to create an ACIS SOLID CYLINDER object. The viewpoint is taken from the point 3,–3,1 looking toward the origin, 0,0,0 (see fig. C.17).

```
Command: CYLINDER (Enter)              Starts CYLINDER command
Elliptical/<center point>              Specifies center of CYLINDER base
 <0,0,0>: 9,5,-3 (Enter)
Diameter/<Radius>: 3 (Enter)           Enters base radius of 3 units
Center of other end/<Height>: 7 (Enter)   Enters height of 7 units
```

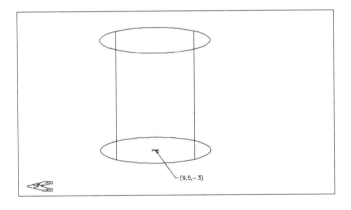

Figure C.17. *An ACIS SOLID CYLINDER object.*

Related Commands
EXTRUDE   INTERFERE   INTERSECTION   SUBTRACT
UNION

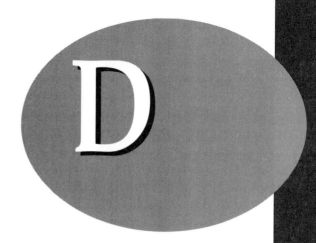

DBLIST

DBLIST (Data Base LIST) provides detailed information on every object in a drawing. DBLIST switches your display to the text screen and then lists the drawing's objects and their properties. To cancel the list, press Escape.

TIP Use the LOGFILEON and LOGFILEOFF commands to capture the information to a file so you can review or print it later.

The DBLIST command does not list drawing status information (see STATUS) or symbol table data.

Example

This example demonstrates the type of information that the DBLIST command returns.

```
Command: DBLIST (Enter)
                LINE       Layer: ARGRIDLINE
                           Space: Model space
                 Handle = EC
        from point, X=5'-6 3/4"   Y=     0'-0"   Z=-1'-4 1/4"
          to point, X=    1'-7"   Y=     0'-0"   Z=-1'-4 1/4"
Extrusion direction relative to UCS:
                 X=    0'-0"   Y=     0'-1"   Z=    0'-0"
         Length =3'-11 7/8",  Angle in XY Plane = 180d0'0"
           Delta X =-3'-11 7/8", Delta Y =      0'-0", Delta Z =      0'-0"

                SOLID      Layer: HVACSUP
                           Space: Model space
                 Handle = F1
        from point, X=2'-6 3/4"   Y=     0'-0"   Z=-3'-4 3/4"
         and point, X=2'-6 5/8"   Y=     0'-0"   Z=-3'-4 3/4"
          to point, X=2'-6 7/8"   Y=     0'-0"   Z=-3'-4 5/8"
         and point, X=2'-6 7/8"   Y=     0'-0"   Z=-3'-4 5/8"
Extrusion direction relative to UCS:
                 X=    0'-0"   Y=     0'-1"   Z=    0'-0"

                TEXT       Layer: HVACSUP
                           Space: Model space
                 Handle = F7
         Style = STANDARD    Font file = SIMPLEX
         start point, X=    4'-6"   Y=     0'-0"   Z=-3'-4 1/2"
         height 0'-0 1/4"
         text 70
         width scale factor    1.000
         obliquing angle 0d0'0"
Extrusion direction relative to UCS:
                 X=    0'-0"   Y=     0'-1"   Z=    0'-0"
```

```
        generation normal
VIEWPORT  Layer: 0
Space: Paper space
              Handle = 2327
                      Status: On but Inactive
                      Scale relative to Paper space:    0.4732xp
          center point, X=   6.1976  Y=   5.0175  Z=   0.0000
              width    5.7762
              height   5.2105
```

Related Commands

LIST   LOGFILEON   LOGFILEOFF   STATUS

DDATTDEF

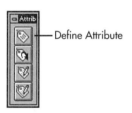
Define Attribute

Toolbar: *Define Attribute, (Attribute)*
Pull-down: *Construct, Attribute...*
Screen: CONSTRUCT, DDatDef:

The DDATTDEF command creates attribute definitions for inclusion in block definitions and insertion into drawings. DDATTDEF is a tool for building nongraphical intelligence into symbol libraries. During block insertion, the attributes are filled with a value unique to that particular insert object.

Attributes are holders of alphanumeric data attached to a block. An unlimited number of attributes can be attached to any block definition. Attributes can contain a constant value or a changeable value. You can control the appearance of attributes individually through the use of text style, height, color, and layer. You also can control the visibility, default values, user prompts, and preset values of attributes.

Attribute data can be extracted for further processing, and is commonly used for component schedule and bill-of-material generation. See the ATTEXT command for a complete description on extracting attributes.

Prompts and Options

The DDATTDEF command displays the Attribute Definition dialog box (see fig. D.1). Enter information into each of the four areas of the dialog box to create an attribute.

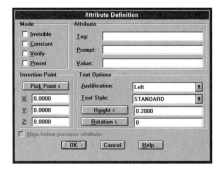

Figure D.1. *The Attribute Definition dialog box.*

The Attribute Definition dialog box presents the options discussed in the following sections.

Mode

Click in one or more of the check boxes to make the attribute invisible, constant, verifiable, or preset. When you open the Attribute Definition dialog box, the modes are set as they were the last time you finished the DDATTDEF command.

Invisible. This option controls attribute visibility. Invisible attributes are normally not visible in the graphics window. Use the ATTDISP command to override the visibility assigned to attributes. Any number of attributes can be visible or invisible.

Constant. This option sets a fixed value for the attribute that cannot be changed. A constant value is used, rather than a variable, when it is important that the attribute value not change. Constant attributes are not attached to insert objects as changeable attributes are. They are displayed as part of the graphical (not attribute) part of the insert.

If the constant check box is selected, the verify, preset, and prompt boxes will be greyed-out. Since constant attributes aren't attached to the insert, these selections do not apply.

Verify. This option instructs AutoCAD to reprompt for the value of the attribute. When inserting a block, you are prompted to enter a value for all nonconstant or nonpreset attributes. After entering a value for each, any attributes that were defined with the verify mode checked will reprompt you to confirm the value entered.

Preset. Select this option to establish a nonconstant attribute with a default value. You will not be prompted for this attribute's value when inserting a block, although you may change its value later. See the DDATTE command for changing the values of attributes.

Attribute

The Attribute section of the dialog box provides three edit boxes in which you enter the attribute's Tag, Prompt, and default Value.

Tag. Enter the name of the tag for this attribute. Attribute tags are used to extract attribute data from the drawing. This name must conform to standard AutoCAD layer naming conventions. Block definitions are allowed to have more than one attribute with the same tag name.

Prompt. Enter the prompt that you want AutoCAD to display when inserting a block with this attribute attached. If you do not enter anything, AutoCAD will prompt with the attribute's tag name when inserting a block with this attribute attached.

Value. Enter a default value for this attribute, if desired. When inserting a block with this attribute attached, AutoCAD will prompt for the value of this attribute, with this default displayed. Press Enter when inserting, and AutoCAD will fill the value of the attribute with this default value.

Insertion Point

Pick a point in the graphics window, or enter the coordinates for the insertion point of the attribute. To pick a point in the graphics window, click on the Pick Pt. button and pick a point. This box is greyed-out if `Align below previous attribute` is checked.

Text Options

Select the text options for the appearance of this attribute. You can set text justification, style, height, and rotation. This box is greyed-out if `Align below previous attribute` is checked.

Justification. Choose a desired justification by clicking on the drop-down list box and selecting from the list of justifications.

Text Style. Choose a desired text style by clicking on the drop-down list box and selecting from the list of currently defined text styles.

Height. Enter the desired height in the edit box to the right of the Height push button. You may also show a height as measured from the insertion point in the graphics window by picking the Height push button.

Rotation. Enter the desired rotation angle in the edit box to the right of the Rotation push button. You may also show a rotation angle as measured from the insertion point in the graphics window by picking the Rotation push button.

Align below previous attribute. Select this check box to place this attribute directly beneath the most previous attribute defined. The attribute will be created with the same height, justification, style, and rotation angle as the previous attribute.

Example

This example creates two attributes placed next to a previously drawn 24" by 36" sink (shown in plan view—see fig. D.2). The first attribute is visible, and the second will normally be invisible. After the attributes are defined, use the BLOCK command to create a block definition, select the sink outline, and then pick the attribute definitions one at a time in the order you want to have them presented when inserting.

Command: **DDATTDEF** (Enter)	Starts DDATTDEF command
Uncheck Invisible, Constant, Verify, or Preset, if any is checked	Specifies normally visible, changeable, not verified and not preset attribute
Enter **MODEL** *in the Tag edit box*	Tag name for this attribute
Enter **Sink model** *in the Prompt edit box*	Prompt for this attribute
Select the Pic**k** Point *push button, and pick ① near the upper right corner of the sink (see fig D.2)*	Specifies insertion point for this attribute
Select Top Left justification, and STANDARD text style	Uses top left justification and standard text style

DDATTDEF

Enter **6.0** in the Height edit box	Specifies a height of 6.0 units for the attribute
Make sure rotation angle is set to 0	To create horizontal text
Pick OK	Creates MODEL attribute
Command: (Enter)	Repeats DDATTDEF command
Check Invisible. The Constant, Verify, and Preset modes are still be unchecked	Specifies normally invisible, changeable, not verified and not preset attribute
Enter **PRICE** in the Tag edit box	Tag name for this attribute
Enter **Sink price** in the Prompt edit box	Prompt for this attribute
Select the Align below previous attribute check box	Places the PRICE attribute immediately below the MODEL attribute
Pick OK	Creates PRICE attribute

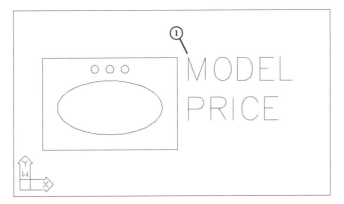

Figure D.2. *Two attributes, before creating a block definition.*

Related Commands

ATTDEF	ATTDISP	ATTEDIT	ATTEXT
ATTREDEF	BLOCK	DDATTE	DDATTEXT
DTEXT			

Related System Variables

AFLAGS   ATTDIA   ATTMODE   ATTREQ

DDATTE

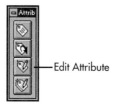

Edit Attribute

Toolbar: *Edit Attribute (Attribute)*
Pull-down: **M**odify, Attri**b**ute, **E**dit
Screen: MODIFY, AttEd:

The DDATTE (Dynamic Dialog ATTribute Edit) enables you to edit nonconstant attribute values using a dialog box. Use the standard edit box editing controls to insert and delete characters, or highlight a group of characters and begin typing to replace the entire group. If an insert has more than eight attributes attached to it, use the Next and Previous push buttons to navigate through groups of eight attributes.

Prompts and Options

Select block Select the block with attribute values you want to edit. If the selected block has no attributes, AutoCAD displays the following prompt:

```
That block has no editable attributes.
```

After a block with attributes is selected, the Edit Attributes dialog box is displayed (see fig. D.3). The block name is displayed at the top, and each attribute's prompt is displayed along with an edit box that enables you to modify the attribute's value. Two push buttons, labeled Next and Previous, are displayed at the bottom.

Previous. This button displays the previous group of eight attributes, if any.

Next. This button displays the next group of eight attributes, if any.

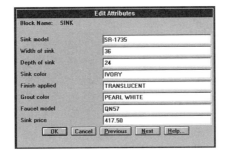

Figure D.3. *The Edit Attributes dialog box.*

Example

This example changes the values of the MODEL and PRICE attributes of a previously drawn 24" by 36" sink (see fig. D.4).

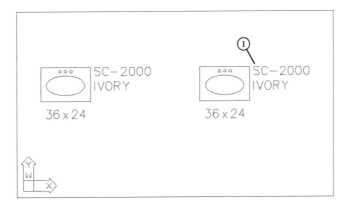

Figure D.4. *The attribute values before editing with DDATTE.*

Command: **DDATTE** (Enter)	Starts DDATTE command
Select block: *Pick the block at* ① *(see fig. D.4)*	Selects the block with attributes to change
Enter **FC-90-9** *in the Sink model edit box*	Changes MODEL attribute to FC-90-9
Enter **GRANITE** *in the Sink color edit box*	Changes COLOR attribute to GRANITE
Enter **179.99** *in the Sink price edit box*	Changes PRICE attribute to 179.99
Pick OK	Updates block attributes (see fig. D.5)

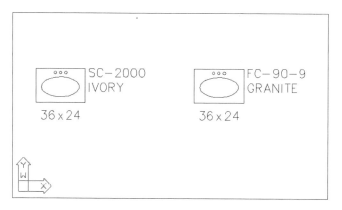

Figure D.5. *The updated attribute values.*

Related Commands

ATTDEF   ATTDISP   ATTEDIT   ATTEXT
ATTREDEF   DDATTDEF   DDATTEXT

Related System Variables

AFLAGS   ATTDIA   ATTMODE   ATTREQ

DDATTEXT

Pull-down: File, Export, Attributes (DOS Only)
Screen: FILE, EXPORT, DDattEx:

The DDATTEXT (Dialog Display ATTribure EXTraction) command extracts attribute information from your drawing and stores it in a text file. You can analyze the extracted attribute data in a spreadsheet program, import it into a database program, or print it as a text report. DDATTEXT extracts information in one of three formats: *Comma Delimited Format* (CDF), *Space Delimited Format* (SDF), or *Drawing Interchange Format* (DXF). Use the format that is accepted by the program in which you want to use the extracted information.

Template Files

To extract attribute information to an external file using the CDF or SDF formats (see the following descriptions), you need to create a template file. This file describes to the DDATTEXT command the types of information you want to extract (attribute values) and the formatting to be used in the output file for storing the attribute information.

The template file consists of two fields on each line. The first is the attribute tag name or block property to extract. The second is a formatting instruction consisting of the letter C or N, followed by two sets of 3-digit numbers (six numbers total).

The letter C or N in the formatting instruction tells the DDATTEXT command to extract the data in either character or numerical format. The first set of 3-digit numbers specifies the output file field width—the number of characters in the output file for this piece of information. If extracting in character format, the second set of 3-digit numbers is ignored. If extracting in numerical format, the second set of 3-digit numbers specifies the precision (the number of decimals to the right of the decimal point) to be used. When specifying the field width of numeric fields, the decimal point takes up one character position, and must be included in the overall field width. If the value to be extracted is too large to fit into the output field width, the output value is truncated, and AutoCAD reports the following:

```
** Field overflow in record X
```

If there is an error is the template file (for example, a line with only an attribute name, and no formatting instruction), AutoCAD will report the error as follows

```
** Invalid field specification:
```

and refuse to continue the extraction.

The recognized attribute tag names will be extracted according to the formatting instructions in the template file. If an attribute tag name is specified that is not found, AutoCAD will fill the output file with spaces (if using the SDF format), or an empty field between two commas (if using the CDF format).

A handy way to insert spaces between numeric or character fields to prevent the fields from running together is to specify a nonexistent attribute tag in the template file. Use a format of character, one or two spaces, and three zeros for the numerical precision.

The recognized block properties that can be extracted are the following:

BL:LEVEL	Block nesting level
BL:NAME	Block name
BL:X	X coordinate of insertion point
BL:Y	Y coordinate of insertion point
BL:Z	Z coordinate of insertion point
BL:NUMBER	Block insertion counter

BL:HANDLE	Block insertion handle
BL:LAYER	Block insertion layer name
BL:ORIENT	Block insertion rotation angle
BL:XSCALE	Block insertion X scale factor
BL:YSCALE	Block insertion Y scale factor
BL:ZSCALE	Block insertion Z scale factor
BL:XEXTRUDE	X component of extrusion vector direction
BL:YEXTRUDE	Y component of extrusion vector direction
BL:ZEXTRUDE	Z component of extrusion vector direction

Use an ASCII text editor to create the template file as a plain ASCII text file. Make sure there is exactly one linefeed after the last line.

When you extract attribute data, AutoCAD prompts for the name of the template file to use and the name of the attribute extract file. You must use different file names for the template and extract files.

Prompts and Options

The DDATTEXT command displays the Attribute Extraction dialog box (see fig. D.6).

Figure D.6. *The DDATTEXT dialog box.*

File Format. Select the desired output file format by selecting one of the three radio buttons marked Comma Delimited File (CDF), Space Delimited File (SDF), or Drawing Interchange File (DXF).

Select Objects. By default, all blocks in the drawing are extracted. Choose the Select Objects button to extract only selected blocks. Select the blocks to be extracted using any object selection method.

Template File. Enter the name of a template file in the edit box to the right of the Template File push button. Alternatively, you can select a template file by clicking on the Template File push button, and using the Template File dialog box to select a file.

Output File. Enter the name of an output file in the edit box to the right of the Output File push button, or click on the Output File button and identify an output file name. If you select an output file that already exists, it will be overwritten.

Example

This example uses a template file to extract all of the attribute values from a drawing. It uses the SINK block similar to the one found in the DDATTE example. Use an ASCII text editor to create a extract template file with the following lines:

```
BL:NAME     C015000
MODEL       C030000
WIDTH       N008002
DEPTH       N008002
PRICE       N007002
```

Make sure there is one and only one linefeed character at the end of the last line. AutoCAD will report an error if blank lines exist in the template file.

Command: **DDATTEXT** (Enter)	Starts the DDATTEXT command
Select the Space Delimited File (SDF) output file format	Specifies SDF output file format
Enter the name of the template file	Specifies template file for SDF extraction
Enter the name of an output file	Specifies output file for attribute data
Click on OK	Performs attribute data extraction
`2 records in extract file.`	

Related Commands

ATTDEF	ATTDISP	ATTEDIT	ATTEXT
ATTREDEF	DDATTDEF	DATTE	

Related System Variables

ATTDIA   ATTMODE   ATTREQ   HIGHLIGHT

DDCHPROP

Screen: MODIFY, Ddchpro: or MODIFY, Change:, DDchprp:

The DDCHPROP command enables you to change drawing objects' (or group of objects) color, layer, linetype, linetype scale, and thickness properties. When you issue the DDCHPROP command, AutoCAD prompts you to select the objects you want to modify. Only after you select these objects does the DDCHPROP dialog box appear (see fig. D.7).

Figure D.7. *The Change Properties dialog box.*

The Change Properties dialog box is featured whenever you choose the Properties button from the Object Properties toolbar and select more than one object.

Dialog Box Items

The Change Properties dialog box contains three buttons and two edit boxes. The buttons display dialog boxes with which to change color, layer, or linetype.

Color. Clicking on the Color button displays the Select Color dialog box (see also DDCOLOR). The Select Color dialog box contains three palette boxes from which to pick a new color. Click on one of the colored squares to pick a new color, or click on the BYLAYER or BYBLOCK buttons to set color by using one of those methods. You also can click on the Color edit box and type a specific color name or number (1–255).

> Setting a color BYLAYER (the default) means that the object inherits the color of the layer on which that object resides. BYBLOCK assigns color 7 (white) to the objects. When you include these objects in a BLOCK and insert them, they inherit the current COLOR setting.
>
> TIP

Layer. To change an object's layer, click on this button to initiate the Select Layer dialog box, which features a list box that contains the names of all of the layers in the drawing (see fig. D.8). A vertical scroll bar appears to the right of the list box if not all the layer names fit on-screen. To select a new layer, double-click on a layer name, or type a layer name in the **S**et Layer Name edit box.

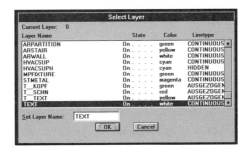

Figure D.8. *The Select Layer dialog box.*

Li̱netype. Click on this button to initiate the Select Linetype dialog box, which lists the currently loaded linetypes (see fig. D.9). If not all linetypes fit in the list box, a vertical scroll bar appears. To select a linetype, double-click on one of the linetype names in the list box or click on the **L**inetype edit box and type a linetype name.

Linetype S̱cale. Click on this edit box and type in a new value (positive integer or real number) to change the linetype scale for the selected objects.

T̲hickness. Click on this edit box and type a new numerical value to change an object's thickness.

Apply DDCHPROP to the example shown in the CHPROP command.

Figure D.9. *The Select Linetype dialog box.*

Related Commands

CHANGE   CHPROP   DDMODIFY

'DDCOLOR

Color control

Toolbar: *Color Control (Object Properties)*
Pull-down: **D**ata, **C**olor

The DDCOLOR command controls the color of new objects. The color value you specify is assigned to each object you create. DDCOLOR displays the Select Color dialog box shown in figure D.10.

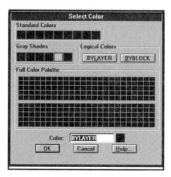

Figure D.10. *The Select Color dialog box.*

> To change the color assigned to existing objects, use the DDMODIFY command.

Dialog Box Items

The Select Color box contains three palette boxes from which to pick a new color. Click on one of the colored squares to pick a new color.

> For best results, keep the color value specified by the COLOR command set to BYLAYER, and use the LAYER's color setting to control object color. This helps to easily identify different layers in your drawing and to redefine the colors of objects assigned to them.

If you select BYLAYER (the default color), the object color defaults to the color assigned to the layer the object resides on.

The BYBLOCK option creates new objects, in the color 7 (white), until they are saved and inserted as a block. When inserted, the objects take on the color value currently set with the COLOR command.

You also can enter a color number or name in the Color edit box. Valid color numbers range from 1 to 255, but what displays on your screen depends on the video board and monitor you are using (see CONFIG). You can assign the first seven colors by number or name, as follows:

Color Number	Color
1	Red
2	Yellow
3	Green
4	Cyan
5	Blue
6	Magenta
7	White

TIP Two AutoCAD slides, CHROMA (located in the \TUTORIAL directory) and COLORWH (located in the \COMMON\SAMPLE directory), display and identify the 256 available colors and their numeric values (see the VSLIDE command).

Apply DDCOLOR to the example used for the COLOR command.

NOTE Plotter pen assignments are usually made by color. To achieve different line or pen widths (or types) on the plotted output, use a different color for each pen—even if you are using a monochrome monitor.

Related Commands
COLOR   DDLMODES

Related System Variable
CECOLOR

DDEDIT

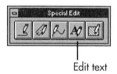

Edit text

Toolbar: *Edit Text (Modify, Special Edit)*
Pull-down: *Modify, Edit Text*
Screen: MODIFY, Ddedit

The DDEDIT (Dynamic Dialog EDIT) command enables you to dynamically edit text objects, attribute definitions, and multiline text objects (see MTEXT). DDEDIT's behavior depends on the type of text object selected. For text objects, the Edit Text dialog box appears. For multiline text objects, the Edit MText dialog box appears. For attribute definitions, the Edit Attribute Definition dialog box appears.

> The DDMODIFY command duplicates the function of DDEDIT with greater control over the object selected. DDMODIFY only changes one selected object at a time, however.

Prompts and Options

`<Select a TEXT or ATTDEF object>/Undo`   The default option edits text objects, mtext objects, or attribute definitions. If you choose an attribute definition, you can change the attribute tag, prompt, and default values.

Enter **U** to select the Undo option. DDEDIT undoes the edits performed on the previous text object.

After you select a text object, mtext object, or attribute definition, a dialog box appears. The dialog box contains an edit box that enables you to modify the text object.

Dialog Box Items

Depending on the type of text object you select, one of three different dialog boxes appear, each of which are covered in the following list.

Edit Text. This dialog box (fig. D.11) contains a single edit box that displays the text you selected. You can edit this text and select OK to change the selected text item, or select Cancel to ignore any changes.

Figure D.11. *The Edit Text dialog box.*

Edit MText. This dialog box has several features, as shown in figure D.12. See the MTEXT command for complete descriptions. The first item in this dialog box is a text box for editing your selected text. You use the other items in the dialog box to assign attributes and properties to the text.

Edit Attribute Definition. As shown in figure D.13, this dialog box contains three edit boxes—one each for the attribute tag, prompt, and default value. See DDATTDEF and ATTDEF for an explanation of these values.

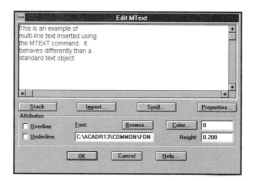

Figure D.12. *The Edit Mtext dialog box.*

Figure D.13. *The Edit Attribute Definition dialog box.*

Related Commands

CHANGE   CHPROP   DDMODIFY   MTPROP
SPELL

'DDEMODES

Object Creation

Toolbar: *Object Creation (Object Properties)*
Pull-down: **D**ata, **O**bject Creation
Screen: DATA, Ddemode:

The DDEMODES command enables you to set the object properties for newly created objects. When you issue the DDEMODES command, the Object Creation Modes dialog box appears (see fig. D.14). You can use this dialog box to set the color, layer, linetype, text style, linetype scale, elevation, and thickness for any new object. The DDEMODES command also is useful for checking the status of these object-creation settings during an editing session.

Figure D.14. *The Object Creation Modes dialog box.*

Dialog Box Items

This command provides a dialog box that features four buttons and three edit boxes described in the following.

Color. Clicking on the Color button displays the Select Color dialog box. See DDCOLOR for an explanation about this dialog box.

Layer. To change an object's layer, click on this button to initiate the Select Layer dialog box, which features a list box that contains the names of all of the layers in the drawing. A vertical scroll bar appears to the right of the list box if not all the layer names fit on-screen. To select a new layer, double-click on a layer name, or type a layer name in the Set Layer Name edit box.

Linetype. Click on this button to initiate the Select Linetype dialog box, which lists the currently loaded linetypes. If not all linetypes fit in the list box, a vertical scroll bar appears. To select a linetype, double-click on one of the linetype names in the list box or click on the Linetype edit box and type a linetype name. See DDLTYPE for a complete discussion of this dialog box.

Text Style. Click on this button to initiate the Select Text Style dialog box, which lists and shows a sample of the currently defined text styles in the Select Text Style dialog box (see fig. D.15). The items within this dialog box are discussed in the following list.

> **Show All.** Select this button to display the Text Style STANDARD Symbol Set dialog box, which shows the entire character set for the text style you select (see fig. D.16).

Figure D.15. *The Select Text Style dialog box.*

Figure D.16. *The Text Style STANDARD Symbol Set dialog box.*

Sample Text. Type characters in this edit box to specify which characters appear in the sample text image tile. To view extended characters, use the %% characters, followed by an ASCII character value. For example, typing %%176 displays a degree symbol.

Style Name. This edit box displays the name you select from the list of styles. You also can type an existing text style name in this box. Use the STYLE command to define a new style. The following text labels display various properties that pertain to the selected text style:

Font.
Height.
Width.
Oblique.
Generation.

Linetype Scale. Use this edit box to assign a linetype scale independent of the LTSCALE setting. This value changes the value for the CELTSCALE system variable.

Elevation. This edit box requires you to enter a valid Z value, or distance above or below the current UCS X,Y plane. By default, new objects are drawn in the X,Y plane of the current UCS at elevation 0.

Thickness. Use this edit box to enter a valid extrusion thickness. Applicable new objects are drawn using the new thickness.

> *Thickness* refers to the extruded depth of an object. Do not confuse it with line width or pen width.

Related Commands

DDLMODES   ELEV   LAYER   LINETYPE
STYLE   XPLODE

Related System Variables

CECOLOR   CELTSCALE CELTYPE   CLAYER
ELEVATION TEXTSTYLE THICKNESS

'DDGRIPS

Pull-down: **O**ptions, **G**rips
Screen: OPTIONS, DDgrips:

Grips are small squares located at strategic points on selected AutoCAD objects and they enable you to quickly select and modify those objects (see fig. D.17). If grips are enabled, grips appear on the objects as you select them while at the command prompt. With grips enabled, the drawing editor crosshairs snap automatically to a grip when the crosshairs pass over the grip. You can use grips to stretch, move, rotate, scale, or mirror the gripped objects. You can use the DDGRIPS command or set the GRIPS system variable to 1 to enable grips. In addition to enabling or disabling grips, the DDGRIPS command enables you to set the grips' color and size (see fig. D.18).

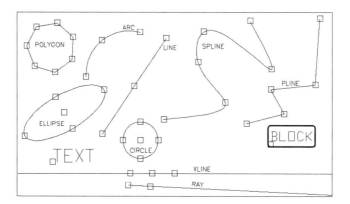

Figure D.17. *Grip locations on various objects.*

Figure D.18. *The Grips dialog box.*

Dialog Box Items

At the top of the DDGRIPS dialog box in the Select Settings area, you see two check boxes. Enable Grips enables or disables grips on primitive objects. Enable Grips Within Blocks enables or disables grips on objects contained within blocks.

Beneath the check boxes, in the Grip Colors area, the Unselected and Selected buttons display the Select Color dialog box (see DDCOLOR), from which you can select colors for unselected and selected grips.

At the bottom of the DDGRIPS dialog box, a scroll bar enables you to dynamically adjust the grips' size in pixels. The small square to the right of the scroll bar grows and shrinks as you drag the scroll box, indicating the grips' size.

Related System Variables

GRIPBLOCK   GRIPCOLOR   GRIPHOT   GRIPS
GRIPSIZE

'DDIM

Dimension Styles

Toolbar: *Dimension Styles (Dimensioning, Dimension Style)*
Pull-down: **D**ata, **D**imension Style...
Screen: DRAW DIM, DDim:

The Dimension Styles dialog box provides a graphical interface for using dimension styles to control AutoCAD's dozens of dimensioning system variables (see fig. D.19). *Dimension styles* are a method of grouping and setting dimension variable settings and saving them under unique names for later recall. Every dimension is associated with a dimension style—even if it is AutoCAD's default Standard style.

Figure D.19. *The Dimension Styles dialog box.*

Dialog Box Items

The Dimension Style area of the dialog box contains a **C**urrent pull-down list box and a **N**ame edit box, in addition to the **S**ave and **R**ename buttons. The **C**urrent list box enables you to display any dimension styles that have been created in the drawing or referenced using an xref. Click on the down arrow to see a complete list. Click on the style name you want to make that style current. You use the **N**ame edit box to create or rename dimension styles. You use the **S**ave button to save all current dimension settings under the style name shown. The **R**ename button enables you to rename the style name shown in the **C**urrent box to that shown in the **N**ame box.

The dimension variables that you adjust in DDIM's subsidiary dialog boxes can also be set directly from the AutoCAD command prompt. Simply type the appropriate variable name and enter the new value. The associative dimension variables DIMSHO and DIMASO can only be set at the command prompt. See your AutoCAD Reference Manual or *Inside AutoCAD Release 13* for an explanation of the dimension variables themselves.

When you use DDIM to change the value of, or override, a dimension variable, AutoCAD creates a new style based on the current style. The new name is the same as the old name, but has a plus sign (+) as a prefix.

The Family area of the Dimension Styles dialog box is used to determine how dimension variable settings are applied to various types of dimensions for a particular dimension style name. The seven radio buttons determine the types of dimensions (with the exception of **P**arent): **P**arent, **L**inear, Ra**d**ial, Ang**u**lar, Dia**m**eter, **O**rdinate, or L**e**ader. The Parent type is considered a "global" setting that controls the other types if they are not specified.

A dimension style can have individual settings for each of these dimension types. For example, a style named OFFICE_STANDARD may have specific settings for linear, angular, and leader dimension types as well as the Parent which would control all the other dimension types.

Geometry

The Geometry button displays the Geometry dialog box (see fig. D.20). Use this dialog box to control the appearance of your dimension objects such as dimension lines, extension lines, arrowheads, and center marks. The available options will depend on the family that is selected. See figure D.21 for an illustration of these dimension features.

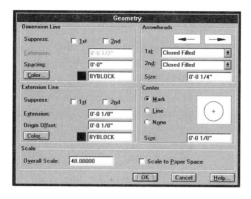

Figure D.20. *The Geometry dialog box.*

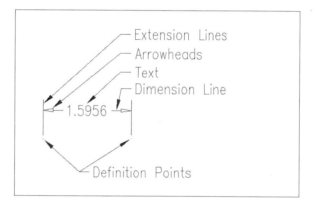

Figure D.21. *Dimension features.*

Dimension Line. This area of the Geometry dialog box contains features that enable you to affect the appearance of the dimension line. The Suppress **1**st and **2**nd check boxes control the visibility of the dimension line on both sides of the text. Use the **E**xtension edit box when you use oblique arrowheads to determine how far the dimension line extends beyond the extension lines. The Sp**a**cing edit box enables you to control the distance between the dimension lines when you use baseline or "stacked" dimensions. To set the color of the dimension line separately, choose the **C**olor button or click on the color swatch to initiate the Select Colors dialog box (see DDCOLOR). You also can type in a color name or number (1–255) in the Color edit box. The default color of BYBLOCK means that the object inherits the color of the layer on which it resides.

Extension Line. You use this section of the Geometry dialog box to control the appearance of extension lines. Use the Suppress 1st and 2nd check boxes to control the visibility of the extension lines. The value in the Extension edit box determines how far the extension line reaches beyond the dimension line. Use the Origin Offset edit box to adjust the gap between the definition point (or the object being dimensioned) and the extension line. The color items perform the same function in the Extension Line section as in the Dimension Line section, as described in the preceding paragraph.

Arrowheads. The two image boxes and 1st and 2nd pull-down list boxes control the type of arrowhead to be drawn on the dimension line. Click on the left image button to cycle through the choices for both left and right arrowheads. Click on the right image button to determine the right arrowhead only. Alternatively, you can select a choice from the pull-down list boxes. The choices are None, Closed, Dot, Closed Filled, Oblique, Open, Origin Indication, Right Angle, and User Arrow. Use the User Arrow option to specify a block name to use for the arrowheads. Use the Size edit box to specify the relative size of the arrowhead.

Center. You use this area of the Geometry dialog box to determine the appearance of center marks for circles and arcs. Choose the Mark, Line, or None radio button, or repeatedly click on the image button to choose the option you want. The Mark option draws a small crosshairs at the center of the circle or arc. The Line option includes center lines. Use the Size edit box to determine the relative size of the center mark.

Scale. The Overall Scale edit box enables you to control the scale factor for the features of your dimensions, such as text height and arrow size. It does not affect the actual measured distance. Activate the Scale to Paper Space check box if you want AutoCAD to automatically calculate the appropriate scale factor, if you are working within a viewport from paper space (TILEMODE=0). These items control the DIMSCALE system variable.

Format

Click on the Format button in the Dimension Styles dialog box to initiate the Format dialog box, which you use to control the placement of dimension text, arrowheads, extension lines, and leader lines (see fig. D.22).

User Defined. Use this check box to define the location of the dimension text—overriding AutoCAD's placement depends on the setting of the dimension variables that control horizontal justification.

Force Line Inside. Use this check box to force AutoCAD to draw a dimension line between the extension lines, even if the text and arrowheads are outside.

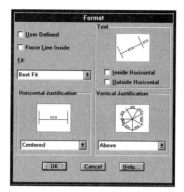

Figure D.22. *The Format dialog box.*

Fit. Use this pull-down list box to determine how AutoCAD places text and arrowheads between extension lines if there is not room for both. The options are Text and Arrows, Text Only, Arrows Only, Best Fit, and Leader.

> If a dimension is created with the Fit option of Leader and there is no room for the text and arrowheads, AutoCAD will draw the dimension text away from the dimension line and draw a leader from the text to the midpoint of the dimension line. If you wish to be able to move the dimension text independently of the dimension line, the dimension has to have been created with the Leader option. This is the same as setting the DIMFIT system variable to 4 prior to dimensioning.

Horizontal Justification. This area of the Format dialog box controls the placement of dimension text horizontally along the dimension line. Select an option from the pull-down list box, or repeatedly click on the image button to cycle through the options. The available options (depending on the specified family type) are Centered, 1st Extension Line, 2nd Extension Line, Over 1st Extension, and Over 2nd Extension.

Text. Use the items in this area of the Format dialog box to control the orientation of the dimension text. Check the Inside Horizontal or Outside Horizontal check boxes. You may also click on the image button to cycle through all possible combinations of whether the text outside or inside the extension lines is horizontal or not.

Vertical Justification. This area of the dialog box is used for controlling the vertical placement of dimension text in relation to the dimension line. The options include Above, Centered, Outside, and JIS (Japanese Industrial

Standards). Choose an option from the pull-down list box, or repeatedly click on the image button to cycle through the options.

 The placement and orientation of dimensions and dimension text are relative to the current UCS (User Coordinate System).

Annotation

The Annotation button in the Dimension Styles dialog box opens the Annotation dialog box used to control the appearance of dimension text (see fig. D.23).

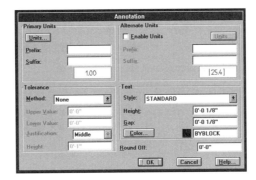

Figure D.23. *The Annotation dialog box.*

Primary Units. You use the <u>U</u>nits button to initiate the Primary Units dialog box, which you use to set the units used for the dimension text (see fig. D.24). The Primary Units dialog box is convenient for specifying the units, precision, scale, and whether to display leading and trailing zeros.

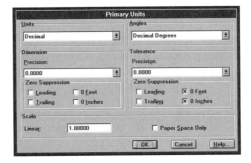

Figure D.24. *The Primary Units dialog box.*

You use the **P**refix and **S**uffix edit boxes to specify text to place before and after the dimension text. The text you specify overrides AutoCAD's built-in prefixes, such as the diameter and radius symbols. The image box displays a sample of what your dimensioning text will look like.

Alternate Units. If you require dual-dimensioning, or an alternate unit of measure (as when dimensioning in English and metric units), use this area of the Annotation dialog box. Check the **E**nable Units check box to use this feature. The Alternate Units area contains the same options as the Primary Units area of the Annotation dialog box.

> If you use metric dimensions, use the **S**uffix edit box in the Annotation dialog box to specify the units. For example, type **mm** in the edit box to specify millimeter dimensions.

TIP

When you check the **E**nable Units box, the U**n**its button becomes enabled. You choose this button to initiate the Alternate Units dialog box (see fig. D.25). This dialog box is similar to the Primary Units dialog box just described, and has all the same options.

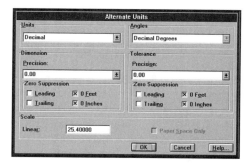

Figure D.25. *The Alternate Units dialog box.*

Tolerance. Use this area of the Annotation dialog box to enable and control the appearance of tolerance and limit dimensions. The various types of tolerances listed in the **M**ethod pull-down list box are None, Symmetrical, Deviation, Limits, and Basic. When appropriate for the type of tolerance dimension, the Upper **V**alue and Lo**w**er Value edit boxes are enabled. Use these to specify the tolerance amounts. The **J**ustification pull-down list box contains three choices for the placement of the tolerance values in relation to the main text: Top, Middle, and Bottom. The He**i**ght edit box enables you to specify the height of the tolerance text in relation to the main dimension text.

Text. This area of the Annotation dialog box provides options that enable you to control the appearance of the dimension text. The Style pull-down list box shows you all the defined text styles within the drawing. Use the Height edit box to specify the relative text height. Use the Gap edit box to control such factors as the amount of space between the text and dimension line and the minimum dimension line length to draw between extension lines. Clicking on the Color button or image tile to the right of the color button initiates the standard Select Color dialog box (see DDCOLOR). You also can specify a valid color name or number (1–255) in the edit box.

Round Off. Use this edit box to specify the rounding value for dimensions. For example, setting this value to 1/2 inch rounds dimension values to the nearest 1/2 inch. This value does not apply to angular dimensions.

Related Commands

DIM   DIMEDIT   DIMOVERRIDE   DIMSTYLE
DIMTEDIT   TOLERANCE

Related System Variables

See your AutoCAD documentation or *Inside AutoCAD Release 13* for a list of dimensioning system variables.

DDINSERT

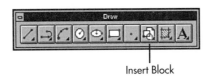

Insert Block

Toolbar: *Insert Block (Draw, Block)*
Pull-down: *D*raw, Inse*r*t, *B*lock
Screen: DRAW 2, DDinsert

You use the DDINSERT command to initiate the Insert dialog box, which you use to insert blocks and draw files into the current drawing (see fig. D.26).

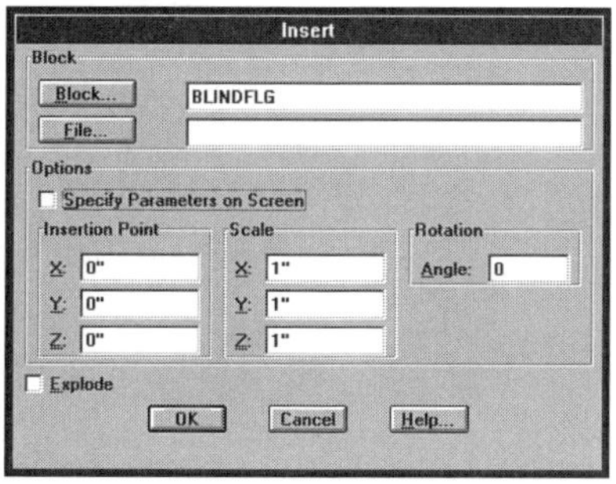

Figure D.26. *The Insert dialog box.*

Dialog Box Items

The first two lines (the Block area) in the Insert dialog box contain buttons and companion edit boxes that you use to select a block or file to insert. You can type specific names in the edit boxes. Clicking on the buttons initiates a second dialog box that you can use to select local blocks or outside drawing files for insertion.

Block

To select a block defined in the current drawing, click on the **B**lock button, which initiates the Defined Blocks dialog box (see fig. D.27). This dialog box contains, at the top, the **P**attern edit box, into which you can type a text pattern that the block name for which you search might contain. Typing F*, for example, lists all block names that begin with the letter F. Below the **P**attern edit box, you see a list box that contains the names of all blocks currently defined in the drawing. If they do not all fit on a single screen, a scroll bar appears to the right of the list box and enables you to scroll through the list until you find the desired block. Below the list box, the **S**election edit box enables you to enter a block name directly.

File

To select a drawing file for insertion, click on the **F**ile button in the Insert dialog box. The Select Drawing File dialog box appears (see fig. D.28). This dialog box begins with a File **N**ame edit box, in which you can type a text pattern that the file you seek might contain. The pattern here, however, must end with the extension DWG, because you can insert only AutoCAD drawing files. For a complete discussion of this and the Browse/Search dialog box features, see the Introduction to this book.

Figure D.27. *The Defined Blocks dialog box.*

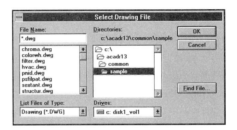

Figure D.28. *The Select Drawing File dialog box.*

In the Options area of the Insert dialog box, you specify the insertion point, scale, and rotation angle of the inserted block or file. The **S**pecify Parameters on Screen check box acts as a toggle that enables you to switch between presetting the insertion point, scale, and rotation values in the dialog box, or specifying them from the command line. It is checked by default, which leaves the edit boxes greyed-out. If you elect to enter the insertion parameters in the dialog box, click on the check box to deactivate it. The edit boxes become active.

Use the Insertion option to specify the **X**, **Y**, or **Z** value for the insertion point. Do the same in the Scale option to specify separate X, Y, and Z scale factors. If you only specify an X scale factor, the Y and Z factors will be changed to match it. Click on the **A**ngle edit box in the Rotation option to enter a rotation angle in degrees. Below the Options portion, a check box lets you specify whether to insert the block exploded into its constituent objects, or as a single block object. You cannot specify unequal X, Y, or Z scale factors and insert a block exploded; however, you may later explode the block if you want using the EXPLODE command.

Inserting a block with a negative X, Y, or Z scale factor effectively creates a mirror image of the block in that axis.

Related Commands

ATTDEF	ATTDISP	ATTEDIT	ATTEXT
BASE	BLOCK	INSERT	MINSERT
WBLOCK	XPLODE		

Related System Variables

INSBASE   INSNAME

'DDLMODES

Layers

    Toolbar: *Layers (Object Properties)*
    Pull-down: **D**ata, **L**ayers
    Screen: DATA, DDlmode:

The DDLMODES command uses the Layer Control dialog box to manage layer settings. You can use this dialog box to create new layers, change color or linetype settings, and rename layers globally or specific to each floating viewport. You can also turn layers on or off, lock or unlock layers, freeze or thaw layers, freeze or thaw viewports, and set a new current layer (see fig. D.29).

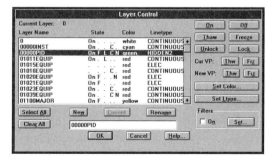

Figure D.29. *The Layer Control dialog box.*

The layer operations lock/unlock, freeze/thaw, current viewport freeze/thaw, on/off, and setting the current layer are also available from the Layer Control list box in the Object Properties toolbar.

Dialog Box Items

DDLMODES provides no command-line prompts. The Layer Control dialog box contains an alphabetical list of the layers in the current drawing (see the MAXSORT system variable in the AutoCAD *Command Reference Manual*) and a group of option buttons. The layer list shows the layer name, state of the layer, and color and linetype assigned to the layer.

Layer names contained in attached or overlaid external references (XREF) are displayed in the form XREFNAME | LAYERNAME. Bound XREF layer names are displayed as DWGNAME0LAYERNAME.

The various layer states that are indicated in the list box are On, Off, Frozen (F), Locked (L), frozen in the current viewport (C), or frozen in new viewports (N), in that order.

The buttons perform the following actions:

On. This option turns selected layers on or off in all viewports.

Off. This option turns selected layers off in all viewports.

Thaw. The Thaw option changes the status of selected layers from Frozen to Thawed. If a layer is thawed, you can turn it on and display it on-screen.

Freeze. This option changes the status of selected layers to Frozen. When a layer is frozen, you cannot display it on-screen.

Unlock. Unlocking a layer reverses the Lock setting and enables you to edit objects on the selected layer(s).

Lock. Locking a layer prevents any editing of objects on the selected layer(s), and prevents any new objects from being placed upon the locked layer.

Cur VP Thw. This option thaws the selected layers in the current viewport only, and applies only to paper-space viewport objects.

Cur VP Frz. This option freezes the selected layers in the current viewport, and applies only to paper-space viewport objects.

New VP Thw. This option controls whether the currently selected layers are thawed in new viewports, and applies only to paper-space viewport objects.

New VP Frz. This option controls whether the currently selected layers are frozen in new viewports, and applies only to paper-space viewport objects.

Set Color. Use this option to change a layer's color. When you select this option, AutoCAD brings up the Select Color dialog box (see DDCOLOR). Any changes you make to the color settings of external reference layers are not saved with the drawing unless the VISRETAIN system variable is set to 1.

Set Ltype. Use this option to change a layer's linetype. When you select this option, AutoCAD brings up the Select Linetype dialog box, which contains linetype options (see DDLTYPE). Any changes you make to the linetype settings of external reference layers are not saved with the drawing unless the VISRETAIN system variable is set to 1.

Select All. This option highlights every layer in the layer list box, which is useful if you want to make changes globally across all drawing layers.

Clear All. This option dehighlights any layer currently highlighted in the layer list box.

New. This option creates a new layer using the name you entered into the edit box below the New button. If you do not enter a name before you choose New, AutoCAD responds `Null entry in edit box`; or, if you do, AutoCAD responds `1 layer name is duplicated`.

Current. This option makes the currently highlighted layer the current drawing layer. All new objects are drawn on this layer. Note that you cannot freeze the current layer from this dialog box, and you cannot make a frozen layer the current drawing layer.

Rename. You can rename a layer by clicking on its existing name and then editing the name. You cannot rename a layer to an existing name, and you cannot rename external reference layer names.

Filters

The Filters option controls which particular layers are displayed in the Layer Control layer list box. This option has two controls which perform the following actions:

On. This check box controls whether the layer name list box displays all the layers within the drawing or only those that match the selected filter set. Check this box to display only the names matching the filter set.

S_et. Choosing this button initiates the Set Layer Filters dialog box (see fig. D.30). This dialog box narrows down the number of layers to be displayed in the Layer Name list box. You can select only the layers that match a certain layer state (On/Off, Frozen/Thawed, Locked/Unlocked, and so on) or layer name/color/linetype.

Figure D.30. *The Set Layer Filters dialog box.*

With this flexibility in filtering layer names and a structured layer naming scheme, you can filter practically any set of layers using a wide variety of criteria. For example, the filter ~FLOORPLN|* would exclude from the layer listing all layer names created by an xref to the FLOORPLN drawing. If you are devising a standard layer naming format that you plan to utilize frequently, it may be worth the initial time and effort to consider groups of layers that you may want to isolate using these wild cards and establish your layer names accordingly. Do not be overwhelmed by the possibilities these wild cards afford. You can probably utilize a few of them to accomplish your filtering needs.

The COLOR, DDCOLOR, DDLTYPE, and LINETYPE commands can override the values of layer color and linetype settings.

Example

This example uses the PNID sample drawing to illustrate how the DDLMODES command works.

'DDLMODES

Choose the Layers tool *from the Object Properties toolbar*	Issues the DDLMODES command
Command: `'ddlmodes`	
Choose the Select All *button*	Highlights all layers in the list
Choose the Off *button*	Turns off all selected layers
Choose the Clear All *button*	Dehighlights or deselects the layers
Select the TEXT *layer*	Highlights the layer
Choose the On *button*	Turns on the layer
Choose the Current *button*	Makes the selected layer current
Choose the Set Ltype *button*	Displays the Select Linetype dialog box
Double-click the CENTER *linetype image*	Selects the linetype to assign to the layer and closes the dialog box
Choose the OK *button*	Terminates the Layer Control dialog box and makes the changes to the drawing

Related Commands

DDCOLOR   DDEMODES   DDLTYPE   LAYER
VPLAYER   XPLODE

Related System Variables

CLAYER   MAXSORT

'DDLTYPE

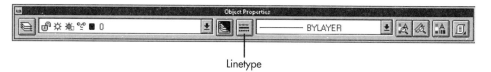

Toolbar: *Linetype (Object Properties, Linetype)*
Pull-down: **D**ata, Li**n**etype
Screen: DATA, DDltype:

The DDLTYPE command displays the Select Linetype dialog box that is used to set the linetype for all new objects (see fig. D.31). Any setting other than BYLAYER overrides the current layer linetype settings. Unlike its command-line equivalent, the LINETYPE command, the Select Linetype dialog box offers a graphic example of each of the available linetypes.

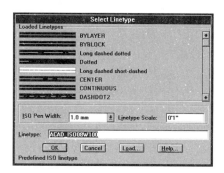

Figure D.31. *The Select Linetype dialog box.*

Dialog Box Items

The Loaded Linetypes area (the main area) of the Select Linetype dialog box displays a column of image buttons graphically showing each linetype and its corresponding name. Standard linetype definitions are stored in the ACAD.LIN file in your AutoCAD support directory. Complex linetypes are stored in the LTYPESHP.LIN file in the support directory. If you load more linetypes than can fit in the list, a vertical scroll bar appears at the right. Clicking on a linetype image selects the linetype and places its name in the **L**inetype edit box. Double-clicking a linetype image makes that linetype current and closes the dialog box. The BYLAYER linetype, AutoCAD's default, means that new objects inherit the linetype of the current layer. The

BYBLOCK option means that if you include the objects on an inserted block, they inherit the linetype that is in effect at the time of the block insertion.

I̲SO Pen Width. When you select an *International Standards Organization* (ISO) linetype pattern, this edit box becomes active. Somewhat of a misnomer, "Pen Width" really should be "Linetype Scaling." This value controls the spacing and scale of the dashes, dots, and lines that make up the linetype, and is stored in the LTSCALE system variable.

> Because the ISO Pen Width setting changes the value of LTSCALE, you should not use a mixture of ISO linetypes and standard AutoCAD linetypes within the same drawing. If you produce an ISO-standard drawing, use only ISO-standard linetypes to avoid confusion in the appearance of the linetypes.

Li̲netype Scale. Use this edit box to specify the global linetype scale (stored in the system variable LTSCALE) for all linetypes except ISO linetypes.

L̲inetype. This edit box reflects the name of your selection from the linetypes as stored in the linetype file, or you can type a linetype name.

> You can customize linetype definitions fairly easily. If you want to experiment, first make a backup copy of the ACAD.LIN file. You also can store your linetypes in another file, or purchase third-party linetypes.

Lo̲ad. Use this button to load a linetype from a linetype file. This button initiates the Load or Reload Linetypes dialog box (see fig. D.32). You use the F̲ile button to bring up the standard file selection dialog box, where you can choose the linetype definition file (ACAD.LIN by default). The list box displays all available linetypes in the specified file. Use the S̲elect All button, and then click on OK, to load all the linetypes.

> Loading unnecessary or unused linetypes increases your drawing's file size. Load only the linetypes you need and later purge any that you do not use.

Figure D.32. *The Load or Reload Linetypes dialog box.*

Example

In the following example, you load the DASHDOT2 linetype from the ACAD.LIN file.

Choose the Linetype tool from the Object Properties toolbar	Issues the DDLTYPE command
Command: '_ddltype	
*Choose the L*o*ad button*	Displays the Load or Reload Linetypes dialog box
*Click on the F*i*le button*	Displays the Select Linetype File dialog box
Double-click on ACAD.LIN	Selects the linetype file to use
Select the DASHDOT2 *linetype*	Selects the linetype to load
Choose OK	Terminates the dialog box
Double-click on DASHDOT2	Determines the current linetype to use

TIP A quick way to specify a loaded linetype is to select a linetype from the Linetype Properties pull-down list box on the Object Properties toolbar.

Related Commands
DDLMODES   LINETYPE   LTSCALE

Related System Variables
CELTSCALE   CELTYPE   LTSCALE   PSLTSCALE

DDMODIFY

Properties

Toolbar: *Properties (Object Properties)*
Pull-down: **E**dit, P**r**operties
Screen: MODIFY, Modify:

The DDMODIFY command enables you to change the specific characteristics of individual objects. The behavior of the Properties tool in the Object Properties toolbar is controlled by the object(s) selected before or after initiating the command. When a single object is selected, the DDMODIFY command is invoked and a dialog box specific to that object's type is opened. When multiple objects are selected (even of the same type), only the Change Properties dialog box is opened (see DDCHPROP).

At the top of a typical DDMODIFY dialog box, three buttons give you access to subsidiary dialog boxes, where you can change the color, layer and linetype settings. In this top section of the dialog box, you also find edit boxes for controlling object thickness and linetype scale, and a listing of the selected objects Handle.

The rest of the DDMODIFY dialog box varies depending on the type of object that you choose to modify. Figure D.33, for example, shows the DDMODIFY dialog box that appears when you modify a line.

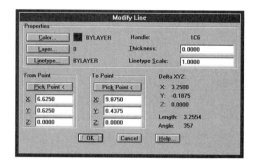

Figure D.33. *The Modify Line dialog box (for editing a line).*

 The DDMODIFY dialog box lists all data contained in the AutoCAD drawing database that pertains to the selected object. Use it in place of the LIST command.

The following list details the types of properties you can change for a particular object type, in addition to the standard properties mentioned above.

3DFace. Corner locations, edge visibility.

3DSolid. You cannot change any additional properties. The normal Thickness option is disabled.

Arc. Center point; radius; start angle and end angle. Also displays the Total Angle and Arc Length values (see fig. D.34).

Figure D.34. *The Modify Arc dialog box.*

Associative Hatch. Displays the Block name and provides access to the Hatchedit dialog box (see HATCHEDIT).

Attribute Definition. Tag; Prompt; Default value; Origin point; Height; Rotation; Width Factor; Obliquing angle; Justification; Style; Upside Down; Backwards; Invisible, Constant, Verify, and Preset.

Block Insertion. Insertion point; X, Y, and Z scale factors; rotation angle; for blocks inserted with MINSERT, the number of columns and rows, and column and row spacing.

> The ELEVATION system variable can be used to control the Z value obtained when using DDMODIFY's pick point feature.

Circle. Center point; radius. Diameter, Circumference, and Area information is also displayed.

Construction Line (XLINE). The Thickness option is disabled. Root point and second point. The Direction Vector X, Y, and Z factors are also displayed.

Dimension. The Thickness option is disabled. The Edit..., Geometry..., Format..., and Annotation... options open supplemental dialog boxes (see DDIM).

Ellipse. The Thickness option is disabled. Center location, Major and Minor Radius, Start and End Angle. Also displays Radius Ratio, Major Axis Vector, and Area information.

External Reference (XREF). Insertion point; X, Y, and Z scale factors; Rotation angle; number of Columns and Rows, and Column and Row Spacing for creating rectangular arrays of the XREF similar to MINSERT. Also displays the Xref Name and Path.

Leader. Geometry, Format, Annotation, Type (Straight or Splined); Arrow controls and whether or not an arrowhead is drawn.

Line. From Point and To Point X, Y, and Z locations. Also displays Delta X, Y, and Z, Length and Angle values. (Refer to fig. D.34.)

Multiline (MLINE). Displays Mline Style (no additional properties can be modified).

Multitext (MTEXT). Insertion point with access provided to additional dialog boxes for editing Contents (Edit MText) and Properties (Mtext Properties). See MTEXT and MTPROP.

Point. Location X, Y, and Z values.

Polyline (PLINE). Display each Vertex location; choose an applicable smoothing method from None, Quadratic, Cubic, Bézier, and Curve Fit; polyline or mesh structure (N or M)—open or closed; Mesh surface approximation factors (U or V); application of linetypes to 2D polylines.

Ray. The Thickness option is disabled. Start Point and Second Point. Also displays Direction Vector information.

Region. No additional properties can be modified.

Shape. Origin Point X, Y, and Z; Size, Rotation, Width Factor, and Obliquing angle.

Solid. Corner point locations X and Y (Z is controlled from the last corner).

Spline. The Thickness option is disabled. No additional properties can be modified. Displays each Control and Data Point Vertex, any weight applied to a control points (its distance from the spline), and the Degree and Properties of the spline.

Text. Edit Text; Origin point; Height; Rotation; Width Factor; Obliquing angle; justification; Style; Upside Down; and Backwards.

Trace. Corner point locations X and Y (Z is controlled from the last corner).

Viewport. The Linetype, Thickness, and Linetype Scale options are disabled. No additional properties can be modified Displays View Center X, Y, and Z location, Vport ID, Width and Height, and Status information.

Related Commands

CHANGE   CHPROP   DDCHPROP   DDEDIT
ELEV   MTPROP   SPELL

Related System Variables

ELEVATION   PICKFIRST

'DDOSNAP

Running Object Snap

Toolbar: *Running Object Snap (Standard Toolbar, Object Snap)*
Pull-down: **O**ptions, Running **O**bject Snap
Screen: OPTIONS, DDosnap: and SERVICE, Osnap:

You use the DDOSNAP command to initiate the Running Object Snap dialog box, which enables you to set AutoCAD's running object snap modes (see fig. D.35). Object snaps enable you to manipulate objects and draw accurately by letting you specify points that correspond to the geometric features of an object you select. To enter a point using object snap, you need only specify an object snap mode and pick any point on an existing object. AutoCAD calculates the precise point coordinates according to the mode you specify and the object selected. You can set one or more modes to be applied to all location selections, or enter them on the fly at AutoCAD's command option prompts.

Figure D.35. *The DDOSNAP dialog box.*

When more than one osnap mode is active, AutoCAD bases the mode to apply on the type(s) of objects found in the aperture box and their proximity. For example, with the mode combination ENDPoint, INTersection, and CENter, if there is more than one object in the aperture box and they intersect, the INTersection mode prevails. If not, one of the following applies to the object nearest the pick point. If it is an arc and the pick is less than the arc's radius from an endpoint, then the ENDPoint mode applies; otherwise, the CENter mode prevails. If it is a circle, the CENter mode is used. If it is a line, the ENDPoint mode is applied.

> CEnter, INTersection, ENDPoint is probably the most useful combination. It will find most of the points you want, and can be overridden in the few cases when you need another mode or no object snapping.
>
> TIP

Other mode combinations are tricky. When you use the ENDPoint mode with the MIDpoint mode, you must pick closer to the end than the middle to indicate which mode you intend. When you combine the PERpendicular and the TANgent modes, proximity distance determines which mode you want applied to an arc or a circle.

Some mode combinations just don't work. The NEArest mode does not combine well with anything because it overpowers everything. Similarly, if you combine the CENter and QUAdrant modes and the radius of a circle or arc is much larger than the aperture, it is impossible to snap to the center. For such large circles and arcs, the distance from the pick point to the center is always greater than the distance to a quadrant point. However, you can still snap to the center of small circles and arcs by placing the crosshairs as close as possible to the center point while picking the circle or arc with the aperture. When in doubt, just override the running mode combination with a mode that you know will work.

Dialog Box Items

The DDOSNAP dialog box is split into two sections. The first is used to specify running osnap mode(s), and the second is used to size the aperture selection box.

Select Settings

Select Settings provides a check box for each object snap mode. Click on one or more of the boxes to select the modes that you wish to remain active.

Endpoint. Snaps to the nearest endpoint of an arc, line, polyline, mesh, elliptical arc, ray, spline, or mline. Endpoint object snap also snaps to the endpoints of extruded edges and corners of 3D faces, traces, or solids.

Midpoint. Snaps to the middle point of a line, arc, elliptical arc, spline, ellipse, solid, ray, xline, or mline. Midpoint also snaps to the midpoint of all four edges of an extruded line or polyline segments and the midpoint of an arc's extruded edge.

Center. Snaps to the center of an arc, circle, ellipse, elliptical arc (you must pick the object on its circumference) , or solid.

Node. Snaps to a point object, including definition points of dimension objects.

Quadrant. Snaps to the nearest 0-, 90-, 180-, or 270-degree quadrant point of an arc, elliptical arc, solid, circle, or ellipse. Quadrant points are relative to the current *User Coordinate System* (UCS).

Intersection. Snaps to the nearest intersection of any combination of lines, polylines, arcs, circles, elliptical arc, ellipses, splines, xlines, rays, or mlines. The intersection point is only found if the objects intersect in three-dimensional space. Intersection also snaps to the corners of solid objects, lines, and extruded polyline segments, or the intersecting edge of two wide objects. If an intersection cannot be found, and the point specified resides on an object, AutoCAD will prompt for a second object to determine the closest intersection. The Intersection and Apparent Intersection modes should not be activated at the same time.

In*s*ertion. Snaps to the insertion point of a block, external reference, shape, attribute, attribute definition, or text object.

Perpen*d*icular. Snaps to a point that is perpendicular from the previous point to the selected object. The resulting point does not have to be located on the selected object.

***T*angent.** Snaps to a point that forms a tangent between a selected circle, arc, ellipse, or spline that is tangent to that object from the last point.

Ne*a*rest. Snaps to the point on a line, arc, circle, polyline, ellipse, mline, spline, ray, xline, viewport, or edge of a solid, trace, or 3Dface that is closest to the crosshairs.

A*p*parent Int. Snaps to the apparent intersection of two objects regardless of whether they actually intersect in 3D space. The Apparent Intersection and Intersection modes should not be activated at the same time.

Q*u*ick. Snaps to the first point found that corresponds to one of the set of currently selected object snap modes. You must have other object snap settings in effect for this option.

C*l*ear All. Clears any active mode selections.

TIP

> Object snap overrides are created by entering the first three letters of the desired osnap mode at the command prompt, or by selecting an option from the cursor menu (also known as the pop-up menu). Access the cursor menu by holding down a shift key and pressing the return button on your pointing device (Shift+right button on a mouse). These momentary osnaps override running osnaps.

Aperture Size

At the bottom of the box, a horizontal scroll bar allows you to dynamically set the size of the *aperture*, a small square that appears at the intersection of the crosshairs when you activate an object snap mode. An object to which you want to snap must cross the boundary of the pick box when you select the object for the object snap to take effect.

A small aperture size finds points faster and more accurately in crowded drawings, but it is harder to line up. A large aperture is easy to line up, but it is slower and less accurate. The 'APERTURE and 'DDOSNAP commands can be issued transparently so you can adjust the aperture size while being prompted for an osnap pick point.

Related Commands
APERTURE   ORTHO   OSNAP

Related System Variables
APERTURE   OSMODE

'DDPTYPE

Pull-down: **O**ptions, **D**isplay, **P**oint Style...
Screen: OPTIONS, Display, DDptype:

Use the DDPTYPE command to specify the size of a point object and how it appears. You must regenerate the drawing before the changes can take effect in the drawing. The DDPTYPE command utilizes the Point Style dialog box (see fig. D.36).

Figure D.36. *The Point Style dialog box.*

Dialog Box Items

The Point Style dialog box displays all possible point display modes in image buttons. Besides the option of creating a single point (or nothing), the display modes offer combinations of various symbols, including points, a plus sign, an × symbol, a vertical tick mark, a circle, and a square. Double-click on an image button to make that mode current for all new point objects.

You use the Point **S**ize edit box to specify the size of the point object. This size is a percentage relative to the drawing screen area or a fixed number of drawing units as indicated by the Set Size **R**elative to Screen radio button or the Set Size in **A**bsolute Units radio button.

Changing the display mode and size of point objects changes all of the points in the current drawing, including points within blocks and external references (XREFs). This can have an undesirable effect if you do not consider with care the placement, size, and appearance of points.

Related Commands

DIVIDE   MEASURE   POINT

Related System Variables

MEASURE   PDMODE   PDSIZE

DDRENAME

Pull-down: **D**ata, **R**ename
Screen: DATA, Rename

You issue the DDRENAME command to initiate the Rename dialog box (see fig. D.37), which enables you to rename blocks, dimension styles, layers, linetypes, text styles, UCS configurations, views, and viewport configurations. You cannot rename an object, however, to an existing name used by the same type of item, nor can you rename colors. In addition, the linetypes BYLAYER, BYBLOCK, or CONTINUOUS, the layer 0, or anonymous blocks such as those created by the HATCH or BHATCH command cannot be renamed.

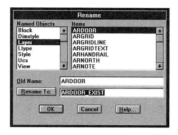

Figure D.37. *The Rename dialog box.*

Dialog Box Items

At the top of the DDRENAME dialog box, as shown in figure D.37, you see two list boxes, as follows:

Named Objects. On the left side, the Named Objects list box shows the categories of objects you can rename. See the list in figure D.37.

> When you rename a linetype, the new name applies only to the current drawing. The linetype name in the ACAD.LIN file remains the same. When a block that was inserted from an external drawing file is renamed, the external file remains unaffected.

Items. On the right side, the Items list box shows the name of each item in the selected category that the current drawing holds. For example, when you click on Layer in the Named Objects box, the Items box shows the name of every layer in the drawing. If the layer names do not all fit on one screen, the scroll bar enables you to view others.

To rename an item, first select the kind of item you want to rename from the Named Objects list box, and then pick a specific item from the Items list box. The name of the item that you choose appears in the **O**ld Name edit box below the two list boxes. Type the item's new name in the **R**ename To edit box. AutoCAD accepts item names up to as many as 31 characters in length, and the names can contain letters, digits, $ (dollar signs), - (hyphens), and _ (underscores). You must choose the **R**ename To button to make the change.

> You can rename groups of items that contain the same text pattern in one fell swoop using the DDRENAME command. If, for example, your drawing contains a series of text styles called SIMPLEX-1, SIMPLEX-2, SIMPLEX-3, SIMPLEX-4, and SIMPLEX-5, and you want to

rename them all to ROMANS-1 . . . ROMANS-5, you would type SIMPLEX* in the **O**ld Name edit box and ROMANS* in the **R**ename To edit box.

Related Command

RENAME

'DDRMODES

Pull-down: **O**ptions, **D**rawing Aids...
Screen: OPTIONS, DDrmode: and SERVICE, DrawAid:

You use the DDRMODES (Dynamic Dialog dRawing MODES) command to initiate the Drawing Aids dialog box, which enables you to control drawing aid settings—ortho, solid fill, quick text, blips, highlight, groups, snap, grid, and isoplane (see fig. D.38). DDRMODES also is useful when you need to check the current status of the various drawing-mode settings.

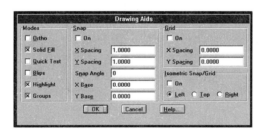

Figure D.38. *The Drawing Aids dialog box.*

Dialog Box Items

DDRMODES provides no command-line prompts. Instead, you select from the dialog box options discussed in the following sections.

Modes

In the Modes area of the Drawing Aids dialog box, the following check boxes are available:

Ortho. You use this check box to turn ortho mode on or off (same as using the F8 key or double-clicking the ORTHO button in the status line).

Solid Fill. You use this check box to notify AutoCAD whether to show solids and thickened polylines or to show only their edges. This box is checked by default.

Quick Text. You use this check box to notify AutoCAD to display text normally or with a boundary box that shows the limits of the text. If you do not activate the box, AutoCAD displays text normally.

Text, solids, and wide polylines add to drawing regeneration time on very large drawings. If your editing does not currently involve these Items, turn off Solid Fill and turn on Quick Text to dramatically decrease regeneration time.

Blips. You use this check box to notify AutoCAD to place "blips" at every point where you pick a point in the drawing editor.

Highlight. You use this check box to notify AutoCAD to display selected objects with a temporary dashed linetype. This is on by default.

Groups. This check box enables you to select objects by groups. For example, if you select an object within a group, you select the entire group. This is on by default.

Snap

You use options in the Snap area to turn snap mode on or off (same as pressing F9 or double-clicking the SNAP button in the status line), change the snap X and Y spacing (the default is 1), snap angle (default 0), and snap base (default 0,0). Snap is off by default.

Grid

You use the options in the Grid area to turn the drawing grid on or off (same as pressing F7 or double-clicking the GRID button in the status line) and change the grid X and Y spacing (the default is 0). The grid is off by default.

Isometric Snap/Grid

You use the options in the Isometric Snap/Grid area to turn isometric drawing mode on or off and determine which isometric plane is currently in use (same as cycling F5). The default value is off.

Example

This example uses the TABLET sample drawing to illustrate how the DDRMODES command works. Figures D.39 and D.40 show a portion of the drawing before and after you turn on Quick Text mode.

Command: **DDRMODES** (Enter)	Issues the DDRMODES command
Click the Quick Text check box	Sets the QTEXT system variable on
Press the OK button	Exits the Drawing Aids dialog box
Command: **REGEN** (Enter)	Regenerates the drawing to make changes evident

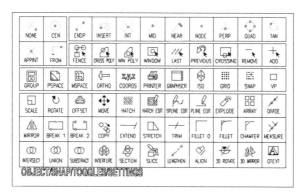

Figure D.39. *The drawing before you turn on Quick Text mode.*

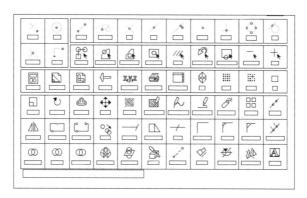

Figure D.40. *The drawing after you turn on Quick Text mode.*

> Before plotting the drawing, turn Quick Text mode off. Plotting with Quick Text on will result in plotting the boundary box instead of text.

Related Commands

BLIPMODE	FILL	GRID	GROUP
ISOPLANE	ORTHO	PICKSTYLE	QTEXT
SNAP			

Related System Variables

BLIPMODE	COORDS	GRIDMODE	GRIDUNIT
HIGHLIGHT	ISOPLANE	ORTHOMODE	SNAPANG
SNAPBASE	SNAPISOPAIR	SNAPMODE	SNAPSTYL
SNAPUNIT			

DDUCS

Named UCS

    Toolbar: *Named UCS (Standard, UCS)*
    Pull-down: <u>V</u>iew, Named U<u>C</u>S...
    Screen: VIEW DDucs:

The *Dynamic Dialog User Coordinate System* (DDUCS) command controls previously saved UCSs using a dialog box. You can restore, delete, or rename a previously saved UCS. You also can list the X, Y, and Z axis directions of any saved UCS with respect to the current UCS (which is identified for you).

Prompts and Options

The DDUCS command displays the UCS Control dialog box (see fig. D.41). The previously saved UCS names are listed at the top, and the C<u>u</u>rrent, D<u>e</u>lete, <u>L</u>ist, and <u>R</u>ename To: push buttons are at the bottom.

Figure D.41. *The UCS Control dialog box.*

The following list describes the options in the UCS Control dialog box:

Current. Restores a previously saved UCS as the current UCS. Select a named UCS from the list box, and then press this push button to restore that UCS as the current UCS.

Delete. Deletes a previously saved UCS. Select a named UCS from the list box, and click on the **D**elete button to delete it. Note that you cannot delete the *WORLD*, *NO NAME*, or *PREVIOUS* coordinate systems.

List. Displays the origin point and X, Y, and Z axis directions of the selected UCS with respect to the current UCS.

Rename To. Renames the selected UCS in the UCS Names list box. Select a named UCS from the list box, enter a new name for this UCS into the edit box next to the **R**ename To: push button, and then click on the **R**ename To: push button. You cannot rename the *WORLD* or *PREVIOUS* coordinate systems.

Example

The following example shows you how to restore a previously saved UCS. Use the UCS command to create the two UCSs shown in figure D.42. The UCS in the left viewport is named RIGHT_SIDE, and the UCS in the right viewport is named FRONT.

```
Command: UCS (Enter)                        Starts UCS command

Origin/ZAxis/3point/OBject/                 Resets World UCS as current UCS
View/X/Y/Z/Prev/Restore/Save/
Del/?/<World>: (Enter)

Command: DDUCS (Enter)                      Starts DDUCS command and opens
                                            the UCS Control dialog box
```

Choose FRONT *from the* UCS Names *list box*	Selects FRONT UCS to control
Choose **C**urrent	Sets FRONT as current UCS
Choose OK	Changes UCS to FRONT
Command: **DDUCS** (Enter)	Starts DDUCS command
Select RIGHT_SIDE *from the* UCS Names *list box*	Selects RIGHT_SIDE UCS to control
Choose **C**urrent	Sets RIGHT_SIDE as current UCS
Choose OK	Changes UCS to RIGHT_SIDE

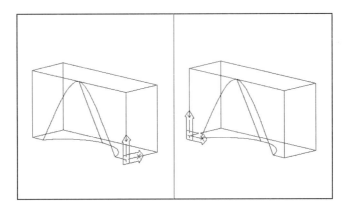

Figure D.42. *Two named UCSs—RIGHT_SIDE and FRONT.*

Related Commands

DDUCSP   ELEV   UCS   UCSICON

Related Variables

UCSFOLLOW   UCSNAME   UCSORG
UCSXDIR   UCSYDIR   WORLDUCS

DDUCSP

Toolbar: *Preset UCS (Standard, UCS)*
Pull-down: <u>V</u>iew, Preset <u>U</u>CS...
Screen: VIEW, DDucsp:

The *Dynamic Dialog User Coordinate System Preset* (DDUCSP) command controls preset orientations for the UCS. These preset orientations are typically 90-degree rotations about one of the existing X, Y, or Z axes. You can restore the World UCS and the previous UCS, and you can change the UCS to match the current view.

Prompts and Options

The DDUCSP command displays the UCS Orientation dialog box (see fig. D.43). Nine image tiles display standard orientations that can be selected, and two radio buttons at the bottom of the dialog box indicate to which UCS the preset orientation references. The red line protruding from the block in each image indicates the direction the Z axis is pointed. The hatched face of the block indicates the X,Y plane.

Figure D.43. *The UCS Orientation dialog box.*

All referrals to rotation follow the "right hand" rule. Refer to the first section in Chapter 11, "Working in Three-Dimensional Space," in the *AutoCAD Users Guide* for an explanation of this convention.

To change to a preset UCS, select the image tile option representing the preset. The following list describes the options in the UCS Orientation dialog box.

World. Restores the World UCS. The **A**bsolute to WCS radio button is not automatically selected.

Top. No change to the UCS if **R**elative to Current UCS is checked. Changes to World UCS if **A**bsolute to WCS is checked.

Back. Rotates the UCS 180 degrees about the Z axis, then 90 degrees about the X axis.

Left. Rotates the UCS –90 degrees about the Z axis, then 90 degrees about the X axis.

Front. Rotates the UCS 90 degrees about the X axis.

Right. Rotates the UCS 90 degrees about the Z axis, then 90 degrees about the X axis.

Current View. The UCS aligns with the current viewing direction. The **A**bsolute to WCS radio button is automatically selected.

Bottom. Rotates the UCS 180 degrees about the X axis.

Previous. Restores the previous UCS. The **R**elative to Current UCS and **A**bsolute to WCS radio buttons are not applicable in this case.

Relative to Current UCS. Rotates the UCS as described in the preceding paragraphs.

Absolute to WCS. Changes the orientation of the UCS relative to the WCS. Basically restores the WCS, then rotates the UCS as described in the preceding paragraphs.

> **TIP** If you are having trouble visualizing the effect of UCS orientation in 3D space, create a 3D cube, label each face, and then try to predict the orientation as you change the UCS.

Example

The following example shows you how to use the DDUCSP command to change from the World UCS to a right side UCS and a front UCS. Use the UCS command to save a front and right UCS. Use the UCS command's Origin option to reset the origin of the UCS, if desired (see fig. D.44).

Command: **UCS** (Enter)	Starts UCS command
Origin/ZAxis/3point/OBject/View/X/Y/Z/Prev/Restore/Save/Del/?/<World>: (Enter)	Resets World UCS as current UCS
Command: **DDUCSP** (Enter)	Starts DDUCSP command and opens the UCS Orientation dialog box
Select the FRONT *image tile*	Selects FRONT rotation
Choose **R**elative to Current UCS	
Choose OK	Rotates UCS 90 degrees about X axis
Command: **DDUCSP** (Enter)	Starts DDUCSP command and opens the UCS Orientation dialog box
Select the RIGHT *image tile*	Selects RIGHT rotation
Choose **A**bsolute to WCS	
Choose OK	Changes UCS back to World orientation, then rotates UCS 90 degrees about the Z axis, then 90 degrees about the X axis

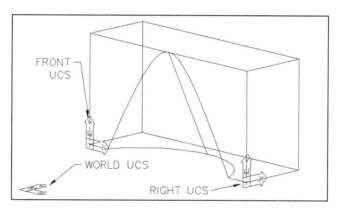

Figure D.44. *Rotating the UCS with the DDUCSP command.*

Related Commands

DDUCS   UCS   UCSICON

Related Variables

UCSFOLLOW   UCSNAME   UCSORG   UCSXDIR
UCSYDIR   WORLDUCS

DDUNITS

Pull-down: **D**ata, Un**i**ts...
Screen: DATA, Units:

AutoCAD allows for the display of coordinates, distances, and angles in several formats, so that, depending on your needs, you can measure and notate in the most appropriate format. You use the DDUNITS command to initiate the Units Control dialog box, which enables you to set the appropriate format (see fig. D.45). The main features of the DDUNITS dialog box are two sets of radio buttons. One set of buttons controls the type of unit used for distances and measurements. The other set is used for specifying angular units.

Figure D.45. *The Units Control dialog box.*

Dialog Box Items

The DDUNITS command Units Control dialog box displays two areas—Units and Angles.

Units

The radio buttons within the Units area determine what Units AutoCAD will use for lengths and distances. You can also specify the precision of the units used. These items are discussed below.

Scientific. Format 0.0000E+01, showing decimal distances with exponent. Each drawing units can be any real-world unit.

De<u>c</u>imal. Format 0.0000, showing distances in decimal. Each drawing unit can be any real-world unit.

<u>E</u>ngineering. Format 0'-0.0000", showing feet and decimal inches. Each unit is assumed to be one inch.

<u>A</u>rchitectural. Format 0'-0/0", showing feet and fractional inches. Each unit is assumed to be one inch.

<u>F</u>ractional. Format 0 0/0, showing fractional distances. Each drawing unit can be any real-world unit.

<u>P</u>recision. Beneath the set of radio buttons, this pull-down list box enables you to set the level of precision you want.

Angles

The radio buttons on the right of the dialog box enable you to choose how AutoCAD measures angles. AutoCAD offers the following choices:

De<u>c</u>imal Degrees. Format 0.0000, simple decimal numbers.

Deg/<u>M</u>in/Sec. Format 0d0'.0000", with 'd' indicating degrees, ' indicating minutes, and " indicating seconds.

<u>G</u>rads. Format 0.0000g, decimal numbers with the appended 'g' indicating grads.

<u>R</u>adians. Format 0.0000r, decimal numbers with the appended 'r' indicating radians.

Sur<u>v</u>eyor. Format N or S 0d0'0.0000" E or W. The angle between N/S and E/W indicates the distance East or West from North or South. When the angle points in a cardinal direction, AutoCAD shows only the compass point, for example E for 0 degrees.

Precisio<u>n</u>. As in the Units area, this pull-down list box beneath the radio buttons enables you to set the precision of the angle's measurement.

At the bottom of the dialog box, you can choose the <u>D</u>irection button to initiate the Direction Control dialog box, which enables you to choose the direction that equals angle 0 (see fig. D.46). You can choose from <u>E</u>ast (default), <u>N</u>orth, <u>W</u>est, <u>S</u>outh, or <u>O</u>ther. If you choose <u>O</u>ther, the <u>A</u>ngle edit box and <u>P</u>ick button highlight. You can type an angle in the <u>A</u>ngle edit box or show an angle that has your pointing device by picking two points on-screen. Beneath the <u>P</u>ick button, two additional radio buttons enable you to choose whether AutoCAD measures angles in the <u>C</u>ounter-Clockwise or C<u>l</u>ockwise direction.

Figure D.46. *The Direction Control dialog box.*

 The angle specified for object rotations is measured independently of the angle zero base. An unrotated object always has a zero rotation. Orientation angles are always measured from the angle zero base. For example, if you choose angle zero to point south, a horizontal line of text is considered to be oriented to 90 degrees.

Related Command

UNITS

Related System Variables

ANGBASE	ANGDIR	AUNITS	AUPREC
LUNITS	LUPREC	UNITMODE	

DDVIEW

Named Views

Toolbar: *Named Views (Standard Toolbar, View)*
Pull-down: <u>V</u>iew, <u>N</u>amed Views...
Screen: VIEW, DDview:

The DDVIEW command controls named views using a dialog box. You can restore a previously saved view, create a new named view, delete existing named views, and display information about a specific view.

Prompts and Options

The DDVIEW command displays the View Control dialog box (see fig. D.47). The previously saved named views are listed at the top of the dialog box, and the **R**estore, **N**ew, **D**elete, and D**e**scription push buttons at the bottom.

Figure D.47. *The View Control dialog box.*

The following list describes the options in the View Control dialog box:

Views. Lists all named views in the drawing. If not all views fit on a single screen, a scroll bar appears so that you can scroll to other view names.

Restore View. Lists the view that will be restored. If no changes have been made, this is the *CURRENT* view.

Restore. Changes the view to restore to match the currently selected named view in the Views list box.

New. Displays the Define New View dialog box (see fig. D.48). Enter the name of the new view in the **N**ew Name edit box. To save the current view in the graphics window, select **C**urrent Display, then **S**ave View.

To save a specific view in the graphics window, select **D**efine Window, and then choose the **W**indow push button from the Define New View dialog box. AutoCAD temporarily hides the Define New View dialog box. Specify the first corner, and then the other corner of the view you want to save. The Define New View dialog box reappears. Select **S**ave View.

Delete. Deletes the currently selected view in the Views list box. You cannot delete the view named *CURRENT*.

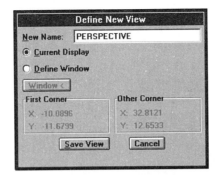

Figure D.48. *The Define New View dialog box.*

Description. Displays the View Description dialog box (see fig. D.49). This dialog box displays information regarding the size, viewing direction, and twist angle of the view. Perspective, lens length, and clipping plane information also are listed. See the DVIEW command for information regarding perspective views, front and back clipping planes, and lens length.

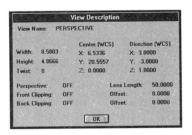

Figure D.49. *The View Description dialog box.*

Example

The following example shows you how to save and restore views using the DDVIEW command.

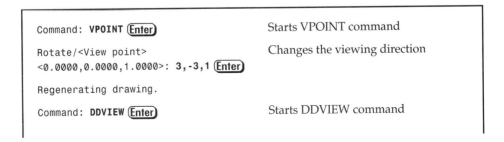

Choose **N**ew	Displays Define New View dialog box
Enter **PERSPECTIVE** *in the* **N**ew *Name edit box*	Specifies PERSPECTIVE as name for view
Choose **C**urrent Display	Saves current display as view
Choose **S**ave View	Returns to View Control dialog box
Choose OK	Exits View Control dialog box
Command: **PLAN** (Enter)	Executes PLAN command
<Current UCS>/Ucs/World: **W** (Enter)	Changes view to plan view of World UCS
Regenerating drawing.	
Command: **DDVIEW** (Enter)	Starts DDVIEW command
Select PERSPECTIVE *from the* Views *list box*	Selects view to control
Choose **R**estore	
Choose OK	Restores view

Related Commands

VIEW   DDVPOINT   MSPACE   PAN
PLAN   PSPACE

Related System Variables

TILEMODE   VIEWCTR   VIEWDIR   VIEWMODE
VIEWSIZE   VIEWTWIST   VSMAX   VSMIN

DDVPOINT

Pull-down: **V**iew, 3D Vi**e**wpoint, **R**otate...

The DDVPOINT command changes the viewing direction using a dialog box. DDVPOINT is disabled while the drawing is in paper space. You can set the viewing direction relative to the current *User Coordinate System* (UCS) or the

World Coordinate System (WCS). To change the viewing direction, specify the viewing angle in the X,Y plane and from the X,Y plane. You also can set the current viewing direction to be a plan view of the current UCS or the WCS.

Prompts and Options

The DDVPOINT command displays the Viewpoint Presets dialog box (see fig. D.50). Two radio buttons at the top of the dialog box indicate which UCS the viewing direction references. Two image tiles are used to graphically describe the angle in the X,Y plane and the angle from the X,Y plane. These angles are indicated in two edit boxes below the image tiles. You also can use the Set to Plan **V**iew push button to set the viewing direction to a plan view.

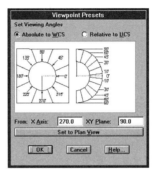

Figure D.50. *The Viewpoint Presets dialog box.*

The following list describes the options in the Viewpoint Presets dialog box:

Absolute to WCS. Changes the viewing direction to be relative to the WCS.

Relative to UCS. Changes the viewing direction to be relative to the current UCS.

From: X Axis. Use this text box to enter the desired viewing direction in the X,Y plane as measured counterclockwise from the X axis. The angle must be a positive angle. From: X **A**xis also displays the selected viewing direction in the X,Y plane, if you use the image tiles to select a viewing direction.

From: XY Plane. Use this text box to enter the desired viewing direction from the X,Y plane. From: XY **P**lane also displays the selected viewing direction from the X,Y plane, if you use the image tiles to select a viewing direction.

Set to Plan View. Changes the viewing direction to a plan view of either the current UCS or the WCS, as determined by the radio buttons at the top of the dialog box.

Image Tiles. Pick a point inside the interior circle of the image tile on the left side of the dialog box to change the viewing direction in the X,Y plane. If you pick more than one, only the last position picked is used.

Pick a point inside the curved band of the image tile on the right side of the dialog box to change the viewing direction from the X,Y plane. If you pick more than one, only the last position picked is used.

The actual angles in the X,Y plane and from the X,Y plane are updated in the edit boxes below the image tiles.

Example

The following exercise shows you how to change the viewing direction using the DDVPOINT command. To help orient your viewing, the objects used in the SUBTRACT example are used as a reference. The screen is split into four viewports, initially with a plan view of the WCS in all four (see fig. D.51).

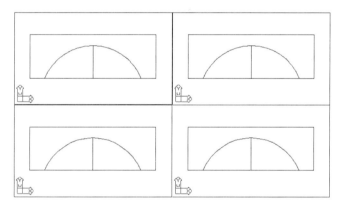

Figure D.51. *The same view in all four viewports.*

Click in the lower left viewport	Activates lower left viewport
Command: **DDVPOINT** (Enter)	Begins DDVPOINT command
Enter **280.0** *in the* From: X **A**xis *edit box and enter* **10.0** *in the* From: XY **P**lane *edit box*	Specifies viewing direction in X,Y plane and from X,Y plane
Choose OK	Changes viewing direction in this viewport (see lower left viewport of fig. D.52)

Click in the lower right viewport	Activates lower right viewport
Command: (Enter)	Repeats DDVPOINT command
Enter **350.0** *in the* From: X **A**xis *edit box and enter* **10.0** *in the* From: XY **P**lane *edit box*	Specifies viewing direction in X,Y plane and from X,Y plane
Choose OK	Changes viewing direction in this viewport (see lower right viewport of fig. D.52)
Click in the upper left viewport	Activates upper left viewport
Command: (Enter)	Repeats DDVPOINT command
Enter **100.0** *in the* From: X **A**xis *edit box and enter* **10.0** *in the* From: XY **P**lane *edit box*	Specifies viewing direction in X,Y plane and from X,Y plane
Choose OK	Changes viewing direction in this viewport (see upper left viewport of fig. D.52)
Click in the upper right viewport	Activates upper right viewport
Command: (Enter)	Repeats DDVPOINT command
Enter **225.0** *in the* From: X **A**xis *edit box and enter* **35.0** *in the* From: XY **P**lane *edit box*	Specifies viewing direction in X,Y plane and from X,Y plane
Choose OK	Changes viewing direction in this viewport (see upper right viewport of figure D.52)

Related Commands

DDVIEW   MSPACE   PLAN   PSPACE
VIEW   VPOINT

Related Variables

WORLDVIEW   TARGET   TILEMODE   VIEWCTR
VIEWDIR   VIEWMODE   VIEWTWIST   VSMAX
VSMIN

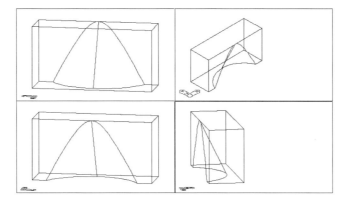

Figure D.52. *The result of changing viewing directions with the DDVPOINT command.*

DELAY

DELAY is a special command that you use with AutoCAD script files. DELAY programs a delay (in milliseconds) in a script. You can cancel the delay by pressing any key.

To use the DELAY command as part of an AutoCAD script, use the following command syntax:

DELAY *number*

In this generic syntax, *number* is the approximate length of the delay in milliseconds. The maximum delay number you can specify is 32,767.

> Use a delay of 1,000 milliseconds for every second you want to pause your script. The maximum delay is slightly more than thirty-two seconds.

Related Command

RESUME   RSRIPT   SCRIPT   LEADER

DIM/DIM1

The DIM and DIM1 commands enable you to enter AutoCAD's dimensioning mode, which you can distinguish from the regular command mode by the Dim: prompt. The dimensioning mode enables you to draw dimensions in your drawings. You should note, though, that Autodesk has replaced the DIM and DIM1 commands in AutoCAD Release 13 with more powerful and enhanced dimensioning commands that you can access from the Command: prompt. The DIM and DIM1 commands are provided only for compatibility with earlier versions of AutoCAD.

When you use the DIM command, you enter dimensioning mode and remain in it until you enter EXIT or press Ctrl+C. When you use the DIM1 command, you remain in dimensioning mode only for a single dimensioning command and then return to normal command mode. When you are in dimensioning mode, AutoCAD's nondimensioning commands (except for transparent commands, such as 'ZOOM and 'PAN) are not available.

You can use any of AutoCAD's dimensioning subcommands while you are in dimensioning mode. These dimensioning subcommands are not covered in detail here. Instead, refer to the new AutoCAD Release 13 dimensioning commands. The following table shows the new AutoCAD Release 13 commands that replace the DIM subcommands.

Table D.1
Release 13 Dimension Commands

Old DIM Command	Release 13 Command
ALIGNED	DIMALIGNED
ANGULAR	DIMANGULAR
APPLY	DIMSTYLE
BASELINE	DIMBASELINE
CENTER	DIMCENTER
CONTINUE	DIMCONTINUE
DIAMETER	DIMDIAMETER
EXIT	Not applicable
HOMETEXT	DIMEDIT
HORIZONTAL	DIMLINEAR
LEADER	LEADER
NEWTEXT	DIMEDIT
OBLIQUE	DIMEDIT
ORDINATE	DIMORDINATE
OVERRIDE	DIMOVERRIDE
RADIUS	DIMRADIUS
REDRAW	REDRAW
RESTORE	DIMSTYLE
ROTATED	DIMLINEAR
SAVE	DIMSTYLE
STATUS	DIMSTYLE
STYLE	DIMSTYLE
TEDIT	DIMTEDIT
TROTATE	DIMEDIT
UNDO	UNDO
UPDATE	Not applicable

DIM/DIM1

Old DIM Command	Release 13 Command
VARIABLES	DIMSTYLE
VERTICAL	DIMLINEAR

If you issue a single UNDO command at AutoCAD's Command: prompt after you exit dimensioning mode, you cancel *all* the commands issued during a single dimensioning session. Therefore, if you enter dimensioning mode, draw several dimensions using dimensioning commands, exit from dimensioning mode, and issue the UNDO command, all the dimensions are undone. You can immediately issue a single REDO command to restore all the undone dimensions before executing another command.

AutoCAD has two types of dimensions: associative and nonassociative. *Associative* dimensions are special blocks that are linked to the objects in your drawing. If you stretch, scale, or modify dimensioned elements, associative dimensions automatically are updated to reflect the new dimension value. You enable associative dimensions by setting the value of the DIMASO variable to 1 (ON—the default setting). *Nonassociative* dimensions are simply arrowheads, lines, and text, and they do not reflect changes you make to the objects in your drawing. You create nonassociative dimensions when you set the DIMASO variable to 0. The DIMASO setting is stored the drawing, not in the dimension style.

Use the DIMASO setting in your prototype drawing (ACAD.DWG by default) to control associative dimensioning.

A few of the dimensioning commands at the Dim: prompt have the same names as regular AutoCAD commands. You should be careful not to confuse these dimensioning commands with the general AutoCAD commands, such as REDRAW, SAVE, STATUS, STYLE, and UNDO. Some of the commands, such as REDRAW and UNDO, perform similar or identical functions in normal drawing mode and dimensioning mode. Others, however, are notably different.

When you use paper space, you should keep associative dimensions in model space. No link exists between objects across the two areas of the drawing. Therefore, if your model changes, AutoCAD does not update dimension objects created in paper space along with your model.

> Associative dimensions are not physically linked to the objects that they dimension. What makes them "associative" is that their definition points lie on the objects dimensioned. When you modify objects, you must be sure your selection set includes the definition points of the dimension before the dimension value can update automatically.

Prompts and Options

After you issue the DIM or DIM1 command, the following prompt appears:

Dim:

At this prompt, enter the name of the DIM subcommand you want to use. The previous table lists the available options.

The Dimension Elements

Each dimension that you use a dimension command to create contains certain elements, independent of whether you create the dimension as associative (DIMASO is set ON) or normal. As shown in figure D.53, a dimension has five distinctive parts, as follows:

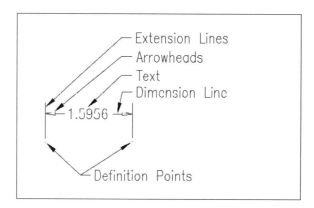

Figure D.53. *The basic dimension and its component parts.*

Dimension Text. Typically, this is the value that the DIMENSION command measures. You can override this text by entering a different value, or you can supplement it by adding prefix and suffix text. You can add prefix or suffix text by entering a new value and the characters "<>". You use these characters to indicate the actual dimension value retrieved by the DIMENSION command.

Dimension Line. This line, or an arc for angular dimensions, is created to delineate the extents of the distance.

Dimension Arrow. These are placed at both ends of the dimension line. You also can use a specialized block or a tick mark for your dimension arrows.

Extension Line. These lines lead from the points you choose to dimension, and extend beyond the dimension line.

Definition Points. These points (nodes) are the measured points that actually define the dimension value or measured distance or angle.

Related Commands

DDIM	DIMALIGNED	DIMANGULAR	DIMBASELINE
DIMCENTER	DIMCONTINUE	DIMDIAMETER	DIMEDIT
DIMLINEAR	DIMORDINATE	DIMOVERRIDE	DIMRADIUS
DIMSTYLE	DIMTEDIT	LEADER	

Related System Variables

For a list of AutoCAD's dimensioning variables, see the DIMSTYLE command. These variables also are explored at length in *Inside AutoCAD Release 13* and your AutoCAD documentation.

DIMALIGNED

Aligned Dimension

Toolbar: *Aligned Dimension, (Dimensioning)*
Pull-down: *Draw, Dimensioning, Aligned*
Screen: DRAW DIM, Aligned:

This dimensioning command draws a linear dimension parallel to a selected object or parallel to two extension line origin points. Use this command when you need to dimension a feature that is not orthogonal and you want extension lines of equal length. When you pick an object to dimension or two origin points, the DIMALIGNED command places the dimension line parallel to the object or points and through a third point that you specify.

To create angled dimensions that have unequal extension lines or that have dimensions at specific angles, use the Rotated option of the DIMLINEAR command to specify a dimension line angle.

Prompts and Options

First extension line origin or RETURN to select Pick a point at one end of the object or feature that you want to dimension. AutoCAD prompts for the Second extension line origin. The extension lines are drawn perpendicular to the angle between the first and second extension line origins.

Select line, arc, or circle This prompt appears if you press Enter at the First extension line origin or RETURN to select: prompt. Select a line, polyline segment, arc, or circle—extension lines are located for you. If you select a line, polyline segment, or arc, AutoCAD dimensions the endpoints. If you select a circle, the diameter is dimensioned from the pick point to the diameter point on the opposite side. AutoCAD dimensions only the selected segment of a polyline.

Second extension line origin Pick a point at the opposite end of the object or feature. The extension lines are drawn perpendicular to the angle between the first and second extension line origin points.

Dimension line location (Text/Angle) Pick the point through which you want the dimension line to pass. AutoCAD uses the point to determine the offset distance between the selected object or pick points and the dimension line.

If you use either of the (Text/Angle) options, one of the following prompts appears:

Enter text angle Your response to this prompt modifies the angle at which the dimension text is drawn. If you press Enter at this prompt, the text is drawn at the default text angle.

DIMALIGNED

Dimension text <default> AutoCAD calculates the distance between the two extension line origin points you pick or between the two points derived from the object you select. AutoCAD then offers the distance (in the current drawing units and precision) as the default dimension text value. You can accept this value (press Enter), specify a new value, suppress any text by typing a space, or apply prefix or suffix text to the value (see the DIM/DIM1 command).

Example

AutoCAD offers two ways to create an aligned dimension: You can select an object or pick both extension line origins. This example uses the drawing shown in figure D.54 to demonstrate both of these methods.

Command: **DIMALIGNED** (Enter)	Issues the DIMALIGNED command
First extension line origin or RETURN to select: (Enter)	Selects object dimensioning method
Select line, arc, or circle: *Pick point ① (see fig. D.54)*	Selects object to dimension
Dimension line location (Text/Angle): *Pick point ②*	Determines location of dimension line
Dimension text <15'-4 1/4">: (Enter)	Accepts measured distance as default for dimension text
Command: (Enter)	Reissues the DIMALIGNED command
DIMALIGNED First extension line origin or RETURN to select: *Pick point ③*	Specifies first definition point
Second extension line origin: *Pick point ④*	Specifies second definition point
Dimension line location (Text/Angle): **A** (Enter)	Selects the text Angle option
Enter text angle: **END** of ③	Specifies first angle point
Second point: **END** of ④	Specifies second angle point
Dimension line location(Text/Angle): *Pick point ⑤*	Specifies location of dimension line
Dimension text <15'-4 1/4">: (Enter)	Accepts default dimension value

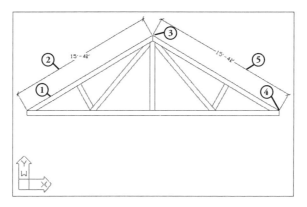

Figure D.54. *The selection points used to create the aligned dimensions.*

Related Commands

DDIM   DIM   DIMSTYLE

Related System Variables

For a list of AutoCAD's dimensioning variables, see the DIMSTYLE command. These variables are also explored at length in *Inside AutoCAD Release 13* or your AutoCAD documentation.

DIMANGULAR

Angular Dimension

Toolbar: *Angular Dimension, (Dimensioning)*
Pull-down: *D̲raw, D̲imensioning, A̲ngular*
Screen: DRAW DIM, Angular:

You use the DIMANGULAR dimensioning command to dimension the angle between two nonparallel lines, the angle swept by an arc or around part of a circle, or the angle between any three points (one of which is a vertex of the angle you want to dimension). The DIMANGULAR command creates a dimension arc rather than a dimension line, using nonparallel extension lines as necessary. You can dimension the inside or outside of major, minor, or complementary angles. Figure D.55 shows examples of angular dimensions.

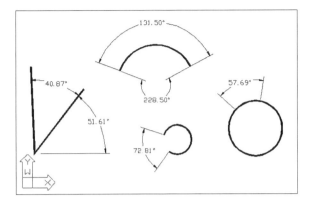

Figure D.55. *Types of angular dimensions.*

Prompts and Options

`Select arc, circle, line, or RETURN` Pick an arc, circle, line, or polyline segment for AutoCAD to dimension. If you select an arc, AutoCAD automatically locates the endpoints for the origin of the extension lines. If you select a circle, the point by which you picked the circle becomes the first extension line origin, and then the `Second angle end point:` prompt appears. If you select a line, AutoCAD considers the line to be one side of an angle you want to dimension, and prompts with `Second line:` for you to pick the second line of the angle to dimension.

Press Enter at the `Select arc, circle, line, or RETURN` prompt to tell AutoCAD that you want to specify three points describing an angle for dimensioning. The three points do not need to be on existing geometry.

`Angle vertex` If you want to dimension an angle by three points, this prompt asks you to enter a point for the vertex of the angle.

`First angle endpoint` This prompt appears when you dimension an angle by three points. Pick a point along one side of the angle to dimension.

`Second angle endpoint` This prompt appears when you dimension an angle by three points or when you pick a circle at the initial prompt. Pick a point along the second side of the angle to dimension.

`Second line` If you pick a line at the initial prompt, this prompt asks you for the second line to describe the angle to dimension.

`Dimension arc line location (Text/Angle)` For all angular dimension methods, pick the point through which you want the dimension line arc to pass. AutoCAD uses the point you pick to calculate the offset distance between your selected object or feature and the dimension line arc.

You can dimension the angle between two lines or the complementary angle (180 degrees, less the angle between the lines), or the inside (minor—under 180 degrees) or outside (major—over 180 degrees) angle of an arc, three points, or points on a circle. The point you pick for the dimension arc location controls which angle is dimensioned.

If you use either of the (Text/Angle) options, you see one of the following prompts:

Dimension text <default> AutoCAD calculates the angle between the two extension line origin points you pick or between the two points derived from the object you select. AutoCAD then offers the angle as the default dimension text value. You can accept this value (press Enter), specify a new value, suppress any text by pressing the spacebar, or apply prefix or suffix text to the value (see the DIM/DIM1 command).

Enter text angle This prompt modifies the angle at which AutoCAD draws the dimension text. If you press Enter, AutoCAD draws the text at the default text angle.

Enter text location (or RETURN) You can locate the text along the dimension arc or place it inside or outside the dimension arc. This prompt enables you to position the text. If you press Enter, the text is placed along the dimension arc.

Examples

These examples demonstrate the steps to perform common angular dimensioning tasks. The drawing in figure D.56 shows the points you pick to create an angular dimension by choosing line objects and by selecting three points that define an angle.

Command: **DIMANGULAR** (Enter)	Issues the DIMANGULAR command
Select arc, circle, line, or RETURN: (Enter)	Chooses the 3-point method
Angle vertex: **END** of ① *(see fig. D.56)*	Specifies the vertex of the angle to dimension
First angle endpoint: **END** of ②	Specifies a point on an imaginary line representing one side of the angle
Second angle endpoint: **END** of ③	Specifies the endpoint of the second side of the angle

```
Dimension arc line location        Specifies location of dimension
(Text/Angle): MID of               line
```
Pick line between ① and ②

```
Command: (Enter)                   Reissues the DIMANGULAR
                                   command
```

```
Select arc, circle, line, or RETURN:   Selects first angle line
```
Pick point ④

`Second line:` *Pick point ⑤*   Selects second angle line

```
Dimension arc line location        Specifies location for
(Text/Angle): ⑤                    dimension line
```

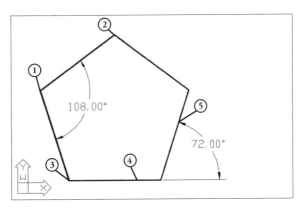

Figure D.56. *Dimensioning inside a minor angle between two lines.*

Related Commands

DDIM   DIM   DIMSTYLE

Related System Variables

For a list of AutoCAD's dimensioning variables, see the DIMSTYLE command. These variables also are explored at length in *Inside AutoCAD Release 13* and your AutoCAD documentation.

DIMBASELINE

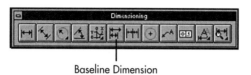
Baseline Dimension

Toolbar: *Baseline Dimension, (Dimensioning)*
Pull-down: *D*raw, *D*imensioning, *B*aseline
Screen: DRAW DIM, Baselin:

The DIMBASELINE dimensioning command enables you to use one existing linear dimension as the basis for one or more new dimensions. All new dimensions are based on the first extension line of the existing dimension. You create each new dimension by specifying a new second extension line origin point. The DIMBASELINE command offsets the new dimension line from the previous one and draws a new extended first extension line over the existing first extension line.

You can create baseline dimensions any time after you create an initial linear dimension. You can select an existing linear dimension for the basis of new baseline dimensions. You must pick the dimension nearest to the end with the extension line you want AutoCAD to use as the first extension line. The BASELINE command offsets each new dimension line by the dimension line increment value stored in the DIMDLI dimension variable.

Prompts and Options

Select next feature or RETURN to select This prompt appears if the last dimension you create is a linear dimension or if you select a base dimension. AutoCAD considers the first extension line of the last dimension to be the first extension line of subsequent dimensions, unless you press Enter to select another extension line. Press Enter if you want to select a dimension other than the last one you created. If you press Enter, you are prompted to Select base dimension.

Select base dimension To select the dimension to use as the base for subsequent dimensions, select it near the end that you want to use for the first extension line. If the object you select is not a dimension, you receive the error message Linear, Ordinate, or Angular associative dimension required. You are then prompted again to select a base dimension.

DIMBASELINE

Second extension line origin or RETURN to select After you establish a base dimension, pick the point for the next extension line origin or press Enter to select the base dimension.

Example

This example demonstrates the steps necessary to create baseline dimensions from an existing horizontal dimension. The points you use to create the dimensions are shown in figure D.57. For this exercise, set your object snap override to ENDpoint.

Choose Linear Dimension (Dimensioning)

`Command: _dimlinear`	Issues the DIMLINEAR command
`First extension line origin or RETURN to select:` *Pick point* ① *(see fig. D.57)*	Specifies the first definition point
`Second extension line origin:` *Pick point* ②	Specifies the second definition point
`Dimension line location (Text/Angle/Horizontal/Vertical/Rotated):` *Pick point* ③	Specifies the location of the dimension
`Command:` *Choose Baseline Dimension (Dimensioning)*	
`Command: _dimbaseline`	Issues the DIMBASELINE command
`Second extension line origin or RETURN to select:` *Pick point* ④	Specifies the next dimension from the base dimension
`Second extension line origin or RETURN to select:` *Pick point* ⑤	
`Second extension line origin or RETURN to select:` *Pick point* ⑥	
`Second extension line origin or RETURN to select:` *Pick point* ⑦	
`Second extension line origin or RETURN to select:` *Pick point* ⑧	
`Second extension line origin or RETURN to select:` *Cancel the command*	Terminates the command
`*Cancel*`	

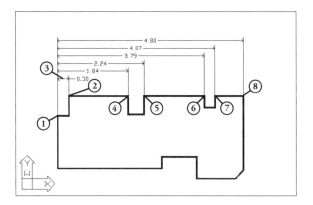

Figure D.57. *Baseline dimensions created using the DIMBASELINE command.*

Related Commands

DDIM   DIM   DIMSTYLE

Related System Variables

For a list of AutoCAD's dimensioning variables, see the DIMSTYLE command. These variables also are explored at length in *Inside AutoCAD Release 13* and your AutoCAD documentation.

DIMCENTER

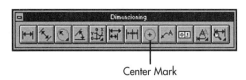

Center Mark

Toolbar: *Center Mark, (Dimensioning)*
Pull-down: **D**raw, **D**imensioning, C**e**nter Mark
Screen: DRAW DIM, Center:

The DIMCENTER dimensioning command enables you to create center marks or center lines at the center points of circles, arcs, or polyline arc segments.

Center marks or lines that you create by using the DIMCENTER command are individual line objects. Center marks are drawn twice the length of the positive value of the dimension variable DIMCEN. If DIMCEN is set to a negative number, center lines also are drawn, extending the length of DIMCEN beyond the circle or arc. If DIMCEN is set to 0, AutoCAD disables center marks or center lines. You can set the value of DIMCEN at the Command: prompt or by using the DDIM dialog box. Figure D.58 illustrates the effect of positive and negative DIMCEN values.

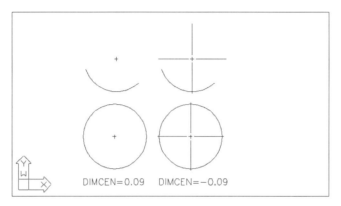

Figure D.58. *The effects of different DIMCEN values on center marks.*

Prompts and Options

Select arc or circle   Select the arc or circle at any point for the placement of the center mark.

Related Commands

DDIM   DIM   DIMSTYLE

Related System Variables

For a list of AutoCAD's dimensioning variables, see the DIMSTYLE command. These variables also are explored at length in *Inside AutoCAD Release 13* and your AutoCAD documentation.

DIMCONTINUE

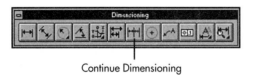

Continue Dimensioning

Toolbar: *Continue Dimension (Dimensioning)*
Pull-down: *D*raw, *D*imensioning, *C*ontinue
Screen: DRAW DIM, Continu:

The DIMCONTINUE dimensioning command enables you to use one existing linear dimension as the basis for a set of dimensions aligned end-to-end (otherwise known as *continuous dimensions*).

You can create continuous dimensions any time after you create an initial linear dimension. If you issue the DIMCONTINUE command immediately after you complete a linear dimension, AutoCAD treats the second extension line origin point of the previous dimension as the first extension line origin point of each new dimension. If you select an existing linear dimension for the basis of new continuous dimensions, you must pick the dimension nearest to the end with the extension line you want to use as the first extension line of subsequent dimensions.

Usually, the DIMCONTINUE command aligns each new dimension line with the last. If the dimension's text would otherwise overwrite the previous continued dimension's text, the CONTINUE command offsets the new dimension line by the dimension line increment value stored in the DIMDLI dimension variable.

Prompts and Options

Second extension line origin or RETURN to select This prompt appears if the last dimension you created is a linear dimension or if you select a base dimension. The second extension line of the last dimension becomes the first extension line of subsequent dimensions, unless you press Enter to select a different extension line. Press Enter if you want to select a dimension other than the last one you created.

Select continued dimension Select the dimension to use as the basis for subsequent dimensions near the end that you want to use for the first extension line. If the object you select is not a dimension, you receive the error message Linear, Ordinate, or Angular associative dimension required. You are then prompted again to select a continued dimension.

Example

This example demonstrates the steps necessary to create continuous dimensions (see fig. D.59). For this exercise, the object snap override is set to ENDpoint.

Choose Linear Dimension (Dimensioning)

`Command: _dimlinear`	Issues the DIMLINEAR command
`First extension line origin or RETURN to select:` *Pick point ①* (*see fig. D.59*)	Specifies the first definition point
`Second extension line origin:` *Pick point ②*	Specifies the second definition point
`Dimension line location (Text/Angle/Horizontal/Vertical/Rotated):` *Pick point ③*	Specifies the location of the dimension

`Command:` *Choose Continue Dimension (Dimensioning)*

`Command: _dimcontinue`	Issues the DIMCONTINUE command
`Second extension line origin or RETURN to select:` *Pick point ④*	Specifies the second definition point
`Second extension line origin or RETURN to select:` *Pick point ⑤*	
`Second extension line origin or RETURN to select:` *Pick point ⑥*	
`Second extension line origin or RETURN to select:` *Pick point ⑦*	
`Second extension line origin or RETURN to select:` *Pick point ⑧*	

Cancel the command

`Second extension line origin or RETURN to select: *Cancel*`	Terminates the DIMCONTINUE command

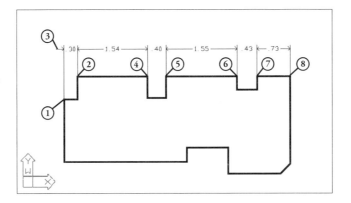

Figure D.59. *Using the DIMCONTINUE command.*

Related Commands

DDIM   DIM   DIMSTYLE

Related System Variables

For a list of AutoCAD's dimensioning variables, see the DIMSTYLE command. These variables also are explored at length in *Inside AutoCAD Release 13* and in your AutoCAD documentation.

DIMDIAMETER

Diameter Dimension

>Toolbar: *Diameter Dimension, (Dimensioning, Radial Dimension)*
>Pull-down: *Draw, Dimensioning, Radial, Diameter*
>Screen: DRAW DIM, Diametr:

The DIMDIAMETER dimensioning command enables you to dimension the diameters of circles, arcs, and polyline arc segments.

AutoCAD can produce several variations of dimensions for diameters, depending on the settings of pertinent dimension variables. You can control these variables most easily by using the DDIM dialog box, but they are mentioned here for reference. These variables are DIMTIX (Text Inside eXtension lines), DIMTOFL (Text Outside, Force dimension Line inside), and DIMCEN (CENter marks and lines). If you set the DIMTOFL and DIMTIX variables to 0 (OFF), AutoCAD draws a leader from the end of the dimension line to the dimension text. AutoCAD draws the leader dynamically so that you can place the text for best readability. When only DIMTOFL is on (set to 1), AutoCAD places the dimension text outside the arc or circle, as in the previous style, and draws a dimension line through the diameter of the object. When DIMTOFL and DIMTIX are on, AutoCAD omits the leader and places the dimension text within the dimension line. Figure D.60 shows some examples of various diameter dimensions.

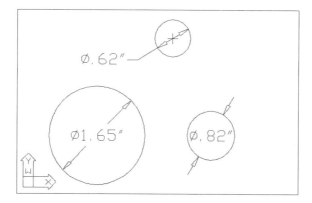

Figure D.60. *Examples of diameter dimensions.*

If the dimension variable DIMCEN is positive, AutoCAD places a center mark at the center point, if DIMCEN is 0, AutoCAD does not place a mark, and if DIMCEN is negative, AutoCAD draws center lines and center marks. If the dimension text is placed at the center of the arc or circle, AutoCAD does not draw the center marks and center lines.

Dimension text for the DIMDIAMETER command always begins with the diameter symbol by default.

Prompts and Options

`Select arc or circle`   Pick the arc or circle to dimension.

`Dimension line location (Text/Angle)`   At this prompt, you can dynamically drag the dimension line to an appropriate location. The text follows accordingly. If you need a leader line, you can dynamically specify its location as well. The `Text` option enables you to customize the dimension value using the MTEXT editor. The `Angle` option prompts you to `Enter text angle` by specifying two points on the screen or by explicitly typing an angle value.

Related Commands

DDIM   DIM   DIMSTYLE

Related System Variables

For a list of AutoCAD's dimensioning variables, see the DIMSTYLE command. These variables also are explored at length in *Inside AutoCAD Release 13* and your AutoCAD documentation.

DIMEDIT

Oblique Dimensions

Toolbar: *Oblique Dimensions, (Dimensioning, Dimension Style)*
Pull-down: *Draw, Dimensioning, Oblique*
Screen: MOD DIM, DimEdit:

You use the DIMEDIT command to edit the text position, text value, text properties, text rotation angle, and dimension obliquing angle of existing dimensions. Figure D.61 illustrates the New, Rotate, and Oblique options on a dimension.

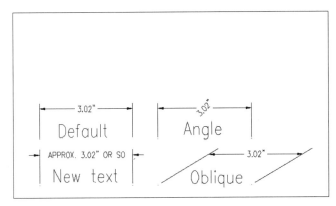

Figure D.61. *Using DIMEDIT to modify a dimension.*

Prompts and Options

When you issue the DIMEDIT command, the following prompt appears:

Dimension Edit (Home/New/Rotate/Oblique) <Home>.

Home Use this default option to move the dimension text back to its default position. When you choose this option, you are asked to select objects. AutoCAD determines which objects within the selection set are dimensions and modifies them accordingly.

New Use this option if you want to use the MTEXT command to change the dimension text. You can add prefixes and suffixes to the dimension text, or completely replace the calculated value. Whenever the angle brackets are used (<>) the actual default measured dimension value is substituted. For example, the string "About <> or so" reads "About 1.8391 or so" for an actual dimension of 1.8391. When you close the MTEXT dialog box, AutoCAD prompts you to select objects. AutoCAD determines which objects within the selection set are dimensions and modifies them accordingly, replacing the text in all of the selected dimensions with the new text you specify.

Rotate Use the Rotate option to rotate the dimension text. You can type in an explicit angle or pick two points to show the angle. When you choose this option, you are asked to select objects. AutoCAD determines which objects within the selection set are dimensions and modifies them accordingly.

> You must use the brackets (<>) to maintain the associativity between the actual measured dimension and the value of the dimension text. The double brackets serve to tell AutoCAD, "Whatever you calculate the actual dimension to be, show it as the dimension value."

Oblique Use this option to create an oblique dimension. By default, AutoCAD draws linear dimensions with the extension line parallel to the dimension line. The Oblique option overrides this feature, because it enables you to specify an angle for the extension lines. AutoCAD first prompts you to select the dimension objects you want to modify. At the Enter obliquing angle (RETURN for none) prompt, enter an angle or pick two points to specify an angle. Pressing Enter at this prompt restores the dimension to its default position with the extension lines perpendicular to the dimension line.

Related Commands

DDIM DIM DIMOVERRIDE DIMTEDIT
DIMSTYLE

Related System Variables

For a list of AutoCAD's dimensioning variables, see the DIMSTYLE command. These variables also are explored at length in *Inside AutoCAD Release 13* and your AutoCAD documentation.

DIMLINEAR

Linear Dimension

> Toolbar: *Linear Dimension, (Dimensioning)*
> Pull-down: *Draw*, *Dimensioning*, *Linear*
> Screen: DRAW DIM, Linear:

The DIMLINEAR command enables you to draw horizontal, vertical, or rotated dimensions. Figure D.62 shows examples of each of these types. DIMLINEAR requires two definition points for the extension lines (see fig. D.62). You can specify these points by picking them on-screen or by selecting an object to dimension. If you select an object (line, arc, circle, or polyline segment), the definition points are automatically specified based on the object.

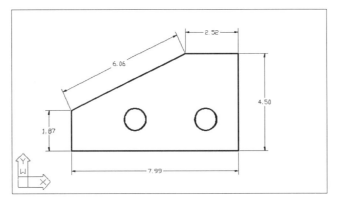

Figure D.62. *Examples of linear dimensions.*

Prompts and Options

`First extension line origin or RETURN to select` Pick two points to specify the distance to dimension. After you pick the first point, AutoCAD prompts you to pick the `Second extension line origin`.

If you dimension a single line, arc, circle, or polyline segment, press Enter to select the object you want to dimension. AutoCAD prompts you `Select object to dimension`. If the object you select is not valid for a linear dimension, AutoCAD prompts `Object selected is not a line, arc, or circle`. You can select objects within a block as long as the block is not mirrored or unequally scaled.

After you define the distance to dimension, AutoCAD shows the following prompt:

`Dimension line location (Text/Angle/Horizontal/Vertical/Rotated):`

Drag the cursor on-screen to locate the dimension line. You can dynamically indicate a horizontal or vertical dimension by dragging the cursor with respect to the definition points. If you drag above or below the points, the dimension becomes horizontal. If you drag to the left or right, the dimension becomes a vertical dimension.

You also can choose one of the other options to change the dimension before you finally locate the dimension on your drawing. These options are explained in detail in the following list.

Text Use this option to change the value of the dimension text. This option utilizes the MTEXT text editor to modify the dimension text.

Angle Use the Angle option to change the angle of the dimension text.

Horizontal Use this option to force the dimension horizontal. This overrides the dynamic vertical orientation of the dimension if you drag the cursor to the left or right (in the X or Y direction) with respect to the definition points. This option issues the prompt, `Dimension line location (Text/Angle)`.

Vertical This option is similar to the Horizontal option that was just described. It forces your dimension to become a vertical dimension. This option issues the prompt, `Dimension line location (Text/Angle)`.

Rotated Use this option to create a rotated dimension. A *rotated dimension* is one in which the dimension line is rotated beyond a vertical or horizontal orientation. The distance measured becomes the distance between the extension lines as they are drawn perpendicular to the dimension line from the definition points. Figure D.63 shows examples of dimensions that have been rotated 45 and 30 degrees. This option issues the prompt, `Dimension line angle <0>`.

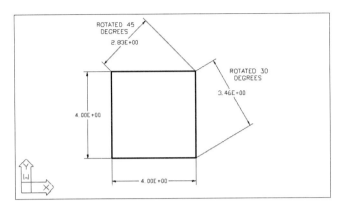

Figure D.63. *Examples of rotated dimensions.*

Example

In the following example, use the DIMLINEAR command to place a horizontal dimension as shown in figure D.64.

Command: **DIMLINEAR**	Issues the DIMLINEAR command
First extension line origin or RETURN to select: _endp of *Pick point ① (see fig. D.64)*	Defines the first extension line origin
Second extension line origin: _center of *Pick point ②*	Defines the second extension line origin
Dimension line location (Text/Angle/Horizontal/Vertical/Rotated): *Pick point ③*	Defines the dimension line location

Related Commands

DDIM   DIMSTYLE

Related System Variables

For a list of AutoCAD's dimensioning variables, see the DIMSTYLE command. These variables also are explored at length in *Inside AutoCAD Release 13* by New Riders Publishing as well as your AutoCAD documentation.

DIMLINEAR

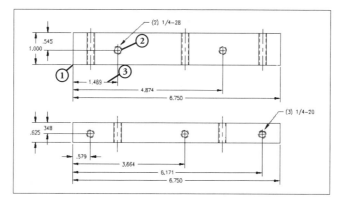

Figure D.64. *Placing linear dimensions.*

DIMORDINATE

Automatic

Toolbar: *Automatic (Dimensioning, Ordinate)*
Pull-down: *Draw, Dimensioning, Ordinate, Automatic*
Screen: DRAW DIM, Ordinat:

The DIMORDINATE dimensioning command enables you to create ordinate dimensions, also called *datum dimensions* (see fig. D.4). Ordinate dimensioning gets its name from the singular X or Y ordinate in an X,Y coordinate pair.

Ordinate dimensions denote the X or Y distance from a common origin (0,0) point. This point is established by reorienting the current UCS origin. Ordinate dimensions consist of dimension text and a leader (without arrowhead) that points to the feature dimensioned. If the angle between the first point (Select Feature:) and the second point (Leader endpoint...) is closest to the angle of the X axis, then the distance along the Y axis is dimensioned. If the angle between the points is closest to the angle of the Y axis, then the distance along the X axis is dimensioned. You can override the ORDINATE command's choice of axes by using the Xdatum or Ydatum option to specify the axis to dimension. The leader and dimension text are aligned perpendicular to the axis being dimensioned. You can enter ordinate dimension leaders more easily if ortho mode is on.

The DIMORDINATE command bases all of its dimensions on the location of the current UCS (User Coordinate System) origin. You must orient the UCS at the desired origin point for the portion of the drawing you are dimensioning.

Prompts and Options

Select Feature   Pick the point you want to dimension. This becomes the start point of the ordinate dimension leader.

Leader endpoint (Xdatum/Ydatum/Text)   Pick an endpoint for the leader or enter an X or Y coordinate to specify the dimension type. With ortho mode off, if you can drag and pick the leader endpoint diagonally, an orthogonal break is automatically drawn in the middle of the leader. If you enter the Xdatum or Ydatum options, the corresponding dimension types are drawn, regardless of the direction or location of the leader endpoint.

It is easier to align the leader endpoints for a neater appearance if you draw a construction line where you want the endpoints to align. Use the perpendicular object snap override to snap to this temporary line for the second leader endpoint.

On the Windows version, choose the Text option to display the Edit Mtext dialog box for customizing the dimension text. On the DOS version, choosing the Text option issues the following prompt.

Dimension text <default>   DOS Version only. AutoCAD calculates the distance between the two extension line origin points you pick or between the two points derived from the object you select. AutoCAD then offers the distance (in the current drawing units and precision) as the default dimension text value. You can accept this value (press Enter), specify a new value, suppress any text by typing a space, or apply prefix or suffix text to the value (see the DIM/DIM1 command).

Example

The following example uses the DIMORDINATE command to dimension the part shown in figure D.65. You define a new UCS for the origin of the ordinate dimensions.

Command: **UCS**	Issues the UCS command
Origin/ZAxis/3point/OBject/View/X/Y/Z/ Prev/Restore/Save/Del/?/<World>: **O** (Enter)	Selects the Origin option for defining the new origin point of the UCS
Origin point <0,0,0>: **END** (Enter)	Defines the new UCS origin
of *Pick point* ① *(see figure D.65)*	
Command: **DIMORDINATE** (Enter)	Issues the DIMORDINATE command
Select feature: **END** (Enter)	Defines the leader start point
of *Pick point* ①	
Leader endpoint (Xdatum/Ydatum/Text): *Pick point* ②	Defines the leader endpoint and terminates the command
Command: (Enter)	Reissues the DIMORDINATE command
DIMORDINATE	
Select feature: **CEN** (Enter)	
of *Pick point* ③	
Leader endpoint (Xdatum/Ydatum/Text): *Pick point* ④	
Command: (Enter)	
DIMORDINATE	
Select feature: **END** (Enter)	
of *Pick point* ⑤	
Leader endpoint (Xdatum/Ydatum/Text): *Pick point* ⑥	

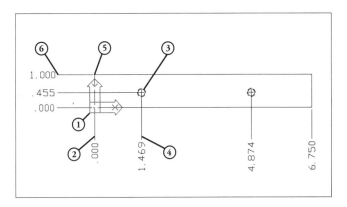

Figure D.65. *Ordinate (datum dimensions) used to locate a part feature.*

Related Commands

DDIM   DIM   DIMSTYLE

Related System Variables

For a list of AutoCAD's dimensioning variables, see the DIMSTYLE command. These variables also are explored at length in *Inside AutoCAD Release 13* by New Riders Publishing as well as your AutoCAD documentation.

DIMOVERRIDE

The DIMOVERRIDE dimensioning command enables you to modify selected dimensions to use new values for one or more dimension variables. This applies to associative dimensions only.

Prompts and Options

`Dimension variable to override (or Clear to remove overrides)`   You enter the name of a dimension variable to change. Use the Clear option to remove any overrides that have been applied to selected dimensions.

`Current value <default> New value`   You enter a new value for each dimension variable specified. Press Enter to proceed with object selection. The variables you override affect only selected dimensions; they do not affect the current dimension style or subsequently created dimensions. The `Dimension variable to override` prompt repeats until you press Enter.

Select objects Use any of AutoCAD's object-selection methods to select the existing associative dimensions you want to override. The settings specified above are applied to each dimension.

Example

This example demonstrates how you can use the DIMOVERRIDE command to adjust selected dimensions within a drawing. Figure D.66 shows the original dimensions and their appearance after you override their DIMTXSTY (DIMension TeXt STYle) original setting.

Command: DIMOVERRIDE **(Enter)**	Issues the DIMOVERRIDE command
Dimension variable to override (or Clear to remove overrides): **DIMTXSTY (Enter)**	Specifies the dimension variable to change for selected dimensions
Current value <STANDARD> New value: **ROMANS (Enter)**	Specifies the new value for the variable
Dimension variable to override: **(Enter)**	Terminates the process of specifying variables to override
Select objects: *Pick point* ① *(see fig. D.66)*	Selects the associative dimensions to modify
Other corner: *Pick point* ②	
3 found	
Select objects: **(Enter)**	Terminates the DIMOVERRIDE command

Related Commands

DDIM   DIM   DIMSTYLE

Related System Variables

For a list of AutoCAD's dimensioning variables, see the DIMSTYLE command. These variables also are explored at length in *Inside AutoCAD Release 13* by New Riders Publishing as well as your AutoCAD documentation.

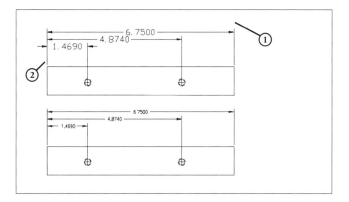

Figure D.66. *Linear dimension before and after overriding DIMTXSTY.*

DIMRADIUS

Radius Dimension

> Toolbar: *Radius Dimension, (Dimensioning, Radial Dimension)*
> Pull-down: **D**raw, **D**imensioning, **R**adial, **R**adius
> Screen: DRAW DIM, Radius

The RADIUS dimensioning command enables you to dimension the radius of circles, arcs, and polyline arc segments (see fig. D.67).

AutoCAD can produce several variations of dimensions for radii. These variations depend on the values of the system variables DIMTIX, DIMUPT, DIMTOFL, DIMFIT, DIMTIH, DIMTOH, DIMJUST, and DIMTAD. The easiest way to set and control these variables is to use the DDIM dialog box.

Dimension text for the RADIUS command always begins with the symbol R (for RADIUS) by default.

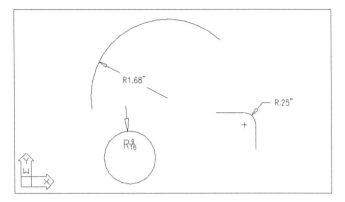

Figure D.67. *Examples of radial dimensions.*

Prompts and Options

Select arc or circle   Pick the arc, circle, or polyline arc segment to dimension.

Dimension line location (Text/Angle)   Use the crosshairs to dynamically drag the dimension line about the circumference of the circle or along the length of the arc. If AutoCAD cannot fit the arrowhead and text inside the object, the program draws a leader line to the text placed outside the object. Pick a point for the location of the dimension line.

The Text option displays the Dimension text <default> prompt on the DOS version of AutoCAD. On Windows systems, the Text option displays the Edit MTEXT dialog box.

Use the Angle option to specify a text angle for the dimension value.

Dimension text <default>   DOS Only. AutoCAD calculates the radius of the object you select. AutoCAD then offers the radius as the default dimension text value. You can accept this value (press Enter), specify a new value, suppress any text by typing a space, or apply prefix or suffix text to the value (see the MTEXT command).

Example

This example creates two types of radial dimensions. Each one is different, due to the size of the selected arc. For this example, decimal units are used with two places of precision, with leading zeros supressed. Figure D.68 shows each type of dimension.

```
Command: DIMRADIUS                              Issues the DIMRADIUS command

Select arc or circle: Pick point ①              Selects the object to dimension
(see figure D.68)

Dimension line location (Text/Angle):           Determines the location for
Pick point ②                                    the dimension

Command: (Enter)                                Reissues the DIMRADIUS command

DIMRADIUS

Select arc or circle: Pick point ③              Selects the object to dimension

Dimension line location (Text/Angle):           Determines the location for
Pick point ③                                    the dimension
```

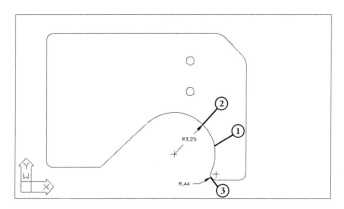

Figure D.68. *Dimensioning with the RADIUS command.*

Related Commands

DDIM   DIM   DIMSTYLE

Related System Variables

For a list of AutoCAD's dimensioning variables, see the DIMSTYLE command. These variables also are explored at length in *Inside AutoCAD Release 13* by New Riders Publishing as well as your AutoCAD documentation.

DIMSTYLE

Screen: MOD DIM, DimStyl:

The DIMSTYLE command is a command-line equivalent of the DDIM command. You use it to control and list the dimensioning variables associated with each dimension style and to create and set dimension styles.

> All dimensions have a dimension style assigned to them. The default dimension style is STANDARD. You can create and modify as many styles as necessary.

Prompts and Options

```
Dimension Style Edit (Save/Restore/STatus/Variables/Apply/?) <Restore>:
```

Save Use this option to create new dimension styles. The current values of all of the dimension variables are saved under the name you specify at the following prompt:

```
?/Name for new dimension style
```

The ? option is available at several prompts and is used to list all currently defined dimension styles in the drawing.

To list the differences between the current dimension style and another defined dimension style, precede the name of the other dimension style with a tilde (~). See the Restore option immediately following.

Restore Use this, the default DIMSTYLE option, to make another dimension style current. The style affects all subsequent dimensions until a new style is restored. You are prompted `?/Enter dimension style name or RETURN to select dimension`. Similar to the prompt for the Variables option, you can list the defined dimension styles in the drawing, type a valid dimension style name, or press Enter to select a dimension that has the style you want to make current. Additionally, you can list the differences between the current dimension style and another dimension style. To do this, precede the dimension style name with a tilde (~) character. For example, if the current dimension style is named ARCH_INCHES and you want to see the differences between it and a dimension style named ARCH_FEET, type **~ARCH_FEET** at the above prompt. Your listing should look similar to the following example:

```
Command: DIMSTYLE (Enter)

dimension style: ARCH_FEET

Dimension Style Edit (Save/Restore/STatus/Variables/Apply/?) <Restore>:
(Enter)

?/Enter dimension style name or RETURN to select dimension: ~ARCH_INCHES
(Enter)

Differences between ARCH_INCHES and current settings:

        ARCH_INCHES      Current Setting
DIMDEC   4                1
DIMTAD   0                1
DIMTIH   On               Off
DIMTOFL  On               Off
DIMTOH   On               Off
DIMZIN   7                2
```

STatus Use the STatus option to list all the current dimension variable overrides and values. If there are any dimension variable overrides, they are listed first. The default STANDARD dimension style variable settings as listed by the STatus option are shown in the following list:

```
DIMALT   Off            Alternate units selected
DIMALTD  2              Alternate unit decimal places
DIMALTF  25.4000        Alternate unit scale factor
DIMALTTD 2              Alternate tolerance decimal places
DIMALTTZ 0              Alternate tolerance zero suppression
DIMALTU  2              Alternate units
DIMALTZ  0              Alternate unit zero suppression
DIMAPOST                Prefix and suffix for alternate text
DIMASO   On             Create associative dimensions
DIMASZ   0.1800         Arrow size
DIMAUNIT 0              Angular unit format
DIMBLK                  Arrow block name
DIMBLK1                 First arrow block name
DIMBLK2                 Second arrow block name
DIMCEN   0.0900         Center mark size
DIMCLRD  BYBLOCK        Dimension line and leader color
DIMCLRE  BYBLOCK        Extension line color
DIMCLRT  BYBLOCK        Dimension text color
DIMDEC   4              Decimal places
DIMDLE   0.0000         Dimension line extension
DIMDLI   0.3800         Dimension line spacing
DIMEXE   0.1800         Extension above dimension line
DIMEXO   0.0625         Extension line origin offset
DIMFIT   3              Fit text
DIMGAP   0.0900         Gap from dimension line to text
```

DIMSTYLE

```
DIMJUST 0              Justification of text on dimension line
DIMLFAC 1.0000         Linear unit scale factor
DIMLIM  Off            Generate dimension limits
DIMPOST                Prefix and suffix for dimension text
DIMRND  0.0000         Rounding value
DIMSAH  Off            Separate arrow blocks
DIMSCALE 1.0000        Overall scale factor
DIMSD1  Off            Suppress the first dimension line
DIMSD2  Off            Suppress the second dimension line
DIMSE1  Off            Suppress the first extension line
DIMSE2  Off            Suppress the second extension line
DIMSHO  On             Update dimensions while dragging
DIMSOXD Off            Suppress outside dimension lines
DIMSTYLE STANDARD      Current dimension style (read-only)
DIMTAD  0              Place text above the dimension line
DIMTDEC 4              Tolerance decimal places
DIMTFAC 1.0000         Tolerance text height scaling factor
DIMTIH  On             Text inside extensions is horizontal
DIMTIX  Off            Place text inside extensions
DIMTM   0.0000         Minus tolerance
DIMTOFL Off            Force line inside extension lines
DIMTOH  On             Text outside horizontal
DIMTOL  Off            Tolerance dimensioning
DIMTOLJ 1              Tolerance vertical justification
DIMTP   0.0000         Plus tolerance
DIMTSZ  0.0000         Tick size
DIMTVP  0.0000         Text vertical position
DIMTXSTY STANDARD      Text style
DIMTXT  0.1800         Text height
DIMTZIN 0              Tolerance zero suppression
DIMUNIT 2              Unit format
DIMUPT  Off            User positioned text
DIMZIN  0              Zero suppression
```

Variables Use this option to list the dimension variable settings and overrides for a selected dimension style. It differs from the STatus option in that the STatus option lists *current* settings whereas the Variables options lists settings for any currently defined dimension style you choose.

After you choose the Variables option, you are prompted ?/Enter dimension style name or RETURN to select dimension. At this point, you can use the ? option to list currently defined dimension styles, type in a dimension style name, or press Enter to select a dimension for listing its variable settings. You also can list the differences between the current dimension style and another defined dimension style by preceding the name of the other dimension style with a tilde (~). See the previously described Restore option for an example of how to use this option.

Apply Use this option to change the dimension style of existing associative dimensions to the current dimension style. When AutoCAD prompts you to select objects, select the dimensions you want to change to the current dimension style.

Related Commands

DDIM	DIM	DIMALIGNED	DIMANGULAR
DIMBASELINE	DIMCENTER	DIMCONTINUE	DIMDIAMETER
DIMEDIT	DIMLINEAR	DIMORDINATE	DIMOVERRIDE
DIMRADIUS	DIMTEDIT	TOLERANCE	

Related System Variables

For a list of AutoCAD's dimensioning variables, see the DIMSTYLE command. These variables also are explored at length in *Inside AutoCAD Release 13* by New Riders Publishing as well as your AutoCAD documentation.

DIMTEDIT

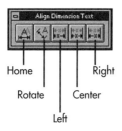

Toolbar: *Align Dimension Text (Dimensioning)*
Pull-down: *Draw, Dimensioning, Align Text (all options except Center)*
Screen: MOD DIM, DimTedt:

The DIMTEDIT command enables you to edit the location or angle of the text of a single existing associative dimension object.

Prompts and Options

Select dimension   Use any of AutoCAD's general object-selection methods to select the dimension you want to edit.

Enter text location (Left/Right/Home/Angle)   Drag the dimension text into the desired position or specify one of the options. If the dimension variable DIMSHO is on (1), the text displays dynamically as you drag it.

> **Left**   The Left option enables you to move the dimension text as far to the left along the dimension line as possible with a two-arrowhead length leader to the left of the text.

Right The Right option moves the dimension text as far to the right along the dimension line as possible with a two-arrowhead length leader to the right of the text.

Home The Home option returns the dimension text to its home position, centered along the length of the dimension line.

Angle The Angle option prompts for a new dimension text angle. If you select this option, the Text angle: prompt appears. This prompt is discussed next.

Enter text angle You enter a new text angle or pick two points to show the angle. The text is rotated about its center point. Angles are measured counterclockwise, according to the standard AutoCAD orientation of 0 degrees in the east direction. If you enter 0, AutoCAD restores the text to its default angle; if you press Enter, AutoCAD leaves the current angle.

Related Commands

DDIM   DIM   DIMSTYLE

Related System Variables

For a list of AutoCAD's dimensioning variables, see the DIMSTYLE command. These variables also are explored at length in *Inside AutoCAD Release 13* by New Riders Publishing as well as your AutoCAD documentation.

'DIST

Toolbar: *Distance (Object Properties, Inquiry)*
Pull-down: **E**dit, In**q**uiry, **D**istance
Screen: ASSIST, INQUIRY, Dist:

Distance

You use the DIST command to measure the distance between two 2D or 3D points. To enter the coordinates of the points, you can use the keyboard or use a pointing device to choose them on-screen. The DIST command also provides information about the angle in the X,Y plane, the angle from the X,Y plane of an imaginary line between the two points, and the difference in X, Y, and Z values between the two points. The distance reported is in the current linear units format and precision.

Prompts and Options

First point At this prompt, specify the first point.

Second point At this prompt, specify the second point.

Example

The following example uses the DIST command to measure the distance between two points.

Command: **DIST** (Enter)	Issues the DIST command
First point: **1,1** (Enter)	Specifies the first point
Second point: **5,5** (Enter)	Specifies the second point

AutoCAD displays the following information:

```
Distance = 5.6569, Angle in XY Plane = 45, Angle from XY Plane = 0
Delta X = 4.0000, Delta Y = 4.0000, Delta Z = 0.0000
```

Use the object snap modes to help measure the distance between specific points on existing objects.

Related System Variable

DISTANCE   LUNITS   LUPREC

DIVIDE

Divide

DIVIDE

Toolbar: *Divide (Draw, Point)*
Pull-down: **D**raw, **P**oint, **D**ivide
Screen: DRAW2, Divide:

The DIVIDE command places point objects or blocks along the length of an object, dividing the object into a specified number of equal segments. You can divide lines, circles, arcs, polylines, and splines. AutoCAD does not, however, divide the object into individual segments.

Prompts and Options

Select object to divide   When AutoCAD displays this prompt, you can use the standard object-selection methods to pick a line, circle, arc, polyline, or spline. The starting point of the segments depends on the type of object. For polylines, for example, whether 3D, closed, or open, the starting segment is at the first vertex. The same applies to splines.

<Number of segments>/Block   At this prompt, you can enter the number of equal segments to create or select the Block option. The Block option enables you to insert a block at the dividing points. Note that the you must define the block in the current drawing before you select the Block option.

When you select the Block option, the following prompts appear:

Block name to insert   Enter the name of a block already defined in the current drawing.

Align block with object? <Y>   If you accept the default answer of yes, AutoCAD aligns the block with the divided object. An aligned block is rotated around its insertion point parallel with the divided object. If you answer **N**, AutoCAD inserts the block with a rotation angle of 0.

Number of segments   At this prompt, enter the number of equal segments to create.

If you use the DIVIDE command to place point objects on the selected object, it helps if you use the DDPTYPE command to change the point type. This makes it easier to see the points. Also, if you intend for these points to be temporary, you can make it easier to erase them later by placing them on a separate layer. Set the desired layer current before you issue the DIVIDE command. The points are automatically placed into the previous selection set.

Example

This example shows the typical way you would use the DIVIDE command in a real-world situation. Figure D.69 shows a wall line that you need to break into seven even sections before you can place any windows. Before you issue the command, use DDPTYPE to select a more visible point type.

Command: **DIVIDE** (Enter)	Issues the DIVIDE command
Select object to divide: *Pick point* ① *(see fig. D.69)*	Selects the object to be divided
<Number of segments>/Block: **7** (Enter)	Specifies the number of segments into which to divide the object

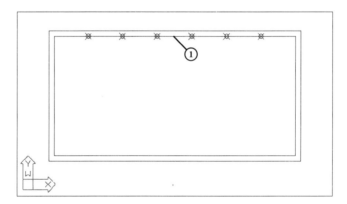

Figure D.69. *Dividing a line segment with the DIVIDE command.*

Related Commands

DDPTYPE   MEASURE

Related System Variables

PDMODE   PDSIZE

DONUT or DOUGHNUT

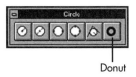
Donut

Toolbar: *Donut (Draw, Circle)*
Pull-down: *Draw, Circle, Donut*
Screen: DRAW1, Donut:

The DONUT command enables you to draw filled rings and circles using wide-polyline arc segments. You must provide the inside diameter, outside diameter, and center point for the polyline.

Prompt and Options

Inside diameter <0.5000>   This prompt requires you to enter a value or two points for the size of the donut's hole. The default value is 0.5 units.

Outside diameter <1.0000>   This prompt requires you to enter a value or two points to create the donut's outer diameter. The outside diameter must be greater than the inside diameter. The default value is 1.0 units.

TIP

> If you want to create a solid dot of any size in your drawing, specify an inside diameter of zero. Specify an outside diameter to match the desired size of the dot.
>
> You also can create donuts and trim them for many useful applications that require wide arc segments. Figure D.70 illustrates some items created from donuts.

Center of doughnut   At this prompt, you specify the donut's center point. You can enter the point's coordinates or pick the point on-screen. This prompt repeats until you press Enter, so you can make multiple donuts of the same size.

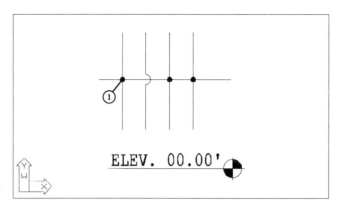

Figure D.70. *Creative uses for the donut.*

Example

The following example creates donut objects using the DONUT command.

Command: **DONUT** (Enter)	Issues the DONUT command
Inside diameter <0.5000>: **0** (Enter)	Specifies the internal diameter of the donut
Outside diameter <1.0000>: **0.2** (Enter)	Specifies the external diameter of the donut
Center of doughnut: *Pick a point* ① *(see fig. D.70)*	Specifies the location of the donut
Center of doughnut: (Enter)	Terminates the DONUT command

Related Commands

FILL   PEDIT   PLINE

Related System Variables

DONUTID   DONUTOD   FILLMODE

DRAGMODE

Screen: OPTIONS, Dragmod:

Some drawing commands (such as CIRCLE, ARC, INSERT, and SHAPE) enable you to drag objects so that you can see the size, shape, or position of the object. Some editing commands, such as MOVE, COPY, and STRETCH, also take advantage of this dragging capability. The DRAGMODE command enables you to control dragging when you draw or move objects.

> Usually, you want to take advantage of AutoCAD's dragging capabilities to facilitate drawing and editing. If you use DRAGMODE during large selection-set manipulations, however, such as when you move or copy complex blocks, screen performance might suffer. On slower systems, turn off DRAGMODE temporarily during such operations for smoother cursor movement.

TIP

You can control DRAGMODE's default setting in new drawings by modifying the state of DRAGMODE in the default prototype drawing. You also can use the DRAGMODE system variable to control dragging.

DIM

Prompts and Options

ON   This option enables object dragging when requested by the user or by a menu macro, and the keyword drag is used at the appropriate prompts.

OFF   This option disables object dragging.

Auto   This option is the default and initiates object dragging automatically for all commands that allow object dragging.

Related System Variables

DRAGMODE   DRAGP1   DRAGP2

'DSVIEWER (Windows Only)

Aerial View

Toolbar: *Aerial View (Standard Toolbar, Tool Windows)*
Pull-down: **T**ools, **A**erial View

For Windows versions only, the DSVIEWER command enables you to display an Aerial View window to facilitate navigation (panning, zooming, and locating objects) within the drawing. Figure D.71 shows a drawing in the Aerial View window. The display driver must be configured for the Accelerated Display Driver by Rasterex (International) a.s for Autodesk, Inc. (See the CONFIG command.) On most systems, using the DSVIEWER command speeds up operations such as zooming and panning. DSVIEWER does not operate in paper space or in a 3D dynamic view (see the DVIEW command).

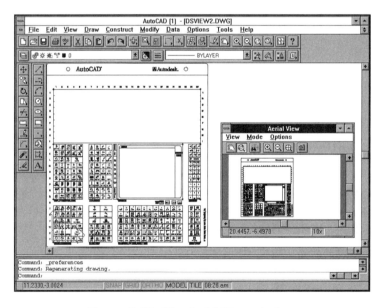

Figure D.71. *The Aerial View window.*

The Aerial View uses what is known as a display list. A *display list* maintains data (in your computer memory) on the way AutoCAD displays objects on-screen, which effectively speeds up display operations such as redraws, panning, and zooming. The display list data is much faster to access in memory than in your drawing file, as happens without a display list.

A display list utilizes your computer's memory. If your system does not have enough *random-access memory* (RAM) for AutoCAD to operate properly and maintain a display list, you might actually see performance suffer. In this scenario, do not utilize a display list processor.

Prompts and Options

The DSVIEWER command does not have command line prompts and options. It operates from a window within the AutoCAD application. See Figure D.72 below.

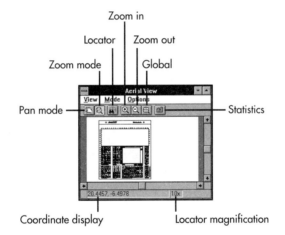

Figure D.72. *The DSVIEWER Aerial View window.*

The DSVIEWER Aerial View window, like any other window, consists of several items. Some of these items, such as the minimize and maximize buttons, the scroll bars, and the ability to resize or move the window are standard Windows features.

Pull-Down Menus

The pull-down menus on the menu bar consist of the View, Mode, and Options menus. Some of the functionality of the pull-down menus is duplicated in the toolbar buttons discussed next. The toolbar provides quicker access to the commands.

View. The View menu consists of the Zoom In, Zoom Out, and Global options. The Zoom In and Zoom Out options, as their names indicate, zoom in or out a preset amount within the aerial view. The Global option shows the entire drawing within the aerial view. These commands do not affect the drawing's view, but rather, affect only the view within the Aerial View window.

Mode. The Mode menu contains two options—Pan and Zoom. A "bullet" marks the option that is active. You can activate only one option at a time. The Pan or Zoom modes determine whether the actions you perform within the Aerial View window pan or zoom the drawing.

Options. The Options menu contains four items: Auto Viewport, Dynamic Update, Locator Magnification, and Display Statistics.

> **Auto Viewport.** Check this option, or turn it on, to automatically update the view within the Aerial View window when you switch model space viewports. If this option is off and you switch model space viewports, you must click on one of the Aerial View window scroll bar buttons to update the aerial view display.
>
> **Dynamic Update.** This option determines whether the aerial view is updated as you edit the drawing.
>
> **Locator Magnification.** This option initiates a dialog box that has a slider control you can use to control the amount of magnification under the cursor when you are in locator mode. You can use a maximum magnification of 32.
>
> **Display Statistics.** Use this option to initiate a dialog box that shows the amount of system memory (RAM) that the display list is using. This is useful for diagnostics if screen performance seems sluggish, indicating a potentially excessively large display list.

Toolbar

Pan Mode. Turning this option on displays a rectangular window in the Aerial View window. The size of this box depends on the last zoom operation. Move the box within the Aerial View window and click on the area to which you want to pan. Your drawing (not the view within the Aerial View window) is updated to reflect the pan operation. Figure D.73 shows the pan window within the Aerial View.

'DSVIEWER (Windows Only)

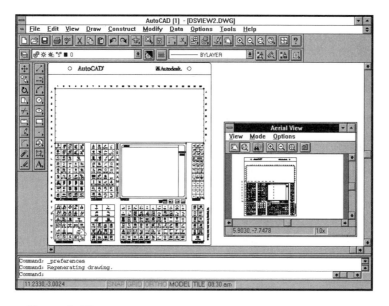

Figure D.73. *The pan window within the Aerial View window.*

Zoom Mode. Use this option to define a zoom window that you can use to change the view of your drawing within the Aerial View window. You can see crosshairs in the Aerial View window for picking two points to define a zoom window. The Aerial View window is not affected by this operation.

Locator. The Locator tool enables you to browse around your drawing without having to zoom in and out several times. You must click and hold this tool as you drag the locator box and cursor around your drawing. Figure D.74 shows the Locator cursor and box. As you drag the Locator cursor around the drawing, the view is dynamically updated within the Aerial View window (see fig. D.75). When you release the mouse button, the drawing view is updated to reflect the view under the locator box (see fig. D.76). Use the Options menu to change the Locator magnification.

Zoom In. See View under "Pull-Down Menus."

Zoom Out. See View under "Pull-Down Menus."

Global. See View under "Pull-Down Menus."

Statistics. See Display Statistics under the Options pull-down menu.

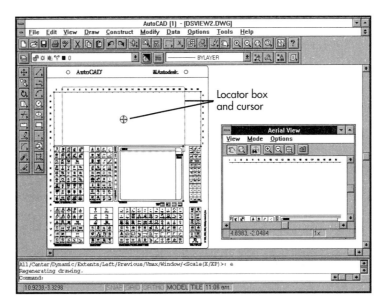

Figure D.74. *The Locator box and cursor.*

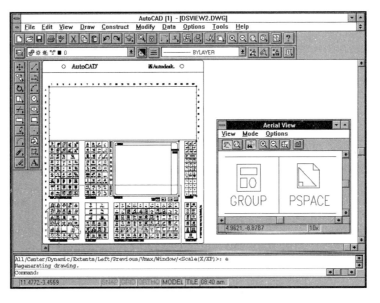

Figure D.75. *Locating objects using the Locator tool.*

'DSVIEWER (Windows Only)

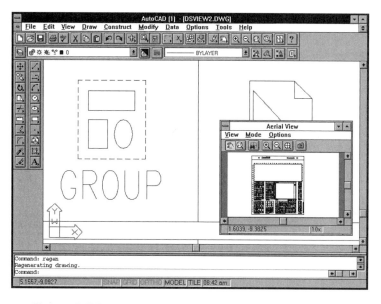

Figure D.76. *Using the Locator to choose a drawing view.*

Status Area

The status area displays two boxes. The left box is a coordinate display for the Aerial View. The right box displays the current magnification of the Locator tool.

Example

Use the TABLET.DWG in the following exercise.

Choose Aerial View from the Standard Toolbar.

Command: `'_dsviewer`	Issues the DSVIEWER command
Choose **O***ptions, Locator* **M***agnification*	Displays the slider bar for changing the locator magnification
Enter **10** *in the Magnification edit box*	Changes the locator magnification
Click on and hold the Locator tool	Activates the Locator function

Move the cursor around the drawing and watch the Aerial View window	Dynamically displays magnified view
Release the mouse button in the desired area of the drawing	Specifies the new view

Related Commands

AV   DDVIEW   PAN   ZOOM

DTEXT

Dtext

Toolbar: *Dtext (Draw, Text)*
Pull-down: *Draw, Text, Dynamic Text*
Screen: DRAW2, DText:

The DTEXT (Dynamic TEXT) command enables you to enter text strings into your drawing. DTEXT produces the same results as the TEXT command, but offers several advantages:

- You can see the text in the drawing as you type.
- You can move the cursor to a different part of the screen to begin a new text line.
- When you begin a second line of text, you press Enter only once, as opposed to when you use the TEXT command and must press Enter twice to begin a second line of text.

The MTEXT command offers more flexibility and capability than the DTEXT or TEXT commands. You might want to consider using MTEXT for all of your text needs in a drawing.

Prompts and Options

`Justify/Style/<Start point>` At this prompt, you have three choices. First, you can select Justify to change the text justification. The default value is left justification. Second, you can select Style to change the current text style. Note that the style must already be defined using the STYLE command. Third, you can enter the starting point of a left-justified text string, which is the default choice at this prompt. If you know the justification option you want to use, you can enter it at this prompt without first selecting Justify. The DTEXT justification options are described later under Justification Options.

`Height` At this prompt, specify the text's height. You see this prompt only when the current style does not have a predefined text height (see the STYLE command).

`Rotation angle` At this prompt, enter the text's rotation angle.

`Text` At this prompt, type the text string. This prompt is repeated so that you can type additional text strings. Press Enter at a blank `Text:` prompt to end the DTEXT command.

If you press Enter again immediately, AutoCAD highlights the last text entered and again prompts `Justify/Style/<Start point>`. If you press Enter at this prompt, you are prompted for a new text string. AutoCAD places the new string directly below the highlighted text and has the same text style, height, and rotation as the highlighted text.

At the Text prompt, you also can pick another start point for text at a new location using the crosshairs. You can repeatedly pick start points throughout your drawing until you press Enter twice to end the command.

If you make a mistake as you add numerous pieces of text to your drawing using the method just described, do not cancel the command. This terminates the DTEXT command prematurely and deletes any text you enter after issuing the command. Instead, press Enter twice to end the command, but keep the entered text. Use the DDEDIT command to edit the text containing errors.

Justification Options

`Align/Fit/Center/Middle/Right/TL/TC/TR/ML/MC/MR/BL/BC/BR.`

You can choose among the following justification options for your text.

Align   You specify the start point and endpoint of the text string. AutoCAD adjusts the text's height so that the text fits proportionally between the two points.

Fit   You specify the start point, endpoint, and height of the text string. AutoCAD fits the text between the two points by adjusting the width factor. AutoCAD does not automatically adjust the height, as it does with the Align justification.

Center   You specify the center of the text string horizontally and the base of the text string vertically.

Middle   You specify the center of the text string horizontally and vertically.

Right   You specify the right endpoint of the text string at the base.

TL (Top Left)   Text justification is at the upper-left corner of the first character's text cell. A *text cell* is the rectangular area into which all characters of a font fit. You can visualize this area by imagining a character that has ascenders and descenders or an uppercase letter that has a descender.

TC (Top Center)   Text justification is at the top of a string's text cells; the string itself is centered horizontally.

TR (Top Right)   Text justification is at the upper right corner of the last text cell of a string.

ML (Middle Left)   Text justification is at the vertical middle of an uppercase text cell and at the left of the first character. Regardless of the text string's composition, ML justification is calculated as if the first character is uppercase and lacks descenders.

MC (Middle Center)   Text justification is at the vertical middle of an uppercase text cell and at the horizontal center of the text string. Regardless of the text string's composition, MC justification is calculated as if the entire string is uppercase and lacks descenders.

MR (Middle Right)   Text justification is at the vertical middle of an uppercase text cell and at the horizontal right of the last character. Regardless of the text string's composition, MR justification is calculated as if the last character is uppercase and lacks descenders.

BL (Bottom Left)   Text justification is at the bottom left of the first character's text cell.

BC (Bottom Center)   Text justification is at the bottom of a string's text cells; the string itself is centered horizontally.

BR (Bottom Right)   Text justification is at the lower right corner of the last text cell of a string.

Figure D.77 illustrates these various justification options.

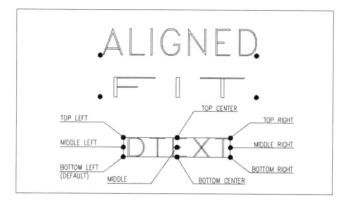

Figure D.77. *Text justification points.*

Related Commands

CHANGE   DDEDIT   MTEXT   QTEXT
SPELL   STYLE   TEXT

Related System Variables

TEXTFILL   TEXTQLTY   TEXTSIZE   TEXTSTYLE

DVIEW

Pull-down: <u>V</u>iew, 3D D<u>y</u>namic View
Screen: VIEW, Dview:

The DVIEW (Dynamic VIEW) command enables you to interactively change the current view of a 3D model. The DVIEW command uses a camera and target metaphor to help you visualize and set up the view. You can change the viewing direction, zoom magnification, and twist angle interactively. You can select perspective or parallel projection mode, and you can set up front and back clipping planes.

Perspective mode displays objects so that they appear larger closer to the camera than the same objects located farther away. When perspective mode is active, the UCS icon in the lower left corner of the graphics windows is replaced by a perspective icon—a cube shown in perspective view. Parallel projection mode displays an object at the same size, regardless of its distance from the camera. The default viewing mode is parallel projection.

The view in the left viewport of figure D.78 illustrates a parallel projection, while that in the right viewport illustrates the same view in a perspective projection. You must be in model space before you can use the DVIEW command. If you try to invoke DVIEW in paper space, AutoCAD responds as follows:

`** Command not allowed in Paper space **`

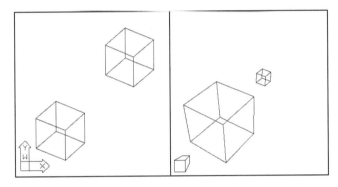

Figure D.78. *The same view in parallel and perspective projection.*

Prompts and Options

Select objects   Select the objects that you want to use as a reference for interactively changing the view. These objects are dynamically displayed (dragged) in the graphics window as you change the view. Selecting many objects can result in sluggish graphics display.

> If no objects are selected, DVIEW will utilize a block named DVIEWBLOCK as the reference object. If DVIEWBLOCK does not exist, AutoCAD will create one that appears as a small house. You may create your own reference DVIEWBLOCK by creating a block scaled to fit into a one-unit cube and aligned with the X, Y, and Z axes of the current UCS.

```
CAmera/TArget/Distance/POints/PAn/Zoom/TWist/CLip/Hide/Off/Undo/<eXit>:
```

Pick a point to use as a rolling view base point, or choose an option. If you pick a rolling view base point, AutoCAD uses the point you pick to measure a direction and magnification angle for rolling the camera point around the target point. The *direction angle* is the angle measured from the twist angle of the current view to establish a plane parallel to the current view. The *magnification angle* is the angle in this parallel plane, as measured from the current camera point.

> This particular method is also not intuitive to use. It's easier to use the CAmera option, which allows you to do basically the same thing.

TIP

CAmera Rotates the camera point about the target. The *camera point* is the position from which the objects are viewed. AutoCAD uses two prompts to determine the way to rotate the camera about the target point:

```
Toggle angle in/Enter angle from XY plane <current>:
```
```
Toggle angle from/Enter angle in XY plane from X axis <current>:
```

Enter the angle from the XY plane, and the angle in the XY plane. Use the T option to change from one prompt to the other.

You also can show the new camera position by picking a point in the graphics window. Position the cursor to the right of the center of the graphics window to indicate a positive angle in the XY plane, and to the left of the center to indicate a negative angle in the XY plane. Position the cursor above the center of the graphics window to indicate a positive angle from the XY plane, and below the center to indicate a negative angle from the XY plane.

TArget Rotates the target point about the camera point. The *target point* is the point toward which the current view is aimed. AutoCAD uses two prompts to request the way to rotate the camera about the target point, as follows:

```
Toggle angle in/Enter angle from XY plane <current>:
```
```
Toggle angle from/Enter angle in XY plane from X axis <current>:
```

Enter the angle from the XY plane, and the angle in the XY plane. Use the T option to change from one prompt to the other.

You also can show the new target position by picking a point in the graphics window. Position the cursor to the right of the center of the graphics window to indicate a positive angle in the XY plane, and to the left of the center to indicate a negative angle in the XY plane. Position the cursor above the center of the graphics window to indicate a positive angle from the XY plane, and below the center to indicate a negative angle from the XY plane.

NOTE The view when you use the DVIEW command always is from the camera point toward the target point. Changing the target point to a point above the XY plane creates a view from the camera point looking up from below.

Distance Enter the distance from the camera to the target. The larger the distance, the farther the camera point is from the target, and the objects appear smaller in the graphics window. A slider bar appears at the top of the graphics window, and you can use it to scale the current distance. If you are not in perspective view, the Distance option switches you from parallel to perspective view.

You cannot invoke the ZOOM, PAN, and SKETCH commands in perspective view. Setting a perspective view distance automatically turns on front clipping, with the clipping plane located at the camera position. Use the OFF option to change from perspective view to parallel view.

POints Enter the target point and the camera point by picking points from the graphics window or typing coordinates. If you currently are in perspective mode, the DDVIEW command switches to parallel mode temporarily while you pick points.

PAn Pick a base point and second point to show a pan displacement. PAn moves both the camera and target points by that displacement parallel to the current view plane. Note that you cannot use object snaps when you use the DVIEW command.

TIP On the other hand, AutoLISP point locations are honored, so you can establish a base point and second point using AutoLISP prior to using the DVIEW command. Use (setq campt (getpoint "camera point")) and (setq tarpt (getpoint "target point")) to save the point locations. Then, when asked for a camera point and target point, use the AutoLISP variable recall operator '!' to provide these locations. Use !campt to recall the camera point and !tarpt to recall the target point. Pans in DVIEW are 3D pans — X, Y, and Z displacement is honored.

Zoom The Zoom option enables you to zoom the image in and out, but does not change the perspective. AutoCAD uses two different prompts, depending on whether the current view mode is parallel or perpendicular, as follows:

```
Adjust zoom scale factor <1>:

Adjust lenslength <50.000mm>:
```

If you are in parallel view mode, enter the zoom scale factor relative to the current zoom magnification. A larger number increases the zoom magnification, and the objects appear larger in the graphics window. This option behaves similarly to ZOOM <Scale>X.

If you are in perspective view mode, enter the lens length. The larger the lens length, the closer the view is to parallel projection. A small lenslength makes the view similar to a camera's wide angle lens.

After you adjust the lenslength in perspective mode, you might need to adjust the camera to target distance. Changing the lenslength changes both the magnitude of perspection and the camera to target distance.

TWist   Enter the twist angle you want, or pick a point in the graphics window to show an angle.

CLip   This option enables you to obscure portions of the drawing by positioning clipping planes. You can use two clipping planes, a front and back, to obscure portions of objects in front of and behind a plane. Each clipping plane is perpendicular to the viewing direction. The front plane obscures objects in front of the plane and the back plane obscures objects behind it.

Select the back cutting plane or the front cutting plane, then enter the cutting plane distance as measured from the target point. You can move, and enable and disable, the front and back cutting planes independently. You can put both in front, both behind, or one in front and one behind.

If the front clipping plane is behind the back clipping plane, and both are enabled, AutoCAD displays no objects. Turn one or both off if you want to see the objects.

The default distance displayed for the front and back clipping plane distance only specifies the distance. It does not turn on front or back clipping if it is not already on. Use the slider bar to position the front or back clipping plane to specify the desired distance and turn on clipping.

Hide   This option enables you to remove hidden lines in the current view.

Off Use this option to turns off perspective mode and turn on parallel projection mode. You cannot invoke the ZOOM, PAN, and SKETCH commands in perspective view.

Undo Use this option to undo the effects of the most recent DVIEW command option.

eXit This option enables you to exit the DVIEW command and regenerate the view based on the DVIEW settings.

Example

This example shows how you can use the DVIEW command to dynamically view the default DVIEWBLOCK. AutoCAD automatically creates the DVIEWBLOCK when you issue the DVIEW command in a new drawing (see fig. D.79).

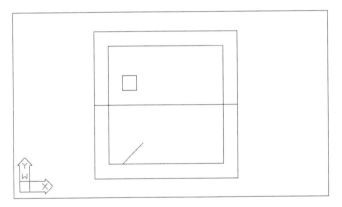

Figure D.79. *The DVIEWBLOCK created by the DVIEW command, seen in plan view.*

Command: **DVIEW** (Enter)	Issues the DVIEW command
Select objects: (Enter)	Selects no objects—creates a block definition called DVIEWBLOCK
CAmera/TArget/Distance/POints/ PAn/Zoom/TWist/CLip/Hide/Off/ Undo/<eXit>: (Enter)	Exits DVIEW command

Insert the DVIEWBLOCK block at the point 0,0,0. Use an X scale factor of 1, a Y scale factor of 1, and a rotation angle of 0. Then use the Extents option of the ZOOM command to zoom tightly around the block.

DVIEW

Command: **DVIEW** (Enter)	Issues the DVIEW command
Select objects: **L** (Enter)	Chooses the DVIEWBLOCK
1 found	
Select objects: (Enter)	Uses just DVIEWBLOCK with DVIEW command
CAmera/TArget/Distance/POints/ PAn/Zoom/TWist/CLip/Hide/Off/ Undo/<eXit>: **Z** (Enter)	Specifies the Zoom option
Adjust zoom scale factor <1>: **.5** (Enter)	Zooms out to make objects appear half as large
CAmera/TArget/Distance/POints/ PAn/Zoom/TWist/CLip/Hide/Off/ Undo/<eXit>: **D** (Enter)	Specifies distance option
New camera/target distance <1.0000>: **5** (Enter)	Sets camera to target distance to 5 and turns on perspective mode
CAmera/TArget/Distance/POints/ PAn/Zoom/TWist/CLip/Hide/Off/ Undo/<eXit>: **CA** (Enter)	Specifies CAmera option
Toggle angle in/Enter angle from XY plane <90.0000>: **25** (Enter)	Rotate camera position to a position 25 degrees above the XY plane
Toggle angle from/Enter angle in XY plane from X axis <-90.00000>: **-120** (Enter)	Rotates camera position to -120 degrees counterclockwise from the X axis (see fig. D.80)
CAmera/TArget/Distance/POints/ PAn/Zoom/TWist/CLip/Hide/Off/ Undo/<eXit>: (Enter)	Exits DVIEW command
Regenerating drawing.	

Related Commands

DDVIEW   HIDE   RENDER   SHADE
VPOINT

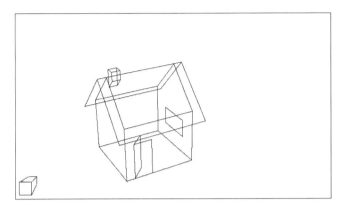

Figure D.80. *The view of DVIEWBLOCK after changing the dynamic view options.*

Related System Variables

BACKZ	FRONTZ	LENSLENGTH	TARGET
TILEMODE	VIEWDIR	VIEWMODE	VIEWSIZE
VIEWTWIST	VSMIN	VSMAX	WORLDVIEW

DXBIN

Pull-down: File, Import, DXB... (DOS Only)
Screen: FILE, IMPORT, DXBin:

The DXBIN command enables you to import DXB files—binary drawing exchange files. DXB files are limited in the types of objects and other drawing data they can contain. Unlike binary DXF files, binary DXB files are not complete representations of the AutoCAD drawing files. Certain programs, such as AutoShade, use DXB files to export simple drawing data, which AutoCAD can then import when you use the DXBIN command.

> DXB files are useful if you want to create flat drawings of three-dimensional models created in AutoCAD. To create a DXB file, configure for plot file output format and select the AutoCAD DXB file output option. A DXB file contains only line objects. In a DXB plot file, circles, arcs, and text are composed of many short lines.

Prompts and Options

When you execute the DXBIN command, the Select DXB File dialog box appears. Select a DXB file, and then choose OK.

Example

The following example shows you how to use the DXBIN command to import a DXB file (see fig. D.81). Create the DVIEWBLOCK object (see the DVIEW command), and then use the PLOT command to create a DXB output file. You might want to create a plotter definition for a DXB output format.

Command: **DXBIN** (Enter)	Issues DXBIN command
Select the DXB output file created using the PLOT *command*	Imports the DXB lines

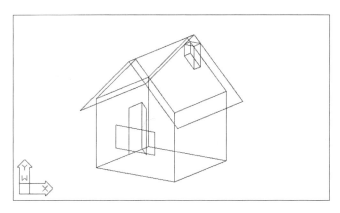

Figure D.81. *The DVIEWBLOCK imported using the DXBIN command.*

Related Commands

ACISIN   DXFIN   GIFIN   IMPORT
PLOT   PCXIN   PSIN   TIFFIN
WMFIN

DXFIN

Pull-down: File, Import, DXF... (DOS Only)
Screen: FILE, IMPORT, DXFin:

The DXFIN command enables you to import a *Drawing Interchange File* (DXF) into the current drawing. The DXF format directly represents all the objects in a drawing, including layers, linetypes, text styles, and block definitions. A DXF file lists this information in three sections, entitled Tables, Blocks, and Entities. DXF files often are used to transfer drawing files between CAD packages.

DXF files cannot contain ACIS SOLID objects. Use the ACISIN and ACISOUT commands to import and export ACIS SOLIDs.

Before you can import a complete DXF file, including any layers, linetypes, text styles, and block definitions, the current drawing must be completely empty. To create an empty drawing, use the NEW command to begin a new drawing, and check the No Prototype check box in the Create New Drawing dialog box. Issue the DXFIN command immediately after AutoCAD generates the new drawing. After the DXFIN command successfully imports a complete DXF file, AutoCAD automatically performs a ZOOM All command.

Some third-party software products automatically create objects upon startup of all new drawings. To prevent this from occurring, repeatedly press Cancel as AutoCAD creates the new drawing.

If a drawing file is not new and empty, DXFIN imports only the Entities section of a DXF file and ignores the Tables and Blocks sections. This ignores all named objects in the DXF file, such as layers, linetypes, text styles, and blocks definitions. A DXF file, however, does not need to be a complete drawing file that contains named definitions—it can be as simple as a single object. Some third-party AutoCAD application programs create new objects as DXF files and use DXFIN to insert them into a drawing.

If you issue the DXFIN command in a drawing that is not new and empty, AutoCAD responds with the following:

```
Not a new drawing - only ENTITIES section will be input.
```

If the DXF file contains insert objects (block references), and these blocks are not previously defined in the drawing, the DXFIN import fails and AutoCAD reports the following:

```
Undefined block BLOCKNAME
```

To add the objects in a DXF file to an existing drawing, create a new drawing that has no prototype. Use the DXFIN command to import the DXF file. Save the drawing under a temporary name. Open the existing drawing to which you want to add the DXF file objects, and use the INSERT or DDINSERT command to insert the temporary file.

Although the DXFIN command checks for errors in the DXF file as it imports it, AutoCAD might not be able to determine the validity of all objects in the DXF file. Use the AUDIT command after executing the DXFIN command to verify that the imported objects are valid.

Prompts and Options

When you execute the DXFIN command, you initiate the Select DXF File dialog box. Select the DXF file you want, and then click on OK. If the system variable FILEDIA is set to 0, type the DXF file name at the prompt.

Example

The following example shows you the way to use the DXFIN command to import a DXF file. The example uses the output file from the DXFOUT command to import simple objects (lines, arcs, circles) into the current drawing (see fig. D.82).

Command: **DXFIN** (Enter)	Invokes DXFIN command
Select the DXF output file created with the DXFOUT *command*	Imports the simple objects

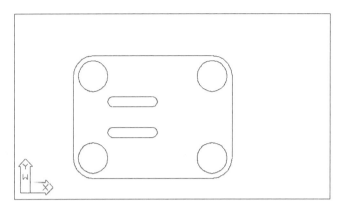

Figure D.82. *Simple objects imported with the DXFIN command.*

Related Commands

ACISIN   DXBIN   DXFOUT   GIFIN
IMPORT   PCXIN   PSIN   TIFFIN
WMFIN

DXFOUT

    Pull-down: File, Export, DXF... (DOS Only)
    Screen: FILE, EXPORT, DXFout:

The DXFOUT command enables you to create a file in the *Drawing Interchange File* (DXF) standard. This file standard directly represents your drawing and often is used to convert AutoCAD files to other CAD-related packages, or to prepare it for machine tool devices or other rendering packages that support the DXF format.

You can create an ASCII DXF, or binary DXF. You can export an entire drawing, or selected objects. If you export a file as an ASCII DXF file, you can select the accuracy of the numerical data.

A DXF file typically takes two to three times more disk space than the original drawing file. The binary format is more compact, efficient, and precise, whereas the default format created by DXFOUT is an ASCII file—the binary format also loads several times faster. Do not confuse the Binary DXF file with a *Drawing Interchange Binary* (DXB) file, which you use with the DXBIN command.

DXFOUT

> **NOTE:** DXF files cannot contain ACIS SOLID objects. Use the ACISIN and ACISOUT commands to import and export ACIS SOLIDs.

By default, the DXFOUT command creates a complete ASCII DXF file that fully describes the drawing. All layers, linetypes, text styles, and blocks definitions are included in the output DXF file. The default precision is six decimal places, which often is sufficient. You can specify the accuracy between 0 and 16 places. The more decimal places you instruct AutoCAD to use, the larger your DXF file is. Binary DXF files are created with the full precision of the AutoCAD drawing.

To output only specific objects, you use the Objects option, then select the objects you want to export. You then specify the accuracy for the output DXF file.

Prompts and Options

When you execute the DXFOUT command, you initiate the Create DXF File dialog box. The default output DXF file name is the same name as the current drawing, with an extension of DXF. Select an existing file to overwrite or specify a new output file name.

`Enter decimal places of accuracy (0 to 16)/Objects/Binary <6>` Press Enter to create an ASCII DXF file that has a precision to six decimal places, or enter a number. The number you enter determines the precision of the output DXF file, and AutoCAD writes a full ASCII DXF file.

Choose the Objects option to output selected objects in DXF format. Select the objects, then enter the number of decimal places of accuracy. The binary option is again available.

The Binary option creates a smaller yet more precise file than the standard ASCII format. This binary file has the same DXF extension as the ASCII format.

`Select objects` Use any of AutoCAD's standard object selection methods to select the objects to write in the DXF output file.

Example

In the following example, you use the DXFOUT command to create a DXF. Create the objects shown in figure D.83. Use only simple lines, circles, and arcs. In this example, you export all the objects in the drawing to the DXF output file.

```
Command: DXFOUT (Enter)                        Invokes the DXFOUT command

Enter the name of a DXF output file            Specifies DXF output file name

Enter decimal places of accuracy               Specifies 12 decimal place
(0 to 16)/Objects/Binary <6>: 12 (Enter)       precision
```

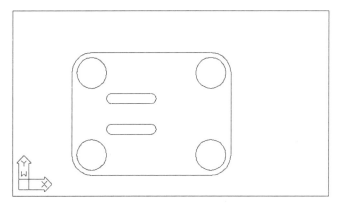

Figure D.83. *Simple objects exported to a DXF file using the DXFOUT command.*

Related Commands

ACISOUT   DXFIN   EXPORT   PLOT
PSOUT   STLOUT

EDGE

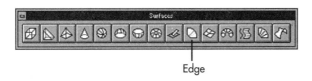
Edge

Toolbar: *Edge (Surfaces)*
Pull-down: *Draw, Surfaces, Edge*
Screen: DRAW2, SURFACES, 3Dface:, Edge:

The EDGE command enables you to hide visible edges of 3D faces, or make visible the invisible edges of 3D faces. The EDGE command interactively changes the visibility of the edges of existing 3D faces. 3D face edges can be visible or invisible.

Prompts and Options

Display/<Select edge> Select the edge of the 3D face to turn invisible. A running object snap of MIDpoint is enabled, with the aperture set to 5 pixels. Select the Display option to view edges of 3D faces that are currently invisible. The edges are turned invisible immediately if you pick them.

Select/<All> Press Enter to show the invisible edges of all 3D faces in the drawing, or choose the Select option to select specific 3D faces to view. If all four of a 3D face's edges are invisible, you cannot select it. Use the All option (the default) in this case to make these 3D faces visible. After you select objects, or choose the All option, AutoCAD displays the invisible edges of 3D faces as highlighted lines, and prints the following:

```
** Regenerating 3DFACE objects...done.
```

Example

The following example changes the visibility of three edges of a 3D face. Create the two 3D faces used in the 3DFACE example (see fig. E.1).

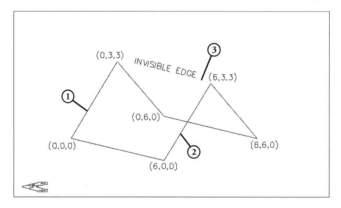

Figure E.1. *3D face edges before changing their visibility.*

Command: **EDGE** (Enter)	Invokes the EDGE command
Display/<Select edge>: **D**	Specifies Display option
Select/<All>: (Enter)	Displays all edges
** Regenerating 3DFACE objects...done.	
Display/<Select edge>: *Pick at* ① (*see fig. E.1*)	Turns left edge invisible
Display/<Select edge>: *Pick at* ②	Turns right edge invisible
Display/<Select edge>: *Pick at* ③	Turns top edge visible
Display/<Select edge>: (Enter)	Exits EDGE command (see fig. E.2)

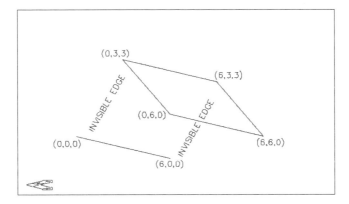

Figure E.2. *Two edges made invisible and one visible using the EDGE command.*

Related Command
3DFACE

Related System Variable
SPLFRAME

EDGESURF

Edge Surface

Toolbar: *Edge Surface (Surfaces)*
Pull-down: *Draw, Surfaces, Edge Surface*
Screen: DRAW2, SURFACES, Edgsurf:

The EDGESURF command enables you to create a four-sided mesh that can be defined by arcs, lines, and open polylines (2D or 3D).

The EDGESURF command approximates a *Coons surface patch* between the four edge objects. The mesh is constructed by dividing the opposing sides into even increments, and creating mesh tabulations along these sides. The two tabulations of the mesh are called the M and N directions of the surface. The system variables SURFTAB1 and SURFTAB2 define the number of tabulation lines along the M and N directions of the surface. The default values for SURFTAB1 and SURFTAB2 create a 6×6 mesh.

> Large SURFTAB1 and SURFTAB2 settings create smoother surfaces at the expense of file size, object regeneration, and hidden-line removal. When you set the variables, consider the application of the mesh. If you need large settings for the final product, construct two meshes using the same boundaries—a temporary mesh that has a moderate number of faces and a final mesh (kept on a frozen layer until needed) that has more faces. By using the temporary mesh, you can save time during the drawing and editing stages of your project. Replace the temporary mesh with the final mesh before final plotting and presentation.

You can use most of AutoCAD's edit commands to edit the completed mesh—for example, you can use the PEDIT command to fit smooth curves through each vertex and to move vertices. If you use the EXPLODE command to break the mesh apart, AutoCAD replaces the mesh with 3D face objects.

The endpoints of the boundary edge objects must intersect, and the objects must form a closed region. If edge n does not intersect the next edge, AutoCAD prints the following message:

```
Edge n does not touch another edge.
```

Prompts and Options

Select edge n Select each of the four boundary edges for the polygon mesh, in any order. The end of the first edge you select, nearest the pick point, is the origin of the mesh, with the M direction extending toward the opposite end of that edge. The other axis of the mesh is the N direction.

Example

In this example, you create a mesh between four objects in 3D space. The objects shown in figure E.3 are a combination of an arc, two lines and one polyline positioned in 3D space. SURFTAB1 and SURFTAB2 are both set to 20 in this example.

```
Command: EDGESURF (Enter)        Issues the EDGESURF command
Select edge 1: Pick at ①        Selects polyline as first
(see fig. E.3)                   boundary edge
Select edge 2: Pick at ②        Selects second boundary edge
Select edge 3: Pick at ③        Selects arc as third boundary edge
Select edge 4: Pick at ④        Selects fourth boundary edge
```

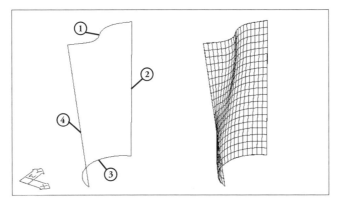

Figure E.3. *The edgesurf edges and the polygon mesh created using EDGESURF.*

Related Commands

3DFACE   3DMESH   PFACE   REVSURF
RULESURF TABSURF

Related System Variables

SURFTAB1 SURFTAB2

ELEV

The ELEV command enables you to set the elevation of the current construction plane for subsequently created drawing objects. This elevation is a distance along the Z axis above or below the current *User Coordinate System* (UCS) origin. The *construction plane* is a plane located at the specified elevation above or below the X,Y plane of the current UCS. The Z coordinates of points and new objects default to lie in the construction plane, unless you specify otherwise when you input the points or create the objects.

The ELEV command also enables you to set the extrusion thickness for subsequently drawn objects. The term *extrusion* refers to the distance an object is projected along the Z axis. An extruded circle, for example, resembles a cylinder when you view it from an oblique viewpoint. Figure E.4 illustrates the elevation and thickness concepts.

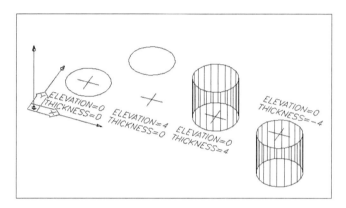

Figure E.4. *Circles at various elevations and thicknesses.*

You can use the DDEMODES command to initiate a dialog box that has edit boxes that enable you to set the elevation and thickness of all new objects, and which you can use transparently within other commands.

You should not use the ELEV command. Setting elevation to a nonzero height is confusing and can lead to errors when combined with a UCS located above or below the WCS origin. It is easier and less confusing to leave the elevation set to zero and use the UCS to control the location of the construction plane. Use the THICKNESS system variable or the DDEMODES dialog box to control extrusion thickness. The ELEV command will probably be purged in a future release of AutoCAD.

Objects not affected by the current thickness setting are meshes, 3D faces, 3D polylines, viewports, dimensions, 3D solids, and text. You can assign a thickness to text after you create it, however, by using the CHANGE or CHPROP command.

Prompts and Options

`New current elevation <0.0000>` At this prompt, you enter a value or pick two points to show a distance to define the new elevation. A positive value specifies an elevation above the current UCS. A negative value specifies an elevation below the current UCS. If you pick a point at this prompt, AutoCAD prompts for a second point.

`New current thickness <0,0000>` You can enter a value or pick two points to show a distance to define the extrusion value for objects. A positive value extrudes objects along the positive Z axis. A negative value extrudes objects along the negative Z axis. If you pick a point at this prompt, AutoCAD prompts for a second point.

Related Commands
DDEMODES   DDUCS

Related System Variables
ELEVATION   THICKNESS

ELLIPSE

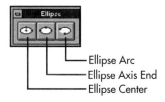
— Ellipse Arc
— Ellipse Axis End
— Ellipse Center

Toolbar: *(Draw, Ellipse)*
Pull-down: *Draw, Ellipse*
Screen: DRAW1, Ellipse:

The ELLIPSE command enables you to draw an ellipse or elliptical arc. If you set the PELLIPSE system variable to 1, the AutoCAD constructs the ellipse of polyline arcs as a single closed polyline. You can use the PEDIT command to modify such an ellipse. This option will be removed in the next release of AutoCAD. The default value for PELLIPSE is zero, so that using the ELLIPSE command creates true ellipse objects. See figure E.5 below.

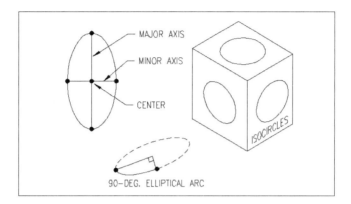

Figure E.5. *Using the ELLIPSE command to create objects.*

You can specify ellipses by any one of several combinations of axis endpoints (the default), axis distances, rotation about an axis, or a center point. If you set the Snap Style option to isometric mode, the ELLIPSE prompt includes an isometric option, which creates an isometric circle in the current isometric plane. See the SNAP command for details on isometric mode.

Prompts and Options

Arc/Center/Isocircle/<Axis endpoint 1>.

This prompt gives you the options discussed in the following three sections.

Arc

Use this option to create elliptical arcs. To create these arcs, follow the same prompts that you do to create a full ellipse. You then are prompted to specify options for the arc.

<Axis endpoint 1>/Center/Isocircle   The default for the Arc option is to specify the endpoint of one of the axes. If you pick a point, the following prompt appears:

Axis endpoint 2:

Specify the other endpoint for the first axis of the ellipse. After you pick this point, the following prompt appears:

`<Other axis distance>/Rotation` At this prompt, AutoCAD draws the ellipse dynamically on-screen, with the endpoint of the second axis passing through the crosshairs. You can specify a point for the second axis endpoint or choose the Rotation option.

If you choose the Rotation option, AutoCAD prompts you for the `Rotation around major axis`. The rotation is an imaginary rotation of a true circle about the axis. You can specify a rotation visually by picking a point, or you can type an explicit angle of rotation. A rotation of zero degrees produces an ellipse object that represents a true circle. A rotation of 90 degrees or multiples of 90 degrees cannot, by definition, be drawn and is invalid. This is due to the rotation being equivalent to viewing the ellipse "on edge," which is not possible. The following prompt for producing an elliptical arc appears after you define the ellipse:

`Parameter/<start angle>:`

Using the `<start angle>` option default, you specify a starting point for the elliptical arc. You can do this by picking a point on the screen, or by typing an explicit angle. Zero degrees is calculated to at the first axis endpoint you specify when you create the ellipse. The Parameter option is discussed later. After you specify the start angle, the following prompt appears:

`Parameter/Included/<end angle>:`

At this prompt, you specify the end angle (the default) by picking a point or explicitly typing an angle. Additionally, you can specify an included angle by using the Included option. If you choose the Included option, type the angle at the `Included angle <default>` prompt.

The Parameter option forces AutoCAD to calculate the elliptical arc using the vector equation:

`p(u) = c + a* cos(u) + b* sin(u)`

where *c* is the center of the ellipse and *a* and *b* are its major and minor axes, respectively. This is just alternate, mathematical way of creating the ellipse or elliptical arc.

The Parameter option displays the following prompts:

`Angle/<start parameter>:`
`Angle/Included/<end parameter>:`

These prompts are similar to the Angle option, in that you specify a beginning angle and an ending angle. The Parameter and Angle options act as a back-and-forth toggle by enabling you to select that option.

Center of Ellipse

The Center option displays this prompt. You specify a point for the center of the ellipse. The ELLIPSE command then prompts for the endpoint of the first axis.

Axis endpoint   If you specify a center point for the ellipse, this prompt displays. You specify a point for one end of the first axis. The point defines the length of the axis from the center point. AutoCAD then displays the <Other axis distance>/Rotation: prompt.

Isocircle

Specifying a point determines the beginning angle of the elliptical arc.

Axis endpoint 2   You enter the second endpoint of the first axis. The axis defined by these two endpoints can be the major or minor axis of the ellipse. The angle of this first axis determines the angle of the ellipse.

<Other axis distance>/Rotation   After you specify the first axis, you enter a distance value or pick a point to show a distance for the endpoint of the other axis of the ellipse. This distance or endpoint is from the center of the ellipse or the midpoint of the first axis you specify. If you enter R for the Rotation option, the ELLIPSE command displays the Rotation around major axis: prompt.

Rotation around major axis   At this prompt, you enter an angle value or pick a point to show the angle to rotate the ellipse around the first axis. The Rotation option is similar to specifying the second axis endpoint by rotating a perfect circle around the first axis in 3D. The Rotation option, however, does not actually rotate the ellipse in 3D. The ellipse is drawn as a two-dimensional object in the current UCS. An angle of 0 degrees creates an ellipse that looks like a circle in plan view.

Example

In the following example, you create an ellipse and an elliptical arc. Use the endpoint object snap when you select points.

Choose Ellipse Axis End (Draw, Ellipse)	Issues the ELLIPSE command
Command: _ellipse	
Arc/Center/<Axis endpoint 1>: endp of *Pick point* ① *(see fig. E.6)*	Specifies first axis endpoint

ELLIPSE

`Axis endpoint 2: _endp of` *Pick point* ②	Specifies second axis endpoint
`<Other axis distance>/Rotation: R` (Enter)	Chooses the Rotation option
`Rotation around major axis: 60`	Specifies the "circle" rotation about the major axis
Choose the Ellipse Arc tool	Issues the ELLIPSE command with the Arc option
`Command: _ellipse`	
`Arc/Center/<Axis endpoint 1>: _a`	
`<Axis endpoint 1>/Center: _endp of` *Pick point* ③	Specifies the first axis endpoint
`Axis endpoint 2: _endp of` *Pick point* ④	Specifies the second axis endpoint
`<Other axis distance>/Rotation: R` (Enter)	Specifies the Rotation option
`Rotation around major axis: 60` (Enter)	Specifies the rotation angle
`Parameter/<start angle>: 0` (Enter)	Determines the start angle for the arc
`Parameter/Included/<end angle>: -180`	Determines the end angle for the arc

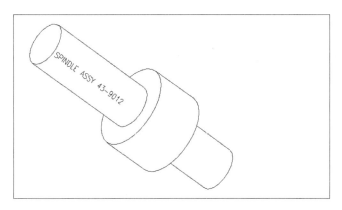

Figure E.6. *Using ellipses in illustrations.*

Related Commands
CIRCLE   ISOPLANE

Related System Variables
ANGDIR   PELLIPSE

END

You use the END command to finish your drawing session by saving your work. If you have an existing drawing in the same directory as the current drawing, and that file has the same name as the current drawing, the existing drawing file is renamed, using a BAK extension. If a file has the same name as the current drawing and a BAK extension already exists in the same directory as the current drawing, the BAK file is deleted. When you END a new un-named drawing, AutoCAD automatically opens the SAVEAS dialog box, prompting you for a name to give the drawing.

Related Commands
QUIT   QSAVE   SAVE   SAVEAS

ERASE

Erase

Toolbar: *Erase (Modify)*
Pull-down: <u>M</u>odify, <u>E</u>rase
Screen: MODIFY, Erase

The ERASE command enables you to delete selected objects from a drawing.

Prompts and Options

Select objects   Use any of AutoCAD's standard object-selection methods to select the objects that you want to erase. Press Enter to terminate object selection and erase the selected objects.

ERASE

TIP

To perform surgical erasures in congested areas or to erase objects off-screen, use the SELECT command to create a selection set of the objects you want erased, and then use ERASE with the **P**revious selection option.

Example

The following example shows how you use the ERASE command to delete objects from a drawing. Figure E.7 shows the results of the ERASE command.

Command: **ERASE** (Enter)	Issues the ERASE command
Select objects: **W** (Enter)	Specifies Window object selection
First corner: *Pick point* ① *(see fig. E.7)*	Defines first corner of object selection window
Other Corner: *Pick point* ②	Defines opposite corner of object selection window
Select objects: (Enter)	Terminates object selection and erases objects

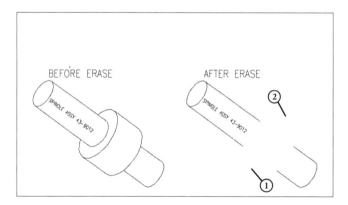

Figure E.7. *Selecting the objects to be erased.*

Related Commands
OOPS   UNDO/U

Related System Variable
UNDOCTL

EXPLODE

Explode

> Toolbar: *Explode (Modify, Explode)*
> Pull-down: <u>M</u>odify, <u>E</u>xplode
> Screen: MODIFY, Explode:

The EXPLODE command enables you to reduce a complex object into its component parts. A *complex object* is an inserted block, polyline, associative dimension, 3D mesh, 3D solid, multiline, polyface mesh, polygon mesh, or region. Complex objects consist of simpler objects such as lines, arcs, text, 3D faces, and other objects.

When you explode polylines, you reduce them into lines and arcs. 2D polylines that are curve-fit or spine-fit lose their original geometry and explode into lines and arcs that approximate the curve or spline. You also lose tangent and width information when you explode polylines. 3D Polylines explode into lines.

Polygon meshes explode into three-dimensional faces. Polyface meshes explode into three-sided faces, lines, and points. If a polyline or mesh contains component parts with differing layers, colors, or linetypes, all component parts receive the layer, color, and linetype of the first component part in the polyline or mesh when they explode.

Multiline objects explode into lines.

With 3D Solids, if any surfaces are planar, they explode into regions. Nonplanar surfaces explode into bodies. You cannot explode a sphere or torus.

Regions explode into lines, arcs, ellipses, or splines.

A body object explodes into single-surface bodies (non-planar surfaces), regions, or curved objects (circles, arcs, ellipses).

Associative dimensions explode into lines, text, and points, and their arrowheads explode into blocks or solids.

Block insertions (inserted blocks) explode into the objects that their block definitions contain. You cannot explode external references (xrefs) and their dependent blocks or blocks that were inserted using the MINSERT command. Attributes in exploded blocks are deleted and replaced with their attribute definition objects.

> If you insert a block with unequal X, Y, or Z scale factors, AutoCAD explodes the block, but you might not expect the resulting final appearance. For example, circles that were a part of the original block are approximated with ellipse objects and arcs become elliptical arcs.

If complex objects are nested, such as a block that contains other blocks or other complex objects, only the outer object explodes. After you explode the outer block, you can select and explode the objects that were contained in it. You can explode only one object at a time if you use the EXPLODE command within a menu, script, or ADS, ARX, or AutoLISP application.

Prompts and Options

Select objects Use any of AutoCAD's standard object-selection methods to select the objects that you want to explode. You can press Enter to terminate object selection and explode the selected objects into their component parts.

Related Commands

BLOCK   INSERT   REGION   UNDO
XPLODE

Related System Variable

EXPLMODE

EXPORT (Windows Only)

Pull-down: <u>F</u>ile, <u>E</u>xport...

The EXPORT command displays a dialog box for selecting an export file type. A variety of export formats, including WMF, ACIS, PFB, TXT, DXF, 3DS, STL, BMP, and native DWG are supported. Once a file has been selected, the appropriate export command (WMFOUT, ACISOUT, PSOUT, 3DSOUT, ATTEXT, DXFOUT, STLOUT, BMPOUT, or WBLOCK) is used to export the selected objects. The file type (the file extension) determines which export command is used. See the individual descriptions of each of these commands for more information on prompts and options available with each command.

Prompts and Options

The EXPORT command displays the Export Data dialog box, which is used to select the desired export file type. Select the List Files of Type drop-down list to select the desired file type, then specify the desired export file name.

Example

The following example creates a Drawing Interchange File (DXF) using the EXPORT command. Create the objects shown in figure E.8. Use only simple lines, circles, and arcs. All of the objects in the drawing are exported to the DXF output file in this example.

Command: **EXPORT** (Enter)	Starts EXPORT command, displays Export Data dialog box
Select the file type **DXF (*.DXF)** *from the List Files of Type drop-down list*	
Select the file **EXPORT.DXF** *from the File Name list box*	
Click on OK	
DXFOUT File name: EXPORT.DXF	Specifies DXF output file name
Enter decimal places of accuracy	Specifies 12 decimal place precision
(0 to 16)/Objects/Binary <6>: **12** (Enter)	

EXPORT (Windows Only)

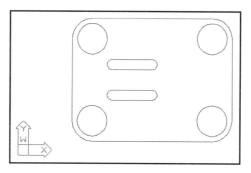

Figure E.8. *Simple objects exported to a DXF file with the EXPORT command.*

Related Commands

ACISIN	ACISOUT	ATTEXT	BMPOUT
DXBING	DXFIN	DXFOUT	GIFIN
PCSIN	PLOT	PSIN	PSOUT
STLOUT	TIFFIN	WBLOCK	WMFOUT

EXTEND

Extend

Toolbar: *Extend (Modify, Trim)*
Pull-down: *Modify, Extend*
Screen: MODIFY, Extend:

The EXTEND command enables you to increase the length of lines, open polylines, splines, rays, elliptical arcs, and arcs so that they intersect a boundary edge. The edge can be any object, such as a line, circle, arc, sketch line, viewport object, or an open or closed polyline (both 2D and 3D). You also can extend associative dimensions; when you extend an associative dimension, AutoCAD automatically updates it. You cannot extend hatch objects, nor can you select a hatch as a boundary edge. Other objects that you cannot extend or use as a boundary edge include blocks, shapes, meshes, 3D faces, text, traces, and points.

AutoCAD enables you to select multiple boundary edges, and you can choose multiple objects to extend by using the fence selection method. The EXTEND command offers an Undo feature, which returns the most recently extended object to its former length.

You also can control extending the object in 3D space. You can extend an object to another object (edge), regardless of whether the objects reside in the same UCS plane, view plane, or would intersect in 3D space.

Prompts and Options

`Select boundary edges: (Projmode = View, Edgemode = No extend) Select objects`   At this prompt, you first select the objects you want to serve as the boundary for other extended objects. In other words, select the objects to which you want to extend other objects. This prompt also shows the current values of the system variables PROJMODE and EDGEMODE, which determine how AutoCAD should extend the subsequently selected objects. You can change these values at the next prompt. Press Enter after you select the boundary objects.

`<Select object to extend>/Project/Edge/Undo`   At this prompt, select the objects you want to extend. You must use individual object selection (pick the objects closest to the end you want to extend toward the boundary objects), or the fence object selection method for multiple objects (the point where the fence intersects the object is used to determine if an edge (boundary) exists in that direction).

At this prompt, you also can change the projection method and edge mode for determining how the objects are extended. If you select the Project option, the `None/Ucs/View <View>` prompt appears.

Use the None option to force AutoCAD to enable you to extend only those objects that actually intersect in 3D space. Use the Ucs option to project the objects onto the current *User Coordinate System* (UCS) plane. AutoCAD extends the objects regardless of whether they actually intersect in 3D space. Use the View option (the default) to extend the objects according to the current view. Again, AutoCAD extends the objects regardless of whether they actually intersect in 3D space.

You select the Edge option to change the way AutoCAD treats boundary edges. You make your choice at the `Extend/No extend <No extend>` prompt. The Extend option treats boundary edges as if they extend infinitely into 3D space. The No Extend option (the default) forces AutoCAD to extend only objects that would actually intersect the selected boundary edges (see fig. E.9). If at any time AutoCAD cannot determine that an object intersects a selected boundary object, you receive the error `Object does not intersect an edge`.

EXTEND

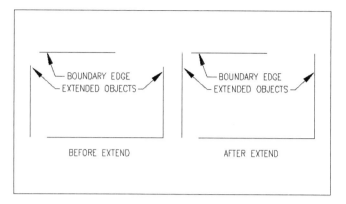

Figure E.9. *The EXTEND command with the Edge option.*

You also can extend boundary objects within the EXTEND command. In figure E.9, you could select all objects as boundary objects, and if you were in edge mode, you could select them all again as objects to extend. This would result in a closed rectangle, and is handy for cleaning up "sketched" drawings.

Example

The following example demonstrates the EXTEND command with the extend mode enabled (see fig. E.10). All the vertical lines are extended in spite of the fact that two of them do not actually intersect the boundary object.

```
Command: EXTEND (Enter)                          Issues the EXTEND command
Select boundary edges:
(Projmode = UCS, Edgemode = No extend)

Select objects: Pick point ①                     Specifies the objects to use as
(see fig. E.10)                                  boundary edges

1 found

Select objects: (Enter)                          Terminates object selection

<Select object to extend>
/Project/Edge/Undo: E (Enter)                    Specifies the Edge option

Extend/No extend <No extend>: E (Enter)          Specifies the Extend option
```

```
<Select object to extend>
/Project/Edge/Undo: F (Enter)         Specifies the Fence object selection
                                      method

First fence point: Pick point ②       Specifies the first fence point

Undo/<Endpoint of line>: Pick point ③ Specifies the second fence point

Undo/<Endpoint of line>: (Enter)      Terminates the fence selection method

<Select object to extend>
/Project/Edge/Undo: (Enter)           Terminates object selection
```

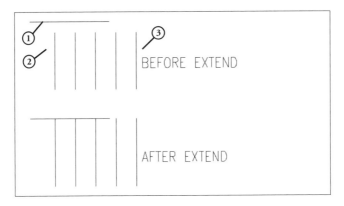

Figure E.10. *Extending lines with the Extend edge mode enabled.*

Related Commands

LENGTHEN   STRETCH   TRIM

Related System Variables

EDGEMODE   PROJMODE

EXTRUDE

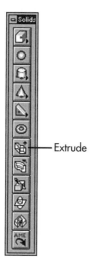
— Extrude

Toolbar: *Extrude (Solids)*
Pull-down: *Draw, Solids, Extrude*
Screen: DRAW2, SOLIDS, Extrude:

The EXTRUDE command enables you to convert 2D objects into ACIS SOLID objects. Valid 2D objects include closed polylines, polygons, circles, ellipses, traces, donuts, and AutoCAD 2D solid objects. Thickness does not matter when you extrude an object.

A polyline must have at least three vertices, no more than 500 vertices, and must not cross itself, before you can extrude one. You extrude wide polylines (and donuts) from their center line.

Prompts and Options

Select objects Select the objects you want to extrude. Use any of AutoCAD's object selection options.

Path/<Height of Extrusion> Enter the height of the extrusion. A positive height creates an extrusion along the positive Z axis, and a negative height creates an extrusion along the negative Z axis. You extrude circles and arcs along their extrusion vector direction. You also can show a positive distance by picking two points in the graphics window. Choose the Path option to select a path object that defines the extrusion direction and length.

Select path Pick an object that defines the extrusion path. AutoCAD extrudes the selected objects along this path. The direction of the path object determines the extrusion direction, and the length of the path object determines the extrusion length. You can use lines, arcs, circles, polyline ellipses, 2D polylines, and open 3D polylines as path objects.

If the selected objects and the path object lie in the same plane, AutoCAD can't extrude them and reports the following:

```
Profile and path are tangential.
Unable to extrude the selected object.
```

If the path does not begin, end, or pass through the object you want to extrude, AutoCAD moves the path to the centroid position of the profile for determining the extrusion path and prints:

```
Path was moved to the center of the profile.
```

If the path contains adjacent segments that are not tangent (a 3D polyline, for example), AutoCAD mitres the extruded solid to join along a plane that bisects the angle between the nontangent segments.

Extrusion taper angle <0> If you have specified an extrusion height, enter the extrusion taper angle at this prompt. An angle of 0 creates an extrusion of uniform cross-section. A positive taper angle creates an extrusion that tapers in from the base to the top. A negative taper angle creates an extrusion that tapers out from base to top. If you use a steep taper angle, you can create an extrusion that tapers to a point before it reaches the full extrusion height.

Example

In the following example, you use the EXTRUDE command to create a three-dimensional tube. Create a 3D polyline, and a circle that has a perpendicular orientation to the first segment of the 3D polyline, as shown in figure E.11.

Command: **EXTRUDE** (Enter)	Begins EXTRUDE command
Select objects: *Pick circle at* ① *(see fig. E.11)*	Selects object to extrude
1 found	
Select objects: (Enter)	Finishes selecting objects to extrude
Path/<Height of Extrusion>: **P** (Enter)	Specifies the Path option
Select path: *Pick 3D polyline at* ②	Specifies extrusion path object

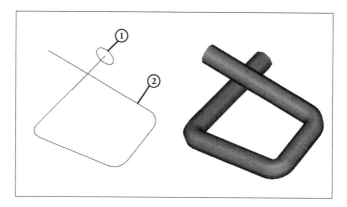

Figure E.11. *The circle and 3D polyline before extruding.*

Related Commands

BOX	CYLINDER	INTERFERE	INTERSECT
REGION	SECTION	SLICE	SUBTRACT
TORUS	UNION	WEDGE	

Related System Variable

THICKNESS

FILEOPEN (Windows Only)

The FILEOPEN command is an undocumented command that is the command-line equivalent of the dialog-based OPEN command. FILEOPEN is used primarily by other Windows applications that utilize *Dynamic Data Exchange* (DDE) or *Object Linking and Embedding* (OLE) functions to interact with AutoCAD.

Prompts and Options

Enter name of drawing <current drawing path and name>   This is the only prompt issued by FILEOPEN. You simply specify the drawing path and name of the file you want to open in AutoCAD. For example, if you have a drawing named TOOLS in the directory named DRAWINGS on your C: drive, your input would look similar to the following:

Enter name of drawing <current drawing path and name>: **C:\DRAWINGS\TOOLS**

Related Commands

NEW   OPEN

Related System Variables

DBMOD   DWGPREFIX   DWGNAME

'FILES

Pull-down: **F**ile, **M**anagement, **U**nlock File...
Pull-down: File, Management, Utilities... (DOS Only)
Screen: FILE, MANAGE, Files:

The FILES command enables you to perform file maintenance from within AutoCAD. You can list drawing files, list other files, delete files, rename files, copy files, and unlock files.

The FILEDIA system variable controls the method of file specification with the FILES command. If FILEDIA is set to 1, each of the command options is performed through dialog boxes (see fig. F.1). If the FILEDIA variable is set to 0, AutoCAD issues the text-only prompts.

Figure F.1. *The File Utilities dialog box.*

You should be careful not to delete any files in use or AutoCAD's temporary files when you are using the FILES command. Temporary files are designated with the extensions $A, $AC, and AC$. Placement of temporary files is controlled from the Operating Parameters menu of the Configuration menu. Files used for file locking are given an extension of ??K. AutoCAD may crash if you delete temporary files. If lock files are deleted, anyone can access the file in use on a network system. A loss of data is inevitable when two people edit the same file on two different machines.

Dialog Box Items

If the FILEDIA variable is set to 1 (the default), each of the five FILES command options (**L**ist files, **C**opy file, **R**ename file, **D**elete file, and **U**nlock file) displays a second dialog box similar to figure F.2. This dialog box is the standard file-selection dialog box and displays available files and the dialog box buttons Cancel and **F**ind File. Sometimes the OK button is displayed.

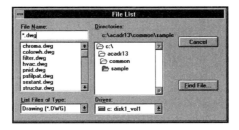

Figure F.2. *The typical FILES command dialog box.*

The FILES command options perform the following operations:

List files. The File List dialog box appears, listing all the drawing files in the current directory. To change the file types displayed in the list box, change the wild-card pattern to the files you want to see. For example, you could change the pattern to *.* to see all the files in the current directory.

Copy file. Initially, the Source File dialog box appears. You should select the file to copy from by navigating the **D**irectories and File **N**ame list boxes. When the file appears, highlight it in the File **N**ame list box and click on OK. You also can type the full path and name of the source file in the File **N**ame edit box.

After selecting the source file, you need to supply a location and name for the copy. The Destination File dialog box appears and requests this information. You can navigate the **D**irectories list box to choose a location for the file. To change the destination file's name, type a new name, including the extension, into the File **N**ame edit box. Click on OK when you are finished. AutoCAD displays the status of the copy at the bottom of the File Utilities dialog box.

Rename file. The Old File Name dialog box appears, requesting the name of the original file. You can select the file name from the **D**irectories and File **N**ame list boxes or type in the full path and name from the File **N**ame edit box. Click on OK when you are finished.

The New File Name dialog box appears next, requesting the new name for the file. You may select the file name from the **D**irectories and File **N**ame list boxes or type the full path and name in the File **N**ame edit box. If you select an existing file name, you are prompted to verify that you want to replace the existing file. Click on OK when you are finished. The success or failure of the operation is reported at the bottom of the File Utilities dialog box.

Delete file. The File(s) to Delete dialog box appears, requesting the names of the files you want erased from your disk. Two additional buttons appear: **S**elect All and **C**lear All. You may select the file names from the **D**irectories and File **N**ame list boxes or type the full path and name in the File **N**ame edit box. If you want to list a specific group of files, such as all the backup drawing files, you can enter the appropriate wild-card pattern at the File **N**ame edit box.

When the files you want to erase are displayed in the File **N**ame list box, you must highlight each file you want to delete. To delete all listed files, click on **S**elect All. To dehighlight a group of files, click on **C**lear All. Click on OK when you are finished. AutoCAD displays the number of files that it deletes at the bottom of the File Utilities dialog box. Any files currently locked by AutoCAD are not deleted.

Unlock file. This option is used to remove the file locks set by AutoCAD in any configuration that has file locking enabled. The Files to Unlock dialog box displays, requesting the names of the files you want to unlock. You specify the names of the actual files you want to unlock, not the names of lock files (#.??K) themselves. You can list specific files by using the Pattern: (DOS) or File **N**ame (Windows) edit box (such as any file matching the *.DWG template). Select the files individually from the Directories and Files list boxes, use the **S**elect all button, or type the names of the exact files you want to unlock.

AutoCAD attempts to unlock any locked files you specify. If a file is already in use by someone, a message appears at the bottom of the dialog box informing you that the file is in use and inquiring if you still want the file to be unlocked. When files are unlocked, AutoCAD displays the total number at the bottom of the dialog box.

Help. This button in the File Utilities dialog box displays the AutoCAD help window.

Ex**it.** This option returns you to the drawing editor.

Prompts and Options

If the FILEDIA variable is set to 0, the FILES command presents the following prompts and options:

```
File Utility Menu
   0.  Exit File Utility Menu
   1.  List Drawing files
   2.  List user specified files
   3.  Delete files
   4.  Rename files
```

```
   5. Copy file
   6. Unlock file
Enter selection (0 to 6) <0>:
```

Exit File Utility Menu   When you select this option, you return to the drawing editor.

List Drawing files   AutoCAD presents a list of all files with the extension DWG in the specified drive or directory. (The list is similar to the results of the DOS command DIR *.DWG /W/P.) After you select this option, AutoCAD displays the following prompt:

```
Enter drive or directory:
```

Press Enter if you want to see a list of the drawing files in the current directory. Otherwise, you can enter an alternative drive or directory.

List user specified files   When you select this option, AutoCAD lists files according to a file-name specification you supply. Wild cards are allowed. You can restrict the list to just the backup files (*.BAK), for example, or to all the drawings with file names beginning with the letter F (F*.DWG). When you select this option, AutoCAD displays the following prompt:

```
Enter file search specification:
```

You should enter a valid file-search specification for your operating system. Include a drive and path prefix if necessary.

Delete files   When you select this option, AutoCAD erases files from a disk. The following prompt appears, asking you to specify the files to be deleted:

```
Enter file deletion specification:
```

You can enter a drive, path, and file-name specification. Wild cards are allowed. If you specify a file that is locked, AutoCAD displays the following messages:

```
Deletion denied, file: filename was locked by login name at time on date
0 files deleted.
Press RETURN to continue:
```

If the file is not in use, you can unlock the file and then delete it.

Rename files   By selecting this option, you can rename existing files from within AutoCAD. This option does not accept wild-card characters. AutoCAD displays the following prompt:

```
Enter current filename:
```

Enter the name of the file to rename. Include a drive and path prefix, if necessary. AutoCAD then prompts for the file's new name, as follows:

```
Enter new filename:
```

You should enter a new name for the file. Do not include a drive or path. If you specify a file that is locked, AutoCAD displays the following messages:

```
Rename denied, file: filename was locked by login name at time on date
0 files renamed.
Press RETURN to continue:
```

If the file is not in use, you can unlock the file and then rename it.

Copy file When you select this option, you can make a copy of one or more specified files from within AutoCAD. The original file is called *source*, and the copy is called *destination*. You can place the copy on a separate drive or in a different directory. AutoCAD displays the following prompts:

```
Enter name of source file:
Enter name of destination:
Copied xxxxxx bytes.
Press RETURN to continue:
```

The *xxxxxx* will be replaced with a number that represents the size of the file copied.

If you specify a file that is locked, AutoCAD displays the following message:

```
Copy denied, file: filename was locked by login name at time on date
0 files copied.
Press RETURN to continue:
```

If the file is not in use, you can unlock the file and then copy it.

Unlock file If you try to open a file that is locked, you receive the following message:

```
Waiting for file: filename.dwg
Locked by user: login name at time on date
Press Ctrl+C to Cancel
```

If you press Ctrl+C, or if 12 attempts to retrieve the file have failed, AutoCAD displays the following prompt:

```
Access denied: filename.dwg is in use.
Press Return to Continue:
```

These prompts indicate that the file is locked. (If a user turns off his computer or if it crashes while editing a locked file, the file remains locked.) If you select the Unlock files option of the Files command, the following prompt appears:

```
Enter locked file(s) specification:
```

You enter the locked drawing's name with the extension DWG, and AutoCAD responds with the following prompt:

```
The file: filename.dwg was locked by login name at time on date.
Do you wish to unlock it <Y>
```

After you verify that the file is not actually in use, press Enter to accept the default of Yes, and the following messages appear:

```
Lock was successfully removed.
1 files unlocked.
Press RETURN to continue:
```

If the drawing file has been deleted, and the lock file still exists, the following messages appear:

```
ORPHAN lock file filename was locked by login name at time on date.
Do you still wish to unlock it? <Y>
```

Example

This exercise demonstrates how to use the FILES command to remove all backup files in the current directory.

Command: **FILES** (Enter)	Issues the FILES command
Click on the Delete file *button*	Chooses the Delete option
Click in the File **N**ame *edit box and enter* ***.BAK**, *then click on* OK	Displays all files matching the selected pattern in the Files list box
Click on the **S**elect all *button to highlight the files*	Selects all files displayed in the Files list box
Click on OK	Deletes the selected files and returns you to the File Utilities dialog box
Click on Exit	Terminates the FILES command

Related Command

SHELL/SH

'FILL

Screen: OPTIONS, DISPLAY, Fill:

The FILL command controls the display of multilines, wide polylines, solids, and traces. The default, On, displays these objects filled in. When FILL is turned off, AutoCAD displays only the outlines of these objects (see fig. F.3).

This setting affects both the screen display and the printed or plotted output. Solid filled objects also display only as outlines when hidden lines are removed with the HIDE command.

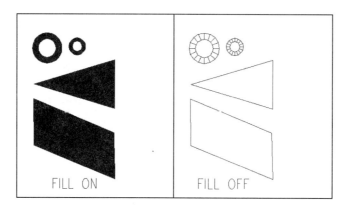

Figure F.3. *Objects shown with FILL on and FILL off.*

Filled objects are regenerated faster when the FILL command is off. A regeneration is necessary to see the results of changing the fill mode setting on existing objects.

Prompts and Options

ON/OFF *<default>* When you specify the On option, AutoCAD displays multilines, wide polylines, solids, and traces as solid (filled in). The objects' extrusion direction must be parallel to the current viewing direction for the fill to be visible. In addition, filled objects will not display when hidden lines are removed. Existing objects are not affected until the next regeneration. When the Off option is specified, AutoCAD displays multilines, wide polylines, solids, and traces as outlines.

> Some displays and plotters take a long time to generate filled objects. For check plots and general editing of drawings that contain many filled objects, it may be advantageous to turn fill off.

Related Commands

DDRMODES   DONUT   PLINE   SOLID
TRACE

Related System Variable
FILLMODE

FILLET

Fillet

Toolbar: *Fillet (Modify, Feature)*
Pull-down: <u>C</u>onstruct, <u>F</u>illet
Screen: Construct, Fillet

The FILLET command joins the closest endpoints of two objects with an arc. The two objects are optionally trimmed or extended so that the arc fits precisely between them. The arc is placed on the current layer if the two objects are on different layers. Otherwise, the arc is placed on the same layer as the objects. The system variable TRIMMODE controls whether the objects are trimmed. You also can control this feature during the FILLET command (see fig. F.4). You also can use the FILLET command on the edges of 3D solids.

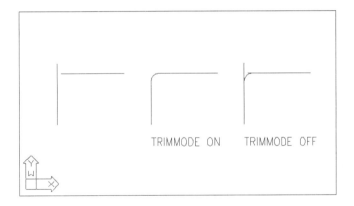

Figure F.4. *A fillet with and without TRIMMODE on.*

The FILLET command can be used only with line, arc, circle, and polyline objects or 3D solids. You can use the FILLET command only when enough distance exists between vertices or endpoints to accommodate the full fillet radius. When used with a fillet radius of 0, the FILLET command is useful for joining objects at their intersection.

You can fillet an entire polyline or two straight, contiguous 2D polyline segments. You cannot fillet one polyline segment with another object.

Prompts and Options

`(TRIM mode) Current fillet radius = 0.0000`
`Polyline/Radius/Trim/<Select first object>` The FILLET command provides an information line above the actual prompt showing the status of the TRIMMODE system variable and the current fillet radius. The default option for the command—`Select first object`—immediately fillets two objects, which can be lines, circles, or arcs. Circles and arcs must be selected by picking or by coordinate entry and are filleted depending on the points you supply. Circles are not trimmed. You can select multiple objects by a window or crossing selection set, but only two objects will be filleted, sometimes with unexpected results. If you select a polyline without first choosing the Polyline option, only the segment you pick will be considered the first object for the FILLET command. You must then select a contiguous segment of the polyline to properly complete the fillet. When the first object is chosen, it is highlighted. You are then prompted to select the second object (see the following discussion), except if the first object you select is the edge of a 3D solid.

If the first object you select for the fillet is the edge of a 3D solid, a different sequence of prompts is issued:

`Chain/Radius/<Select edge>` The default `Select edge` prompt issues the prompt, `Enter radius <default>`, to specify the radius of the rounded edge of the solid. The following prompt is repeated until you press Enter, enabling you to pick as many edges of the solid as desired for the fillet.

`Chain/Radius/<Select edge>:`

When you press Enter, AutoCAD fillets the edges and informs you of how many edges were filleted. For example, `2 edges selected for fillet`. If you cancel the command, AutoCAD prompts, `No fillet to be computed`.

`Chain` The Chain option is used to fillet sequential and tangential edges automatically for the fillet. For example, you might use the Chain option to fillet all the edges of the top of a 3D solid cube (see fig. F.5). After choosing this option you are prompted, `Edge/Radius/<Select edge chain>`. You can toggle back to edge mode (selecting individual edges) with the Edge option and specify a new radius for an edge using the Radius option (see Radius later in this section). Figure F.6 illustrates filleted edges using the Edge option.

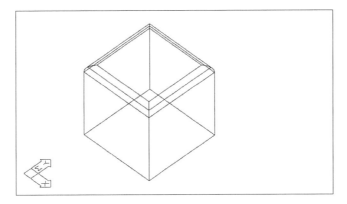

Figure F.5. *Using the Chain option to fillet the top edges of a 3D solid cube.*

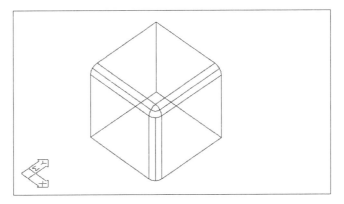

Figure F.6. *Using the Edge option to fillet edges of a 3D solid cube.*

Select second object   You select the second object to be filleted. The two objects are optionally trimmed or extended until they intersect the fillet arc. You can "fillet" parallel lines as AutoCAD attempts to draw the proper fillet radius between the two endpoints of the lines.

> Early versions of AutoCAD Release 13 do not distinguish between the Chain and Edge options of the FILLET command when filleting a 3D solid.

NOTE The desired location for the fillet depends a great deal on the point you use to select the objects. AutoCAD always attempts to fillet the objects closest to the endpoints of the pick point on the side of the two objects' intersection. Figure F.7 illustrates the effect of pick point locations on producing a fillet between two lines. Each column in the illustration shows the original lines at the top and the pick points used to produce the fillet below.

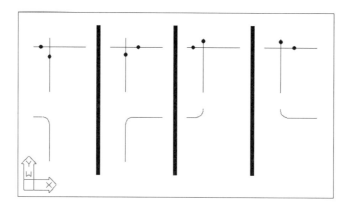

Figure F.7. *Effect of object selection points on the FILLET command.*

Polyline This option fillets all the valid vertices of a 2D polyline. The fillet radius is applied to each vertex. Vertices that have enough distance between the following and preceding vertices are filleted with the set radius. The command reports the number of vertices that could or could not be filleted. This option prompts you to Select 2D polyline.

Radius Use this option to specify the radius of the arc used to join the selected objects. You are prompted to Enter fillet radius <*default*>. A value of 0 forces the objects' endpoints to intersect each other. A positive value joins the chosen objects with an arc.

Trim The Trim option is used to change the value of the TRIMMODE system variable. The prompt, Trim/No trim <Trim>, enables you to specify whether the objects you choose to fillet are trimmed to the arc.

Example

The following example shows how the FILLET command can be used on lines, polylines, and solids (see fig. F.8).

Command: **FILLET** (Enter)	Issues the FILLET command
(NOTRIM mode) Current fillet radius = 0.4000Polyline/Radius/ Trim/<Select first object>: **R** (Enter)	Specifies the Radius option
Enter fillet radius <0.4000>: **0** (Enter)	Specifies a zero radius for the fillet
Command: (Enter)	Reissues the FILLET command
FILLET (NOTRIM mode) Current fillet radius = 0.0000 Polyline/Radius/ Trim/<Select first object>: **T** (Enter)	Selects the Trim option
Trim/No trim <No trim>: **T** (Enter)	Turns on trim mode
Polyline/Radius/Trim/ <Select first object>: *Pick point* ① *(see fig. F.8)*	Selects the first object for filleting
Select second object: *Pick point* ②	Selects the second object to fillet
Command: (Enter)	Reissues the FILLET command
FILLET (TRIM mode) Current fillet radius = 0.0000 Polyline/Radius/ Trim/<Select first object>: **R** (Enter)	Specifies the Radius option
Enter fillet radius <0.0000>: **.5** (Enter)	Specifies a 0.5 unit radius for the fillet
Command: (Enter)	Reissues the FILLET command
FILLET (TRIM mode) Current fillet radius = 0.5000 Polyline/Radius/ Trim/<Select first object>: *Pick point* ③	Selects the first object to fillet
Chain/Radius/<Select edge>: Enter radius <0.5000>: (Enter)	Specifies the radius for the edge
Chain/Radius/<Select edge>: *Pick point* ④	Selects another edge to fillet
Chain/Radius/<Select edge>: *Pick point* ⑤	

```
Chain/Radius/<Select edge>:
Pick point 6

Chain/Radius/<Select edge>: Enter      Terminates edge selection and
                                       FILLET command

4 edges selected for fillet.

Command: Enter                         Reissues the FILLET command

FILLET (TRIM mode) Current fillet      Selects the Polyline option
radius = 0.5000 Polyline/Radius/
Trim/<Select first object>: P Enter

Select 2D polyline: Pick point 7

4 lines were filleted
```

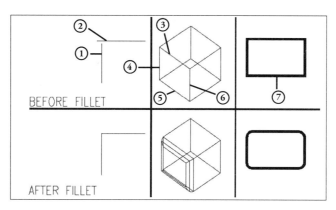

Figure F.8. *The objects before and after using the FILLET command.*

Related Command
CHAMFER

Related System Variables
FILLETRAD   TRIMMODE

'FILTER

Selection Filters

Toolbar: *Selection Filters (Standard Toolbar, Select Objects)*
Pull-down: Edit, Select Objects, Selection Filters...
Screen: ASSIST, Filter:

The FILTER command displays the Object Selection Filters dialog box, as shown in figure F.9, and enables you to create filters to aid in creating select sets. FILTER can be used at the Command: prompt to create select sets for later use, or it can be used transparently at a Select objects prompt to select objects for the current command. FILTER creates a list of properties that an object must have to be selected. Object properties include color, linetype, layer, object type, coordinates, and so forth.

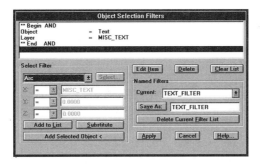

Figure F.9. *The Object Selection Filters dialog box.*

> **NOTE**
> For the FILTER command to filter objects by color and linetype, object color and linetype must be assigned directly to an object with the COLOR, LINETYPE, or CHPROP commands. Objects with properties set to BYLAYER are not filtered for these properties.

The Object Selection Filters dialog box is divided into three groups of options: the Object Selection Filter list box, the Select Filter group, and the Named Filters group. FILTER enables you to use relational operators (<, >, <=, >=, =, !=, and *) and Boolean operators (AND, OR, XOR, and NOT) when defining filters.

Dialog Box Items

The list box at the top of the Object Selection Filters dialog box is for displaying and editing the filter criteria.

Select Filter. This area of the dialog box contains features for specifying the filter criteria for object selection.

Select Filter drop-down list box. This list displays a list of all the filter types available. If you are editing an existing filter, this option shows the current filter's type.

Select. This button displays a dialog box with all the available items of the filter type being edited. Valid types for select are Xdata ID, Block Name, Color, Dimension Style, Layer, Linetype, or Text Style Name (see fig. F.10).

Figure F.10. *Specifying objects using the Select button.*

X. This drop-down list box displays the relational operators from which you can choose. The relational operators are =, !=, <, <=, >, >=, and *. X displays an X coordinate value in the edit box when working with coordinates, such as the starting point of a line. X displays the selected attribute when working with properties such as the color of a layer.

Y. Y displays the relational operators from which you can choose. The relational operators are =, !=, <, <=, >, >=, and *. This option displays a Y coordinate value in the edit box when working with coordinates.

Z. Z displays the relational operators from which you can choose. The relational operators are =, !=, <, <=, >, >=, and *. This option displays a Z coordinate value in the edit box when working with coordinates.

Add to List. This button adds the current Select Filter settings to the Filters list box above the highlighted filter.

Substitute. This button replaces the filter highlighted in the Filter list box with the current Select Filter settings.

Add Selected Object. This button adds the properties of a selected object to the Filter list box. The dialog box is temporarily cleared from the screen while you select an object in your drawing.

Edit Item. This option moves the filter highlighted in the Filters list box to the Select Filter group for editing.

Delete. This option deletes the filter highlighted in the Filters list box.

Clear List. This option deletes all the filters in the Filters list box.

The Named Filters group contains the following options:

Current. This drop-down list box displays a list of the available named filter.

Save As. This button saves the current set of filters in the Filter list box to the name entered in the Save As edit box. This creates a named filter list. You can have up to 18 named filters, each up to 25 characters in length, stored in the FILTER.NFL file.

TIP

If you have a complicated selection filter that you want to use in other drawings, type a name in the Save As edit box and click on the Save As button. Your filter will be stored in the FILTER.NFL file in your AutoCAD directory. Use the Current drop-down list box to choose your saved filter and apply it.

Delete Current Filter List. This button deletes the current filter from the list of available named filters in the FILTER.NFL file.

Apply. This button exits the Object Selection Filters dialog box and applies the filters to all items you select. You are prompted to Select objects.

Select Objects You select the objects to which you want to apply the filter. This prompt appears after you click on **A**pply in the Object Selection Filters dialog box. You can use any valid object selection method. Use ALL to apply the filter to all objects in the drawing. AutoCAD reports how many objects were found and how many were filtered out.

Example

The following example uses FILTER on the sample PNID.DWG drawing to select block objects to ERASE.

Choose Erase	
`Command: _ERASE`	Issues the ERASE command
Choose Selection Filters (Object Selection)	
`Select objects: '_filter`	Issues the FILTER command transparently
Choose Block Name *from the Select Filter drop-down list box.*	Specifies the object type to filter from the drawing
Click on the Select *button*	Displays the Select Block Name(s) dialog box
Select the block name ACON *from the list*	Specifies which block to filter
Click on OK	Closes the Select Block Name(s) dialog box
Click on Add to List	Adds the block name to the filter list
Click on Apply *button*	Closes the Object Selection Filters dialog box and prompts for object selection.
`Applying filter to selection.` `Select objects: ALL` (Enter)	Specifies that all objects will be selected for filtering
`2281 found` `2178 were filtered out.`	
`Select objects:` (Enter)	Terminates filtered object selection
`Exiting filtered selection. 103 found`	
`Select objects:` (Enter)	Terminates object selection for the ERASE command

After an item is selected using a filter, you can change the filter without affecting the selected objects.

Related Commands

GROUP   SELECT

GIFIN

Pull-down: File, Import, Raster, GIF... (DOS Only)
Screen: FILE, IMPORT, GIFin:

The GIFIN command enables you to import a *Graphics Interchange Format* (GIF) raster file into AutoCAD. AutoCAD scans the raster image and creates a block that consists of a rectangular, colored solid for each pixel in the GIF file.

After you import a raster image into AutoCAD, you can trace over the raster image with AutoCAD geometry to create an AutoCAD drawing of the raster image. After you finish, you can erase the raster image. You can scale, mirror, and rotate raster images like regular blocks.

You also can use raster images to represent images you obtain by scanning photographs, logos, and artwork.

Do not explode the block representation of a raster file—the resulting objects use large quantities of disk space and memory.

You import raster images as anonymous blocks. If you reimport the same image multiple times, you create a new block each time.

Before you import any raster images, you need to set the system variables that control raster image conversion. These system variables begin with the letters RI, affect the GIFIN, PCXIN, and TIFIN commands, and you can change them directly at the AutoCAD Command: prompt.

RIASPECT. Enter a real number to control the aspect ratio of the raster image. To display VGA or MCGA images in CGA 320×200 mode, use a RIASPECT of 0.8333.

RIBACKG. Enter the AutoCAD color number of your graphics background. You use this system variable to set the background color of the raster image. Areas of the raster image that are the same color as RIBACKG are not converted to solid objects in the block and reduce the size of an imported image.

RIEDGE. You use RIEDGE to control the amount of the image that AutoCAD imports. Enter 0 (the default) to disable edge detection and import the entire image. Enter a larger number, 1–255, to increase edge detection. Edge detection is the determination of an edge, where one color stops and another begins. The higher you set RIEDGE, the more prominent an image's color change must be before AutoCAD imports it. Use a larger RIEDGE to import just the edges of an image if you want to trace over it with vectors.

RIGAMUT. You use RIGAMUT to control the number of colors AutoCAD imports from a raster image. The value reflects the number of colors, from 0 (black) through 256. Valid values are 8–256. If you enter 8, you import the eight basic color areas (black, red, yellow, green, cyan, blue, magenta, and white) of the raster file. Use RIEDGE and RITHRESH to control importing on a monochrome display.

RIGREY. If you set RIGREY to a nonzero number, AutoCAD imports the raster file in shades of gray. If you set RIGREY to 0 (the default), AutoCAD imports the raster images in color.

RITHRESH. You use RITHRESH to control the amount of raster image AutoCAD imports based on the brightness of the image area. The default is 0, which disables brightness threshold checking. Enter a number to import only pixels with a brightness over the number. See the following example for an illustration of changing RITHRESH.

GRIPBLOCK. Set the system variable GRIPBLOCK to 0 if you don't want to highlight all the solid objects in the block with grips.

Prompts and Options

`GIF file name`   Enter the name of the GIF file to import. A file selection dialog box is not available. You do not have to include the GIF extension, because, if necessary, the GIFIN command adds it.

`Insertion point <0,0,0>`   Pick a point in the graphics window, or enter the coordinates of the insertion point for the raster image.

`Scale Factor`   Enter a number or pick a point in the graphics window to show a distance. If you pick a point in the graphics window, AutoCAD uses the distance from the insertion point as the scale factor.

`New length`   If you press Enter at the Scale Factor prompt, AutoCAD reprompts you (this is that prompt) to enter a new scale factor or to pick a point to show a distance for the scale factor.

Example

The following example imports a GIF file created from the Torus option of the 3D command. It was rendered and saved as a GIF file. It is first imported as outline image by setting RIEDGE to 25, then inserted as a rendered image by setting RIEDGE to 0 (see fig. G.1). Set RIBACKG to your graphics window background color first.

Command / Prompt	Description
Command: **RIEDGE** (Enter)	Issues RIEDGE command to change system variable RIEDGE
Raster input edge detection <0>: **25** (Enter)	Specifies new value for RIEDGE
Command: **RIBACKG** (Enter)	Issues RIBACKG command to change system variable RIBACKG
Raster input screen background color <0>: **7** (Enter)	Specifies new value for RIBACKG; Color 7 specifies a white background
Command: **GIFIN** (Enter)	Issues GIFIN command
GIF file name: **TORUS** (Enter)	Specifies file name TORUS.GIF
Insertion point<0,0,0>: (Enter)	Accepts default insertion point
Scale factor: **1** (Enter)	Specifies scale factor of 1
Command: **RIEDGE** (Enter)	Issues RIEDGE command to change system variable RIEDGE
Raster input edge detection <25>: **0** (Enter)	Specifies new value for RIEDGE
Command: **GIFIN** (Enter)	Invokes GIFIN command
GIF file name: **TORUS** (Enter)	Specifies file name TORUS.GIF
Insertion point<0,0,0>: **1,0,0** (Enter)	Specifies insertion point of 1, 0, 0
Scale factor: **1** (Enter)	Specifies scale factor of 1

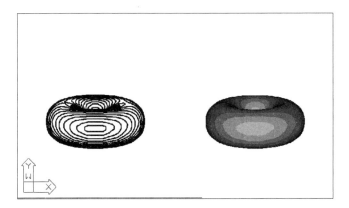

Figure G.1. *A rendered torus imported as raster images with GIFIN command.*

Related Commands

ACISIN   DXBIN   DXFIN   FILL
IMPORT   PCXIN   PSIN   TIFFIN
WMFIN

Related System Variables

FILLMODE   GRIPBLOCK   RIASPECT   RIBACKING
RIEDGE   RIGAMUT   RIGREY   RITHRESH

'GRAPHSCR

The GRAPHSCR command switches a single-screen AutoCAD system from the text screen to the graphics screen. On systems with windowing environments, the switch is between the graphics window and the text window. You can press F1 (on DOS systems) or F2 (on Windows systems) to switch between the two types of screen display. This command has the opposite effect of the TEXTSCR command. Neither of these commands affects an AutoCAD system running with dual screens. The GRAPHSCR command often is used within AutoLISP routines to return to the drawing editor after commands such as LIST, STATUS, TIME, or TYPE are invoked.

Related Commands

SCRIPT   TEXTSCR

Related System Variable
SCREENMODE

GRID

Pull-down: <u>E</u>dit, <u>G</u>rid
Screen: ASSIST, Grid:

The GRID command displays a rectangular array of reference points, which are aligned with the current UCS. You can turn the grid on or off by pressing F7, double-clicking the GRID button in the status line (Windows), or pressing Ctrl+G. You can change the grid's spacing in both axes, set the spacing so that it equals the current Snap increment, and adjust the grid aspect ratio for special needs (such as isometric drafting). You also can turn the grid on and off and alter its appearance for each viewport. The grid is a visual tool on the display and, therefore, is not plotted nor is it considered a part of your drawing.

Prompts and Options

`Grid spacing(X) or ON/OFF/Snap/Aspect <0.0000>` The default option is to enter a number at this prompt. AutoCAD sets the grid spacing to the drawing units specified. If you enter a number followed by an X, the grid spacing is adjusted to a multiple of the current snap spacing. If you set the snap, for example, to a spacing of one drawing unit, you can display a grid point at every ten snap points by entering **10X**. If you specify a distance of zero, the grid spacing is set to the current snap spacing. If the grid is turned on but cannot be seen because the spacing between dots is not great enough, you see the prompt, `Grid too dense to display`.

ON and OFF The On and Off options are used to set the display of the grid. The most recent settings for spacing and aspect are used. You can turn the grid on and off by pressing Ctrl+G or F7 or by double clicking the GRID button in the status line.

Snap The Snap option sets the grid spacing to the current snap increment value.

Aspect The Aspect option enables you to display a grid that has different X and Y spacing. This feature is detailed in the following example.

Example

In this example, a grid is displayed with an X (horizontal) spacing value of .5 drawing units and a Y (vertical) spacing of 1 drawing unit. The grid that AutoCAD draws is shown in figure G.2.

`Command: GRID` (Enter)	Issues the GRID command
`Grid spacing(x) or ON/OFF/Snap/Aspect <0.0000>:` **A** (Enter)	Selects the Aspect option
`Horizontal spacing(x) <0.0000>:` **.5** (Enter)	Specifies the grid spacing between columns of grid dots
`Vertical spacing(x) <0.0000>:` **1** (Enter)	Specifies the grid spacing between rows of grid dots

Figure G.2. *The grid set so that the X and Y aspects have different values.*

Related Commands

DDRMODES   ISOPLANE   LIMITS   SNAP

Related System Variables

GRIDMODE   GRIDUNIT   LIMMAX   LIMMIN

-GROUP

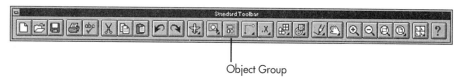

Object Group

Pull-down: <u>E</u>dit, <u>G</u>roup Objects
Screen: ASSIST, Group

The GROUP command creates named selection sets of objects within the drawing. This enables you to manipulate and edit objects as a group rather than individual items. By default, when you select an object within a group, the entire group is selected. An object may belong to more than one group. You can assign names and descriptions to groups or let AutoCAD assign an anonymous name to any new groups you create. Groups should not be confused with AutoCAD block objects. A block insertion is a collection of objects considered to be one object that cannot easily be edited. A group, on the other hand, is a collection of individual objects that retain their own identity and capability to be edited. The GROUP command is a powerful tool for manipulating a set of objects at one time.

Dialog Box Items

As shown in figure G.3, the Object Grouping dialog box contains four basic areas: the Group Name list box, the Group Identification area, the Create Group area, and the Change Group area.

Figure G.3. *The Object Grouping dialog box.*

Group Name List Box

This list box contains the names of all the groups defined within the drawing and whether they are selectable. *Selectable* means that if you select any one object within a group, the entire group is selected. Selectability is determined when you create a group and also can be changed at any time using the Selectable button.

Group Identification

This area of the Object Grouping dialog box is used for assigning new names and descriptions to a group and for finding a group name from a list of groups.

Group Name. The Group Name edit box is used for entering the name of a new group to create or showing the name of the highlighted group in the Group Name list box. Group names can be up to 31 characters in length, but cannot contain any spaces. AutoCAD converts the names to uppercase.

Description. Use this edit box to type an optional description of the group. Descriptions can be up to 64 characters in length and can contain spaces.

Find Name. Use the Find Name button to list the groups that any one selected object belongs to. The Find Name button prompts you to pick a member of a group. If the object you select is not a member of a group, AutoCAD prompts you as such. If you select an object that belongs to a group, the Group Member List dialog box appears, listing all the groups that include the selected object (see fig. G.4).

Figure G.4. *The Group Member List dialog box.*

Highlight. The Highlight button is used to highlight all the objects in a drawing that belong to the selected group. First select the desired group in the Group Name list box, and then select the Highlight button.

Include Unnamed. Use this check box to cause AutoCAD to display all group names, regardless of whether they are assigned an explicit name. All group names assigned by AutoCAD begin with *A*n where *n* is a sequential number. (See the following Unnamed check box.)

> When you copy a group, the copy is defined as an unnamed group. Use the Include Unnamed option to list such groups and then use the Change Group options to rename them, explode them, change their selection status, etc.

TIP

Create Group

This area of the Object Grouping dialog box is used for creating and selecting new groups.

New. Use the **N**ew button to define a selection set for a new group. You must have a valid name entered in the **G**roup Name edit box unless the **U**nnamed check box is checked. Selecting the objects for the group is the last step in defining a group. Be sure you have entered the name and description for the group before clicking on New.

Selectable. This check box only affects newly created groups and determines whether the new group will be selectable. Selectability means that the entire group is selected if any one object within a group is selected.

Unnamed. Use this check box to specify whether or not you can create unnamed groups.

Change Group

This area of the Object Grouping dialog box is used for changing the items within a group or their order within the group.

Remove. Use this button to remove items from a group. You are prompted to `Select objects to remove..` If an object belongs to more than one group, it is only removed from the current group.

Add. Use this button to add items to the current group. You are prompted to `Select objects to add..` If an object already belongs to other groups and any of those groups are selectable, the entire group is added to the current group.

Renam**e.** Use this button to rename a group. Highlight the group you want to rename in the Group Name list box. Type over the name in the **G**roup Name edit box and click on the Rena**m**e button.

Re-o**rder.** Objects are added to groups in the order you select them. If it is important to have them in a specific order, use the Re-**o**rder button. When you select this button, an Order Group dialog box is displayed (see fig. G.5). This dialog box provides functions for changing the position of objects within a group.

Figure G.5. *The Order Group dialog box.*

The Order Group dialog box contains the following options:

Group Name. This list box displays the names of the groups defined in the drawing.

Description. This text area lists the description, if any, of a selected group.

Remove from position (0 - *nnn*). Object numbering with a group begins with zero. This edit box label shows the number of items within the selected group, starting at zero. In this edit box, enter the number of the item you want to move within the group.

Replace at position (0 - *nnn*). Use this edit box to determine to what position within the group the item in the Remove from position edit box gets moved.

Number of objects (1 - *xxx*). Use this edit box to enter a value or range of values to specify how many objects within the group will be moved to the new position.

Re-order. This button performs the re-ordering of the objects within the group as specified earlier.

Highlight. Use this button to selectively highlight individual objects within a group. When you select this button, the Object Grouping Highlight dialog box appears (see fig. G.6). This dialog box contains a Next and Previous button as well as a text label showing the current position of the highlighted object within the group. Use the buttons to work forward or backward through a group as AutoCAD highlights the object occupying that position within the group.

Figure G.6. *Dialog box for highlighting individual objects within a group.*

Reverse Order. Use this button to totally reverse the positions of objects within a group. In other words, the last becomes first and the first becomes last.

Description. This button in the Object Grouping dialog box is used to change a group description for an existing selected group. Type the new description in the Description edit box and click on the Description button to effect the change.

Explode. Use this button to destroy a group, removing the objects from the group. The objects are not erased—they simply have their individual identity restored. The group name is deleted from the drawing.

Selectable. This button turns the selectability of the highlighted group on or off.

Prompts and Options

The command-line equivalent of the GROUP command (-GROUP) has options that correlate closely with the dialog items discussed previously:

`?/Order/Add/Remove/Explode/REName/Selectable/<Create>:`

? This option lists groups defined in the drawing. You are prompted, `Groups(s) to list <*>`, at which point you press Enter to list all groups or use a wild-card pattern to selectively list groups. AutoCAD switches to the text window and lists the groups in a format similar to the following:

```
Defined groups.                 Selectable
   ALL                             Yes
   CIRCLES                         Yes
   CIRCLES_AND_SQUARES             Yes
   SQUARES                         Yes
   TRIANGLES                       Yes
```

Order Use the Order option to reorder the objects within a group. See reorder in the preceding discussion of dialog box items. The prompt issued with this option, `Group name (or ?)`, needs the name of an existing group. Use the ? option if you are unsure of the names of the groups. The next prompt, `Reverse order/Remove from position <0 - 11>`, enables you to specify whether to reverse the order of the group or move objects from one position to another. If you choose the latter, enter a position value at this prompt. The next prompt, Replace at position <0 - 11>, also requests a position value. You are then prompted Number of objects to re-order <1 - 12> to specify how many objects to reposition within the group. See the preceding Re-order section.

Add   The Add option is used to add objects to a specified group. You are first prompted for a valid group name at the prompt, Group name (or ?). You are then asked to Select objects to add and prompted to Select objects.

Remove   Use the Remove option to remove items from a group. You are first prompted for a valid group name at the prompt, Group name (or ?). You are then asked to Select objects to remove and prompted to Remove objects.

Explode   The Explode option deletes the group name and returns the objects within that group to their individual status. The objects are not erased. If the objects were included in more than one group, they remain within those groups until those groups are also exploded. You are prompted for the valid name of a group at the prompt, Group name (or ?).

REName   Use the REName option to change the name of an existing group. You are prompted for the Old group name (or ?) and then the New group name (or ?).

Selectable   The Selectable option changes the selectability of a group. You are first prompted for a valid group name at the prompt, Group name (or ?). You are then informed of the status of the group and asked if you want to change it. For example, you might see the following prompt:

This group is selectable. Do you wish to change it? <Y>

<Create>   This, the default option for the -GROUP command, is used for creating new groups. You are first prompted Group name (or ?) for a valid group name. You are then asked for an optional Group description. Next, you are asked to select objects for inclusion in the newly created group.

Related Commands

BLOCK   DDRMODES   FILTER   SELECT
SHAPE

Related System Variable

PICKSTYLE

HATCH

The HATCH command fills areas of your drawing with non-associative patterns. In the crosshatching process, you select a boundary that AutoCAD fills with the pattern you specify. The resulting hatch region is saved as an unnamed block definition that can be moved, copied, colored, and manipulated in much the same manner as other blocks. Hatches, like all other AutoCAD 2D objects, can be created in any definable construction plane. This versatility makes hatches very desirable for adding textures to three-dimensional models such as buildings. The BHATCH (Boundary HATCH) command has essentially replaced the HATCH command. BHATCH enables you to define a hatch boundary with as little as a single pick, and has the option of creating associative hatch patterns. With BHATCH, you also can see a sample of the available hatch patterns and preview your hatch pattern while you are still able to make adjustments.

The HATCH command also enables you to create simple patterns directly at the Command: prompt.

Prompts and Options

Refer to the BHATCH command's discussion of command-line prompts and options.

Related Commands

BHATCH   BOUNDARY   EXPLODE   HATCHEDIT

Related System Variables

HPANG   HPBOUND   HPDOUBLE   HPNAME
HPSCALE HPSPACE   SNAPBASE

-HATCHEDIT

Edit Hatch

Toolbar: *Edit Hatch (Modify, Special Edit)*
Pull-down: *Modify, Edit Hatch*
Screen: MODIFY, HatchEd:

The HATCHEDIT command is used to edit associate hatch patterns that have been applied using the BHATCH command. With it, you can modify the hatch pattern and its properties such as pattern, scale, rotation, and others.

Dialog Box Options

When the HATCHEDIT command is issued, you are prompted to Select hatch object. The Hatchedit dialog box appears. Notice that it duplicates the Boundary Hatch (BHATCH) dialog box except that nonrelevant buttons have been grayed out (see fig. H.1).

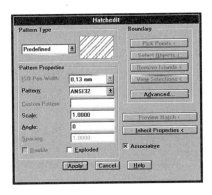

Figure H.1. *The Hatchedit dialog box.*

-HATCHEDIT

For information concerning the dialog box items for HATCHEDIT, refer to the BHATCH command.

Prompts and Options

Using the -HATCHEDIT command-line version, you are prompted to Select hatch object. The following prompt is displayed:

Disassociate/<Properties>:

Disassociate This option removes any associativity of the hatch pattern with its boundaries. The hatch pattern becomes an anonymous block consisting of line segments rather than an "intelligent" hatch pattern that retains its pattern name and properties and boundary set. This option responds with the following:

Analyzing associative hatch...
Hatch associativity removed

For more on hatch pattern associativity, see the BHATCH command.

<Properties> For the Properties options, see the BHATCH command.

> To view examples of the supplied hatch patterns, use the BHATCH command, locate the pattern you want and note its name, cancel, and then run HATCHEDIT.

Related Commands

BHATCH   EXPLODE   HATCH

Related System Variables

HPANG   HPBOUND   HPDOUBLE   HPNAME
HPSCALE HPSPACE   SNAPBASE

'HELP

Help

Pull-down: **H**elp
Screen: HELP

The HELP command provides information on the commands available within the AutoCAD program. In Windows, you can access HELP with the F1 key. You can issue the HELP command transparently by preceding the command with an apostrophe ('HELP). A question mark (?) also invokes help, but not transparently. If 'HELP is used transparently during a command, it provides information about the command.

When you enter **HELP** at the Command: prompt, AutoCAD displays the Help dialog box. This dialog box displays a comprehensive index from which you can select help for specified commands. The Help information is cross-referenced to the *AutoCAD Reference Manual*.

Windows Systems

The HELP command for Windows systems utilizes a standard Windows Help File format utilizing text links, icons, and so on. To display the Contents screen, press F1 at the Command: prompt. You may transparently invoke help during a command or while a dialog box is active by pressing F1 during the command. You may also invoke help for a pull-down menu item by first selecting the menu item and then pressing F1. The Help screen displays information pertaining to that menu item.

DOS Systems

The AutoCAD Help dialog box contains a row of buttons at the top for navigating through the Help file.

Contents. The **C**ontents button displays main topics of interest in double brackets in the Help dialog list box, as follows:

```
<<Pull-down Menus>>
<<Commands>>
<<System Variables>>
<<Definition of Terms>>
```

Choose one of these topics to access a submenu of headings pertaining to that topic.

Search. The **S**earch button displays the AutoCAD Help Search dialog box for searching through the Help index for a particular topic. Type a topic name in the edit box or choose a topic from the list box and then choose the **S**how Topics button. Subtopics are displayed in the list box below the **S**earch button. Choose a subtopic and then choose the Go To button to display help information about that topic.

Back. Use the **B**ack button to go back one level at a time through the Help dialog boxes.

History. The **H**istory button displays the AutoCAD HELP History dialog box listing all the options you have made during the HELP command. Choose a topic from the list box and then choose the Go To button.

He**lp.** Use the H**e**lp button for information on how to use the HELP command.

The Help list box. The HELP command displays information in the list box. "Hot" topics, or words, that reference additional information are surrounded by double brackets (<< >>). Double-click or highlight the word; then choose the **G**o To button to jump to that topic. If more than one topic is shown on a line, use the **N**ext Topic button to cycle through the choices.

HIDE

Hide

Toolbar: *Hide (Render)*
Pull-down: **T**ools, H**i**de
Screen: TOOLS, Hide:

The HIDE command temporarily suppresses the display of any lines or edges hidden behind a surface. A *surface* can be a circle, solid, trace, wide polyline, polygon mesh, extruded edge, or 3D face. The HIDE command gives an opaque top and bottom face to extruded circles, solids, traces, and wide polylines. This command typically is used to present a three-dimensional model. HIDE also is useful for verifying the accuracy of a model's surfaces.

The command is completely automatic. A hidden-line removal may take time, depending on the complexity of the model. You can reduce this time by using the ZOOM command to fill the display with only the desired geometry. AutoCAD hides only the information that appears within the boundaries of the current display. The HIDE command also works more quickly if unneeded layers are frozen.

After hidden lines are removed, the entire drawing can be displayed only after a regeneration of the drawing, caused by using any display command. To save a hidden-line view for later display, use the MSLIDE command.

The HIDE command affects only the current viewport, and you can hide only one viewport at a time. Also, only objects on layers that are turned on and thawed are considered for hidden-line removal. Displays made by the command are lost after the drawing session ends or the viewport is regenerated. The SHADE command performs similar results by filling the faces with color. The SHADE command is quicker than the HIDE command, but not always as accurate. The HIDE command does not affect plotting. The PLOT command includes an option for hiding objects. The MVIEW command contains an option for hiding lines within a paper space model view during plotting.

> Two system variables, FACETRES and DISPSILH, can be used to improve the display generated from the HIDE command. FACETRES (FACET RESolution) determines the smoothness of the objects. The default value is 0.5. A higher value results in smoother objects, but will require more memory and time to generate. DISPSILH (DISPlay SILHouette) controls the display of the edges, or silhouette, of the objects. The default value is 0, meaning that all face edges will be shown. Change the value to 1 to show only the edges of the entire object without its constituent faces. See figure H.2 for examples.

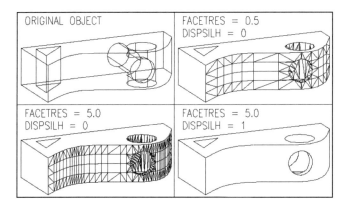

Figure H.2. *The effects of DISPSILH and FACETRES on the HIDE command.*

Related Commands

DVIEW   MSLIDE   RENDER   SHADE

Related System Variables

DISPSILH   FACETRES

'ID

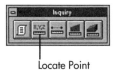

Locate Point

Toolbar: *Locate Point (Object Properties, Inquiry)*
Pull-down: *Edit, Inquiry, Locate Point*
Screen: ASSIST, INQUIRY, ID:

The ID command identifies the absolute X,Y,Z coordinates of a single point within 3D space. You pick a point within the drawing editor, and AutoCAD displays the point's coordinates. The point listed is in the current UCS coordinate system. The Z value is the current elevation unless a point on an object is selected using an object snap setting. The ID command is useful for finding the location of points along objects that do not lie parallel to the WCS.

Prompts and Options

Point You specify a point in the drawing editor for which you want to retrieve the coordinates. You can use object snap overrides or any other method of point selection. The point data is returned similar to the following example:

```
X = 4.5796      Y = 2.8369      Z = 4.0000
```

Related System Variable

LASTPOINT

IMPORT (Windows Only)

Pull-down: *File, Import...*

The IMPORT command displays a dialog box for selecting a graphics file to import into AutoCAD. Graphics file formats of WMF, ACIS, EPS, PCX, TIF, GIF, and 3DS can be imported. Once a file has been selected, the appropriate import command (WMFIN, ACISIN, PSIN, PCXIN, TIFIN, GIFIN, or 3DSIN) is used to import the file. The file type (the file extension) determines which import command is used. See the individual descriptions of each of these commands for more information on prompts and options available with each command.

Prompts and Options

The IMPORT command displays the Import File dialog box, which is used to select the desired graphics file to import. Select the List Files of Type drop-down list to select the desired file type, then select the graphics file to import.

Each of the raster image settings (see the GIFIN command for a full explanation of the various raster image settings) must be set prior to importing the graphics file with the IMPORT command.

Example

The following example imports a GIF file created from the Torus option of the 3D command. It was rendered and saved as a GIF file. It is first imported as an outline image by setting RIEDGE to 25, then inserted as a rendered image by setting RIEDGE to 0 (see fig. I.1). Set RIBACKG to your graphics window background color first.

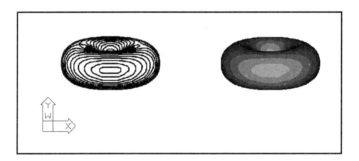

Figure I.1. *A rendered torus imported as raster images with IMPORT command.*

Command: **RIEDGE** (Enter)	Issues RIEDGE command to change system variable RIEDGE
Raster input edge detection <0>: **25** (Enter)	Specifies new value for RIEDGE
Command: **RIBACKG** (Enter)	Issues RIEDGE command to change system variable RIBACKG
Raster input screen background colour <0>: **7** (Enter)	Specifies new value for RIBACKG Color 7 specifies a white background

IMPORT (Windows Only)

Command: **IMPORT** (Enter)	Starts IMPORT command, displays Import File dialog box
Select the file type **GIF (*.GIF)** *from the List Files of Type drop-down list*	
Select the file **TORUS.GIF** *from the File Name list box*	
Click on OK	
GIFIN GIF file name: TORUS.GIF Insertion point<0,0,0>: (Enter)	Accepts default insertion point
Scale factor: **1** (Enter)	Specifies scale factor of 1
Command: **RIEDGE** (Enter)	Issues RIEDGE command to change system variable RIEDGE
Raster input edge detection <25>: **0** (Enter)	Specifies new value for RIEDGE
Command: **IMPORT** (Enter)	Starts IMPORT command, displays Import File dialog box
Select the file type **GIF (*.GIF)** *from the List Files of Type drop-down list*	
Select the file **TORUS.GIF** *from the File Name list box*	
Click on OK	
GIFIN GIF file name: TORUS.GIF Insertion point<0,0,0>: **1,0,0** (Enter)	Specifies insertion point of 1,0,0
Scale factor: **1** (Enter)	Specifies scale factor of 1

Related Commands

ACISIN	DXBING	DXFIN	GIFIN
INSERT	PCSIN	PCXIN	PSIN
TIFFIN	TIFIN	WMFIN	

Related System Variables

FILLMODE   GRIPBLOCK

INSERT

Screen: DRAW, Insert

The INSERT command places blocks created with the BLOCK command or external drawing files into the current drawing. It is the command-line version of the DDINSERT command. INSERT enables you to specify how blocks are located, scaled, and rotated when added to your drawing. If a block name that you specify is not currently defined in the drawing, INSERT attempts to load an external drawing file.

Prompts and Options

`Block name (or ?) <default>` At this prompt, enter a block name to insert or accept the default name of the last block inserted. If the name you supply is not a block defined in the current drawing, the program attempts to find a file with a matching name along the AutoCAD search path. If no match is found, the command is aborted, and you receive an error message. To see a list of the blocks defined in the current drawing, enter a question mark at this prompt. Enter a tilde (~) to display the Select File dialog box.

You can replace an existing block with another drawing stored on disk by redefining the current block. You do this by specifying the old block name (current block name) followed by an equal sign (=) and then the name of the drawing stored on disk. For example:

`Block name (or ?) <default>: OLDBLOCK=C:\BLOCKS\NEWBLOCK`

This method also can be used to rename an inserted drawing file from disk to a new block name within the drawing. In the preceding example, if the block OLDNAME did not already exist in the drawing, the inserted drawing NEWBLOCK would become a block name OLDBLOCK.

> If you type an asterisk before the name of the block to insert, AutoCAD automatically explodes the block when it places it into your drawing.

`Insertion point` You specify an insertion point for the block. This insertion point is used to place, scale, and rotate the block in the drawing editor.

Until you specify a point for the block you insert, the block is highlighted so that you can drag it on-screen and have an idea of how the block will look when placed. If you know in advance the various insertion parameters (X, Y, and Z scales and rotation), you can preset the parameters so that the highlighted image is more accurate before being inserted. You can enter these preset parameters at this prompt before you choose the insertion point. A description of each parameter option follows:

Scale. The Scale option presets the scale in each axis (X, Y, and Z) to the same value. The highlighted block is updated, and then you can choose its insertion point. After the block is located in the drawing, you are not prompted to enter a value for the scale factors.

Xscale. The Xscale option presets the scale in the X axis only. Insertion then proceeds as with Pscale (see the following Note).

Yscale. The Yscale option presets the scale in the Y axis only. Insertion then proceeds as with Pscale.

Zscale. The Zscale option presets the scale in the Z axis only. Insertion then proceeds as with Pscale.

Rotate. The Rotate option presets the block rotation value. The highlighted block is updated, and insertion can proceed. After the block is located, this angle is used and you are not prompted to supply this value.

The following five options enable you to preset the highlighted block's values, but then you must answer the INSERT command's usual prompts about scale factors and rotation.

Pscale. The Pscale option presets all three axes' scales, but after the block is located, you still are prompted for a block scaling factor.

Pxscale. The Pxscale option presets the block's X axis scale factor, but after the block is located, you still are prompted for the scale along this axis.

Pyscale. The Pyscale option presets the block's Y axis scale factor, but after the block is located, you still are prompted for the scale along this axis.

Pzscale. The Pzscale option presets the block's Z axis scale factor, but after the block is located, you still are prompted for the scale along this axis.

Protate. The Protate option presets the highlighted block's rotation. After the block is located in the drawing editor, you again are prompted for a final rotation angle.

`X scale factor <1>/Corner/XYZ` Enter a number for the X scale factor, accept the default value, or enter an option. You receive this prompt when none of the scale factors are preset. A positive scale factor creates an inserted block in the same orientation as the original block definition. If you enter a negative value, the block appears mirrored about the Y axis. You also can specify a scale factor by dragging your pointing device or by using the Corner option.

For either of these choices, the distance between the two specified points is used as the scale factors for both the X and Y axes.

Y scale factor (default=X)   Enter a number for the Y-scale factor or accept the default. By default, this value is the same as the X-scale factor.

Rotation angle <0>   At this prompt, enter a number for the rotation angle to be used when inserting the block. You can specify a point either by coordinates or by dragging the pointing device, and the angle between this point and the insertion point is used as the rotation angle.

X scale factor <1>/Corner   This prompt appears if you use the XYZ option. You are prompted for scale factors for each of the three axes, beginning with the X axis. The corner option works the same as in the first prompt.

Y scale factor (default=X)   This second prompt of the XYZ option enables you to specify a scale factor for the Y axis. By default, this value is set to the same scale as the one for the X axis.

Z scale factor (default=X)   This last prompt of the XYZ option enables you to specify a scale factor for the Z axis. By default, this value is set to the same scale as that for the X axis.

> **NOTE:** To change the scale factors of a block after it is inserted, use the DDMODIFY command.

Example

The following example uses the INSERT command to insert a block of a table as illustrated in figure I.2. This exercise demonstrates the effects that uneven scale factors can have upon a block.

Command: **INSERT** (Enter)	Issues the INSERT command
Block name (or ?): **TABLE** (Enter)	Specifies the name of the block to insert
Insertion point: *Pick point* ①	Determines the placement of the block
X scale factor <1> / Corner / XYZ: (Enter)	Determines the X scale factor of the block
Y scale factor (default=X): (Enter)	Determines the Y scale factor of the block

`Rotation angle <0>:` *Enter*	Determines the rotation angle of the block
`Command:` *Enter*	Reissues the INSERT command

```
INSERT Block name (or ?) <TABLE>:
Enter
Insertion point: Pick point ②
X scale factor <1> / Corner / XYZ: 2
Enter
Y scale factor (default=X): 1 Enter
Rotation angle <0>: 90 Enter
```

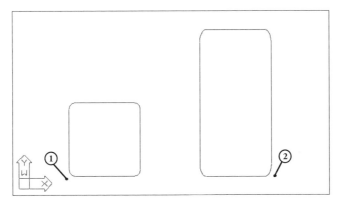

Figure I.2. *A table block inserted with different scaling and rotation factors.*

Related Commands

ATTDEF	ATTDISP	ATTEDIT	ATTEXT
BASE	BLOCK	COPY	DDINSERT
EXPLODE	IMPORT	MINSERT	WBLOCK
WMFIN	XREF		

Related System Variables

INSBASE   INSNAME

INSERTOBJ (Windows Only)

Pull-down: <u>E</u>dit, <u>I</u>nsert Object...

Use INSERTOBJ to take advantage of the *Object Linking and Embedding* (OLE) features of Microsoft Windows. Since AutoCAD is both an OLE client and server, the INSERTOBJ command takes advantage of AutoCAD's OLE server capabilities. The INSERTOBJ command supports embedding but not linking documents or objects into AutoCAD from Windows applications that support OLE version 1.0. Figure I.3 illustrates a word processing document and a spreadsheet that have been embedded in an AutoCAD drawing.

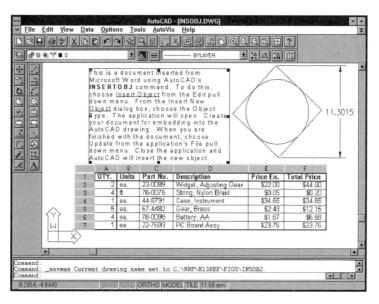

Figure I.3. *A word processing document and spreadsheet embedded as OLE objects.*

Embedding occurs when the inserted object is no longer associated with the application that created it. For example, if you embed a word processing document containing specifications for a drawing, you can change the document from within AutoCAD (using the application that created it) without affecting the original. Linking, on the other hand, occurs when changing the object within AutoCAD also changes the original. You would use linking if the object is referenced in several drawings. You could then change the original and have it automatically update all links to other drawings or applications. See the commands PASTECLIP, PASTESPEC, COPYLINK, and OLELINKS for more information concerning linking.

OLE objects appear on your screen and can be manipulated as other OLE objects (see your Windows documentation). You can print or plot drawings containing OLE objects using a Windows system driver. You cannot print or plot using a device that cannot be configured as a Windows system printer. If a drawing containing OLE objects is opened in the DOS or Unix version of AutoCAD, the OLE objects will not appear.

Dialog Box Items

The INSERTOBJ command uses only one simple dialog box for selecting the type of object to embed, the Insert New Object dialog box (see fig. I.4).

Figure I.4. *The Insert New Object dialog box.*

The Insert New Object dialog box lists applications installed on your system that support OLE. Select an application to create an object to embed into your AutoCAD drawing. Once you make your selection, the application opens. Create your document and save it. Closing the application or choosing Update from the applications File pull-down menu inserts the object into AutoCAD. If you close the application without first updating the OLE connection, you are presented with a Windows dialog box warning you of such action (see fig. I.5). After the object is inserted, you can then move, size, or scale the object using the object's control frame (not to be confused with AutoCAD's grips). The OLE object is not transparent and hides all AutoCAD objects underneath it. OLE objects might not display properly when viewed through a floating model space viewport from paper space.

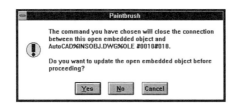

Figure I.5. *The Windows warning to update OLE objects before inserting.*

TIP Since most OLE objects most likely will be related to drawing annotation, place OLE objects in paper space. Be sure they do not overlap viewports or otherwise obscure other AutoCAD objects.

AutoCAD provides two methods to remove an OLE object from the drawing. The first is to highlight the object's control frame by clicking on the object, then use the ERASE command. The other option is to click on the object with the mouse return button to display a pop-up menu. Choose Clear to remove the object from the drawing. The other options on this pop-up menu are Cut, Copy, Undo, and Edit. Use Cut to remove the object to the Windows Clipboard. Use Copy to copy the object to the Windows Clipboard, leaving the original intact. Use Undo to cancel the last edit operation. Use Edit to open the application that created the OLE object or double-click on the OLE object.

Example

The following example will embed an object created using Windows Paintbrush into an AutoCAD drawing.

Choose **I**nsert Object *from the* **E**dit *pull-down menu*	Issues the INSERTOBJ command
Choose Paintbrush Picture *from the* Insert New Object *dialog box*	Specifies the application to create the new OLE object
Create a picture. (see fig. I.6 for an example)	Creates the OLE object
Choose **U**pdate *from the application's* **F**ile *menu*	Inserts the OLE object into AutoCAD (see fig. I.7)
`Command: _insertobj`	Issued by the applications Update command
Change to your AutoCAD window. The object is inserted.	

INSERTOBJ (Windows Only)

Figure I.6. *Creating an OLE object for embedding.*

Figure I.7. *The OLE object embedded in AutoCAD.*

Related Commands

OLELINKS   PASTECLIP   PASTESPEC

INTERFERE

Interfere

Toolbar: *Interfere (Solids)*
Pull-down: *D̲raw, So̲lids, Interference*
Screen: DRAW2, SOLIDS, Interfer:

The INTERFERE command identifies the volume where two ACIS SOLIDS overlap in space. INTERFERE highlights the two ACIS SOLIDS that overlap and can create an object representing the overlap volume. When creating the overlapping volume, the INTERFERE command operates exactly the same as INTERSECT. If no interference is found, AutoCAD responds with the following:

```
Solids do not interfere.
```

Prompts and Options

Select the first set of solids   Select a set of ACIS SOLIDS to act as a primary set. You may either check for the interference between all SOLIDS in this set, or check for the interference between each SOLID in this set and each SOLID in a second set.

Select the second set of solids   Press Enter (without selecting any solids) to check for the interference between all SOLIDS in the first selection set. AutoCAD will report the following:

```
No solids selected.
Comparing n solids with each other.
```

Or, select a set of ACIS SOLIDS to act as a second set. If at least one solid is selected, AutoCAD checks for the interference between each solid in the first set and each solid in the second set.

AutoCAD performs the interference check, and reports the following:

```
Comparing n solids against y solids.
Interfering solids (first  set): n
                  (second set): y
Interfering pairs             : z
```

Create interference solids ? <N> If an interference is found, AutoCAD highlights the interfering solids. Enter **Y** to create an ACIS SOLID object for all interference volumes found.

Highlight pairs of interfering solids ? <N> If more than one pair of interfering solids was found, enter **Y** to highlight the pairs one at a time. This aids you in determining exactly which solids are interfering with each other.

eXit/<Next pair> Press Enter to highlight the next pair of interfering solids. You may view all interfering pairs of SOLIDS, one pair at a time. When you reach the end of the set of interfering pairs, press Enter to go back to the first pair. Enter **X** or **E** to finish the INTERFERE command.

Example

The following example shows you how to check the interference between two ACIS SOLIDS, a box and a cone (see the BOX and CONE commands, respectively). An interference volume is created where these two objects interfere (see fig. I.8). The viewpoint is from 3,2,1.

Command: **INTERFERE** (Enter)	Starts the INTERFERE command
Select the first set of solids:	
Select objects: *Pick* ① *(see fig. I.8)*	Selects box object
Select objects: *Pick* ②	Selects cone object
Select objects: (Enter)	Finishes selecting objects
Select the second set of solids:	
Select objects: (Enter)	Compares all objects in first set against each other
No solids selected.	
Comparing 2 solids with each other.	
Interfering solids: 2	
Interfering pairs : 1	
Create interference solids ? <N>: Y (Enter)	Creates third solid representing intersection between cone and box

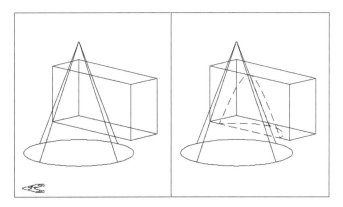

Figure I.8. *The box and cone, before and after checking for interference.*

Related Commands

BOX	CONE	CYLINDER	EXTRUDE
INTERSECT	REGION	SECTION	SLICESPHERE
SUBTRACT	TORUS	UNION	WEDGE

INTERSECT

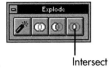

Intersect

Toolbar: *INTERSECT (Modify, Explode)*
Pull-down: *Construct, Intersection*
Screen: DRAW2, SOLIDS, Intrsec:

The INTERSECT command determines the common volume between ACIS SOLID objects or the common area between ACIS REGIONs. INTERSECT creates an ACIS SOLID object representing the volume common to all selected SOLIDS or a region representing the area common to all selected regions.

Existing solids are replaced by the intersecting volume. To retain the existing solids and produce the intersecting volume, use the INTERFERE command. If no intersecting volume exists between the selected SOLIDS, AutoCAD deletes the solids and reports the following:

```
Null solid created - deleted
```

Existing regions must be coplanar, and are replaced by the common area region. If regions are not coplanar, all regions on the same plane are grouped together for intersecting comparison. If no intersecting areas are between the regions, AutoCAD deletes the regions and reports the following:

```
Null region created - deleted
```

Prompts and Options

Select objects Select the ACIS SOLIDs and REGIONs to be checked for overlapping volumes or areas. You may select both SOLIDs and REGIONs. SOLIDs are checked against other SOLIDs, and REGIONs against other REGIONs.

Example

The following example shows you how to create an intersection region from two overlapping regions (see fig. I.9). See the BOX and CONE commands for creating these objects. The viewpoint is from 3,2,1.

Command: **INTERSECT** (Enter)	Starts INTERSECT command
Select objects: *Pick* ① *(see fig I.9)*	Selects box
Select objects: *Pick* ②	Selects cone
Select objects: (Enter)	Produces intersecting solid from box and cone

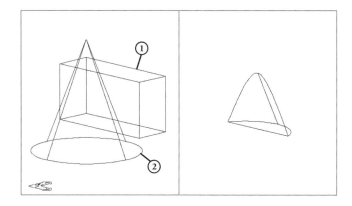

Figure I.9. *The box and cone, before and after using the INTERSECT command.*

Related Commands

BOX	CONE	CYLINDER	EXTRUDE
INTERFERE	REGION	SECTION	SLICE
SPHERE	SUBTRACT	TORUS	UNION
WEDGE			

'ISOPLANE

The ISOPLANE command is used in conjunction with the Style option of the SNAP command to create 2D isometric drawings that resemble 3D objects. The ISOPLANE command is a drawing aid (similar to the GRID, SNAP, and ORTHO commands) that enables you to draw in the three isometric drafting planes. All the ISOPLANE command options are available from the DDRMODES dialog box.

Setting the Style option of the SNAP command to Isometric forces the crosshair cursor to align with the 30-, 90-, and 150-degree axes used in isometric drafting. If grid mode is turned on, it too displays as isometric. When Ortho mode is on in isometric mode, lines can be drawn only in the two axes of the current isometric plane.

Figure I.10 demonstrates how a 2D isometric drawing appears to be three-dimensional. The figure contains three distinct isometric planes at 30, 90, and 150 degrees. The ISOPLANE command enables you to specify which plane to work in and should be used in conjunction with the ORTHO command to restrict drawing to a single plane at one time. When you are drawing in one of the isometric planes, the crosshairs align parallel to that plane.

Use the Ctrl+E key sequence to quickly switch between the three isometric planes.

Prompts and Options

The ISOPLANE command presents you with the following options:

Left/Top/Right/<Toggle>

Left The Left option sets the current isometric plane to the left plane. After you select this or any other option at this prompt, the crosshairs are rotated to reflect the plane you chose.

Right The Right option sets the current isometric plane to the right plane.

Top The Top option sets the current isometric plane to the top plane.

<Toggle> Accepting the default option, Toggle, cycles among the left, top, and right isometric planes. If your current plane is top, it is changed to right, and so on. After pressing Enter at the prompt, you return to AutoCAD's Command: prompt.

Example

This example demonstrates how to use the ISOPLANE and SNAP commands to prepare to draw in the left isometric plane. The drawing in figure I.10 shows the crosshairs aligned to the left plane.

```
Command: SNAP (Enter)                          Issues the SNAP command

Snap spacing or                                Specifies the Style option
ON/OFF/Aspect/Rotate/Style
<1.0000>: S (Enter)

Standard/Isometric <S>: I (Enter)              Sets the snap to Isometric style

Vertical spacing <1.0000>: (Enter)             Determines the snap increments

Command: ISOPLANE (Enter)                      Issues the ISOPLANE command

Left/Top/Right/<Toggle>: (Enter)               Toggles the isometric plane to the
                                               next plane

Current Isometric plane is: Top
```

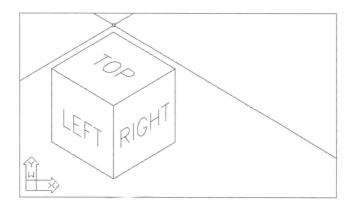

Figure I.10. *An illustration of the three isoplanes.*

Related Commands

DDRMODES   ELLIPSE   GRID   SNAP

Related System Variable

SNAPISOPAIR   SNAPSTYL

'LAYER

The LAYER command enables you to control layers used for the drawing, displaying, and plotting of objects. Use it transparently to set the color, linetype, and visibility of each layer, make new layers, set the current layer, freeze or thaw layers, or lock and unlock layers.

TIP You also can use the DDLMODES command to modify layer properties. Instead of working from the command line, as the LAYER command works, the DDLMODES command uses a dialog box to display all layers and modify their properties.

Prompts and Options

The following prompt presents all the LAYER command's options, which are discussed in the following paragraphs. For more detail on each of the options, see the DDLMODES command.

?/Make/Set/New/ON/OFF/Color/Ltype/Freeze/Thaw/LOck/Unlock:

? The ? option lists all the layers defined within the current drawing. This list contains the full name of the layer, its state of visibility, and its color and linetype. When using this option, you get an additional prompt, Layer name(s) to list <*>:, that enables you to specify which layer name(s) you want listed. The default lists all the layers, but if you are looking for information about particular layers only, you can type each layer's name, separated by commas, or use wild-card searches to narrow down the layers listed. Wild-card options are listed in the Introduction.

TIP Use the LAYER command's ? option in combination with the LOGFILEON command to capture a list of a drawing's layers to a text file. With Windows, you also can use the Cut editing option to capture the layer information from the text screen.

Make Use the Make option to create a new layer and make the new layer the current layer. The Make option issues the following prompt:

New current layer <default>

Enter the name of the layer you want to create and set as the current layer. If the layer name you enter does not exist, the layer is created. If the layer name already exists in your drawing, the Make option simply sets it as the current layer.

Set Use the Set option to make an existing layer the current layer. The Set option issues the following prompt:

New current layer <default>

Enter the name of an existing layer you want to make current. The layer cannot be frozen. If the layer name does not exist, you see the following prompt and are prompted again for the new current layer:

```
Cannot find layer XXXXX.
```

New The New option prompts you to enter the names of new layers that you want to add to the current drawing. The new option issues the following prompt:

```
New layer name(s):
```

With most of the LAYER command options, you can enter more than one layer name by separating each name with a comma.

OFF The LAYER command warns you if you attempt to turn off the current layer. The OFF option issues the following prompt:

```
Layer name(s) to turn Off:
```

ON Enter the names of layers to turn on at the following prompt:

```
Layer name(s) to turn On:
```

Color Enter a color number or name for layers you specify. The color you enter can be any valid color number (1 - 255) for your graphics card, or the name of one of the first seven colors: red, yellow, green, cyan, blue, magenta, or white. Then, at the Layer name(s) for color *number* <default> prompt, enter the name(s) of the layers to which you want that color assigned.

Ltype Use this option to assign a linetype name to layers you specify. If you use the ? option, a list of the linetypes currently loaded in the current drawing is displayed. The Ltype option issues the following prompt:

```
Linetype (or ?) <CONTINUOUS>:
```

After you specify a linetype, you must indicate which layers that linetype is to be used for, at the Layer name(s) for linetype *name* <default>: prompt. The default sets the current layer to the new linetype, but you also can enter other layer names as needed.

Freeze Use this option to enter the name(s) of layers to freeze. The Freeze option issues the following prompt:

```
Layer name(s) to Freeze:
```

Thaw Use this option to enter the name(s) of layers to thaw. Thawing a layer reverses the freezing process. The Thaw option issues the following prompt:

```
Layer name(s) to Thaw:
```

LOck Enter the name(s) of layers to lock at the prompt, as follows:

```
Layer name(s) to Lock:
```

Unlock Enter the name(s) of layers to unlock at the prompt, as follows:

```
Layer name(s) to Unlock:
```

Example

This example uses the LAYER command to change the linetype of the objects on the LINES layer, which is shown in figure L.1.

Command: **LAYER** (Enter)	Issues the LAYER command
?/Make/Set/New/ON/OFF/Color/Ltype/Freeze/Thaw/LOck/Unlock: **LT** (Enter)	Selects the LType option
Linetype (or ?) <CONTINUOUS>: **HIDDEN** (Enter)	Specifies the linetype for the layer(s)
Layer name(s) for linetype HIDDEN <0>: **LINES** (Enter)	Specifies the layers for the new linetype
?/Make/Set/New/ON/OFF/Color/Ltype/Freeze/Thaw/LOck/Unlock: (Enter)	Exits the LAYER command
Regenerating drawing.	

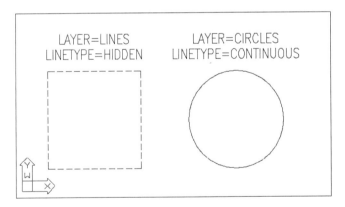

Figure L.1. *Using the LAYER command to set the linetype of a layer.*

Related Commands
DDEMODES   DDLMODES   VPLAYER

Related System Variables
CECOLOR   CELTYPE   CLAYER   MAXSORT

LEADER

Leader

Toolbar: *Leader (Dimensioning)*
Pull-down: ***D**raw*, ***D**imensioning*, *Lea**d**er*
Screen: DRAW DIM, Leader:

The LEADER command provides a method of annotating features of a drawing by connecting text, tolerances, or blocks via a leader line. The leader line can be straight or splined with or without an arrowhead. The annotation is not associated with the leader line. Leader lines and their associated arrowheads are considered one AutoCAD object, regardless of the number of segments the leader line may contain. Hook lines are drawn if the angle of the last segment of the leader line exceeds 15 degrees from horizontal. You cannot use a user-defined arrowhead for leaders but you can use any of the arrowhead types supplied with AutoCAD (see DDIM). Figure L.2 illustrates various types of leaders.

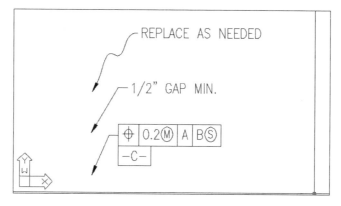

Figure L.2. *Various leaders' formats and annotations.*

Prompts and Options

From point   You are initially prompted for the first point of the leader line. This point determines the placement of the arrowhead for the leader line.

To point   This prompt determines the opposite endpoint for the first segment of the leader line.

To point (Format/Annotation/Undo)<Annotation>   This prompt repeats as long as you define points for the leader line segments. The other options are discussed in the following paragraphs.

Format   Use the Format option to specify whether the leader will be a spline curve, straight, or have an arrowhead. The Format option issues the following prompt:

Spline/STraight/Arrow/None/<Exit>

> **Spline**   The Spline option enables you to specify the controlling points on a spline curve similar to the SPLINE command. It repeats the To point (Format/Annotation/Undo)<Annotation> prompt until you choose one of its other options.
>
> **STraight**   Use the STraight option to draw straight line segments for the leader line. Each point becomes a vertex of the leader line. Straight leader lines are the AutoCAD default.
>
> **Arrow**   Use this option to have arrowheads placed on the leader lines. The first point picked for the leader line determines the location of the arrowhead. Arrowheads are drawn by default.
>
> **None**   Use this option to turn off arrowheads.

Annotation   This default option of the LEADER command determines the type of annotation that will be placed at the end of the leader line. You can use multiline text (MTEXT), blocks, or tolerances (control frames) for annotation. The Annotation option initially prompts for a line of MTEXT at the prompt, Annotation (or RETURN for options). If you type a line of text and then press Enter, you are prompted for another line of text at the prompt, MText. You can enter another line of text or press Enter to terminate the LEADER command. Options for annotation are presented by the following prompt and are discussed in the following paragraphs:

Tolerance/Copy/Block/None/<Mtext>

> **Tolerance**   The Tolerance option creates geometric dimensioning and tolerancing control frames containing tolerance symbols and values. These are created through the use of the same dialog boxes used for the TOLERANCE command.
>
> **Copy**   Use the Copy option to copy an existing text, mtext, block, or feature control frame containing geometric tolerances. The copied object

is connected to the end of the leader line. At the Select object prompt, select the object to copy. The system variable DIMGAP determines the location of text and mtext objects. Tolerance objects and blocks are located at the end of the leader line. After the object is placed, the command terminates.

Block Use this command to insert a block at the end of the leader line. AutoCAD issues the same prompts as the INSERT command. The block is placed at an offset from the end of the leader line.

None Use the None option to terminate the LEADER command without adding any annotation to the leader.

A practical example of the None option is when multiple leaders reference the same annotation.

TIP

Mtext Use this default option to display the Edit Mtext dialog box (DOS: The DOS text editor). The text entered is attached to the leader line and centered vertically. The command terminates after the text is placed.

Undo The Undo option undoes the last segment of the leader line. The prompt, To point (Format/Annotation/Undo)<Annotation>, is displayed.

Example

The following example places a splined leader with multiline text (MTEXT) annotation (see fig. L.3).

Choose the Leader *tool.*	
Command: _leader	Issues the LEADER command
From point: *Pick point* ① *(see fig. L.3)*	Specifies the first point of the leader (see fig. L.3)
To point: *Pick point* ②	Specifies the next vertex of the leader line
To point (Format/Annotation/Undo) <Annotation>: **F** (Enter)	Selects the Format option
Spline/STraight/Arrow/None/<Exit>: **S** (Enter)	Selects the Spline option

`To point (Format/Annotation/Undo)` `<Annotation>:` *Pick point* ③	Selects the next leader line vertex
`To point (Format/Annotation/Undo)` `<Annotation>:` *Pick point* ④	
`To point (Format/Annotation/Undo)` `<Annotation>:` (Enter)	Terminates leader line placement
`Annotation (or RETURN for options):` (Enter)	Displays annotation options
`Tolerance/Copy/Block/None/<Mtext>:` (Enter)	Selects the default Mtext option

Enter the text as shown in fig. L.3.
Text should be 0.125 units high. Click
on OK.

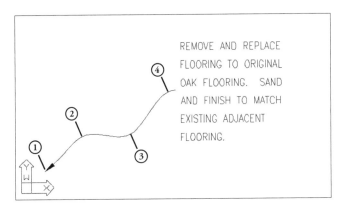

Figure L.3. *Drawing a leader with multiline text annotation.*

Related Commands

DIM   MTEXT   SPLINE   TOLERANCE

Related System Variables

DIMASZ   DIMBLK   DIMBLK1   DIMCLRD
DIMGAP   DIMSCALE   DIMTAD   DIMTOH

LENGTHEN

Lengthen

Toolbar: *Lengthen (Modify, Resize)*
Pull-down: *Modify, Lengthen*
Screen: MODIFY, Lengthn:

The LENGTHEN command changes the total length (longer or shorter) of an object and the included angle of arcs. You can specify a delta length, percentage, total length, or dynamically drag the length. Closed objects cannot be lengthened. There are no restrictions on the object's relative position to the current User Coordinate System.

Prompts and Options

The LENGTHEN command presents the following options:

`DElta/Percent/Total/DYnamic/<Select object>`

Select object Use this default option to display the length and included angle of the object if applicable:

`Current length: 3.5633, included angle: 205.6419`

This is used for obtaining a reference length and angle only and does not necessarily define the selection set to be lengthened.

> The spline object can typically be shortened, but cannot be lengthened.

DElta Use the DElta option to lengthen or shorten an object by a specified increment. Specify a non-negative value to lengthen an object or a negative value to shorten the object. You can specify a length or an angle. The object is lengthened or shortened by the specified amount from the endpoint closest to the pick point used to select the object. The DElta option issues the following prompt:

`Angle/<Enter delta length (0.0000)>`

    Angle Use the Angle option to incrementally change the included angle of an arc. Enter a positive or negative angle value at the prompt,

Enter delta angle <0.0000>; and select an object to modify at the prompt <Select object to change>/Undo. The Undo option reverses the change made to the last object.

Enter delta length This is the default option for the DElta method. Enter a positive or negative value at this prompt and select the object to modify at the prompt <Select object to change>/Undo. The Undo option reverses the change made to the last object.

Percent Use the Percent option to specify a percentage change for the object. For example, a 50 percent change would result in the object being shortened by half. A 200 percent change would double the length of the object. This option changes the included angle of an arc by the specified percentage. The percentage must be a positive value greater than zero. The Percent option issues the prompt:

Enter percent length <0.0000>:

Enter the percent change and select an object to modify at the prompt <Select object to change>/Undo. The Undo option reverses the change made to the last object.

Some early versions of AutoCAD Release 13 display the default or last-used percentage improperly when the units are set to anything but decimal units. You still can type in a valid percentage, though, with no adverse affect.

Total Use the Total option to set an explicit length of an object from a fixed endpoint. For an arc, the Total option determines the total included angle of the arc. The Total option issues the prompt:

Angle/<Enter total length (0.0000)>:

Angle The Angle option is used to specify the total included angle of an arc. Enter a value at the prompt, Enter total angle <0.0000>; and select an object to modify at the prompt <Select object to change>/Undo. The Undo option reverses the change made to the last object.

Enter total length (0.0000) At this prompt, enter the total length of the object and select an object to modify at the prompt, <Select object to change>/Undo. The Undo option reverses the change made to the last object.

DYnamic Use this option to dynamically drag the length of the selected object. The endpoint closest to the pick point of the object is dragged to the desired length or included angle (for an arc), while the other endpoint remains fixed.

The DYnamic option issues the prompt, `<Select object to change>/Undo`. The Undo option reverses the change made to the last object. You cannot use the Dynamic option with Spline objects.

Example

In the following example, the included angle of an arc is shortened. Figure L.4 illustrates a door swing in an architectural drawing before and after shortening the arc and rotating the door.

Choose the Lengthen *tool.*

Command	Description
`Command: _lengthen`	Issues the LENGTHEN command
`DElta/Percent/Total/DYnamic/<Select object>:` **T** (Enter)	Selects the Total option
`Angle/<Enter total length (1.0000)>:` **A** (Enter)	Selects the Angle option
`Enter total angle <57.2958>:` **45** (Enter)	Specifies the total included angle of the arc
`<Select object to change>/Undo:` *Pick point* ① *(see fig. L.4)*	Specifies the object to lengthen (or shorten)
`<Select object to change>/Undo:` (Enter)	Terminates the LENGTHEN command

Rotate the door -45 degrees

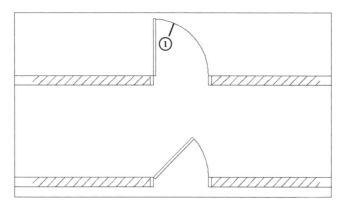

Figure L.4. *Using the LENGTHEN command to modify an arc.*

Related Commands

EXTEND   STRETCH   TRIM

LIGHT

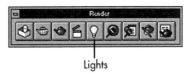
Lights

Toolbar: *Lights (Render)*
Pull-down: <u>T</u>ools, <u>R</u>ender, <u>L</u>ights...
Screen: TOOLS, RENDER, Lights:

The LIGHT command specifies, places, and controls lighting for rendering. You can place point, distant, or spotlights anywhere in model space. You also can control the amount of ambient light that shines on all surfaces.

You can control the light position, color, and intensity of all types of lighting.

Prompts and Options

The LIGHT command displays a series of dialog boxes for controlling the different types of lights. The Lights dialog box is used to create new lights, select specific lights to modify, and to change ambient lighting characteristics. The New Point Light, New Distant Light, and New Spotlight dialog boxes are used to define new lights of these types.

The Modify Point Light, Modify Distant Light, and Modify Spotlight dialog boxes are used to change the features of existing lights of these types. The Show Light Position dialog box displays the light location and target location (if applicable). The Color dialog box changes a color assigned to a light. The Select Color dialog box is used to select a standard AutoCAD color.

The Lights Dialog Box

The Lights dialog box lists the existing lights in the drawing and creates new point, distant, and spot lights (see fig. L.5). You also can change the ambient lighting characteristics with the Lights dialog box, which has the following options:

Lights. The Lights list box displays the names of the existing lights in the current drawing.

Modify. Select an existing light from the Lights list box to modify; then click on the **M**odify button. This displays the Modify Point Light, Modify Distant Light, or Modify Spotlight dialog box, according to the type of light selected. The **M**odify button enables you to change the parameters of the selected light. If you double-click on a light name in the Lights list box, the Modify Point Light, Modify Distant Light, or Modify Spotlight dialog box automatically appears. The features and options of the Modify dialog boxes are identical to the New dialog box discussed later.

Delete. Select an existing light from the Lights list box to delete, and then click on the **D**elete button. The selected light is then deleted from the drawing.

Select. The **S**elect button causes the Lights dialog box to disappear, enabling you to pick a light icon from the graphics window. After successfully selecting a light from the drawing, that light is highlighted in the Lights list box.

New. The **N**ew button creates a new light. Select either Point Light, Distant Light, or Spotlight from the drop-down list box next to the **N**ew button; then click on **N**ew to open the New Point Light, New Distant Light, or New Spotlight dialog box. When you create a new light, AutoCAD places a light block describing the properties of the new light in the drawing.

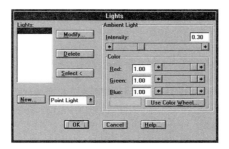

Figure L.5. *The Lights dialog box.*

New lights are positioned at the center of the current viewpoint and, in the case of distant lights and spotlights, are parallel to the current line of sight.

A *point* light emits beams uniformly in all directions. A point light is analogous to a bare light bulb. The intensity attenuates (falls off) as the distance from the light to the object increases.

A *distant* light emits parallel beams from a plane at the light source. A distant light behaves similarly to sunlight. Distant lights do not have intensity attenuation.

A *spotlight* emits beams in the shape of a cone originating at the light source, pointed towards a target. The spread of the beam, as well as the radial and linear attenuation, can be changed to alter the characteristics of the spotlight.

Specifying a light type and clicking <u>N</u>ew displays one of three different New dialog boxes (specifying an existing light opens an identical Modify dialog box) depending upon what type of light was specified. For example, if you specify a point light, the New Point Light (or the Modify Point Light) dialog box is displayed (see fig. L.6).

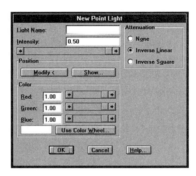

Figure L.6. *The New Point Light dialog box.*

Specifying a distant light displays the New Distant Light dialog box (see fig. L.7), whereas selecting a spotlight displays the New Spotlight dialog box (see fig. L.8).

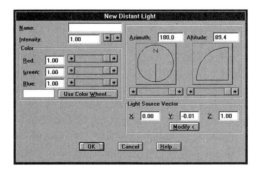

Figure L.7. *The New Distant Light dialog box.*

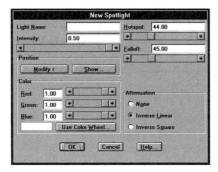

Figure L.8. *The New Spotlight dialog box.*

Each of these dialog boxes displays an edit box in which you can enter or change the light name, an edit box and scroll bar for changing the light's intensity, and a color group for changing the light's color. In addition, each dialog box displays options specific to that type of light.

Light Name. Enter the name for the new light or edit the name of the existing light. Light names are limited to eight characters.

Intensity. Enter the intensity for this light in the edit box or use the slider bar to interactively specify a value. The value range for distant lights is from zero (off) to one (brightest), whereas the range for point lights and spotlights depends on both the selected attenuation and the size of the current drawing's extents. For these types of lights, the range is from zero to a value approximately half the distance from minimum extents to maximum extents for inverse linear attenuation. The maximum for inverse square attenuation is the square of the maximum for the linear attenuation. If the attenuation is off, the maximum is 1.

Color. Edit the color values for the Red, Green, and Blue primary colors to change the color of this light. All the options for changing the color of a specific light are the same as the options for changing the color of ambient light (see the preceding discussion).

Position. Select the Modify button to change the location of a point light or a spotlight by picking a point in the graphics window. For spotlights, clicking this button also enables changing the target point of the spotlight. This option is not available for distant lights. Use the Light Source Vector option for distant lights to change their position.

Select the Show button to display the Show Light Position dialog box (see fig. L.9). This dialog box displays the light location and the target position for spotlights.

Figure L.9. *The Show Light Position dialog box.*

The Point Light Dialog Box

In addition to the light name, intensity, and color, a point light has a rate of attenuation over distance. The Point Light dialog box enables you to change this also.

Attenuation. Select the desired attenuation for the point light or spotlight. *Attenuation* is the decrease in intensity of the light as the distance from the light increases. Clicking on the None button disables attenuation for this light; all objects are illuminated uniformly, regardless of distance from the point light source. Intensity attenuation is also called *falloff*. Distant lights do not attenuate.

Select Inverse Linear to cause a point light's or spotlight's intensity to fall off inversely to the distance from the light source. This means that an object that is 10 units from a point light source will be illuminated at 1/10 the intensity of the source.

Select Inverse Square to force a point light's or spotlight's intensity to fall off inversely to the square of the distance from the light source. This means that an object that is 10 units from a point light source will be illuminated at 1/100 the intensity of the source.

The Distant Light Dialog Box

In addition to the light name, intensity, and color, a distant light has a location specified by either a vector, or an azimith and altitude. The Distant Light dialog box enables you to change this also.

Azimuth. Enter the azimuth value for the location of this distant light in the Azimuth edit box, use the slider bar to interactively specify a value, or pick a position inside the Azimuth image tile. The *azimuth* is the angle in the XY plane for this distant light, as measured from the north. A clockwise angle is a *positive azimuth*, whereas a counterclockwise angle is *negative azimuth*. Valid azimuths range from –180 to 180 degrees. Changes to the azimuth of the distant light also are reflected in the Light Source Vector coordinates (discussed later in this section).

Altitude. Enter the altitude value for the location of this distant light in the Altitude edit box, use the slider bar to interactively specify a value, or pick a position inside the A<u>l</u>titude image tile. The *altitude* is the angle from the XY plane for this distant light. A *positive altitude* is an angle above the XY plane, whereas a *negative altitude* is an angle below the XY plane. Valid azimuths range from –90 to 90 degrees. Note that it is not possible to specify a negative altitude using the A<u>l</u>titude image tile—you must use the edit box to enter a negative altitude. Changes to the altitude of the distant light also are reflected in the Light Source Vector coordinates (see the following paragraph).

Light Source Vector. Edit the <u>X</u>, <u>Y</u>, and <u>Z</u> coordinate values to locate the distant light. The values in these edit boxes are updated when using the <u>A</u>zimuth and A<u>l</u>titude image tiles to position the distant light.

Select the <u>M</u>odify button to change the light direction by specifying the TO and FROM points for the light. AutoCAD switches to the graphics screen and issues prompts for specifying the TO and FROM points.

The Spotlight Dialog Box.

In addition to the light name, intensity, and color, a spotlight has a hotspot angle and falloff angle. The spotlight dialog box enables you to change this also.

Hotspot. Edit the <u>H</u>otspot angle, also known as the cone angle, to adjust the divergence angle of the spotlight beam. The <u>H</u>otspot angle is the angle from the outer edge of bright beam on one side to the other. Use the slider bar to interactively specify a value. The value range for the <u>H</u>otspot angle is from zero (no divergence) to 160.

Falloff. Edit the <u>F</u>alloff angle to adjust the amount of radially attenuated light from the spotlight beam. The <u>F</u>alloff angle must be equal to or larger than the <u>H</u>otspot angle, and this angle also is measured from the outer edge of beam on one side to the other. Use the slider bar to interactively specify a value. The value range for the <u>F</u>alloff angle is from zero to 160.

Ambient Light

The Ambient Light group controls the amount of background light that shines on all object surfaces. Edit the Intensity edit box to increase or decrease the amount of ambient light, or use the slider bar to interactively specify a value. The value range for ambient light is from zero (off) to one (brightest).

Color. Edit the color values for the Red, Green, and Blue primary colors to change the color of ambient light. You also can use the slider bars next to each primary color to interactively specify a primary color value. The range is from zero (color off) to one (color fully on). Note that primary colors can be combined to produce other colors: red, blue, and green fully on produce white. Green and blue fully on produce cyan, green and red fully on produce yellow, red and blue fully on produce magenta.

Clicking on the Use Color **W**heel button displays the Color dialog box. Select either RGB or HLS from the Color System drop-down list box, then edit the individual values for the color's *red, green, and blue* (RGB) values, or *hue, luminance, and saturation* (HLS) values. The current color is displayed in the Color Selected box. You also may select from the standard AutoCAD colors by clicking on **S**elect from ACI, which displays the standard AutoCAD Select Color dialog box.

Example

The following example uses the LIGHT command to create two new point light sources in the drawing EX09 (supplied with AutoCAD). The difference in rendering with no lights (seen in the left viewport) and with the two lights created in this example (seen in the right viewport) is shown in figure L.10.

Open the drawing EX09 and turn off paper space by setting tilemode to one. Use the DVIEW command to turn off perspective view. Use the RENDER command to perform an initial render, and note the uniformity of the color density of the rendering.

Command	Description
Command: **LIGHT** (Enter)	Starts the LIGHT command
Click on the New drop-down list, and select Distant Light	Selects Distant Light to create
Click on the New *button*	Opens New Distant Light dialog box
Enter **DIST1** *in the* **N**ame *edit box*	Specifies name of DIST1 for this light
Enter **90** *in the* **A**zimuth *edit box*	Locates light along the X axis
Enter **25** *in the* **Al**titude *edit box*	Locates light 25 degrees above the XY plane
Click on OK	Closes New Distant Light dialog box
Click on the **N**ew *drop-down list and select* Spotlight	Selects Spotlight to create
Click on the **N**ew *button*	Opens New Spotlight dialog box
Enter **SPOT1** *in the* **N**ame *edit box*	Specifies name of SPOT1 for this light
Enter **8** *in the* **I**ntensity *edit box*	Specifies an intensity of 8 for this light

Click on the Modify button	Temporarily removes New Spotlight dialog box to specify target and light locations
`Enter light target <current>:` **8.64,2.79,4.13** `(Enter)`	Specifies new target location as center of lens turntable
`Enter light location <current>:` **11.95,-6.19,7.03** `(Enter)`	Specifies new light location ten units away from lens turntable along current viewing direction
Click on OK	Closes New Spotlight dialog box
Click on OK	Closes Lights dialog box
`Command:` **RENDER** `(Enter)`	Starts the RENDER command
Click on Viewport as the destination	
Click on Render Scene	Begins rendering to current viewport
`Using current view. Default scene selected.`	

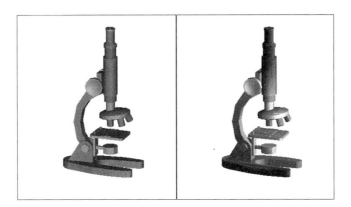

Figure L.10. *Rendering with no lights, and with one spot and one distant light.*

Related Commands

RENDER   RENDERUNLOAD   SCENE

Related System Variables

TARGET   VIEWDIR

'LIMITS

Pull-down: **D**ata, Dr**a**wing Limits
Screen: DATA, Limits:

The LIMITS command defines a rectangular boundary in the *World Coordinate System* (WCS) within which you can draw. You can exceed or redefine the boundary at any time. The boundary limits have a lower left corner and an upper right corner in the X-Y plane, but no limit in the Z axis.

The drawing's limits also are used for displaying the extent of the grid when grid mode is turned on and as an area specification for plotting. Model space and paper space each have their own drawing limits—when you issue the ZOOM command's All option, ZOOM displays the drawing's limits or extents, whichever is greater.

Prompts and Options

The LIMITS command presents the user with the following options:

`ON/OFF/<Lower left corner><0.0000,0.0000>:`

ON The On option turns on limits checking. While turned on, any coordinate entry that does not fall within the drawing limits is not accepted. If you try to enter coordinates outside these boundaries, the following message appears:

`**Outside limits.`

Note that this checking is only for points you specify. For example, you can define a circle whose perimeter exceeds the drawing's limits by specifying its center point within the limits but typing in a radius that would draw portions of the circle outside the limits.

Off The Off option disables limits checking. Limits checking is off by default, even after you set the drawing's limits.

Lower left corner The Lower left corner option is the default and defines the lower left corner of a rectangular area that represents the drawing's limits. Enter a 2D coordinate or pick a point on-screen. The default is 0,0 unless otherwise specified in a prototype drawing.

Upper Right Corner<12.0000,9.0000> After specifying the lower left corner of the drawing's limits, you are prompted for the upper right corner. This point represents the opposite corner of the rectangular area of the drawing's limits. The default setting is governed by the prototype drawing.

Related Commands
GRID   PLOT   ZOOM

Related System Variables
LIMCHECK   LIMMAX   LIMMIN

LINE

Line

Toolbar: *Line (Draw, Line)*
Pull-down: *Draw, Line*
Screen: DRAW1, Line:

The LINE command draws straight lines between two specified points. These points may have any 2D or 3D coordinate location. The command repeats, enabling many lines to be created, until you press Enter or Ctrl+C. After lines have been drawn, you can type **C** to create a closed polygon. You can draw lines at right angles by using Ortho mode. You also can use the TRACE or POLYLINE commands for wide lines.

Prompts and Options

From point Specify a starting point for the line segment. The point can have any X, Y, and Z coordinates and can be preceded with any Osnap overrides or point filters. If you press Enter at this prompt, AutoCAD begins the line by using the endpoint of the last line or arc created. If the last object was an arc, the line is drawn from the arc endpoint tangent to the arc.

To point Enter an endpoint for the segment, and a line is drawn. This prompt repeats until you press Enter or Ctrl+C.

    Close Enter **C** at any To point: prompt to connect the end of the last line with the beginning of the first line and complete the command. You must have drawn at least two previous line segments to use the Close option.

> **NOTE:** The Close option only closes lines drawn while within the current LINE command. You cannot use the Close option to include lines drawn prior to issuing the current LINE command.

Undo   Enter **U** while within the command to remove the last endpoint specified. You can use the Undo option to remove previous line segments back to the initial start point.

Example

This example shows the simplicity of using the LINE command. The lines drawn are shown in figure L.11.

Choose the Line *tool*

Command: **_LINE**	Issues the LINE command
From point: *Pick ① (see fig. L.11)*	Specifies the start point for the first line segment
To point: *Pick ②*	Specifies the endpoint of the line segment
To point: *Pick ③*	
To point: **C** (Enter)	Closes the polygon from the last point to the original start point

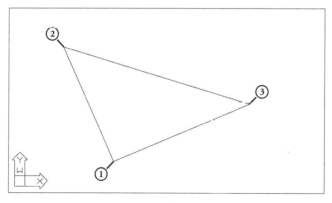

Figure L.11. *Simple shape drawn with the LINE command.*

Related Commands

MLINE   PLINE   RAY
SKETCH   TRACE   XLINE

Related System Variables

CELTYPE   LASTPOINT   LTSCALE   ORTHOMODE

LINETYPE

The LINETYPE command is used to load and list the linetypes available in the current drawing. You also can create new linetypes with this command and choose a new linetype for subsequent objects. The default linetype is BYLAYER, which new objects display in the linetype assigned to the layer on which they are created. The DDLTYPE command offers easier control over linetypes from a dialog box.

Prompts and Options

The LINETYPE command presents the user with the following options:

```
?/Create/Load/Set:
```

? When you choose the ? option, the Select Linetype File dialog box appears. By default, the ACAD.LIN file is highlighted. Complex linetypes are stored in the file LTYPESHP.LIN in the SUPPORT directory. Pressing Enter lists all the linetypes in the highlighted file. Use the Directories and Files list boxes to select another file to list. The descriptive text example of each linetype also is shown. If the system variable FILEDIA is set to 0, you see the prompt `File to list <ACAD>`, instead of the dialog box.

Create Choosing the Create option enables you to create a simple linetype definition (using dashes, dots, and spaces) from within the AutoCAD drawing editor. Enter the name you want to give the linetype at the following prompt. The name can be up to 31 characters long but cannot contain any spaces.

```
Name of linetype to create:
```

After entering the name of the linetype you want to create, the Create or Append Linetype File dialog box appears. It enables you to add the linetype to the ACAD.LIN file or create a new file for storing the linetype. At the following prompt,

```
Descriptive text:
```

enter up to 47 characters and spaces to describe the linetype you are about to create. Dashes, underscores, periods, and spaces are used semi-graphically to depict what the linetype actually looks like. This text is displayed next to the linetype name, when you list linetypes. You will then see the following prompt:

```
Enter pattern (on next line)
   A,
```

A simple linetype pattern is a series of dashes or spaces of different lengths and dots that make up one complete linetype pattern, which is repeated between the line endpoints according to the current linetype scale. A positive number indicates the length of a line segment; a negative number indicates a space. If you want a dot in the linetype definition, use the value zero (0). For example, the definition 2,-.5,0,-.5 produces a line segment of two units, a space of one-half unit, a dot, and then another space of one-half unit before repeating.

Load The following prompt appears when you choose the Load option:

```
Linetype(s) to load:
```

At this prompt, enter the names of the linetypes you want added to the drawing. To enter more than one name, separate each name by a comma. You also can use wild cards. For example, typing **HIDDEN*** would load all the linetype definitions beginning with the letters HIDDEN. By default, the Select Linetype File dialog box selects the ACAD.LIN file from which to load linetypes.

If you have several linetypes that are common in your drawings, load them into your prototype drawing, and they will be automatically included in all your new drawings.

AutoCAD includes linetypes for generating *International Standards Organization* (ISO) drawings. These linetypes begin with the name ACAD_ISO. There are also several examples of complex linetypes included in the file LTYPESHP.LIN.

If the linetype name you specified is already loaded in the drawing, you receive the following prompt.

```
Linetype linetype name is already loaded. Reload it? <Y>
```

The PURGE command is used to remove linetypes that were loaded and unused.

LINETYPE

Set If you choose the Set option, enter the name of a linetype currently loaded into the drawing. You can type **?** to list the linetypes currently loaded in the drawing. The Set option issues the following prompt:

```
New object linetype <default>:
```

Example

This example shows the process for loading a new linetype from the ACAD.LIN file and making it the default linetype used for drawing new objects. The linetypes included in the ACAD.LIN and LTYPESHP.LIN files are shown in figures L.12 and L.13.

Command: **LINETYPE** (Enter)]	Issues the LINETYPE command
?/Create/Load/Set: **L** (Enter)]	Selects the Load option
Linetype(s) to load: **DASHDOT** (Enter)	Specifies the name of the linetype to load
Select ACAD.LIN *in the dialog box and choose* OK.	
Linetype DASHDOT loaded.	
?/Create/Load/Set: **S** (Enter)	Selects the Set option
New object linetype (or ?) <BYLAYER>: **DASHDOT** (Enter)	Specifies the name of the linetype to set
?/Create/Load/Set: (Enter)	Terminates the LINETYPE command

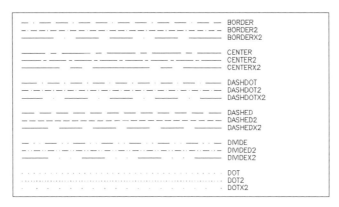

Figure L.12. *Linetypes loaded from the ACAD.LIN file.*

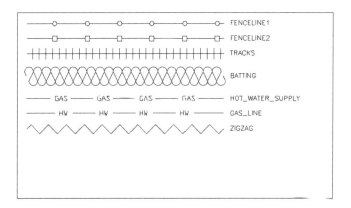

Figure L.13. *Linetypes loaded from the LTYPESHP.LIN file.*

Related Commands

CHANGE   CHPROP   DDCHPROP   DDEMODES
DDMODIFY

Related System Variables

CELTSCALE   CELTYPE   FILEDIA   LTSCALE
PSLTSCALE

LIST

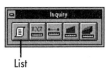
List

Toolbar: *List (Object Properties, Inquiry)*
Pull-down: *Edit, Inquiry, List*
Screen: ASSIST, INQUIRY, List:

The LIST command displays all the information about selected objects as stored in the drawing database. The properties include information such as line lengths, the layer in which an object resides, or scaling factors of blocks. If the information is too lengthy and begins to scroll off the screen, press Ctrl+S to pause scrolling, then press any key to resume. Press Ctrl+C to cancel the command. You can turn on the log file (LOGFILEON) to write the information to a file for later viewing or printing.

LIST

> For listing individual objects, the DDMODIFY command is a much more elegant and readable method for displaying the object's database information.
>
> **TIP**

Prompts and Options

Select objects Choose the objects about which you want information displayed.

Example

This example invokes the LIST command to view the properties of a line.

```
Command: LIST (Enter)                    Issues the LIST command


Select objects:
    LINE             Layer: 0
                     Space: Model space
    from point, X=  16.6089   Y=    4.4457   Z=    0.0000
      to point, X=  -7.9727   Y=   -8.1630   Z=    0.0000
Length =  27.6267,  Angle in XY Plane  =    207
         Delta X = -24.5816, Delta Y = -12.6087, Delta Z = 0.0000
```

Related Commands

AREA	DBLIST	LOGFILEOFF	LOGFILEON
STATUS	TREESTAT		

Related System Variables

AREA   PERIMETER

LOAD

Pull-down: **D**ata, **S**hape File...
Screen: DATA, Load:

The LOAD command is used to load compiled shape definition files for use by the SHAPE command. Shape definitions are stored in external files, and these files must be accessible every time you open the drawing. Compiled shape files have the extension .SHX—the same extension as compiled font files. You cannot load a compiled font file using the LOAD command—use the STYLE command instead to load a compiled font file.

Prompts and Options

The LOAD command displays the Select Shape File dialog box. Select the desired shape file. If the file selected is a compiled font file, AutoCAD advises the following:

```
complex.shx is a normal text font file, not a shape file.
```

You then are reprompted to select a shape file.

Example

The following example uses the PC.SHX shape file (supplied with AutoCAD) to draw standard shapes. These shapes are then connected with lines to create a simple wiring diagram.

Command: **LOAD** (Enter)	Starts the LOAD command
Name of shape file to load (or ?): **\R13\COMMON\SAMPLE\PC** (Enter)	Specifies shape file to load (PC.SHX is supplied with AutoCAD)
Command: **SHAPE** (Enter)	Begins the SHAPE command
Shape name (or ?): **DIP14** (Enter)	Specifies shape to insert
Starting point: **1,1** (Enter)	Location for shape
Height <1.0000>: (Enter)	Accepts default height
Rotation angle <0>: (Enter)	Accepts default rotation, draws shape (see fig. L.14)
Command: **SHAPE** (Enter)	Starts SHAPE command
Shape name (or ?) <DIP14>: **DIP8** (Enter)	Specifies shape to insert
Starting point: **2,.7** (Enter)	Location for shape
Height <1.0000>: (Enter)	Accepts default height
Rotation angle <0>: **90** (Enter)	Specifies rotated 90 degrees counterclockwise; draws shape (see fig. L.14)

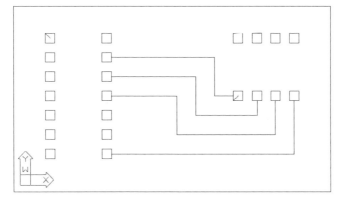

Figure L.14. *A simple wiring diagram created with shapes from PC.SHX.*

Related Commands
COMPILE   SHAPE   STYLE

Related System Variable
SHPNAME

LOGFILEOFF

The LOGFILEOFF command stops recording the text window and closes the log file.

The Preferences dialog box Environment tab contains items for changing the name, location, and status of the log file. See the LOGFILEON command for details.

Related Commands

DBLIST	LIST	LOGFILEON	PREFERENCES
STATUS	TIME	TREESTAT	

LOGFILEON

AutoCAD has the capability of recording the contents of the text window to a log file. The default name for this file is ACAD.LOG. The LOGFILEON command opens the log file specified in the Preferences dialog box and starts recording all text sent to the text window.

The Preferences dialog box **E**nvironment contains items for changing the name, location, and status of the log file (see fig. L.15). Enter the path and name of the log file in the **L**og File edit box. Checking the Log File check box has the same effect as LOGFILEON. Clear the box to turn the log file off. When the log file is on, it remains on for each AutoCAD session until turned off. Each recorded session is separated by the date, time, and a dashed line in the log file.

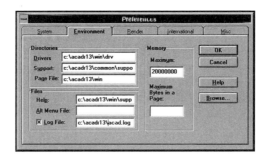

Figure L.15. *Log file settings in the Preferences dialog box.*

The following is a portion of an ACAD.LOG file:

```
[ AutoCAD - Fri Dec 16 14:17:59 1994 ]----------------------------------------
Command: style
Text style name (or ?) <STANDARD>: romans
New style. Height <0.0000>:
Width factor <1.0000>: .8
Obliquing angle <0>:
Backwards? <N>
Upside-down? <N>
Vertical? <N>
ROMANS is now the current text style.
Command: z
ZOOM
All/Center/Dynamic/Extents/Left/Previous/Vmax/Window/<Scale(X/XP)>: e
Drawing extents undefined.  Zooming to limits.
Regenerating drawing.
Drawing extents undefined.  Zooming to limits.
Command: logfileoff
```

Related Commands

DBLIST	LIST	LOGFILEOFF	PREFERENCES
STATUS	TIME	TREESTAT	

'LTSCALE

Pull-down: **O**ptions, Li**n**etypes, **G**lobal Linetype Scale
Screen: OPTIONS, DISPLAY, LTscale:

The LTSCALE command controls the LTSCALE system variable that determines the display and plot of noncontinuous linetypes. The LTSCALE system variable can also be controlled from the Select Linetype dialog box accessed by the DDLTYPE command. The LTSCALE setting is a global linetype scale setting. It affects objects with linetype scales set independently using the CELTSCALE system variable set with the Linetype Scale option of the DDMODIFY or DDCHPROP dialog boxes.

Each noncontinuous linetype is a pattern of dashes, dots, and spaces, and the pattern has a fixed size. By setting the LTSCALE value, you can adjust the scale of the linetype pattern in order to closely match the scale at which you are plotting.

In a large drawing, if the linetype scale is set to a low number, screen regeneration speed can be affected. You can improve screen regeneration speed by assigning a high value to the linetype scale (minimizing the number of dots and dashes displayed) until you are ready to plot the drawing.

Prompts and Options

`New scale factor <1>`   The current linetype scale factor is shown in angle brackets. Enter any positive number at the prompt. Decimal fractions are enabled. After the next screen regeneration, the display reflects the new linetype scale. Figure L.16 illustrates the CENTER linetype at a linetype scale of 0.5, 1.0, and 2.0.

Related Commands

DDLTYPE   LINETYPE

Related System Variables

CELTSCALE   LTSCALE   PSLTSCALE

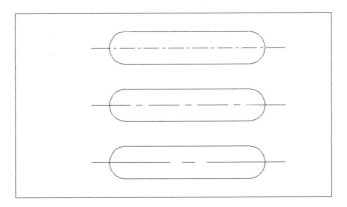

Figure L.16. *The Center linetype at a LTSCALE factor of 0.5, 1, and 2.*

MAKEPREVIEW

The MAKEPREVIEW command is used to create a preview image of a drawing. Its primary function is to create preview images of drawings created in earlier releases of AutoCAD. Use this command to create the preview if you do not want to save the older drawing in Release 13 format, but still want to be able to preview it in the Select File dialog box. MAKEPREVIEW creates a compressed BMP file of the current drawing view and stores it in the same directory as the drawing file.

There are no prompts or options for the MAKEPREVIEW command. This command is unnecessary for Release 13 drawings since AutoCAD automatically creates the preview image (depending on the RASTERPREVIEW system variable setting) during the SAVE or SAVEAS commands. If the RASTERPREVIEW system variable is set to 0 (the default value), AutoCAD creates a BMP format image. If RASTERPREVIEW is set to 1 or 2, AutoCAD creates a WMF format image. If RASTERPREVIEW is set to 3, no preview image is saved. You can use the Raster Preview Options in the Render section of the PREFERENCES dialog box to determine the type of preview image to create. The MAKEPREVIEW command will only create a compressed BMP file.

> **TIP** Setting the RASTERPREVIEW system variable to a non-zero value saves a small amount of disk space at the expense of having a distorted or non-existent preview image.

Related Commands

OPEN   SAVE   SAVEAS   SAVEASR12

Related System Variable

RASTERPREVIEW

MASSPROP

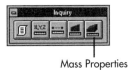

Mass Properties

Toolbar: *Mass Properties (Object Properties, Inquiry)*
Pull-down: *Edit, Inquiry, Mass Properties*
Screen: ASSIST, INQUIRY, MassPro:

MASSPROP is an inquiry command that reports the physical properties of selected ACIS SOLIDs and REGIONs. The bounding box and centroid are reported for both ACIS SOLIDs and REGIONs, as well as information specific to each. You can save the information to a file.

Additional information provided for ACIS SOLIDs includes the mass, volume, moments of inertia, products of inertia, radii of gyration, and principal axes and principal moments of inertia.

For ACIS REGIONs, the area and perimeter are also reported. If the X,Y plane of the first selected REGION is coplanar with the current UCS, MASSPROP also calculates the moments of inertia, products of inertia, radii of gyration, and principle axes and principal moments of inertia.

Prompts and Options

Select objects   Select the objects to list the physical properties. Any object that is not an ACIS SOLID or a REGION is ignored. If you select no ACIS SOLIDs or REGIONs, AutoCAD reports the following:

No solids or regions selected.

All selected SOLIDs are reported as if they were one large mass. The center of gravity of two non-connected SOLIDs can be calculated in this manner. Any REGIONs that are not coplanar with the first REGION selected are ignored, and AutoCAD reports the following:

region ignored.

Write to a file? <N>   Enter **Y** to save the calculations to a file for later inspection, or **N** to finish the command. If you choose **Y**, the Create Mass and Area Properties File dialog box appears. Select an existing file to overwrite, or specify a new file to create. The default file extension is MPR.

Example

The following example analyzes the physical properties of an interrupted tube oriented along the Z axis using the MASSPROP command (see fig. M.1).

```
Command: MASSPROP (Enter)                       Starts the MASSPROP command
Select objects: Pick the SOLID                  Specifies ACIS SOLID object
at (1)                                          to inspect
Select objects: (Enter)                         Finishes selecting objects
- - - - - - -       SOLIDS    - - - - - - -
Mass:                   1.7907
Volume:                 1.7907
Bounding box:       X: -1.0000   —   1.0000
                    Y: -1.0000   —   1.0000
                    Z:  0.0000   —   4.0000
Centroid:           X: -0.2019
                    Y: -0.2017
                    Z:  2.0000
Moments of inertia: X: 10.3608
                    Y: 10.3610
                    Z:  1.6208
Products of inertia: XY: -0.1720
                     YZ: -0.7224
                     ZX: -0.7230
Radii of gyration:  X: 2.4054
                    Y: 2.4054
                    Z: 0.9514
Principal moments and X-Y directions about centroid:
                    I: 2.8801 along [0.7071 -0.7071 -0.0001]
                    J: 3.3700 along [0.7071  0.7071  0.0000]
                    K: 1.4749 along [0.0001  0.0000  1.0000]
Write to a file ? <N>: (Enter)                  Don't save results
```

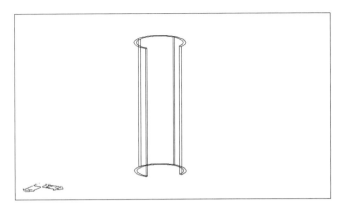

Figure M.1. *Calculating physical properties using MASSPROP.*

Related Commands

AREA   REGION   REVOLVE   SECTION
SLICE

MATLIB

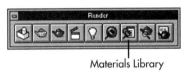

Materials Library

Toolbar: *Materials Library (Render)*
Pull-down: *Tools, Render, Materials Library...*
Screen: TOOLS, RENDER, MatLib:

The MATLIB command (Materials Library) controls rendering material definitions. You can import material definitions from a file into the current drawing, save existing material definitions into a material file, and remove unused material definitions from the drawing.

Render material definitions are stored in a standard block—named RM-SDB—placed at the origin of the WCS. Use the RMAT command to create new rendering material definitions.

Prompts and Options

The MATLIB command displays the Materials Library dialog box (see fig. M.2). Selecting the Materials **L**ibrary push button from the RMAT command also displays this dialog box, which has the following options.

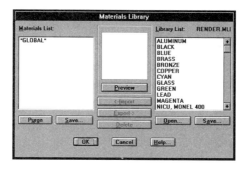

Figure M.2. *The Materials Library dialog box.*

Materials List. Lists the currently loaded render materials in the current drawing. Select one or more materials to save to a file or export to a material library file.

Purge. Deletes all unused (unreferenced) materials from the current drawing. A dialog box confirms the purge.

Save. Saves all currently loaded render materials from the current drawing into a materials library file. Select a file to overwrite, or specify a new file to save the material definitions into. The file extension defaults to MLI.

Library List. Lists the material definition names from a materials library file. The current file is displayed to the right of the Library List label. Select one or more materials to import into the drawing, delete from the library file, or save to a different library file. Select only one to preview.

Open. Closes the current materials library file and opens a different one. The file extension defaults to MLI.

S**a**ve. Saves all material definitions from the current library file into a new library file. Select a file to overwrite, or specify a new file to save the material definitions into. The file extension defaults to MLI.

Preview. Displays the selected material, if exactly one material is selected. The material is displayed in the image tile above the Preview push button.

Import. Copies the selected material definitions from the library file into the current drawing. Use the Delete option to remove them from the drawing. An RM-SDB block is inserted into the currect drawing for each material imported.

Export. Copies the selected material definitions from the drawing into the current materials library file. Material definitions can be transferred from one drawing to another by exporting to a library file from one drawing, then importing from the library file into another drawing.

Delete. Deletes the selected material definitions from either the current drawing or the current library file. If the selected materials are being used in the current drawing, a warning dialog box is displayed, and the material definition is deleted.

Example

This example imports the material definitions for all metals found in the sample materials definition file RENDER.MLI into the current drawing.

Command: **MATLIB** (Enter)	Starts the MATLIB command
Select ALUMINUM, BRASS, BRONZE, COPPER, LEAD, NICU MONEL 400, STAINLESS STEEL, *and* STEEL *from the Library List box*	Specifies material definitions to copy from materials library file into current drawing
Click on **I**mport	Copies material definitions from library file into current drawing
Click on OK	Creates RM-SDB blocks and inserts them for each new material

Related Commands

RENDER   RENDERUNLOAD   RMAT

MEASURE

Measure

MEASURE

Toolbar: *Measure (Draw, Point)*
Pull-down: *D̲raw*, *Poi̲n̲t*, *M̲easure*
Screen: DRAW2, Measure:

The MEASURE command places equally spaced points along an object at a specified distance. Blocks can be substituted for points if the blocks are already defined within the drawing with the BLOCK command. You can measure arcs, circles, lines, splines, and 2D or 3D polylines.

Prompts and Options

Select object to measure Pick the object to mark at equal distances. The MEASURE command works with only one object at a time. The starting location for the placement of points or blocks is the endpoint closest to the point used to pick the object. From the endpoint, measure points are calculated at equal intervals until no more will fit. You can use the Previous selection set option to select all the points or blocks placed along the object. Use the DDPTYPE command to alter the visual appearance of the points.

> The point objects placed by the MEASURE command are automatically placed into the Previous selection set. To quickly delete the points, use the ERASE command with the Previous selection set. You must do this, however, before creating any other selection sets.

<Segment length>/Block At this prompt, specify a distance or pick two points to show a distance for measuring the object. If you enter **B** to invoke the Block option, you must enter a block name already defined within the drawing at the prompt, Block name to insert. If you enter a block name, the following prompt appears:

Align block with object? <Y>:

Answer **Y** to rotate the inserted blocks about their insertion points so that they are aligned with the object being measured.

> If the PDMODE system variable is set to zero (PDMODE controls the appearance of point objects), the points placed by the MEASURE command are placed on the object but may not be visible. It is usually best to choose another point style (through DDPTYPE) so that you can see where the measurement marks are.

Example

This example shows how the MEASURE command draws points at even spacings along a spline. The object shown in figure M.3 contains points placed at eight-foot intervals.

Choose the Measure *tool*

Command: _measure	Issues the MEASURE command
Select object to measure: *Pick point* ① *(see fig. M.3)*	Chooses the object to measure
\<Segment length>/Block: **8'** (Enter)	Specifies the distance between points or blocks

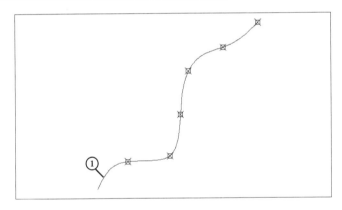

Figure M.3. *Blocks placed along a polyline with the MEASURE command.*

Related Commands

DDPTYPE   DIVIDE   POINT

Related System Variables

PDMODE   PDSIZE

MENU

Pull-down: *Tools, Menus...* (DOS Only)
Screen: TOOLS, Menu:

MENU

The MENU command enables you to load alternative menu files into the AutoCAD drawing editor. AutoCAD is supplied with the menu ACAD.MNU, which includes menu selections for each command supplied with the software. The ACADFULL.MNU file (Windows platform) expands the pull-down menu selection to more closely duplicate the DOS menu. Typically, add-on packages that increase the functionality of AutoCAD have a customized menu for accessing their functions. For example, when you install AutoVision, the ACAD.MNU file is modified so that you can have menu access to AutoVision commands.

Prompts and Options

By default, the MENU command displays a file dialog box that enables you to select the menu file you want to use. If the FILEDIA variable is set to 0, you see instead the `Menu File name or . for none <ACAD>:` prompt, where you enter the name of a valid menu file. The Select Menu File dialog box initially displays the names of any files with an MNU extension. If the file you want to load is in the list, you can highlight it and click on OK. You also can navigate the Directories: list box if the file is in a different drive or directory.

Related Commands

MENULOAD   MENUUNLOADT   PREFERENCES

Related System Variables

FILEDIA   MENUECHO   MENUNAME

MENULOAD (Windows Only)

Pull-down: _Tools_, Customize _M_enus...

The MENULOAD command enables you to add partial menu files to the existing main menu file (ACAD.MNU). Each menu file has a group name through which you can access the pull-down menu for that menu file. This command affects pull-down menus only. You can customize the menu bar by adding or removing predefined pull-down menus from the menu bar.

Dialog Box Items

The MENULOAD command displays the Menu Customization dialog box, which has the following options:

Menu Groups. The Menu Groups section of the Menu Customization dialog box (see fig. M.4) contains the following items:

Menu Groups. This list box lists the menu groups currently loaded.

File Name. Use this edit box to enter the name of a menu file to load when the Load button is selected. You optionally can use the Browse button to select a file from the Select Menu File dialog box.

Replace All. Use this check box to unload all existing menu groups from the drawing when you load a new menu file.

Unload. Use this button to remove the highlighted menu group from the Menu Groups list box.

Load. Use this button to load the file name entered in the File Name edit box.

Browse. Use this button to display the Select Menu File dialog box to select a menu file to load.

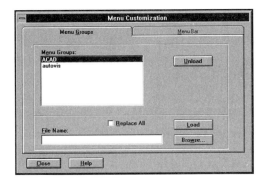

Figure M.4. *The Menu Groups section of the Menu Customization dialog box.*

Menu Bar. The Menu Bar section of the Menu Customization dialog box provides items for modifying the menu bar for pull-down menus in Windows (see fig. M.5).

Menu Group. This drop-down list box displays the menu file selected in the Menu Groups list box in the Menu Groups section.

Menus. This list box displays all the pull-down menu sections available in the menu group selected in the Menu Group drop-down list box.

Menu Bar. This list box displays all the pull-down menus currently loaded in AutoCAD. The list reads from top-to-bottom corresponding to the left-to-right order of the menus in the menu bar.

Insert. The Insert button inserts the highlighted menu from the Menus list box above the highlighted menu in the Menu Bar list box. If you have not highlighted a menu bar in the Menu Bar list, the menu is inserted at the top of the list, or at the far left of the menu bar. If your AutoCAD menu bar is visible, you can see the menu bar reflect the change you made.

Remove. The **R**emove button removes the highlighted menu in the Menu **B**ar list box from the menu bar.

Remove All. Use this button to remove all menus except **F**ile and **H**elp from the menu bar in AutoCAD.

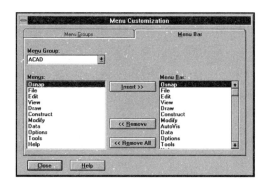

Figure M.5. *The Menu Bar section of the Menu Customization dialog box.*

Prompts and Options

When the system variable FILEDIA is set to zero, MENULOAD displays the following prompt:

`Menu file name or . for none <C:\ACADR13\WIN\SUPPORT\ACAD.MNC>:`

Example

The following example adds the Osnap pull-down menu to the AutoCAD menu bar (see fig. M.6). Note the change in the AutoCAD menu bar as you proceed.

Command: **_MENULOAD**	Issues the MENULOAD command
Select the **M***enu Bar section*	Displays the **M**enu Bar section
Choose Osnap *in the* **M***enus list box*	Selects the menu to add
Highlight File *in the* Menu **B***ar list box*	Determines placement of the menu in the menu bar

Choose **I**nsert	Inserts the Osnap menu above the File menu
Choose **C**lose	Closes the Menu Customization dialog box

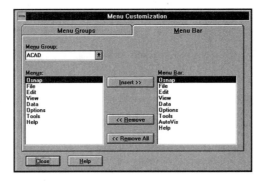

Figure M.6. *Adding a menu to the AutoCAD menu bar.*

Related Commands

MENU   MENUUNLOAD

MENUUNLOAD (Windows Only)

MENUUNLOAD provides the capability of removing a menu group when the FILEDIA system variable is set to zero. By default, the MENUUNLOAD command functions the same as the MENULOAD command in displaying the Menu Customization dialog box.

Prompts and Options

If the system variable FILEDIA is set to zero, the following prompt is displayed:

```
Enter the name of the MENUGROUP to unload :
```

Related Commands

MENU   MENULOAD

Related System Variable

FILEDIA

MINSERT

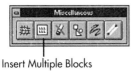

Insert Multiple Blocks

Toolbar: *Insert Multiple Blocks (Miscellaneous)*
Pull-down: *D*raw, Inse*r*t, *M*ultiple Blocks
Screen: DRAW2, Minsert:

The MINSERT (Multiple INSERT) command inserts a block multiple times in a rectangular pattern. This command combines the INSERT and ARRAY commands into a single command. After the MINSERT command has been used, the array of blocks becomes a single object that cannot be exploded. As a single object, it takes up less space in the drawing database. If you need to modify any of the individual blocks, use the INSERT and ARRAY commands instead.

While you cannot explode a minsert object, you can change any of its option settings at any time using the DDMODIFY command.

Prompts and Options

Block name (or ?) At this prompt, enter the name of a block defined in the current drawing or in the AutoCAD library search path. You may not precede a block with an asterisk (*) to insert it as pre-exploded, as you can with the INSERT command. You can enter a question mark to display a list of defined blocks, or enter a tilde (~) to display the Select Block dialog box to insert a drawing from disk.

Insertion point Specify the insertion point for the multiple arrayed block. This point is the location where the first block will be inserted in the array.

NOTE: You can use the same preset options that are available with the INSERT command.

X scale factor <1>   At this prompt, enter a scale factor for the block in the current X axis.

Y scale factor (default=X)   Enter a scale factor for the block in the current Y direction. By default, the Y scale factor is set to the same value as the X-axis scale factor.

Rotation angle   At this prompt, enter a non-zero number to rotate the array. This has the same effect as using the ROTATE command on an array of blocks.

Number of rows (—)   At this prompt, enter any positive, non-zero number for the number of rows of the array.

Number of columns (¦¦¦)   At this prompt, enter any positive, non-zero number for the number of columns of the array.

Unit cell or distance between rows (—)   Enter a number for the distance between rows of the block array. A positive number creates rows along the positive Y axis; a negative value creates rows along the negative Y axis. Specify a point to indicate that you want to show AutoCAD both the distance between rows and the distance between columns by defining a unit cell rectangle. The width of the rectangle becomes the column spacing; the height of the rectangle specifies the row spacing.

Other corner   Specify a unit cell rectangle corner point opposite the point specified above.

Distance between columns (¦¦¦)   Enter a number for the distance between columns of the array.

Example

This example demonstrates how to create an arrayed insertion of a chair block, as shown in figure M.7.

Choose the Minsert *tool*

Command: minsert	Issues the MINSERT command
Block name (or ?): **CHAIR** (Enter)	Specifies the block name to insert

```
Insertion point: Pick point ①      Specifies the start point of the array
(see fig. M.7)

X scale factor <1> / Corner / XYZ:  Accepts the default X-scale factor of 1
Enter

Y scale factor (default=X): Enter   Accepts the default Y-scale factor
                                    equal to the X-scale factor

Rotation angle <0>: Enter           Accepts the default rotation angle of 0

Number of rows (-—) <1>: 2 Enter    Specifies the number of rows in the
                                    array

Number of columns (|||) <1>: 4 Enter  Specifies the number of columns in
                                      the array

Unit cell or distance               Specifies the distance between rows
between rows (-—): 60 Enter         of blocks

Distance between columns (|||):     Specifies the distance between
30 Enter                            columns
```

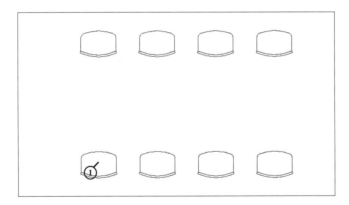

Figure M.7. *A 2 x 4 array of the chair block.*

Related Commands
ARRAY   BLOCK   DDINSERT   INSERT

Related System Variables
INSBASE   INSNAME

MIRROR

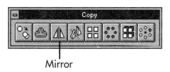
Mirror

Toolbar: *Mirror (Modify, Copy)*
Pull-down: <u>C</u>onstruct, <u>M</u>irror
Screen: CONSTRCT, Mirror:

The MIRROR command creates copies of selected objects symmetrically about a temporary mirror line. You can opt to remove the original objects from the drawing after the mirrored objects are created or leave the original objects intact.

Text, attribute, and attribute definition objects specified in a MIRROR selection set are literally mirrored to create new copies; they read backwards or upside-down depending on the angle of the mirror line. Associative dimension text is not affected. To mirror text, attributes, and attribute definitions so that the text reads correctly, set the MIRRTEXT system variable to zero. Text and constant attributes within a block will be inverted regardless of the value of MIRRTEXT.

In Release 13, you *can* explode a mirrored block.

Prompts and Options

Select objects   Select the objects to be mirrored.

First point of mirror line   Specify one endpoint of a rubber-band line, which can be of any length, that will serve as the line about which the objects will be mirrored.

Second point   Specify the second endpoint of the mirror line. The objects selected will be mirrored after you select this point.

Delete old objects? <N> If you press Enter at this prompt, the original objects remain in the drawing. If you answer **Y** to this prompt, the original objects will be erased after your mirrored objects are created.

You also can use the grip edit mirror mode. See the *AutoCAD User's Guide* for details.

Example

This example demonstrates the effects of using the MIRROR command. The points used to create the mirror line and the new objects created are shown in figure M.8.

Choose the Mirror *tool*

Command: mirror (Enter)	Issues the MIRROR command
Select objects: W (Enter)	Specifies the Window selection method
First corner: *Pick point* ① *(see fig. M.8)*	Specifies the first window point
Other corner: *Pick point* ②	Specifies the opposite window point
4 found	
Select objects: (Enter)	Terminates object selection
First point of mirror line: *Pick point* ③	Specifies the first mirror line endpoint
Second point: *Pick point* ④	Specifies the second mirror line endpoint
Delete old objects? <N> (Enter)	Determines whether original objects will be deleted

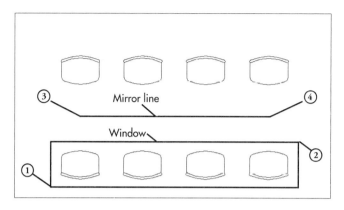

Figure M.8. *The mirrored objects.*

Related Command

COPY   ROTATE

Related System Variable

MIRRTEXT

MIRROR3D

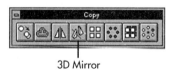

3D Mirror

Toolbar: *3D Mirror (Modify, Copy)*
Pull-down: *Construct, 3D Mirror*
Screen: CONSTRCT, Mirro3D:

The MIRROR3D command creates the mirror image of objects through a plane oriented in three-dimensional space.

Prompts and Options

Select objects Select the objects you want to mirror. You can use any of the AutoCAD object selection methods.

Plane by Entity/Last/Zaxis/View/XY/YZ/ZX/<3points> Specify the method of identifying the mirror image plane.

Entity The Entity option specifies the construction plane of a 2D object as the mirroring plane.

Pick circle, arc, or 2D-polyline segment Select an arc, circle, or 2D polyline to define the mirror plane.

Last The Last option specifies the last 3D mirroring plane. If there is no last plane, you are warned and reprompted with the original prompt. This method enables you to repeat the MIRROR3D command with different objects at different times.

Zaxis The Zaxis option specifies the mirroring plane as a point on a plane and a point on the Z axis normal to the plane.

Point on plane Pick a point in the graphics window, or enter the coordinates of a point that lies on the desired mirror plane.

Point on Z-axis (normal) of the plane Pick a point in the graphics window, or enter the coordinates of a point on the normal to the desired mirror plane. This defines the Z axis of the mirror plane.

View The View option aligns the mirroring plane with the current viewing plane through a selected point.

Point on view plane <0,0,0>: Pick a point in the graphics window, or enter the coordinates of a point that lies on the desired mirror plane. The current viewing direction defines the Z axis of the mirror plane.

XY, YZ, ZX The XY, YZ, and ZX options align the mirroring plane with either the XY, YZ, or ZX plane, respectively, that passes through a selected point.

Point on XY, YZ, or ZX plane <0,0,0> Pick a point in the graphics window, or enter the coordinates of a point for the mirroring plane to pass through.

3points This option specifies a mirroring plane that passes through three selected points. The 3points option has three prompts:

> **1st, 2nd, 3rd point on plane** Pick a point in the graphics window, or enter the coordinates of the first, second, and third points of the mirroring plane.
>
> **Delete old objects <N>** Enter **Y** to delete the object in its current location; enter **N** to duplicate the object in its mirrored location.

Example

The following example mirrors a cylinder about a three-dimensional plane using MIRROR3D. Create a cylinder with a center base at 10,0,5, radius of 2, and another center point at 10,10,5. The viewpoint is taken from the point 3, 2, 1, as seen in figure M.9.

Command: **MIRROR3D** (Enter)	Starts the MIRROR3D command
Select objects: *Pick cylinder at* ①	Selects cylinder for 3D mirroring
Select objects: (Enter)	Finishes selecting objects
Plane by Entity/Last/Zaxis/View/XY/YZ/ZX/<3points>: **10,10,3** (Enter)	Specifies first point on mirror plane
2nd point on plane: **8,9,5** (Enter)	Specifies second point on mirror plane
3rd point on plane: **12,9,5** (Enter)	Specifies third point on mirror plane
Delete old objects? <N> (Enter)	Retains old objects

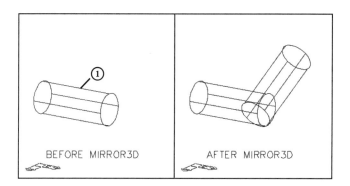

Figure M.9. *Creating the mirror image of a cylinder using MIRROR3D.*

Related Commands
MIRROR   ROTATE3D

Related System Variable
MIRRTEXT

MLEDIT

Edit Multiline

Toolbar: *Edit Multiline (Modify, Special Edit)*
Pull-down: *M*odify, Edit *M*ultiline...
Screen: MODIFY, Mledit:

The MLEDIT (MultiLine EDIT) command is used to perform simple editing of multiline objects. Multiline cross or tee intersections can be cleaned up, vertices can be added or removed, and corner intersections can be created, similar to the FILLET command.

Prompts and Options

As shown in figure M.10, the MLEDIT command displays the Multiline Edit Tools dialog box, which has the following options:

Closed Cross. Creates a closed cross intersection from the intersection of two multilines. At a closed cross intersection, the first multiline remains intact, and the second is trimmed away from the first.

Open Cross. Creates an open cross intersection from the intersection of two multilines. At an open cross intersection, the first multiline remains intact, and the outer lines of the second multiline are trimmed where they intersect those of the first. The inner lines of the second multiline remain intact.

Merged Cross. Creates a merged cross intersection from the intersection of two multilines. At a merged cross intersection, all lines of the first and second multilines are trimmed where they intersect.

Closed Tee. Creates a closed tee intersection from the intersection of two multilines. The first multiline is trimmed or extended to meet the second multiline. The second multiline remains intact.

Open Tee. Creates an open tee intersection from the intersection of two multilines. The first multiline is trimmed or extended to meet the second multiline. The second multiline's outer line is trimmed where it intersects those of the first.

Merged Tee. Creates a merged tee intersection from the intersection of two multilines. The first multiline is trimmed or extended to meet the second multiline. All lines of the second multiline on the side where they intersect the first are trimmed.

Corner Joint. Creates a corner joint of two multilines by extending or trimming the multilines until they meet at a corner. This is similar in operation to the FILLET command used on single lines with a fillet radius of zero.

Add Vertex. Inserts a vertex into the selected multiline at the point picked. The vertex is added in the line of the current multiline and is not immediately apparent.

Delete Vertex. Deletes the multiline vertex closest to the point picked. This has the effect of "straightening out" a multiline with bends in it.

Cut Single. Introduces a visible break on one line of a multiline between two picked points.

Cut All. Introduces a visible break on all lines of a multiline between two picked points.

Weld All. Removes all visible breaks from multilines between two picked points. Note that this will not join two separate multilines into one.

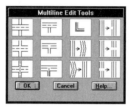

Figure M.10. *The Multiline Edit Tools dialog box.*

Once you have selected an option and clicked on OK or pressed Enter, MLEDIT issues the following command line prompts:

```
Select first mline
Select second mline
Select first mline(or Undo)
```

Example

The following example trims the intersection of a pair of multilines to meet in an open tee, as seen in figure M.11.

Command: **MLEDIT** (Enter)	Starts the MLEDIT command
Select the Open Tee icon	Specifies tee intersection cleanup
Click on OK	

```
Select first mline: Pick ①        Specifies minor multiline (multiline
(see fig. M.11)                    that ends at tee)
Select second mline: Pick ②       Specifies major multiline (multiline
                                   that breaks one side open at tee)
Select first mline(or Undo): Enter  Finishes MLEDIT command
```

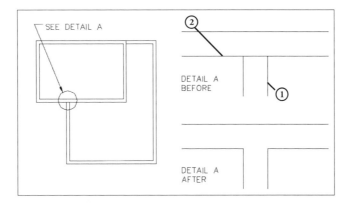

Figure M.11. *Cleaning up intersections of multilines with the MLEDIT command.*

Related Commands

EXTEND   FILLET   MLINE   MLSTYLE
PEDIT   TRIM

Related System Variables

CMLJUST   CMLSCALE   CMLSTYLE

MLINE

Toolbar: *Multiline (Draw, Polyline)*
Pull-down: *Draw, Multiline*
Screen: DRAW1, Mline:

The MLINE command creates multiple parallel lines. The lines can have separate color and linetype properties. Also, the distance between lines can vary, depending on the multiline style (see MLSTYLE). The MLINE command enables you to specify the justification (or offset) from the cursor as you draw. You also can specify the scale and style of the multiline to use. MLINEs can contain up to sixteen elements per style. The MLINE command cannot create arc segments.

Prompts and Options

The MLINE command presents the user with the following options:

```
Justification = Top, Scale = 1.00, Style = STANDARD
Justification/Scale/STyle/<From point>:
```

From point As with the LINE command, you specify a start point for the multiline. Once a point is specified, the <To point> prompt appears for the endpoint of the first segment of the multiline. The prompt, Undo/<To point>, appears for the endpoint of the second multiline segment. Entering **U** undoes the previous segment. When two MLINE segments have been drawn, the prompt, Close/Undo/<To point>, appears. Enter **Close** to create a closed MLINE object.

Justification The Justification option determines the position of the MLINE offset relative to the points you specify for the endpoints. See MLSTYLE for determining positive and negative offsets. This option issues the following prompt:

```
Top/Zero/Bottom <top>:
```

> **Top** The Top option draws the multiline such that the line with the most positive offset is drawn through the points you specify for the endpoints.
>
> **Zero** Use the Zero option to draw the multiline with its 0.0 offset at the points you specify.
>
> **Bottom** This option draws the multiline such that the line with the most negative offset is at the points you specify.

Figure M.12 illustrates the three justification options. The endpoints specified have been emphasized for clarity.

MLINE 425

Figure M.12. *Multiline top, zero, and bottom justification options.*

Scale   The Scale option affects the width of the multiline as it is defined in its style. A scale factor of 2 produces a multiline twice as wide as defined in its style. A negative scale factor reverses the order of offsets in the style, effectively mirroring the offsets. A zero scale factor reduces the multiline to a single line. Figure M.13 illustrates a five-line multiline at scale factors of 1, 2, and -1.5.

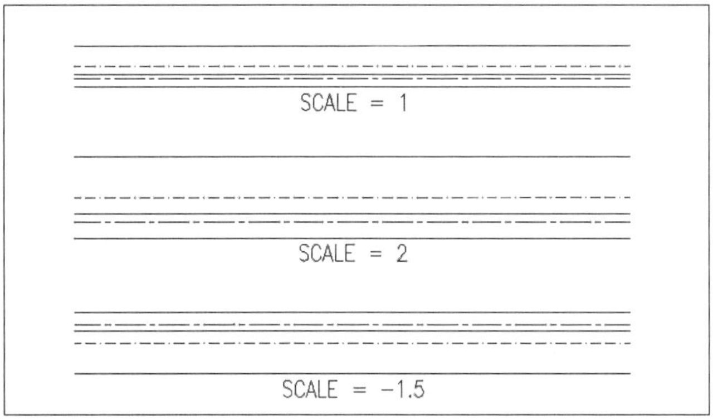

Figure M.13. *The effects of various scale factors on multilines.*

STyle   Use the STyle option to define the multiline style to use. This option issues the prompt, `Mstyle name (or ?)`. Type in a valid style name. The style name must be one already loaded in the drawing or contained in the standard Multiline Style library file ACAD.MLN. If you enter a **?**, AutoCAD lists the multiline styles defined in the drawing:

```
Loaded multiline styles:
     Name           Description
 _____        _____
STANDARD
```

Example

The following example creates a box using the STANDARD multiline style (see fig. M.14).

```
Choose the Multiline tool.

Command: _mline                              Issues the MLINE command

Justification = Top,                         Selects the Justification option
Scale = 1.00, Style = STANDARD
Justification/Scale/STyle/
<From point>: J (Enter)

Top/Zero/Bottom <top>: Z (Enter)             Selects zero justification

Justification = Zero,                        Specifies the start point of the MLINE
Scale = 1.00, Style = STANDARD
Justification/Scale/STyle/
<From point>: 2,2 (Enter)

<To point>: @12<0 (Enter)                    Specifies the endpoint of the first
                                             segment

Undo/<To point>: @8<90 (Enter)               Specifies the next endpoint

Close/Undo/<To point>: @12<180 (Enter)

Close/Undo/<To point>: C (Enter)             Closes the multiline and exits the
                                             command
```

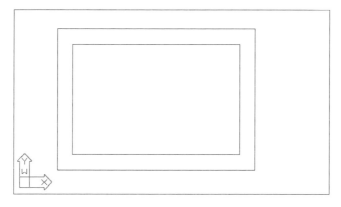

Figure M.14. *Using the MLINE command.*

Related Commands

LINE   MLEDIT   MLSTYLE

Related System Variables

CMLJUST   CMLSCALE   CMLSTYLE

MLSTYLE

Toolbar: *Multiline Style (Object Properties)*
Pull-down: **D**ata, **M**ultiline Style...
Screen: DATA, MLstyle:

The MLSTYLE command creates, modifies, loads, and saves multiline style definitions. Multilines consist of one or more parallel lines. Each line can have its offset distance, color, and linetype independently controlled. The joints of multilines can be displayed, and the end caps can be drawn flat, angled, curved, or omitted.

The last modified multiline style remains the current multiline style after exiting the MLSTYLE command. New multiline objects drawn with the MLINE command are drawn in that style. Use the PURGE command to remove defined multiline styles.

Prompts and Options

The MLSTYLE command displays a series of dialog boxes for controlling the different features of multiline styles.

The Multiline Styles Dialog Box

The Multiline Styles dialog box displays the name and description of the current multiline style (see fig. M.15). Additional multiline styles can be selected from the Current drop-down list box. You can also load multiline style definitions from a file, save the definitions from the current drawing to a file, add a new definition, or rename an existing definition. An image tile in the center of the dialog box displays the image of the current multiline style.

Figure M.15. *The Multiline Styles dialog box.*

Current. Specify a current multiline style by selecting from the available multiline styles listed in the drop-down list.

Name. Lists the name of the current multiline style.

Description. Lists the user-defined description of the current multiline style.

Load. Displays the Load Multiline Styles dialog box (discussed later). Use this dialog box to load a multiline style definition from an external file.

Save. Saves all of the multiline styles defined in the current drawing in a multiline style definition file. The file extension for a multiline style definition file is MLN. The multiline style definitions are saved in a format very similar to the DXF format in this file. Specify the file name to save the multiline style definitions in.

Add. Creates a new multiline style definition in the current drawing. Enter a new name in the Name edit box, and an optional description in the Description edit box, then click on the Add button.

Rename. Changes the name of an existing multiline style definition in the current drawing. Select the existing multiline style definition to be changed in the Current drop-down list, and enter a new name in the Name edit box. Then click on the Rename button.

Element Properties. Displays the Element Properties dialog box (discussed later) for adding or removing lines, or changing the offset, color, or linetype of lines in the current multiline style.

Multiline Properties. Displays the Multiline Properties dialog box (discussed later) for changing the joint display, end cap style, or fill mode of lines in the current multiline style.

The Load Multiline Styles Dialog Boxes

Once invoked from the previous Load option, the Load Multiline Styles dialog box is used to select a multiline style defined in a file for loading into the current drawing (see fig. M.16).

Figure M.16. *The Load Multiline Styles dialog box.*

File. Specify the multiline style definition file from which to load a specific multiline style(s). The styles available in the file are listed in the list box in the center of the dialog box. Select the multiline style(s) to load, and click on OK. If the selected multiline style is already loaded, an Invalid name error message is displayed.

The Element Properties Dialog Boxes

The Element Properties dialog box is opened from the previous Element Properties push button (see fig. M.17). It is used to add and remove lines from a multiline style, set the offset distance for each line, and set the color and linetype of each line.

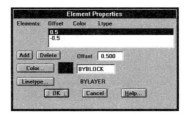

Figure M.17. *The Element Properties dialog box.*

Elements. Lists the lines defined in the current multiline style. The offset, color, and linetype assigned to each line is specified in the list box. Select a line to modify, and then click on the Add, Delete, Color, or Linetype push button(s).

Add. Click on the Add button to create a new line. The offset distance is set by the distance in the offset edit box.

> **NOTE:** You must specify the joint, end cap, and fill mode before adding a new multiline style. See the following Multiline Properties section.

Delete. Select the line to delete, and click on the Delete button to delete one of the lines from the current multiline style. You can delete all but the last line in the style.

Color. Click on the Color button to set the color of the currently selected line. The standard Select Color dialog box will be displayed. Select the desired color for the line, and click on OK. The current color is displayed in a color box to the right of the Color button.

Linetype. Click on the Linetype button to set the linetype of the currently selected line. The standard Select Linetype dialog box will be displayed. Select the desired color for the line, and click on OK. Use the LINETYPE command to load linetypes from a linetype definition file, or to create new linetypes on-the-fly. The current linetype is displayed to the right of the Linetype push button.

The Multiline Properties Dialog Boxes

Once invoked from the previous Multiline Properties option, the Multiline Properties dialog box is used to turn on or off the joint display, specify the type of end caps to be used, and to turn on and off the multiline fill (see fig. M.18).

Figure M.18. *The Multiline Properties dialog box.*

Display Joints. Check the Display Joints check box to display the joints of a multiline by drawing a continuous line across the multiline from one side to another. If the end caps are angled, the joint angle is the average of the start and end-cap angles.

> Displaying joints can be helpful in locating vertices of multilines where the two segments of the multiline are going the same direction. Without displaying the joints, this multiline appears as if no vertex exists.

TIP

Caps. Check the Line Start or Line End check boxes to close the ends of the multilines with a straight line. Check the Outer arc Start or Outer arc End check boxes to close the ends of the outermost pair of multilines with a semicircle arc. Check the Inner arc Start or Inner arc End check boxes to close all of the ends of the inner multilines with a semicircle arc. Specify an angle for the Start Angle or End Angle to draw the closing caps at a specific angle.

It is possible to have both line and arc end caps enabled simultaneously.

Fill. Check the Fill check box to fill the multiline with a specific color. The entire multiline is filled in, including any end caps.

Example

The following example creates a new multiline style called bevel using the MLSTYLE command. The bevel multiline style is comprised of three parallel lines, has the outer end caps drawn as semicircles, and is filled in with red.

Command: **MLSTYLE** (Enter)	Starts MLSTYLE command, displays Multiline Styles dialog box
Click on Multiline Properties	Displays Multiline Properties dialog box
Check the Outer arc Start *check box*	Draws multiline with semicircle closing starting end
Check the Outer arc End *check box*	Draws multiline with semicircle closing ending end
Check the Fill On *check box*	Draws multiline filled with a color
Click on Color	Displays Select Color dialog box
Specify standard color red	Selects color red for filling multiline
Click on OK	Closes Select Color dialog box
Click on OK	Closes Multiline Properties dialog box

Click on Element Properties	Displays Element Properties dialog box
Click on Add	Adds another line, at default offset 0.0
Edit the Offset to -.25	Changes offset of new line to -.25 from center of multiline
Click on OK	Closes Element Properties dialog box
Enter **BEVEL** in the Name edit box	Specifies name of new multiline style
Click on OK	Closes Multiline Styles dialog box

Related Commands

MLINE   MLEDIT

Related System Variables

CMLJUST   CMLSCALE   CMLSTYLE

MOVE

Move

Toolbar: *Move (Modify)*
Pull-down: <u>M</u>odify, M<u>o</u>ve
Screen: MODIFY, Move:

The MOVE command relocates objects to another position in a drawing. The MOVE command works both in 2D or 3D.

Prompts and Options

`Select objects`   Select the objects to be moved using AutoCAD's standard object selection methods.

`Base point or displacement`   Specify a base point for the move in the current User Coordinate System (UCS). The base point need not be on any selected object. Alternatively, you can enter an XYZ distance to move the current

MOVE

selection set. You can specify a 2D or 3D point, and the point's XYZ values will be considered the displacement for the selected objects in each of those axes.

Second point of displacement   After you specify a base, enter a second point to move the object or objects toward. You can enter a location by picking the point, entering a relative location, or giving an absolute XYZ location. If you press Enter at this prompt, the first point you specified is used as a relative XYZ displacement.

> For easier editing, use the grip edit move mode. See the *AutoCAD User's Guide* for details.

TIP

Example

This example shows a typical application of the MOVE command using relative displacement. The selected objects shown in figure M.19 are moved ten units in the positive X direction to a new location, as displayed in the figure.

Choose the Move *tool.*

Command: _move	Issues the MOVE command
Select objects: *Pick point* ① *(see fig. M.19)*	Specifies the first window corner
Other corner: *Pick point* ② 3 found	Specifies the opposite window corner
Select objects: **Enter**	Terminates object selection
Base point or displacement: **10,0**	Specifies a relative displacement
Second point of displacement: **Enter**	Moves the objects and terminates the command

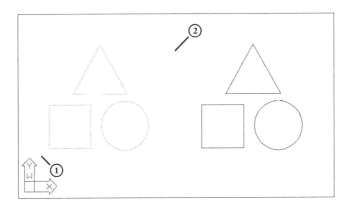

Figure M.19. *Using relative displacement to move objects.*

Related Commands

ALIGN   COPY   ROTATE   ROTATE3D
STRETCH

Related System Variable

GRIPS

MSLIDE

Pull-down: **T**ools, Sli**d**e, **S**ave...
Screen: TOOLS, Mslide:

The MSLIDE command creates slide files. Slides are raster images of the current screen display (like snapshots). The command-line area, screen menu area, status line, crosshairs, and UCS icon are not included in the slide image. Although slides cannot be edited like normal drawing files, they have the advantages of taking up little space on your disk and loading quickly. You can use slide files and libraries for image items in image menus, for referencing other drawings, and for creating presentations of your work.

AutoCAD is shipped with a utility for creating slide libraries called SLIDELIB.EXE. It is installed in the AutoCAD support directory.

Slide libraries store many slides more compactly and in a more organized fashion than individual slide files.

Prompts and Options

`Slide file <default>`   By default, the MSLIDE command displays a dialog box that enables you to enter the name of the slide file to create. If the FILEDIA variable is set to zero, you receive instead the `Slide file <default>` prompt, where you should enter the name to give the slide file. The Create Slide File dialog box initially displays the names of any current slide files. You can navigate the Directories list box if you want to save the slide in a different drive or directory.

The slide file is given the extension SLD. After you enter a valid file name, AutoCAD redraws the screen and creates the image file. Slides made in model space contain only the image in the current viewport. Slides made in paper space include all visible viewport objects and their contents. To make a slide, adjust your screen display with the AutoCAD display commands ZOOM, PAN, VIEW, and so on to achieve the view you want. Then execute the MSLIDE command.

You can create an automated slide show by using a script file in AutoCAD. See the SCRIPT and VSLIDE commands for more information.

Related Commands

SCRIPT   DELAY   HIDE   VSLIDE

MSPACE

  Screen: VIEW, Mspace:

The MSPACE command switches from paper space to model space and works only when paper space is active and at least one viewport has been created in paper space. In Windows, you can switch between model space and paper space by double-clicking the MODEL/PAPER area in the AutoCAD status bar. Model space is indicated by the presence of the crosshairs in only one of the viewports, called the *active* or *current viewport*. The model space UCS icon (see the icon in the lower left viewport in fig. M.20) is visible if the UCSICON command is on. The MSPACE command is not allowed if TILEMODE is set to 1.

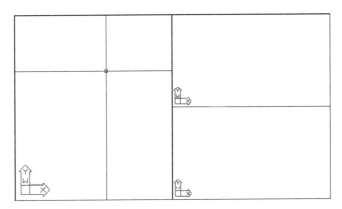

Figure M.20. *The left model space viewport activated using the MSPACE command.*

Example

This example demonstates changing from paper space to model space using the MSPACE command.

Command: **TILEMODE** (Enter)	Starts the SETVAR command to change TILEMODE
New value for TILEMODE <1>: **0** (Enter)	Changes to paper space
Entering Paper space. Use MVIEW to insert Model space viewports.	
Regenerating drawing.	
Command: **MVIEW** (Enter)	Starts the MVIEW command to create viewports
ON/OFF/Hideplot/Fit/2/3/4/ Restore/<First Point>: **3** (Enter)	Specifies the three viewport option
Horizontal/Vertical/Above/ Below/Left/<Right>: **L** (Enter)	Creates three viewports: one large one on left side of graphics window, with two smaller ones on right side
Fit/<First Point>: **F** (Enter)	Fits three new viewports into graphics window
Regenerating drawing.	
Command: **MSPACE** (Enter)	Changes from paper space to model space

Related Commands

DDVIEW   DDVPOINT   MVIEW   MVSETUP
PSPACE   UCSICON

Related System Variables

MAXACTVP   PSLTSCALE   TILEMODE   UCSICON
VISRETAIN

-MTEXT

Text

    Toolbar: *Text (Draw, Text)*
    Pull-down: *Draw, Text, Text*
    Screen: DRAW2, Mtext:

The MTEXT command creates paragraph text. You define a boundary for the text that specifies the width and alignment of the text. MTEXT objects are considered one object, regardless of how many lines of text it contains. You can manipulate the width, height, and placement of the paragraph text by manipulating its boundary box. Figure M.21 illustrates the same paragraph text before and after repositioning using its boundary box.

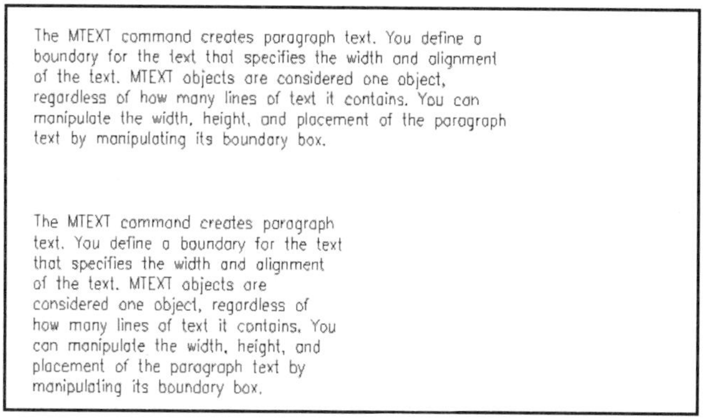

Figure M.21. *Manipulating MTEXT objects using the boundary box.*

On Windows systems, AutoCAD uses an internal MTEXT editor for creating and editing MTEXT objects. You can specify a different editor in the Preferences dialog box Misc. section. On DOS and Unix platforms, the MTEXT command uses an external text editor. On DOS systems, the default installation uses the MS-DOS EDIT.COM text editor.

Prompts and Options

`Attach/Rotation/Style/Height/Direction/<Insertion point>:`

`<Insertion point>` The default Insertion point option is used for specifying the first point of a boundary box for the text. The point you choose becomes the alignment point and starting point for the text. Once you specify this point, the following prompt is displayed:

`Attach/Rotation/Style/Height/Direction/Width/2Points/<Other corner>:`

`<Other corner>` At this prompt, specify the opposite corner of the boundary box for the text. The point you specify determines the size of the boundary box—not necessarily the placement of the text. It is important to note that the first point specified determines the placement and alignment of the text.

After you specify the size of the boundary box, AutoCAD displays the Edit Mtext dialog box (Windows systems) or the external text editor (DOS/Unix systems). The Edit Mtext dialog box is discussed in a later section.

Attach Use this option to control how the text boundary box is aligned with the insertion point of the text. The option selected determines the justification of the text within the boundary box as well as how the text flows (direction) within the boundary box. This option displays the following prompt showing the alignment options available. These options are discussed in detail in the DTEXT command section.

`TL/TC/TR/ML/MC/MR/BL/BC/BR:`

Rotation Use the Rotation option to specify the rotation angle of the text boundary box.

Style The Style option is used to specify the name of an existing text style to use for the paragraph text. This option displays the following prompt:

`Style name (or ?) <STANDARD>:`

After specifying a style name, AutoCAD repeats the previous prompt.

Height Use the Height option to specify the text height of uppercase text. At the following prompt, enter a positive value. AutoCAD will then return to the previous prompt, `Attach/Rotation/Style/Height/Direction/Width/2Points/<Other corner>.`

`Height <0.2000>:`

Direction Use this option to specify whether the text is drawn from left-to-right (horizontal) or top-to-bottom (vertical). This option displays the following prompt:

Horizontal/Vertical:

After you specify an option, AutoCAD will return to the previous prompt.

Width Use this option instead of the <Other corner> option to specify the width of the boundary box for the text.

2Points This option is similar to the Width option except that you specify the width of the text boundary box by picking two points.

Dialog Box Items

As shown in figure M.22, the Edit Mtext dialog box contains the text box for editing your selected text. Position the cursor in the edit box and begin typing your text. The text will automatically wrap to the next line as you type. Where the text line breaks in the edit box is not necessarily an indication of where the line breaks will be in the drawing.

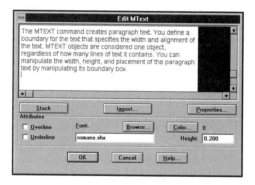

Figure M.22. *The Edit Mtext dialog box.*

AutoCAD uses the Unicode character encoding standard, which greatly increases the number of characters any one font file can contain. The Unicode standard was established to handle the large character sets of other languages. This capability of handling many characters was not available and was a limitation in earlier releases of AutoCAD. Unicode fonts can include as many as 65,535 characters. To enter a character that is not available from the keyboard, such as the degree symbol, the plus/minus tolerance symbol, and the diameter symbol, you must use a Unicode escape sequence. In Windows, you must use the percent sign (%) followed by a backslash U (\U) then a plus sign (+) and a hexadecimal number for the Unicode character. For example, you would type **180%\U+00B0F** for 180 degrees Fahrenheit. (In DOS systems, do not enter the percent (%) symbol.) The following escape codes are used in Unicode.

- %\U+00B0 degree symbol
- %\U+00B1 plus/minus tolerance symbol
- %\U+2205 diameter symbol

Table M.1 lists the Unicode hexadecimal code ranges and the corresponding character sets (adapted from *The Unicode Standard - World-Wide Character Encoding - Version 1.0* published by Addison Wesley).

Table M.1
Unicode Hexadecimal Code Ranges

Hexadecimal Code	Character Set
0000 - 007F	ASCII
0080 - 00FF	Latin1 Characters
0100 - 017F	European Latin
0180 - 01FF	Extended Latin
0200 - 024F	<Bad unicode range>
0250 - 02AF	Standard Phonetic
02B0 - 02FF	Modifier Letters
0300 - 036F	Generic Diacritical Marks
0370 - 03FF	Greek
0400 - 04FF	Cyrillic
0500 - 052F	<Bad unicode range>
0530 - 058F	Armenian
0590 - 05FF	Hebrew
0600 - 06FF	Arabic
0900 - 1FFF	<not specified in table>
2000 - 206F	General Punctuation
2070 - 209F	Superscripts & Subscripts
20A0 - 20CF	Currency Symbols

Hexadecimal Code	*Character Set*
20D0 - 20FF	Diacritical Marks for Symbols
2100 - 214F	Letterlike Symbols
2150 - 218F	Number Forms
2190 - 21FF	Arrows
2200 - 22FF	Mathematical Operators
2300 - FFFF	<not specified in table>

The font files supplied with AutoCAD support Unicode character encoding to a certain extent. As noted in the previous table, Unicode characters 0000 through 007F hex (0–127 decimal) are standard ASCII characters that can be accessed through the keyboard. For other characters, you will need to use the Unicode escape sequence. The following charts show most of the Unicode character codes used in the AutoCAD font file ROMANS.SHX. The charts show three columns. The first is the decimal equivalent of the hexadecimal character code shown in the second column. The third column is the character generated by the Unicode sequence in AutoCAD.

33	0021	!	57	0039	9	81	0051	Q	105	0069	i
34	0022	"	58	003A	:	82	0052	R	106	006A	j
35	0023	#	59	003B	;	83	0053	S	107	006B	k
36	0024	$	60	003C	<	84	0054	T	108	006C	l
37	0025	%	61	003D	=	85	0055	U	109	006D	m
38	0026	&	62	003E	>	86	0056	V	110	006E	n
39	0027	'	63	003F	?	87	0057	W	111	006F	o
40	0028	(	64	0040	@	88	0058	X	112	0070	p
41	0029	)	65	0041	A	89	0059	Y	113	0071	q
42	002A	*	66	0042	B	90	005A	Z	114	0072	r
43	002B	+	67	0043	C	91	005B	[	115	0073	s
44	002C	,	68	0044	D	92	005C	\	116	0074	t
45	002D	-	69	0045	E	93	005D	]	117	0075	u
46	002E	.	70	0046	F	94	005E	^	118	0076	v
47	002F	/	71	0047	G	95	005F	_	119	0077	w
48	0030	0	72	0048	H	96	0060	`	120	0078	x
49	0031	1	73	0049	I	97	0061	a	121	0079	y
50	0032	2	74	004A	J	98	0062	b	122	007A	z
51	0033	3	75	004B	K	99	0063	c	123	007B	{
52	0034	4	76	004C	L	100	0064	d	124	007C	|
53	0035	5	77	004D	M	101	0065	e	125	007D	}
54	0036	6	78	004E	N	102	0066	f	126	007E	~
55	0037	7	79	004F	O	103	0067	g	127	007F	?
56	0038	8	80	0050	P	104	0068	h			

Figure M.23. *Unicodes 0021 through 007F in ROMANS.SHX.*

161	00A1	¡	200	00C8	È	228	00E4	ä	260	0104	Ą	353	0161	š
162	00A2	¢	201	00C9	É	229	00E5	å	261	0105	ą	356	0164	Ť
163	00A3	£	202	00CA	Ê	230	00E6	æ	262	0106	Ć	357	0165	ť
164	00A4	?	203	00CB	Ë	231	00E7	ç	263	0107	ć	366	016E	Ů
165	00A5	¥	204	00CC	Ì	232	00E8	è	268	010C	Č	367	016F	ů
167	00A7	§	205	00CD	Í	233	00E9	é	269	010D	č	368	0170	Ű
170	00AA	ª	206	00CE	Î	234	00EA	ê	270	010E	Ď	369	0171	ű
171	00AB	«	207	00CF	Ï	235	00EB	ë	271	010F	ď	377	0179	Ź
176	00B0	°	209	00D1	Ñ	236	00EC	ì	280	0118	Ę	378	017A	ź
177	00B1	±	210	00D2	Ò	237	00ED	í	281	0119	ę	379	017B	Ż
181	00B5	µ	211	00D3	Ó	238	00EE	î	282	011A	Ě	380	017C	ż
186	00BA	º	212	00D4	Ô	239	00EF	ï	283	011B	ě	381	017D	Ž
187	00BB	»	213	00D5	Õ	241	00F1	ñ	321	0141	Ł	382	017F	ž
188	00BC	¼	214	00D6	Ö	242	00F2	ò	322	0142	ł			
189	00BD	½	216	00D8	Ø	243	00F3	ó	323	0143	Ń			
190	00BE	?	217	00D9	Ù	244	00F4	ô	324	0144	ń			
191	00BF	¿	218	00DA	Ú	245	00F5	õ	327	0147	Ň			
192	00C0	À	219	00DB	Û	246	00F6	ö	328	0148	ň			
193	00C1	Á	220	00DC	Ü	247	00F7	÷	336	0150	Ő			
194	00C2	Â	221	00DD	Ý	248	00F8	ø	337	0151	ő			
195	00C3	Ã	223	00DF	ß	249	00F9	ù	344	0158	Ř			
196	00C4	Ä	224	00E0	à	250	00FA	ú	345	0159	ř			
197	00C5	Å	225	00E1	á	251	00FB	û	346	015A	Ś			
198	00C6	Æ	226	00E2	â	252	00FC	ü	347	015B	ś			
199	00C7	Ç	227	00E3	ã	253	00FD	ý	352	0160	Š			
						255	00FF	ÿ						

Figure M.24. *Unicodes 00A1 through 017E in ROMANS.SHX.*

1040	0410	А	1064	0428	Ш	1088	0440	р	8359	20A7	₧
1041	0411	Б	1065	0429	Щ	1089	0441	с	8486	2126	Ω
1042	0412	В	1066	042A	Ъ	1090	0442	т	8709	2205	∅
1043	0413	Г	1067	042B	Ы	1091	0443	у	8734	221E	∞
1044	0414	Д	1068	042C	Ь	1092	0444	ф	8804	2264	≤
1045	0415	Е	1069	042D	Э	1093	0445	х			
1046	0416	Ж	1070	042E	Ю	1094	0446	ц			
1047	0417	З	1071	042F	Я	1095	0447	ч			
1048	0418	И	1072	0430	а	1096	0448	ш			
1049	0419	Й	1073	0431	б	1097	0449	щ			
1050	041A	К	1074	0432	в	1098	044A	ъ			
1051	041B	Л	1075	0433	г	1099	044B	ы			
1052	041C	М	1076	0434	д	1100	044C	ь			
1053	041D	Н	1077	0435	е	1101	044D	э			
1054	041E	О	1078	0436	ж	1102	044E	ю			
1055	041F	П	1079	0437	з	1103	044F	я			
1056	0420	Р	1080	0438	и						
1057	0421	С	1081	0439	й						
1058	0422	Т	1082	043A	к						
1059	0423	У	1083	043B	л						
1060	0424	Ф	1084	043C	м						
1061	0425	Х	1085	043D	н						
1062	0426	Ц	1086	043E	о						
1063	0427	Ч	1087	043F	п						

Figure M.25. *Unicodes 0410 through 2264 in ROMANS.SHX.*

> **NOTE**
>
> Release 13 still supports the older %% escape sequences for generating symbols. For example, %%C generates the diameter symbol, %%D the degree symbol, and %%P the plus/minus symbol. This feature, however, will be dropped in future releases of AutoCAD.

In addition to the Unicode character sequences previously described for generating special characters, AutoCAD uses special formatting codes for underlining, overlining, color, height, stacking, tracking, obliquing, width, and ending paragraphs. Use these codes if you are using the DOS or Unix versions of AutoCAD or are using an external text editor on the Windows platform. Formatting text on the Windows platform can be done through the Edit Mtext dialog box. The following chart lists the format codes and their descriptions. Note that case is important when typing format codes.

Table M.2
Descriptions of Format Codes

Format code	Description
\O	Overline on
\o	Overline off
\L	Underline on
\l	Underline off
\~	Inserts a non-breaking space for keeping words together on the same line
\\	Inserts a backslash
\{	Inserts an opening curly brace {
\}	Inserts a closing brace }
\C*nnn*	Changes the subsequent characters to the specified color number
\F*file name;*	Changes the subsequent characters to the specified font file
\H*nnn*	Changes the subsequent characters to the specified text height
\S...^...	Stacks the subsequent text at the ^ or \ symbol
\T*nnn*	Adjusts character spacing (values range from .75 to 4 times)
\Q*nnn*	Changes the oblique angle of the subsequent text
\W*nnn*	Changes the width factor of the subsequent text
\P	Ends the paragraph

You can use curly braces to format text only within the braces. Braces can be nested up to eight levels deep.

The other items in the Edit Mtext dialog box are used for assigning attributes and properties to the text.

Stack. This button is used to create stacked fractions, tolerances, or for placing a piece of text above another. To stack text, insert a forward slash (/) at the point in the text where you would like the horizontal line drawn separating the text. Next, highlight the text to stack (upper and lower portion) and choose the **S**tack button.

NOTE: Early shipments of AutoCAD Release 13 exhibit problems displaying stacked text.

Import. This button displays the Import Text File dialog box. Use this option to import an ASCII text file into your drawing. The text is displayed in the Edit Mtext dialog box edit box.

Properties. This button displays the Mtext Properties dialog box (see fig. M.26). Use this button to change the text style, height, direction, point of attachment, width of the text box, and rotation.

Figure M.26. *The Mtext Properties dialog box.*

The Mtext Properties dialog box duplicates the functionality of the previous command-line prompts. The Contents section contains the following three items:

- Text **S**tyle pull-down list box for specifying the text style for any new or selected text.
- Text Hei**g**ht edit box for entering a positive real number for the height of any new or selected text.
- **D**irection pull-down list box for specifying a Left-to-Right or Top-to-Bottom direction for drawing the text paragraph.

The Object section of the Mtext Properties dialog box also contains three items, as follows:

- **A**ttachment pull-down list box for specifying the justification of the text paragraph in relation to the text boundary box. See the Attach option.
- **W**idth edit box for entering a positive real number to specify the width of the text boundary box.
- **R**otation edit box for entering a real number to specify the rotation angle of the text boundary box.

The following Edit Mtext dialog box items are included in the Attributes section of the dialog box.

Overline. If this check box is checked, any new text entered at the current cursor position in the edit box or any selected text in the edit box is overlined.

Underline. If this check box is checked, any new text entered at the current cursor position in the edit box or any selected text in the edit box is underlined.

Font. The font name specified in this edit box becomes the new font for new text entered at the current cursor position or any selected text. Use the **B**rowse button to display the Change Font dialog box for selecting a font file.

Browse. The Browse button displays the Change Font dialog box for selecting font files (see the Font option).

Color. Use the Color button to display the Select Color dialog box. The selected color becomes the color for new text or any selected text.

Height. Use the Height edit box to enter a positive real number for the height of new text or any selected text.

Example

The following example illustrates the use of the MTEXT command.

Choose the Text *tool.* *Tool:* [Text](Draw, Text)	Issues the MTEXT command
`Command: mtext`	

`Attach/Rotation/Style/Height`
`/Direction/<Insertion point>:`
Pick point ① *(see fig. M.27)*
	Specifies the insertion point of the text

`Attach/Rotation/Style/Height`
`/Direction/Width/2Points`
`/<Other corner>:` *Pick point* ②
	Specifies the opposite corner of the boundary box

Enter **ALL DIMENSIONS +.005/-.005 UNLESS NOTED OTHERWISE** *in the dialog box edit box*	Enters paragraph text
Highlight +.005/-.005 *and choose* **S**tack	Stacks the selected text at the "/" character
Choose OK	Closes the Edit Mtext dialog box and places text on drawing

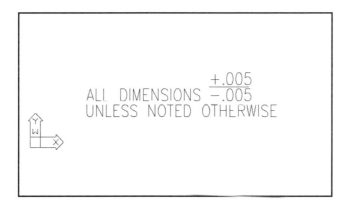

Figure M.27. *Creating paragraph text with stacked text.*

Related Commands

DTEXT	LEADER	MTPROP	PREFERENCES
QTEXT	SPELL	STYLE	TEXT

Related System Variables

FONTALT FONTMAP MTEXTED

MTPROP

The MTPROP command enables you to change the properties of paragraph text that was created using the MTEXT or LEADER commands. You can change the style, height, and direction of the text as well as the alignment point, width of the boundary box, and rotation. The MTPROP command duplicates the functionality of the Properties button in the Edit Mtext dialog box when MTEXT is selected for the DDMODIFY command. The MTPROP command displays the Mtext Properties dialog box, shown in figure M.28.

Figure M.28. *The Mtext Properties Dialog box.*

Prompts and Options

`Select an MText object`   Select a multiline text object. The Mtext Properties dialog box is displayed, listing the current properties of the selected multiline text object.

Dialog Box Items

See the Dialog Box Items section of the MTEXT command for discussions concerning the Mtext Properties dialog box functions.

Example

The following example uses the MTPROP command to modify an existing multiline text object. The original MText object (see the upper left Mtext object of fig. M.29) has its justification changed to TopCenter and its width increased to 9.0 (see the lower Mtext object of fig. M.29).

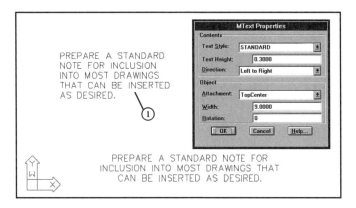

Figure M.29. *The multiline text object, before and after modification using MTPROP.*

Command: **MTPROP** (Enter)	Starts MTPROP command
Select an MText object: *Select* ① *(refer to fig. M.29)*	Selects Mtext object to modify, displays Mtext Properties dialog box
Click on the **A***ttachment drop-down list, select* TopCenter	Selects TopCenter justification
Enter **9.0** *in the* **W***idth edit box*	Specifies new width for Mtext object
Click on OK	Updates Mtext object with new properties

Related Commands

DDEDIT   DDMODIFY   MTEXT   PREFERENCES
STYLE

Related System Variables

FONTALT   FONTMAP   MTEXTED

MULTIPLE

MULTIPLE is a command modifier for issuing another command many times in succession. Enter **MULTIPLE** at the Command: prompt, followed by the name of the command to be repeated. The command is repeated until you cancel it by pressing Ctrl+C or Escape. You can use MULTIPLE with any command except PLOT, QUIT, END, and any dialog-based commands. MULTIPLE is an invalid argument for the AutoLISP COMMAND function.

The MULTIPLE command does not function the same as the Multiple option of the COPY or SELECT commands. The MULTIPLE command does not remember any of the specified command's options. If you specify MULTIPLE INSERT, for example, you must answer all the INSERT command's prompts each time the command is repeated.

MVIEW

Pull-down: **V**iew, Floating Viewports
Screen: VIEW, Mview:

The MVIEW command controls the creation and display of viewports in paper space. MVIEW creates new viewports, turns on and off existing viewports, and controls hidden line removal on a per-viewport basis. The TILEMODE system variable must be set to 0 (off) in order to use the MVIEW command. If model space is active, AutoCAD switches to paper space to perform the MVIEW command. The maximum number of active viewports varies from system to system. For DOS and Windows, it is 48. Set the MAXACTVP system variable to the number of viewports you want to activate at any one time.

Prompts and Options

<First point>   Specify the first corner of an area to enclose the viewport(s).

Other corner   Specify the opposite corner of the area to enclose the viewport(s). After you specify the second point, the current model space view is displayed in the newly created viewport(s).

Fit   This creates a viewport the same size as the graphics window. Use the ZOOM command, .9x option, to see the viewport just created.

ON   The ON option enables the display of model space objects within the selected viewports. Select the viewports by picking the viewport border(s). Any model space objects visible in the viewport are then displayed.

OFF   The OFF option disables the display of all model space objects within the selected viewport(s). If you select all the viewports, AutoCAD advises you

```
Really want to turn off all active viewports? <N>
```

If you enter **N**, the MVIEW command finishes without altering the visibility of any of the selected viewports.

Hideplot   Hideplot controls whether hidden lines are removed in the selected viewport(s) when paper space is plotted. You can turn on or turn off removal of hidden lines on a viewport-by-viewport basis. Turning on hidden-line removal plots the viewport with hidden lines removed. Turning off hidden-line removal plots the viewport without removing hidden lines.

2   Creates two equal-size paper space viewports either side-by-side or one directly over the other. Horizontal creates a horizontal division between the two viewports—the two viewports are created one directly over the other. Vertical (the default) creates a vertical division—the two viewports are created side-by-side. Choose either Horizontal or Vertical orientation and specify the viewport area using the Fit or First point option.

3   Creates three viewports, either three the same size side-by-side, three the same size one above another, or one large and two small.

Horizontal/Vertical/Above/Below/Left/<Right> Choose Horizontal or Vertical to create three viewports the same size. Horizontal places them one above the other. Vertical places them side-by-side. Choose Above, Below, Left, or Right to create three viewports, with one large one above, below, to the left, or to the right, respectively, of two smaller ones. Specify the viewport area using the Fit or First point option.

4 Creates four equal-size paper space viewports. Specify the viewport area using the Fit or First point option.

Restore Creates a paper space viewport configuration equivalent to a model space viewport configuration saved with the VPORTS command. The Restore option is an effective way to transfer views created for modeling purposes to paper space for plotting.

?/Name of window configuration to insert <default> Enter the name of the viewport configuration to retrieve into paper space, or enter **?** to list the saved viewport configurations within the current drawing. Specify the viewport area using the Fit or First point option.

Example

The following example uses MVIEW to create three viewports, a large one below two smaller ones, within paper space (see fig. M.30).

Command: **MVIEW** (Enter)	Starts the MVIEW command
ON/OFF/Hideplot/Fit/2/3/4/ Restore/<First Point>: **3** (Enter)	Specifies the three viewport option
Horizontal/Vertical/Above/ Below/Left/<Right>: **B** (Enter)	Creates new viewports with large one below two smaller ones
Fit/<First Point>: *Pick point at* ① *(see fig. M.30)*	Specifies lower left corner for viewports
Second point: *Pick point at* ②	Specifies upper right corner for viewports
Regenerating drawing.	

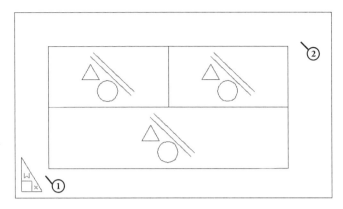

Figure M.30. *Three viewports created with the MVIEW command.*

Related Commands

MSPACE   MVSETUP   PSPACE   VPLAYER
VPORTS

Related System Variables

CVPORT   MAXACTVP   PSLTSCALE   TILEMODE
VISRETAIN

MVSETUP

Pull-down: <u>V</u>iew, Floating Viewports, MV <u>S</u>etup

The MVSETUP AutoLISP program provides automated drawing setup for AutoCAD. It supports both paper space and model space. If you want to use only model space, the MVSETUP routine performs the drawing setup as the SETUP command did in versions of AutoCAD prior to Release 11. If you want to use both paper space and model space, however, MVSETUP enables you to define, align, and scale viewports, as well as to place a title block in paper space within which the model space viewports can be arranged.

The MVSETUP program has two branches to the setup routine. The model space only branch executes the setup routine that AutoCAD used in pre-Release 11 versions. This routine is limited to setting the proper units and scale, and to inserting a border scaled to the paper size on which you will be plotting. The paper space branch invokes the paper space setup routine that places a drawing border in paper space and enables you to define viewports to display your model space entities. To use the pre-Release 11 model space setup option, answer **N** at the `Enable paper space? (No/<Yes>):` prompt.

The pull-down menu selection automatically enables paper space.

Prompts and Options

`Enable paper space? (No/<Yes>)`   The type of setup performed depends on whether paper space is activated. If you answer **N**, the following model space setup routine is used. If you activate paper space, the paper space setup routine is performed. AutoCAD displays this prompt only if TILEMODE is set to 1; the paper space setup routine is executed if TILEMODE is set to 0 when the MVSETUP command is issued.

The Model Space Setup Routine Prompts and Options

`Units type (Scientific/Decimal/Engineering/Architectural/Metric)`   Choose the units option for the units you want to use. MVSETUP displays a sampling of common scales for that type of units:

```
Decimal Scales          Metric Scales           Architectural Scales
==============          =============           ====================
(4.0)   4 TIMES         (5000)  1:5000          (480)   1/40"=1'
(2.0)   2 TIMES         (2000)  1:2000          (240)   1/20"=1'
(1.0)   FULL            (1000)  1:1000          (192)   1/16"=1'
(0.5)   HALF            (500)   1:500           (96)    1/8"=1'
(0.25)  QUARTER         (100)   1:100           (48)    1/4"=1'
                        (75)    1:75            (24)    1/2"=1'
                        (50)    1:50            (16)    3/4"=1'
                        (20)    1:20            (12)    1"=1'
                        (10)    1:10            (4)     3"=1'
                        (5)     1:5             (2)     6"=1'
                        (1)     FULL            (1)     FULL
```

`Enter the scale factor`   Enter a scale factor, as listed in the left column from the preceding lists. The scale factors listed earlier are examples of the most commonly used scale factors for decimal, metric, and architectural use. MVSETUP accepts any real number at this prompt.

`Enter the paper width:, Enter the paper height`   Enter the desired paper width and height. AutoCAD sets the limits of the drawing to a rectangle (paper width×scale factor) by (paper height×scale factor) and inserts a polyline border around these limits. The LTSCALE system variable is not changed.

The Paper Space Setup Routine

The paper space setup routine is executed if you answer yes to the `Enable paper space? (No/<Yes>):` prompt or if the TILEMODE system variable is set to 0 when the MVSETUP command is issued. When paper space is activated, the MVSETUP command automates the process of inserting a title block, creating paper space viewports, scaling paper space viewports, and aligning the views of paper space viewports.

`Align/Create/Scale viewports/Options/Title block/Undo`   Select the Align option to align the views between viewports. Select the Create option to create new viewports. Select the Scale option to change the view scale factor in selected viewports. Select the Options option to control limits, title block layer, drawing units, and title block insertion method, either XREF or INSERT. Select the Title block option to control the available title blocks and to insert a title block into the drawing. Select the Undo option to reverse the effects of the previous MVSETUP option. Each of these options, except Undo, has its own series of prompts, discussed in the following sections.

Align

`Angled/Horizontal/Vertical alignment/Rotate view/Undo`   If you select the Align option, MVSETUP presents this prompt. Select the Angled option to pan the view in one viewport to a position a specific distance and direction from a basepoint in another. Select the Horizontal or Vertical options to align the views in two viewports either horizontally or vertically. Select the Rotate option to rotate the view in a viewport. All four options present the following prompts:

`Basepoint`   Specify a reference point in a viewport. For the Angled option, this establishes the basepoint for the pan view location. For the Horizontal or Vertical options, this establishes the first reference point. For the Rotate option, this is the base point for the rotation.

`Other point`   Specify a "target" point in a different viewport. If the Horizontal option was chosen, MVSETUP pans this viewport up or down to align the base point and this target point. If the Vertical option was chosen, MVSETUP pans this viewport left or right to align the target point with the base point. If the Angled option was chosen, this is the destination reference point in the second viewport, and AutoCAD prompts

```
Specify the distance and angle to the new alignment point
in the current viewport where you specified the basepoint.
```

Distance from basepoint Enter the desired paper space distance from the base point to the target point.

Angle from basepoint Enter the desired paper space angle from the base point to the target point. Note that if the angle is either 0 or 180 degrees, this option has the same effect as Horizontal. If the angle is either 90 or 270 degrees, this option has the same effect as Vertical.

> After aligning different views, it may be necessary to resize the viewport without altering the view location. Use the STRETCH command to stretch the corners of the viewports without altering their views.

Specify in which viewport the view is to be rotated... Basepoint This prompt appears if the Rotated option is chosen from the Angled/Horizontal/Vertical alignment/Rotate view/Undo: prompt. Select the basepoint for rotating the view.

Angle from basepoint Pick a point in the viewport or enter an angle to rotate the view.

Create

Delete objects/Undo/<Create viewports> If you select the Create option, MVSETUP presents this prompt. Select the Delete option to erase viewport objects. Select the Create option to create new viewports.

Create viewports Creates new viewports, using one of three possible layouts. The three supplied viewport layout options are the following:

```
Available Mview viewport layout options:
    0:      None
    1:      Single
    2:      Std. Engineering
    3:      Array of Viewports
```

Redisplay/<Number of entry to load> Enter a number, 0–3, representing the viewport layout to create, or enter **R** to choose to redisplay the viewport layout options. Entering **0** (the None option) returns you to the previous prompt. Entering **1** creates a single viewport, within the bounding area specified next. Entering **2** creates four viewports of equal size within the bounding area. The lower left viewport is a front view; the lower right is a right side view; the upper left is a top view; and the upper right is an isometric view. Entering **3** creates a rectangular array of viewports that you define by entering the number of rows and columns.

MVSETUP

> The number of active viewports permitted in paper space varies from system to system. Both the DOS and Windows verstions of AutoCAD allow up to 48 active viewports. If you need more than this number of viewports, you must turn off some viewports to allow others to be turned on. Use the MVIEW command to turn on and off viewports. Set the system variable MAXACTVP to the number of viewports you want to have active at any one time.

Bounding area for viewports. Default/<First point > Specify the first point of the bounding area for the viewport(s). If a title block has not yet been inserted, the Default option is not available. If a title block has been inserted, selecting the Default option places the viewports at predetermined positions within the title block.

Other point Specify the location of the opposing corner of the bounding area for the viewport(s).

Distance between viewports in X, Y. <0.0> Enter a gap distance to be placed between adjacent viewports. The X distance is the distance between adjacent columns, and the Y distance is the distance between adjacent rows.

Number of viewports in X, Y. <1> Enter the number of columns (viewports in X) and the number of rows (viewports in Y) to create. You can create an array of one row and one column if you want. Entering a negative number for both creates just one viewport, below and to the left of the bounding area. Entering a negative number for X and a positive value for Y creates one viewport to the left of the bounding area. Entering a positive number for X and a negative value for Y creates one viewport below the bounding area.

Select the objects to delete... Select objects Select any objects you want to delete. MVSETUP does not filter for viewport objects only—any AutoCAD object can be deleted with this option.

Scale Viewports

Select the viewports to scale... Select objects If you select the Scale option, MVSETUP presents this prompt. Select the viewport objects to adjust the model space scale factor.

Set zoom scale factors for viewports. Interactively/<Uniform> If you selected more than one viewport at the preceding prompt, you are presented with this prompt. Select the Interactively option to set the model space scale factor viewport by viewport. Select the Uniform option to apply one scale factor to all the selected viewports. MVSETUP prompts:

```
Enter the ratio of paper space units to model space units...
```

For each viewport that you scale, you must define the ratio of paper space units to model space units.

Number of paper space units. <1.0> Enter the number of paper space units per model space unit. For example, if the desired plotting scale is 1/4" = 1', enter **1/4**. For an eighth scale mechanical drawing, the desired plotting scale is 1:8, so enter **1** here.

Number of model space units. <1.0> Enter the number of model space units per paper space unit. For example, if the desired plotting scale is 1/4" = 1', enter **1'** (or **12**). For an eighth scale mechanical drawing, the desired plotting scale is 1:8, so enter **8** here.

> MVSETUP scales the viewports by a factor determined by dividing the model space units by the paper space units. Entering **1/4** for the paper space and **12** for the model space is equivalent to entering **1** for the paper space and **48** for the model space.

Options

Set Layer/LImits/Units/Xref If you select the Options option, MVSETUP presents this prompt. Select the Layer option to enter a layer for the title block, or the LImits option to set drawing limits. Select the Units option to define the type of paper space units, or the Xref option to insert the title block as a standard block or an Xref.

Layer name for title block or . for current layer Enter the name of a layer on which to place the title block created by MVSETUP. Enter a period to place the title block on the current layer. If the layer does not exist, it is created by MVSETUP.

Set drawing limits? <N> Enter **Y** at this prompt to automatically set the paper space limits to the size of the title block.

Paperspace units are in Feet/Inches/MEters/Millimeters? <in> Choose the unit type for paper space units. The default is inches.

Xref Attach or Insert title block? <Insert> Enter the insertion method for the title block. If you specify Insert, the title block will be inserted as a block in your drawing. If you specify Xref, the title block will be attached as an external reference.

Title Block

Delete objects/Origin/Undo/<Insert title block> If you select the Title block option, MVSETUP presents this prompt. Select the Delete objects option to erase paper space objects. Select the Origin option to change the insertion point of the title block. Select the Insert title block option to insert or attach an external reference title block.

Insert title block Controls insertion of a title block from a list of available title blocks. You may add and remove title blocks from the list. MVSETUP prints the list of available title blocks, which initially appears as:

```
Available title block options:
     0:      None
     1:      ISO A4 Size(mm)
     2:      ISO A3 Size(mm)
     3:      ISO A2 Size(mm)
     4:      ISO A1 Size(mm)
     5:      ISO A0 Size(mm)
     6:      ANSI-V Size(in)
     7:      ANSI-A Size(in)
     8:      ANSI-B Size(in)
     9:      ANSI-C Size(in)
    10:      ANSI-D Size(in)
    11:      ANSI-E Size(in)
    12:      Arch/Engineering (24 x 36in)
    13:      Generic D size Sheet (24 x 36in)
```

Add/Delete/Redisplay/<Number of entry to load> Enter a number, **0–13**, representing the title block to insert, or choose an option. Select the Redisplay option to print the list of available title blocks again. Select the Add option to add a custom title block to the list. Select the Delete option to remove a title block from the list. Entering **0** (the None option) returns you to the previous prompt.

Entering a number **1-13** draws a title block, if a drawing of that name cannot be found. If a drawing with that name is found, it is inserted or attached as an external reference. Use the Options option of the main MVSETUP command to select the import method of the title block. If a drawing with that name is not found, after AutoCAD draws in the title block, you can create the drawing.

Create a drawing named title.dwg? <Y> If a drawing with the name of the title block inserted is not found, AutoCAD prompts you to create one. Enter **Y** to create a title block drawing with this name.

TIP After the drawing has been created, you can customize it for use as a title block in other drawings.

Select the objects to delete... Select objects Select any objects you want to delete. MVSETUP does not filter for viewport objects only—any AutoCAD object can be deleted with this option.

New origin point for this sheet Pick a point or enter the paper space coordinates for the lower left corner of the title block.

Title block description If you select the Add option of the Add/Delete/Redisplay/<Number of entry to load>: prompt, MVSETUP presents this prompt. Enter a brief description to appear in the list of available title blocks.

Drawing to insert (without extension) Enter the full path and file name of the title block drawing to insert. The drawing will be inserted into paper space, and the description and location of the file are saved to a file named MVSETUP.DFS.

Specify default usable area? <Y> Enter Y if you want to specify a viewport boundary area in the new drawing. This area will be used as the default viewport boundary area when creating standard engineering viewports.

Lower left corner, Upper right corner Pick a point, or enter the coordinates for the lower left and upper right corners of the viewport boundary area in the new title block drawing.

Example

The following example uses the MVSETUP command to set up a title block in paper space, display the drawing in multiple scaled viewports, and then align the object between viewports.

Command: **MVSETUP** (Enter)	Starts the MVSETUP command
Enable paper space? (No/<Yes>): (Enter)	Selects paper space setup
Regenerating drawing.	
Align/Create/Scale viewports/ Options/Title block/Undo: **O** (Enter)	Specifies Options option
Set Layer/LImits/Units/Xref: **LI** (Enter)	Selects limits control

MVSETUP

```
Set drawing limits? <N>: Y (Enter)
```
Resets limits to paper size

```
Set Layer/LImits/Units/Xref: X (Enter)
```
Selects title block insertion control

```
Xref Attach or Insert title
block? <Insert>: X (Enter)
```
Specifies to attach title block as external reference

```
Set Layer/LImits/Units/Xref: (Enter)
```
Exits Options option

```
Align/Create/Scale viewports/
Options/Title block/Undo: T (Enter)
```
Specifies Title block option

```
Delete objects/Origin/Undo/
<Insert title block>: (Enter)
```
Selects Insert title block option

```
Available title block options:
0:   None
1:   ISO A4 Size(mm)
2:   ISO A3 Size(mm)
3:   ISO A2 Size(mm)
4:   ISO A1 Size(mm)
5:   ISO A0 Size(mm)
6:   ANSI-V Size(in)
7:   ANSI-A Size(in)
8:   ANSI-B Size(in)
9:   ANSI-C Size(in)
10:  ANSI-D Size(in)
11:  ANSI-E Size(in)
12:  Arch/Engineering (24 x 36in)
13:  Generic D size Sheet (24 x 36in)

Add/Delete/Redisplay/
<Number of entry to load>: 9 (Enter)
```
Specifies ANSI-C Size (in) title block

```
Create a drawing named ansi-c.dwg?
<Y>: (Enter)
```
Creates drawing of title block

```
Align/Create/Scale viewports/
Options/Title block/Undo: C (Enter)
```
Selects Create option

```
Delete objects/Undo/<Create
viewports>: (Enter)
```
Specifies Create viewports option

```
Available Mview viewport layout
options:
0:   None
1:   Single
2:   Std. Engineering
3:   Array of Viewports
```

```
Redisplay/
<Number of entry to load>: 2 (Enter)
```
Specifies Standard Engineering viewport layout

```
Bounding area for viewports.
First point: 2,2 (Enter)
```
Specifies lower left corner of viewport area

```
Other point: 15,14 (Enter)
viewport area
```
Specifies upper right corner of

```
Distance between viewports in X.
<0.0>: (Enter)
```
Specifies no gap between viewport columns

```
Distance between viewports in Y.
<0.0>: (Enter)
```
Specifies no gap between viewport rows, creates viewports (see fig. M.31)

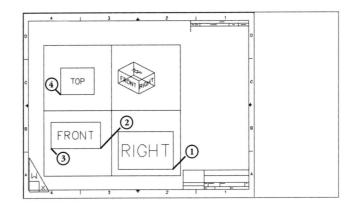

Figure M.31. *The title block and standard engineering viewports.*

```
Align/Create/Scale viewports/
Options/Title block/Undo: S (Enter)
```
Specifies Scale viewports options

```
Select the viewports to scale...
Select objects:
```

Select all four viewports just created

```
Select objects: (Enter)
```

```
Set zoom scale factors for
viewports. Interactively/<Uniform>:
(Enter)
```
Selects Uniform option

```
Enter the ratio of paper space units
to model space units...
```

MVSETUP

`Number of paper space units.` `<1.0>:` (Enter)	Selects 1.0 paper space units
`Number of model space units.` `<1.0>:` (Enter)	to 1.0 model space units. Viewports will be viewed full scale
`Align/Create/Scale viewports/` `Options/Title block/Undo: A` (Enter)	Specifies Align option
`Angled/Horizontal/Vertical` `alignment/Rotate view/Undo: H` (Enter)	Specifies horizontal alignment
`Basepoint: INT` (Enter) of *Pick point* ① *(see fig. M.32)*	Base point of horizontal alignment is lower left endpoint in lower right viewport
`Other point: INT` (Enter) of *Pick point* ②	Target point of horizontal alignment is lower right endpoint in lower left viewport
`Angled/Horizontal/Vertical` `alignment/Rotate view/Undo: V` (Enter)	Specifies vertical alignment
`Basepoint: INT` (Enter) of *Pick point* ③	Base point of vertical alignment is lower left endpoint in lower left viewport
`Other point: INT` (Enter) of *pick point* ④	Target point of vertical alignment is lower left endpoint in upper right viewport
`Angled/Horizontal/Vertical` `alignment/Rotate view/Undo:` (Enter)	Exits Align option
`Align/Create/Scale viewports/` `Options/Title block/Undo:` (Enter)	Exits MVSETUP command.

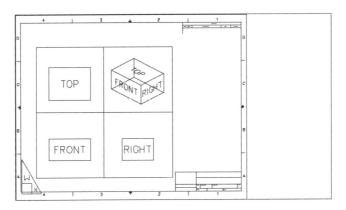

Figure M.32. *The scaled and aligned viewports, inside the title block.*

Related Commands

DDUNITS   MSPACE   MVIEW   PSPACE

Related System Variables

ACADPREFIX   LTSCALE   PSLTSCALE   TILEMODE

NEW

New

    Toolbar: *New (Standard Toolbar)*
    Pull-down: File, New
    Screen: FILE, New:

The NEW command begins and initializes a new drawing in the drawing editor. If you have made any modifications to the current drawing, you can save them, discard them, or cancel the NEW command. The Create New Drawing dialog box is displayed for you to specify a new file name and prototype drawing (see fig. N.1).

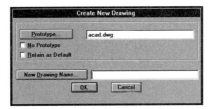

Figure N.1. *The Create New Drawing dialog box.*

Dialog Box Items

NEW displays no command-line prompts. Instead, you make selections from the following dialog boxes and options.

The Create New Drawing dialog box offers the following options:

Prototype. This button is enabled if the No Prototype check box below it is not checked. Clicking on the Prototype button displays the Prototype Drawing File dialog box, in which you can select a prototype for the new drawing (see fig. N.2). Alternatively, you can enter the name of a known file in the text box to the right of the button. The new drawing inherits all the objects and settings of the prototype. When a prototype drawing has been selected, its name appears in the text box. If no prototype file is selected, AutoCAD uses defaults from the configured default prototype drawing file.

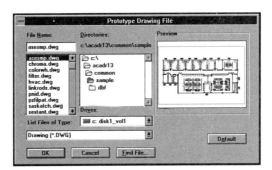

Figure N.2. *The Prototype Drawing File dialog box.*

No Prototype. If this box is checked, the new drawing uses no prototype file, and AutoCAD's default settings, as shipped, are used.

Retain as Default. Checking this box causes AutoCAD to store the name of the prototype drawing file selected above as the default for subsequent new drawings.

New Drawing Name. Clicking on this button displays the Create Drawing File dialog box. You can use this dialog box to select a destination directory and specify a file name for the new drawing. After selecting a directory and file name, they appear in the text box to the right of the button. Alternatively, you can simply enter a new file name in the text box, and the drawing is placed in the default directory. By entering a new file name followed by the equal sign (=) and the name of an existing file, you can specify both the new name and the prototype AutoCAD should use. For example, entering **WIDGET=GADGET** would create a new drawing named WIDGET with all the objects and settings from a drawing named GADGET. You also can omit the prototype name in this method to specify no prototype. If you omit the new drawing name, AutoCAD creates an unnamed drawing.

> If you enter the name of an existing drawing file in the New Drawing Name edit box, you will be prompted if you want to overwrite the existing file. If you answer **Yes**, the new prototype based file will totally replace the existing file with no hope of recovering the original file's information.

Related Commands
FILEOPEN   OPEN

Related System Variable
ACADPREFIX

OFFSET

Toolbar: *Offset (Modify,Copy)*
Pull-down: *Construct, Offset*
Screen: CONSTRCT, Offset:

The OFFSET command creates a copy of an object parallel to the original object in any direction. You can offset arcs, circles, lines, splines, and two-dimensional polylines. When used on circles and arcs, the new object has the same center point as the original. If the OFFSET command is used to copy a polyline, the new polyline has the same width(s) as the original, and the vertices of the polyline are offset in the direction selected.

The OFFSET command works only on one object at a time. To offset a single object many times, use the ARRAY command.

Prompts and Options

Offset distance or Through: <Through>   Enter a distance to offset the object that you select at the next prompt. You can pick two points that define the distance you want to use, or select the Through (default) option, which instructs AutoCAD to offset the object through a chosen point.

Select object to offset   Pick the object to be offset.

Through point   This prompt appears if you specified the Through option at the first prompt. The point supplied at this prompt provides AutoCAD with the direction and offset distance for the new object.

Side to offset?   If a distance is supplied for the OFFSET command, AutoCAD asks on which side of the original to place the new object.

When offsetting polyline or spline objects, AutoCAD attempts to offset each vertex or control point by the specified amount. Unexpected results may occur if the new points are calculated to be on the opposite side of the original object than you selected for the placement of the offset (for example outside a closed polyline instead of inside). This is particularly true if you try to offset to the inside of an acute angle in a spline or polyline.

Example

The following example offsets polyline and circle objects shown in figure O.1.

Choose the Offset *tool*	
Command: _offset	Issues the OFFSET command
Offset distance or Through <Through>: **.25** (Enter)	Specifies the distance between the original and the offset object
Select object to offset: *Pick point* ① *(see fig. O.1)*	Selects the object to offset

Side to offset? *Pick point* ②	Specifies where to place the offset
Select object to offset: *Pick point* ③	Selects the object to offset
Side to offset? *Pick point* ④	Specifies where to place the offset

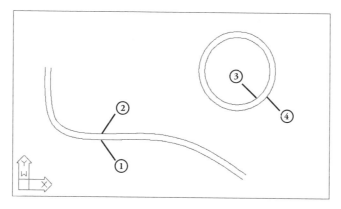

Figure O.1. *Duplicate objects created by the OFFSET command.*

Related Commands

COPY   XLINE

Related System Variable

OFFSETDIST

OLELINKS (Windows Only)

Pull-down: <u>E</u>dit, <u>L</u>inks

The OLELINKS command controls Object Linking and Embedding (OLE) links in the current drawing. When objects are inserted using the INSERTOBJ or PASTESPEC commands, links to the original object are retained. The

OLELINKS command updates, deletes, and changes these links. The OLELINKS command also can launch the application that created the linked object to edit the object.

Prompts and Options

The OLELINKS command displays the Links dialog box (see fig. O.2). If no links exist, the command exits without opening the Links dialog box.

Figure O.2. *The Links dialog box.*

Links. Lists the embedded objects in the drawing that have links. Select an object to control.

Update. Changes updating of the selected object to either automatic or manual. When updating is manual, you must select the object in the **L**inks list box and click on the **U**pdate Now button. Automatically updated objects are updated when AutoCAD opens the drawing.

Update Now. Updates the embedded object in the drawing to reflect the current state of the object. Note that AutoCAD automatically updates all objects whose link specifies automatic updating when the drawing is opened. Use this option to update an embedded object that has changed since the drawing was opened.

Cancel Link. Deletes the link to the selected object. The object remains in the drawing and can be edited like any other embedded object.

Change Link. Changes the directory or file name for the source object.

Activate. Launches the object, if it can be launched. For example, activating a sound object plays that sound through your sound card and speakers.

Edit. Launches the parent application of the embedded object, with the embedded object as the opened document. Edit the document using the parent application; then save and exit. Use the **U**pdate Now option to update the AutoCAD object to reflect the changes made.

Example

This example demonstrates changing the location of the Microsoft Windows document used in the PASTESPEC example. Move the notes document to a different location; then open the drawing that has a link to it (refer to fig. O.2).

Command: **OLELINKS** (Enter)	Starts the OLELINKS command
Select the Microsoft Word 6.0 document from the Links list box	Specifies which object to control
Click on Change Link	Specifies what to control
Select the file from its new location using the Change Link dialog box	Specifies new file location
Click on Update Now	Updates the object in the drawing
Click on Done	Updates link information

Related Commands

COPYCLIP COPYEMBED COPYLINK CUTCLIP
INSERTOBJ PASTECLIP PASTESPEC

OOPS

Oops!

Toolbar: *Oops! (Miscellaneous)*
Pull-down: *Modify, Oops!*
Screen: MODIFY, Oops:

The OOPS command restores objects removed from the drawing by the last ERASE, BLOCK, or WBLOCK commands. The OOPS command only restores the last set of objects removed.

TIP The OOPS command provides a function not available with the UNDO command. If you have problems selecting the correct objects for an edit command, erase the troublesome objects and then perform the edit on the remaining objects. You then can use the OOPS command to restore the erased objects back to their original condition.

Related Commands

ATTREDEF   BLOCK   ERASE   U
UNDO   WBLOCK

OPEN

Open

Toolbar: *Open (Standard)*
Pull-down: File, Open
Screen: FILE, Open:

The OPEN command loads a drawing into the drawing editor. If you have made any modifications to the current drawing, you can save them, discard them, or cancel the OPEN command. The Select File dialog box displays to enable you to specify a file name (see fig. O.3).

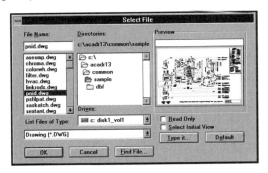

Figure O.3. *The Select File dialog box.*

Dialog Box Items

The OPEN command does not display command-line prompts. Instead, you can make selections from the following options available in the Select File dialog box. See the Introduction to this book for a discussion of the file dialog boxes.

Related Commands

FILEOPEN   MAKEPREVIEW   NEW   RECOVER

Related System Variables

DWGWRITE   ACADPREFIX

'ORTHO

Pull-down: *E*dit, Ort*h*o
Screen: ASSIST, Ortho:

The ORTHO command is a drawing aid that constrains subsequent point selections to angles of 0, 90, 180, and 270 degrees relative to the current UCS. You can press Ctrl+O or F8 to turn Ortho on or off. In Windows, the word ORTHO is displayed on the status bar, and double-clicking it toggles Ortho mode. You also can turn Ortho mode on or off through a check box in the DDRMODES dialog box. Ortho is affected by the current UCS and Snap rotation angle. Any coordinate entry from the keyboard and any use of Object Snap overrides ortho mode.

Prompts and Options

ON/OFF<Off>   Turns orthogonal mode on or off.

Related Commands

DDOSNAP   DDRMODES   OSNAP   SNAP
UCS

Related System Variables

ORTHOMODE   OSMODE   SNAPANG

'OSNAP

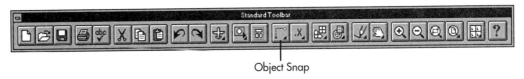

Object Snap

Toolbar: *(Standard, Object Snap)*
Pull-down: *E*dit, Object S*n*ap
Screen: * * * * and ASSIST, Osnap:

The OSNAP (Object SNAP) command causes AutoCAD to use a specific geometric point on an existing object when a command requests point entry. Twelve different geometric modes are available and are described in the following section. The OSNAP command can be set to one or more running object snap settings. You also can temporarily activate any of the object snap modes within a command by entering the first three letters of the snap mode before you pick a point. This is known as *Object Snap Override* and is active only for the single point selection.

Prompts and Options

Object snap modes   You can specify one or more object snap modes by typing the first three letters of the mode. More than one mode can be requested by separating each mode with a comma. For a description of the osnap modes, see the DDOSNAP command.

Example

The following example uses object snap overrides to choose specific points on the objects shown in figure O.4.

Command: **LINE** (Enter)	Issues the LINE command
From point:	
Choose the Snap to Midpoint *tool*	
_mid of: *Pick point* ① *(see fig O.4)*	Specifies the MIDpoint object snap
To point:	
Choose the Snap to Perpendicular *tool*	

_per to *Pick point* ②	Specifies the PERpendicular object snap
To point: (Enter)	Terminates the LINE command

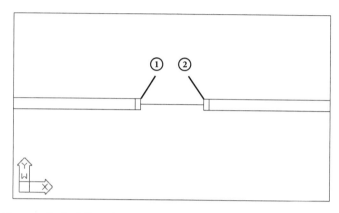

Figure O.4. *A line drawn with the help of object snap overrides.*

Related Commands

APERTURE   DDOSNAP   ORTHO

Related System Variables

APERTURE   OSMODE

'PAN

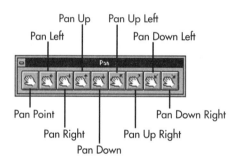

Toolbar: *(Standard, Pan)*
Pull-down: View, Pan
Screen: View, Pan:

The PAN command shifts the view of your drawing currently to another location without changing its size. The PAN command is typically used to view adjacent areas of your drawing. You can use the PAN command transparently (preceded by an apostrophe) if the requested view does not require a screen regeneration. The toolbar, pull-down, and screen menus offer preset pan options that pan approximately half the screen width in the direction(s) indicated.

> **TIP** If the view you need to pan to is more than one screen away, use the DSVIEWER or ZOOM (Dynamic) command instead.

Prompts and Options

Displacement   At this prompt, select a starting point that serves as a reference to shift the view of the current drawing.

Second point   At this prompt, enter the second point for moving the display. If you press Enter at this prompt, a relative displacement is used based on the point you enter at the `Displacement:` prompt.

Related Commands

DDVIEW   DSVIEWER   VIEW   ZOOM

Related System Variables

VIEWCTR   VSMAX   VSMIN

PASTECLIP (Windows Only)

Paste

Toolbar: *Paste (Standard Toolbar)*
Pull-down: **E**dit, **P**aste

The PASTECLIP command copies the objects from the Clipboard into the drawing. If the object in the Clipboard is an AutoCAD graphic, it is inserted as a block into the drawing. If the object in the Clipboard was created with another application, it is inserted as an OLEFRAME object. If the object in the Clipboard is text, it is inserted as an MTEXT object.

> **NOTE** OLEFRAME objects cannot be selected in AutoCAD. They do affect the drawing extents, however.

PASTECLIP (Windows Only)

AutoCAD objects can be copied from one drawing to another by copying to the Clipboard with the COPYCLIP command, and then pasting into another drawing using the PASTECLIP command.

Prompts and Options

If the Clipboard objects consist solely of text, the text is inserted in the upper left corner of the graphics window as an MTEXT object. If the Clipboard objects consist of an application image (such as a Paintbrush image), the image is inserted in the upper left corner of the graphics window as an OLEFRAME object.

If the Clipboard objects consist of AutoCAD objects that have been copied there with the COPYCLIP or CUTCLIP commands, AutoCAD forms a block out of them and inserts the block with the following prompts. (See the INSERT command for a complete description.)

Insertion point   Pick a point in the graphics window or enter the coordinates for the insertion point of the block.

X scale factor <1> / Corner / XYZ   Enter the desired X scale factor for the block, or pick a point in the graphics window to show the X and Y scale factors.

Y scale factor (default=X)   Enter the desired Y scale factor for the block if you did not pick a point in the graphics window to show an X and Y scale factor.

Rotation angle <0>   Enter the desired rotation angle, or pick a point to show the rotation angle as measured from the insertion point of the block.

Example

This example shows you how to use the PASTECLIP command to copy images from Paintbrush into an AutoCAD drawing (see fig. P.1).

Launch Microsoft Paintbrush

Create some simple geometric shapes

Choose E*dit,* C*opy to copy them to the clipboard*

Launch AutoCAD

Command: **PASTECLIP** (Enter)   Pastes Paintbrush image into AutoCAD

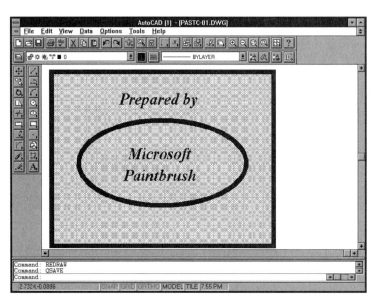

Figure P.1. *Copying objects from the clipboard using the PASTECLIP command.*

Related Commands

INSERTOBJ   PASTESPEC

PASTESPEC (Windows Only)

Pull-down menu: **E**dit, Paste **S**pecial

The PASTESPEC command copies the Clipboard objects and their links into the drawing. If the object in the Clipboard was created by an application that doesn't support links, the PASTESPEC command behaves exactly the same as the PASTECLIP command. If the object in the Clipboard is an AutoCAD graphic, it is inserted as a block into the drawing. If the object in the Clipboard is text, it is inserted as an MTEXT object.

If the object in the Clipboard was created with another application, it is inserted as an OLEFRAME object, and a link is created to the original file. Use the OLELINKS command to control the links from the pasted objects in the AutoCAD drawing to the original file.

OLEFRAME objects cannot be selected in AutoCAD. They do affect the drawing extents, however.

AutoCAD objects can be copied from one drawing to another by copying to the Clipboard with the COPYCLIP command, and then pasting into another drawing using the PASTESPEC command.

Prompts and Options

The PASTESPEC command displays the Paste Special dialog box (see fig. P.2), which has the following options:

Source. The application that created the object in the Clipboard, along with the object's file name, is displayed. To the right of the object's file name is the link type, if any. If no links are available for this object, the Paste Link radio button will be grayed out.

Paste/Paste Link. Select Paste to insert a static image of the Clipboard object into the drawing. When Paste is selected, the PASTESPEC command behaves exactly the same as the PASTECLIP command.

Select Paste Link to insert a dynamic image into the drawing. When a link is active, the object in the drawing updates whenever the original file is changed. Updating can be either automatic or manual. See the OLELINKS command for instructions on updating images with links.

As. Select the desired object type to import from the Clipboard. The native application object type is listed first, if a link is available. If Picture is selected, the Convert check box becomes available, and the Clipboard object is inserted as a graphic object. If Text or OEM Text is listed, the Clipboard object is inserted as an MTEXT object and is not linked.

If the Clipboard object consists of an application image (such as a Microsoft Word document), it is inserted in the upper left corner of the graphics window as an OLEFRAME object, and a link to the original file is established.

Convert. If the selected object type is Picture, check the Convert box to convert the original image to AutoCAD objects. The object is converted to a block and inserted into the current drawing with the following prompts. See the INSERT command for a complete description.

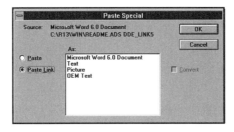

Figure P.2. *The Paste Special dialog box.*

Insertion point Pick a point in the graphics window or enter the coordinates for the insertion point of the block.

X scale factor <1> / Corner / XYZ Enter the desired X scale factor for the block, or pick a point in the graphics window to show the X and Y scale factors.

Y scale factor (default=X) Enter the desired Y scale factor for the block if you did not pick a point in the graphics window to show an X and Y scale factor.

Rotation angle <0> Enter the desired rotation angle, or pick a point to show the rotation angle as measured from the insertion point of the block.

Example

This example shows you how to use the PASTESPEC command to copy images from Microsoft Word into an AutoCAD drawing (see fig. P.3).

Launch Microsoft Word

Create the drawing notes as shown (see fig. P.3)

Choose Edit, Copy *to copy them to the Clipboard*

Launch AutoCAD

Command: **PASTESPEC** (Enter)	Starts the PASTESPEC command
Select the native object type from the As *box, Microsoft Word 6.0 Document*	Selects object type that supports links
Click on Paste Link	Specifies pasting with link
Click on OK	Inserts object from Clipboard
Position the linked object at the desired location using the cursor	Positions object

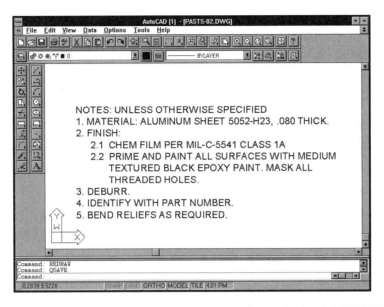

Figure P.3. *Linking drawing notes from Microsoft Word using PASTESPEC.*

Related Commands

COPYEMBED	COPYLINK	CUTCLIP	DDINSERT
INSERT	INSERTOBJ	PASTECLIP	PASTESPEC

PCXIN

Pull-down: File, Import, Raster, PCX... (DOS Only)
Screen: FILE, IMPORT, PCXin:

The PCXIN command imports a Zsoft PCX raster file into AutoCAD. AutoCAD scans the raster image and creates a block consisting of a rectangular colored solid for each pixel in the PCX file.

When a raster image is imported into AutoCAD, you can trace over the raster image with AutoCAD geometry to create an AutoCAD drawing of the raster image. When you are through, you can erase the raster image. Raster images can be scaled, mirrored, and rotated like regular blocks.

Raster images also can be used to represent images obtained by scanning photographs, logos, and artwork.

Do not explode the block representation of a raster file. If you do, the resulting objects will use large quantities of disk space and memory.

Raster images are imported as anonymous blocks. If you reimport the same image multiple times, a new block is created each time you import.

Before importing any raster images, it is important to set the system variables that control raster image conversion. The related system variables are named RIBACKG, RIEDGE, RIGAMUT, RIGREY, and RITHRESH. See the GIFIN command for a full description of each of these. Set the system variable GRIPBLOCK to 0 to avoid highlighting all the solid objects in the block with grips.

Prompts and Options

PCX file name   Enter the name of the PCX file to import. A file selection dialog box is not available. You do not have to include the PCX extension because the PCXIN command adds it, if necessary.

Insertion point <0,0,0>   Pick a point in the graphics window, or enter the coordinates of the insertion point for the raster image.

Scale Factor   Enter a number or pick a point in the graphics window to show a distance. If you pick a point in the graphics window, the distance from the insertion point is used as the scale factor.

New length   If you press Enter at the Scale Factor prompt, you will be reprompted to enter a new scale factor, or to pick a point to show a distance for the scale factor.

Example

The following example imports a PCX file created using the PFACE command. It was rendered and saved as a PCX file. It is first imported as an outline image by setting RIEDGE to 5, and then inserted as a rendered grayscale image by setting RIEDGE to 0 and RIGREY to 1 (see fig. P.4). Set RIBACKG to your graphics window background color first.

Command: **RIEDGE** (Enter)	Issues the RIEDGE command to change system variable RIEDGE
Raster input edge detection <0>: **5** (Enter)	Specifies new value for RIEDGE
Command: **RIBACKG** (Enter)	Issues the RIBACKG command to change system variable RIBACKG
Raster input screen background color <0>: **7** (Enter)	Specifies new value for RIBACKG Color 7 specifies a white background
Command: **PCXIN** (Enter)	Starts the PCXIN command
PCX file name: **ELBOW** (Enter)	Specifies file name ELBOW.PCX
Insertion point<0,0,0>: (Enter)	
Scale factor: **1** (Enter)	Specifies scale factor of 1
Command: **RIEDGE** (Enter)	Issues the RIEDGE command to change system variable RIEDGE
Raster input edge detection <25>: **0** (Enter)	Specifies new value for RIEDGE
Command: **RIGREY** (Enter)	Issues the RIGREY command to change system variable RIGRAY
Raster input grayscale mode <0>: **1** (Enter)	Specifies new value for RIGREY
Command: **PCXIN** (Enter)	Starts the PCXIN command
PCX file name: **ELBOW** (Enter)	Specifies file name ELBOW.PCX
Insertion point<0,0,0>: **1,0,0** (Enter)	Specifies insertion point of 1,0,0
Scale factor: **1** (Enter)	Specifies scale factor of 1

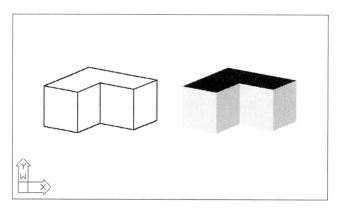

Figure P.4. *A rendered rectangular elbow imported as raster images with the PCXIN command.*

Related Commands

ACISIN	DXBIN	DXFIN	GIFIN
IMPORT	PSDRAG	PSIN	TIFFIN
WMFIN			

Related System Variables

FILLMODE	GRIPBLOCK	PSQUALITY	RIBACKG
RIEDGE	RIGAMUT	RIGREY	RITHRESH

PEDIT

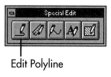

Edit Polyline

Toolbar: *Edit Polyline (Modify, Special Edit)*
Pull-down: *Modify, Edit Polyline*
Screen: MODIFY, Pedit:

The PEDIT command edits 2D and 3D polylines and polygon meshes. Each of these objects is a variation of the basic polyline object; thus, the PEDIT command performs a variety of manipulations of these objects. The PEDIT command responds differently for each type of polyline object. The next section explains the prompts and options for each type of object.

Prompts and Options

Select polyline   At this prompt, select a polyline for editing by using any of the standard AutoCAD object selection methods. If the selected object is not a polyline or mesh, the following message appears:

`Entity selected is not a polyline`

If the selected object is a line or an arc, it will be highlighted and you will receive the following prompt:

`Do you want to turn it into one? <Y>`

The PEDIT command can change a "normal" line into a 2D polyline. If you decide not to transform the object, the PEDIT command terminates.

2D Polylines

The following prompts and options appear when you use the PEDIT command to edit 2D polyline objects:

`Close/Join/Width/Edit vertex/Fit/Spline/Decurve/Ltype gen/Undo/eXit <X>:`

Close   The Close option creates a closing polyline segment from the end of the polyline back to its beginning. If the ending segment is an arc, the Close option creates a closing arc segment. After the polyline is closed, this option changes to Open. The Open option removes closing polyline segments.

Join   When you specify the Join option, you see the `Select objects:` prompt. You can select line, arc, and polyline segments to add to the current polyline. Each segment chosen must meet the adjacent segment at its endpoint, forming a continuous chain. After performing the join operation, the PEDIT command reports how many segments were added.

Width   The Width option enables you to set a constant width for all segments of the polyline. If individual segments have tapered widths, this value overrides the previous width information. When you choose the Width option, you receive the following prompt:

`Enter new width for all segments:`

Edit vertex   The Edit vertex option presents the following new prompt line of options. These options are used to edit a polyline on a vertex-by-vertex basis. When you edit vertices, the PEDIT command marks the current vertex with an X. Each of the options that has additional prompts is described with its prompts. The options without additional prompts are described in the following paragraphs.

`Next/Previous/Break/Insert/Move/Regen/Straighten/Tangent/Width/eXit <X>:`

Next The Next option enables you to move the vertex marker (the X) to the next polyline vertex. The Previous option moves the vertex marker to the preceding vertex.

Regen When you make vertex edits, you can easily obscure the current shape of the polyline. The Regen option forces a regeneration of only the polyline so that you can view it in its current form.

Break and **Straighten** If you select either the Break or Straighten options, you are presented with the prompt Next/Previous/Go/eXit <N>:. The Break option removes the section of the polyline between the specified vertices. The Straighten option removes all the vertices between the two specified vertex points and replaces them with one polyline segment. With either option, the current position of the vertex marker is considered the starting point for breaking or straightening.

Next, Previous, Go, and **eXit** The Next or Previous options locate the ending vertex for your edit. After that vertex is located, use the Go option to execute the break or straighten actions. The eXit option returns to the previous prompt without performing any editing.

Insert The Insert option enables you to specify the coordinates of a new polyline vertex to be created. The Insert option issues this prompt: Enter location of new vertex:.

Move The Move option enables you to alter the location of the current polyline vertex by supplying a new location for the current vertex. The Move option issues the following prompt: Enter new location:.

Tangent The Tangent option enables you to determine the tangent direction used by fitted curves at the current vertex. The Tangent option issues the prompt: Direction of tangent:. The tangent direction is indicated by an arrow through the Edit vertex mode's Xs.

Fit The Fit option creates a continuous smooth curve composed of arcs among all the polyline's vertices. If you specify any tangent directions for vertices (under the Edit vertex option), the directions are used to compute the curve direction at the vertices. If you explode a curve-fit polyline or use the BREAK or TRIM commands on the polyline, a pair of arcs appears between each vertex.

Spline The Spline option uses the existing polyline vertices to form the frame for fitting either a quadratic B-spline or a cubic B-spline curve (based on the value of the SPLINETYPE variable) along the polyline. The resolution (number of lines or arcs between each pair of vertices) is set by the value of the SPLINESEGS system variable. If SPLINESEGS is positive, the spline uses lines; if negative, the spline uses arcs to create the B-spline.

Decurve The Decurve option removes any curve-fitting or spline-fitting arc segments from the polyline.

Ltype gen By default, when AutoCAD displays polylines with noncontinuous linetypes, the pattern begins and ends at each vertex. Setting Ltype gen ON forces linetypes to be rendered between endpoints, ignoring intermediate vertices.

Undo The Undo option reverses the last action performed on the polyline. If you make many changes in the Edit vertex option, all the changes can be reversed by a single undo.

eXit The eXit option terminates the polyline editing and returns you to the `Command:` prompt.

Width The Width option enables you to vary the width of the polyline segment between the current vertex and next vertex. The Width option displays the following prompt: `Enter starting width <default>:`. Enter a value to be used for the starting width and the ending width. If the polyline has a width currently assigned, that width appears as the default. The polyline does not show the effects of the change in width until you use the Regen option, or if you exit to the main PEDIT prompt line.

3D Polylines

The following prompt and options appear when you use the PEDIT command to edit 3D polyline objects:

`Close/Edit vertex/Spline curve/Decurve/Undo/eXit <X>:`

Close The Close option creates a closing polyline segment from the end of the polyline back to its beginning. When the polyline is closed, this option changes to Open in the prompt line. The Open option removes a closing polyline segment.

Spline curve The Spline curve option works the same as for 2D polylines except that the curve is generated in 3D space and consists of straight line segments only, regardless of the value of SPLINESEGS.

Decurve The Decurve option removes any spline-fitting and restores the polyline to its original state.

Undo and **Regen** The Undo and Regen options function the same as for 2D polylines.

Edit vertex The Edit vertex option displays the following prompt. Each option edits vertices in the same manner as in 2D polyline editing, except that now you can supply a 3D location for the polyline's vertices.

`Next/Previous/Break/Insert/Move/Regen/Straighten/eXit <X>:`

Polygon Meshes

The following prompt appears when you use the PEDIT command to edit polygon meshes:

```
Edit vertex/Smooth surface/Desmooth/Mclose/Nclose/Undo/eXit <X>:
```

Edit vertex The Edit vertex option displays the following prompt, which enables you to relocate the position of each of the vertices of the polygon mesh. The prompt displays the current position of the vertex you are editing in both the M and N directions.

```
Vertex (m,n). Next/Previous/Left/RIght/Up/Down/Move/REgen/eXit <X>:
```

For meshes generated by commands affected by the SURFTAB1 and SURFTAB2 system variables, the M direction corresponds to the SURFTAB1 setting, and the N direction corresponds to the SURFTAB2 setting. The options Next, Previous, Left, Right, Up, and Down all move the current vertex X marker through the mesh.

> **Move** The Move option of Edit vertex enables you to relocate the current polyline vertex by specifying a new coordinate anywhere within 3D space. The Move option displays the prompt: Enter new location:.

Smooth surface The Smooth Surface option fits a smooth surface to the framework of the mesh by using one of three smoothing options based on the value of the SURFTYPE variable. If the variable is equal to 5, quadratic B-spline surface smoothing occurs. If its value is 6, a cubic B-spline smoothing routine is used. If the variable value is 8, the surface is smoothed with a Bezier curve equation. The density of the smoothed surface is controlled by the SURFU system variable in the M direction and by the SURFV system variable in the N direction. The surface does not pass through the vertex (control) points of the mesh, but is controlled by them—as in spline-fitting a 2D or 3D polyline.

Desmooth The Desmooth option reverses any smoothing and restores the original polygon mesh.

Mclose and **Nclose** The Mclose and Nclose options close the polygon mesh in the M or N directions. If the polygon mesh is currently closed in either the M or N direction, the Close option for that direction is replaced with Mopen or Nopen.

Undo The Undo option reverses the previous action performed on the mesh. If you make many changes in the Edit vertex option, all the changes can be reversed by a single undo.

Exit The Exit option terminates editing and returns to the Command: prompt.

Example

The following example uses the PEDIT command to edit a 2D polyline, shown in figure P.5, by changing its width.

Choose the Polyline Edit *tool.*

Command: _pedit	Issues the PEDIT command
Select polyline: *Select a polyline*	Specifies the polyline to change
Close/Join/Width/Edit vertex/Fit/ Spline/Decurve/Ltype gen/Undo/ eXit <X>: **W** (Enter)	Selects the Width option
Enter new width for all segments: **.3** (Enter)	Specifies the new width for the polyline
Close/Join/Width/Edit vertex/Fit/ Spline/Decurve/Ltype gen/Undo/ eXit <X>: (Enter)	Terminates the PEDIT command

---

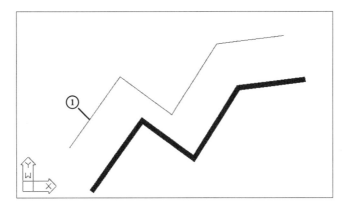

Figure P.5. *The polyline before and after changing the width.*

Related Commands

3D	DMESH	DPOLY	LINE
SPLINE	SPLINEDIT	SURFTYPE	

Related System Variables

SPLFRAME   SPLINESEGS   SPLINETYPE

PFACE

Screen: DRAW2, SURFACES, Pface:

The PFACE command creates a polygon mesh by first locating points in 3D space and then connecting these points to form a face. Virtually any number of points (called *vertices*) can be defined. Many different faces can be created from these vertices.

No matter how many faces are created, they are linked together as one object. Each face can be given a separate color or can be placed on a different layer as it is created. The edges of a face can be made invisible. Faces on frozen layers are not displayed. If the polygon mesh's layer is frozen, the entire polygon mesh is not displayed.

This command was designed for use with AutoLISP programs and ADS applications, so input for this command can be quite complicated. The polygon mesh object that is created cannot be modified using the PEDIT command.

Prompts and Options

Vertex x   Pick a point in the graphics window, or enter the coordinates for the vertex location. This prompt continues until you press Enter, signifying the end of the vertex definition.

Face x, Vertex x   Define each face by entering the vertex number of the vertices around the edges of the face. Enter the vertex numbers either clockwise or counterclockwise around the face. Enter each vertex using the vertex number defined when locating the vertex. After all vertices for the face are identified, press Enter to define the next face. Press Enter at the first vertex prompt of any face to complete the command and create the polyfaces. Enter a vertex number preceded by a minus sign to make the edge of the face from that vertex invisible, such as -3.

You also can enter **Color** and **Layer** at this prompt. These two options specify a separate face color or layer, respectively. When you change the color or layer of a face, all faces subsequently defined use that color and layer.

Example

This example creates a simple polyface object, a rectangular elbow, shown in figure P.6, using the PFACE command. The viewpoint is taken from 3,2,1. Create a script file called ELBOW.SCR using an ASCII text editor (see *Command Scripts* in *Chapter 6, Programming Interfaces* of the *AutoCAD Release 13 Customization Guide* for more information regarding scripts). Make sure there are two hard returns after the last line. Then use the SCRIPT command to run the ELBOW.SCR script and create the elbow.

```
; Start PFACE command:
PFACE
; Locate twelve vertices for elbow:
0,0,0 4,0,0 4,2,0 2,2,0 2,4,0 0,4,0
0,0,2 4,0,2 4,2,2 2,2,2 2,4,2 0,4,2

; Vertices for first face:
1 7 8 2

; Vertices for second face:
2 8 9 3

; Vertices for third face:
3 9 10 4

; Vertices for fourth face:
4 10 11 5

; Vertices for fifth face:
5 11 12 6

; Vertices for sixth face:
6 12 7 1

; Vertices for seventh face:
1 2 3 4 5 6

; Vertices for last face:
7 8 9 10 11 12
```

Command: **SCRIPT** (Enter)	Executes SCRIPT command, displays Select Script File dialog box
Select the file ELBOW.SCR	Creates rectangular elbow using PFACE command instructions from script file

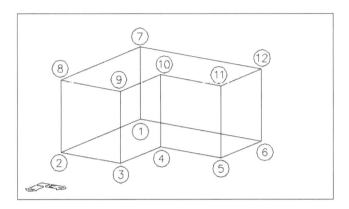

Figure P.6. *A simple rectangular elbow polygon mesh created with the PFACE command.*

Related Commands

3DFACE   3DMESH   EDGESURF   REVSURF
RULESURF   TABSURF

Related System Variable

SPLFRAME

PLAN

Pull-down: **V**iew, 3D V**i**ewpoint Presets, **P**lan View
Screen: VIEW, Plan:

The PLAN command sets the view to the plan view of one of three possible coordinate systems. When you are working in model space, the plan view is a view where the X axis is oriented horizontally along the bottom of the graphics window, and the Y axis is oriented vertically along the left edge of the graphics window.

The PLAN command provides a quick method of setting your viewpoint to 0,0,1 of the selected UCS. The PLAN command is not allowed in paper space.

PLAN

Invoking the PLAN command when perspective mode is enabled (see the DVIEW command) disables perspective mode.

Prompts and Options

<Current UCS>/UCS/World   Select an option to change the viewing direction. The default option, <Current UCS>, changes the view to the plan view of the current UCS. The World option changes the view to the plan view of the WCS. The UCS option changes the view to the plan view of a previously saved UCS.

?/Name of UCS   Enter the name of a saved User Coordinate System, or enter **?** to display a list of currently saved User Coordinate Systems.

UCS name(s) to list <*>   Enter the UCS name pattern to match, or press Enter to view a list of all defined User Coordinate Systems.

Example

This example shows how to use the plan view to change the viewing direction in viewports. Create the object shown in the upper right viewport of figure P.7 (see the PFACE command). The WCS is shown in the upper right viewport. Save a UCS called RIGHT, defined as shown in the upper left viewport.

Command: **PLAN** (Enter) *Select the lower right viewport*	Starts the PLAN command
<Current UCS>/UCS/World: **W** (Enter)	Changes to plan view of World UCS
Command: **PLAN** (Enter) *Select the lower left viewport*	Executes PLAN command
<Current UCS>/UCS/World: **U** (Enter)	Specifies UCS option
?/Name of UCS: **RIGHT** (Enter)	Changes to plan view of UCS named RIGHT

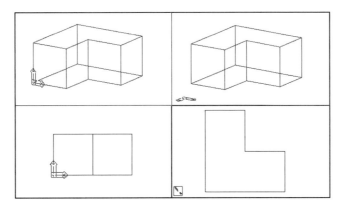

Figure P.7. *Four views of the same object after using the PLAN command to change the view.*

Related Commands

DDUCS   DDUCSP   DDVPOINT   DDVIEW

Related System Variables

UCSFOLLOW   UCSNAME   VIEWCTR   VIEWDIR
VIEWSIZE   VIEWTWIST   VSMAX   VSMIN

PLINE

Polyline

>Toolbar: *Polyline (Draw, Polyline)*
>Pull-down: **D**raw, **P**olyline
>Screen: DRAW1, Pline:

The PLINE command draws polyline objects. Polylines are complex objects that are a combination of line and arc segments, but are treated by AutoCAD as a single object. As a complex object, 2D polylines have great flexibility to meet special needs in an AutoCAD drawing—from custom leader lines to hatch boundaries.

> Polylines are ideal for re-creating company logos and other freeform shapes. The width and arc options enable you to be creative unlike most any other AutoCAD object.

Prompts and Options

`From point`   At this prompt, enter the starting point of the polyline.

`Arc/Close/Halfwidth/Length/Undo/Width/<Endpoint of line>`   This prompt contains all the major options of the PLINE command.

Arc

This option presents this additional prompt:

`Angle/CEnter/CLose/Direction/Halfwidth/Line/Radius/Second pt/Undo/Width/<Endpoint of arc>:`

Each of the possible polyline arc options is discussed in the following paragraphs.

Angle   This option asks you to enter the included angle of the arc. The Angle option issues the `Included angle` prompt. After you have entered the value for the included angle, you receive the prompt, `Center/Radius/<Endpoint>`. Enter the center point for the arc, the arc's radius, or use the default option to specify an endpoint for the arc.

CEnter   This option displays the prompt `Center point`, at which you enter the arc's center point. By default, the PLINE command draws arcs tangent from the last segment and automatically locates the arc's center point. This option enables you to override the default action of the PLINE command.

`Angle/Length/<End point>`   If you used the Center option displayed previously, enter the additional information needed to create the arc. You can enter the included angle, a value for the chord length, or simply specify the arc's endpoint (the default option).

Close   This option draws a polyline arc segment back to the beginning of the polyline.

Direction   This option enables you to specify the direction that the arc will be drawn from the arc's starting point. The Direction option issues the `Direction from starting point` prompt. The PLINE command draws the arc tangent to the starting point by default. If you want to override this default, pick a point in the drawing editor to indicate the arc's new direction.

End point After the polyline arc direction has been entered, locate the endpoint of the arc by specifying a point.

Halfwidth This option enables you to enter a value for the width of a polyline segment based on the width from the center of the polyline to its edge. The actual width of the polyline segment will be double the value you enter at the following prompt:

```
Starting half-width <0.000>:
Ending half-width <0.000>:
```

The ending polyline half-width is the same as its starting half-width by default. This gives the polyline segment a uniform width. If you want the width tapered from the beginning to the end, enter an ending half-width that differs in value from the starting half-width.

Line This option returns you to the Line mode prompt.

Radius This option accepts a value for the radius of an arc.

Angle/<End point> After you enter the radius, locate an ending point at this prompt to create the arc or enter a value for the arc's included angle.

Second point Polyline arc segments can be created similar to a standard three-point arc with this option. Enter the second of three points that will describe the arc.

End point After the second point of the polyline arc is located, specify the endpoint at this prompt to properly create the polyline arc.

Undo This option undoes individual segments one at a time.

Width The Width option works in the same manner as the half-width option. It enables you to assign a width at the Starting width <0.000> prompt for the current polyline segment. The difference is that the width is measured from the edges of the polyline, not from the center to the edge.

```
Ending width <0.000>:
```

The ending polyline width is the same as its starting width by default. This gives the polyline segment a uniform width. If you want the width to taper from beginning to end, enter an ending width at the preceding prompt that differs from the starting width.

Endpoint of arc The default option, enables you to select the endpoint for an arc that is drawn tangent to the last segment.

Following are the remaining PLINE line mode options.

Close

This option works in the same manner as the Close option of Arc mode, except that it draws a straight segment back to the beginning of the polyline.

Halfwidth/Undo/Width

These options work the same as when you draw polyline arc segments.

Length

Enter a value for the length of the next segment. The segment will be drawn at the same angle as the previous segment. If no segment exists, an angle of 0 degrees is used to draw the next segment.

Endpoint of line

This option, which is the default, enables you to specify the location for another segment endpoint.

Example

This example demonstrates using some of the PLINE command's options to create the polyline shown in figure P.8.

Choose the Polyline *tool.*

`Command: _pline`	Issues the PLINE command
`From point:` *Pick point* ① *(see fig. P.8)*	Specifies the start of the polyline
`Current line-width is 0.0000`	
`Arc/Close/Halfwidth/Length/Undo/Width/<Endpoint of line>:` **W**	Specifies the Width option
`Starting width <0.0000>:` (Enter)	Specifies the starting width
`Ending width <0.0000>:` **.5**	Specifies the ending width
`Arc/Close/Halfwidth/Length/Undo/Width/<Endpoint of line>:` *Pick point* ②	
`Arc/Close/Halfwidth/Length/Undo/Width/<Endpoint of line>:` **W** (Enter)	
`Starting width <0.5000>:` **.1** (Enter)	
`Ending width <0.1000>:` (Enter)	

```
Arc/Close/Halfwidth/Length/Undo/Width/
<Endpoint of line>: Pick point ③

Arc/Close/Halfwidth/Length/Undo/Width/    Terminates the PLINE command
<Endpoint of line>: Enter
```

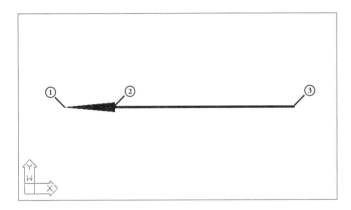

Figure P.8. *A polyline created with various width options.*

Related Commands

EDIT	FILL	LINE	SKETCH
SPLINE	SPLINEDIT	TRACE	

Related System Variables

PLINEGEN   PLINEWID

PLOT

Print

Toolbar: *Print (Standard)*
Pull-down: **F**ile, **P**rint...
Screen: FILE, Print:

The PLOT command produces a hard copy of your drawing on an installed and configured plotting device. The PLOT command outputs only the current drawing. You can specify one of several different drawing areas to plot, including the most recent display view, the extents of the drawing, the limits as established by the LIMITS command, a named view, or a user-specified window. Each plot can be directed either to the configured plotter or to a file on disk.

Prompts and Options

The Plot Configuration dialog box, shown in figure P.9, displays each of the plotting options in a series of radio buttons, check boxes, and option buttons, divided into logical groups. The functions of each of these groups are described in the following paragraphs.

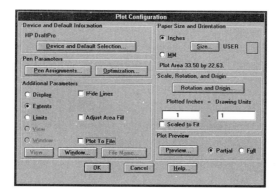

Figure P.9. *The Plot Configuration dialog box.*

The Plot Configuration dialog box is controlled by the CMDDIA system variable. If CMDDIA is set to zero, then no dialog box will be shown, and command prompts will be displayed. This setting is most useful if you need to perform plotting from a script file.

The Device and Default Information group has a single button described next.

Device and Default Selection

This button displays the Device and Default Selection dialog box (see fig. P.10). This dialog box contains a list box of the defined plotter configurations. You can choose from up to 29 predefined printer and plotter configurations. Both printer plotter and pen plotter configurations can be placed in this list to use as your output device. You must use the CONFIG command to create plotter configurations. To make one of the configurations active, highlight it and click on the OK button. If you click on the Cancel button, any modifications you have made in the dialog box are removed. This dialog box also contains the following buttons:

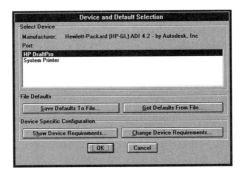

Figure P.10. *Device and Default Selection dialog box.*

Save Defaults To File. This button enables you to save all the plotting parameters you have chosen from the Configuration Plot dialog box, to a plot configuration file. This file can be used at a later time to restore all the defaults you have chosen. Plot configuration files have an extension of PCP.

Get Defaults From File. This button retrieves any previously saved plotter configuration file and updates the current plot parameters.

Show Device Requirements. This option displays additional configuration information about the plotter. If this button is grayed, there are no additional requirements for this particular plotting device.

Change Device Requirements. This option enables you to change plotter configuration values if the selected plotter has any additional possible values. If this button is grayed, no other values are possible.

Pen Parameters

The Pen Parameters group is used to specify information specific to the type of plotter you have selected. This group has the following two buttons:

Pen Assignments. This button is used to assign AutoCAD color numbers to plotter pens. This button displays the Pen Assignments dialog box, which is used to define which AutoCAD color is assigned to each plotter pen number, and also assign such attributes as hardware linetype, pen speed, and pen width (see fig. P.11). Click on the Feature Legend button to display which of these attributes can be assigned using the current plotter.

PLOT

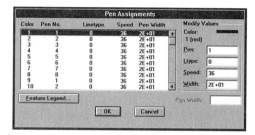

Figure P.11. *The Pen Assignments dialog box.*

It is usually best to let AutoCAD use its own linetypes and features rather than use hardware features. You will most likely rarely need to use the built-in hardware features of your output device. The AutoCAD drivers usually provide all the capability needed to produce professional-looking plots.

Optimization. Use this button to display the Optimizing Pen Motion dialog box (see fig. P.12). At plot time, AutoCAD optimizes the plot information so that your plotter does not waste time. The items checked in the dialog box depend on the plotting device currently selected. Checking each successive item includes all the previous items except No Optimization. You will rarely have to modify these settings. In fact, excessive optimization may actually increase plotting time.

Figure P.12. *The Optimizing Pen Motion dialog box.*

Additional Parameters

The Additional Parameters group determines what information in your drawing gets sent to the plotter. The group of radio buttons enables you to plot out the current display, the drawing's extents, the drawing's limits, a named view, or a windowed area of your drawing. You also can choose to hide lines that may be obscured in a 3D drawing, adjust the fill area based on the width of the pen in use, or send all the plot information to a file. The items in this group perform the following functions:

View. If you choose to plot a named view, this button displays the View Name dialog box. This box contains a list of all the named views within the current drawing. To plot one of the views, highlight the name in the list box, and click on the OK button.

Window. If you choose to plot a windowed area of your drawing, this button displays the Window Selection dialog box. This box enables you to enter the absolute X and Y locations for the window's corners, or you pick the window by clicking on the pointing device pick button.

File Name. You can choose to plot the drawing to a file, instead of the plotter. Typically, the default plot file name is set with the CONFIG command, but you can use this button to select a different file name for the plot file. This button is only active if the Plot to File check box is checked. You specify the plot file name in the Create Plot File dialog box.

Hide Lines. Use the Hide Lines button to remove hidden lines in model space viewports. When you plot from paper space with this option on, AutoCAD will process each viewport in the drawing to remove hidden lines according to its Hideplot setting made with the MVIEW command. When plotting from model space, all viewports are processed regardless.

Adjust Area Fill. Use this option for greater accuracy when plotting filled areas. AutoCAD will take the pen width into consideration when plotting filled areas by adjusting the fill boundary inward by one-half the pen width. This option is unnecessary except when extreme accuracy is required.

Plot to File. Use this check box to create a file containing instructions for your output device. This is commonly used in network situations or when a spooling application is used. The spooling application will intercept the plot file and direct it to the appropriate output device. The default extension for a plot file is PLT. The plot file generated is for the current selected device. Some devices may not permit plotting to a file.

Paper Size and Orientation

The Paper Size and Orientation group features are used to tell AutoCAD the size of the output for your plot. The radio buttons in this group determine which type of units, Inches or Millimeters (**M**M), are used for displaying the size of the plot.

Size. The Size button enables you to choose the size of plotted output for the current plot. The Paper Size dialog box displays a list of possible paper sizes based on the current plotter configuration (see fig. P.13). You also can specify custom plot sizes by filling in the User edit boxes. The current plot orientation (landscape or portrait mode) is displayed.

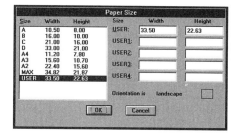

Figure P.13. *The Paper Size dialog box.*

Scale, Rotation, and Origin

The Scale, Rotation, and Origin group is used to determine the final plot parameters before output. You can directly enter the scale for the plot in the supplied edit boxes, or you may choose to fit the plot within the boundaries of the paper you have chosen by checking the Scaled to Fit check box.

Rotation and Origin. This button enables you to rotate the plotted output and locate the starting point on the paper where the plot will begin. This button displays the Plot Rotation and Origin dialog box (see fig. P.14).

Figure P.14. *The Plot Rotation and Origin dialog box.*

In the Plot Rotation and Origin dialog box, specify the rotation of the plot on the paper by choosing one of the radio buttons. The choices are 0, 90, 180, and 270 degrees. Use the X Origin and Y Origin edit boxes to specify the plot position on the paper.

If you wish to plot many small plots on a larger sheet, use the origin edit boxes to specify a different origin for each plot. For example, if you want to plot 8-1/2"x11" plots in landscape orientation, you might use a 0,0 origin for the first plot. Use an origin of 0,8-1/2 to place the second plot above the first one.

> The origin edit boxes can also be used to adjust the plot on plotters that have a tendency to "chop" or cut off the plot on one or two edges.

Plot Preview

The final group of plot options is the Plot Preview group. It enables you to perform an on-screen preview before any information is sent to the plotter. This has the advantage of displaying any possible problem with the plot before actually putting any information down on paper. The two options, Part*i*al or F*u*ll, determine the amount of detail shown when you click on the P*r*eview button.

When you perform a partial preview, you see an accurate rendering of the paper size you are plotting to, along with an indicator of the amount of space needed to plot the drawing. This preview shows no drawing geometry and is quick. A full preview, on the other hand, shows exactly what will plot in the area that is assigned. This method takes longer to preview due to the greater amount of detail required (see figs. P.15 and P.16).

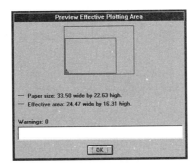

Figure P.15. *Partial plot preview.*

Example

This example of the PLOT command shows you how to set plot parameters and perform a full plot preview. When shown in preview mode, the drawing looks similar to figure P.16.

PLOT

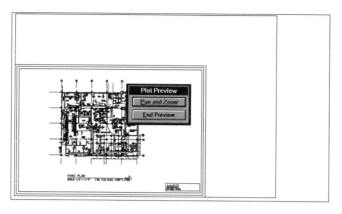

Figure P.16. *Full plot preview.*

From the **F***ile pull-down menu, choose* **P***rint*	Issues the PLOT command
`Command: _plot`	
Click on the **Ex***tents radio button*	Specifies plotting of all objects within the drawing's extents
Click on the **S***ize button*	Displays the Paper Size dialog box
Select "D" size from the list box, then click on OK	Specifies a D-size sheet Closes the Paper Size dialog box
Set the scale to 1=1	Specifies a 1-to-1 plot scale
Click on the **Fu***ll button, then click on the* **P***review button*	Specifies a Full preview
Click on the **E***nd Preview button*	Terminates plot preview and returns to the Plot Configuration dialog box
Click on the Cancel *button*	Cancels the PLOT command.

Related Commands

CONFIG	DXBIN	DXFOUT	LIMITS
PREFERENCES	PSOUT	QTEXT	STLOUT

Related System Variables

CMDDIA	PLOTID	PLOTROTMODE	PLOTTER

POINT

Point

Toolbar: *Point (Draw, Point)*
Pull-down: *Draw, Point, Point*
Screen: DRAW2, Point:

The POINT command creates a point object in your drawing. You can enter a point coordinate from the keyboard, or you can pick a point on the screen. If you enter 2D coordinates, the Z elevation defaults to the current construction plane. Point objects can be used for object snap points when you use the NODe object snap mode.

You can alter the style and size of point display by using the PDMODE and PDSIZE system variables. You can modify these variables directly, or graphically through the DDPTYPE command Point Style dialog box. After you change these variables, all subsequently created points reflect the new settings. Existing points do not display in the new style and size until the drawing is regenerated.

AutoCAD also creates points when you create associative dimensions. These dimension definition points are placed on a layer named DEFPOINTS. If you move these points, AutoCAD automatically updates the associated dimension. These definition points are not affected by the settings of the PDMODE and PDSIZE variables.

Prompts and Options

Point At this prompt, specify the new point object's location.

Related Commands

DDPTYPE   MEASURE

Related System Variables

PDMODE   PDSIZE

POLYGON

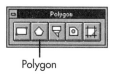
Polygon

Toolbar: *Polygon (Draw, Polygon)*
Pull-down: *Draw, Polygon, Polygon*
Screen: DRAW1, Polygon:

The POLYGON command creates a multisided regular polygon as a polyline object. Each object has sides of equal length and spacing around the center. Polygons are closed polyline objects made up of at least three segments (up to 1,024 segments).

Prompts and Options

Number of sides <4>   At this prompt, specify the number of sides for the polygon. Enter any number from 3 to 1,024. The default creates a square.

Edge/<Center of polygon>   When you specify an edge, you draw one side of the polygon. The other edges are drawn using the same length. If you want to draw the polygon by using a circle as a guide, specify the circle's center point.

> **First endpoint of edge**   This Edge option's first prompt requests the starting point for the polygon face.
>
> **Second endpoint of edge**   At this prompt, specify a point to define the endpoint of the polygon's first edge.

Inscribed in circle/Circumscribed about circle (I/C) <I>   This prompt appears after you specify the polygon's center point. You define the polygon by inscribing or circumscribing it about an imaginary circle. Figure P.17 illustrates the difference between an inscribed polygon and a circumscribed one.

Enter **I** if you want to specify the polygon by inscribing it within a circle. When the polygon is inscribed in the circle, the circle's radius defines the distance from the center to the vertex of the sides.

Enter **C** if you want to specify the polygon by using a circle to circumscribe it. If the object is circumscribed about the circle, the radius measures the distance from the center of the circle to the midpoint of the edges.

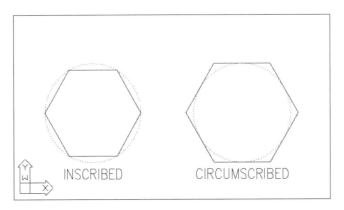

Figure P.17. *Inscribed and Circumscribed polygons.*

Because polygons are in actuality polyline objects, you cannot use the CENter object snap mode to snap to the center of an existing polygon object.

Radius of circle   At this prompt, enter a distance for the radius or pick a point to indicate the radius, and the polygon is created using that point to set its size and orientation.

Example

This example creates a polygon with eight sides. The results are shown in figure P.18.

Command: **POLYGON** (Enter)	Issues the POLYGON command
Number of sides <4>: **8** (Enter)	Specifies the number of sides
Edge/<Center of polygon>: *Pick point ① (see fig. P.18)*	Specifies the center of the polygon
Inscribed in circle/ Circumscribed about circle (I/C) <I>: **C** (Enter)	Selects the Circumscribed option
Radius of circle: **4** (Enter)	Specifies the distance between the center and midpoint of the edges

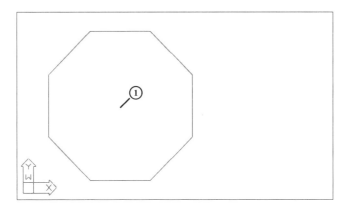

Figure P.18. *An octagon drawn with the POLYGON command's Circumscribed option.*

Related Commands
LINE   PEDIT   RECTANG

Related System Variables
PLINEGEN   POLYSIDES

PREFERENCES

Pull-down: **O**ptions, **P**references

The Preferences command enables you to customize various AutoCAD settings. It displays one of two dialog boxes, depending on your system. On DOS and Unix platforms, you can only specify the units of measurement (English or metric) and the prototype drawing to use. On Windows platforms, options are available for customizing your setup, changing the AutoCAD environment (support files and memory settings), rendering environment, system of measurement, and miscellaneous functions such as font mapping, text editor (for paragraph text), and start-up parameters.

Dialog Box Items

The Preferences dialog box items for the Windows platform are discussed in this section (see fig. P.19). For information on the Preferences dialog for DOS and Unix platforms see your AutoCAD documentation.

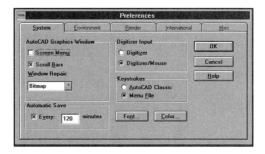

Figure P.19. *The Preferences dialog box.*

System

The **S**ystem tab of the Preferences dialog box has four areas for specifying options to your AutoCAD setup. These are the AutoCAD Graphics Window, the Automatic Save option, the Digitizer Input option, and the Keystrokes options. Also included in the System tab are the Fo**n**t and **C**olor buttons, used to specify the font and color in AutoCAD operations.

AutoCAD Graphics Window. This option enables the user to turn on or off the Screen Men**u** and Scroll **B**ars. Figure P.20 shows an AutoCAD setup with the screen menu displayed and the scroll bars turned off, and figure P.21 shows a setup with no screen menu displayed and the scroll bars turned on. The default configuration is with no screen menu.

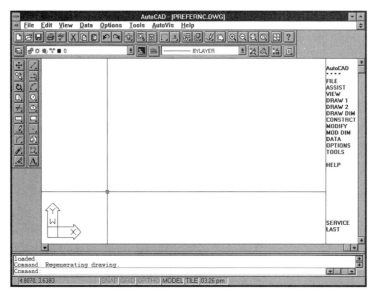

Figure P.20. *Using the AutoCAD screen menu and scroll bars.*

PREFERENCES 511

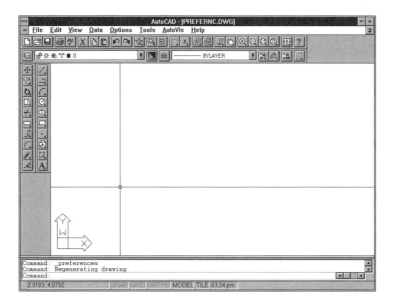

Figure P.21. *An AutoCAD setup without a screen menu and scroll bars.*

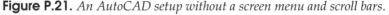

Use of the screen menu on the Windows platform might be useful for those users migrating to the Windows environment from the DOS platform.

The AutoCAD Graphics Window area also contains a pull-down list for **W**indow Repair that lists choices for determining how AutoCAD repaints the screen image when an overlying widow is removed. If you use the display driver that ships with AutoCAD, the only option is Bitmap. If you purchase and use a third-party display driver, other choices can be listed.

Automatic Save. This area of the dialog box determines whether your drawing is automatically saved, and how often. If automatic save is enabled, AutoCAD will periodically save your drawing to a file named AUTO.SV$ in the default drawing directory. You can change the name and location of this file by reconfiguring the automatic-save feature under the operating parameters section of the CONFIG command.

E*v*ery. When this check box is checked, AutoCAD will perform an automatic save. Use the minutes edit box to specify how often AutoCAD automatically will save your drawing.

Digitizer Input. This area in the **S**ystem tab of the Preferences dialog box determines how AutoCAD accepts input from the pointing device. You either can select Digiti**z**er or Di**g**itizer/Mouse in this option.

> **Digiti*z*er.** Choosing this radio button indicates that AutoCAD will accept input from the digitizing device it is configured for. If there is no digitizer configured, AutoCAD will accept input from the mouse.
>
> **Digitizer/Mouse.** When you choose this button, AutoCAD will accept input from the last device that sent data to AutoCAD. This option is on by default and has no effect if only one device is used for AutoCAD input.

Keystrokes. AutoCAD on the Windows platform permits the definition of "accelerator" keystrokes in the ACAD.MNU AutoCAD menu file. Accelerator keys are standard Windows keystrokes. For example, Ctrl+C in Windows copies selected data to the Windows Clipboard. You can override these accelerator keys by reverting to the "AutoCAD Classic" keystroke definition of older releases.

> **A**utoCAD Classic. Choose this radio button to ignore accelerator keys that may be defined in the AutoCAD for Windows menu file. Select the Menu **F**ile radio button to allow the accelerator keys to take precedence over older AutoCAD keystroke combinations.
>
> **Menu F**ile. Choosing this radio button allows accelerator keys to take precedence over older AutoCAD keystroke combinations.

> If you absolutely cannot get used to using the Esc key instead of the Ctrl+C used in older AutoCAD releases for canceling commands, you may want to consider using the AutoCAD Classic keystroke definitions. This enables you to use Ctrl+C for canceling commands, overriding the Windows Copy function.

The following table lists the accelerator keystroke combinations used in the stock Windows CAD and ACADFULL menu files.

Table P.1
Accelerator Keys Used For Windows Functions

Function	*Keystrokes*
Ctrl+O (Ortho mode)	[Ctrl+L]
Ctrl+V (switch viewports)	[Ctrl+R]

Function	Keystrokes
Undo	[Ctrl+Z]
Cut	[Ctrl+X]
Copy	[Ctrl+C]
Paste	[Ctrl+V]
Open	[Ctrl+O]
Print	[Ctrl+P]
New	[Ctrl+N]
Save	[Ctrl+S]

Font. This button displays the Font dialog box in figure P.22. Use this box to specify the font used in the graphics area (screen menu, for example) and text window. Use the **G**raphics or **T**ext buttons within the Font dialog box to specify fonts for that particular area.

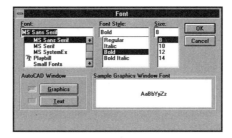

Figure P.22. *The Font dialog box.*

The Font dialog box does not change or override the fonts used for standard Windows objects such as pull-down menu labels and tooltip fonts. Use the Windows Control Panel to change Windows fonts.

Color. Use the **C**olor button to display the AutoCAD Window Colors dialog box for specifying colors for specific elements of the AutoCAD screen area (see fig. P.23).

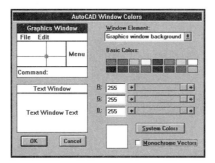

Figure P.23. *The AutoCAD Window Colors dialog box.*

In the AutoCAD Window Colors dialog box, you can specify colors for graphics screen background, text screen background, and text background color and text color for both screens. You can click on a specific area shown in the image tiles or select an area from the Window Element pull-down list box. For specifying a color, you can choose a color from the Basic Colors swatches or specify red, green, and blue values using the slider bars. The color changes in the sample image box at the bottom of the dialog box. Use the System Colors button to default to colors defined in the Windows Control Panel color settings. Check the Monochrome Vectors check box to display all object colors in either black or white (depending on the background color). Monochrome Vectors were used in creating the illustrations in this book.

Environment

The Environment tab of the Preferences dialog box is used to specify the directories for AutoCAD's driver, support, and paging files (see fig. P.24). It also has other features for specifying log file parameters, memory settings, and other file settings. The default settings are set up for you when you install AutoCAD. These settings become effective immediately after closing the Preferences dialog box.

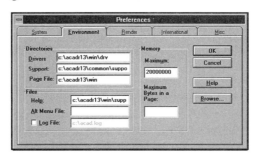

Figure P.24. *The Environment tab of the Preferences dialog box.*

Directories. This section is used to specify the location of AutoCAD's support file. It contains **D**rivers, S**u**pport, and P**a**ge File edit boxes.

Drivers. This edit box is used to specify the location for the ADI drivers that AutoCAD uses to communicate with your display, printers, plotters, digitizers, and other peripherals. This value is stored in the environment variable ACADDRV.

Support. This edit box specifies the location of support files used by AutoCAD such as fonts, menus, AutoLISP files, linetypes, and hatch patterns. This value is stored in the ACAD environment variable.

Page File. This edit box sets the environment variable ACADPAGEDIR for specifying the directory for the page file. A page file is created when AutoCAD runs out of physical memory and must write data to the hard drive. By default, page files are placed in the current directory.

TIP

Specify a drive and directory with plenty of free space for the location of the page file. A good location for the file would be the directory Windows uses to store its temporary files. To find out which directory this is, type SET, then press Enter at a DOS prompt (you could open an MS-DOS window to do this). Look for the line that begins "TEMP=". Specify this directory for the page file. You should make sure no data or program files are stored in this directory and periodically delete any temporary files left there after leaving AutoCAD and Windows.

Files. This area of the Environment tab specifies the location of the help, alternate menu, and log files.

Help. The file name in this edit box is stored in the environment variable ACADHELP and specifies the name of the help file AutoCAD uses. AutoCAD for Windows can read older-style AutoCAD help files as well as any help file in Windows help-file format.

Alt **Menu File**. Use this edit box if you have a digitizer and want to swap another menu file with the standard AutoCAD tablet menu. This value is stored in the environment variable ACADALTMENU.

Log **File**. Check the check box to have AutoCAD generate a log file using the location and name specified in the edit box. This value is stored in the ACADLOGFILE environment variable.

Memory. The Memory option determines how AutoCAD utilizes your system's memory. AutoCAD divides your drawing file into "page" (see Page

Filr) while Windows allocates space for the pages in your system's RAM. When the system RAM is used up, AutoCAD writes portions of your drawing to disk.

Because of AutoCAD's and Window's extensive use of temporary and paging files, it is vitally important that you do not delete any temporary or paging files while using Windows or AutoCAD. Exit both applications to return to DOS before deleting these files. Failure to do so will result in data loss and possibly crash your system.

Maximum. Use this edit box to specify the amount of RAM in bytes that the AutoCAD pager can receive from Windows. Setting this value equal to the amount of RAM your system has ensures that AutoCAD utilizes all of the RAM it can before paging to disk—which results in dramatically decreased performance. Set the value lower for compatibility with applications that require more RAM than Windows would normally allocate. This value is stored in the environment variable ACADMAXMEM.

Maximum Bytes in a Page. This edit box is used to specify the maximum number of bytes used for the first page file. If there is no value specified, AutoCAD will write to the page file until the disk is full. If you are limited on hard drive space, you should set this limit to allow for some space remaining on your hard drive. This value is stored in the environment variable ACADMAXPAGE.

PSDRAG

Pull-down: File, Import, PostScript, Display (DOS Only)
Pull-down: File, Options, PostScript Display (Windows Only)
Screen: FILE, IMPORT, PSdrag:

PSDRAG controls the display of PostScript images while they are placed and scaled by the PSIN command.

Prompts and Options

`PSIN drag mode <0>` Enter **0** to display only the boundary of PostScript images while inserting and scaling with the PSIN command. Enter **1** to display the rendered PostScript image.

PSDRAG 517

> The PSIN drag mode has no effect if the PSQUALITY system variable is set to 0—only boundaries are displayed.

Example

This example describes using the PSDRAG command to change the display of rendered PostScript images when importing with the PSIN command, as shown in figure P.25.

Command: **PSDRAG** (Enter)	Starts the PSDRAG command
PSIN drag mode <0>: **1** (Enter)	Displays full PostScript images when importing

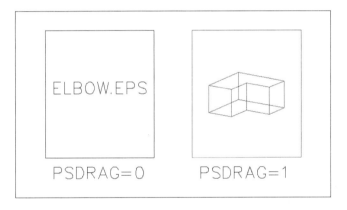

Figure P.25. *Importing a PostScript image with PSDRAG set to 0 or 1.*

Related Commands

PSFILL   PSIN

Related System Variable

PSQUALITY

PSFILL

PostScript Fill

Toolbar: *PostScript Fill (Draw, Hatch)*
Pull-down: *Draw, Hatch, PostScript Fill*
Screen: CONSTRCT, PSfill:

The PSFILL command fills areas enclosed by 2D polylines with a PostScript pattern. The fill pattern is visible only on hard-copy output and is not drawn in the graphics window. PSFILL uses patterns defined in the AutoCAD PostScript support file ACAD.PSF.

Prompts and Options

Select polyline Pick the polyline to fill with a PostScript pattern. The new pattern is assigned to the area within the polyline.

PostScript fill pattern (. = none) <.>/?: ? Enter the name of a fill pattern to assign to the selected area, or enter ? to view a list of PostScript patterns defined in the ACAD.PSF file. Enter the pattern name preceded with an asterisk to prevent printing of the solid polyline outline on hard copy; only the fill pattern is plotted.

If the polyline already has an assigned PostScript pattern fill, that pattern name becomes the default. To remove a PostScript pattern fill, enter a single period (.) for none.

Fill patterns included with Release 13 include Grayscale, RGBcolor, Allogo, Lineargray, Radialgray, Square, Waffle, Zigzag, Stars, Brick, and Specks.

Specific Options Each different PostScript fill pattern has different required options. Options such as scale factors, line width, levels, cycles, angles, separation, frequency, foreground gray shade, and background gray shade are all possible.

Example

This example fills three rectangular polylines with three different PostScript fill patterns using the PSFILL command (see fig. P.26). Each polyline measures roughly five units wide by four units tall. For larger or smaller areas, adjust the scale factor accordingly. The pattern fills are shown below the polylines, although they don't display in the graphics window.

Command: **PSQUALITY** (Enter)	Starts the SETVAR command to change PSQUALITY
New value for PSQUALITY <75>: **75** (Enter)	Sets PSQUALITY to display only outlines
Command: **PSFILL** (Enter)	Starts the PSFILL command
Select polyline: *Pick* ① *(see fig. P. 26)*	Specifies polyline to fill
PostScript fill pattern (. = none) <.>/?: **ZIGZAG** (Enter)	Specifies PostScript fill pattern
Scale <1.0000>: (Enter) LineWidth <1>: (Enter) ForeGroundGray <50>: (Enter) BackGroundGray <0>: (Enter)	Accepts default options
Command: **PSFILL** (Enter)	Starts the PSFILL command
Select polyline: *Pick* ②	Specifies polyline to fill
PostScript fill pattern (. = none) <.>/?: **STARS** (Enter)	Specifies PostScript fill pattern
Scale <1.0000>: (Enter) LineWidth <1>: (Enter) ForegroundGray <100>: (Enter) BackgroundGray <0>: (Enter)	Accepts default options
Command: **PSFILL** (Enter)	Starts the PSFILL command
Select polyline: *Pick* ③	Specifies polyline to fill
PostScript fill pattern (. = none) <.>/?: **BRICK** (Enter)	Specifies PostScript fill pattern
Scale <1.0000>: (Enter) LineWidth <1>: (Enter) BrickGray1 <100>: (Enter) BrickGray2 <50>: (Enter) BackGroundGray <0>: (Enter)	Accepts default options

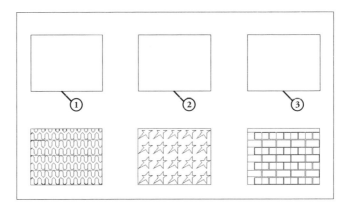

Figure P.26. *Three different PostScript fill patterns.*

Related Commands

PSIN   PSDRAG   PSOUT

Related System Variable

PSQUALITY

PSIN

Pull-down: File, Import, PostScript, Import... (DOS Only)
Screen: FILE, IMPORT, PSin:

The PSIN command imports an existing Encapsulated PostScript (EPS) file into the current drawing. You can drag the image on-screen and place it by picking.

If PSDRAG is set to 0 (or if PSQUALITY is set to 0), AutoCAD displays the image as a box with the file name of the image within the box. If PSDRAG is set to 1, and PSQUALITY is not zero, AutoCAD displays the image as it drags it into position in the graphics window. AutoCAD imports the EPS image as an anonymous (unnamed) AutoCAD block.

The original PostScript data is appended to the block as extended object data in case the image is output back to an EPS file with the PSOUT command.

Prompts and Options

The PSIN command first displays the Select Postscript File dialog box. Select an existing *Encapsulated PostScript* (EPS) file to import.

Insertion point <0,0,0> Pick a point in the graphics window, or enter the coordinates of the insertion point for the raster image.

Scale Factor Enter a number or pick a point in the graphics window to show a distance. If you pick a point in the graphics window, the distance from the insertion point is used as the scale factor.

New length If you press Enter at the Scale Factor prompt, you are reprompted to enter a new scale factor or to pick a point to show a distance for the scale factor.

Example

This example uses the Encapsulated PostScript file created by PSOUT to insert into a new drawing (see fig. P.27).

```
Command: PSIN (Enter)                    Starts the PSIN command
Insertion point <0,0,0>: (Enter)         Specifies insertion point at 0,0,0
Scale factor: 1 (Enter)                  Specifies scale factor of 1
```

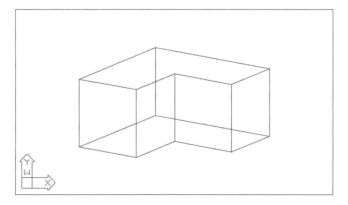

Figure P.27. *Importing an Encapsulated PostScript image with the PSIN command.*

Related Commands

ACISIN	DXBIN	DXFIN	GIFIN
IMPORT	PCXIN	PSOUT	TIFFIN
WMFIN			

Related System Variable

PSQUALITY

PSOUT

Pull-down: File, Export, PostScript, Export... (DOS Only)
Screen: FILE, EXPORT, PSout:

The PSOUT command exports the current drawing as an *Encapsulated PostScript* (EPS) file. The EPS file can then be imported into another graphics or desktop publishing program. A user-selectable resolution screen image can be included for previewing the file within other programs.

> If any blocks exist in the drawing with PostScript information in extended object data, such as created by PSIN, that information is output to the EPS file as well.

AutoCAD outputs the drawing objects using the PostScript support file ACAD.PFS to determine fill patterns, font definitions, and stroke characteristics. You can add prologue definitions to this file using an ASCII text editor and reference them by setting the PSPROLOG system variable to the new definition.

Prompts and Options

The PSOUT command displays the Create PostScript File dialog box. Specify a file name to contain the Encapsulated PostScript output, with an extension of EPS.

What to export - Display, Extents, Limits, View or Window <D> Enter an option for the area of the current drawing to export.

The Display option exports an area equivalent to the current graphics window. The Extents option exports an area containing all the objects in the current space on nonfrozen layers. The Limits option exports an area equivalent to the current drawing's limits as set by the LIMITS command.

PSOUT

The View option exports an area defined by an existing view created by the VIEW command. The Window option exports an area bounded by a window specified in the graphics window.

First corner, Other corner If you select the Window option, these prompts appear. Pick a point in the graphics window, or enter the coordinates for two opposing corners of a window to export.

Include a screen preview image in the file? (None/EPSI/TIFF) <None> Enter the type of screen preview to include within the EPS file or accept the default, None. EPSI-type preview images are predominantly used by the Macintosh platform. TIFF previews are usually necessary for DOS. If you specify a preview image type, the following prompt appears.

Screen preview image size (128x128 is standard)? (128/256/512) <128> Enter a number for the resolution of the screen preview image. Smaller sizes display faster than larger ones. Higher-resolution images display with more detail.

Size units (Inches or Millimeters) <Inches> Enter **Inches** or **Millimeters** to determine output units.

Specify scale by entering: Output Inches=Drawing Units or Fit or ? <Fit> Specify the output scale factor.

Enter the Size or Width,Height (in Inches) <USER> Specify the paper size by either entering a letter from the list that AutoCAD presents or by entering the width and height (separated by a comma) of a user size of paper.

Example

The following example creates an EPS file of the rectangular elbow created with the PFACE command (see fig. P.28).

Command: **PSOUT** (Enter) *Enter the file name in the edit box*	Starts the PSOUT command Specifies output EPS file
What to plot -- Display, Extents, Limits,View, or Window <D>: (Enter)	Specifies output current display areas in graphics window
Include a screen preview image in the file? (None/EPSI/TIFF) <None>: T (Enter)	Includes screen preview image, of TIFF type
Screen preview image size (128x128 is standard)? (128/256/512) <128>: (Enter)	Specifies size of preview image is 128×128 pixels

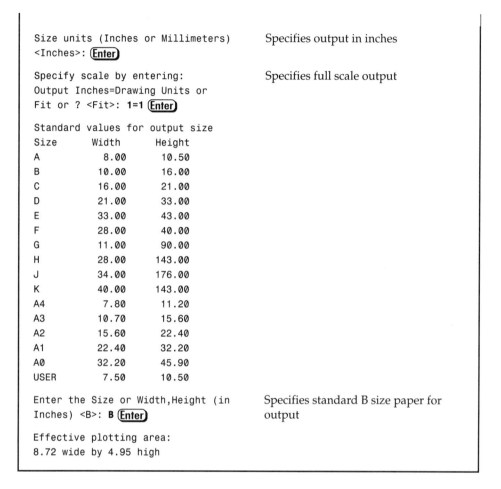

Size units (Inches or Millimeters) <Inches>: **(Enter)**	Specifies output in inches	
Specify scale by entering: Output Inches=Drawing Units or Fit or ? <Fit>: **1=1 (Enter)**	Specifies full scale output	

```
Standard values for output size
Size     Width     Height
A         8.00      10.50
B        10.00      16.00
C        16.00      21.00
D        21.00      33.00
E        33.00      43.00
F        28.00      40.00
G        11.00      90.00
H        28.00     143.00
J        34.00     176.00
K        40.00     143.00
A4        7.80      11.20
A3       10.70      15.60
A2       15.60      22.40
A1       22.40      32.20
A0       32.20      45.90
USER      7.50      10.50
```

Enter the Size or Width,Height (in Inches) <B>: **B (Enter)**	Specifies standard B size paper for output

```
Effective plotting area:
8.72 wide by 4.95 high
```

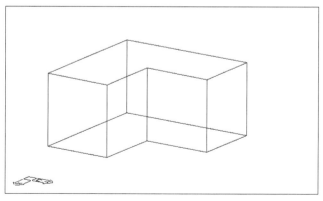

Figure P.28. *Exporting the rectangular elbow as an Encapsulated PostScript image.*

Related Commands

DXFOUT   EXPORT   PLOT   PSIN

Related System Variables

PSPROLOG   PSQUALITY

PSPACE

Paper Space

Toolbar: *Paper Space (Standard Toolbar, Space)*
Pull-down: <u>V</u>iew, Paper <u>S</u>pace
Screen: VIEW, Pspace:

The PSPACE command switches from model space to paper space and works only when paper space is active and at least one viewport has been created in paper space. Paper space is indicated by the presence of the crosshairs across the entire graphics window, and in Windows, by the keyword *PAPER* on the status line. In Windows, you can toggle between model and paper space by double clicking the name in the status line. The Paper space UCS icon (see the icon in the lower left corner of figure P.29) is visible if the UCSICON command is on. The PSPACE command is not allowed if TILEMODE is set to 1; AutoCAD responds:

```
** Command not allowed unless TILEMODE is set to 0 **
```

If you issue the PSPACE command while in paper space, AutoCAD responds:

```
Already in paper space.
```

You must make paper space active to create or edit paper space objects. Model space must be active if you want to work on model space objects or to pan, zoom, or modify the viewport contents. Use the MSPACE command to make model space active.

Example

This example demonstrates changing from paper space to model space using the PSPACE command.

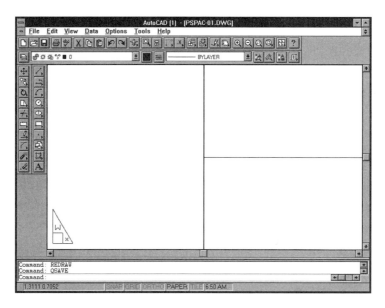

Figure P.29. *Switching to paper space from a model space viewport with the PSPACE command.*

Command: **TILEMODE** (Enter)	Starts the SETVAR command to change TILEMODE
New value for TILEMODE <1>: **0** (Enter)	Changes to paper space
Entering Paper space. Use MVIEW to insert Model space viewports.	
Regenerating drawing.	
Command: **MVIEW** (Enter)	Starts MVIEW command to create viewports
ON/OFF/Hideplot/Fit/2/3/4/ Restore/<First Point>: **3** (Enter)	Specifies the three viewport option
Horizontal/Vertical/Above/ Below/Left/<Right>: **L** (Enter)	Creates three viewports, one large one on left side of graphics window, with two smaller ones on right side
Fit/<First Point>: **F** (Enter)	Fits three new viewports into graphics window
Regenerating drawing.	

Command: **MSPACE** (Enter)	Changes from paper space to model space
Command: **PSPACE** (Enter)	Changes from model space to paper space

Related Commands

DDVIEW   DDVPOINT   MSPACE   MVIEW
UCSICON   VPLAYER

Related System Variables

MAXACTVP   PSLTSCALE   TILEMODE
UCSICON   VISRETAIN

PURGE

    Pull-down: **D**ata, **P**urge
    Screen: DATA, Purge:

The PURGE command selectively removes from the drawing unreferenced definitions of blocks, dimension styles, layers, linetypes, shapes, text styles, application identifiers (for add-on ADS, ARX, or AutoLISP applications), and multiline styles. By using the PURGE command to remove unused definitions, you can reduce the size of the drawing and speed up the loading of drawings. You can use the PURGE command at any time during a drawing session.

Named definitions that are nested, such as blocks, are purged only one level per execution of the PURGE command. For example, you may have a block definition that references another block. Therefore you must purge the highest level first then issue the PURGE command repeatedly to purge the nested items. You may have to do this procedure several times to purge all unused items if they are deeply nested.

Prompts and Options

`Purge unused`
`Blocks/Dimstyles/LAyers/LTypes/SHapes/STyles/APpids/Mlinestyles/All`   At this prompt, enter the capital letter(s) of the definition type to purge. Enter an **A** to purge unreferenced definitions of all types.

Purge *item* **NAME? <N>**   If any unreferenced definitions of the specified type exist (listed in the prompt), the PURGE command displays each unreferenced definition's name (in the prompt) and asks if you want to remove it. PURGE continues to prompt for all unreferenced items of that type. If you specify the All option, PURGE prompts individually for all unreferenced definitions of each of the types.

Example

This example uses the PURGE command to remove a block definition named CHAIR from the drawing.

Command: **PURGE** (Enter)	Issues the PURGE command
Purge unused Blocks/Dimstyles/LAyers/LTypes/ SHapes/STyles/APpids/Mlinestyles/ All: **B** (Enter)	Selects the Block option
Purge block CHAIR? <N> **Y** (Enter)	Removes the block definition from the drawing database

Related Commands

BLOCK   STYLE   SHAPE   WBLOCK

QSAVE

Save

Toolbar: *Save (Standard)*
Pull-down: **F**ile, **S**ave
Screen: FILE, Save:

The QSAVE command works the same way as the SAVE command, saving any changes to the current drawing to disk without exiting the drawing editor. The difference between QSAVE and SAVE is that QSAVE does not prompt for a file name; the current drawing is saved to the default file name without hesitation. If the current drawing has not yet been named or was opened in read-only mode, the Save Drawing As dialog box appears so that you can specify a file name.

TIP Use the QSAVE command to save your work periodically. It saves changes to the default drawing quickly.

Related Commands

END   QUIT   SAVE   SAVEAS   SAVESR12

Related System Variables

DBMOD   DWGNAME   DWGPREFIX

QTEXT

Pull-down: **O**ptions, **D**isplay, **T**ext Frame Only
Screen: OPTIONS, DISPLAY, Qtext:

The QTEXT command turns quick text mode on and off. When quick text mode is on, any text object is redisplayed as boxes that indicate the approximate size of the text object, instead of text characters. The screen regenerates and redraws much faster with quick text mode on, especially if the drawing contains much text or uses a complex font. New text displays as text characters until the next screen regeneration. Quick text mode does not affect the text editing commands CHANGE, DDATTE, and DDEDIT. You may also use the DDRMODES Drawing Aids dialog box to turn the QTEXT mode on and off. Figure Q.1 illustrates the QTEXT OFF and ON modes.

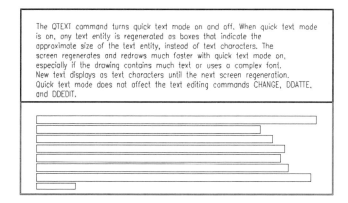

Figure Q.1. *QTEXT OFF (above) and ON (below).*

Prompts and Options

ON/OFF Enter **ON** to turn on quick text mode. After the next regeneration, the display shows all existing text as boxes.

Enter **OFF** to disable quick text mode. After the next regeneration, all text displays normally.

Example

The following example shows the effect of quick text mode on existing text in a drawing (refer to fig. Q.1).

```
Command: QTEXT (Enter)            Issues the QTEXT command

On/Off <Off>: ON (Enter)          Specifies the ON option

Command: REGEN (Enter)            Regenerates the drawing to effect the
                                  QTEXT change
```

Related Commands

| DDRMODES | DTEXT | MTEXT | PLOT |
| REGEN | TEXT | | |

Related System Variable

QTEXTMODE

QUIT

Pull-down: <u>F</u>ile, E<u>x</u>it
Screen: FILE, Exit:

The QUIT command exits AutoCAD. If the drawing has been modified since the last SAVE, a dialog box appears, prompting you to save or discard changes before exiting AutoCAD.

Related Commands

| END | QSAVE | SAVE | SAVEAS |
| SAVEASR12 | | | |

Related System Variable

DBMOD

RAY

Ray

Toolbar: *Ray (Draw, Line)*
Pull-down: **D**raw, **R**ay
Screen: DRAW1, Ray:

The RAY command draws straight lines starting at one point and extending to infinity along a specified direction. The direction is specified by selecting a second point to draw the ray through. The starting and through points can be any 2D or 3D coordinate location.

The command repeats, enabling many rays to be created from the same starting point, until you press Enter or Cancel. You can draw rays at right angles by turning on ortho mode. Use the XLINE command to draw rays extending to infinity in both directions.

Rays are used as construction lines and do not affect the extents of the drawing.

Prompts and Options

From point   Specify a starting point for the ray. The point can have any X, Y, and Z coordinates and can be selected with any object snap overrides or point filters.

Through point   Pick a point in the graphics window or enter the coordinates for a point to draw the ray through. This prompt repeats until you press Enter or Cancel.

Example

This example demonstrates using the RAY command to draw rays from the centers of two circles. The rays are drawn in different directions to calculate an intersection (see fig. R.1).

Command: **CIRCLE** (Enter)	Starts the CIRCLE command
3P/2P/TTR/<Center point>: **4,2** (Enter)	Specifies center point of circle
Diameter/<Radius>: **1** (Enter)	Specifies radius distance of circle
Command: **CIRCLE** (Enter)	Starts the CIRCLE command
3P/2P/TTR/<Center point>: **10.35,2** (Enter)	Specifies center point of circle
Diameter/<Radius> <1.0000>: (Enter)	Repeats previous radius distance
Command: **RAY** (Enter)	Starts RAY command
From point: **CEN** (Enter)	Specifies object snap CENter
of *Pick* ① *(see fig. R.1)*	Selects center of left circle to draw from
Through point: **@1<35** (Enter)	Specifies ray direction
Through point: (Enter)	Finishes RAY command
Command: **RAY** (Enter)	Starts the RAY command
From point: **CEN** (Enter)	Specifies object snap CENter
of *Pick* ②	Selects center of right circle to draw from
Through point: **@1<100** (Enter)	Specifies RAY direction
Through point: (Enter)	Finishes RAY command

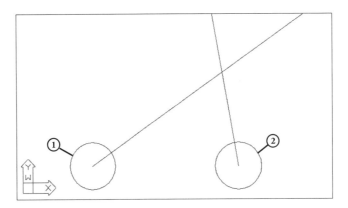

Figure R.1. *Finding an intersection using two rays.*

Related Commands
LINE   XLINE

Related System Variable
CECOLOR   CELTSCALE   CELTYPE   CLAYER
LASTPOINT

RCONFIG

Pull-down: **O**ptions, **R**ender Configure
Screen: TOOLS, RENDER, Config:

The RCONFIG (Render CONFIGure) command changes the configured display and hard copy rendering devices used by the RENDER command. All other AutoCAD display and output are through devices configured by the CONFIG command. AutoCAD switches focus to the text window and then displays the current rendering device configuration. The configuration menu has four options.

Prompts and Options

`Enter selection <0>`   Enter one of the following four configuration menu options at this prompt.

`0. Exit to drawing editor`   Exits the RCONFIG command and returns to the drawing editor. You first are prompted to save or discard the changes made to the configuration.

1. Show current configuration   Displays the opening screen of the RCONFIG command, showing the current configuration.

2. Configure rendering device   Displays the currently available rendering and combined rendering/display devices, and enables you to configure them. The prompts and options vary depending on the device. Consult the *AutoCAD Release 13 Installation Guide for DOS* and your rendering driver's documentation for more information. The Windows version of AutoCAD does not have any configuration changes available.

3. Configure hard copy rendering device / Render Window   Displays the currently available hard copy rendering devices and enables you to configure them. The prompts and options vary depending on the device. Consult the *AutoCAD Release 13 Installation Guide for DOS* and your rendering driver's documentation for more information. The Windows version of AutoCAD does not have any configuration changes available.

Related Commands

CONFIG   RENDER   RPREF

RECOVER

Pull-down: File, Management, Recover...
Screen: File, MANAGE, Recover:

The RECOVER command attempts to repair damaged drawing files. Drawing files can become corrupted or damaged in any number of ways, including power outages, power surges, disk errors, and so on. AutoCAD drawing files seem particularly sensitive to damage due to their complexity. In the Recover Drawing File dialog box, select the file name of the damaged drawing. The RECOVER command displays the results of the recovery process on the text screen. The AutoCAD OPEN command performs an automatic recovery on the drawing being loaded into the AutoCAD editor. The following is an example of the drawing recovery report:

```
Command: RECOVER (Enter)
Drawing recovery.
Drawing recovery log.
Scanning completed.
Validating objects in the handle table.
Valid objects 49     Invalid objects 0
Validating objects completed.
Used contingency data.
    Salvaged database from drawing.
```

```
   2      Blocks audited
Pass 1 11      objects audited
Pass 2 11      objects audited
Total errors found 0 fixed 0
Regenerating drawing.
```

Related Commands

AUDIT   OPEN

RECTANG

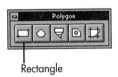

Rectangle

Toolbar: *Rectangle (Draw, Polygon)*
Pull-down: **D**raw, Polygon, **R**ectangle
Screen: DRAW1, Rectang:

RECTANG enables you to draw orthogonal rectangles by picking any two opposing corners. The rectangle is a closed polyline, and as such, can be edited with the PEDIT command, solidified, or extruded. The angle of the rectangle depends upon the current *User Coordinate System* (UCS).

> If your User Coordinate System is not parallel and at right angles to your current view, the drag box used to pick two points to specify the opposite corners of the rectangle will not be accurate. In this scenario, you must at least type in the coordinates or displacement for the second point, if not both points.

Prompts and Options

First corner   Specify the first corner of the rectangle. You can enter coordinates, pick a point, or use the object snap modes.

Other corner   Specify the second corner of the rectangle. You can enter coordinates, pick a point, or use the object snap modes.

Example

The following example draws a rectangle.

From the Draw menu, choose Polygon, then Rectangle

Command: _rectang	Issues the RECTANG command
First corner: **4,3** (Enter)	Specifies one corner of the rectangle
Second corner: **8.5,6** (Enter)	Specifies the opposite corner of the rectangle

---

Related Commands
PLINE   POLYGON

Related System Variable
PLINEGEN

REDEFINE

The REDEFINE command reverses the UNDEFINE command by restoring an AutoCAD command to its original action. The UNDEFINE command disables AutoCAD commands so they cannot be used. You can use AutoLISP or ADS to define a custom command to replace an undefined command. For example, you can define a replacement CIRCLE command that asks you to specify the radius distance before the center location.

If you do not want to redefine the command, but you still need to use it with its original actions, you can enter the command name preceded by a period at the Command: prompt. For example, if CIRCLE is undefined, you can still use it by typing **.CIRCLE** at the Command: prompt.

Prompts and Options

Command name   Enter the name of the AutoCAD command to restore.

Example

The following example uses the UNDEFINE command to disable the ELEV command. The REDEFINE command is then used to restore the ELEV command back to its original action.

Command: **UNDEFINE** (Enter)	Starts the UNDEFINE command to remove a command definition
Command name: **ELEV** (Enter)	Specifies the ELEV command to undefine
Command: **ELEV** (Enter)	Attempts to start the ELEV command
Unknown command "ELEV". Type ? for list of commands.	
Command: **.ELEV** (Enter)	Starts ELEV command by preceding command with a single period
New current elevation <0.0000>: *Press Cancel*	Cancels the ELEV command
Cancel	
Command: **REDEFINE** (Enter)	Starts the REDEFINE command
Command name: **ELEV** (Enter)	Specifies the ELEV command to restore
Command: **ELEV** (Enter)	Starts the restored ELEV command
New current elevation <0.0000>: *Press Cancel*	Cancels the ELEV command
Cancel	

Related Command

UNDEFINE

REDO

Redo

Toolbar: *Redo (Standard Toolbar)*
Pull-down: **E**dit, **R**edo
Pull-down: Assist Redo (DOS only)
Screen: ASSIST Redo:

The REDO command reverses the effects of the UNDO or U command. REDO only works if the immediately preceding command was UNDO (or U).

Related Commands

U   UNDO

Related System Variables

UNDOCTL   UNDOMARKS

'REDRAW

Redraw View

Toolbar: *Redraw View (Standard Toolbar, Redraw)*
Pull-down: **V**iew, Redraw **V**iew
Screen: VIEW, Redraw:

The REDRAW command redisplays the image in the current viewport. Blips are removed from the display. Use this command to refresh the display after you erase objects that overlap, or to return to the current drawing after viewing a slide with the VSLIDE command.

REDRAW is substantially faster than the REGEN command, which also refreshes the displayed image. The REGEN command, however, regenerates the current view in addition to redrawing it.

NOTE: REDRAW will restore a view that has been rendered, but a REGEN is required to restore a view after using the HIDE command.

The current viewport automatically redraws when a layer is turned on or off, or the grid is turned off. Note that the grid's density affects the speed of the redraw. Objects on layers turned off or frozen layers reduce the time required to redraw. You can stop a redraw operation by pressing Ctrl+C. In this case, you can select only displayed objects until a complete redraw takes place.

Related Commands

REDRAWALL   REGEN   REGENALL   REGENAUTO

Related System Variable

REGENMODE

'REDRAWALL

Redraw All

Toolbar: *Redraw All (Standard Toolbar, Redraw)*
Pull-down: **V**iew, Redraw **A**ll
Screen: VIEW, RedrwAl:

The REDRAWALL command is identical to the REDRAW command, except that it redisplays the images in all active viewports on the screen, not just the current viewport.

Related Commands

REDRAW   REGEN   REGENALL   REGENAUTO
VPORT

Related System Variable

REGENMODE

REGEN

Screen: TOOLS, SHADE, Regen:

The REGEN command regenerates the geometry of all objects within the drawing and redisplays the image in the current viewport. AutoCAD rereads all the objects from within the drawing database on disk (except those objects on frozen layers). It then recalculates the screen coordinates for properly displaying the objects in your drawing. You cannot use this command transparently. If you make modifications to a drawing, you may need to issue the REGEN command to ensure that the modifications are displayed correctly.

A regeneration occurs automatically when the drawing is loaded into memory with the OPEN command. Certain command options, such as ZOOM All always regenerate the drawing. Other actions, such as redefining a block or text style, resetting linetype scale, or LAYER Freeze/Thaw automatically regenerate the drawing unless automatic regenerations have been turned off. Automatic regeneration by such commands is controlled by the REGENAUTO command. The REGEN command also smoothes out arcs and circles that look segmented due to the current zoom factor.

To speed up the regeneration process, freeze or turn off layers not in use. You can stop the screen regeneration by pressing Ctrl+C. In this case, any objects not displayed may not be selected or redrawn until a completed regeneration takes place.

Related Commands
QTEXT   REDRAW   REGENALL   REGENAUTO
VIEWRES   ZOOM

Related System Variables
EXPERT   QTEXT   REGENMODE   TXTQLTY

REGENALL

The REGENALL command regenerates the entire drawing and redisplays the current views in all active viewports. The REGENALL command differs from the REGEN command in that REGENALL regenerates every active viewport. If you have only one active viewport, the REGENALL command works exactly the same as the REGEN command.

Related Commands

REGEN REDRAWALL REGENAUTO VIEWRES VPLAYER

Related System Variables

QTEXT REGENMODE TXTQLTY

'REGENAUTO

The REGENAUTO command controls automatic screen regenerations caused by commands such as BLOCK, STYLE, LTSCALE, LAYER, and ZOOM, which automatically cause a screen regeneration.

Prompts and Options

ON/OFF <On> When REGENAUTO is on, AutoCAD executes a screen regeneration when certain commands require it.

If REGENAUTO is OFF, AutoCAD disables automatic regeneration caused by certain actions. With some commands, this forces AutoCAD to prompt you to verify that you want a screen regeneration. If you execute such a command, the following prompt appears:

```
About to regen, proceed? <Y>
```

AutoCAD displays the following prompt during a transparent command if regeneration is required:

```
Regen queued
```

Note that you can suppress this prompt by setting the EXPERT system variable to a value of 1 or more.

Related Commands

ATTDISP REDRAW REDRAWALL REGEN REGENALL ZOOM

Related System Variables

EXPERT REGENMODE

REGION

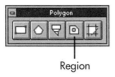
Region

Toolbar: *Region (Draw, Polygon)*
Pull-down: *C*onstruct, *R*egion
Screen: CONSTRUCT, Region:

The REGION command converts 2D objects into ACIS REGION objects. Valid 2D objects include closed polylines, polygons, circles, ellipses, traces, donuts, closed splines, and AutoCAD 2D solid objects. Groups of contiguous lines, arcs, and open 2D polylines also can be converted into regions, if they do not cross themselves. Objects lose any thickness when converting to a region.

Polylines, to be converted to a region, must have at least three vertices and must not cross themselves. Wide polylines (and donuts) are converted to a region from their center line. If you attempt to form a region out of a polyline that crosses itself, AutoCAD responds:

```
1 loop rejected.  Self intersections: 1 loop.
```

If more than one object is selected, the conversion to regions is performed in two steps. First, all closed 2D polylines are converted to regions. Then, all coplanar objects are grouped together and converted. Objects do not need to be in the current UCS in order to be converted to regions.

Prompts and Options

Select objects Select the objects you want to convert to regions. Use any of AutoCAD's object selection options.

Example

The following example shows how to create a region from a trimmed polyline and arc. Use the RECTANG command to create a polyline from 2,2 to 8,6. Use the CIRCLE command to create a circle centered at 8,6 with a radius of 2.5, and use the TRIM command to trim the two objects as shown in figure R.2.

```
Command: REGION (Enter)              Begins the REGION command
Select objects: W (Enter)            Specifies window option for selecting
                                     objects
First corner: Pick ①                 Specifies first corner of selection
(see fig R.2)                        window
Other corner: Pick ②                 Specifies opposing corner of window
3 found
Select objects: (Enter)              Finishes selecting objects
1 loop extracted.
1 Region created.
```

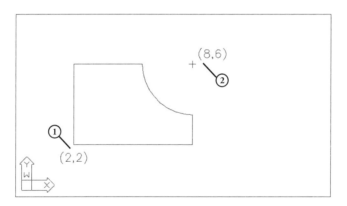

Figure R.2. *The trimmed circle and polyline before converting into a REGION.*

Related Commands

BOUNDARY   EXPLODE   EXTRUDE   INTERFERE
INTERSECT MASSPROP   SUBTRACT   UNION

Related System Variable

THICKNESS

REINIT

Pull-down: **T**ools, Reinitiali**z**e
Screen: TOOLS, Reinit:

The REINIT command reinitializes the peripherals with which AutoCAD communicates. Use REINIT when operation of your display, digitizer, or plotter has been lost or interrupted by another program, or by disconnecting and reconnecting the peripheral. You also can use REINIT to reload the ACAD.PGP file after changes have been made during the current editing session.

Prompts and Options

The REINIT command displays the Re-initialization dialog box (see fig. R.3), which has the following options:

I/O Port Initialization. Check either or both the **D**igitizer or **P**lotter check box to re-initialize communications with your system's input and output ports. Checking one of these options might not necessarily re-establish communications with the peripheral attached to the specified port. See the Device and File Initialization options below.

Device and File Initialization. Check the Di**g**itizer check box to initialize the configured digitizer. If the I/O port itself, to which the digitizer is connected, has been reset by other software, I/O port initialization may need to be performed. See the preceding I/O Port Initialization options.

Figure R.3. *The Re-initialization dialog box.*

Check the Di**s**play check box to initialize the configured display. Both the AutoCAD graphics screen and text screen are completely redrawn. Use this option if another program executed from within AutoCAD does not restore the screen contents upon exiting.

Check the PGP **F**ile check box to reload the ACAD.PGP file. Any changes made to ACAD.PGP do not take effect until the file is loaded by the REINIT command or when AutoCAD is started.

Example

The following example shows how to reinitialize the drawing editor after making an addition to the ACAD.PGP file. Add an alias for the EXTEND command to the ACAD.PGP file and create a line to extend to another line, as shown in figure R.4.

Command: **X** (Enter)	Attempts to start nonexistent command X
`Unknown command "X".` `Type ? for list of commands.`	
Edit the ACAD.PGP file to include the following new alias:	Adds command alias for EXTEND command as the X command
`X,     *EXTEND`	
Command: **REINIT** (Enter)	Starts the REINIT command
Check the PGP File check box	Selects ACAD.PGP for reloading
Click on OK	Reloads ACAD.PGP
Command: **X** (Enter)	Starts the X command, an alias for EXTEND

`EXTEND`
`Select boundary edges: (Projmode = UCS,`
`Edgemode = No extend)`	

`Select objects:` *Pick* ① *(see fig. R.4)*	Selects boundary edge
`1 found`	
`Select objects:` (Enter)	Finishes selecting boundary edges
`<Select object to extend>/Project/` `Edge/Undo:` *Pick* ②	Selects line to extend to boundary edge
`<Select object to extend>/Project/` `Edge/Undo:` (Enter)	Finishes selecting objects to extend

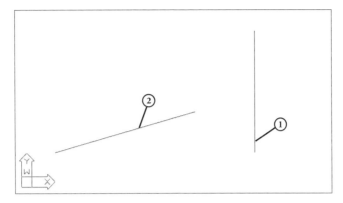

Figure R.4. *The two lines before reinitializing and extending.*

Related Command

CONFIG

Related System Variable

RE-INIT

RENAME

The RENAME command changes the names of named objects such as dimension styles, layers, views, and text styles. See DDRENAME.

> The new DDRENAME dialog box is much easier to use than the RENAME command when you are renaming defined items.

Prompts and Options

Block/Dimstyle/LAyer/LType/Style/Ucs/VIew/VPort   This prompt contains a list of the named items that you can rename. Type the uppercase letter(s) for the item type you want to rename.

Old item name   At this prompt, enter the current name of the item that you want to rename. If the name you enter does not belong to a current item, the command exits and the prompt `Old item NAME not found` appears.

New item name At this prompt, enter a new name for the item. The new name is subject to the standard limitations on name length and valid characters used by AutoCAD for all other item names.

Example

The following example renames a layer named DOOR-2 to UNUSED_DOORS.

Command: **RENAME** (Enter)	Issues the RENAME command
Block/Dimstyle/LAyer/LType/Style/Ucs/VIew/VPort: **LA** (Enter)	Selects the LAyer option
Old layer name: **DOOR-2** (Enter)	Specifies the existing layer to rename
New layer name: **UNUSED_DOORS** (Enter)	Specifies the new name

Related Commands

BLOCK   DDRENAME

RENDER

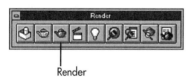
Render

Toolbar: *Render (Render)*
Pull-down: *Tools, Render, Render*
Screen: TOOLS, RENDER, Render:

The RENDER command creates a realistically shaded image of 3D surface or solid objects within AutoCAD. Surface materials, lighting, scene, and rendering preference information is used to produce the shaded image. The rendered image can be output to a viewport, a DOS hard-copy device, or a file. The AutoCAD for Windows Render Window also can be used for viewing of multiple rendered images, and enables saving a rendered image to a file, copying to the clipboard, or printing.

RENDER

> The RENDER commands options also are available from the LIGHT, RPREF, and SCENE commands. For more detail on the various options, refer to these commands.

Prompts and Options

The RENDER command displays a series of dialog boxes for controlling the rendering procedure. The Render dialog box is used to choose the rendering type and select the rendering scene (see fig. R.5). The Screen Palette, Rendering Options, Destination options, and Render Scene and Render Objects selection options also are available and can be preset from the RPREF command.

Rendering Type. Select the desired rendering method. AutoCAD Render is supplied with AutoCAD. Additional rendering methods (such as Autodesk AutoVision) appear in this list when installed.

Scene to Render. Select the desired view to render. If no scenes are yet defined (see the SCENE command), only the current view is available for rendering. Each scene defines a view with lights. If no scenes are defined, the current view is rendered using all lights in the drawing. If there are no lights, the rendering is produced using a single default distant light, located at the viewing position directed along the current viewing direction.

Screen Palette. Select the color map desired for rendering images. The three available selections are Best Map/No Fold, Best Map/Fold, and Fixed ACAD Map.

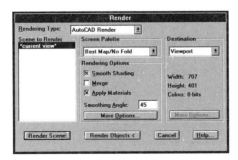

Figure R.5. *The Render dialog box.*

TIP If the Skip Render dialog option is checked in the Render Preferences dialog box (see the RPREF command), then the dialog box is not displayed. Use this control to create preset rendering options that execute without prompting the instant you invoke the RENDER command.

Rendering Options

Check **S**mooth Shading to cause the transition between adjacent polygon mesh surfaces to appear smooth when rendered. Check **M**erge to enable multiple image merging in the frame buffer. Check **A**pply Materials to control the application of defined surface materials. See the RMAT command for a complete description of surface materials.

The More **O**ptions button accesses the options available for the currently selected rendering type.

Render Scene. Select Render Scene to render all of the objects visible in the currently selected scene.

Render Objects. Select Render Objects to select specific objects to render from the graphics window. You can use any standard AutoCAD object selection method to select the objects for rendering.

Destination. Select either Viewport, Render Window, or File from the Destination drop-down list box.

The AutoCAD for Windows Render Window

The Render Window (available only when using the Windows version of AutoCAD) displays, views, saves, and prints rendered images. It is a separate window generated when you start an AutoCAD Render application. The window will close automatically when AutoCAD exits. Images are displayed in client windows within the Render Window. Select the desired scan line interlacing, if supported for the currently selected output file type.

Open. Opens an existing image file. Valid file types include Windows Bit Map files (BMP), Windows Metafiles (WMF), Windows Clipboard files (CLP), Device Independent Bitmap (DIB) files, and Run Length Encoded (RLE) files. Choosing Open, from either the Open icon or the **F**ile menu, displays the Render Open file dialog box. Select the desired file to open and click on OK. If Reuse Window is not checked in the **W**indow menu, a new client window is created to hold the image. If Reuse Window is checked, the image file opened replaces the current image.

The REPLAY command is used to open other image files, such as GIF, TIFF, and TGA files.

> **WARNING**
> In some early versions of Release 13, it can be difficult to close the Render Window. If you use the End Task option from the Task List feature of Windows, the window will close, but AutoCAD will not perform any more rendering unless you change to the File Destination option.

Save. Saves the current image to a file, using the WMF format. Choosing Save, from either the Save icon or the File menu, displays the Save BMP file dialog box. Specify the desired file to save and click on OK.

Print. Prints the current image to the current default Windows printer. Choosing Print, from either the Print icon or the File menu, displays the Print dialog box. Select the number of copies desired, specify tiling the image across multiple pages (if desired), and click on OK.

Options. Changes the bitmap size (the number of horizontal and vertical pixels) and the color depth. Choosing Options, from either the Options icon or the File menu, displays the Windows Render Options dialog box (see fig. R.6).

Figure R.6. *The AutoCAD for Windows Render Window.*

Specify the size in pixels for the image, using either standard VGA (640×480) or 1024×768. The image also can be scaled to fit the viewport, or a custom size can be entered by selecting User and entering the horizontal and vertical pixel sizes in the edit boxes.

Specify the number of colors (8-bit is 256 colors; 24-bit is 16 million colors), and specify whether to scale the image to fill the window. Images scaled to fit the window will not have their aspect ratio changed to match the window. As a result, the image might have a background visible on either the right and left sides, or the top and bottom, depending upon the window shape.

Copy. Copies the current image to the Windows Clipboard. Choosing Copy, from either the Copy icon or the <u>E</u>dit menu, copies the image to the Clipboard as a device-independent bitmap. The image can then be imported as a bitmap image into other Windows applications.

Reuse Window. Determines if an image file replaces an existing image, or if a new window is created for an image file opened with the Open command. If Reuse Window is not checked in the Window menu, a new client window is created to hold the image file. If Reuse Window is checked, the image file opened replaces the current image.

Example

The following example uses the RENDER command to render all viewports in the microscope drawing EX09 (supplied with AutoCAD). See figure R.7 for the rendered views.

Click in the upper left viewport	Activates upper left viewport
Command: **RENDER** (Enter)	Starts the RENDER command
Click on Render Scene	Specifies rendering of current viewport
Click in the middle left viewport	Activates middle left viewport
Command: **RENDER** (Enter)	Starts the RENDER command
Click on Render Scene	Specifies rendering of current viewport
Click in the lower left viewport	Activates lower left viewport
Command: **RENDER** (Enter)	Starts the RENDER command
Click on Render Scene	Specifies rendering of current viewport
Click in the large right viewport	Activates large right viewport
Command: **RENDER** (Enter)	Starts the RENDER command
Click on Render Scene	Specifies rendering of current viewport

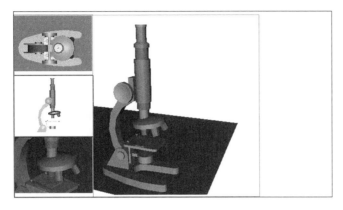

Figure R.7. *Four views of the microscope, rendered using the RENDER command.*

Related Commands

DVIEW	HIDE	LIGHT	MATLIB
PREFERENCES	RENDSCR	RENDERUNLOAD	REPLAY
RMAT	RPREF	SAVEIMG	SCENE
SHADE	STATS		

Related Variables

PSQUALITY   SHADEDGE

RENDSCR

The RENDSCR (RENDering SCReen) command redisplays the last rendered image on single-monitor DOS systems. After an image is displayed on the full screen, you can press any key to return to the current drawing. The F1 key continues to work normally, flipping between the drawing editor and text display. The RENDSCR command has no effect in the Windows version of AutoCAD.

Related Commands

RCONFIG	RENDER	RENDERUNLOAD	REPLAY
SAVEIMG	VSLIDE		

Related System Variable

SCREENMODE

RENDERUNLOAD

The RENDERUNLOAD command removes the AutoCAD Render application from memory if it is currently loaded. The AutoCAD render commands are dynamically loaded—if they are not yet loaded, the first time a render-related command is issued, all the AutoCAD render commands automatically are loaded. The RENDERUNLOAD command is used to remove them from memory and improve performance on systems with limited memory.

Related Commands

LIGHT	MATLIB	RENDER	RENDSCR
REPLAY	RMAT	RPREF	

REPLAY

Pull-down: Tools, Image, View...
Screen: TOOLS, Replay:

The REPLAY command displays raster image files on the configured rendering display, or in the Render Window. You can display GIF, TGA, or TIFF files.

Any rectangular area of a GIF, TGA, or TIFF file can be displayed by specifying an image offset location (in pixels) and an image size (in pixels). The area can then be placed anywhere on the rendering screen by specifying a screen offset location (in pixels). This process is useful if the image file was created by a system with a different rendering display resolution. In the Windows version of AutoCAD, the replayed image is displayed in the Render Window. See the RENDER command for more information regarding the Render Window.

Prompts and Options

The REPLAY command displays the Replay file dialog box, which is used to select an existing file of GIF, TIFF, or TGA format. After a file of the appropriate type has been specified, the REPLAY command displays the Image Specifications dialog box (see fig. R.8), which has the following options:

IMAGE. The size of the saved image is displayed in the image tile as two small "x"es. Pick two points to specify the lower left and upper right corners of the image to display. The Image Offset and Image Size values update as the corners are picked. The size of the image file (in pixels) is displayed above the image tile.

Image Offset. Specify the X and Y Image Offset locations in the edit boxes. This is the lower left corner of the image to display, in pixels. Values for the X and Y image offset must be positive and cannot exceed the entire image size. The specified values are updated in the image tile above as the lower left corner point.

Image Size. Specify the Image Size, in pixels, in the edit boxes. This is the distance, in pixels, that the upper right corner of the image area rectangle is located from the X and Y image offset. Values for the X and Y image size must be positive and cannot exceed the image size minus the image offset distances.

SCREEN. The center of the screen is displayed in the image tile as a small x. Pick a point to specify the center of the screen to display the image. The Screen Offset values update as the center is picked. The size of the screen (in pixels) is displayed above the image tile.

Screen Offset. Specify the X and Y Screen Offset locations in the edit boxes. This is the lower left corner of the screen, in pixels, at which the image is displayed. Values for the X and Y image offset must be positive and cannot exceed the entire screen size. The specified values are updated in the image tile above as the lower left corner point.

Screen Size. The X and Y values displayed show the actual size of the image area that will be displayed. The values will be equal to the Image Size up to a maximum of the screen size minus the screen offset.

Reset. The Reset button sets all image offset, image size, and screen offset parameters back to the defaults.

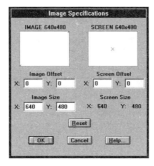

Figure R.8. *The Image Specifications dialog box.*

Example

This example uses the image saved using the RPREF command as a GIF file (see the RPREF command), as seen in figure R.9.

Command **REPLAY** (Enter)	Starts the REPLAY command; displays the Replay file dialog box
Select the GIF *file saved using the* RPREF *command, and click* OK	Selects GIF file to replay; displays Image Specifications dialog box
Click on OK	Closes Image Specifications dialog box; displays image in Render Window

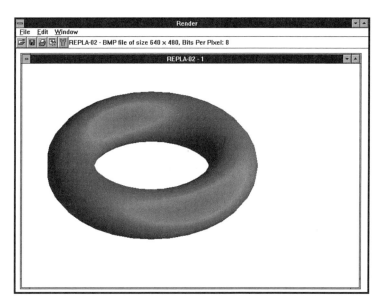

Figure R.9. *The replayed torus, as seen in the Render Window.*

Related Commands

RENDER   RENDERUNLOAD   RENDSCR   SAVEIMG

'RESUME

The RESUME command continues a script file that has been halted or interrupted. If you stop a script file by pressing Backspace, enter **RESUME** at the Command: prompt to restart it at the next line of the script. If you stop the script with Ctrl+C as it executes a command, you can use the RESUME command transparently by entering **'RESUME**.

Related Commands

DELAY   RSCRIPT   SCRIPT

REVOLVE

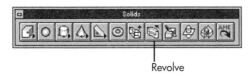

Revolve

Toolbar: *Revolve (Solids)*
Pull-down: *D*raw, *S*olids, Re*v*olve
Screen: DRAW2, SOLIDS, Revolve:

The REVOLVE command converts 2D objects into ACIS SOLID objects by revolving them around an axis. Valid 2D objects include closed polylines, polygons, circles, ellipses, traces, closed splines, regions, and AutoCAD 2D solid objects. The axis of revolution can be specified by picking two points, picking an object, or using the X or Y axis of the current UCS. A complete revolution can be created, as can a partial revolution.

The REVOLVE command does not work with DONUT objects.

If more than one object is selected, only the first object selected is revolved. Objects lose any thickness when converting to an ACIS SOLID.

Prompts and Options

Select objects Select the object to revolve. While any selection method can be used, only the first object found is revolved. If the first object found is invalid, the command fails.

Axis of revolution - Object/X/Y/<Start point of axis>   Pick the first point of the axis of revolution, or choose an option to specify an axis of revolution. The X and Y options use the X or Y axis of the current UCS as an axis of revolution. The Object option enables you to select an object to define an axis of revolution.

Select an object   If you choose the Object option to specify an axis of revolution, this prompt appears. Select either a line or a polyline with exactly one segment. If you select a polyline with more than one segment, AutoCAD responds:

```
That polyline does not define an axis.
```

Angle of revolution<full circle>   Press Enter to create a fully revolved ACIS SOLID, or enter the angle of revolution. A positive angle creates a counter-clockwise revolution, whereas a negative angle creates a clockwise revolution, according to the positive direction of the axis of revolution (see the "Direction of Revolution" discussion that follows). You also can show an angle by picking two points in the graphics window—the angle from the first point to the second is used as the angle of revolution.

Direction of Revolution

The direction of revolution is determined by the direction of the axis of revolution. If two points are picked for the axis, the first point picked becomes the base of the vector that defines the axis of revolution. If either the X or Y option is chosen, the origin of the current UCS becomes the base of the vector. If the Object option is chosen, the endpoint of the line or polyline segment closest to the pick point becomes the base of the vector that defines the axis of revolution. The opposite end becomes the top. If you look from the top of the vector to the base, a positive included angle constructs the ACIS SOLID in the counterclockwise direction, whereas a negative angle constructs a clockwise ACIS SOLID.

Example

The following example uses the REVOLVE command to construct an ACIS SOLID object shaped like a bottle. Create a 2D polyline and an axis of revolution, as shown in the left viewport (see fig. R.10). The right viewport displays the rendered revolution.

Command: **REVOLVE** (Enter)	Starts the REVOLVE command
Select objects: *Pick* ① *(see fig R.10)*	Selects 2D polyline to revolve

REVOLVE

```
1 found
Select objects: (Enter)                Finishes selecting objects to
                                        revolve

Axis of revolution - Object/X/Y/       Specifies Object option to use an
<Start point of axis>: O (Enter)       existing object as the axis of
                                        revolution

Select an object: Pick ②               Selects dashed line as axis of
                                        revolution

Angle of revolution                    Specifies full circle of revolution
<full circle>: (Enter)
```

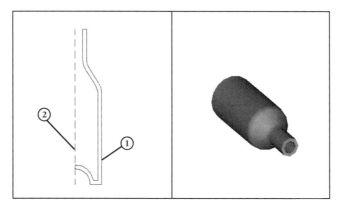

Figure R.10. *The 2D polyline before and after revolving.*

Related Commands

EXPLODE   EXTRUDE   INTERFERE   INTERSECT
MASSPROP   SUBTRACT   UNION

Related System Variable

EXTRUDE   MASSPROP

REVSURF

Revolved Surface

Toolbar: *Revolved Surface (Surfaces)*
Pull-down: *Draw, Surfaces, Revolved Surface*
Screen: DRAW2, SURFACES, Revsurf:

The REVSURF command creates a polygon mesh defined by rotating a profile object (path curve) around an axis of rotation. The REVSURF command is useful for creating objects that are radially symmetrical about one axis, such as a wine goblet. This command can create surfaces that are open like a vase, closed like a spindle, or hollow like a tire. The SURFTAB1 and SURFTAB2 system variables are used to control the M and N densities of the mesh.

The SURFTAB1 and SURFTAB2 system variables must be set before the REVSURF command is used, as there is no option for changing them within the command.

Prompts and Options

Select path curve Select one object as the path curve. The path curve can be an arc, circle, line, 2D polyline, or 3D polyline. The path curve defines the N direction of the mesh. If the path curve is a circle or closed polyline, the polygon mesh produced by the REVSURF command will be closed in the N direction. If you select an invalid object for the path curve, AutoCAD responds:

`Object not usable to define surface of revolution.`

Select axis of revolution Select a line, open 2D polyline, or open 3D polyline. If you choose an object other than a line or an open polyline, AutoCAD responds:

`Object not usable as rotation axis.`

The same object cannot be both the curve path and the axis of revolution. If you select the same object for the axis of revolution as the path curve, AutoCAD responds:

`You already picked that object!`

When a curved or multisegmented polyline is selected as the axis of revolution, the vector from the first vertex to the last vertex defines the actual axis of revolution. The pick point used to select the axis of rotation influences the rotation angle. See the following discussion about the direction of revolution. The axis of revolution defines the M direction of the polygon mesh.

Start angle <0> Press Enter to create the polygon mesh starting at the location of the path curve. If you specify an angle other than 0 degrees, the mesh is offset from the path curve by that angle.

Included angle (+=ccw, -=cw) <Full circle> Press Enter to create a fully revolved polygon mesh, or enter an angle for a partially revolved mesh. The included angle determines the extent to which the path curve sweeps around the axis of revolution. If the default Full circle option is used, the resulting mesh is closed in the M direction. A positive included angle causes the mesh to be generated in a counterclockwise direction. The mesh generates with respect to the pick point that you used to select the axis of revolution.

Direction of Revolution

The direction of revolution is determined by the pick point used for selecting the axis of revolution and the included angle specification. The endpoint of the axis of revolution closest to the pick point becomes the base of the vector that defines the axis of revolution. The opposite end becomes the top. If you look from the top of the vector to the base, a positive included angle constructs the polygon mesh in the counterclockwise direction, offset by the start angle.

Example

The following example uses the REVSURF command to construct an open polygon mesh to form a tire shape, as shown in figure R.11. The left viewport shows the original path curve (an open 2D polyline) and the axis of revolution (a line). The right viewport displays the completed mesh with hidden lines removed.

```
Command: SURFTAB1 (Enter)
```
Starts the SETVAR command to change value of SURFTAB1 system variable

```
New value for SURFTAB1 <6>: 24 (Enter)
```
Specifies 24 for new value of SURFTAB1

Command: **SURFTAB2** (Enter)	Starts the SETVAR command to change value of SURFTAB2 system variable
New value for SURFTAB2 <6>: **12** (Enter)	Specifies 12 for new value of SURFTAB1
Command: **REVSURF** (Enter)	Starts the REVSURF command
Select path curve: *Pick* ① *(see fig. R.11)*	Selects polyline to use as path object
Select axis of revolution: *Pick* ②	Selects line to use as axis of revolution
Start angle <0>: (Enter)	Specifies no start angle offset
Included angle (+=ccw, -=cw) <Full circle>: (Enter)	Specifies fully revolved mesh

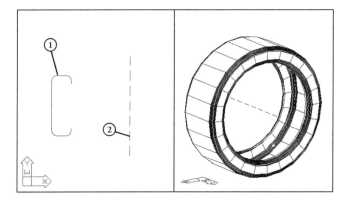

Figure R.11. *A tire created using REVSURF.*

Related Commands

3DFACE   3DMESH   EDGESURF   PFACE   RULESURF
TABSURF

Related System Variables

SURFTAB1   SURFTAB2

RMAT

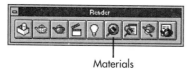

Materials

Toolbar: *Materials (Render)*
Pull-down: *T*ools, R*e*nder, *M*aterials...
Screen: TOOLS, RENDER, Mater'l:

The RMAT (Render MATerials) command assigns and controls surface finish materials of three-dimensional objects for rendering. You can control the name, color, ambiance, reflectivity, and roughness of surface finish materials. Use the MATLIB command to import and export surface finish materials to and from drawings.

A material is assigned to an object in one of three ways. A material can be assigned directly to an object, to all objects on a particular layer, or to all objects of a specific color. This last method uses the standard *AutoCAD Color Index* (ACI) to force all objects with the same color to share the same finish.

Prompts and Options

The RMAT command displays a series of dialog boxes for controlling the different properties of surface finish materials. The Materials dialog box is used to create new materials, access the materials library, select materials to modify, assign specific objects a selected material, and assign materials to layers and standard AutoCAD colors.

The New Standard Material and Modify Standard Material dialog boxes are used to define the properties of new materials and change the properties of existing materials. The Attach by AutoCAD Color Index and Attach by Layer dialog boxes attach the selected material to a standard AutoCAD color or an existing layer. The Color dialog box changes the color assigned to a material. The Select Color dialog box is used to select a standard AutoCAD color.

The Materials Dialog Box

As shown in figure R.12, the Materials dialog box lists the existing materials in the drawing, previews selected materials, and accesses the materials library (see the MATLIB command). In addition, the Materials dialog box selects materials from objects, and attaches and detaches materials from objects interactively.

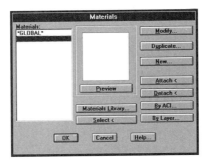

Figure R.12. *The Materials dialog box.*

Materials. The Materials list box displays the names of the current materials in the drawing. The *GLOBAL* material is the default material for all objects that do not have any other material assigned.

Preview. Previews the selected material, using a sphere, in the image tile above the Preview button. This is useful for quickly checking the effect of changes made to a specific material definition.

Materials Library. Displays the Materials Library dialog box for importing, exporting, and deleting materials. See the MATLIB command for more information.

Select. The Select button causes the Materials dialog box to disappear, enabling you to pick an object from the graphics window. After successfully selecting an object from the drawing, that object's assigned material is highlighted in the Materials list box.

Modify. Select an existing material from the Materials list box to modify, then click the Modify button. This displays the Modify Standard Materials dialog box, which is discussed in the next section. The Modify button enables you to change the properties of the selected material. If you double-click on a material name in the Materials list box, the Modify Standard Materials dialog box automatically appears.

Duplicate. Select an existing material from the Materials list box to copy, then click the Duplicate button. A new material is created, using the properties of the selected material. This new material can then be modified as desired.

New. The New button creates a new material, and displays the New Standard Material dialog box, which is discussed in the next section. New materials are assigned a primary color, ambient color, reflective color, and roughness size. The following section also describes each of these material attributes in more detail.

Attach. The **A**ttach button causes the Materials dialog box to disappear, enabling you to select objects from the graphics window. The currently selected material will be attached to all the selected objects.

Detach. The **D**etach button causes the Materials dialog box to disappear, enabling you to select objects from the graphics window. Any material currently attached to the selected objects will be detached from them. The objects will then take on the default material of *GLOBAL*.

By ACI. Clicking on the **B**y ACI button displays the Attach by AutoCAD Color Index dialog box (see fig. R.13). The **B**y ACI button enables you to assign materials to standard AutoCAD colors, remove material assignments from standard AutoCAD colors, and preview materials in an image tile.

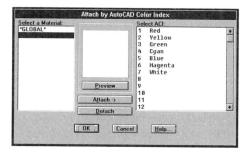

Figure R.13. *The Attach by AutoCAD Color Index dialog box.*

Attaching a material to a standard AutoCAD color assigns that material to all objects that appear in that color, and that do not have another material assigned directly to them. If a layer has a material assigned to it, and objects on that layer have a material assigned to their color, the objects are rendered according to their color, not their layer. All objects that have the same color will thus be assigned the same material.

To attach a material to one or more standard AutoCAD colors, select the desired material in the Select a Material list, select the desired color(s) from the Select ACI list, and click A**t**tach. To remove material assignments from one or more standard AutoCAD colors, select the desired color(s) from the Select ACI list, and click **D**etach. To preview, select the desired material from the Select a material list and click on the **P**review button.

By Layer. Clicking on the B**y** Layer button displays the Attach by Layer dialog box (see fig. R.14). The B**y** Layer button enables you to assign materials to layers, remove material assignments from layers, and preview materials in an image tile.

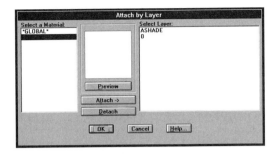

Figure R.14. *The Attach by Layer dialog box.*

Attaching a material to a layer assigns that material to all objects that are on that layer, do not have another material assigned to them by color, and do not have another material assigned directly to them. All objects on the same layer will thus be assigned the same material. If a layer has a material assigned to it, and objects on that layer have a material assigned to their color, the objects are rendered according to their color, not their layer.

To attach a material to one or more layers, select the desired material in the Select a Material list, select the desired layer(s) from the Select Layer list, and click Attach. To remove material assignments from one or more layers, select the desired layer(s) from the Select Layer list, and click Detach. To preview, select the desired material from the Select a material list and click on the Preview button.

New and Modify Standard Material Dialog Boxes

Clicking the New button, or selecting a material type and clicking Duplicate from the Materials dialog box displays the New Standard Material dialog box (see fig. R.15). Selecting an existing material and clicking Modify from the Materials dialog box displays the Modify Standard Material dialog box.

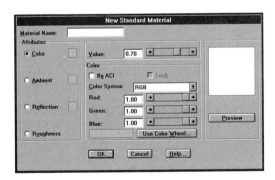

Figure R.15. *The New Standard Material dialog box.*

Each of these dialog boxes displays an edit box to enter or change the material name, and an attributes group for selecting a render attribute to change. In addition, a color group for changing the selected attribute's value and color, and a Preview image tile and button are displayed.

Material Name. Enter the name for the new material or edit the name of the existing material. Material names are limited to sixteen characters.

Attributes. Select one of the attributes to change. If the Roughness attribute is selected, the Color controls are unavailable. Selecting By ACI matches the selected attribute's color with the object's color. Also, if either the Ambient or the Reflection attribute is selected, locking the attribute ties that attribute color to the primary color, and the color controls are unavailable.

The Color attribute determines the primary color of the material. This is the color the object appears in the absence of any directed lights (see the LIGHT command). This is also called the diffuse color of the material.

The Ambient attribute determines the ambient color of the material. This is the surface color of the object on surfaces that are not directly illuminated by lights (see the LIGHT command). This color is mixed with the primary material color to create the shadow color of the material.

The Reflection attribute determines the reflected color of the material. This is the color the object appears when illuminated with a light (see the LIGHT command). This is also called the *highlight color* of the material.

The Roughness attribute determines the relative size of reflective patches on the surface of the material. A large roughness causes a large reflective surface to appear, while a small roughness causes a small reflective surface to appear. Use the Preview button to quickly see the effect of changing the roughness value.

Each of the four attributes is independent of any other. Changing them individually can yield quite unusual results, such as blue spheres that radiate yellowish shadows with green highlights.

Value. Enter a value for the selected attribute, in the range from zero (off) to one (maximum). Note that reducing the primary color value of a material displays it with more gray color, while reducing the ambient and reflection attributes soften the effects of these attributes on the rendered surface.

Color. Check the By ACI check box to force the attribute's color to match the object's color. It is then possible, for example, to have the same material display different colored reflective patches if the reflective attribute is checked as colored By ACI.

Check the Lock check box to lock the attribute's color to the material's primary color. Only the Ambient and Reflection attributes can be locked to the primary color.

Edit the color values for the Red, Green, and Blue primary colors to change the color of the selected attribute. You can also use the slider bars next to each primary color to interactively specify an attribute color value. The range is from zero (color off) to one (color fully on). Note that primary colors can be combined to produce other colors: red, blue, and green fully on produce white. Green and blue fully on produce cyan, green and red fully on produce yellow, red and blue fully on produce magenta.

Clicking on the Use Color **W**heel button displays the Color dialog box (see fig. R.16). Select either RGB or HLS from the Color System drop-down list box, then edit the individual values for the color's *red, green, and blue* (RGB) values, or *hue, luminance, and saturation* (HLS) values, or pick a color visually from the color wheel. If you select a color from the color wheel, AutoCAD will update the red, green, and blue (or hue, luminance, and saturation) values to reflect the chosen color. The current color is displayed in the Color Selected box. You also can select from the standard AutoCAD colors by clicking on **S**elect from ACI. This displays the standard AutoCAD Select Color dialog box (see fig. R.17).

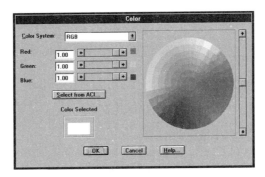

Figure R.16. *The Color dialog box.*

Click on the **P**review button to preview the material in the image tile, which displays a sphere. This is useful for quickly checking the effect of changes made to a specific material definition.

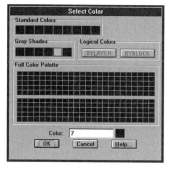

Figure R.17. *The Select Color dialog box.*

Example

This example of the RMAT command uses a torus and a single directed light to create and apply a copper material to the torus, as seen in figure R.18. Use the MATLIB command to import the material copper.

Command **RMAT** (Enter)	Invokes the RMAT command
Select COPPER *in the Materials list box, then click on Modify*	Selects COPPER as the material to modify
Select Color *from the attributes group*	Specifies changing primary material color
Edit the Value to **0.80**	Changes intensity to .80
Select Ambient *from the attributes group*	Specifies changing material ambient color
Edit the Value to **0.80**	Changes intensity to .80
Select Reflection *from the attributes group*	Specifies changing reflected color
Change the Red color to **1.00**	Changes red intensity to maximum
Change the Green color to **0.00**	Changes green intensity to minimum
Change the Blue color to **0.00**	Changes blue intensity to minimum
Select Roughness *from the attributes group*	Specifies roughness (reflected spot size) to change

Edit the Value to **1.00**	Changes spot size to maximum
Click on OK	Closes Modify Standard Material dialog box
Click on Attach	Temporarily closes Materials dialog box
`Select objects to attach "COPPER" to:`	Selects torus to attach COPPER material
Select the torus	
`1 found`	
`Select objects:` (Enter)	Finishes selecting objects to attach COPPER material, restores Materials dialog box
Click on OK	Closes Materials dialog box
Use the RENDER *command to render the torus and view the new finish*	Renders current scene

Figure R.18. *The Rendered torus.*

Related Commands

LIGHT   MATLIB   RENDER   RENDERUNLOAD
RPREF

ROTATE

Rotate

Toolbar: *Rotate (Modify, Rotate)*
Pull-down: <u>M</u>odify, Rot<u>a</u>te
Screen: MODIFY, Rotate:

The ROTATE command rotates selected objects about a fixed point in the current construction plane. After you choose the fixed point, AutoCAD asks you for the amount, in degrees, that you want to rotate the objects. The new orientation of the objects is based on the rotation value entered or picked.

> ROTATE is also available as an option to the Grips selection edit feature.

Prompts and Options

Select objects Use any object selection method to choose all the objects you want to rotate.

Base point The base point is the location about which the objects are rotated. After you enter the rotation value, the chosen objects are rotated about the Z axis of the base point. The base point does not necessarily have to reside on the objects selected for rotation.

<Rotation angle>/Reference At this prompt, enter a value with which to rotate the objects. A positive number changes the objects' orientation in a counter-clockwise direction. A negative number rotates the objects in a clockwise direction. A rubber-band line appears between the base point and the crosshairs. The objects being rotated are highlighted and dragged as you move the crosshairs.

Reference angle <0> The Reference option enables you to define the angle of rotation by specifying a reference angle and a new angle. This is useful in situations in which the objects need to be rotated relative to other objects.

New angle The selected objects are rotated by the difference between the reference angle and the new angle that you specify at this prompt.

Example

This example demonstrates how to use the ROTATE command to change the orientation of a group of objects shown in figure R.19.

From the Modify *menu, choose* Rotate

`Command: _rotate`	Issues the ROTATE command
`Select objects:` *Pick point* ① *(see fig. R.19)*	Specifies the first corner of a selection window
`Other corner:` *Pick point* ②	Specifies the opposite corner of a selection window
`Base point:` *Pick point* ③	Specifies the rotation base point
`<Rotation angle>/Reference:` **-90** (Enter)	Specifies the rotation angle

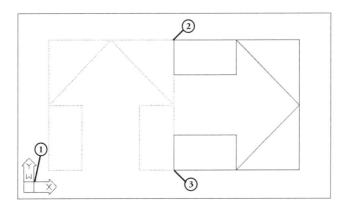

Figure R.19. *Rotating a group of objects.*

Related Commands

ALIGN   MIRROR   ROTATE3D

Related System Variables

DRAGMODE   GRIPS   HIGHLIGHT

ROTATE3D

Toolbar: *3D Rotate (Modify, Rotate)*
Pull-down: <u>C</u>onstruct, *3D Rotat<u>e</u>*
Screen: CONSTRCT, Rotat3D:

The ROTATE3D command rotates objects about a 3D axis. The axis of rotation can be defined by selecting a line, circle, arc, or 2D polyline segment. The axis of rotation also can be defined by selecting the X, Y, or Z axis of the current UCS, by picking two points, or by specifying the current viewing direction.

Prompts and Options

Select objects Select the objects you want to rotate about a 3D axis, using any of the standard AutoCAD object selection methods.

Axis by Entity/Last/View/Xaxis/Yaxis/Zaxis/<2point> Choose an option to specify the axis of rotation, pick a point in the graphics window, or enter the coordinates of the first point on the axis of rotation. Choose the Entity option to use an existing object to define the axis of rotation. Choose the Last option to re-use the previous axis of rotation. Choose the View option to rotate the objects using the current viewing direction as the axis of rotation, or choose the Xaxis, Yaxis, or Zaxis option to use one of the axes of the current UCS as the axis of rotation.

Pick a line, circle, arc or 2D-polyline segment If you choose the Entity option, this prompt appears. If you select a line or 2D polyline segment, the axis of rotation is defined by the direction of the line or 2D polyline segment. If you select a circle or arc, the extrusion vector direction of the arc or circle is used as the rotation axis. If you select any other kind of object, AutoCAD responds:

Improper type of entity picked.

Last The Last option uses the previous axis of rotation. If there is no previous axis, you are warned and reprompted with the Axis prompt.

Point on view direction axis <0,0,0> If you select the View option, this prompt is displayed. The View option aligns the axis of rotation with the current viewing direction passing through a selected point. Pick a point in the graphics window, or enter the coordinates of a point for the axis of rotation to pass through.

Point on X, Y, or Z axis <0,0,0> The Xaxis, Yaxis, or Zaxis option aligns the axis of rotation with the specified axis, passing through a selected point. Pick a point in the graphics window, or enter the coordinates of a point for the axis of rotation to pass through. The other end of the axis of rotation will be aligned parallel to the selected X, Y, or Z axis.

1st point on axis, 2nd point on axis Pick a point in the graphics window, or enter the coordinates for two points to define the axis of rotation.

<Rotation angle>/Reference Enter the degree of rotation about the 3D axis or specify the Reference option to enter the current angle and a new angle. The direction of rotation is determined by the orientation of the axis of rotation. If you look from the top of the axis to the base, a positive rotation angle rotates the objects in the counterclockwise direction, whereas a negative rotation angle rotates them clockwise. The Reference option displays the following prompts:

Reference angle <0> Enter the current degree of rotation of the selected objects.

New angle Enter the new angle for the selected entities.

Example

The following example uses the ROTATE3D command to rotate a 4×4 stud about a 3D rotation axis, which passes through the base of the stud. The stud is shown before and after the rotation (see fig. R.20).

Command: **ROTATE3D** (Enter)	Issues the ROTATE3D command
Select objects: *Pick* ① (see fig. R.20)	Selects object to rotate
1 found	
Select objects: (Enter)	Finishes selecting objects to rotate
Axis by Entity/Last/View/Xaxis/Yaxis/Zaxis/<2points>: **END** (Enter)	Specifies ENDpoint object snap
of *Pick* ②	Selects first endpoint for rotation axis
2nd point on axis: **END** (Enter)	Specifies ENDpoint object snap
of *Pick* ③	Selects second endpoint for rotation axis
<Rotation angle>/Reference: **90** (Enter)	Rotates 90 degrees counterclockwise

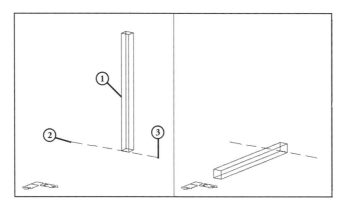

Figure R.20. *The 4×4 stud before and after a 3D rotation.*

Related Commands

ALIGN   MIRROR3D   ROTATE

Related System Variable

VIEWDIR

RPREF

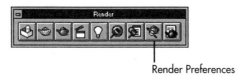

Render Preferences

Toolbar: *Render Preferences (Render)*
Pull-down: *T*ools, R*e*nder, Preferences...
Screen: TOOLS, RENDER, Prefer:

The RPREF command controls rendering preferences. The rendering type, color map, render destination, and RENDER command options are set with the RPREF command. In addition, the RPREF command determines the type of rendering, the shading smoothness, whether to apply materials to rendered surfaces, and whether to overwrite or merge the rendered image with the current display.

Prompts and Options

The RPREF command displays a series of dialog boxes for controlling the different rendering preferences. The Rendering Preferences dialog box is used to select the rendering type, set the rendering color map, and set the RENDER command options (see fig. R.21). It also is used to set the shading smoothness, to determine whether to apply materials definitions, and to determine whether to merge the rendered image with the current screen or overwrite it. In addition, the rendered image destination of either the current viewport, the render window, the currently configured hard-copy device (DOS versions only), or a file can be selected.

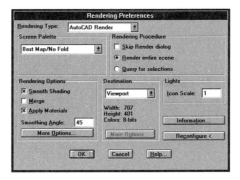

Figure R.21. *The Rendering Preferences dialog box.*

The AutoCAD Render Options dialog box is used to specify the quality of rendering from the currently selected rendering type. The File Output Configuration dialog box specifies the options for writing a rendered image to a file, whereas the Render Information dialog box displays information about the currently selected rendering type.

The Rendering Preferences Dialog Box

Rendering Type. Select the desired rendering method. AutoCAD Render is supplied with AutoCAD. Additional rendering methods (such as Autodesk AutoVision) appear in this list when installed.

Screen Palette. Select the color map desired for rendering images. The three available selections are Best Map/No Fold, Best Map/Fold, and Fixed ACAD Map. The current Destination setting can affect the availability of this option.

The Best Map/No Fold option maintains a separate color map for each rendering viewport and does not change the AutoCAD colors 9-255 to the closest color in the 1-8 color range. Object colors in nonrendering viewports are altered according to the color map of the rendering viewport.

The Best Map/Fold option maintains a separate color map for each rendering viewport and changes the AutoCAD colors 9-255 to the closest color in the 1-8 AutoCAD color range. This means that all objects with AutoCAD color values higher than 8 in nonrendering viewports are changed to the closest color in the 1-8 AutoCAD color range. This prevents object colors from changing after rendering in another viewport.

The Fixed ACAD Map option uses the standard AutoCAD color map for both nonrendering and rendering viewports. Results from this option are usually poor renderings and inconsistent results.

Rendering Procedure. Check **S**kip Render dialog to force the RENDER command to immediately render the current screen to the currently selected destination. This option affects the operation of the RENDER command. If **S**kip Render dialog is checked, no dialog box is presented for the RENDER command. The RENDER command either renders the current scene (or view if no scene is defined) or selected objects. If **S**kip Render dialog is checked, select either **R**ender entire scene or **Q**uery for selections. If **S**kip Render dialog is unchecked, the **R**ender entire scene and **Q**uery for selections options are ignored.

Rendering Options. Check **S**mooth Shading to cause the transition between adjacent polygon mesh surfaces to appear smooth when rendered. If **S**mooth Shading is unchecked, polygon mesh surfaces have a faceted appearance. The Smoothing **A**ngle determines the maximum angle between adjacent faces to attempt to smooth.

Check **M**erge to enable multiple image merging in the frame buffer. If merging is unchecked, the frame buffer is cleared before each rendering. If a complex drawing is changed in one area, that area can be rendered and merged with the original image without requiring a complete re-rendering. Images can be overlaid upon one another, or an image can be rendered onto a background.

> Merging two or more rendered images can be quite useful in constructing assembly views or overlaying designs on top of existing backgrounds. Use the Render Window to import a background first, then merge an AutoCAD rendered image to overlay it on the background.

Check **A**pply Materials to control the application of defined surface materials. If **A**pply Materials is off, all entities are rendered with the default *GLOBAL* material. If **A**pply Materials is checked, the different materials applied to each object (either directly, or through color or layer) are applied to the rendering. See the RMAT command for a complete description of surface materials.

The More Options button accesses the options available for the currently selected rendering type. If the currently selected rendering type is AutoCAD Render, then the AutoCAD Render Options dialog box is displayed (see fig. R.22). This dialog box changes the rendering quality and controls the rendering of back faces.

Figure R.22. *The AutoCAD Render Options dialog box.*

Two kinds of rendering quality, Gouraud and Phong, are offered in the AutoCAD Render Options dialog box. The default Gouraud algorithm calculates the color at all vertices of a mesh face and then blends the color across the face. The Phong algorithm creates a more realistic rendering by calculating the color at each pixel and takes longer to perform.

Back face rendering is controlled by selecting Discard Back Faces and Back Face Normal is Negative. Checking Discard Back Faces speeds up the rendering process by discarding any faces hidden from the current view. Checking Back Face Normal is Negative (the default) identifies faces drawn counterclockwise as front faces and those drawn clockwise as back faces. If the Back Face Normal is Negative is unchecked and Discard Back Faces is checked, the rendered without the front faces shown. This reverses the rendered image by rendering light faces dark and dark faces light.

Destination. Select either Viewport, Render Window, or File from the Destination drop-down list box. If File is selected, the More Options button can be clicked to display the File Output Configuration dialog box.

Selecting Viewport renders the selected scene or objects to the active viewport. Selecting Render Window (if using the Windows version of AutoCAD) renders the selected scene to the AutoCAD for Windows Render Window—a separate Window opened when the RENDER command is initialized. Selecting Hard-copy (if using the DOS version of AutoCAD) renders the image to the currently configured hard-copy device. Images rendered to a viewport or to the Render Window can be saved to a file using the SAVEIMG command.

Selecting File renders the selected scene or objects to a specified file. Standard image file formats supported include BMP, PCX, TGA, TIFF, PostScript, and others. Images rendered to a file can be displayed using image viewing programs or the AutoCAD REPLAY command.

If File is selected, the More Options button can be clicked to display the File Output Configuration dialog box (see fig. R.23). The File Output Configuration dialog box specifies the options for writing a rendered image to a file.

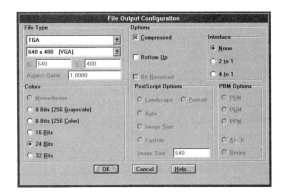

Figure R.23. *The File Output Configuration dialog box.*

Lights. Enter a scale factor for light icons in the Icon Scale edit box. The scale factor specifies the scale to apply to rendering light blocks named OVERHEAD, DIRECT, and SH_SPOT. Set the icon scale factor to the same scale as other symbols in your drawing. See the LIGHT command for more information on creating and modifying light blocks.

Information. Click on the Information button to display the Render Information dialog box (see fig. R.24). This dialog box displays the currently selected rendering type's copyright notice and configuration information.

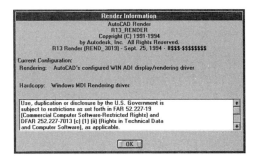

Figure R.24. *The Render Information dialog box.*

Reconfigure. Click the Reconfigure button to reconfigure the rendering device and hard-copy output device. See the RCONFIG command for more information.

The File Output Configuration Dialog Box

File Type. Select the desired output file type from the drop-down list box. Supported file types include BMP, FAX G III (Group III Facsimile), FITS, GIF, IIF, PBM, PCX, PostScript, TGA, TIFF, SUN, and X11. Select the desired resolution from the drop-down list box beneath the file type. The available resolutions include most standard resolutions from 320×200 to the maximum user-defined size of 4096×4096.

If the selected resolution is user-defined, enter the horizontal and vertical sizes of the image in the <u>X</u> and <u>Y</u> edit boxes, respectively. The Aspect <u>R</u>atio edit box changes the aspect ratio of the saved image.

Colors. Select the desired bit depth for the image color. Not all file types support all bit depths. For example, both BMP and PCX support a maximum of 8-bit color depth, or 256 colors.

Options. Check <u>C</u>ompressed to compress the output image, if the selected file type supports compression. Select Bottom <u>U</u>p to reverse the scan line order in the saved image. By default, many file types write the image from top to bottom. Checking Bottom <u>U</u>p writes the image from bottom to top. Select Bit <u>R</u>eversed (available only for the file type FAX G III) to reverse the black and white pixels.

PostScript Options. If PostScript is the currently selected file type, these options are available. Select either <u>L</u>andscape or <u>P</u>ortrait to orient the image. Select either A<u>u</u>to or Image <u>S</u>ize or C<u>u</u>stom to size the image. A<u>u</u>to automatically scales the image to fit the selected file type resolution. Image <u>S</u>ize uses the image pixels, whereas C<u>u</u>stom scales the image to fit a particular resolution, entered in the <u>I</u>mage Size edit box.

Interlace. Select the desired scan line interlacing, if supported for the currently selected output file type.

PBM Options. IF *Portable Bit Map* (PBM) is the currently selected file type, these options are available. Select either P<u>B</u>M, P<u>G</u>M, or PP<u>M</u>. Select either <u>A</u>SCII or <u>B</u>inary.

Example

This example uses the RPREF command to change the render preferences to output a rendering to a GIF file. Create a torus and a single direct light (see the LIGHT command), as shown in figure R.25.

Command **RPREF**    Starts the RPREF command, displays
                                         the Rendering Preferences dialog box

Click on More **O**ptions *from the Rendering Options group*	Displays the AutoCAD Render Options dialog box
Select **P**hong *from the Render Quality group*	Selects best quality AutoCAD Render method
Check **D**iscard Back Faces *from the Controls group*	Does not calculate rendering of *Face back faces*
Click on OK	Closes AutoCAD Render Options dialog box
Select File *from the Destination drop-down list box*	Changes render destination to output file, rather than viewport or Render Window
Click on More O**p**tions *from the Destination group*	Displays File Output Configuration dialog box
Select GIF *from the File Type list box (it's at the top of the list)*	Selects GIF standard output file drop-down format
Click on OK	Closes File Output Configuration dialog box
Click on OK	Closes Rendering Preferences dialog box

Use the RENDER command to render the torus and save the image to a file. When prompted for an output file name using the Rendering File (GIF 640x480:8) dialog box; enter a file name with the same base name as the drawing.

Figure R.25. *Saving a rendered torus as a GIF file using the RPREF command.*

Related Commands

RCONFIG   RENDER   RENDERUNLOAD   STATS

RSCRIPT

The RSCRIPT command causes a script to repeat itself from the beginning. You can execute the RSCRIPT command only from a script file. The script continues to repeat until you press Ctrl+C or Backspace.

Related Commands

DELAY   RESUME   SCRIPT

SAVE

The SAVE command displays the Save Drawing As dialog box, requests a file name, and saves the current drawing as a file with the extension DWG. If the system variable FILEDIA is set to zero, entering a tilde (~) at the Save current changes as: prompt displays the Save Drawing As dialog box. You can enter the drawing name in the File edit box or select a name from the Files list box. Do not include the DWG extension; it is assumed. If the drawing has already been named, SAVE uses that name as a default in the File edit box. Each time you use SAVE, the previous saved drawing is renamed as the backup (BAK) drawing.

Save your drawing regularly during a drawing session to avoid data loss due to system failure or power loss. Use the SAVETIME system variable to set the number of minutes between automatic saves. Setting SAVETIME to zero disables the Autosave feature.

Related Commands

END	MAKEPREVIEW	QSAVE	QUIT
SAVEAS	SAVEASR12		

Related System Variables

DWGNAME	DWGPREFIX	DWGTITLED	FILEDIA
MAXSORT	SAVEFILE	SAVENAME	SAVETIME
TDUPDATE	WGWRITE		

SAVEAS

Pull-down: **F**ile, Save **A**s
Screen: FILE, SaveAs:

The SAVEAS command works like the SAVE command—saving any changes to the current drawing to disk without exiting the drawing editor—except that this command asks for a new file name. SAVEAS leaves the original file intact, saves your changes to the new name, and makes that new name your current or default drawing. The Save Drawing As dialog box and the current drawing name are the default. Clicking on OK accepts your file name choice.

Use the QSAVE command to periodically save your work. QSAVE automatically saves changes to the default drawing name and bypasses the dialog box.

Prompts and Options

Refer to the Introduction for more information on the File Selection dialog box options.

Related Commands

END   MAKEPREVIEW   QSAVE   QUIT
SAVE   SAVEASR12

Related System Variables

DBMOD   DWGNAME   DWGPREFIX   DWGTITLED
FILEDIA   MAXSORT   SAVEFILE   SAVENAME
SAVETIME   TDUPDATE

SAVEASR12

Screen: FILE, EXPORT, SaveR12:

The SAVEASR12 command saves the current drawing in AutoCAD Release 12 format. The Release 13 file is saved as a backup file with the same file name and a BAK extension. When saving as a Release 12 drawing, some drawing data specific to Release 13 will be lost. A log file will be listed on the text screen listing all information that will be lost or changed. A sample log file is as follows:

```
Command: saveasr12
Save as release 12 drawing log.
Writing drawing header.
Writing objects database.
Changed MTEXT to release 12 objects.  1 found.
Changed SPLINE to release 12 objects.  1 found.
Changed ELLIPSE to release 12 objects.  2 found.
Writing layer table.
Writing text font and shape table.
Writing linetype table.
Writing view table.
Writing coordinate system table.
Writing viewport table.
Writing registered application table.
Writing dimension style table.
Writing viewport object table.
Writing block definition table.
```

Table S.1 summarizes the Release 13 objects or features that are affected by the SAVEASR12 command and how they are treated when converting to Release 12 format.

Table S.1
Release 13 Object Conversion to Release 12

Feature	Conversion
3D Solid	Converted to lines, arcs, circles, 3D polylines, 3D faces
ASE	Ignores ASE link information
Body	Converted to lines, arcs, circles, 3D polylines, 3D faces
Dimensions	Text converted to text objects; additional dimstyles and their system variable settings are ignored
Ellipse	Converted to polylines, circles
Object Visibility	Ignored
Groups	Ignored
Hatch Patterns	No longer associative
Leader	Converted to lines or polylines; arrows converted to circles, polygons, or polylines
Linetype	Ignores CELTSCALE setting
Linetype Tables	Shapes are ignored
Multiline	Converted to lines, polylines, arcs, polygons, filled arcs, filled polygons; color and/or linetype may vary for each polyline or filled polygon
Multiline Styles	Ignored
Mtext	Converted to text objects; formatting may be lost
OLE objects	Ignored
Overlays (Xrefs)	Ignored
Preview	Ignored
Ray	Converted to line; length determined by limits or extents of drawing; discarded if length does not cross extents
Region	Converted to lines, arcs, circles, 3D polylines, 3D faces
Render	Ignores ASI material assignments

Feature	Conversion
Spline	Converted to polylines
TrueType Fonts	Converted to TXT.SHX font
New System Variables	Ignored
Tolerances	Converted to polylines and text
Xline	see Ray

Related Commands

END	MAKEPREVIEW	QSAVE	QUIT
SAVE	SAVEAS		

Related System Variables

DBMOD	DWGNAME	DWGPREFIX	DWGTITLED
FILEDIA	MAXSORT	SAVEFILE	SAVENAME
SAVETIME	TDUPDATE		

SAVEIMG

Pull-down: **T**ools, Ima**g**e, **S**ave...
Screen: TOOLS, SaveImg:

The SAVEIMG command saves the current viewport, drawing area, or full-screen image to a TGA, TIFF, or GIF file. You can view saved images by using the REPLAY command or other graphics applications.

One of two Save Image dialog boxes (see figs. S.1 and S.2) displays when the SAVEIMG command is issued, depending on the rendering destination specified in the RPREF command. If you have the rendering destination specified as a viewport, the Portion group shows three options for specifying the area of the screen to save. If you have the rendering destination specified as either the Render Window or to a file, the Portion group displays an image tile, enabling you to interactively specify the area of the screen to save. The Save Image dialog box for viewport rendering is shown in figure S.1, and the Save Image dialog box for rendering to the Render Window or to a file is shown in figure S.2.

Figure S.1. *The Save Image dialog box, when configured for rendering to a viewport.*

Figure S.2. *The Save Image dialog box, when configured for rendering to the Render Window or to a file.*

Prompts and Options

The Save Image dialog boxes contain the following options:

TGA. The TGA option of the Format group saves the image file in 32-bit RGBA Truevision V2.0 format. TGA files have the TGA extension. The TGA file can be either compressed or uncompressed, depending on the settings of the TGA Options dialog box (see fig. S.3). Access the TGA Options dialog box through the Options button.

Figure S.3. *The TGA Options dialog box.*

TIFF. The TIFF option of the Format group saves the image file in 32-bit Tagged Image File Format. The TIFF file extension is TIF. The TIFF file can be compressed (using one of two methods), or it can be uncompressed, depending on the settings of the TIFF Options dialog box (see fig. S.4). Access the TIFF Options dialog box through the Options button.

Figure S.4. *The TIFF Options dialog box.*

GIF. The GIF option of the Format group saves the image file in Graphics Interchange Format, which was developed by CompuServe Information Service. The saved image file has a GIF extension.

Portion. If the rendering destination is either to the Render Window or to a file, the Portion group displays an image tile, enabling you to interactively choose the area of the rendered image to save. Pick two opposite corner points in the image tile to define the area to be saved, or use the Offset and Size edit boxes to enter the two corners of the image.

If the rendering destination is to the current viewport, the Portion group displays three options for specifying what part of the image to save: Active Viewport, Drawing Area, and Full Screen. The Active Viewport option saves only the area of the current viewport.

The Drawing Area option saves the entire drawing area, not including the command area, screen menu, or pull-down menu bar. The Full Screen option saves the entire screen including command area, screen menu, and pull-down menu bar. In the Windows version of AutoCAD, the Full Screen and Drawing Area options save only the drawing area.

Options. Displays the TGA Options dialog box (refer to fig. S.3) or the TIFF Options dialog box (refer to fig. S.4), depending on the image file format selection. The TGA Options dialog box enables you to choose between no compression and RLE (run length encoded) compression for TGA files. The TIFF Options dialog box enables you to choose from no compression or PACK (packbits) and LZW (Lempel-Ziv and Welch) compression.

Reset. The Reset button sets all image offset and image size parameters back to the defaults.

Offset. Specify the X and Y image offset locations in the edit boxes. This is the lower left corner of the image to save, in pixels. Values for the X and Y image offset must be positive and cannot exceed the entire image size. If the current rendering destination is either a file, or the Render Window, the specified values are updated in the image tile above as the lower left corner point.

Size. Specify the image size, in pixels, in the edit boxes. This is the distance, in pixels, the upper right corner of the image area rectangle is located from the X and Y image offset. Values for the X and Y image size must be positive and cannot exceed the image size minus the image offset distances.

Default. Displays the maximum image area size in pixels.

Example

This example saves the rendered perspective view in the right viewport of the EX09 sample drawing (supplied with AutoCAD), as seen in figure S.5.

Command **MSPACE:** (Enter)	Changes to model space if paper space is active
Click in the right viewport	Activates the right viewport
Command **RENDER:** (Enter)	Starts the RENDER command; displays the Render dialog box
Select Viewport from the Destination group	Selects rendering destination
Click on Render Scene	Renders current viewport
Command **SAVEIMG:** (Enter)	Starts the SAVEIMG command; displays the Save Image dialog box
Choose **G**IF *from the Format group*	Selects GIF file to save
Click on OK	Displays Image file dialog box
Specify the GIF file to save	
Click on OK	Saves active viewport as GIF file

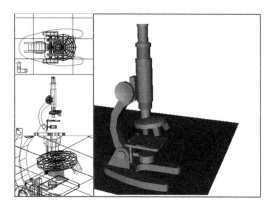

Figure S.5. *The microscope before saving the rendered perspective view in the right viewport.*

Related Commands

RENDER   RENDSCR   REPLAY

SCALE

Scale

Toolbar: *Scale (Modify, Resize)*
Pull-down: *M̲odify, Scal̲e*
Screen: MODIFY, Scale:

The SCALE command enlarges or reduces selected objects by a specified value. You can specify the new size by entering a numeric scale factor or by specifying a reference length, typically using a new length relative to a reference length. The SCALE command scales objects equally in the X, Y, and Z directions.

> Use the SCALE grip edit mode to scale an object without issuing the SCALE command. The SCALE grip edit mode allows for multiple copies of scaled items.

TIP

NOTE: You can scale a viewport in paper space to increase or decrease the amount of model space visible in the viewport.

Prompts and Options

`Select objects`   Choose all the objects you want to enlarge or reduce by means of any of the object selection methods.

`Base point`   Enter a base point in the current coordinate system around which to scale objects. When the scaling occurs, all points on selected objects move closer to the base point or farther away from the base point as their scale is reduced and enlarged.

TIP: Choose a base point that relates to the object or objects being scaled and positions them correctly after scaling. You generally pick a corner or the center of the object being scaled.

After you select the objects for scaling and specify a base point, the following prompt appears:

`<Scale factor>/Reference.`

`<Scale factor>`   Specify a scale factor by which to scale objects. A number greater than one enlarges the objects; a number between zero and one reduces the objects. You can enter a number or pick a point to show a distance. If you pick a point, a rubber-band line appears between the base point and the crosshairs. The objects to be scaled are highlighted and dragged as you move the crosshairs.

`Reference`   Enter an **R** for the Reference option if you want to define the scale factor in reference to a length, such as the size of an existing object.

NOTE: You cannot scale the X, Y, or Z values independently.

`Reference length <1>`   If you specify the Reference option, the scale factor is defined by the ratio of the two lengths that you specify. You can enter a real number or distance. You also can pick two points, usually on an existing object, to show the reference length.

New length Enter the new length to scale the reference length to. The selected objects are then scaled by the ratio between the reference length and the new length. You also can pick one point to show the new length as a distance from the base point. As you move the cursor to pick the new length, AutoCAD shows a rubber-band line from the base point.

Example

This example uses the SCALE command to enlarge an object using a reference length. The before and after results are shown in figure S.6.

Choose the Scale *tool.*	Issues the SCALE command
`Command: _scale`	
`Select objects:` *Pick point* ① *(see fig. S.6)*	Selects the object to scale
`1 found`	
`Select objects:` Enter	Terminates object selection
Choose the ENDPOINT *tool*	Specifies the endpoint object snap
`Base point: _end` `of` *Pick point* ②	Specifies the base point for scaling the objects
`<Scale factor>/Reference: R` Enter	Specifies the Reference option
Choose the ENDPOINT *tool*	
`Reference length <1>: end` `of` *Pick point* ②	Specifies the first point defining the reference distance to use
`Second point:` *Pick point* ③	Specifies the reference length
Choose the ENDPOINT *tool*	
`New length: _end of` *Pick point* ④	Specifies the new length

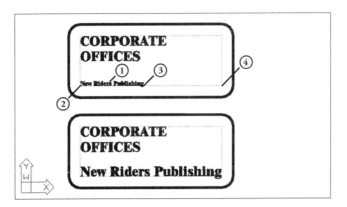

Figure S.6. *The text before and after the SCALE command.*

Related Commands

CHANGE   STRETCH

SCENE

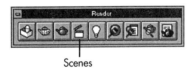

Toolbar: *Scenes (Render)*
Pull-down: *T*ools, R*e*nder, *S*cenes
Screen: TOOLS, RENDER, Scenes:

Used for generating renderings, the SCENE command enables you to create, name, restore, modify, and delete combinations of multiple views and related lighting that produce a specific image. One or more lights assigned to a single view define a scene. Lights not associated with a scene are not considered when the scene is rendered.

Dialog Box Items

The SCENE command has three dialog boxes. The first Scenes dialog box accesses the New Scene and Modify Scene dialog boxes. Figure S.7 shows the Scenes dialog box.

SCENE

Figure S.7. *The Scenes dialog box.*

The Scenes Dialog Box

The Scenes dialog box has the following options:

Scenes. The Scenes list box displays the currently defined scenes and specifies the scene to be modified, deleted, or rendered. If the *NONE* scene is selected, the current view and all lights are used for rendering. You can highlight a scene and exit the dialog box by clicking on OK to specify the scene to be rendered by the RENDER command.

New. The New button accesses the New Scene dialog box, enabling you to add a new scene to your drawing. This dialog box is similar to the Modify Scene dialog box.

Modify. The Modify button accesses the Modify Scene dialog box, as shown in figure S.8, enabling you to change scene parameters including scene name, view for scene, and associated lights. To modify a scene, highlight a scene name in the Scenes list box and then click on Modify.

Figure S.8. *The Modify Scene dialog box.*

Delete. The Delete button removes a scene from the drawing. To delete a scene, highlight a scene name in the Scenes list box and then click on the Delete button.

The New Scene and Modify Scene Dialog Boxes

Because the New Scene and Modify Scene dialog boxes have identical features, they are discussed together.

Scene Name. The Scene Name edit box enables you to specify or change the name of the scene. The scene name must be eight characters or fewer; long names are truncated to eight characters.

Views. The Views list box displays all the saved views in the drawing. The highlighted view is the scene view. To change the view for a scene, highlight a different view. The *CURRENT* view is the view in the current active viewport.

Lights. The Lights list box displays all the defined lights in your drawing and enables you to select the lights for the scene. The highlighted lights are selected for the current scene. Click on a light name to highlight it and add it to the scene. Click on a highlighted light name to remove that light from the scene. The *ALL* light name uses all the defined lights in the scene.

Related Commands
LIGHT   RENDER

Related System Variables
TARGET   VIEWDIR

'SCRIPT

Pull-down: *Tools*, *R*un Script
Screen: TOOLS, Script:

The SCRIPT command displays the Select Script File dialog box and invokes the selected script file. If the FILEDIA system variable is set to zero, you are prompted with `Script file <drawing name>:` at the command prompt.

A *script file* is a set of steps to execute AutoCAD commands and options, similar to a batch (BAT) file in DOS. You must create this file in ASCII format and save it with the SCR extension. AutoCAD interprets and executes the contents of a script file exactly as if you were entering the characters at the keyboard. Therefore, any extra spaces, returns, blank lines, or typographical errors cause problems. You can undo the effects of the SCRIPT command by issuing a single UNDO. You can stop scripts by pressing Ctrl+C. You can use the EXPERT system variable to eliminate conditional prompts in scripts.

You also can execute a script file automatically when you load AutoCAD by putting the script's file name after the drawing's file name. For example, you can type the following (for DOS systems):

`C:\> ACAD DRAWING1 SCRIPT1`

For Windows systems, you can modify the program item properties for the AutoCAD icon in Windows Program Manager. In the Program Manager, choose File, Properties and enter the drawing name followed by the script name after ACAD.EXE in the Command Line edit box in the Program Item Properties dialog box. You also can drag the script file name from the Windows File Manager window to the AutoCAD screen. This automatically executes the script.

If a script file contains a SCRIPT command, the current script is stopped, and the specified script becomes current.

> **NOTE:** Scripts are often used to display slide shows, plot drawings, and reset system variables. If you change drawing standards and need to update existing drawings, use script files to do the work.

Prompts and Options

`Script file <drawing name>` If the system variable FILEDIA is set to zero, SCRIPT displays this prompt. Enter the name of the script file you want to run—do not enter the SCR extension. Preface the file name with a drive and a path specification if needed. The default script file name is the same as the drawing name. Enter a tilde (~) to display the Select Script File dialog box. See the Introduction for more information on File Selection dialog boxes.

Related Commands

DELAY	GRAPHSCR	MSLIDE	RESUME
RSCRIPT	TEXTSCR	VSLIDE	

Related System Variables

EXPERT   FILEDIA

SECTION

Section

Toolbar: *Section (Solids)*
Pull-down: *D̲raw, So̲lids, Se̲ction*
Screen: DRAW2, SOLIDS, Section:

The SECTION command creates an ACIS REGION section view from an ACIS SOLID. The section view is created by determining the outer boundary of the ACIS SOLID object projected onto a section plane. The section plane can be defined by three points; be parallel to the current XY, YZ, or XZ planes; or be defined by a 2D object such as a circle, ellipse, arc, spline, or 2D polyline segment. The section plane also can be defined to be perpendicular to the current viewing direction or by defining a normal vector to the section plane.

The ACIS REGION is placed inside the ACIS SOLID it is sectioning, on the current layer. The SECTION command does not draw crosshatching on the ACIS REGION created. See the HATCH or BHATCH commands for more information on creating crosshatching on the section. It may be necessary to align the UCS with the ACIS REGION to produce the desired crosshatching.

Prompts and Options

Select objects Select the objects you want to section. These must be ACIS SOLID objects. Each ACIS SOLID is sectioned using the plane defined in the next prompt, and an ACIS REGION object is created to represent the section.

Section plane by Object/Zaxis/View/XY/YZ/ZX/<3points> Press Enter, pick the first of three points in the graphics window, or enter the coordinates of the first of three points to define a section plane. You also can choose one of the options for defining a section plane.

Object Select a circle, arc, ellipse, spline, or 2D polyline to define the section plane. A 3D object (such as a 3D face) does not have an associated plane of orientation. If you select a 3D object, AutoCAD responds:

```
Unable to extract the plane of the selected object.
```

Zaxis Aligns the section plane perpendicular to the axis specified, passing through the first point picked. At the Point on plane: prompt, pick a point in the graphics window or enter the coordinates of a point through which to pass the section plane. At the `Point on Z-axis (normal) of the plane:` prompt, pick a point in the graphics window or enter the coordinates of a point on the positive Z axis of a normal to the section plane.

View Aligns the section plane perpendicular to the current viewing direction. At the `Point on view plane <0,0,0>:` prompt, pick a point in the graphics window or enter the coordinates of a point through which to pass the section plane.

XY, YZ, or ZX Defines a section plane parallel to the current XY, YZ, or ZX planes. At the `Point on XY, YZ, or ZX plane <0,0,0>:` prompt, pick a point in the graphics window or enter the coordinates of a point through which to pass the section plane.

Example

The following example shows how to create a section from an ACIS SOLID consisting of a box with a subtracted cone and cylinder (see fig. S.9). The section was then hatched with the HATCH command. See the BOX, CONE, and CYLINDER commands for more information on creating ACIS SOLID primitive objects. See the SUBTRACT command for more information on subtracting ACIS SOLIDs from each other.

Command: **SECTION** (Enter)	Starts the SECTION command
Select objects: *Pick* ① *(see fig. S.9)*	Selects ACIS SOLID to section
1 found	
Select objects: (Enter)	Finishes selecting objects to section
Section plane by Object/Zaxis/View/ XY/YZ/ZX/<3points>: **MID** (Enter)	
of *Pick* ②	Specifies midpoint of lower right edge
2nd point on plane: **MID** (Enter)	
of *Pick* ③	Specifies midpoint of upper right edge
3rd point on plane: **MID** (Enter)	
of *Pick* ④	Specifies midpoint of upper left edge

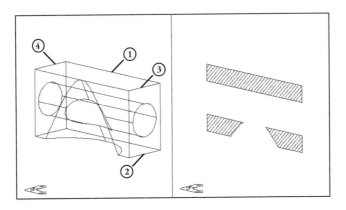

Figure S.9. *The ACIS SOLID before and after sectioning with the SECTION command.*

Related Commands

EXTRUDE   INTERFERE   INTERSECT   MASSPROP
SLICE   SUBTRACT   UNION

Related System Variable

VIEWDIR

SELECT

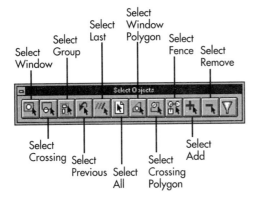

Toolbar: *(Standard, Select Objects)*
Pull-down: *Edit, Select Objects*
Screen: ASSIST, Select:

SELECT

The SELECT command enables you to create a selection set to use with another command. At the subsequent command's `Select objects:` prompt, you can enter **P** to specify the selection set established with the SELECT command.

Some of AutoCAD's menu selections use the SELECT command for object selection. You may notice the SELECT command being invoked during the command. When you finish selecting the objects and press Enter, AutoCAD passes the selection set to the actual command you wanted to invoke.

If the PICKFIRST system variable is on, you can select objects with the cursor and then issue the SELECT command to add the objects to the selection set. If PICKFIRST is off, you cannot preselect objects; you must issue SELECT, and then select the objects using the options described in the following section.

You cannot select objects from paper space that were created in model space, and vice versa.

Prompts and Options

Select objects Select all the objects that you want in your selection set. You can use any of the following selection methods:

> **A point** Picks the object passing through the specified point.
>
> **ALL** Selects all the objects in the drawing within the current space (paper space or model space).
>
> **Add (A)** Adds objects to the selection set.
>
> **Auto (AU)** If a pick fails to select an object, the selection method becomes the BOX option.
>
> **BOX** Pick a point to define the first corner of a rectangular box. If you move the crosshairs to the right, it becomes a window—to the left it becomes a crossing window.
>
> **Crossing Polygon (CP)** Selects all objects crossing or enclosed in a user-defined irregular polygon.
>
> **Crossing** Selects objects crossing or enclosed in a rectangular window area.
>
> **Fence** Selects objects that cross the fence line.

Group Selects all objects within a group name specified at the prompt, `Enter group name`.

Last (L) Selects the most recently created object that is currently visible.

Multiple (M) Enables you to pick multiple points on-screen before SELECT searches for objects. Press Enter to proceed.

Previous (P) Selects the previous selection set.

Remove (R) Removes specified objects from the selection set.

SIngle (SI) Selects the first object found and completes the selection set.

Undo (U) Removes the last group of selected objects.

Window (W) Selects objects enclosed within a rectangular window area.

Window Polygon (WP) Selects all objects completely enclosed in a user-defined irregular polygon.

Ctrl+C cancels the selection process without creating the selection set.

Example

The following example uses the SELECT Fence method to create a selection set (see fig. S.10).

From the pull-down menu, choose **E***dit,* **S**e*lect Objects*	Issues the SELECT command
`Command: _select`	
`Select objects:` **F** (Enter)	Chooses the Fence object selection method
`First fence point:` *Pick point* ① *(see fig. S.10)*	Specifies endpoints for the fence
`Undo/<Endpoint of line>:` *Pick point* ②	
`Undo/<Endpoint of line>:` *Pick point* ③	
`Undo/<Endpoint of line>:` *Pick point* ④	
`Undo/<Endpoint of line>:` *Pick point* ⑤	

```
Undo/<Endpoint of line>:
Pick point ⑥

Undo/<Endpoint of line>: (Enter)        Terminates fence selection

5 found

Select objects: (Enter)                 Terminates object selection
```

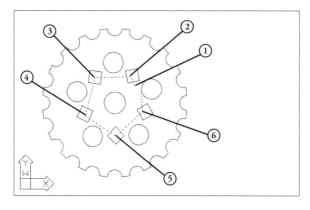

Figure S.10. *Using the Fence option to select objects.*

Related Commands
DDSELECT   GROUP

Related System Variables
HIGHLIGHT   PICKADD   PICKAUTO   PICKFIRST
PICKDRAG

'SETVAR

Pull-down: *O*ptions, S*y*stem Variables
Screen: OPTIONS, Sys Var:

The SETVAR (SET VARiable) command modifies and lists the settings of AutoCAD system variables. System variables store values used to control the behavior of AutoCAD commands. These values can be text strings, integers, real numbers, or coordinates. Variables that cannot be modified are called *read-only* variables. Almost all string variables are read-only.

You can directly access most system variables by entering the name of the variable at the Command: prompt. You can use SETVAR transparently to modify a variable setting while using another command, by prefacing SETVAR with an apostrophe ('SETVAR).

Prompts and Options

`Variable name or ? <variable name>` Enter the name of the variable you want to modify or enter a question mark (?) to list variables.

`Variable(s) to list <*>` Enter the name(s) of the variables you want to list. If you press Enter, AutoCAD displays a list of all the variables, one page at a time on the text screen. You can specify more than one variable by separating each with a comma or by using wild-card characters such as a question mark (?) or an asterisk (*).

`New value for VARIABLE <current value >` Enter a new value for the variable or press Enter to leave the current value unchanged. If the specified variable is read-only, the variable is displayed with the current value, and the New value for: prompt does not display.

Example

The following example demonstrates setting an AutoCAD variable.

Command: **SETVAR**	Issues the SETVAR command.
Variable name or ?: **EXPERT**	Specifies the system variable to change
New value for EXPERT <0>: **2**	Specifies the new value for the variable

Related System Variables

A complete list of AutoCAD system variables and dimension variables is featured in *Inside AutoCAD Release 13*, as well as the *AutoCAD Command Reference*.

SHADE

Shade

Toolbar: *Shade (Render)*
Pull-down: *T*ools, S*h*ade
Screen: TOOLS, SHADE, Shade:

The SHADE command generates a simple rendering of a 3D model by filling every face in the current viewport with a color. The color displayed is based on the entity's color, the angle of the face from the current viewpoint, the setting of the SHADEDGE and SHADEDIF system variables, and your display hardware's capabilities. You cannot select or plot the image, but you can make a slide of it using the MSLIDE command.

AutoCAD calculates the shading as if the objects were illuminated by a single light source directly behind you as you face the screen. The ratio of diffuse reflection from the light source to ambient (background) light is controlled by the SHADEDIF system variable. The SHADEDGE system variable controls the color in which edges are drawn. Regenerate the drawing to remove shading. Set SHADEDGE to zero or one to shade the faces with different colors, according to the angle the face forms with the current viewing direction, on 256-color systems.

> The time required for the SHADE command is reduced by freezing unnecessary layers, excluding irrelevant objects from the view, and minimizing the size of the viewport in which the shading is performed.

Example

The following example shades the ACIS SOLID object shown in the left viewport of figure S.11. See the SUBTRACT command for information on creating the ACIS SOLID.

Activate the right viewport by clicking anywhere inside it.	Makes right viewport current
Command: **SHADE** (Enter)	Starts the SHADE command
Regenerating Drawing. Shading XX% done. Shading complete.	

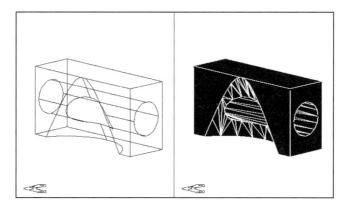

Figure S.11. *The right viewport displays the shaded entities of the left viewport.*

Related Commands

DVIEW   HIDE   RENDER

Related System Variables

FACETRES   SHADEDGE   SHADEDIF   VIEWDIR

SHAPE

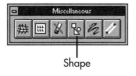

Shape

Toolbar: *Shape (Miscellaneous)*
Pull-down: *D̲raw, Inse̲rt, S̲hape*
Screen: DRAW2, Shape:

SHAPE

The SHAPE command inserts a shape object into a drawing at a specified location. Shapes are objects that you can define or are supplied from third-party vendors in a file (*.SHP) using lines, arcs, and subshapes. Shape objects can be inserted into the drawing similar to blocks. Shape definitions, however, do not become part of the drawing. The actual shape objects that become part of the drawing contain only the object's location and size and a reference to the shape definition file. AutoCAD uses shape definitions in creating complex linetypes.

Newly created shape definitions must be compiled with the COMPILE command and loaded with the LOAD command before they can be inserted. You can use the Insert object snap mode to snap to a shape's insertion point. When you load a drawing file, AutoCAD loads the compiled definition file corresponding to any inserted shapes.

If you modify a shape definition file, you must recompile it or AutoCAD continues to use the old shape definition.

TIP

You can use Xrefs instead of shapes if you need the efficiency and automatic updating provided by external definitions. Xrefs are easy to create and modify. Note, however, that shapes in an externally referenced drawing (xref) are not available in the drawing to which the xref is attached. You could also create and use blocks instead of shapes. Xrefs and blocks offer more flexibilty than shapes.

Prompts and Options

Shape name (or ?) <default>   Enter the name of a shape to insert. It must be already loaded into the drawing. Enter a question mark (**?**) to see a list of all currently loaded shapes.

Shape(s) to list <*>   Press Enter to list all the shapes currently loaded in the drawing. You also can enter more than one name to list by separating each name with a comma or use a wild-card search string to list only shapes that match the wild-card pattern.

Starting point   Enter a point in the drawing to locate the origin of the shape.

Height <1.0>   Enter a value to use as a multiplier for the shape's height. The shape's height initially is based on its definition in the shape file. You also can pick two points to define the height.

Rotation angle <0.0> Enter the angle you want to rotate the shape around its starting point. The shape's initial orientation is defined in the shape file. You also can pick two points to define the rotation angle.

Example

This example first loads a shape file from one of AutoCAD's sample shape files. After the shape file is loaded, its shape names are listed and then a shape is inserted into the drawing.

Command: **LOAD** (Enter)	Issues the LOAD command to make the shapes available for inserting
Specify the PC.SHX *file in the AutoCAD SAMPLE directory in the* Select Shape File *dialog box*	Specifies the name of the shape file to load
Command: **SHAPE** (Enter)	Issues the SHAPE command
Shape name (or ?): **?** (Enter)	Lists the loaded shape names
Shape(s) to list <*>: (Enter)	Lists all loaded shape names
Available Shapes: File: C:\ACAD\SAMPLE\PC.shx FEEDTHRU DIP8 DIP14 DIP16 DIP18 DIP20 DIP24 DIP40	
Command: (Enter)	Reissues the SHAPE command
SHAPE Shape name (or ?): **DIP24**	Specifies the name of the shape to insert
Starting point: *Pick a point*	Specifies the insertion point for the shape
Height <1.0>: **2** (Enter)	Specifies the relative shape height
Rotation angle <0>: **90** (Enter)	Specifies the relative shape rotation angle

Related Commands

BLOCK   COMPILE   GROUP   LOAD
PURGE   XREF

Related System Variable
SHPNAME

SHELL/SH

The SHELL command (or the SH abbreviation) enables you to run other programs or temporarily exit to the operating system prompt without ending the current drawing session. When you execute SHELL, the prompt, OS Command, is displayed. After issuing one operating system command, AutoCAD opens a DOS window, executes the command, closes the DOS window, and returns to AutoCAD. If you press Enter at the OS Command prompt, a DOS window is opened and remains there until you type **EXIT** at the DOS prompt. You are returned to the drawing editor, and AutoCAD resumes.

You may encounter memory problems with the SHELL command and larger programs. If so, you are prompted with Shell error: insufficient memory for command.

> Do not use the SHELL command to perform any of the following tasks:
> - Delete any files having extensions of ??K, AC, AC, or $A. These are files in use by AutoCAD.
> - Run the CHKDSK command with an /F option on DOS, Windows, or OS/2 systems.
> - Execute programs that reset serial ports (avoid Microsoft BASIC and programs compiled with it) on DOS, Windows, or OS/2 systems.
> - Run programs that write to the same graphics memory as AutoCAD.
> - Swap drawing disks.
> - Execute *Terminate and Stay Resident* (TSR) programs on DOS systems unless the programs are loaded before you load AutoCAD.

Remember to save your drawing file before you temporarily exit the drawing editor.

Prompts and Options

OS Command Enter the name of the single command or program you want to run, or press Enter and an operating system prompt appears.

If you press Enter to get an operating system prompt, you can then execute any number of programs or operating system commands. Issue the EXIT command to return to the drawing editor.

> Make sure that you exit the SHELL command from the same directory as you entered.

Example

The following example uses the SHELL command to list the drawing files in the SAMPLE directory, using the DOS DIR command.

Command: **SHELL**	Issues the SHELL command
OS Command: **DIR C:\ACADR13\COMMON\SAMPLE*.DWG**	Specifies the operating system command to execute

The list varies depending on the files in your directory and the version of DOS you are running.

Related Command

FILES

SKETCH

Sketch

Toolbar: *Sketch (Miscellaneous)*
Pull-down: <u>D</u>raw, S<u>k</u>etch
Screen: DRAW1, Sketch:

SKETCH

The SKETCH command creates a contiguous series of lines as you move the cursor. This feature enables you to draw freehand or to trace curves on a paper drawing in tablet mode. If you set the AutoCAD system variable SKPOLY to 1, each group of individual lines converts to a single polyline when the command is completed. A common application of this command is to trace contour lines from a site plan.

If the current thickness is set to a non-zero value, the sketched lines or polylines are not extruded until they are placed in the drawing with the Record or eXit option. The SKETCH command is affected by the current snap, ortho, and tablet settings.

The length of the individual SKETCH lines is controlled by the record increment. If the record increment (saved in system variable SKETCHINC) is set to 0.2 units, a new line is generated each time the cursor moves to more than 0.2 units. The length of the SKETCH lines is also affected by the speed at which the cursor is moved across the screen. If you move the cursor, the segments created may be longer than the length specified by the record increment.

You cannot turn tablet mode on and off while sketching.

The SKETCH command creates temporary lines that can be edited before they are placed on the drawing. If you create more temporary objects than can be stored in memory, AutoCAD prompts you to stop sketching objects and writes them to the disk. If you do not pause while AutoCAD writes to disk, input is lost and accuracy suffers.

You must use the continuous linetype when sketching.

Prompts and Options

Record increment *<value>*   Enter the length for each line segment. After the pointing device is moved this distance, the temporary segment is created on-screen. Use the largest value that produces sufficient detail. After specifying a record increment, the following prompt appears:

```
Sketch. Pen eXit Quit Record Erase Connect.
```

Select one of the following options. These options control how and when the SKETCH lines are drawn. The options also list the corresponding buttons on the pointing device that can be used.

You can use the following options with the SKETCH command:

. (period) Button 1. Draws a single line segment from the last point to the current pointing device location. Record increment does not affect the line length.

Pen Pick Button. This option turns the sketching on and off by placing the pen "up" and "down" on the drawing. When the pen is down, you can record lines.

eXit Button 3. Records temporary line segments and exits the SKETCH command.

Quit Button 4. Discards temporary line segments and returns to the Command prompt.

Record Button 2. Records temporary line segments and remains in the SKETCH command.

Erase Button 5. Erases temporary line segments in the opposite order from which they were entered as you move your pointing device back over the line segments.

Connect Button 6. By moving your pointing device close to the endpoint of the last temporary line segment, you can connect to that endpoint and continue sketching. If you enter Connect while the pen is down, you get the prompt `Connect command meaningless when pen down`. You can abort the connect by pressing Ctrl+C or entering any other option.

Example

The following example shows you how to draw polylines using the SKETCH command.

`Command:` **`SKPOLY`**	Issues the SKPOLY command
`New value for SKPOLY <0>:` **`1`** (Enter)	Sets SKPOLY to 1 for recording polylines
`Command:` **`SKETCH`** (Enter)	Issues the SKETCH command
`Record increment <0.1000>:` (Enter)	Accepts default sketch increment

SKETCH

```
Sketch.                                 Puts pen down
Pen eXit Quit Record Erase
Connect . P Enter
<Pen down>
```

Begin creating the line at ① by dragging the pointing device to ② (see fig. S.12)

```
P Enter                                 Takes pen up
<Pen up>

Sketch.                                 Records the polyline and exits the
Pen eXit Quit Record Erase              SKETCH command
Connect . X Enter
1 polyline with XX edges recorded.
```

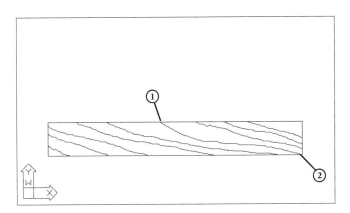

Figure S.12. *Using SKETCH to draw connecting lines.*

Related Commands

LINE   PLINE

Related System Variables

SKETCHINC   SKPOLY

SLICE

Slice

Toolbar: *Slice (Solids)*
Pull-down: *D̲raw, S̲olids, Sl̲ice*
Screen: DRAW2, SOLIDS, Slice:

The SLICE command modifies an existing ACIS SOLID by slicing away one portion or splitting the ACIS SOLID into two solids along a slicing plane. The slicing plane can be defined in three ways: by three points, as parallel to the current XY, YZ, or XZ planes, or by a 2D object such as a circle, ellipse, arc, spline, or 2D polyline segment. The slicing plane also can be defined to be perpendicular to the current viewing direction or by defining a normal vector to the slicing plane.

The SLICE command trims an ACIS SOLID up to a slicing plane. Use the SECTION command to simply create a section view through a specified section plane.

Prompts and Options

Select objects Select the objects you want to slice. These must be ACIS SOLID objects. Each ACIS SOLID is sliced using the plane defined in the next prompt.

Slicing plane by Object/Zaxis/View/XY/YZ/ZX/<3points> Press Enter, pick the first of three points in the graphics window, or enter the coordinates of the first of three points to define a slicing plane. You also can choose one of the options for defining a slicing plane.

> **Object** Select a circle, arc, ellipse, spline, or 2D polyline to define the slicing plane. A 3D object (such as a 3D face) does not have an associated plane of orientation. If you select a 3D object, AutoCAD responds:
> Unable to extract the plane of the selected object.
>
> **Zaxis** Aligns the slicing plane perpendicular to the axis specified, passing through the first point picked. At the Point on plane: prompt, pick a point in the graphics window or enter the coordinates of a point through which to pass the slicing plane. At the Point on Z-axis (normal) of the plane: prompt, pick a point in the graphics window or enter the coordinates of a point on the positive Z axis of a normal to the slicing plane.

View Aligns the slicing plane perpendicular to the current viewing direction. At the `Point on view plane <0,0,0>:` prompt, pick a point in the graphics window or enter the coordinates of a point through which to pass the slicing plane.

XY, YZ, or ZX Defines a slicing plane parallel to the current XY, YZ, or ZX planes. At the `Point on XY, YZ, or ZX plane <0,0,0>` prompt, pick a point in the graphics window or enter the coordinates of a point through which to pass the slicing plane.

`Both sides/<Point on desired side of the plane>:` Select a point on the side of the slicing plane to retain or choose the Both option to split the ACIS SOLID into two pieces along the slicing plane. If you pick a point in the graphics window or enter the coordinates of the point to retain, the portion of the original ACIS SOLID on the other side of the slicing plane is deleted. This trims the ACIS SOLID up to the slicing plane.

Example

The following example shows how to create a slice from an ACIS SOLID consisting of a box with a subtracted cone and cylinder (see fig. S.13). See the BOX, CONE, and CYLINDER commands for more information on creating ACIS SOLID primitive objects. See the SUBTRACT command for more information on subtracting ACIS SOLIDs from each other.

Command: **SLICE** (Enter)	Starts the SLICE command
Select objects: *Pick* ① *(see fig. S.13)*	Selects ACIS SOLID to slice
1 found	
Select objects: (Enter)	Finishes selecting objects to slice
Slicing plane by Object/Zaxis/View/ XY/YZ/ZX/<3points>: **MID** (Enter)	
of *Pick* ②	Specifies midpoint of lower right edge
2nd point on plane: **MID** (Enter)	
of *Pick* ③	Specifies midpoint of upper right edge
3rd point on plane: **MID** (Enter)	
of *Pick* ④	Specifies midpoint of upper left edge

```
Both sides/<Point on desired
side of the plane>: MID (Enter)
```

of *Pick* ⑤   Specifies midpoint of upper back edge
                                           to retain that side of ACIS SOLID

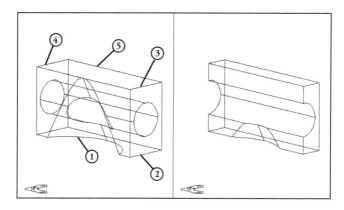

Figure S.13. *The ACIS SOLID before and after slicing with the SLICE command.*

Related Commands

EXTRUDE   INTERFERE   INTERSECT   MASSPROP
SECTION   SUBTRACT   TRIM   UNION

Related System Variable

VIEWDIR

'SNAP

Pull-down: *E̲dit, Sn̲ap*
Screen: ASSIST, Snap:

SNAP restricts the movement of the crosshairs to specified increments, enabling you to accurately enter points in the drawing area. You can alter the snap spacing in the X and Y directions, reset the base point of the snap and grid, and rotate the snap and grid about a point in the drawing. You also can use SNAP in Isometric mode to create drawings that appear to be three-dimensional but are actually two-dimensional. Each viewport may have individual snap settings. You can override any snap settings with keyboard input or object snap modes.

> You can also toggle snap mode by pressing Ctrl+B or F9. Within Windows, snap mode can be toggled by double clicking SNAP in the status bar.

Prompts and Options

`Snap spacing or ON/OFF/Aspect/Rotate/Style <1.000>`   Enter a new snap increment or enter one of the options described as follows to configure the SNAP command. Enter a number or pick two points to specify the snap increment.

`ON`   This option turns on SNAP. You also can turn it on with the F9 key or Ctrl+B.

`OFF`   This option turns off SNAP. You also can turn it off with the F9 key or Ctrl+B.

`Aspect`   This option enables you to set different X and Y axis values for the snap spacing. The following prompts appear:

`Horizontal spacing <1.0000>:`

You can enter a number or pick two points to specify a distance.

`Vertical spacing <1.0000>:`

You can enter a number or pick two points to specify a distance.

`Rotate`   This option enables you to rotate the snap and the crosshairs in the drawing. This rotation also affects the grid and ortho mode. After you specify the Rotation option, the following prompts appear:

`Base point <0.0000,0.0000>:`

You can enter coordinates or pick a point.

`Rotation angle <0>:`

You can enter an angle of rotation or pick a point to define the angle of rotation.

> Resetting the rotation of the snap and grid does not affect the origin or orientation of the current UCS. It is generally better to use the UCS command than to rotate or offset SNAP.

If you want to create an ARRAY at an angle, rotate the snap angle.

Style This option enables you to set the snap style to either Standard (the default) or Isometric. Style displays the following prompt:

Standard/Isometric <current>:

Standard resets the snap style to the default setting. Isometric enables isometric drafting, based on snap angles of 30, 90, 150, 210, 270, and 330. After you specify Isometric, AutoCAD displays the prompt:

Vertical spacing <1.0000>:

Specify the distance between the snap points.

You can check current SNAP settings by using the STATUS and DDRMODES commands.

Example

Follow this example to adjust the horizontal and vertical spacing of the SNAP command and to specify a rotation angle.

Command: **SNAP**	Issues the SNAP command
Snap spacing or ON/OFF/Aspect/Rotate/Style <1.000>: **A**	Selects the Aspect option
Horizontal spacing <1.0000>: **.5** (Enter)	Specifies the horizontal distance between snap increments
Vertical spacing: <1.0000> **1** (Enter)	Specifies the vertical snap increment distance
Command: **SNAP** (Enter)	Issues the SNAP command
Snap spacing or ON/OFF/Aspect/Rotate/Style <A>: **R** (Enter)	Selects the Rotate option
Base point: <0.0000,0.0000>: (Enter)	Specifies a rotation base point

`Rotation angle <0>: 25` **Enter**	Specifies the rotation angle for the snap grid
`Command:` **GRID**	Issues the GRID command
Grid spacing(X) or `ON/OFF/Snap <0.0000>:` **S**	Selects the Snap option

Related Commands

DDRMODES GRID ISOPLANE ORTHO OSNAP

Related System Variables

SNAPANG SNAPBASE SNAPMODE SNAPSTYL SNAPUNIT

SOLID

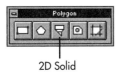

2D Solid

Toolbar: *2D Solid (Draw, Polygon)*
Pull-down: *Draw, Polygon, 2D Solid*
Screen: DRAW1, Solid:

SOLID draws solid-filled areas. These areas are defined by three or four corner points, entered in an edge-to-edge order. The first two points are the endpoints of a starting edge. The next two points (called the third and fourth points) are the endpoints of the opposing edge.

AutoCAD fills in the area bounded by the lines from the first to the second point, the second to the fourth point, the fourth to the third point, and the third to the first point. If no fourth point is entered, AutoCAD creates a fourth point at the same location as the third point. Use the FILL command to turn on or off filled area display, or set the FILLMODE system variable to one or zero, respectively. If FILLMODE is one, the areas are filled.

> **TIP** To save time during regenerations and redraws, use the FILL command to turn off area fill display. To see the results of turning FILL on or off, regenerate the drawing.

Do not confuse the SOLID command, which creates 2D solid filled areas, with the ACIS SOLID objects created by the BOX, CONE, CYLINDER, SPHERE, or WEDGE commands.

Prompts and Options

First point Pick a point in the graphics window or enter the coordinates of the first point of the solid-filled area object.

Second point Specify the second point of the solid-filled area object.

Third point For creating a four-cornered solid, the direction in which you select the third point determines the appearance of the solid. If points are selected in a clockwise or counterclockwise direction, the solid appears as a bow tie. See the solid-filled area in the upper left of figure S.14 for an example.

Fourth point Pick a point to draw a four-sided solid. You do not have to specify a point at this prompt—if you press Enter, AutoCAD creates a three-sided solid by creating a fourth point at the same location as the third point. The SOLID command continues with a prompt for the third point of the next solid. The next solid uses the third and fourth points of the previous solid as the first and second points of the new solid.

Example

The following example creates four solid filled areas, as shown in figure S.14.

Command: **SOLID** (Enter)	Starts the SOLID command
First point: *Pick point* ① (see fig. S.14)	Specifies first corner
Second point: *Pick point* ②	Specifies second corner
Third point: *Pick point* ③	Specifies third corner
Fourth point: *Pick point* ④	Specifies fourth corner
Third point: (Enter)	Creates bow tie solid filled area

```
Command: SOLID (Enter)              Starts the SOLID command
First point: Pick point ⑤           Specifies first corner
Second point: Pick point ⑥          Specifies second corner
Third point: Pick point ⑦           Specifies third corner
Fourth point: Pick point ⑧          Creates rectangular solid filled area
Third point: (Enter)                Finishes SOLID command
Command: SOLID (Enter)              Starts the SOLID command
First point: Pick point ⑨           Specifies first corner
Second point: Pick point ⑩          Specifies second corner
Third point: Pick point ⑪           Specifies third corner
Fourth point: Pick point ⑫          Creates rectangular solid filled area
Third point: Pick point ⑬           Specifies third corner
Fourth point: (Enter)               Creates fourth corner at same
                                    location as third corner, results in
                                    triangular solid
Third point: (Enter)                Finishes SOLID command
```

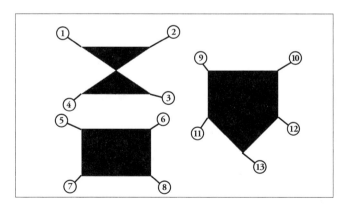

Figure S.14. *Creating solids with FILL on.*

Related Command
FILL

Related System Variable
FILLMODE

SPELL

Spelling

Toolbar: *Spelling (Standard)*
Pull-down: **T**ools, **S**pelling
Screen: TOOLS, Spell:

The SPELL command adds spell-checking capability to AutoCAD. The SPELL command attempts to correct the spelling of text objects created with the TEXT, DTEXT, or MTEXT commands. It also corrects the spelling of default values in attribute definitions. It does not correct spelling of text within dimensions or attributes.

Prompts and Options

Select Objects   You can use any valid AutoCAD object selection method for selecting text objects. You may enter ALL to select all objects in the current space (model space or paper space). AutoCAD filters out the text objects and searches for a misspelled word or a word not in its dictionary. If such a word is found, the Check Spelling dialog box is displayed (see fig. S.15). If no misspelled words are found, an alert box is displayed stating Spelling check complete.

SPELL

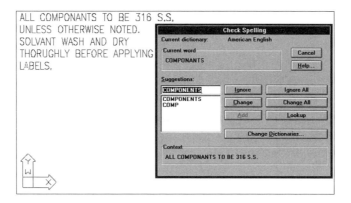

Figure S.15. *Checking the spelling on drawing text.*

Dialog Box Items

Current dictionary. This text label displays the name of the dictionary the SPELL command is currently using. You can specify another main dictionary (British spelling, for example) or specify or create a custom dictionary using the Change **D**ictionaries button discussed later. The name of the main dictionary is stored in the system variable DCTMAIN. The system variable DCTCUST stores the name of the current custom dictionary.

Current word. The text box displays the current word not listed in the dictionary. You have the option of changing the word or ignoring it.

Suggestions. The dictionary word most closely matching the current word is listed in the **S**uggestions edit box. Other possible words may be listed in the list box below it. These words come from the main dictionary and any custom dictionary you may have active at the time. If one of these words is correct, you can select it, replacing the suggested word with your choice. You can also edit the word and select the **C**hange or Chang**e** All button to change the current word.

Ignore. The **I**gnore button skips the current word and proceeds to the next word, if any.

Ignore All. Use the I**g**nore All button to skip over the current word and all other words in the text selection that match it.

Change. Selecting the **C**hange button changes the current word to that in the **S**uggestions edit box (see **S**uggestions, discussed previously).

Change All. Use the Chang**e** All button to change the current word and all subsequent words that match it to that in the **S**uggestions edit box.

Add. If a custom dictionary has been defined (see Change **D**ictionaries discussed later), you can add the current word to it as is.

> If your company or discipline uses technical terms not commonly listed in dictionaries, add these words to the custom dictionary when you run the spell checker. Once these words are added to the dictionary, subsequent spell checks will bypass them.

Lookup. Use the **L**ookup button to check the spelling of the word in the **S**uggestions edit box. This is handy if you change or edit the word and are unsure of its spelling. After you are satisfied with its spelling, use the **C**hange or Chang**e** All button to change the current word.

Change Dictionaries. Use this button to display the Change Dictionaries dialog box, illustrated in figure S.16. This dialog box allows you to select another main dictionary or define a custom dictionary.

Figure S.16. *The Change Dictionaries dialog box.*

Main dictionary. This pull-down list box lists language-specific versions of main dictionaries you may use. The U.S. version of AutoCAD lists three choices: American English, British English (ise), and British English (ize).

Custom dictionary. Use this edit box to specify the name of a custom dictionary to create or use. **C**ustom dictionary files have the extension CUS. You may use the **B**rowse button to select a custom dictionary file. You may have any number of custom dictionaries, but only one can be used by the spell checker at any one time. If no custom dictionaries are specified, the **A**dd button on the Check Spelling dialog box is disabled.

Add. Use this button to add the word shown in the edit box to the custom dictionary specified above. If the word already exists in the dictionary, the text "Could not add word" is displayed at the lower left corner of the dialog box.

Delete. The **D**elete button removes the word in the edit box from the custom dictionary specified above.

Context. The context text box, the last button in the Check Spelling dialog box, displays the line of text containing the current word. This is useful if you are unsure where in the drawing the particular word is located and need to know the context it was used in.

Related Commands

ATTDEF   CHANGE   DDATTDEF   DDEDIT
DDMODIFY   DTEXT   MTEXT   STYLE
TEXT

Related System Variables

DCTCUST   DCTMAIN

SPHERE

Sphere

Tool: *Sphere (Solids)*
Pull-down: *Draw, Solids, Sphere*
Screen: DRAW2, SOLIDS, Sphere:

The SPHERE command creates a 3D ACIS SOLID shaped like a SPHERE. The SPHERE is placed parallel to the current UCS by specifying the center point of the SPHERE. The size of the SPHERE can be specified by either radius or diameter.

Prompts and Options

`Center of sphere<0,0,0>`   Specify the center point of the SPHERE by picking a point in the graphics window or entering coordinates.

Diameter/<Radius>   Specify a value or pick a point to show a distance for the radius of the SPHERE, or enter **D** if you prefer to specify a value for the diameter of the SPHERE.

Diameter   Enter a value or pick a point to show a distance for the diameter of the SPHERE.

Example

This example shows how to create an ACIS SOLID SPHERE object (see fig. S.17).

Command: **SPHERE** (Enter)	Starts the SPHERE command
Center of sphere<0,0,0>: **8,7,4** (Enter)	Specifies center of sphere
Diameter/<Radius> of sphere: **1** (Enter)	Specifies sphere radius of 1.0

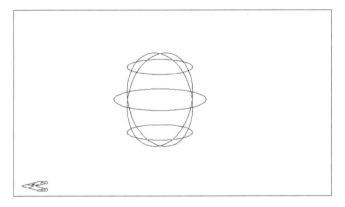

Figure S.17. *An ACIS SOLID SPHERE object.*

Related Commands

INTERFERE   INTERSECTION   SUBTRACT   UNION

SPLINE

Spline

Toolbar: *Spline (Draw, Polyline)*
Pull-down: *Draw, Spline*
Screen: DRAW 1, Spline:

The SPLINE command creates a *non-uniform rational B-spline* (NURBS). This is a smooth curve fit to a sequence of points. You specify the control points for the curve and the start and end point tangencies to create the spline. The SPLINE command can create a true spline object from a spline-fit 2D or 3D polyline (see PEDIT). Splines are mathematically more accurate and consume less system memory and disk space than polylines. You can control the tolerance, or how closely the spline fits the control points, while you are drawing the spline. Splines, unlike spline-fit polylines, are easily edited using grips or with the SPLINEDIT command while maintaining their mathematical accuracy.

Prompts and Options

```
Object/<Enter first point>.
```

<Enter first point>   Specify the starting or first point for the spline. You are then prompted to Enter point for the second point. After the second point is specified, the following prompt appears:

```
Close/Fit Tolerance/<Enter point>:
```

> **<Enter point>**   Enter all points necessary to define the spline object. Press U to go back to the previous point. Press Enter to terminate point specification. You are issued the following prompt:
> ```
> Enter start tangent:
> ```
>
> At this prompt, you specify a point for the tangency of the spline at the starting point. Press Enter to force AutoCAD to calculate the default tangency. Tangency determines the direction of the curve. You are then prompted with the following:
> ```
> Enter end tangent:
> ```

At this prompt, you specify a point for the tangency of the spline at the ending point. Press Enter to force AutoCAD to calculate the default tangency. You may use object snaps to make the spline tangent with other objects in the drawing.

Close Use this option to create a closed spline curve. The last point and the starting point are at the same location. You are then issued the following prompt:

```
Enter tangent:
```

Specify a point for the tangent vector or press Enter to accept the default tangency.

Fit tolerance The Fit tolerance option is used to define how close or accurately the curve passes through the control points. The default tolerance of 0 (zero) means that the curve will pass through the control points. The following prompt appears:

```
Enter Fit tolerance <0.0000>:
```

Enter a positive value for the tolerance. Figure S.18 illustrates the effect of a zero tolerance versus a tolerance of two.

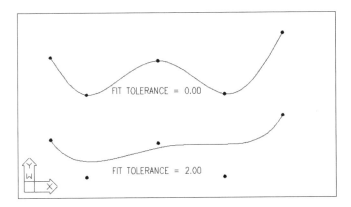

Figure S.18. *The effect of tolerance on a spline.*

Object Use this option to create a spline object from a spline-fit 2D or 3D polyline. If the system variable DELOBJ is set to 0, the original polyline object is not deleted. Select the 2D or 3D spline-fit polylines at the prompt, `Select objects`. Figure S.19 illustrates a 2D polyline that has been spline-fit with the PEDIT command and finally converted to a spline object with the SPLINE command.

SPLINE

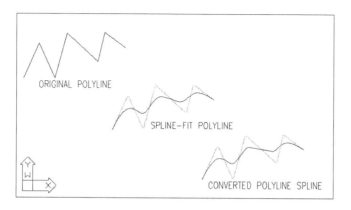

Figure S.19. *Converting 2-D spline-fit polylines to spline objects.*

Example

The following example illustrates how to draw a simple spline object.

Choose the SPLINE *tool.* *Tool:* [Spline](Draw, Polyline)	Issues the SPLINE command
Command: _spline	
Object/<Enter first point>: 1,1 (Enter)	Specifies the first point of the spline
Enter point: 3,3 (Enter)	Specifies a control point for the spline
Close/Fit Tolerance/ <Enter point>: 7,2 (Enter)	
Close/Fit Tolerance/ <Enter point>: 9,5 (Enter)	
Close/Fit Tolerance/ <Enter point>: 13,2 (Enter)	
Close/Fit Tolerance/ <Enter point>: (Enter)	Specifies the endpoint of the spline
Enter start tangent: (Enter)	Specifies the tangent direction
Enter end tangent: (Enter)	

Related Commands

PEDIT   PLINE   SPLINE   SPLINEDIT

SPLINEDIT

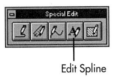

Edit Spline

Toolbar: *Edit Spline (Modify, Special Edit)*
Screen: MODIFY, SplinEd:

The SPLINEDIT command provides methods for modifying a NURBS spline object. You can add, move, and delete control and fit points. You can apply more weight or pull to control points. You can modify the fit data for a spline. The splines can be opened or closed and the start and end tangents modified. You can increase the order of the spline, adding more control points for more control of the curve. Finally, you can reverse the order or direction of the points defining a spline. In addition to the SPLINEDIT command, you can perform a limited amount of spline editing using grips.

Prompts and Options

Select spline   Select the SPLINE object you want to edit. Control points appear in the same color as grips. If the SPLINE has fit data, the fit points also appear (see fig. S.20).

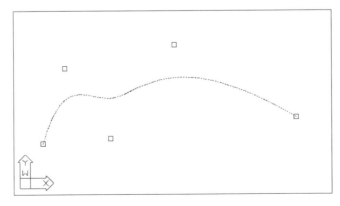

Figure S.20. *Selecting a spline for editing.*

```
Fit Data/Close/Move Vertex/Refine/rEverse/Undo/eXit <X>:
```
Fit Data This option is only available if the spline selected has fit data. Fit data can only be applied during the SPLINE command by choosing a spline-fit polyline object or by specifying a fit tolerance or tangents.

> Fit data will be removed from a spline if any of the following conditions are met:
> - The Fit Data Purge option of the SPLINEDIT command is used.
> - The spline is refined.
> - The spline has a tolerance applied and its control points are moved.
> - The spline has a tolerance applied and it is opened or closed.

The Fit Data option issues the following prompt for an open spline. For a closed spline, the Close option shown below becomes Open.

```
Add/Close/Delete/Move/Purge/Tangents/toLerance/eXit <X>:
```

> **Add** Use the Add option to add fit points to a spline (see fig. S.21). You are prompted to Select point. When you select a fit point, AutoCAD highlights the next fit point and draws a rubber band line at the Enter new point prompt. If you pick the start point, AutoCAD prompts, After/<Before>, to specify adding a point before or after the start point. As you specify new fit points, AutoCAD redraws the spline throughout the new points and continues highlighting the next point and prompting for a new fit point until you press Enter. When you press Enter, the Select point prompt reappears, enabling you to specify another fit point. Press Enter to return to the original Fit Data option prompt.
>
> **Close** Use the Close option to close an open spline. AutoCAD will make the tangents at the start and end points continuous or smooth.
>
> **Open** The Open option is used to open a closed spline. If the endpoints of the spline were the same before it was closed, the endpoints lose their tangency when opened. If the endpoints of the spline were not coincident before closing the spline, the endpoints are restored with their original tangency.
>
> **Delete** Use this option to remove fit points from the spline. The spline is redrawn through the remaining points. You are prompted to Select point to specify the point to remove. This prompt repeats until you press Enter.

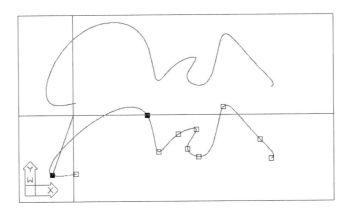

Figure S.21. *Adding a fit point to a spline.*

Move Use this option to move change the location of a fit point. The Move option issues the following prompt:

`Next/Previous/Select Point/eXit/<Enter new location> <N>:`

The Move option highlights the first or starting point of the spline. The Next option highlights the subsequent fit point. The Previous option highlights the fit point previous to the one currently highlighted. Use the Select Point option to specify any fit point on the spline. The default option to `Enter new location` draws a rubber band line from the highlighted point. Specify the new location for the highlighted point. The spline will be redrawn through this point. The preceding prompt repeats until you select the eXit option or press Enter.

> You may also use grips to relocate points defining a spline.

Purge Use the Purge option to remove the spline's fit data. The Fit Data option will be removed from the SPLINEDIT main prompt. Do not confuse this Purge option with AutoCAD's PURGE command.

Tangents This option enables you to modify the start and end tangents of a spline. You can allow AutoCAD to calculate the default tangent or specify a new tangent. The following two prompts appear in order for an open spline. The prompt, `System Default/<Enter tangent>`, appears for closed splines. Press Enter to leave the current tangent unmodified.

`System Default/<Enter start tangent>:`
`System Default/<Enter end tangent>:`

toLerance The toLerance option is used to specify a new fit tolerance for the existing fit points. A fit tolerance of zero means that the spline will pass through the fit points. The toLerance option issues the following prompt:
```
Enter fit tolerance<0.0000>
```

eXit Use this option to return to the main SPLINEDIT prompt.

Close See the Close option under Fit Data in the preceding.

Open See the Open option under Fit Data in the preceding.

Move Vertex Use this option to move the spline's control points. It issues the same prompts and options as the Fit Data Move option above.

Refine Use the Refine option to add more control to the appearance of the spline curve. You can add more control points, increase the order of the spline, and add more weight to specific control points. The Refine option issues the following prompt:
```
Add control point/Elevate Order/Weight/eXit <X>:
```

Add control point Use this option to add a new control point on the spline. This gives more control over the spline. You are prompted to Select a point on the spline. Pick any point on the spline. AutoCAD will add a new control point between the two points controlling that portion of the spline close to your pick point.

Elevate Order This option increases the number of control points uniformly across the spline. This gives you many more control points for finely controlling the appearance of the spline curve. The maximum value of the order is 26. The following prompt is displayed with this option and shows the current order of the spline: Enter new order <current>. You must enter an integer value greater than the current order but less than 27. You cannot lower the order of a spline once you have elevated it.

Weight Use this option to apply more weight or pull to a particular control point on the spline. A greater weight applied to a point will force the spline curve closer to that point. The Weight option issues the following prompt:
```
Next/Previous/Select Point/eXit/<Enter new weight> <1>:
```

The Weight option highlights the first or starting point of the spline. The Next option highlights the subsequent fit point. The Previous option highlights the fit point previous to the one currently highlighted. Use the Select Point option to specify any fit point on the spline. The default option to Enter new weight asks for a new weight to apply to the highlighted point. The spline will be redrawn using this new weight applied to this point. This prompt repeats until you select the eXit option or press Enter.

eXit   This option returns to the main SPLINEDIT prompt.

rEverse   Use this option to reverse the order of points controlling the spline. In other words, what was the start point becomes the endpoint and all the points in-between are reversed. Some third-party applications such as software that generates numerical control data for machining can require points to be in a certain order.

Undo   This option will undo the most recent editing operation performed in the SPLINEDIT command.

eXit   Use this option to exit the SPLINEDIT command.

Example

Use the SPLINEDIT command to add a control point to a spline and move it.

Command: **SPLINEDIT** (Enter)	Issues the SPLINEDIT command
Select spline: *Select the spline object*	Specifies the object to edit
Fit Data/Close/Move Vertex/Refine/ rEverse/Undo/eXit <X>: **R** (Enter)	Selects the Refine option
Add control point/Elevate Order/ Weight/eXit <X>: **A** (Enter)	Selects the Add control point option
Select a point on the spline: *Pick point* ①	Specifies where to add the control point (see fig. S.22)
Select a point on the spline: (Enter)	Exits the Add control point option
Add control point/Elevate Order/ Weight/eXit <X>: **X** (Enter)	Exits the Refine option

SPLINEDIT

`Close/Move Vertex/Refine/rEverse/` `Undo/eXit <X>:` **M**	Selects the Move Vertex option
`Next/Previous/Select Point/eXit/` `<Enter new location> <N>:` **S** (Enter)	Selects the Select Point option
`Select point:` *Pick point* ①	Specifies the control point to move

`Next/Previous/Select Point/eXit/`
`<Enter new location> <N>:`
Pick point ②
	Specifies the new location for the control point

`Next/Previous/Select Point/eXit/` `<Enter new location> <N>:` X	Exits the Move Vertex option
`Close/Move Vertex/Refine/` `rEverse/Undo/eXit <X>:` **X**	Exits the SPLINEDIT command

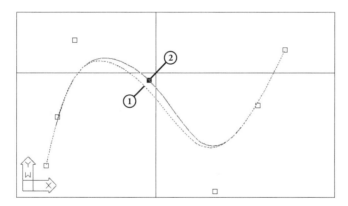

Figure S.22. *Adding and moving a spline control point.*

Related Commands

PLINE   SPLINE

STATS

Statistics

Toolbar: *Statistics (Render)*
Pull-down: *T*ools, R*e*nder, S*t*atistics...
Screen: TOOLS, RENDER, Stats:

The STATS command displays statistical information about the last rendering and enables you to save the statistics as a file.

Dialog Box Items

The STATS command displays the Statistics dialog box shown in figure S.23 below. Its main feature is a list box containing the rendering data.

Figure S.23. *The rendering Statistics dialog box*

Save **Statistics to File.** The Save Statistics to File check box and edit box enable you to write the statistical information to a file. First, place a check in the check box, and then enter a file name, including the extension, in the edit box. The resulting file is an ASCII file, which you can display by using any text editor or the DOS TYPE command. If the file name you enter already exists, the information is appended to that file. The following is a sample of the output generated from the STATS command.

```
Statistics for rendering begun Fri Jan 20 16:40:26 1995

Rendering Type:         AutoVision
Scene Name:             *current view*

Total Time:             16 Seconds

Initialization Time:    1 Second
Traversal Time:         2 Seconds
Render + Display Time:  13 Seconds
Cleanup Time:           0 Seconds

Total Faces:            448
Total Triangles:        768

Width:                  707
Height:                 401
Colors:                 8-bits
Color palette:          Best Map/No Fold

Sub Sampling:           1:1
Smoothing:              On
Smoothing Angle:        45.00
Apply Materials:        On
Shadows:                Off
Anti-aliasing Level:    Minimal
Texture Map Sampling:   Linear Sample
Discard Back Faces:     Off
Back Face Normal is:    Negative
```

Related Command

RENDER

'STATUS

Pull-down: **D**ata, Stat**u**s
Screen: DATA, Status:

The STATUS command provides detailed information about the current drawing and AutoCAD's memory usage. Information that STATUS provides includes the number of objects in the drawing; the drawing's limits and whether they are being exceeded; the current color, layer, and linetype; and the status of drawing aids, such as snap and ortho modes. STATUS also displays information on disk and memory usage. The number format is controlled by the UNITS command.

TIP Use the STATUS command to monitor your free disk space. If the disk fills up, AutoCAD cannot continue.

The following listing is a sample STATUS output. Each section is discussed after the listing:

```
11226 objects in C:\ACADR13\COMMON\SAMPLE\PNID
Model space limits are X:    0.0000   Y:    0.0000  (Off)
                       X:   12.0000   Y:    9.0000
Model space uses       X:    0.0000   Y:    0.0000 **Over
                       X:   41.3267   Y:   27.5511 **Over
Display shows          X:    0.0000   Y:    0.0000
                       X:   48.1128   Y:   30.3830
Insertion base is      X:    0.0000   Y:    0.0000  Z:    0.0000
Snap resolution is     X:    1.0000   Y:    1.0000
Grid spacing is        X:    0.0000   Y:    0.0000

Current space:         Model space
Current layer:         0
Current color:         BYLAYER — 7 (white)
Current linetype:      BYLAYER — CONTINUOUS
Current elevation:     0.0000   thickness:    0.0000
Fill on  Grid off  Ortho off  Qtext off  Snap off  Tablet off
Object snap modes:     None
Free disk (dwg+temp=C:): 67551232 bytes
Free physical memory: 0.0 Mbytes (out of 18.8M).
Free swap file space: 30.5 Mbytes (out of 69.6M).
Virtual address space: 38.8 Mbytes.
```

The first line of the STATUS output displays the total number of objects in the drawing and the path and drawing name.

Model space limits or **Paper space limits**   This section shows the coordinates defining the drawing limits set by the LIMITS command. The first line in this section shows the limit's lower left X and Y values. These are stored in the system variable LIMMIN. The second line shows the limit's upper right X and Y values as stored in the system variable LIMMAX. The comment (Off) indicates that limit checking is off and reflects the value of the system variable LIMCHECK. Limits checking can be set through the LIMITS command.

Model space uses or **Paper space uses**   This section of the STATUS listing displays data concerning the extents of the drawing. The extents include all objects in the AutoCAD drawing database and may or may not exceed the drawing limits. The first line in this section shows the extents lower left X and Y values. These are stored in the system variable EXTMIN. The second line shows the extents' upper right X and Y values as stored in the system variable EXTMAX. The comment **Over indicates that the objects extend beyond the limits of the drawing.

Display shows This section of the STATUS listing shows what portion of the drawing extents are visible in the current viewport. The first line shows the coordinates of the lower left corner of the display and the second line of the upper right corner.

Insertion base is This line of the STATUS listing shows the X, Y, and Z values of its insertion base point as stored in the INSBASE system variable and set by the BASE command. This point is used as the insertion point if this drawing is inserted as a block or Xref into another drawing.

Snap resolution is This line shows the current snap spacing in the X and Y directions. This is set by the SNAP command and is stored in the system variable SNAPUNIT.

Grid spacing is This line displays the current grid spacing in the X and Y directions as stored in the system variable GRIDUNIT and set by the GRID command.

Current space This line shows whether model space or paper space is currently active. AutoCAD determines this by the values stored in the system variables TILEMODE and CVPORT.

Current layer This line shows the name of the current layer as stored in the system variable CLAYER and set by the LAYER, CLAYER, or DDLMODES commands.

Current color This line shows the current color as stored in the CECOLOR system variable and set by the COLOR or DDEMODES command.

Current linetype This line shows the current linetype as set by the LINETYPE or DDEMODES command. This value is stored in the system variable CELTYPE.

Current elevation This line lists the current elevation (Z value relative to the current UCS). This value is stored in the ELEVATION system variable. This value can be set through the ELEVATION or DDEMODES commands.

Current thickness This line displays the current thickness (extrusion in the Z axis) as stored in the system variable THICKNESS. The thickness can be set through the ELEV, THICKNESS, or DDEMODES commands.

The next line in the STATUS listing shows the On/Off status of fill, grid, ortho, qtext, snap, and tablet modes. These values are stored in the system variables FILLMODE, GRIDMODE, ORTHOMODE, QTEXTMODE, SNAPMODE, and TABMODE, respectively.

Object snap modes This line of the STATUS listing shows what running object snap modes have been set by the SNAP or DDOSNAP commands. These values are stored in the system variable OSMODE.

Free disk (dwg+temp=C) This line shows the amount of free space available on the drive configured for the AutoCAD temporary files.

Free physical memory This line lists the amount of free installed memory (RAM) on your system.

Free swap file space This line shows the amount of free space available in the swap file.

Virtual address space This line shows the total amount of system resources (RAM plus swap file space) available for use. This does not list free space available, but the total amount, regardless of whether in use.

Related Commands

DBLIST	LIST	LOGFILEOFF	LOGFILEON
TIME	TREESTAT		

Related System Variables

CLAYER	CECOLOR	CELTYPE	CVPORT
ELEVATION	EXTMAX	EXTMIN	FILLMODE
GRIDMODE	INSBASE	LIMCHECK	LIMMAX
LIMMIN	LUNITS	ORTHOMODE	OSMODE
QTEXTMODE	RIDUNIT	SNAPMODE	SNAPUNIT
TABMODE	THICKNESS	TILEMODE	

STLOUT

Pull-down: File, Export, Stereolithography (DOS Only)
Screen: FILE, EXPORT, STLout:

The STLOUT command exports a single ACIS SOLID object to a file in the STereo-Lithography (STL) standard. This file format is used by a Stereo-Lithography Apparatus (SLA) to create a 3D part from your ACIS SOLID model. The STL file contains a description of all the facets used to construct the boundary model of the ACIS SOLID, in either ACSII or binary format. The ACIS SOLID to be extracted must have all of its boundaries located in the positive X, positive Y, and positive Z octant of the world coordinate system.

Prompts and Options

Select a single solid for STL output, Select objects   Select only a single ACIS SOLID for exporting to an STL file. Any objects that are not ACIS SOLIDs are ignored. If you select more than one ACIS SOLID for extraction, AutoCAD responds:

`Only one solid per file permitted.`

If no ACIS SOLIDs are selected for extraction, AutoCAD responds:

`No solids selected.`

Create a binary STL file ? <Y>   Press Enter to create a binary STL file; enter **N** to create an ASCII STL file. If you selected an ACIS SOLID that does not lie in the first 3D octant (positive X, Y, and Z coordinates), AutoCAD responds:

`The solid does not lie in the positive XYZ octant.`

After successfully selecting a single ACIS SOLID in the first 3D octant, the STLOUT command displays the Create STL File dialog box. Pick an existing STL output file to overwrite or specify a new STL output file name and click on OK.

Example

The following example creates an STL file from a single ACIS SOLID created by subtracting a cone and cylinder from a box (see the SUBTRACT command for more information). The ACIS SOLID is shown in figure S.24.

Command: **STLOUT** (Enter)	Starts the STLOUT command
Select a single solid for STL output:	
Select objects: *Pick* ① *(see fig. S.24)*	Selects ACIS SOLID object for extracting
1 found	
Select objects: (Enter)	Finishes selecting objects
Create a binary STL file ? <Y>: (Enter)	Specifies binary rather than ASCII STL output file contents; displays Create STL File dialog box
Enter the name of an STL output file	Specifies STL output file name
Click on OK	Creates STL output file

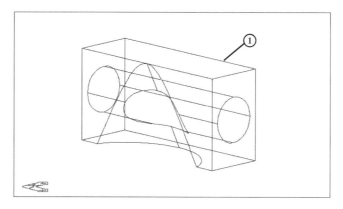

Figure S.24. *Extracting an ACIS SOLID to an STL file with the STLOUT command.*

Related Commands

ACISOUT   DXFOUT   EXPORT   PLOT
PSOUT

Related System Variable

FACETRES

STRETCH

Stretch

    Toolbar: *Stretch (Modify, Resize)*
    Pull-down: <u>M</u>odify, Stret<u>c</u>h
    Screen: MODIFY, Stretch:

The STRETCH command moves and stretches objects by relocating the points that define the objects. To select objects for STRETCH, drag a crossing window or crossing polygon. Objects within the window are moved; objects that cross the edge of the window are stretched. Only the points within the selection window are moved. You cannot stretch some objects, such as circles, shapes, text, blocks, and points. You can move these objects, however, if their primary definition point is located within the crossing window.

STRETCH

> Use the grip edit stretch mode for quicker stretching and as a copy option. You can also stretch a circle's radius with the grip edit stretch mode.

TIP

Prompts and Options

Select objects to stretch by crossing-window or -polygon...
Select objects At this prompt, you must use a crossing window or crossing polygon to select objects. AutoCAD accepts only one selection window. The STRETCH command ignores multiple selection sets, using the last one only. Use the BOX crossing option, Crossing window (C), or the Crossing Polygon (CP) object selection method to select the objects for stretching. You can use the Remove (R) option to remove objects from the selection set. You cannot use the Add (A) option, however, as AutoCAD ignores objects other than those originally selected using a crossing option. The prompt repeats until your selection set is complete. Press Enter to terminate object selection.

Base point or displacement Enter the base point of displacement or a coordinate amount of displacement.

Second point of displacement Enter the new point for the stretched objects.

Example

The following example uses STRETCH on the window shown in figure S.25 to widen the window by one foot.

Choose the Stretch *tool*.	Issues the STRETCH command
Command: _stretch	
Select objects to stretch by crossing-window or -polygon...	
Select objects: *Pick point* ① *(see fig. S.25)*	Specifies the first corner of a crossing box
Other corner: *Pick point* ②	Specifies the opposite corner of the crossing box
7 found	
Select objects: (Enter)	Terminates object selection

Base point or displacement: *Pick any point*i*	Specifies the reference point for STRETCH
Second point of displacement: @1'<0 (Enter)	Determines stretch direction and distance

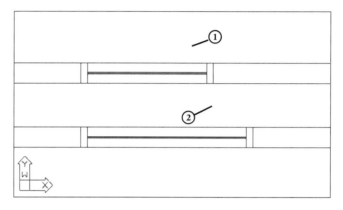

Figure S.25. *A window before and after STRETCH.*

Related Commands

EXTEND   LENGTHEN   MOVE   SCALE
TRIM

'STYLE

Pull-down: **D**ata, **T**ext Style
Screen: DATA, Style:

The STYLE command loads fonts that you can use with the TEXT, DTEXT, MTEXT, ATTDEF, and dimensioning commands to create text. In addition, STYLE enables you to define the look of a text font in the drawing. The STYLE command enables you to specify a font file and its properties to be assigned to a style name. You can assign a style using any of the supplied or third-party compiled shape files (.SHX), PostScript files (.PFB or .PFA), or TrueType fonts (.TTF). AutoCAD is installed with a STANDARD style name using the TXT.SHX font file.

If you change a style, all text created with that style is changed upon the next screen regeneration.

Prompts and Options

`Text style name (or ?) <STANDARD>` Enter the desired name for the text style. Each unique text style must have its own name. The default name for the text style is the name of the file that contains the font. Use the question mark option (?) to obtain a list of the currently defined styles in the drawing.

The LIST and DDMODIFY commands display the STYLE settings of a text object.

If you choose the question mark option (?), you can specify which style(s) you want to view at the prompt, `Text style(s) to list <*>`. If you press Enter, all loaded text styles are listed. You also can enter a wild-card search string to list only styles that match the wild-card pattern.

If you enter a style name, the Select Font File dialog box is displayed (see fig. S.26). Enter the name of the file that contains the font definition. This file has an SHX, TTF, PFA, or PFB extension. You can define the types of files to list using the List Files of Type drop-down list box in the Select Font File dialog box. If you press Enter, the style is based on the font file of the current style.

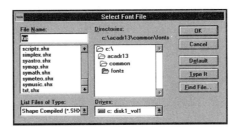

Figure S.26. *The Select Font File dialog box.*

> **TIP** The style name you use can and should be descriptive. The style name does not have to relate to the font file name. For example, you can have any number of style names, all using the ROMANS.SHX font file. Each style may have differing heights, oblique angles, or width factors.

Height <0.0> Specify a height of 0.0 if you want the TEXT, DTEXT, and MTEXT commands to prompt for a text height each time you use them. Enter the default height for the style if you want all text created with this style to have a uniform height.

Width factor <1.0> The width factor expands or compresses the amount of space taken up by each letter. A default value of 1.0 uses the text as defined in the font file. A value smaller than 1 compresses the text; a value greater than 1 expands the text.

Obliquing angle <0> Enter an angle that forces the font to be slanted. A positive value slants the text forward by the specified degree; a negative value slants the text backward. The oblique angle must be between -85 and 85 degrees.

Backwards? <N> A backward font is a horizontal mirror image of normal text.

Upside-down? <N> An upside-down font is a vertical mirror image of normal text.

Vertical? <N> This prompt appears only if the vertical option is enabled in the font file definition. A font entered vertically is drawn with each letter below the previous one.

> **NOTE** Unlike blocks, font files are stored externally. Unique font files must accompany the drawing file in drawing exchanges.

Example

The following example defines a text style using the ROMANS font file.

```
Command: STYLE                          Issues the STYLE command

New Style. Text style name              Specifies the name of the new text
(or ?) <STANDARD>: ROMANS               style to create and displays the Select
                                        Font File dialog box.
```

Choose ROMANS.SHX *from the File
Name list box in the* Select Font File
dialog box

```
Height <0.000>: (Enter)                 Specifies the default height for the font

Width factor <1.00>: (Enter)            Specifies how narrow or wide the
                                        characters are drawn

Obliquing angle <0> (Enter)             Specifies the slant of the characters

Backwards? <N> (Enter)                  Determines whether the characters will be
                                        drawn reversed

Upside-down? <N> (Enter)                Determines whether the characters will be
                                        drawn upside down

Vertical? <N> (Enter)                   Determines whether the characters will be
                                        drawn in a vertical orientation

ROMANS is now the current text style.
```

Related Commands

COMPILE	DDEMODES	DTEXT	LOAD
MTEXT	MTPROP	PURGE	TEXT

Related System Variables

FILEDIA	TEXTFILL	TEXTQLTY	TEXTSIZE
TEXTSTYLE			

SUBTRACT

Subtract

Tool: *Subtract (Modify, Explode)*
Pull-down: *Construct, Subtract*
Screen: DRAW2, SOLIDS, Subtrac:

The SUBTRACT command performs a Boolean subtraction operation. SUBTRACT removes one or more ACIS SOLIDs from a selected group of ACIS SOLIDs, or removes one or more ACIS REGIONs from a selected group of ACIS REGIONs.

The first selection set defines the source object(s). You can select more than one ACIS SOLID or REGION for the source objects. If two or more source objects overlap in 3D space, they are unioned together to form a single object from which to subtract. The second selection set defines the object(s) to be subtracted from the source objects. You can select more than one ACIS SOLID or REGION to subtract from the source objects. Each object in the second selection set is subtracted from each object in the source selection set.

ACIS REGIONs to be subtracted from must be coplanar. If regions are not coplanar, all regions on the same plane are grouped together for subtracting comparison.

Prompts and Options

Select solids and regions to subtract from... Select objects Pick the source ACIS SOLIDs and REGIONs you want to subtract from at this prompt. If you select an object that is not an ACIS SOLID or REGION, it is ignored.

Select solids and regions to subtract... Select objects Pick the ACIS SOLIDs and REGIONS you want to subtract from the first selection set. If the ACIS REGIONs to subtract are not coplanar, all regions on the same plane are grouped together for subtraction from the source regions on the same plane. If there are no intersecting volumes between solids in the selection set to subtract, the solids to be subtracted are deleted.

If there are no regions in the selection set to subtract that intersect with regions in a source selection set, the regions in the selection set to subtract are deleted. If there are no regions in the selection set to subtract that are coplanar with a source selection set, the source selection set is rejected, and the regions remain in the drawing.

Example

The following example subtracts a cone and cylinder from a box. Create a box, located at 5,5,1, with a length of 6, width of 2, height of 3. Create a cone, located at 8,4,0, with a base radius of 3 and a height of 6. Create a cylinder with a radius of .75 from 12,6,2.5 to 4,6,2.5. See the BOX, CONE, and CYLINDER commands for more information. The box, cone, and cylinder are shown before and after the subtraction in figure S.27.

Command: **SUBTRACT** (Enter)	Starts the SUBTRACT command
Select solids and regions to subtract from...	
Select objects: *Pick box at* ① *(see fig. S.27)*	Selects box as source to subtract from
1 found	
Select objects: (Enter)	Finishes selecting source objects
Select solids and regions to subtract...	
Select objects: *Pick cone at* ②	Selects cone to subtract from box
1 found	
Select objects: *Pick cylinder at* ③	Selects cylinder to subtract from box
1 found	
Select objects: (Enter)	Finishes selecting objects to subtract from box

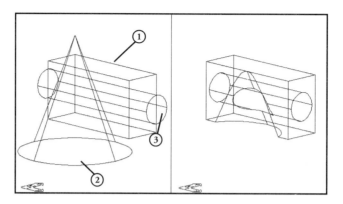

Figure S.27. *The box, cone, and cylinder before and after the SUBTRACT command.*

Related Commands

BOX	CONE	CYLINDER	EXTRUDE
INTERFERE	INTERSECT	REGION	SECTION
SLICE	SHERE	TORUS	UNION
WEDGE			

SYSWINDOWS (Windows Only)

The SYSWINDOWS command controls window display in the Windows version of AutoCAD. Windows can be cascaded or tiled horizontally or vertically, and minimized window icons can be rearranged. The SYSWINDOWS command provides functionality similar to that found on the **W**indow pull-down menu in the Program Manager application. See your Windows User's Guide for more information.

It is possible to draw and edit the current drawing when its window is displayed as a minimized icon, but you will not see the effects of the drawing and editing commands.

Prompts and Options

`Cascade`   Resizes and layers all open windows one on top of another, so that the title bar of each is clearly visible. The first window is placed in the upper left corner of the graphics area; the next is placed on top of the first, located slightly down and to the right, so that the title bar of the first is still visible. Subsequent windows are placed in a similar fashion, down and to the right of the preceding one. Does not affect minimized window icons.

`tileHorz`   Resizes and places all open windows side-by-side. The border of each open window does not overlap with any other window. Does not affect minimized window icons.

`tileVert`   Resizes and places all open windows one above another. The border of each open window does not overlap with any other window. Does not affect minimized window icons.

`Arrangeicons`   Reorders and adjusts the spacing between all minimized window icons. If a window is not minimized, its minimized location will still be rearranged. The change to the minimized location is only apparent when the window is later minimized to an icon.

Example

The following example rearranges the minimized window icon using the SYSWINDOWS command. The icon before the rearranging is shown in figure S.28.

Minimize the current drawing by clicking on the minimize button (see the Windows Guide for more information). Move the icon to the center of the graphics window, as shown in figure S.28.

| Command: **SYSWINDOWS** (Enter) | Starts the SYSWINDOWS command |
| Cascade/tileHorz/tileVert/ Arrangeicons: **A** (Enter) | Specifies Arrangeicons option; rearranges minimized window icons |

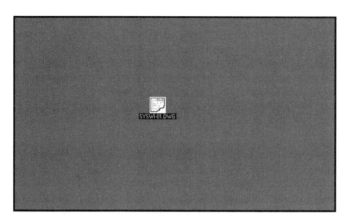

Figure S.28. *Rearranging the minimized window icon with the SYSWINDOWS command.*

TABLET

    Pull-down: **O**ptions, **T**ablet
    Screen: OPTIONS, Tablet:

The TABLET command prepares AutoCAD to receive input from a digitizer tablet. It also prepares a tablet menu to supply command input. The TABLET command enables you to synchronize the drawing editor's coordinate tracking with a paper (or other media) drawing that you want to digitize (trace) accurately into AutoCAD. You cannot use a mouse or other relative pointing device as a tablet.

Prompts and Options

The TABLET command presents the user with the following options:

`Option (ON/OFF/CAL/CFG)`

ON/OFF Enter the full two- or three-character option desired. The CAL and CFG options are discussed in the following prompts. The ON and OFF options turn tablet mode on and off. When tablet mode is on (and the tablet has been calibrated), the tablet is used for digitizing a paper drawing. When tablet mode is off, the tablet is used for screen pointing and tablet menu selection. A shortcut is to press Ctrl+T, which turns tablet mode on or off.

Setting the system variable TABMODE to zero or one turns the tablet off or on, respectively.

CAL The CAL option (short for CALibrate) enables you to synchronize a paper drawing—that is attached to a digitizer tablet—with points in the drawing editor. The number of coordinates you use determines the accuracy of the coordinates in the drawing editor. First you pick the point on the paper drawing, and then you are prompted for its coordinates.

```
Digitize point #number: Digitize point

Enter coordinates point #number:
```

Enter the known coordinate for the point you digitized. When you have chosen all the points that you want to digitize, press Enter. AutoCAD reports on the success or failure of establishing a successful coordinate transformation and prompts, as follows:

```
Select transformation type...
Orthogonal/Affine/Projective/<Repeat table>:
```

Enter the type of coordinate transformation you want to use when digitizing the current drawing. Press Enter to display the table showing the success or failure of establishing a proper coordinate transformation.

AutoCAD enables you to use up to four points when calibrating AutoCAD's coordinate space with a paper drawing. The location of these points determines the type of coordinate transformation used by AutoCAD when interpreting digitized information.

If only two points are used for the calibration, AutoCAD performs an *Orthogonal* transformation of the information you are digitizing. This is a uniform interpretation of the coordinates entered, and is most useful for drawings considered accurate.

For drawings that may have uneven scaling in the two axes, AutoCAD enables you to digitize three points to assign an *Affine* transformation to the coordinates. This type of transformation corrects for the uneven scaling in both axes.

Drawings that are actually two-dimensional perspective images should use four digitizing points. AutoCAD performs a *Projective* transformation of the information entered and tries to correct for the uneven scaling and lack of parallel lines in any axis.

CFG If you choose the CFG option (short for ConFiGure), you can define the screen pointing area and the areas used by a tablet menu for entering commands. The following prompt is displayed:

```
Enter number of tablet menus desired (0-4) <4>:
```

The default AutoCAD tablet menu uses four separate areas that define executable commands. If the tablet you are using has a different number of areas, enter that number here. The maximum number of tablet menu areas is four.

```
Do you want to realign tablet menu areas? <N>
```

This prompt appears if you currently are using a tablet menu and you accepted the default number of menu areas at the previous prompt. This prompt enables you to change the location of the areas. If you do not want to change the location, press Enter at this prompt. The following prompt appears for specifying the screen pointing area:

```
Digitize upper left corner of menu area menu #number:
```

For each of the menu areas, you must pick three points (upper left, lower left, and lower right) that define the pointing area for the menu's commands. The *number* shown in the prompt is a digit from 1 to 4, specifying which tablet menu area you are configuring. The preceding prompt asks for the first point of that area. The following prompts complete the sequence necessary for configuring each menu section for use by AutoCAD. The last prompt is discussed following.

```
Digitize lower left corner of menu area #number:
Digitize lower right corner of menu area #number:
Enter number of columns for menu area #number:
```

Each tablet menu is divided into a series of rows and columns. Each box in this array can correspond to a menu item to execute. Enter the number of columns in the tablet menu area (*#number*). AutoCAD's default template has menu areas defined with the following numbers of rows and columns: area 1 is 25×9; area 2 is 11×9; area 3 is 9×13; and area 4 is 25×7.

```
Do you want to respecify the screen pointing area?:
```

This prompt enables you to define an area on the digitizer tablet that corresponds to the drawing area in the drawing editor. This area should not overlap any of the defined menu areas, but otherwise it can be as large or as small as you want within the confines of the tablet, of course.

```
Digitize lower left corner of screen pointing area:
```

Pick the first point of the rectangular area that you want to use for picking points in the drawing editor.

```
Digitize upper right corner of screen pointing area:
```

Pick the second point of the rectangular area that you want to use to pick objects in the drawing editor. After you enter this point, the tablet menu becomes active.

Example

The following example shows you how to configure the supplied AutoCAD tablet menu ACAD.MNU. Use figure T.1 as a guide.

`Command:` **`TABLET`** (Enter)	Issues the TABLET command
`Option (ON/OFF/CAL/CFG):` **`CFG`** (Enter)	Specifies the CFG option
`Enter the number of tablet menus desired (0-4) <0>:` **`4`** (Enter)	Specifies the number of areas on the tablet
`Digitize the upper left corner of menu area 1:` *Pick point* ① *(see fig. T.1)*	This and following points specify the corners of each menu area
`Digitize the lower left corner of menu area 1:` *Pick point* ②	
`Digitize the lower right corner of menu area 1:` *Pick point* ③	
`Enter the number of columns for menu area 1:` **`25`** (Enter)	Specifies the number of cells in each row of the tablet area
`Enter the number of rows for menu area 1:` **`9`** (Enter)	Specifies the number of cells in each column of the tablet area
`Digitize the upper left corner of menu area 2:` *Pick point* ②	
`Digitize the lower left corner of menu area 2:` *Pick point* ④	
`Digitize the lower right corner of menu area 2:` *Pick point* ⑤	
`Enter the number of rows for menu area 2:` **`11`** (Enter)	
`Digitize the upper left corner of menu area 3:` *Pick point* ⑥	

```
Digitize the lower left corner
of menu area 3: Pick point ⑦

Digitize the lower right corner
of menu area 3: Pick point ⑧

Enter the number of columns for
menu area 3: 9 (Enter)

Enter the number of rows for menu
area 3: 13 (Enter)

Digitize the upper left corner
of menu area 4: Pick point ④

Digitize the lower left corner
of menu area 4: Pick point ⑨

Digitize the lower right corner
of menu area 4: Pick point ⑩

Enter the number of columns for
menu area 4: 25 (Enter)

Enter the number of rows for
menu area 4: 7

Do you want to respecify the screen    Determines whether to configure the
pointing area (Y) (Enter)               screen pointing area on the tablet

Digitize lower left corner of screen
pointing area: Pick point ⑤

Digitize upper right corner of screen
pointing area: Pick point ⑥
```

Related Command

CONFIG

Related System Variable

TABMODE

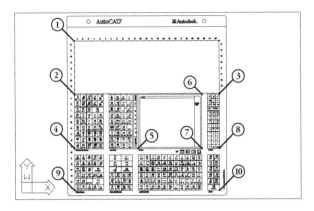

Figure T.1. *Pick points for configuring the standard AutoCAD tablet menu.*

TABSURF

Extrude Surface

Toolbar: *Extruded Surface (Surfaces)*
Pull-down: *Draw, Surfaces, Tabulated Surface*
Screen: DRAW2, SURFACES, Tabsurf:

The TABSURF command creates a polygon mesh defined by extending a profile object (path curve) along the length of a direction object (direction vector).

The path curve may be an arc, circle, line, ellipse, spline, or an open or closed polyline (either 2D or 3D). The endpoint nearest your pick point becomes the start of the point mesh. The direction vector is defined by the first and the last endpoints of a selected line or open polyline. The endpoint nearest your pick point is the starting point of the direction vector.

The SURFTAB1 variable determines the density of the polygon mesh in the N direction. The polygon mesh projects from the starting point to the other endpoint along the direction vector in the M direction. The original objects used to define the path curve and direction vector are unchanged by TABSURF. If you use the EXPLODE command on the polygon mesh, the polygon mesh breaks into individual 3D faces.

Prompts and Options

Select path curve Select one object as the path curve. The path curve can be an arc, circle, line, ellipse, spline, 2D polyline, or 3D polyline. The path curve defines the N direction of the mesh. If the path curve is a circle, ellipse, closed spline, or closed polyline, the polygon mesh produced by the TABSURF command is closed in the N direction. If you select an invalid object for the path curve, AutoCAD responds with the following:

```
Path curve object not usable to define tabulated surface.
```

Select direction vector Select a line, open 2D polyline, or open 3D polyline to define the distance and direction of the desired projection. The endpoint closest to the pick point of the object determines the beginning of the polygon mesh. If you select a polyline, AutoCAD uses the first and last vertices to calculate the distance and direction. If you choose an object other than a line or an open polyline, AutoCAD responds with the following:

```
Object not usable as direction vector.
```

The same object cannot be both the curve path and the direction vector. If you select the same object for the direction vector as the path curve, AutoCAD responds with the following:

```
You already picked that object!
```

Example

The following example uses the TABSURF command to construct an open polygon mesh, as shown in figure T.2. The upper viewport shows the original path curve (an open 2D polyline) and the direction vector (a line). The lower viewport displays the completed mesh with hidden lines removed.

Command: **SURFTAB1** (Enter)	Starts the SETVAR command to change value of SURFTAB1 system variable
New value for SURFTAB1 <6>: **12** (Enter)	Specifies 12 for new value of SURFTAB1
Command: **TABSURF** (Enter)	Starts the TABSURF command
Select path curve: Pick ① (see fig. T.2)	Selects polyline to use as path object
Select direction vector: Pick ②	Selects line to use as direction vector

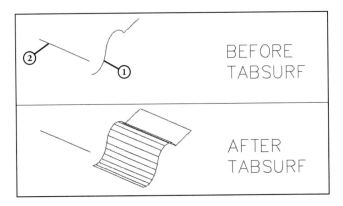

Figure T.2. *A polygon mesh created using TABSURF.*

Related Commands

3DFACE   3DMESH   EDGESURF   PFACE
REVSURF   RULESURF

Related System Variable

SURFTAB1

TBCONFIG (Windows Only)

Pull-down: **T**ools, Customize Tool**b**ars...

The TBCONFIG (Toolbar CONFIG) command displays the Toolbar dialog box used to customize the AutoCAD for Windows toolbars. Toolbars can be created or deleted, displayed or hidden, and their displayed size can be changed. The buttons and flyouts on a toolbar can be added, changed, or deleted. TBCONFIG does not affect the location of a toolbar (see the TOOLBAR command).

> In the Windows ACAD or ACADFULL menus, the Toolbar dialog box is displayed when you right click on a toolbar button.

Toolbar definitions are stored in the AutoCAD menu files. See *Inside AutoCAD for Release 13* or the *AutoCAD Release 13 Customization Guide* for more information on the AutoCAD menu files.

TBCONFIG (Windows Only)

The TBCONFIG command operates as a child window. After issuing the TBCONFIG command, the Command: prompt returns, enabling you to continue entering commands while the Toolbar dialog box remains displayed. Note that the actions of the toolbar buttons are disabled while the TBCONFIG command is active.

The TBCONFIG actions affect the menu file on disk and cannot be undone with the UNDO command. If you make a change to the toolbars that you do not want to keep, you must manually change it back. If you want to experiment, back up your menu files first.

Prompts and Options

The TBCONFIG command uses a series of dialog boxes to customize the toolbars and buttons. As shown in figure T.3, the Toolbars dialog box is the starting point from which you can create new toolbars, modify or delete existing toolbars, and turn tooltips on and off.

Figure T.3. *The Toolbars dialog box.*

The Toolbars Dialog Box

The Toolbars dialog box lists the existing toolbars, creates new toolbars, and deletes selected toolbars. It also controls the large or small button display and turns tooltip the display on or off. In addition, the Customize Toolbars and Toolbar Properties dialog boxes are accessed through the Toolbars dialog box.

Toolbars. The Toolbars list box displays the names of the toolbars in the current menu. When you open the Toolbars dialog box through a right click on a toolbar button, that toolbar's name is highlighted.

Close. Exits the TBCONFIG command, updates the current menu file, and returns to the Command: prompt.

New. Displays the New Toolbar dialog box used to define new toolbars (see fig. T.4). Enter a new toolbar name in the **T**oolbar Name edit box and select a menu group for the new toolbar from the **M**enu Group drop-down list. Click on OK to complete the operation. For more information on menu groups, see the *AutoCAD Release 13 Customization Guide*.

Figure T.4. *The New Toolbar dialog box.*

Delete. Removes an existing toolbar from the menu file.

Deleted toolbars are not displayed in the drawing editor and must be re-created manually. Because toolbar definitions are stored in the AutoCAD menu files, create a backup copy of your menu files before deleting toolbars. The original AutoCAD menus are available from your installation disks.

Customize. Displays the Customize Toolbars dialog box, discussed in the following section.

Properties. Select a toolbar from the **T**oolbars list and click on the **P**roperties button to change the properties of the toolbar. This displays the Toolbar Properties dialog box (see fig. T.5). The toolbar name and the help string displayed at the bottom of the application window can both be changed. The current AutoCAD menu alias (an internal reference used by AutoCAD) is listed, along with a checkbox enabling you to hide or display the toolbar. To display the toolbar, make sure that the Hi**d**e checkbox is unchecked.

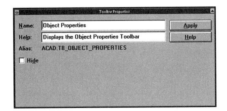

Figure T.5. *The Toolbar Properties dialog box.*

Large Buttons. Displays large (32×32 pixel) buttons if checked; small (16×16 pixel) buttons if unchecked. Button icons can be changed through the Button Editor dialog box. See the following section on button icon editing for more information.

Show Tooltips. Displays tooltips if checked; does not display them if unchecked. A *tooltip* is a short description of the button that displays when the pointer is held motionless on top of the button for a short time.

Tooltips can be changed through the Button Properties dialog box or the Flyout properties dialog box. See the following sections on button and flyout properties for more information.

Tooltips are defined in the ACAD.MNS file. It is also possible to edit the ACAD.MNS file and change the desired tooltip.

The Customize Toolbars Dialog Box

The Customize Toolbars dialog box displays available buttons, and is used to add or remove buttons in new and existing toolbars. While the Customize Toolbars dialog box is displayed, you can also move or copy buttons from one toolbar to another. The Customize Toolbars dialog box lists the toolbar categories and the buttons associated with each category (see fig. T.6).

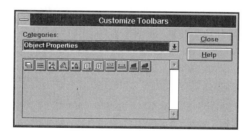

Figure T.6. *The Customize Toolbars dialog box.*

The **C**ategories drop-down lists displays the button categories. Below the currently selected category is an icon list box displaying the icons included in the category. The Custom category has blank icons available.

To add buttons to a toolbar. Select a category to locate a specific icon, and drag the icon over the desired toolbar, and release it over the toolbar to which you want to copy the button. The button inserts itself at the location at which it is released within the toolbar. Both flyout button sets and regular buttons can be copied in this manner.

> If a button is dragged from the Customized Toolbars dialog box and released over an open portion of the graphics display, a new toolbar will be created for the button.

To remove buttons from a toolbar. With the Customize Toolbars dialog box displayed, drag a button from a toolbar and release it over an open portion of the drawing or the Customize Toolbars dialog box.

With the Customize Toolbars dialog box displayed, click and drag a button from the source toolbar to the destination toolbar and release it. The release point determines the button's location in the destination toolbar.

To copy buttons from one toolbar to another. This operation is performed in the same way as moving a button except that you hold the Ctrl key down as you click and drag the button from the source toolbar to the destination toolbar.

Change the action(s) of a button. Position the pointer over the button to change, and click the right mouse button. The Customize Toolbars dialog box must be displayed for this to occur. If the button to change is a regular button, the Button Properties dialog box is displayed. If the button to change is a flyout button, the Flyout Properties dialog box is displayed.

The Button and Flyout Properties Dialog Boxes

As shown in figure T.7, the Button Properties dialog box is used to change a button's name (and tooltip) and the help string displayed at the bottom of the application window, icon, and the invoked by the button. Specify the action (specific commands and options) taken when the button is clicked in the Macro section. The current Button Icon is displayed within a scrolling list of the other icons available. An Edit button enables you to customize the icon as desired.

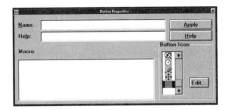

Figure T.7. *The Button Properties dialog box.*

The Flyout Properties dialog box is used to change a flyout button's name (tooltip), the help string displayed at the bottom of the application window, default icon, and the name of the toolbar displayed by the flyout button (see fig. T.8). A *flyout* is simply a button that displays another toolbar. A flyout button has a small triangle pointing to the right in the lower right corner. A scrolling list of icons enables you to select from a list of available icons. An Edit button enables you to customize the icon as desired.

Figure T.8. *The Flyout Properties dialog box.*

Name. Enter a name for the button. This appears as the tooltip beneath the button, if tooltips are enabled.

Help. Enter a help string for the button. The help string is displayed in the status line at the bottom of the application window, when the pointer is held motionless over the button.

Macro. For a regular button, the Macro edit box contains the instructions to perform if the button is pushed. Most standard AutoCAD menu macro instructions can be entered here. See the *AutoCAD Release 13 Customization Guide* for more information on menu macros.

Button Icon. Select the icon to display on this button from the scrolling list of icons.

Edit. Displays the Button Editor dialog box, enabling you to customize the icon. See the following section on button icon editing for more information.

Associated Toolbar. A flyout button displays another toolbar. The default toolbar selected in the Associated Toolbar list is the toolbar displayed when the flyout button is clicked. To display a different toolbar when clicking the flyout, select the desired toolbar, and click on **A**pply. Because each toolbar has a different icon, the icon displayed in this flyout button changes with the toolbar. The icon can then be changed as desired. The icon will not change if Sho**w** This Button's Icon is checked.

Show This Button's Icon. Locks the button's icon to the currently selected icon from the Button Icon list, if checked. If unchecked (the default), the flyout button changes to show the icon of the last button clicked. If Sho**w** This Button's Icon is checked, the flyout's icon is the only icon displayed, even after other buttons are chosen from the flyout.

> Leaving the Sho**w** This Button's Icon check box unchecked allows a toolbar to customize itself to the way it is being used. As this can speed up command selection, you should probably leave this box unchecked.

The Button Editor Dialog Box

The Button Editor dialog box is a pixel editor used to change the individual pixels that appear in a button icon (see fig. T.9). Button icons can be modified and new button icons can be created. Images can be edited by adding colored pixels, lines of colored pixels, and ellipses or circles of colored pixels. Pixels can have their coloring removed, and the images can be saved for later use.

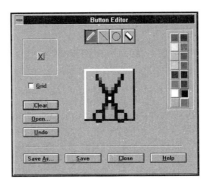

Figure T.9. *The Button Editor dialog box.*

Button Image. Displays the current full-size image of the button in an image tile in the upper left corner of the Button Editor dialog box.

Grid. Displays a grid between each pixel in the editing area, if checked.

Clear. Removes all color from all pixels in the editing area.

Open. Selects an existing icon file, using the Open Bitmap File dialog box. Icon files are saved as bitmap files and have a BMP extension.

Undo. Reverses the effects of the last operation. The Button Editor can undo only the last operation, not preceding ones.

Pencil. Colors an individual pixel in the editing area. Position the pointer over the pixel to color, and click and release the pick button. Click and drag the pointer across the editing area to sketch a series of colored pixels. Select the current pixel color from the Color Palette to the right of the editing area.

Line. Colors a line of pixels in the editing area. Position the pointer over the beginning pixel of the line; click and drag the pointer across the editing area to the ending pixel of the line. Then release the pointer. Select the current line color from the Color Palette to the right of the editing area.

Ellipse/Circle. Colors an ellipse or circle of pixels in the editing area. Position the pointer over the center of the ellipse or circle; click and drag the pointer across the editing area to one of the diagonal corners of the desired ellipse or circle. Then release the pointer. Select the current ellipse or circle color from the Color Palette to the right of the editing area.

Erase. Removes the color from an individual pixel in the editing area. Position the pointer over the pixel to clear, then click and release the pointer. Click and drag the pointer across the editing area to clear a series of pixels.

Editing Area. A 16×16 grid (if small buttons are displayed) or 32×32 grid (if large buttons are displayed) of pixels in the center of the Button Editor dialog box. Color the pixels using the pencil, line, and ellipse/circle tools. Erase the pixels using the erase tool, or the Clear button. Display a grid between the pixels using the Grid checkbox.

Color Palette. Displays the 16 primary colors. The currently selected color has a shadow box around it. Color 8 (light gray) is the same as the background color for the icons.

Save. Saves the current image as a bitmap file. The file has a BMP extension. If the current image was opened as a BMP file (rather than an existing AutoCAD icon), the image is saved with the same file name. Use the Save As option to save the file with a different name.

Save As. Saves the current image as a bitmap file. The file has a BMP extension. If the current image was opened as a BMP file (rather than an existing AutoCAD icon), use this option to save the image with a different name.

Example

This example of the TBCONFIG command shows you how to create a new toolbar and insert seven buttons into it. The actions of one of the buttons is customized, and one of the buttons is discarded. See figure T.10 for the layout of the toolbar and the TBCONFIG dialog boxes.

Command: **TBCONFIG** (Enter)	Invokes the TBCONFIG command; displays Toolbars dialog box
Click on **N***ew*	Displays New Toolbar dialog box
Enter **AllPurpose** *in the Toolbar Name edit box*	Do not include any spaces in the name
Click on OK	Creates small empty toolbar somewhere on-screen

Drag the AllPurpose toolbar to upper left of graphics window, and drag the Toolbars dialog box to the upper right corner, as shown in figure T.10.

Click on C**u***stomize*	Displays Customize Toolbars dialog box
Select the Standard category from the Customize Toolbars dialog box	Selects group of icons to choose from

Drag the Zoom Window icon (see the completed toolbar in fig. T.9) from the Customize Toolbars dialog box to the AllPurpose toolbar. The Zoom Window icon is in the third row from the top. Then drag the Zoom Previous icon to the AllPurpose toolbar. Zoom Previous is the first icon in the last row (use the scroll bar).

Select the Draw category from the Customize Toolbars dialog box	Selects group of icons to choose from

Drag the Text flyout icon (located in the first row) to the AllPurpose toolbar. Then drag the Line icon (near the end of the first row—not the Line flyout) and the Circle/center/radius icon (third row) to the AllPurpose toolbar.

Select the Modify category from the Customize Toolbars dialog box	Selects group of icons to choose from
Drag the Move icon and the Erase icon (both located in the first row) to the AllPurpose toolbar	

Position the pointer over the Line icon and note that the tooltip says Line. Click the right (or Enter) button of the pointer, and the Button Properties dialog box appears (shown in the lower left corner in figure T.10).

Enter **One Segment** *in the* Name edit *box*	Changes name of tooltip for this button
Enter **Creates one straight line segment** *in the* Help edit *box*	Changes help string displayed at bottom of application window for this button
Edit the macro to say **^C^C_line;\\;**	There should be no spaces in the macro
Click on **A**pply	Effects changes onto button

Position the pointer over the Line icon, and note that the tooltip now says One Segment. To remove an unwanted button from the toolbar, drag it from the toolbar and release it over an empty portion of the drawing. Drag the Text Flyout (the icon with the letter A) from the AllPurpose toolbar to an empty portion of the graphics window and release it.

Click on **C**lose *in the Customize Toolbars dialog box*	Closes Customize Toolbars dialog box
Click on **C**lose *in the Toolbars dialog box*	Closes Toolbars and Button Properties dialog boxes

Figure T.10. *Adding a custom toolbar with the TBCONFIG command.*

Related Commands

CONFIG   PREFERENCES   TOOLBAR

Related System Variable

TOOLTIPS

TEXT

 — Single-Line Text

Toolbar: *Single-Line Text (Draw,Text)*
Pull-down: *Draw*, *Text*, *Single-Line Text*

The TEXT command adds a single line of text to the drawing. Characters display on the screen after you type the string and press Enter at the Text: prompt. This command is similar to the DTEXT command except that the DTEXT command displays the text string on the drawing as you type it and accepts multiple lines of text. You can justify the text string with one of 15 options. You also can enhance the text by underlining it, or include such special characters as degree symbols, plus or minus symbols, or diameter symbols.

See the DTEXT command for an explanation of the prompts and options.

Related Commands

ATTDEF   DTEXT   MTEXT   QTEXT
SPELL   STYLE

Related System Variables

MIRRTEXT   TEXTEVAL   TEXTFILL   TEXTQLTY
TEXTSIZE   TEXTSTYLE

'TEXTSCR

The TEXTSCR command causes the text screen or window to display on single-monitor systems. Pressing F1 (F2 on Windows systems) also flips between the text and graphics screens. The purpose of the TEXTSCR command is to provide a method for macros, AutoLISP routines, and scripts to flip to the text screen. It is also useful for viewing long listings from commands such as LIST, DBLIST, and so on. The TEXTSCR command has the opposite effect of the GRAPHSCR command. Neither command has any effect on an AutoCAD system running with dual monitors.

Related Commands

GRAPHSCR SCRIPT

Related System Variable

SCREENMODE

TIFFIN

Pull-down: File, Import, Raster, TIFF... (DOS Only)
Screen: FILE, IMPORT, TIFFin:

TIFFIN imports a Tagged Image File Format raster file into AutoCAD. AutoCAD scans the raster image and creates a block consisting of a rectangular colored solid for each pixel in the TIFF file.

When a raster image is imported into AutoCAD, you can trace over the raster image with AutoCAD geometry to create an AutoCAD drawing of the raster image. When you are finished, you can erase the raster image. Raster images can be scaled, mirrored, and rotated like regular blocks.

Raster images also can be used to represent images obtained by scanning photographs, logos, and artwork.

Do not explode the block representation of a raster file. If you do, the resulting objects will use large quantities of disk space and memory.

Raster images are imported as anonymous blocks. If you reimport the same image multiple times, a new block is created each time you import.

Before importing any raster images, it is important to set the system variables that control raster image conversion. These system variables are named RIASPECT, RIBACKG, RIEDGE, RIGAMUT, RIGREY, and RITHRESH. See the GIFIN command for a full description of each of these. Set the system variable GRIPBLOCK to 0 to avoid highlighting all the solid objects in the block with grips.

Prompts and Options

TIFF file name   Enter the name of the TIFF file to import. A file selection dialog box is not available. You do not have to include the TIF extension; the TIFFIN command adds it if necessary.

Insertion point <0,0,0> Pick a point in the graphics window, or enter the coordinates of the insertion point for the raster image.

Scale Factor Enter a number or pick a point in the graphics window to show a distance. If you pick a point in the graphics window, the distance from the insertion point is used as the scale factor.

New length If you press Enter at the Scale Factor prompt, you are reprompted to enter a new scale factor, or to pick a point to show a distance for the scale factor.

Example

The following example imports a TIFF file created using the PFACE command. It was rendered and saved as a TIFF file. It is first imported as an outline image by setting RIEDGE to 5; then inserted as an image by setting RIEDGE to 0 (see fig. T.11). Set RIBACKG to your graphics window background color first.

Command: **RIEDGE** (Enter)	Issues the RIEDGE command to change system variable RIEDGE
Raster input edge detection <0>: **5** (Enter)	Specifies new value for RIEDGE
Command: **RIBACKG** (Enter)	Issues the RIEDGE command to change system variable RIBACKG
Raster input screen background colour <0>: **7** (Enter)	Specifies new value for RIBACKG; Color 7 specifies a white background
Command: **TIFFIN** (Enter)	Starts the TIFFIN command
TIFF file name: **ELBOW** (Enter)	Specifies file name ELBOW.TIF
Insertion point<0,0,0>: (Enter)	Accepts default insertion point
Scale factor: **1** (Enter)	Specifies scale factor of 1
Command: **RIEDGE** (Enter)	Issues the RIEDGE command to change system variable RIEDGE
Raster input edge detection <5>: **0** (Enter)	Specifies new value for RIEDGE
Command: **TIFFIN** (Enter)	Starts the TIFFIN command
TIFF file name: **ELBOW** (Enter)	Specifies file name ELBOW.TIF
Insertion point<0,0,0>: **1,0,0** (Enter)	Specifies insertion point of 1,0,0
Scale factor: **1** (Enter)	Specifies scale factor of 1

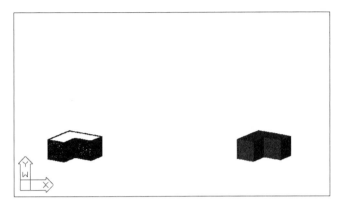

Figure T.11. *A rendered rectangular elbow imported as raster images with the TIFFIN command.*

Related Commands

ACISIN	BMPOUT	DXBIN	DXFIN
GIFIN	IMPORT	PCXIN	PSIN
WMFIN			

Related System Variables

FILLMODE	GRIPBLOCK	RIASPECT	RIBACKG
RIEDGE	RIGAMUT	RIGREY	RITHRESH

'TIME

Pull-down: **D**ata, Tim**e**
Screen: DATA, Time:

The TIME command displays information regarding the current time and date, date and time of the last modification to the drawing, total time spent in the drawing editor, elapsed time, and the time until the next automatic save. (The interval between automatic saves is controlled by the system variable SAVETIME and also can be set from the Preferences dialog box.)

The time and date of the last modification to the drawing are updated when the END command or the SAVE command is used. The total time spent in the drawing editor is continuously updated. The current editing session's time, however, is lost if you quit the drawing. The elapsed timer is similar to a stopwatch.

Only the elapsed timer can be turned on, off, or reset to zero. The computer's clock provides the current time and date. All AutoCAD time values display in military, 24-hour format. Accuracy is displayed to the nearest millisecond, but is dependent on the accuracy of your system's internal clock.

The following is a sample listing generated by the TIME command.

```
Current time:           Monday, 26 Dec 1994 at 11:12:45:780 am
Times for this drawing:
  Created:              Friday, 28 Oct 1994 at 01:00:01:950 pm
  Last updated:         Monday, 31 Oct 1994 at 05:51:59:890 pm
  Total editing time:   0 days 00:40:45.940
  Elapsed timer (on):   0 days 00:40:45.940
  Next automatic save in: 0 days 01:35:00.810
Display/ON/OFF/Reset:
```

Prompts and Options

Display Displays all the current time information.

ON Turns on the elapsed timer. The timer is on by default.

OFF Turns off the elapsed timer.

Reset Resets the elapsed timer to zero.

Related Commands

LOGFILEOFF   LOGFILEON   STATUS

Related System Variables

CDATE   DATE   SAVETIME   TDCREATE
TDINDWG   TDUPDATE   TDUSRTIMER

TOLERANCE

Tolerance

Toolbar: *Tolerance (Dimensioning)*
Pull-down: **D**raw, **D**imensioning, **T**olerance
Screen: DRAW DIM, Toleran:

TOLERANCE

The TOLERANCE command is used to generate geometric dimensioning and tolerance control frames. These tolerances control the maximum variation of form, profile, orientation, location, and runout from the theoretical ideal dimensions and features in a drawing. AutoCAD automatically generates the feature control frames containing the appropriate symbols, tolerances, modifiers, datum references, and so on. The feature control frame and its data, as illustrated in figure T.12 below, is constructed as one object and cannot be exploded. Use the DDEDIT or DDMODIFY command to edit a TOLERANCE object. You can also place feature control frames using the LEADER command.

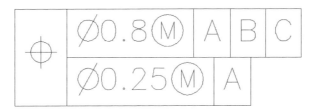

Figure T.12. *A feature control frame generated with the TOLERANCE command.*

Dialog Box Items

The TOLERANCE command first displays the Symbol dialog box (see fig. T.13). This dialog box displays symbols for geometric characteristics, as illustrated in figure T.14. You select the symbol you want to use in the first cell of the feature control frame. After making your selection, the symbol is placed in the Sym image box of the Geometric Tolerance dialog box displayed when you exit the Symbol dialog box.

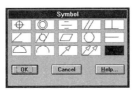

Figure T.13. *The Symbol dialog box.*

> This discussion of the TOLERANCE command is not meant to be a tutorial for Geometric Dimensioning and Tolerancing. It is assumed

that you are familiar with the application and proper use of GDT feature control frames and their related annotations. The U.S. standard for Geometric Dimensioning and Tolerancing is ANSI Y14.5M.

Symbol	Meaning	Symbol	Meaning
—	STRAIGHTNESS	Ⓜ	AT MAXIMUM MATERIAL CONDITION
⌀	FLATNESS	Ⓛ	AT LEAST MATERIAL CONDITION
○	CIRCULARITY	Ⓢ	REGARDLESS OF FEATURE SIZE
⌭	CYLINDRICITY	Ⓟ	PROJECTED TOLERANCE ZONE
⌒	PROFILE OF A LINE	⌀	DIAMETER
⌓	PROFILE OF A SURFACE	▷	CONICAL TAPER
∠	ANGULARITY	⌲	SLOPE
⊥	PERPENDICULARITY	⊔	COUNTEBORE/SPOTFACE
∥	PARALLELISM	∨	COUNTERSINK
⊕	POSITION	↧	DEPTH
◎	CONCENTRICITY	□	SQUARE
≐	SYMMETRY	⌒	ARC LENGTH
↗	CIRCULAR RUNOUT		
↗↗	TOTAL RUNOUT		

Figure T.14. *Geometric dimensioning and tolerance symbols and their meanings.*

The Geometric Tolerance dialog box is laid out in such a way to resemble the feature control frame it creates (see fig. T.15). You specify the symbols or data to fill the desired cells of the tolerance frame.

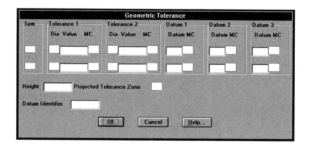

Figure T.15. *The Geometric Tolerance dialog box.*

Sym. This image tile contains the symbol, if any, you selected from the Symbol dialog box. Selecting this tile redisplays the Symbol dialog box.

Tolerance 1. This area of the Geometric Tolerance dialog box is used to create the first tolerance value in the feature control frame. You can include a diameter symbol and material condition modifier in this frame. The data in this frame controls the amount by which the referenced geometric characteristic can vary from ideal.

Dia. Select this image tile to insert a diameter symbol in the tolerance frame.

Value. Use this edit box to enter the tolerance value.

MC. Select this image tile to display the Material Condition dialog box, as shown in figure T.16, for specifying a material condition modifier symbol.

Figure T.16. *The Material Condition dialog box.*

Tolerance 2. This area of the Geometric Tolerance dialog box creates the second tolerance value in the feature control frame. Use the same procedure as for Tolerance 1.

Datum 1. Use this area of the Geometric Tolerance dialog box to specify a primary datum reference in the control frame. You can specify a value in the edit box and/or a modifying symbol.

Datum. Specify the datum reference value in this edit box.

MC. Selecting this box displays the Material Condition dialog box described earlier.

Datum 2; Datum 3. These areas create secondary and tertiary datum references in the same manner as the Datum 1 area described previously.

Height. Use this edit box to specify a projected tolerance zone value in the feature control frame. This value controls the height of fixed perpendicular objects such as studs or bolts and restrains the dimensions to those specified by the positional tolerances.

Projected Tolerance Zone. Selecting this image tile displays the projected tolerance zone symbol and appends it in the feature control frame to the projected tolerance zone value specified previously.

Datum Identifier. Use this edit box to enter the datum identifier consisting of an uppercase letter preceded and followed by a dash. You must type in the dashes.

After you are satisfied with your data for the tolerance feature control frame and you select OK, you will be prompted as follows:

```
Enter tolerance location:
```

The point you specify is the upper left corner of the feature control frame. AutoCAD will draw the frame and contents after you pick a point.

TIP AutoCAD uses the font file GDT.SHX for generating the symbols used in feature control frames. You may want to create a text style using this font file (stored in the AutoCAD support directory). Use the DDIM command to make this style active for creating your tolerances. Be sure to use uppercase letters when typing data in the Geometric Tolerance dialog box.

If you want to access the geometric dimensioning and tolerancing symbols in the GDT.SHX font file, figure T.17 shows a chart of the symbols and the keys used to produce them. The GDT.SHX font file must be used in the current text style to be able to type the symbols.

Figure T.17. *Geometric dimensioning and tolerancing symbols stored in the GDT.SHX font file.*

Example

The following example will produce a geometric dimensioning and tolerancing control frame similar to the one shown in figure T.18.

Choose the Tolerance *tool.* *Tool:* [Tolerance](Dimensioning)	Issues the TOLERANCE command
`Command: _tolerance`	
Enter the data shown in *figure T.18.*	Specifies the data for the feature control frame
`Enter tolerance location:` *Pick any point*	Specifies the upper left corner of the feature control frame

TOLERANCE

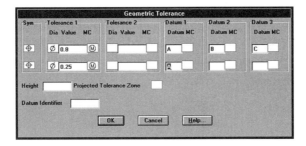

Figure T.18. *Entering data in the Geometric Tolerance dialog box.*

Related Commands

DDIM   LEADER   STYLE

Related System Variables

See Dimensioning Variables

TOOLBAR (Windows Only)

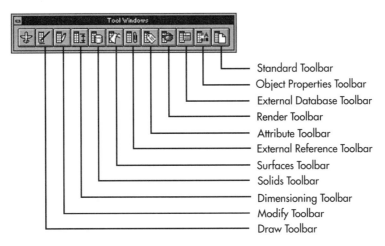

Toolbar: *(Standard Toolbar, Tool Windows)*
Pull-down: **T**ools, **T**oolbars

The TOOLBAR command controls the display and positioning of toolbars. Toolbars can be turned on (show) or off (hide). Floating toolbars can be positioned anywhere on the graphics screen. Floating toolbars have a title bar.

Docked toolbars have no title bars and are attached to the bottom, top, right, or left edges of the application window. You cannot undo the TOOLBAR command.

Prompts and Options

Toolbar name (or ALL)   At this prompt, enter the name of the toolbar you want to show, position, or hide. You may enter the toolbar name as shown in the TBCONFIG dialog box, substituting the underscore character (_) for spaces in the toolbar name. Typing the ACAD prefix is optional. Additionally, you may specify the toolbar alias name as listed in the ACAD.INI file. For example, to specify the Tool Windows toolbar, any of the following names are acceptable:

- Tool_Windows
- ACAD.TOOL_WINDOWS
- ACAD.TB_TOOL_WINDOWS
- TB_TOOL_WINDOWS

Upper- or lowercase makes no difference.

The following table lists all the AutoCAD toolbars as shipped and their corresponding alias names as listed in the ACAD.INI file and ACAD.MNU menu files. Also, refer to the inside cover illustrations which identify the available toolbar menus.

Table T.1
Toolbar Names and Their Aliases

Toolbar Name	Toolbar Alias
ACAD.Standard Toolbar	ACAD.STANDARD_TOOLBAR
ACAD.Arc	ACAD.TB_ARC
ACAD.Attribute	ACAD.TB_ATTRIBUTE
ACAD.Bind	ACAD.TB_BIND
ACAD.Block	ACAD.TB_BLOCK
ACAD.Box	ACAD.TB_BOX
ACAD.Break	ACAD.TB_BREAK
ACAD.Circle	ACAD.TB_CIRCLE
ACAD.Cone	ACAD.TB_CONE

TOOLBAR (Windows Only)

Toolbar Name	Toolbar Alias
ACAD.Copy	ACAD.TB_COPY
ACAD.Cylinder	ACAD.TB_CYLINDER
ACAD.Dimensioning	ACAD.TB_DIMENSIONING
ACAD.Ordinate	ACAD.TB_DIMORDINATE
ACAD.Radial Dimension	ACAD.TB_DIMRADIAL
ACAD.Dimension Style	ACAD.TB_DIMSTYLE
ACAD.Align Dimension Text	ACAD.TB_DIMTEXT
ACAD.Draw	ACAD.TB_DRAW
ACAD.Ellipse	ACAD.TB_ELLIPSE
ACAD.Explode	ACAD.TB_EXPLODE
ACAD.External Database	ACAD.TB_EXTERNAL_DATABASE
ACAD.External Reference	ACAD.TB_EXTERNAL_REFERENCE
ACAD.Feature	ACAD.TB_FEATURE
ACAD.Hatch	ACAD.TB_HATCH
ACAD.Inquiry	ACAD.TB_INQUIRY
ACAD.Line	ACAD.TB_LINE
ACAD.Miscellaneous	ACAD.TB_MISCELLANEOUS
ACAD.Modify	ACAD.TB_MODIFY
ACAD.Object Properties	ACAD.TB_OBJECT_PROPERTIES
ACAD.Object Snap	ACAD.TB_OBJECT_SNAP
ACAD.Pan	ACAD.TB_PAN
ACAD.Polyline	ACAD.TB_PLINE
ACAD.Point	ACAD.TB_POINT
ACAD.Point Filters	ACAD.TB_POINT_FILTERS
ACAD.Polygon	ACAD.TB_POLYGON
ACAD.Redraw	ACAD.TB_REDRAW
ACAD.Render	ACAD.TB_RENDER

continues

Table T.1, Continued
Toolbar Names and Their Aliases

Toolbar Name	Toolbar Alias
ACAD.Resize	ACAD.TB_RESIZE
ACAD.Rotate	ACAD.TB_ROTATE
ACAD.Select Objects	ACAD.TB_SELECT_OBJECTS
ACAD.Solids	ACAD.TB_SOLIDS
ACAD.Space	ACAD.TB_SPACE
ACAD.Special Edit	ACAD.TB_SPECIAL_EDIT
ACAD.Surfaces	ACAD.TB_SURFACES
ACAD.Text	ACAD.TB_TEXT
ACAD.Tool Windows	ACAD.TB_TOOL_WINDOWS
ACAD.Trim	ACAD.TB_TRIM
ACAD.UCS	ACAD.TB_UCS
ACAD.View	ACAD.TB_VIEW
ACAD.Wedge	ACAD.TB_WEDGE
ACAD.Zoom	ACAD.TB_ZOOM

Typing **ALL** for the toolbar name displays the prompt, Show/Hide. The Show option displays all toolbars at their last location. The Hide option turns all the toolbars off.

```
Show/Hide/Left/Right/Top/Bottom/Float:   <Show>:
```

<Show>   This, the default option for the TOOLBAR command, displays the specified toolbar at its last default location.

Hide   The Hide option closes the toolbar.

Left   This option docks the toolbar at the left side of the screen. It issues the prompt, Position <0,0>, for specifying a relative horizontal, vertical position within the docking area. Pressing return places the toolbar at the top left corner of the docking area, to the right of any existing docked toolbars.

The position value is formatted as <Column, Row>. 0 is the first position value. You cannot use the position value to reposition a

TOOLBAR (Windows Only)

toolbar within the same screen area, or place it in a location occupied by another toolbar except to displace it. You cannot create an empty toolbar location; remaining toolbars are repositioned when one is removed.

TIP If you click and hold the menu arrow pointer in the border of a toolbar you can drag the toolbar to a new location. When you reach a toolbar screen area (left, right, top or bottom), the shape of the toolbar changes to suit that area.

Right This option docks the toolbar to the right of the screen. The default position is at the top of the docking area to the right of any existing docked toolbars. It issues the same Position <0,0> prompt as the Left, Top, and Bottom options.

Top This option docks the toolbar at the top of the screen. The default position is at the top left of the docking area, moving any existing toolbars to the right to accommodate the new toolbar. This option also issues the Position <0,0> prompt as the Left, Right, and Bottom options.

Bottom This option docks the toolbar to the bottom of the screen. The default position is at the top left corner of the docking area, moving any existing toolbars to the right to accommodate the new one. This option also issues the Position <0,0> prompt as the Left, Right, and Top options.

Float Use the Float option to place a floating toolbar at a specific location on your graphics screen. You also can specify how many rows the toolbar will have when floating. At the prompt, Position <0,0>, enter the horizontal, vertical position in screen pixels for the top left corner of the floating toolbar. The top left corner of the graphics screen is position 0,0. On a screen at 800×600 pixels resolution, the bottom right corner position would be 800,600. The position coordinates are not necessarily relative to your AutoCAD application window. For example, if your Windows screen resolution is 1024×768 pixels and your AutoCAD application window is only 800×600, it is possible to place toolbars outside the AutoCAD window. The second prompt, Rows <1>, is for determining how many rows the toolbar will have. Figure T.19 shows the Render toolbar positioned at 400,300 with two rows.

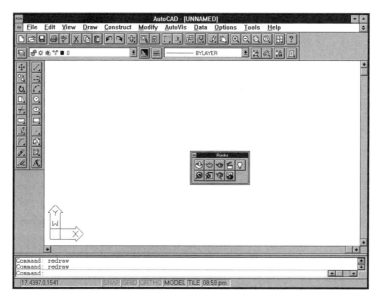

Figure T.19. *Positioning a toolbar with the Float option of the TOOLBAR command.*

 AutoCAD stores the Rows value specified for each toolbar. Use the TOOLBAR commands Float option to control this value.

Example

In this example, you re-create the appearance and placement of the Render toolbar in figure T.19.

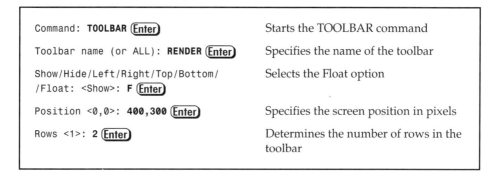

Command: **TOOLBAR** (Enter)	Starts the TOOLBAR command
Toolbar name (or ALL): **RENDER** (Enter)	Specifies the name of the toolbar
Show/Hide/Left/Right/Top/Bottom/ /Float: <Show>: **F** (Enter)	Selects the Float option
Position <0,0>: **400,300** (Enter)	Specifies the screen position in pixels
Rows <1>: **2** (Enter)	Determines the number of rows in the toolbar

Related Command
TBCONFIG

Related System Variable
TOOLTIPS

TORUS

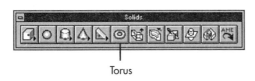
Torus

Toolbar: *Torus (Solids)*
Pull-down: **D**raw, S**o**lids, **T**orus
Screen: DRAW2, SOLIDS, Torus:

The TORUS command creates a three-dimensional ACIS SOLID shaped like a torus (a donut-shaped solid object). The torus is placed parallel to the current UCS by specifying the center point, major diameter, and minor diameter of the torus. The major diameter and minor diameter can be specified by either diameter or radius.

Prompts and Options

Center of torus<0,0,0> Specify the center point of the torus by picking a point in the graphics window or entering coordinates. The torus is placed parallel to the current UCS.

Diameter/<Radius> of torus Specify a value or pick a point to show a distance for the radius of the torus, or enter **D** if you prefer to specify a value for the diameter of the torus. This distance is the major diameter of the torus.

Diameter/<Radius> of tube Specify a value or pick a point to show a distance for the radius of the tube, or enter **D** if you prefer to specify a value for the diameter of the tube. This distance is the minor diameter of the torus.

Diameter Enter a value or pick a point to show a distance for the diameter of the torus or tube.

Example

This example shows how to create an ACIS SOLID TORUS object (see fig. T.20).

Command: **TORUS** (Enter)	Starts the TORUS command
Center of torus<0,0,0>: **10,7,2** (Enter)	Specifies center of torus
Diameter/<Radius> of torus: **8** (Enter)	Specifies torus radius of 8, or a major diameter of 16
Diameter/<Radius> of tube: **3** (Enter)	Specifies tube radius of 3, or a minor diameter of 6

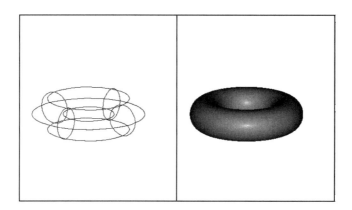

Figure T.20. *An ACIS SOLID TORUS object.*

Related Commands

EXTRUDE   INTERFERE   INTERSECT   SUBTRACT   UNION

TRACE

Trace

Toolbar: *Trace (Miscellaneous)*
Screen: DRAW2, Trace:

The TRACE command creates solid filled lines similar to polyline segments with width. TRACE segments are similar to polyline segments in that the endpoints are mitered to meet each other. They are much more limited than polylines, however. The miter angles are calculated for both ends of each segment before it is drawn. Thus, a segment is drawn after the angle of the following segment is known. You cannot use the following editing commands on a trace object: CHANGE, EXPLODE, EXTEND, OFFSET, and TRIM.

You cannot execute UNDO when you are drawing the trace segments, nor does the TRACE command have a Close option. The appearance of the completed trace object is solid if the FILL mode is on; otherwise, only the outline of the object displays.

Prompts and Options

`Trace width <0.0500>`   You can alter the default width of .05 units by entering any value you choose. The value becomes the default for the next use of TRACE.

`From point`   This point is the starting location of the trace object.

`To point`   Enter the second point of the trace. The preceding segment is not drawn until the subsequent segment endpoint is chosen. This prompt repeats until you press Enter or Ctrl+C.

Related Commands
FILL   LINE

Related System Variables
FILLMODE   TRACEWID

TREESTAT

TREESTAT displays the status of the current drawing's spatial index. The information displayed by TREESTAT can be used to improve system performance. AutoCAD indexes all drawing objects spatially using a tree structure. TREESTAT uses two main branches, a 2D branch for paper space (quad-tree), and a 2D or 3D branch (oct-tree) for model space. The TREESTAT command displays two particularly important pieces of information, the number of nodes and the average objects per node.

Use the TREEDEPTH system variable to increase or decrease the length of the tree to attain the best possible performance. The oct-tree structure is more effective if there are fewer objects per node. Therefore, a deep tree with many nodes is preferable. Each node takes about 80 bytes of memory, so too many nodes will consume memory and force disk swapping. Usually, you do not need to tune AutoCAD's performance unless you are working with an extremely large drawing. The ideal setting depends on your system's configuration and the size of the drawing. The default depth limits are 30 for model space and 20 for paper space. This value is stored as 3020 in the system variable TREEDEPTH.

The following listing is a sample report generated using the TREESTAT command:

```
Model-space branch
-----------------
Oct-tree, depth limit = 30
Objects on frozen layers: 54
Objects with undefined extents: 3
Subtree containing objects with defined extents:
    Nodes: 218   Objects: 202   Maximum depth: 30
    Average objects per node: 0.93
    Average node depth: 19.40   Average object depth: 16.94
    Objects at depth 5: 24   6: 13   29: 4   30: 8
    Nodes with population 0: 144   1: 40   12: 1   24: 1
Total nodes: 221   Total objects: 259

Paper-space branch
-----------------
Quad-tree, depth limit = 20
Objects with undefined extents: 1
Subtree containing objects with defined extents:
    Nodes: 1   Objects: 1   Maximum depth: 5
    Average objects per node: 1.00
 Average node depth: 5.00   Average object depth: 5.00
    Objects at depth 5: 1
    Nodes with population 1: 1
Total nodes: 4   Total objects: 2
```

> **TIP** A negative tree depth makes AutoCAD ignore the Z coordinates of objects and use a quad-tree for model space indexes.

Example

The following example displays and resets the tree depth using the TREESTAT command and the TREEDEPTH system variable.

```
Command: TREESTAT (Enter)                  Issues the TREESTAT command
```
The resulting display varies depending on your system and drawing. Notice the tree depth in both model space and paper space.
```
Command: TREEDEPTH (Enter)                 Displays the TREEDEPTH system
                                           variable settings
New value for TREEDEPTH <3020>:            Specifies the tree depth for model
4030 (Enter)                               space/paper space
Command: TREESTAT (Enter)
```
The tree depth is now 40 for model space and 30 for paper space.

Related Commands
LIST   LOGFILEOFF   LOGFILEON   STATUS

Related System Variables
TREEDEPTH   TREEMAX

TRIM

Trim

Toolbar: *Trim (Modify, Trim)*
Pull-down: <u>M</u>odify, T<u>r</u>im
Screen: MODIFY, Trim:

The TRIM command edits the length of lines, open or closed 2D and 3D polylines, arcs, circles, ellipses, elliptical arcs, rays, splines, and construction lines to match a cutting edge(s). The cutting edge(s) can be any object except blocks, meshes, 3D faces, text, mtext, traces, shapes, or points. To trim a circle, you must intersect cutting edges in at least two places.

You can select multiple cutting edges. Objects to be trimmed must be picked one at a time unless you use the Fence object selection method. The same object can be both a cutting edge and an object to trim. The TRIM command cuts polylines to the center of the polyline, with the ends remaining squared. If you select an associative dimension to trim, AutoCAD trims and updates the dimension. Note that you cannot split a dimension object in two.

You can trim in 3D space using implied edges (regardless of whether they actually intersect the object to be trimmed). You also can trim in 3D space using any of the following three projection methods:

- **None.** Trims objects only if they intersect the cutting edges in 3D space.
- **UCS.** Trims objects as if they were projected onto the current UCS plane, regardless of whether the objects intersect the cutting edges in 3D space.
- **View.** Trims objects as if they were projected onto the current viewing plane, regardless of whether the objects intersect the cutting edges in 3D space.

Prompts and Options

`Select cutting edges: (Projmode = UCS, Edgemode = No extend)`
Select objects This prompt displays the current projection mode and Edgemode for the TRIM command. These can be changed at subsequent prompts. Select the objects that you want to use as the cutting edges for the command using any object selection method. If the view plan is not aligned with the current UCS, you see the warning, `View is not plan to UCS. Command results may not be obvious.`

After you have selected the objects to use as cutting edges, the following prompt appears:

`<Select object to trim>/Project/Edge/Undo:`

<Select object to trim> Pick the object to trim. Only one object can be picked at one time unless you use the Fence object selection method. The prompt, `<Select object to trim>/Project/Edge/Undo,` repeats until you press Enter. If no intersection can be found between the object to trim and the cutting edge, the prompt, `Object does not intersect an edge,` appears.

Project This option of the TRIM command enables you to specify the mode of projection for trimming subsequent options. The default mode is UCS. The Project option displays the following prompt:

`None/Ucs/View <Ucs>:`

> **None** This options specifies that no projection will be used for trimming. This means that the objects to be trimmed must intersect with the cutting edges in order to be trimmed. Figure T.21 shows objects before trimming. The circle in the drawing is two units in the positive Z direction above the other object. Figure T.22 shows the objects trimmed using no projection.

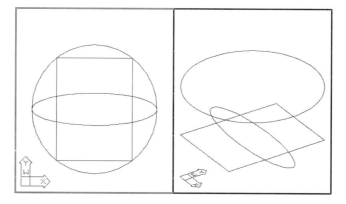

Figure T.21. *Objects shown in two views before trimming.*

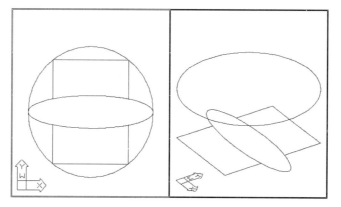

Figure T.22. *Objects shown in two views after trimming using no projection.*

ucs This default projection method means that AutoCAD will project the objects to be trimmed and cutting edges onto the current UCS X,Y plane. The objects projected do not have to intersect the cutting edges in 3D space to be trimmed. Figure T.23 illustrates this projection method.

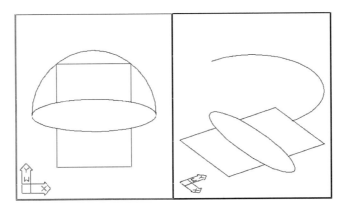

Figure T.23. *Objects shown in two views after trimming using UCS projection.*

View This projection method projects the objects onto the current viewing plane along the current view direction. The objects do not necessarily have to intersect the cutting edges in 3D space to be trimmed. Figure T.24 illustrates this projection method.

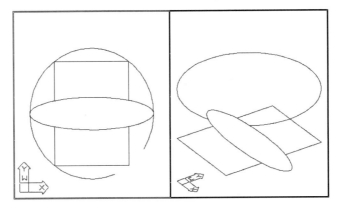

Figure T.24. *Objects shown in two views after trimming using View projection.*

Edge The Edge option of the TRIM command determines whether the objects trimmed are trimmed to the implied cutting edges, or only to the cutting edge if it actually intersects in 3D space.

Extend This option extends the cutting edge through 3D space for trimming objects that may intersect it.

No Extend This default option ensures that the objects to be trimmed are trimmed only if they intersect the actual cutting edges selected.

Undo Use the Undo option of the TRIM command to reverse the most recent trim operation. You can Undo to the start of selecting objects to trim.

Example

The following example demonstrates the command by trimming existing objects, as shown in figure T.25.

Choose TRIM (Modify, Trim)	Issues the TRIM command
`Command: _trim`	

`Select cutting edges:`
`(Projmode = None, Edgemode = No extend)`
`Select objects:` *Pick point* ①
(see fig. T.25)
	Selects objects to use as trimming edges

`Other corner:` *Pick point* ②	
`6 found`	
`Select objects:` (Enter)	
`<Select object to trim>` `/Project/Edge/Undo:` **F** (Enter)	Selects the Fence option for selecting objects
`First fence point:` *Pick point* ③	
`Undo/<Endpoint of line>:` *Pick point* ④	
`Undo/<Endpoint of line>:` *Pick point* ⑤	
`Undo/<Endpoint of line>:` *Pick point* ⑥	
`Undo/<Endpoint of line>:` *Pick point* ⑦	
`Undo/<Endpoint of line>:` *Pick point* ⑧	
`Undo/<Endpoint of line>:` (Enter)	Terminates Fence object selection
`<Select object to trim>` `/Project/Edge/Undo:` (Enter)	Terminates the TRIM command

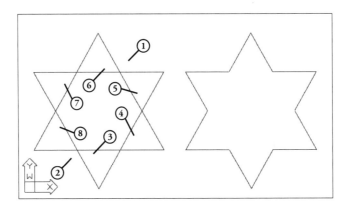

Figure T.25. *Before and after images of objects to be trimmed.*

Related Commands

BREAK   CHAMFER   EXTEND   FILLET
LENGTHEN   SLICE   STRETCH

Related System Variable

TRIMMODE

U

Undo

Toolbar: *Undo (Standard Toolbar)*
Pull-down: **E**dit, **U**ndo
Screen: SERVICE, Undo

The U command is an abridged version of the UNDO command. It is the same as entering **UNDO 1**. The U command reverses the effects of the previous command. The U command has no effect if the drawing has just been loaded, or if the previous command was PLOT, SH, SHELL, or other operations external to the drawing. You can disable the U command with the UNDO command's Control option. Undo options are available in the object selection mode and some commands such as EXTEND, LINE, PLINE, and TRIM. You can reverse all the effects of running a script by executing a single U command. Any transparent commands executed during the previous command are also reversed by executing the U command.

AutoCAD presents the following prompt if the U command cannot be executed:

Everything has been undone.

Related Commands

REDO   OOPS   UNDO

Related System Variable

UNDOCTL

UCS

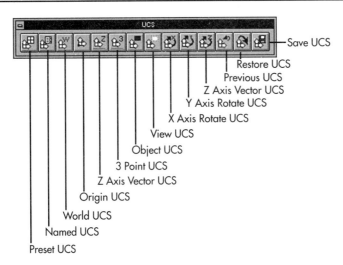

Toolbar: *(Standard Toolbar, UCS)*
Pull-down: **V**iew, **S**et UCS
Screen: VIEW, UCS:

The UCS command defines a working coordinate system. Using a different coordinate system can make constructing objects much easier. A *User Coordinate System* (UCS) is defined relative to the *World Coordinate System* (WCS). AutoCAD uses the current coordinate system when you pick points in the graphics window or enter any coordinate locations. You also can set and modify the UCS with a dialog box—see the DDUCS command for more information.

Two-dimensional objects, such as circles, arcs, text, and 2D polylines, are always created parallel to the current UCS. To properly position these objects in 3D space, it is often necessary to define an appropriate UCS beforehand. Use the UCS icon as a visual guide for determining the current orientation of the UCS—see the UCSICON command for more information.

TIP

> The UCSFOLLOW system variable controls the display of the drawing when changing the UCS. When UCSFOLLOW is set to 0 (the default), the display is unaffected by a change to the UCS. When set to 1, the display is automatically reoriented to keep the origin in the lower left with the positive Z axis outward. This can be very helpful when working in oblique 3D space.

The right-hand rule is used to determine positive axis direction of all AutoCAD coordinate systems. If you place the thumb of your right hand along the positive axis direction, the direction your fingers curl around your thumb is the positive (counterclockwise) rotation direction. If you point the first finger of your right hand along the positive X axis and align the second finger of your right hand perpendicular to the first along the positive Y axis, the direction of your extended thumb, perpendicular to both of your other fingers, is along the positive Z axis.

Prompts and Options

The UCS command presents the user with the following options:

`Origin/ZAxis/3point/OBject/View/X/Y/Z/Prev/Restore/Save/Del/?/<World>:`

Origin Defines a new UCS by specifying a different origin point relative to the current UCS. You can specify a point relative to the WCS by preceding the coordinates with an asterisk (*). The current UCS origin (0,0,0) is moved, while the direction of the existing X, Y, and Z axes are maintained.

ZAxis Select a new origin and a point in the positive direction of the Z axis of the desired coordinate system. The orientation of the X and Y axes is determined through the use of the arbitrary axis algorithm.

> The *arbitrary axis algorithm* is a method to determine an X axis based upon an arbitrary Z axis. The arbitrary Z axis is checked to see if it lies within 1/64 of the Z axis of the WCS (in other words, if the arbitrary Z axis is within about one degree of the Z axis of the WCS). If so, the vector cross product of the WCS Y axis and the arbitrary Z axis determines the arbitrary X axis. If the arbitrary Z axis does not lie within 1/64 of the Z axis of the WCS, the cross product of the WCS Z

TIP

> axis and the arbitrary Z axis determines the arbitrary X axis. If the arbitrary Z axis is very close to the WCS Z axis, this results in a UCS nearly parallel to the WCS.

If you press Enter at the `Point on positive portion of Z-axis` prompt, the directions of the X, Y, and Z axes remain unchanged. This option then has the same effect as the Origin option.

3point Specify a new origin location, a point on the positive X axis, and point in the positive direction on the desired XY plane. The Y axis does not necessarily pass through the Y axis point picked—the point is used only as a reference to orient the XY plane.

Object Select an object to define a new UCS. The new UCS is oriented to be coplanar with the selected object with the Z axis the same as was used to create the object. The type of object selected determines the new UCS as follows:

> **Point.** The UCS origin is moved to the points location while the orientation of the X, Y, and Z axes are maintained.
>
> **Line.** The UCS origin is positioned at the lines endpoint nearest the selection point and the X axis is aligned with the line.
>
> **Circle.** The positive X axis is directed through the selection point while the UCS origin is positioned at the center of the circle.
>
> **Arc.** The positive X axis is directed to the arc's endpoint nearest the selection point. The UCS origin is positioned at the center of the arc.
>
> **Polyline (2D Only).** The X axis is oriented from the start point of the polyline through the first vertices. The UCS origin is located at the polylines start point.
>
> **Inserted objects.** This includes standard text and attributes, Block insertions and Shapes. The UCS origin is located at the insertion point and the X axis follows the objects rotation angle.
>
> **Dimension.** The X axis is oriented parallel to the UCS that was used to create the dimension with the origin positioned at the center of the dimension text.
>
> **2D Solid.** The X axis is oriented from the first point of the 2D solid through the second. The UCS origin is located at the first point.
>
> **Trace.** The UCS origin is located at the start point of the trace segment selected while the X axis is oriented along the selected segments centerline.

3D Face. The X axis extends from the first point through the second point. The Y axis extends from the first point through the fourth point. The origin is placed at the first point.

You cannot select certain objects, such as ACIS solids or regions, ellipses, splines, rays, xlines, leaders, mtext, mlines, 3D polylines, polygon meshes, or paper space viewports as these objects do not define a unique UCS.

View   Reorients the UCS so that it is parallel to the current view. The X axis is parallel to the bottom of the view; the Y axis is parallel to the left side. Does not change the origin point.

X/Y/Z   Rotates the UCS around the specified axis. The right-hand rule determines the positive rotation direction. This option is handy for creating a UCS from the existing UCS, such as making a side UCS from a plan UCS.

Previous   Restores the previously defined UCS. You can step back up to ten User Coordinate Systems with this option. If the variable TILEMODE is set to zero, the ten previous UCSs in both paper space and model space are saved. The previous UCS for the current space is restored.

Restore   Retrieves a previously saved UCS. At the ?/Name of UCS to restore: prompt, enter the name of a previously saved UCS, or use the ? option to list the names of the saved UCSs. See the Save option for more information.

Save   Saves the currently defined UCS in the drawing. The origin and X, Y, and Z axes directions are saved. At the ?/Desired UCS name: prompt, enter the name to save the current UCS under. The name can be between 1 and 31 characters long, and letters, numbers, "$," "-," and "_" are all valid characters. Enter ? at the ?/Desired UCS name: prompt to list the names of the previously save UCSs.

Delete   Removes a saved User Coordinate System from the drawing. Enter the name(s) of the previously saved UCSs to delete. Multiple UCSs can be deleted by separating the names with commas.

?   Lists the User Coordinate Systems that have been saved in the drawing. At the UCS name(s) to list <*>: prompt, enter a name pattern to match or press enter to list all saved UCSs. The saved information includes the UCS name, origin, and X, Y, and Z axes directions.

World   Press Enter to accept the default option of World. AutoCAD restores the *World Coordinate System* (WCS).

Example

The following example uses the UCS command options to define two new User Coordinate Systems and save them (see fig. U.1). Use the UCSICON command to display the UCS icon at the origin of the current UCS.

Command	Description
Command: **UCS** (Enter)	Invokes the UCS command
Origin/ZAxis/3point/OBject/View/ X/Y/Z/Prev/Restore/Save/Del/?/ <World>: **3** (Enter)	Specifies 3 Point option
Origin point <0,0,0>: **END** (Enter)	Selects endpoint object snap
of *Pick* ① *(see fig. U.1)*	Pick new UCS origin
Point on positive portion of the X-axis<12.0000,5.0000,-1.0000>: **END** (Enter)	Selects endpoint object snap
of *Pick* ②	Pick new X axis point
Point on positive-Y portion of the UCX XY plane <10.0000,5.0000, -1.0000>: **END** (Enter)	Selects endpoint object snap
of *Pick* ③	Pick new Y axis point
Command: **UCS** (Enter)	Starts the UCS command
Origin/ZAxis/3point/OBject/View/ X/Y/Z/Prev/Restore/Save/Del/?/ <World>: **S** (Enter)	Specifies Save option
?/Desired UCS name: **RIGHT** (Enter)	Saves current UCS with the name RIGHT
Command: **UCS** (Enter)	Executes UCS command
Origin/ZAxis/3point/OBject/View/ / X/Y/Z/Prev/Restore/Save/Del/?/ <World>: **Y** (Enter)	Specifies Y axis rotation option
Rotation angle about Y axis <0>: **-90** (Enter)	Rotate 90 degrees clockwise about current Y axis
Command: **UCS** (Enter)	Starts the UCS command
Origin/ZAxis/3point/OBject/View/ X/Y/Z/Prev/Restore/Save/Del/?/ <World>: **O** (Enter)	Specifies Origin option
Origin point <0,0,0>: **END** (Enter)	Selects endpoint object snap

of *Pick* ④	Pick new UCS origin
Command: **UCS** (Enter)	Starts the UCS command
Origin/ZAxis/3point/OBject/View/ X/Y/Z/Prev/Restore/Save/Del/?/ <World>: **S** (Enter)	Specifies Save option
?/Desired UCS name: **FRONT** (Enter)	Saves current UCS with the name Front
Command: **UCS** (Enter)	Issues the UCS command
Origin/ZAxis/3point/OBject/View/ X/Y/Z/Prev/Restore/Save/Del/?/ <World>: (Enter)	Restores World Coordinate System

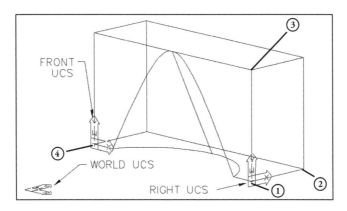

Figure U.1. *Defining two new UCSs with the UCS command.*

Related Commands

CSICON   DDUCS   DDUCSP   ORTHO

Related System Variables

UCSFOLLOW UCSICON UCSNAME UCSORG
UCSXDIR   UCSYDIR WORLDUCS

UCSICON

Pull-down: **O**ptions, **U**CS
Screen: OPTIONS, UCSIcon:

The UCSICON command controls the display of the graphical icon for the current coordinate system. The UCS icon indicates the orientation of the current coordinate system and whether the current coordinate system is the *World Coordinate System* (WCS) or a *User Coordinate System* (UCS). The shape of the icon indicates the drawing is currently in model space, or paper space. This UCS icon also indicates whether you are viewing the drawing from above (positive Z), from below (negative Z), or from edge on (zero). Figure U.2 shows six examples of UCS icons.

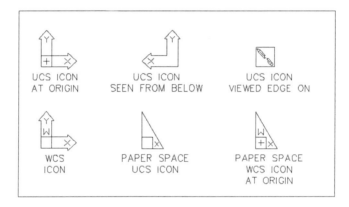

Figure U.2. *Coordinate system icons.*

You can turn the UCS icon on or off and set it to display at the origin (when it fits in the viewport) or at the lower left corner of the viewport. The icon display can be set independently in each viewport.

When viewed from above, the icon contains a square in the corner (see the WCS icon in the lower left corner of fig. U.2). When viewed from below, the icon does not contain the square (see the UCS icon in the upper middle of fig. U.2).

> When determining whether the icon can be displayed at the origin and still fit in the viewport, AutoCAD considers the size of the icon to be a few pixels larger than the displayed icon itself.

Prompts and Options

The UCSICON command presents the user with the following options:

ON/OFF/All/Noorigin/ORigin

ON Turns on the display of the UCS icon in the current viewport.

OFF Disables the display of the icon in the current viewport.

All Applies the settings made by the current UCSICON command to all active viewports. The ON/OFF/Noorigin/ORigin prompt repeats.

Noorigin Displays the UCS icon in the lower left corner of the viewport. This option is the opposite of the ORigin option.

ORigin Displays the UCS icon at the current coordinate system's origin. The UCS icon is displayed with a small cross in the lower left corner (see the upper left icon example in fig. U.2). If this origin point is located off the screen, or if the location of the origin would force part of the icon off the screen, the icon is displayed instead in the lower left corner of the viewport.

Example

This example disables the UCSICON in the current viewport.

Command: **UCSICON** (Enter)	Starts the UCSICON command
ON/OFF/All/Noorigin/ORigin <ON>: **OFF** (Enter)	Turns off UCS icon display in current viewport

Related Commands

DDUCS   DDUCSP   MSPACE   PSPACE
UCS

Related System Variables

TILEMODE   UCSFOLLOW   UCSICON   UCSORG
VIEWDIR   WORLDUCS

UNDEFINE

The UNDEFINE command disables specified AutoCAD commands so that they cannot be executed in the normal manner.

An undefined command can still be executed by prefacing its name with a period. For example, if SAVE is undefined, you can still use it by typing **.SAVE** at the Command: prompt. Use the REDEFINE command to restore undefined commands.

Prompts and Options

Command name   Enter the name of the AutoCAD command that you want to disable.

Example

See the example given for the REDEFINE command.

Related Command

REDEFINE

UNDO

Screen: Assist, Undo:

The UNDO command reverses the effects of previous commands or groups of commands. You can set markers during the editing session and later automatically undo all the commands back to these markers. The effects of an UNDO can be reversed with the REDO command. The U command is a simpler version of the UNDO command that only reverses the previous single command.

The following commands and system variables are not affected by the UNDO command:

ABOUT	AREA	ATTEXT	COMPILE
CONFIG	CVPORT	DBLIST	DELAY
DIST	DXFOUT	END	FILES

GRAPHSCR	HELP	HIDE	ID
IGESOUT	LIST	MSLIDE	NEW
OPEN	PLOT	PSOUT	QSAVE
QUIT	RECOVER	REDRAW	REDRAWALL
REGEN	REGENALL	REINIT	RESUME
SAVE	SAVEAS	SHADE	SHELL
STATUS	TBCONFIG	TEXTSCR	

Prompts and Options

The UNDO command presents the user with the following prompt:

`Auto/Control/BEgin/End/Mark/Back/<Number>:`

<Number> You can enter a number to tell AutoCAD to undo the last *number* of commands issued.

Auto Causes UNDO to interpret menu picks as one command. After you select this option, the following prompt appears:

`ON/OFF <default>:`

When set to ON, UNDO reverses the effects of a menu selection, no matter how many steps it includes. For example, if a menu selection changes layers, inserts a block, and rotates it as needed, one execution of UNDO treats all these steps as one. If the Auto option is set to OFF, each step is removed individually. The *default* displays the current setting. If the Control option has been turned off or limited the UNDO command in some way, the Auto option is not available.

Control Enables the normal UNDO, disables it, or limits it to one step or command. If you select this option, the following options appear:

`All/None/One <All>:`

> **All** The All option enables the UNDO command fully to operate.
>
> **None** The None option disables completely the UNDO and U commands. If you select this option and then later enter the UNDO command, the `Control:` prompt immediately displays.
>
> **One** This option restricts U and UNDO to a single step. You cannot perform multiple UNDO commands if you select this option. When this mode is active, UNDO displays the following prompt instead of the standard UNDO prompt, `Control /<1>`. Press Enter to UNDO a single action, or enter **C** to modify the settings.

BEgin The BEgin and End options work together to group a sequence of commands together into one UNDO operation. Undo End is required to close a group. This option treats a sequence of commands as one command. These commands are usually entered at the keyboard. Precede the commands with **BEgin**, finish the set with **End**, and then you can use a single U command to undo all the commands. If a group is not properly Ended, the next BEgin option starts a new group, discarding the previous one. Also, issuing UNDO will not back up past the UNDO BEgin point. If an Undo Mark exists, it disappears inside the group.

Back Instructs AutoCAD to undo all commands until a mark is found. You can use the Mark option (explained later) to place multiple marks throughout the drawing. If no mark is in the drawing, AutoCAD displays the following prompt:

```
This will undo everything. OK? <Y>
```

End This option closes a group of commands since the BEgin option was issued.

Mark This option works in conjunction with the Back option. You can place marks periodically as you enter commands. Then you can use Undo Back to undo all the commands that have been executed since the last mark. Marks can be thought of as "bookmarks"—holding your place for a subsequent UNDO operation.

> If you have several design considerations and want to be able to revert to a certain point in your drawing to try another design option, use the Undo Mark option to hold your place.

AutoCAD may present the following prompt if the U command cannot be executed:

```
Everything has been undone.
```

Related Commands

ERASE   EXPLODE   OOPS   REDO
U

Related System Variable

UNDOCTL UNDOMARKS

UNION

Union

Toolbar: *Union (Modify, Explode)*
Pull-down: *Construct*, *Union*
Screen: DRAW2, SOLIDS, Union:

The UNION command joins two or more coplanar regions into a composite region and two or more solids into a composite solid (see figures U.3 and U.4). The regions or solids do not have to share a common area or volume to be joined by the UNION command.

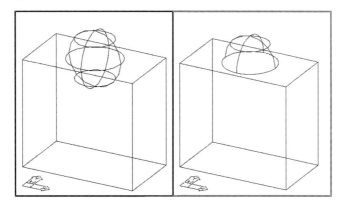

Figure U.3. *Solids before and after joining with the UNION command.*

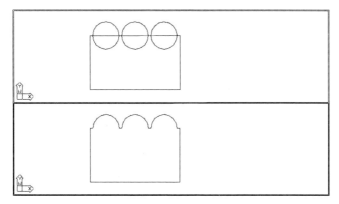

Figure U.4. *Regions before and after joining with the UNION command.*

Prompts and Options

If the objects you select cannot be joined, AutoCAD displays the following prompt:

At least 2 solids or coplanar regions must be selected.

Related Commands

BOX	CONE	CYLINDER	INTERFERE
INTERSECT	REGION	SECTION	SLICE
SPHERE	SUBTRACT	TORUS	WEDGE

'UNITS

The UNITS command specifies the units that AutoCAD uses when it reports and accepts numeric information. Use the UNITS command to tell AutoCAD what type of distance and angle formats to use. If you are drawing a building floor plan, for example, you can use architectural units; if you are designing a printed circuit board, you may want to specify decimal units.

> The UNITS command exists to provide backward compatibility to menus and support programs written for previous releases of AutoCAD. The DDUNITS command enables easier setting of the various drawing units by means of a dialog box.

Prompts and Options

For an explanation of the available Units settings, see the DDUNITS command.

Related Command

DDUNITS

Related System Variables

ANGBASE	ANGDIR	AUNITS	AUPREC
LUNITS	LUPREC	UNITMODE	

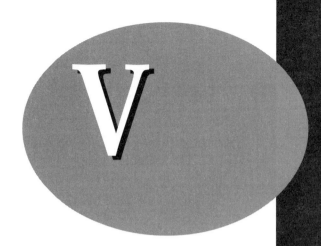

VIEW

The VIEW command saves and restores the display of the current drawing. Each view is saved with a name, which can be later restored. If a view created for paper space is restored while the drawing editor is in model space (or vice versa), AutoCAD switches to the correct space. When AutoCAD saves a view, it stores information about the current view, not the objects in the view. This is different from saving current viewport display with the MSLIDE command.

NOTE: The VIEW command exists to provide backward compatibility to menus and support programs written for previous releases of AutoCAD. The DDVIEW command enables easier access and editing of named views by means of a dialog box.

The saved view information includes the center, size, and twist angle of the view, the 3D viewpoint, and perspective (if perspective viewing is on). When you restore the view, AutoCAD uses the information to display that portion of your drawing quickly.

The VIEW command can be issued transparently, providing that no other transparent command is currently active (transparent commands cannot interrupt other transparent commands). Fast zooms (see the VIEWRES command) must be turned on for the VIEW command to be executed transparently. Also, the VIEW command cannot restore a VIEW transparently that requires a drawing regeneration.

When working with viewports, the viewport must be activated (by clicking with the pointer anywhere inside it) before issuing the VIEW command.

TIP: Views can greatly speed the process of moving between different areas of your drawing. Defining views can make setting up paper space viewports much easier. Views are saved in the drawing and can aid in plotting. Should the same area of a drawing be plotted often, save that area of the drawing as a view and plot the view when needed.

Prompts and Options

Issuing the VIEW command presents the following options:

`?/Delete/Restore/Save/Window`

? Lists the views that have been saved in the drawing. At the `View(s) to list <*>:` prompt, enter a name pattern to match or press Enter to list all saved views. The saved information listed includes the view name and the space (model or paper).

Delete Removes a saved view from the drawing. Enter the name(s) of the previously saved view(s) to delete. Multiple views can be deleted by separating the names with commas. If the name entered does not match a saved view, the VIEW command reports:

`No matching view names found.`

Restore Retrieves a previously saved view. At the `View name to restore:` prompt, enter the name of a previously saved view. If the name entered does not match a saved view, the VIEW command reports:

```
Cannot find view ...
```

Save Saves the view in the current viewport in the drawing. The center of the view, height and width of the view, the viewing direction, and the twist angle (the angle of the view relative to the bottom of the viewport) are saved. In addition, if perspective viewing is on (see the DVIEW command), the front and back clipping planes and the lens length are saved.

At the `View name to save:` prompt, enter the name to save the current view under. The name can be between 1 and 31 characters long, and letters, numbers, "$", "-", and "_", are all valid characters. If you specify an existing view name, it is overwritten without warning.

Window Saves a portion of the view in the current viewport in the drawing. See the Save option for the information saved and the valid view-naming criteria.

Specify the portion of the view to save by picking two corners of the view in the graphics window (or by entering coordinates).

Example

This example saves a view of the current drawing with the Window option in one viewport and restores it in another (see fig. V.1).

Click in the left viewport	Activates left viewport
`Command:` **VIEW** (Enter)	Starts the VIEW command
`?/Delete/Restore/Save/Window:` **W** (Enter)	Specifies Window option
`View name to save:` **DETAIL** (Enter)	Specifies name to save view under
`First corner:` *Pick* ① *(see fig. V.1)*	Specifies lower left corner of view
`Other corner:` *Pick* ②	Specifies upper right corner of view
Click in the right viewport	Activates right viewport
`Command:` **VIEW** (Enter)	Issues the VIEW command
`?/Delete/Restore/Save/Window:` **R** (Enter)	Specifies Restore option
`View name to restore:` **DETAIL** (Enter)	Specifies name of previously saved view to restore

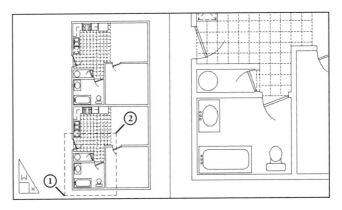

Figure V.1. *Defining a view and restoring it with the VIEW command.*

Related Commands
DDVIEW   PAN   ZOOM

Related Command
TILEMODE   VIEWCTR   VIEWDIR   VIEWMODE
VIEWSIZE   VIEWTWIST   VSMAX   VSMIN

VIEWRES

Screen: OPTIONS, Viewres:

The VIEWRES command controls the display resolution of circles and arcs. AutoCAD calculates and displays arcs and circles as series of short, straight line segments. Splines and ellipses are unaffected by the VIEWRES setting. VIEWRES also controls whether most zooms can be performed at redraw speed instead of requiring a regeneration. If VIEWRES is set for *fast zooms*, most pans and zooms execute at redraw speed. The VIEWRES Circle zoom percent setting controls the resolution of arcs and circles. A setting of 100 always regenerates with sufficient line segments to approximate smooth circles and arcs. As you zoom into the drawing, the line segments become apparent unless you have the fast zoom feature turned off. A higher circle zoom percent enables you to zoom farther in before the line segments become apparent; a lower setting makes them apparent at lower levels of zoom magnification, or even at each regeneration.

The circle zoom percent affects only the displayed image. Any printed or plotted output is created at the highest resolution possible by the printer or plotter.

Prompts and Options

Do you want fast zooms? <Y> If you answer no at this prompt, AutoCAD forces a screen regeneration after any PAN, ZOOM, or VIEW Restore; thus, any attempt at a transparent zoom is useless. If you answer Yes, AutoCAD zooms at redraw speed whenever possible. Zooms outside the current virtual screen area or significantly small zoomed views still require a screen regeneration.

Enter circle zoom percent (1-20000) <100> Your response to this prompt determines the accuracy for the display of circles and arcs, including any arcs in font styles. The higher the number, the more segments are displayed for an arc or circle, and the smoother the arc or circle appears. The disadvantage to a higher number is an increase in screen display time. The default of 100 is sufficient for most purposes. On faster systems with less complicated drawings, you can set the circle zoom percent higher with little loss of performance.

Example

The following example uses the VIEWRES command to initiate fast zooms and to set the circle zoom percent to 16 in one viewport and to 200 in another. The example assumes that two viewports are active, with a circle visible in each, as shown in figure V.2.

```
Command: VIEWRES (Enter)                    Issues the VIEWRES command
Do you want fast zooms? <Y>: (Enter)        Specifies whether ZOOM, PAN, or
                                            VIEW Restore perform at REDRAW
                                            speed

Enter circle zoom percent                   Controls the appearance of arcs and
(1-20000) <100>: 16 (Enter)                 circles
Regenerating drawing
```
Click on the right viewport to make it current.

```
Command: VIEWRES Enter
Do you want fast zooms? <Y>: Enter
Enter circle zoom percent
(1-20000) <16>: 200 Enter
Regenerating drawing
```

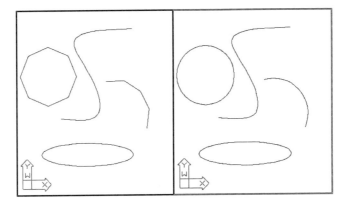

Figure V.2. *The effect of different VIEWRES settings on object appearance.*

Related Commands
REGEN   ZOOM

VLCONV

The VLCONV command converts Visual Link data to a form usable by AutoVision. Visual Link is an Autodesk product. The Visual Link data converted includes lights, cameras, material assignments, and mapping. Visual Link cameras are converted to named views in AutoCAD. Camera path data is not converted. Material assignments are only applied to objects selectable within AutoCAD.

Dialog Box Items

The VLCONV command displays the Visual Link Data Conversion dialog box that contains only one check box item (see fig. V.3).

Figure V.3. *The Visual Link Data Conversion dialog box.*

Overwrite AutoVision Material and Mapping Assignments. If this check box is not checked, existing AutoVision mapping and material assignments are retained. If this box is checked, existing AutoVision assignments are overwritten by Visual Link assignments. If there is a name conflict, the Visual Link name has a sequence number appended to the name. The VLCONV command does not change Visual Link data.

VPLAYER

Pull-down: <u>D</u>ata, <u>V</u>iewport Layer Controls
Screen: DATA, VPlayer:

The VPLAYER (ViewPort LAYER) command controls the freeze or thaw status of layers within individual floating viewports. The TILEMODE system variable must be set to zero. The VPLAYER command works in both paper space and model space. If layers are frozen or turned off with the LAYER command, they are invisible in every viewport, regardless of the settings made with the VPLAYER command.

You may freeze or thaw layers in all the current viewports. To disable a layer in all but one viewport, it is easier to quickly freeze the layer in all the viewports and then thaw it in the viewport in which it is to be visible. Individually selecting many viewports in which to freeze a layer can be time-consuming.

Prompts and Options

The VPLAYER command presents the following options:

```
?/Freeze/Thaw/Reset/Newfrz/Vpvisdflt
```

? Lists the layers frozen within the selected viewport. If you are working within model space, AutoCAD temporarily switches to paper space to select a viewport. At the `Select a viewport:` prompt, pick a viewport.

Freeze Freezes one or more layers within a selected viewport. At the `Layer(s) to Freeze:` prompt, enter one or more layer names to freeze. Separate each layer name with a comma. You also can use wild-card characters for specifying layer names.

Press Enter at the `All/Select/<Current>:` prompt to affect only the current viewport. Use the Select option to select more than one viewport to freeze layers in. If you select the All option, the layer(s) is frozen in all the current viewports, including paper space viewports that have their displays turned off by the MVIEW command.

Thaw Reverses the effect of the Freeze option. Note that if a layer is frozen globally with the LAYER command, this command has no effect on that layer. At the `Layer(s) to Thaw:` prompt, enter one or more layer names to thaw. Separate each layer name with a comma. You also can use wild-card characters for specifying layer names.

After specifying the layer(s) to thaw, you are prompted to choose which viewports are to be affected. See the Freeze option for a description about selecting viewports.

Reset Restores the default visibility of a layer as defined by the Vpvisdflt option. At the `Layer(s) to Reset:` prompt, enter one or more layer names to reset. Separate each layer name with a comma. You also can use wild-card characters for specifying layer names.

After specifying the layer(s) to reset, you are prompted to choose which viewports are to be affected. See the Freeze option for a description about selecting viewports.

Newfrz Creates new layers that are frozen in all viewports. This option is most useful for making layers intended to be displayed in only one viewport. At the `New viewport frozen layer name(s):` prompt, enter one or more layer names to create. Separate each layer name with a comma. You also can use wild-card characters for specifying layer names.

The created layers are frozen in all existing viewports and in any new viewports created with the MVIEW command. Use the Thaw option of this command to display the layer(s) in the desired viewport(s).

Vpvisdflt Specifies the default visibility, frozen or thawed, for specific layer(s) in subsequently created viewports. This option does not affect existing viewports. At the `Change default viewport visibility to Frozen/<Thawed>:` prompt, enter one or more layer names to thaw in subsequently created viewports. Use the Frozen option to specify layer names to freeze in subsequently created viewports. Separate each layer name with a comma. You also can use wild-card characters for specifying layer names.

This feature is useful for modifying layers that contain text or annotation that should not be displayed in subsequently created viewports.

Example

The following example shows the effects of changing a layer's visibility from thawed to frozen in a viewport. The same drawing is shown in two floating viewports after freezing a layer in figure V.4.

`Command: VPLAYER (Enter)`	Starts the VPLAYER command
`?/Freeze/Thaw/Reset/Newfrz/Vpvisdflt: F (Enter)`	Specifies Freeze option
`Layer(s) to Freeze: DIMS (Enter)`	Specifies DIMS layer to freeze
`All/Select/<Current>: S (Enter)`	Specifies Select option
`Switching to Paper space.`	
`Select objects:` *Pick lower viewport*	Selects lower viewport to freeze DIMS layer
`1 found`	
`Select objects: (Enter)`	Finishes selecting viewports to freeze DIMS layer
`Switching to Model space.`	
`?/Freeze/Thaw/Reset/Newfrz/Vpvisdflt: (Enter)`	Finishes VPLAYER command; regenerates drawing
`Regenerating drawing.`	

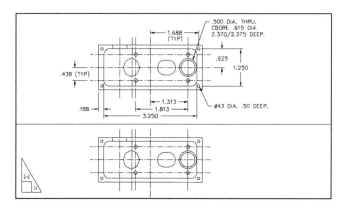

Figure V.4. *Freezing the DIMS layer in the lower viewport using VPLAYER.*

Related Commands

LAYER   DDLMODES   DDVIEW   DDVPOINT
MVIEW   PSPACE

Related System Variables

TILEMODE   VISRETAIN

VPOINT

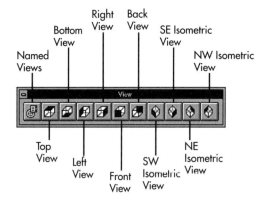

Pull-down: **V**iew, 3D Vi**e**wpoint
Pull-down: **V**iew, 3D V**i**ewpoint Presets
Screen: VIEW, Vpoint:

VPOINT

The VPOINT command changes the view of your drawing to view from any location in 3D space. You can specify a 3D coordinate for the viewpoint, rotate the current view by specifying an angle in the XY plane and an angle from the XY plane, or interactively specify a viewpoint by using two graphical aids.

The view is constructed by displaying the extents of the drawing within the current viewport, as seen from the viewpoint looking toward a target point. The default target point is the origin of the World Coordinate System. Use the DVIEW command to change the target point.

The WORLDVIEW system variable controls the reference used in determining a display specified by the DVIEW or VPOINT commands. Set to 1 (the default) all viewpoints are taken relative to the World Coordinate System. Changing WORLDVIEW to 0 causes the viewpoint to be taken relative to the current UCS.

VPOINT displays images in parallel projection. For the dynamic selection of a 3D view, or for perspective projection, use the DVIEW command.

Prompts and Options

Rotate/<View point> <current>   Enter the coordinates, or pick a point in the graphics window for the new viewing point. The target point remains unchanged. Press Enter to use the compass and axis tripod options (see the following View point option description), or select the Rotate option to specify a viewing point using two angles.

<current>   The point location listed in default brackets is the current viewing location. Pick a point in the graphics window, or enter the coordinates of a new viewing location. Press Enter to use the compass and axis tripod options, and press Enter again to retain the current viewing location.

Turn off any running object snaps before picking a point in the graphics window. If a running object snap is active, the viewing location could be snapped to an object, resulting in an unexpected viewpoint.

Rotate   Rotates the viewing location by specifying two rotation angles. Enter the first angle, measured from the X axis of the WCS, at the Enter angle in XY plane from X axis<*current*>: prompt. Enter the second angle, measured from the XY plane of the WCS, at the Enter angle from XY plane<*current*>: prompt.

View point If you press Enter at the Rotate/<View point> <current>: prompt, a pair of icons (see fig. V.5) appear on-screen. These icons are used to specify a new viewpoint interactively. The icon located in the upper right corner, called the *compass icon*, symbolizes a flattened globe that represents all possible 3D viewing locations. The center point of the icon is the north pole (looking down), the middle ring shows the equator, and the outer circle represents the south pole.

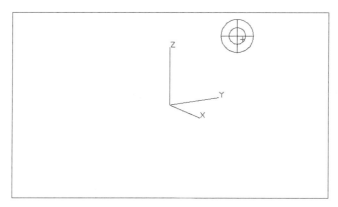

Figure V.5. *Using the axis tripod and compass to interactively specify a viewing location.*

As the cursor is moved around this globe, the axis tripod icon rotates to show the orientation of the X, Y, and Z axes for this viewpoint. The model can be viewed from below, if the cursor is placed between the equator ring (the inner ring) and the south pole ring (the outer ring). Position the cursor at the desired compass location, verify that the axis tripod has the desired orientation, and pick the point in the compass icon. If you press Enter, the previous viewing location remains unchanged.

Example

The following example creates four views: top, front, right side, and isometric by using VPOINT options. Each view is displayed in a viewport, as seen in figure V.6.

Click in the upper right viewport	Activates upper right viewport
Command: **VPOINT** (Enter)	Starts the VPOINT command
Rotate/<View point>	Specifies new viewing location

```
<0.0000,0.0000,1.0000>: -1,1,8 (Enter)
Regenerating drawing.
Command: DVIEW (Enter)                          Starts the DVIEW command
Select objects: ALL (Enter)                     Selects all objects for dynamic
                                                viewing
1 found
Select objects: (Enter)                         Finishes selecting objects for dynamic
                                                viewing
CAmera/TArget/Distance/POints/PAn/              Specifies TWist option, to twist view
/Zoom/TWist/CLip/Hide/Off/Undo/
<eXit>: TW (Enter)
New view twist <0.00>: 225 (Enter)              Specifies new twist angle
CAmera/TArget/Distance/POints/PAn/              Finishes the DVIEW command
/Zoom/TWist/CLip/Hide/Off/Undo/
<eXit>: (Enter)
Regenerating drawing.
```
Click in the lower right viewport   Activates lower right viewport

```
Command: VPOINT (Enter)                         Issues the VPOINT command
Rotate/<View point>                             Specifies new viewing location
<0.0000,0.0000,1.0000>: -1,-12,1
(Enter)
Regenerating drawing.
```
Click in the lower left viewport   Activates lower left viewport

```
Command: VPOINT (Enter)                         Starts the VPOINT command
Rotate/<View point>                             Specifies new viewing location
<0.0000,0.0000,1.0000>: 10,-1,1
(Enter)
Regenerating drawing.
```
Click in the upper left viewport   Activates upper left viewport

```
Command: VPOINT (Enter)                         Executes VPOINT command
Rotate/<View point>                             Specifies new viewing location
<0.0000,0.0000,1.0000>: 3,-3,1
(Enter)
Regenerating drawing.
```

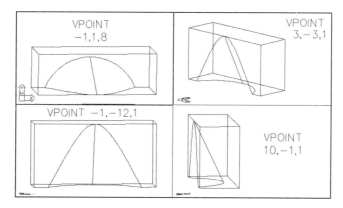

Figure V.6. *Four views of the same drawing obtained with the VPOINT command.*

Related Commands
DDVIEW

Related System Variables
WORLDVIEW   TARGET   VIEWDIR

VPORTS

Pull-down: **V**iew, Tile**d** Viewports
Screen: VIEW, Vports:

The VPORTS (or VIEWPORTS) command controls multiple concurrent views in model space. Viewports can be split, combined, saved, and restored. The TILEMODE system variable must be set to one. The VPORTS command creates and restores tiled viewports. Use the MVIEW command with TILEMODE set to one to create floating viewports. A maximum of 48 tiled viewports can be created, each no smaller than 1/64 of the graphics window.

Each viewport displays a view of your drawing. These views are updated automatically as changes to the drawing are made. The current viewport is identified by a heavy outline around its border. The crosshairs are displayed only in the current viewport. While the pointer is over other viewports, it appears as a small arrow. Only one of the viewports can be current. To switch between viewports, click in another viewport.

You can begin almost any command in the current viewport and switch focus between viewports as needed while still within the command. You can select objects, pick points, and specify options in different viewports, while within one command. Some commands affect only the current viewport. These commands include DVIEW, GRID, PAN, SNAP, UCSICON, VIEW, VPOINT, and ZOOM. Most of these commands do not accept a change to another viewport while they are active. To successfully use these commands, activate the desired viewport before issuing the command. Use the REDRAWALL and REGENALL commands to redraw or regenerate all the viewports.

Objects are highlighted and dragged only in the viewport in which they were selected. However, if you click in another viewport to make it current while dragging, objects being dragged are highlighted in the new current viewport.

Prompts and Options

The VPORTS command presents the user with the following options:

`Save/Restore/Delete/Join/SIngle/?/2/<3>/4:`

Save Saves the current viewport configuration in the drawing. The number of viewports, their sizes, locations, and view displayed within each are saved. The perspective view information and front and back clipping planes are saved for each viewport that has them active. See the DVIEW command for more information. In addition, grid spacing, snap spacing, snap origin, snap aspect ratio, UCS icon, and view resolution information for each viewport are saved.

At the `?/Name for new viewport configuration:` prompt, enter the name to save the current viewport configuration under. The name can be between 1 and 31 characters long; and letters, numbers, and the characters "$", "-", and "_", are all valid. Enter **?** at the `?/Name for new viewport configuration:` prompt to list the names of the previously saved viewport configurations.

When listing names of previously saved viewport configurations, the 2D screen coordinates for the lower left corner and upper right corner of each viewport are displayed. The screen coordinate values range from 0,0 (lower left) to 1,1 (upper right). The current configuration is always displayed first, with the current viewport listed at the top.

Use the Retrieve option of the VPORTS command to retrieve a previously saved model space viewport configuration in model space. Use the Retrieve option of the MVIEW command to retrieve a previously saved model space viewport configuration in paper space.

Restore Retrieves a previously saved viewport configuration. At the `?/Name of viewport configuration to restore:` prompt, enter the name of a previously saved viewport configuration, or use the **?** option to list the names of the saved viewport configurations. See the Save option for more information.

Delete Removes a saved viewport configuration from the drawing. Enter the name of the previously saved viewport configuration to delete.

Join Merges two displayed viewports into one. The boundaries of the two define the new viewport's boundary. The resulting viewport must be rectangular for the join to take effect. At the `Select dominant viewport <current>:` prompt, click in the viewport for which you want to provide the settings for the combined viewport. See the list of settings saved under the Save option for more information. At the `Select viewport to join:` prompt, click in the second viewport to combine it with the dominant viewport.

SIngle Returns the display to a single viewport. A single viewport fills the graphics window, using the settings from the current viewport.

2 Splits one viewport into two smaller viewports. Specify Horizontal to place a horizontal dividing bar between the two viewports. Specify Vertical to place a vertical dividing bar between the two viewports.

3 Splits one viewport into three smaller viewports, in one of six different possible configurations. Specify Horizontal to place a horizontal dividing bar between each of the three equal-sized viewports. Specify Vertical to place a vertical dividing bar between each of the three equal-sized viewports.

Specify Above, Below, Left, or Right to split the current viewport into three smaller ones, resulting in a larger viewport either above, below, to the left, or to the right of two smaller ones.

Example

The following example uses the VPORTS command to split one large viewport into three smaller ones, with a large viewport on the left of two smaller ones. Figure V.7 shows the viewports after the VPORTS command.

Command: **VPORTS** (Enter)	Starts the VPORTS command
Save/Restore/Delete/Join/ SIngle/?/2/<3>/4: **3** (Enter)	Specifies 3 option, to split viewport into three smaller ones
Horizontal/Vertical/Above/ Below/Left/<Right>: **L** (Enter)	Specifies Left option, to split viewport with large viewport on left of two smaller ones
Regenerating drawing.	

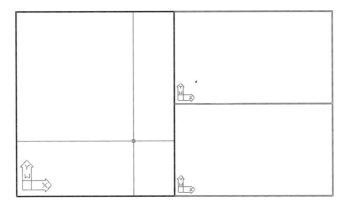

Figure V.7. *Creating three tiled (non-overlapping) model space viewports.*

Related Commands
MVIEW   REDRAWALL   REGENALL

Related System Variables
CVPORT   MAXACTVP   TILEMODE

VSLIDE

Pull-down: **T**ools, Sli**d**e, **V**iew
Screen: TOOLS, Vslide:

The VSLIDE command displays previously created slide files. Slide files (extension SLD) can be used to create presentations of your work. Slides are only snapshots; they contain no object information, so they load much more quickly than drawings. They cannot be edited, however. Slides take up very little space and are therefore excellent for showing highlights of your work.

Multiple slide files can be compiled into a slide library (extension SLB) by using the SLIDELIB.EXE program that accompanies AutoCAD. The ACAD.SLB file contains slides used by icon items in icon menus. When a slide is displayed, the current drawing is concealed but still active.

TIP You can create an automated slide show by using a script within AutoCAD. See the SCRIPT and DELAY commands for more information.

Prompts and Options

The options for viewing slide images are outlined as follows:

Slide file <default>   Enter the name of the slide file (without the extension) you want to display on-screen. If the FILEDIA system variable is set to one (on), a file dialog box displays instead of this prompt. If so, use the dialog box to specify the file name.

The default name for the slide file is the same name as the current drawing. After you enter the appropriate file name, AutoCAD displays the image saved in the slide file in the current viewport. To redisplay your drawing, invoke the REDRAW command.

The VSLIDE command also can display slides stored in slide file libraries. To view slides stored within slide file libraries, you must put the slide file name in parentheses after the name of the library. To view the file showing the Romans text style out of the ACAD.SLB file, for example, you would enter ACAD(ROMANS) as the slide name. If the Select Slide File dialog box is displayed, you must choose the **T**ype It button before typing the name of a slide file within a slide library.

Example

The following example uses VSLIDE to view both an individual slide file and a slide stored within a slide file library. The example assumes that the COLORWH.SLD and ACAD.SLB files are in the AutoCAD program directory or another directory in AutoCAD's search path. The system variable FILEDIA is set to zero.

Command: **VSLIDE** (Enter)	Issues the VSLIDE command
Slide file <default>: **COLORWH** (Enter)	Specifies the name of the slide file to display
Command: **VSLIDE** (Enter)	Issues the VSLIDE command
Slide file <default>: **ACAD(CONE)** (Enter)	Specifies the name of the slide library/slide name

Related Commands

MSLIDE   RENDSCR   SCRIPT

Related System Variable

FILEDIA

WBLOCK

Pull-down: File, Export, Block... (DOS Only)
Screen: FILE, EXPORT, Wblock:

The WBLOCK command copies a block definition or selection set to an external drawing file. This file can be edited like any other drawing file. The file then can be inserted in another drawing with the INSERT command. The file created by the WBLOCK command inherits all the drawing settings and definitions used by the selected block or objects in the current drawing. Named views, UCSs, and viewport configurations are not copied. The current UCS in the current drawing becomes the WCS of the new drawing.

Prompts and Options

The WBLOCK command displays the Create Drawing File dialog box. Specify the name for the new file (without the extension). The extension DWG is added for you. If the file already exists, AutoCAD asks whether you want to overwrite the existing file. After entering the file name, the dialog box disappears and the following Block name prompt is displayed.

Block name Enter the name of the block to copy as a drawing file. If you enter an equal sign (=), AutoCAD looks for, and uses if found, a block name that is the same as the file name you supplied in the Create Drawing File dialog box above. If you enter an asterisk (*) here, AutoCAD copies all the objects of the current drawing. If you press Enter at this prompt, you can select the objects that you want copied to a separate file.

> If you enter an asterisk (*) for the block name, AutoCAD copies all the objects in the drawing. Unused information such as unreferenced block names, layers, linetypes, text styles, and dimension styles are not included in the new drawing file. This is an excellent means of reducing file size should the drawing contain additional, unused data. This is especially applicable when you archive completed drawings. When doing this, however, be sure to QUIT the current drawing without saving. Because you wrote all object information out using the (*) option, ending or saving the drawing overwrites this file.

Insertion point This prompt appears if you press Enter at the Block name prompt. Specify the insertion base point for the new drawing file, relative to the objects you select. This is similar to choosing an insertion point for a block.

Select objects This prompt appears if you press Enter at the Block name prompt. Select each of the objects you want copied to the new file. You can use any appropriate selection method. The selected objects are erased from the current drawing. Use the OOPS or U command to restore them, if desired.

Example

The following example demonstrates how to create a new drawing that contains specific objects.

Command: **WBLOCK** (Enter)	Issues the WBLOCK command
File name: **DETAIL** (Enter)	Specifies the name of the new drawing file to create
Block name: (Enter)	Allows for specifying objects to include in the new drawing file

Insertion base point: *Pick a point*	Specifies the new drawing's base or insertion point
Select objects: *Select the objects*	Specifies the objects that will be included in the new file

The objects are copied to the DETAIL drawing file and removed from the current drawing. To restore the objects back to the drawing, use the OOPS or UNDO command.

Related Commands

BLOCK   DDINSERT   EXPORT   INSERT
OOPS

Related System Variable

INSBASE

WEDGE

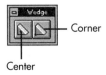
Corner
Center

Toolbar: *(Solids, Wedge)*
Pull-down: *D*raw, S*o*lids, *W*edge
Screen: DRAW2, SOLIDS, Wedge:

The WEDGE command creates a three-dimensional ACIS SOLID shaped like a wedge. The wedge is placed parallel to the current UCS. To create a rotated wedge, rotate the UCS and then use the WEDGE command to create the wedge. The size of the wedge can be specified by length, width, and height, or by picking two opposite base corners and entering a height. A wedge with the same height, width, and length also can be created.

NOTE: Don't confuse the WEDGE command with the 3D command's Wedge option. The WEDGE command creates an ACIS SOLID object, whereas the 3D command's Wedge option creates a polygon mesh surface object.

Prompts and Options

`Center/<Corner of wedge><0,0,0>` Specify the first corner of the wedge by entering a coordinate or by picking a point in the graphics window. You also can choose the Center option to specify the centroid position of the wedge. The default places the corner of the wedge at the origin of the current UCS.

`Center of wedge <0,0,0>` Pick a point in the graphics window or enter the coordinates for the center point of the wedge. The default places the center of the wedge at the origin of the current UCS.

`Cube/Length/<other corner>` Pick a point or enter the coordinates of the other corner of the wedge. If the other corner lies in the same construction plane as the first corner, you are prompted to enter the height of the wedge. If the other corner lies above or below the first corner, the difference in elevation is used as the height. If the other corner lies directly above the first corner, AutoCAD responds with the following:

```
Wedge of zero length not permitted.
```

and you are re-prompted to pick the other corner. You can choose the Cube option to specify a wedge having the same length, width, and height (a 45-degree wedge). Choose the Length option to specify a differing length, width, and height.

`Length` Enter the length of the wedge along the X axis. You also can pick two points in the graphics window to show the distance. If you have chosen the Cube option, this length also is used for the width and height.

`Width` Specify the width of the wedge along the Y axis, either by picking two points to show a distance, or entering a number.

`Height` Specify the height of the wedge along the Z axis. You also can pick two points in the graphics window to show the distance.

Example

The following example shows you how to create an ACIS SOLID wedge object. Figure W.1 shows the creation of the wedge with a view taken from a viewpoint of 3,-3,1 looking toward the origin, 0,0,0.

```
Command: WEDGE (Enter)                    Starts the WEDGE command
Center/<Corner of wedge><0,0,0>:          Specifies first corner of wedge
4,3,2 (Enter)
Cube/Length/<other corner>:               Specifies other corner of wedge,
9,5,5 (Enter)                             creates wedge with length 5,
                                          width 2, height 3
```

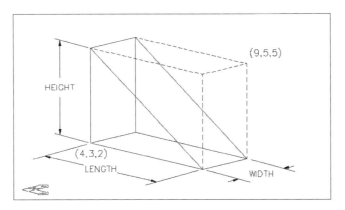

Figure W.1. *An ACIS SOLID wedge.*

Related Commands

EXTRUDE   INTERFERE   INTERSECT   SUBTRACT
UNION

WMFIN (Windows Only)

The WMFIN command imports a Windows MetaFile (WMF) vector file into AutoCAD. AutoCAD scans the vector file and creates a block definition consisting of lines, 2D polylines, and 2D solid objects. The block is then inserted with a name beginning with WMF and ending in a number. The Windows MetaFile is scaled to fill the current viewport.

Windows MetaFiles contain information in vector format and can be scaled and rotated without loss of resolution. If the block is exploded, the individual objects comprising the block can be edited as any regular AutoCAD line, polyline, or 2D solid object. Set the WMF file import options using the WMFOPTS command before importing the WMF file.

NOTE: Windows MetaFiles are imported as blocks with sequential names. If you reimport the same file multiple times, a new block is created each time you import.

When importing large Windows MetaFiles, AutoCAD displays a dialog box indicating the MetaFile loading progress.

Prompts and Options

The WMFIN command displays the Import WMF file dialog box. Select a Windows MetaFile to import. A preview image tile displays the contents of the WMF file. The WMFIN command does not honor the FILEDIA setting, and always displays the file dialog box. After selecting a WMF file to import, a block is created, and you are prompted to insert it with each of the prompts found in the INSERT command.

`Insertion point` Pick a point in the graphics window, or enter the coordinates of the insertion point for the WMF block. The WMF block is constructed such that the insertion point is up and to the left of all the objects. The insertion point is the upper left corner of the block representing the WMF file.

`X scale factor <1> / Corner / XYZ` Enter a number or pick a point in the graphics window to show the first point of a window. If you pick a point in the graphics window, the point is used as a base point for a window. If you choose the Corner option, the insertion point is used as a base point for a window. The second point of the window determines the X and Y scale factors for the WMF block. The distance from the second point to the first point along the X axis is the X scale factor; whereas the distance from the second point to the first point along the Y axis is the Y scale factor. Specify the XYZ option to specify a separate X, Y, and Z scale factor.

`Y, Z scale factor (default=X)` Enter a number for the Y or Z scale factor. This prompt appears if you entered a number for the X scale factor or chose the XYZ option. Press Enter to specify the same Y or Z scale factor as the X scale factor.

`Rotation angle <0>` Enter a rotation angle for the WMF block, or press Enter to accept the default of 0.

Example

The following example imports a WMF file created using the WMFOUT command, scaled 1 unit along the X axis and .8 units along the Y axis (see fig. W.2).

WMFIN (Windows Only)

```
Command: WMFIN (Enter)              Issues the WMFIN command
Insertion point: 0,9 (Enter)        Specifies insertion point
X scale factor <1> / Corner / XYZ:  Accepts default X scale factor of 1
(Enter)
Y scale factor (default=X): .8 (Enter)  Specifies Y scale factor of .8
Rotation angle <0>: (Enter)         Accepts default rotation angle of 0
```

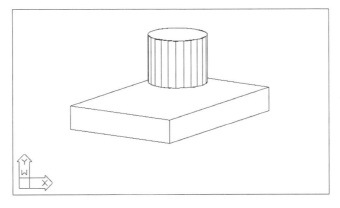

Figure W.2. *Importing a WMF file with the WMFIN command.*

Related Commands

ACISIN	DXBIN	DXFIN	GIFIN
IMPORT	INSERT	PCXIN	PSIN
TIFFIN	WMFOPTS	WMFOUT	

Related System Variable

GRIPBLOCK

WMFOPTS (Windows Only)

Pull-down: **F**ile, Op**t**ions, WMF Op**t**ions...

The WMFOPTS (Windows MetaFile OPTions) command sets the import options for the WMFIN command. Two options, wide lines and wire frame, can be turned on or off. The WMFOPTS command displays the WMF Import Options dialog box (see fig. W.3). The current WMF import options are saved in the ACAD.INI file, under the [WMF] section.

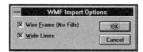

Figure W.3. *The WMF Import Options dialog box.*

Prompts and Options

Wire Frame (No Fills). Check the Wire Frame box to convert area fills within the WMF file to wire frame outlines when importing. If the Wire Frame box is unchecked, 2D solid objects are created to approximate the area fills in the WMF file.

Wide Lines. Check the Wide Lines box to retain wide (filled) lines when importing a WMF file. Wide lines are converted to 2D solids upon importing. If the Wide Lines box is unchecked, all lines are imported as zero width lines.

Example

The following example sets the WMF import options to retain both filled areas and wide lines.

Command: **WMFOPTS** (Enter)	Starts the WMFOPTS command
Check the Wire Frame (No Fills) *check box*	Sets conversion of filled areas to on
Check the Wide Lines *check box*	Retains wide lines when importing WMF files
Click on OK	Finishes the WMFOPTS command

Related Commands
WMFIN   WMFOUT

WMFOUT (Windows Only)

The WMFOUT command exports selected objects as a Windows MetaFile (WMF) file. The WMF file can then be imported into another graphics or desktop publishing program. Objects are exported to a WMF file in vector format and do not experience a loss of resolution when importing into other programs as raster images may.

Prompts and Options

The WMFOUT command displays the Create WMF File dialog box. Specify a file name to contain the Windows MetaFile output. (AutoCAD adds an extension of WMF.)

Select objects Select the desired objects to export to the WMF File. The visible portion of any object selected is exported. Any portion of an object obscured (such as the result of the HIDE command) is not exported. All 3D information is converted into a 2D WMF format.

Example

The following example exports a hidden view of an AutoCAD drawing. Use the 3D command to create a box and a cylinder, as shown in figure W.4.

Command: **HIDE** (Enter)	Creates hidden view of current drawing
Command: **WMFOUT** (Enter)	Starts the WMFOUT command
Specify an output file name in the Create WMF File dialog box	Specifies output file name
Select objects: **ALL** (Enter)	Specifies all objects in drawing
2 found.	
Select objects: (Enter)	Finishes selecting objects

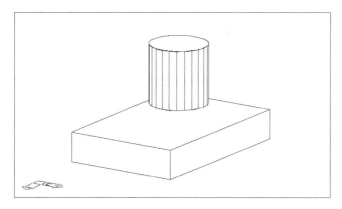

Figure W.4. *Exporting a 3D box and cylinder with the WMFOUT command.*

Related Commands

ACISOUT   DXFOUT   EXPORT   PLOT
PSOUT   WMFIN   WMFOPT

XBIND

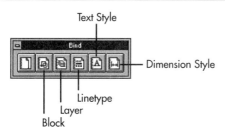

Toolbar: *(External Reference, Bind)*
Pull-down: *F*ile, *B*ind
Screen: FILE, Xbind:

The XBIND (eXternal BIND) command permanently attaches dependent symbols of an external reference drawing (XREF) to the current drawing database. A *dependent symbol* is a block, layer, linetype, dimension style, or text style found in the XREF. Normally, none of the information stored within XREFs is made a permanent part of the drawing database. If you need to use some of the XREF's dependent symbols, such as dimension styles or blocks, you must add them to the database with XBIND. Otherwise, the XREF might be detached, and those objects no longer would be available for your use.

Prompts and Options

`Block/Dimstyle/LAyer/LType/Style` Dependent objects from XREFs must be bound one at a time using the XBIND command. Enter the option for the object type that you want to bind. To bind all the dependent symbols from one or more XREFs, see the Bind option of the XREF command.

`Dependent symbol name(s)` Enter a name pattern to match to permanently attach dependent symbols. Dependent symbol names are identified by the name of the XREF drawing followed immediately by the vertical bar (also called the *pipe* character), followed by the external reference symbol name. You can use wild-card characters (listed in the introduction) in specifying the symbol name(s). Separate more than one name or name pattern with commas.

> The pipe character is replaced by a dollar sign, a number, and another dollar sign when binding. The number is incremented each time a symbol with the same name is attached from the same XREF. Depending upon the number, at least two additional characters are added to the symbol name. The symbol name may not exceed 31 characters after it has been converted, or the XBIND operation will fail.

If a block from an XREF is bound, and this block references layers, linetypes, text styles, or dimension styles in the XREF, these additional dependencies are also bound. If the block contains an XREF, all symbols from this XREF are bound. If a layer that depends on a linetype other than continuous is bound, the dependent linetype is also bound.

Example

In the following example, two blocks belonging to an external reference file are bound into the current drawing. Create a sample drawing called BOX.DWG with two blocks, named CUBE and CYLINDER, as shown in figure X.1—then start a new drawing.

`Command: XREF` (Enter)	Issues the XREF command
`?/Bind/Detach/Path/Reload/` `Overlay/<Attach>:` (Enter)	Specifies default option, Attach
Select the drawing BOX.DWG *from the Select file to attach dialog box*	Specifies drawing to attach as an external reference

```
Attach Xref XREF1: BOX.DWG
BOX loaded.
```

`Insertion point: 0,0,0` (Enter)	Specifies insertion point of XREF
`X scale factor <1> / Corner / XYZ:` (Enter)	Accepts default of X scale factor of 1
`Y scale factor (default=X):` (Enter)	Accepts default of Y scale factor of 1
`Rotation angle <0>:` (Enter)	Accepts default of rotation angle of 0
`Command: XBIND` (Enter)	Starts the XBIND command
`Block/Dimstyle/LAyer/LType/Style:` `B` (Enter)	Specifies Block option
`Dependent layer name(s):` `BOX¦CUBE,BOX¦CYLINDER` (Enter)	Specifies block names to bind

```
Scanning...
2 Block(s) bound.
```

`Command: BLOCK` (Enter)	Issues the BLOCK command to check current block status
`Block name (or ?): ?` (Enter)	Specifies ? option to list blocks
`Block(s) to list <*>:` (Enter)	Lists all blocks

```
Defined blocks.
BOX$0$CUBE
BOX$0$CYLINDER
User      External      Dependent    Unnamed
Blocks    References    Blocks       Blocks
  2           0             0           0
```

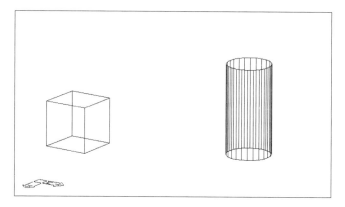

Figure X.1. *The BOX drawing with two blocks, CUBE and CYLINDER.*

Related Commands
XREF   XREFCLIP

Related System Variable
XREFCTL

XLINE

Construction Line

    Toolbar: *Construction Line (Draw, Line)*
    Pull-down: *D̲raw, Con̲struction Line*
    Screen: DRAW1, Xline:

The XLINE command provides a method of creating construction lines in a drawing. Construction lines are similar to AutoCAD's line objects except that they have no defining endpoints (refer to the LINE command). Construction lines can have various object properties in terms of color, layer, linetype, and so on, as most other AutoCAD objects. When a construction line is trimmed at one end, it becomes a Ray object. If the other end is trimmed as well, the object becomes a Line. Construction lines are ignored when AutoCAD calculates the extents of a drawing as in ZOOM Extents.

Prompts and Options

The following prompt displays when the XLINE command is executed:

`Hor/Ver/Ang/Bisect/Offset/<From point>:`

These options provide various methods of placing the construction lines.

Hor   The Hor (Horizontal) option creates construction lines through a specified point that are parallel to the X axis of the current UCS. At the following prompt, pick a point for the construction line to pass through and then press Enter to terminate the command. The use of AutoCAD's object snaps are permitted and encouraged.

`Through point:`

Ver   The Ver (Vertical) option is similar to the Horizontal option except that all lines are parallel to the Y axis of the current UCS. At the following prompt, pick a point for the construction line to pass through and then press Enter to terminate the command:

`Through point:`

Ang   The Angle option asks you to specify the placement of a construction line by one of two methods. You can specify a reference or "base angle" or specify an explicit angle. The Angle option displays the following prompt:

`Reference/<Enter angle (0.0000)>:`

>   **Reference**   This option asks you to select a line or polyline line segment that will become the zero-degree reference for the angle of the construction line. This option displays the following prompt:
>
>   `Select a line object.`
>
>   The `Enter angle` prompt displayed next is for specifying the angle of the construction line relative to the reference line selected earlier.
>
>   The `Through point` prompt asks you to specify the point that the angled construction line will pass through. This prompt repeats until you press Enter.

Bisect   The Bisect (Bisector) option of the XLINE command permits the placement of construction lines bisecting specified angles. The angles to be bisected are specified by the vertex and a point on each of the two lines (real or imaginary) that form the angle. The following prompt asks you to specify the vertex of the angle to be bisected. By nature, it is also the point through which the construction line will pass.

`Angle vertex point.`

The next prompt asks you for a point that lies on a line that crosses through the vertex, forming one leg of the angle. This point can be any point in the drawing and does not necessarily have to reside on an AutoCAD object.

`Angle start point.`

The last prompt displayed asks you for a point that will lie on the opposite leg of the angle that passes through the vertex. This prompt repeats until you press Enter.

`Angle end point.`

Offset The Offset option of the XLINE command operates in the same manner as the OFFSET command. You must specify an offset distance or through point that the offset line will pass through. The first prompt for the Offset option asks for an offset distance or a point specification.

`Offset distance or through:`

If you enter a distance using the keyboard or by picking two points, the `Select a line object` prompt appears. You then select a line or polyline line segment. The `Side to offset` prompt asks you to pick a point on either side of the selected object to determine on which side of the object the construction line will be drawn. A construction line is then drawn parallel to the selected object at the distance specified. The direction of offset is determined by the current UCS.

If a through point is specified in response to the prompt, `Offset distance or through`, the same prompts appear as discussed earlier, enabling you to select a line object and side to offset.

<From point> The From point option is the default option for the XLINE command. Specify the first of a pair of points that the construction line will pass through. After you specify the `From point`, a construction line is drawn through the point, with the other point passing through the AutoCAD crosshairs. The `Through point` prompt awaits a second point specification to draw the construction line. The `Through point` prompt repeats until you press Enter.

Example

The following example uses the XLINE command to place construction lines. Use the LINE command to draw a figure similar to the view in the lower left corner shown in figure X.2. Use ENDPOINT object snap when specifying points.

Choose the Construction Line *tool*.

Command: _xline	Issues the XLINE command
Hor/Ver/Ang/Bisect/Offset/ <From point>: H (Enter)	Specifies the Horizontal option
Through point: *Choose the* Snap to Endpoint *tool*	Specifies ENDpoint object snap
endp of *Pick point* ① *(see fig. X.2)*	Specifies the location of the construction line
Through point: _Choose the Snap to Endpoint *tool*	
endp of *Pick point* ②	
Through point: (Enter)	Terminates the XLINE command

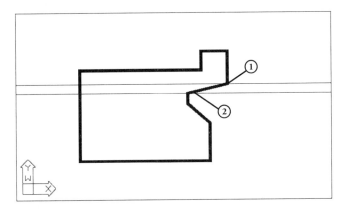

Figure X.2. *Creating construction lines.*

Related Commands

LINE RAY OFFSET

Related System Variables

LASTPOINT OFFSETDIST

XPLODE

The XPLODE command enhances the EXPLODE command by enabling you to explode multiple compound objects while optionally changing the color, layer, and linetype of each object within the block. You can change these properties globally for the selection set or individually for each compound object in the selection set. Additionally, you can assign a specific layer, linetype, and color or these properties can be inherited from the object being exploded.

Prompts and Options

Select objects At this prompt, you select the objects you want to explode. AutoCAD prompts you with the number of objects selected and how many valid objects can be exploded. If more than one valid object is selected, the following prompt appears:

```
XPlode Individually/<Globally>:
```

<Globally> This option applies the changes to all the selected objects. The following prompt is then displayed when this option is chosen:

```
All/Color/LAyer/LType/Inherit from parent block/<Explode>:
```

> **<Explode>** This option performs the same task as the EXPLODE command, breaking an object into its component parts.
>
> **All** This option enables you to change the color, layer, and linetype of each of the component objects after they are exploded. The prompts associated with each of the next three options are then displayed.
>
> **Color** Use this option to set the color of the exploded objects. When this option is chosen, AutoCAD displays the following prompt:
>
> ```
> Red/Yellow/Green/Cyan/Blue/Magenta/White/BYLayer/BYBlock <BYLAYER>:
> ```
>
> Enter the color name or a valid color number (1 - 255) or the BYBlock or BYLayer option. The BYLayer option forces the component objects to inherit the color of the exploded object's layer. The BYBlock option causes the component objects to inherit the same color as the block itself.
>
> **LAyer** Use this option to set the layer of the component objects. This option displays the following prompt:
>
> ```
> XPlode onto what layer? <0>:
> ```
>
> Enter the name of an existing layer. The default is the current layer.

LType Use this option to set the linetype of each component object after you explode them. This option prompts as follows:

`Enter new linetype name. <BYLAYER> :`

Enter the name of an existing linetype, BYLAYER, or BYBLOCK. The BYLayer option forces the component objects to inherit the linetype of the exploded object's layer. The BYBlock option causes the component objects to inherit the same linetype as the block itself.

Inherit from parent block Use this option to set the color, layer, and linetype of the component objects to that of the exploded block if it resides on layer 0 and its linetype and color are assigned BYBLOCK.

XPlode Individually This option makes changes to selected objects one at a time, issuing the following prompt for each object:

`All/Color/LAyer/LType/Inherit from parent block/<Explode>:`

Each of these options is discussed under Globally earlier.

Related Commands

| BLOCK | DDEMODES | DDINSERT | DDLMODES |
| EXPLODE | | | |

Related System Variables

| CECOLOR | CELTYPE | CLAYER | EXPLMODE |

XREF

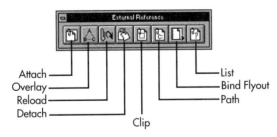

Toolbar: *(External Reference)*
Pull-down: *File*, External *R*eference
Screen: FILE, Xref:

The XREF (eXternal REFerence) command manages references to external drawings. An *external reference* is similar to a block, except that no part of the external reference resides within the drawing database. After an external reference is attached to a drawing, only a reference to the external file is placed in the drawing database.

An external reference has two advantages over a block—it takes up less space within a drawing file, and it cannot be edited from within the drawing into which it was inserted. The external reference is similar to any other drawing file. The next time the file containing the external reference is loaded into AutoCAD, or plotted with the PLOT command, the current version of the external reference is loaded.

The XREF command attaches and detaches XREFs, binds dependent symbols (symbols contained in the external reference, such as blocks and layers), and can reload an XREF during an editing session. The XREF command also is used to change the path to an external reference, should the external reference be moved from one directory to another.

Prompts and Options

The XREF command presents the following options:

`?/Bind/Detach/Path/Reload/Overlay/<Attach>:`

? Lists external references attached to the current drawing. At the `Xref(s) to list <*>:` prompt, enter a name pattern to list. Press Enter to list all external references.

Bind Permanently attaches all dependent symbols from an external reference to the current drawing. Dependent symbols are blocks, layers, linetypes, dimension styles, and text styles. Dependent symbols have names that combine the name of the external reference file, the vertical bar (also called the "pipe") character and a specific symbol name.

The external reference is bound as a block, and all dependent symbol names are converted to names that combine the name of the original external reference file, a dollar sign, a number, another dollar sign, and then the name of the original dependent symbol. This procedure ensures that the names used in the external reference are not confused with any similarly named objects within the current drawing.

NOTE: The pipe character is replaced by a dollar sign, a number, and another dollar sign when binding. The number is incremented each time a symbol with the same name is bound from the same external reference. Depending upon the number, at least two additional characters are added to the symbol name. The symbol name may not exceed 31 characters after it has been converted, or the bind operation will fail.

At the Xref(s) to bind: prompt, enter the name or name pattern of external references that you want placed in the drawing database. If you are binding multiple external references, separate each name with a comma.

TIP: If you only want to bind some of the external references' dependent symbols, use the XBIND command.

Detach Removes a reference to an external drawing. At the Xref(s) to detach: prompt, enter the name or name pattern of the external reference(s) that you want removed from the drawing. If you are removing multiple external references, separate each name with a comma.

Path Changes the path to an external reference. The path to each external reference is stored in the current drawing. If the external reference is moved from one directory to another, it will not be found until the path is changed, or the external reference is detached and reattached. At the Edit path for which Xref(s): prompt, enter the name of the external reference whose path has changed. The old path will be displayed, and at the New path: prompt, enter the current path for the external reference.

Reload Updates an external reference without having to exit AutoCAD or reopen the current drawing. This option is especially convenient when used in a network environment in which other users might be making modifications to an external reference that you have attached to your drawing. After they have completed and saved their changes, you can use the Reload option to update your copy of the external reference. At the Xref(s) to reload: prompt, enter a name or name pattern of the external reference(s) to be reloaded.

Overlay Attaches an external reference into the current drawing file. This attached external reference is not referenced if the drawing in which it is attached is itself referenced by another drawing. See the following description of the Attach option.

<Attach> Attaches an external reference into the drawing file. At the `Xref to attach <current XREF name >:` prompt, enter the name of the drawing file you want to attach to the drawing. After specifying the name of the external reference to attach, AutoCAD inserts a reference to the external drawing and prompts you with each of the prompts found in the INSERT command. See the INSERT command for more information. The external reference, for all intents and purposes, acts as an insert object to a block that cannot be edited or exploded or changed from within the current drawing.

If the drawing being attached contains an attached external reference to a third drawing, that third drawing is also attached as an external reference. If the drawing being attached contains an overlaid external reference to a third drawing, the third drawing is ignored. If the drawing being attached contains an external reference to the current drawing, a situation known as a *circular reference* occurs. AutoCAD will not attach an external reference if the external reference drawing references the current drawing.

If the drawing being attached is currently attached, AutoCAD simply inserts another reference to the external drawing and prompts with each of the prompts found in the INSERT command.

The layers 0 and DEFPOINTS and the linetype CONTINUOUS are common to both the current and external reference drawings. Objects on these layers in external references are controlled by setting the layer in the current drawing. If the DEFPOINTS layer does not exist in the current drawing, but exists in an attached external reference, it is bound to the current drawing with the name DEFPOINTS.

Example

The following example attaches a reference to an external drawing using the Attach option of the XREF command. Create a bathroom layout drawing called BATH.DWG, a kitchen layout drawing called KITCHEN.DWG, and a floor plan drawing. Open the floor plan drawing (see fig. X.3).

Command: **XREF** `Enter`	Starts the XREF command
`?/Bind/Detach/Path/Reload/Overlay/<Attach>:` `Enter`	Accepts default option of Attach
Select the drawing BATH.DWG *from the Select File to Attach dialog box*	Specifies external drawing to attach
`Attach Xref BATH: BATH.DWG` `BATH1 loaded.`	

Insertion point: **END** (Enter)	Specifies Endpoint object snap
of *Pick* ① *(see fig. X.3)*	Specifies attachment point for XREF
X scale factor <1> / Corner / XYZ: (Enter)	Accepts X scale factor of 1
Y scale factor (default=X): (Enter)	Accepts Y scale factor of 1
Rotation angle <E>: (Enter)	Accepts rotation angle of 0
Command: **XREF** (Enter)	Issues the XREF command
?/Bind/Detach/Path/Reload/Overlay/<Attach>: (Enter)	Accepts default option of Attach
Select the drawing **KITCHEN.DWG** *from the Select file to Attach dialog box*	Specifies external drawing to attach
Attach Xref KITCHEN: KITCHEN.DWG KITCHEN loaded.	
Insertion point: **END** (Enter)	Specifies Endpoint object snap
of *Pick* ②	Specifies attachment point for XREF
X scale factor <1> / Corner / XYZ: (Enter)	Accepts X scale factor of 1
Y scale factor (default=X): (Enter)	Accepts Y scale factor of 1
Rotation angle <E>: (Enter)	Accepts rotation angle of 0

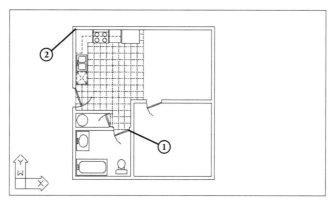

Figure X.3. *The floor plan after referencing the bath and kitchen drawings.*

Related Commands

BASE	BLOCK	DDLMODES	INSERT
LAYER	LINETYPE	STYLE	XBIND
XREFCLIP			

Related System Variable

XREFCTL

XREFCLIP

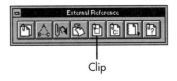

Clip

Toolbar: *Clip (External References)*
Pull-down: *F̲ile, External R̲eference, C̲lip*

The XREFCLIP (eXternal REFerence CLIP) command attaches and clips references to external drawings.

The XREFCLIP command is an AutoLISP program that freezes all layers, attaches an external reference on a new layer, and creates a new floating viewport of model space.

The XREFCLIP command requires you to change to paper space (set the TILEMODE system variable to zero). If you are not in paper space when you start the command, it will enable paper space after prompting you.

TIP

> The AutoLISP file that defines this command is loaded the first time you invoke the command. Once loaded, you can abbreviate the XREFCLIP command with XC until you exit the drawing.

Prompts and Options

Xref name   Enter the name of the XREF to attach. A dialog box is not available.

> **WARNING**
> Do not enter a file name with the extension DWG in capitol letters. The XREFCLIP command examines the file name to see whether it has an extension of lowercase dwg, and, if so, it is stripped from the file name. A lower case dwg is appended to the file name, and the directory is searched. If you enter a file name with the extension DWG, a lowercase dwg is appended to it and The file will not be found, even if the file name entered is correct.

Clip onto what layer? Enter a new layer name. The XREFCLIP command creates two new layers—one with the name entered here, and one by appending -VP to the name entered here.

> **WARNING**
> Do not enter a layer name with more than 28 characters. The maximum number of characters a layer name can have is 31. The XREFCLIP command appends three more characters to the layer name entered. If the appended layer name has more than 31 characters, the XREFCLIP command will halt execution half-way through.

The layer name must not already exist. If it does, the XREFCLIP command responds with the following:

`Layer exists.`

and reprompts for a layer name.

After entering a new, nonexistent layer name, the layer is created. The XREF is attached onto that layer using the XREF command, at an insertion point of 0,0, at the current elevation, with a scale factor of 1, and a rotation angle of 0.

> **TIP**
> If you need the XREF attached at a different insertion point in model space, complete the XREFCLIP command and then switch to model space to relocate the XREF. You can move, scale, rotate, and mirror the XREF in model space. You may have to change the paper space viewport after making such changes.

A new layer is created by appending -VP to the layer name entered. A temporary floating viewport is created on that layer, and all other existing layers are frozen. The new temporary viewport is sized to fit the current display, and the XREF appears in the temporary viewport such that the entire extents of the XREF are visible. The default visibility for these new layers is set to frozen in subsequently created viewports using the VPLAYER command.

Setting the system variable MAXSORT to a larger value slows down the freezing of layers, by forcing AutoCAD to sort the layers. Best performance is achieved by setting MAXSORT to zero before running the XREFCLIP command.

On a Pentium 90 MHz computer with 64 MB of RAM, a drawing with 200 layers takes approximately three minutes to freeze or thaw the layers with MAXSORT set to a value larger than 200. If MAXSORT is set to zero, the same computer can freeze or thaw the layers in under two minutes.

First corner of clip box Enter the coordinates, or pick a point from the graphics window of the first corner of the area of the XREF to clip.

If other floating viewports existed before the XREFCLIP command was issued, and these other viewports had their UCS icons visible, the icons for these viewports (but not the viewports themselves) will be visible on-screen.

Other corner Enter the coordinates, or pick a point from the graphics window of the opposing corner of the area of the XREF to clip. The size of the clipping area is calculated based on the distance from the first to the second clipping points.

Enter the ratio of paper space units to model space units... Number of paper space units <1.0> Enter a number for the distance in paper space. You may not show a distance in the graphics window. The viewport is sized according to the ratio of model space units to paper space units. To clip an XREF at half scale, enter **2.0** for the paper space units and **1.0** for the model space units.

Number of model space units <1.0> Enter a number for the distance in model space. You may not show a distance in the graphics window. The viewport is sized according to the ratio of model space units to paper space units. To clip an XREF at full scale, enter **1.0** for both the paper space and model space scale factors. To clip an XREF at a scale of 1/4"=1' (or 1"=48"), enter **48.0** for the paper space units and **1.0** for the model space units.

NOTE: You must enter both the paper space units and model space units using an integer or real number. You cannot enter a distance using architectural units, even if your units are set to architectural using the UNITS or DDUNITS commands.

After entering the viewport scale, the previously existing layers in the drawing are thawed.

Insertion point for clip Pick the lower left corner of the clipped viewport. This creates the new viewport, in which the clipped view of the XREF is visible. The view in the viewport changes to the plan view of the WCS (see the PLAN command). The view is resized to fit the viewport at the scale entered earlier. If the resulting viewport is located off the screen, or if too many viewports have been created to display the contents of this viewport (see the MAXACTVP system variable), the XREFCLIP command responds with this somewhat inaccurate response:

```
Viewport is too small.
```

This message also occurs if the viewport object information is incorrect, such as a missing status field code. If the viewport is visible on-screen, and the number of active viewports has not been exceeded, use the AUDIT command to repair any damage to the AutoCAD drawing.

Example

The following example attaches and clips a portion of a floor plan (see the XREF command for a more detailed description on using external references). The clipped external reference is shown in figure X.4.

Command	Description
Command: **XREFCLIP** (Enter)	Starts the XREFCLIP command
Xref name: **FLOORPLN** (Enter)	Specifies external reference drawing named FLOORPLN to attach
Clip onto what layer? **TEMP** (Enter)	Specifies layer name to create
First corner of clip box: *Pick* ① *(see fig. X.4)*	Locates lower left corner of clipping box
Other corner: *Pick* ②	Identifies upper right corner of clipping box

XREFCLIP

```
Enter the ratio of paper space         Specifies 2 paper space units
units to model space units...
Number of paper space units <1.0>:
2 (Enter)

Number of model space units <1.0>:     Accepts the default of 1 model
(Enter)                                space unit

Insertion point for clip:              Locates lower left corner of
Pick ③                                 viewport

Viewport is too small.                 Inaccurate error message from
                                       XREFCLIP
```

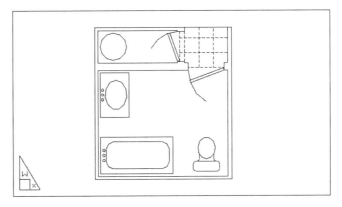

Figure X.4. *The clipped external reference, attached using the XREFCLIP command.*

Related Commands

AUDIT	DDUNITS	LAYER	PLAN
UCSICON	UNITS	VPLAYER	XBIND
XREF			

Related System Variables

MAXSORT   MAXACTVP   TILEMODE   UCSICON

'ZOOM

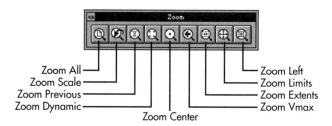

Toolbar: *(Standard Toolbar, Zoom)*
Pull-down: <u>V</u>iew, <u>Z</u>oom
Screen: VIEW, Zoom:

The ZOOM command enlarges or reduces the display of the drawing to aid in drafting and editing. If more than one viewport is active, the display seen in each viewport can be zoomed independently.

To optimize the ZOOM command, use the VIEWRES command to enable fast zooms and turn automatic screen regenerations off with the REGENAUTO command.

If used in model space with paper space enabled, the Zoom Scale XP option enables a paper space viewport to be scaled relative to paper space. The Vmax option makes the view as large as possible without causing a screen regeneration.

Prompts and Options

The following is the main ZOOM prompt, at which you enter an option or scale factor:

`All/Center/Dynamic/Extents/Left/Previous/Vmax/Windows/<Scale (X/XP)>:`

All   If the current display is the plan view of the World Coordinate System (WCS), this option zooms to the greater of the drawing's extents or limits. If the display shows a view of a 3D model, this option displays the model's extents. The All option always causes a screen regeneration.

Center   Specify the center and magnification of the zoomed view. You receive the `Center point:` prompt, at which you specify the center of the view to be zoomed. AutoCAD then presents the `Magnification or Height <default>:` prompt, at which you enter the height of the view in drawing units. The default value shows the current magnification. Selecting a smaller value increases the screen's magnification. If the number is followed by an X, the new view is based relative to the current display. Type **4** at this prompt, for example, to create a view four units high; type **4X** to create a view four times as large as the current display. You also can type **XP** after a number to scale the current display relative to paper space.

Dynamic   This option enables you to indicate graphically the desired view. The Zoom Dynamic screen appears after you select the Dynamic option. On color displays, the outermost box indicates the drawing limits, the box indicated by the red corner brackets shows the currently generated information, the green dashed box indicates the current view, and the gray box with an X indicates the view to be zoomed.

You can resize the X box by clicking the pick button. The X turns into an arrow, indicating that the window can be resized. Click the pick button again to return to the X. Press Enter to accept the new view. If the X box is moved outside the currently generated area, an hourglass appears in the lower left corner of the screen to indicate that a regeneration is taking place.

On Windows systems, the Aerial View (DSVIEWER) replaces the Dynamic option of the ZOOM command and provides additional functionality. On all platforms, third-party display drivers may provide their own zoom functions to enhance AutoCAD's zoom functions.

Extents   ZOOM Extents creates a view that fills the display with the drawing's objects. This is unlike ZOOM Limits (described in following paragraphs) because the limits of a drawing can be far greater than the area used by the objects.

Left   This option is similar to the Center option discussed earlier. Specify a point that is to be the lower left corner of the new view at the Lower left corner point: prompt. AutoCAD then prompts for the size of the zoomed view with the Magnification or Height <default>: prompt. Enter the number of drawing units for zoom height at this prompt.

Previous   This option zooms to the previous view that was on the display within that specific viewport. This command displays the previous view, whether it was created with the PAN, VIEW, or ZOOM commands. The last ten views are saved for each viewport. The view created with this command may differ from the time it was last seen if the drawing has been modified, but the display shows the same area.

Vmax This option creates the largest available view that does not require a regeneration. This command usually provides the view needed at a redraw speed. As such, ZOOM All, which forces a regeneration, should be used only after finding that the view created by ZOOM Vmax is undesirable.

Window If a point is selected or coordinates given, the ZOOM command then defaults to the Window option. Window also can be selected by entering the Window option. The ZOOM Window option is the most common way to create the desired view. You are asked to drag a window around the area to zoom in on with the following prompts:

```
First corner:

Other corner:
```

Scale This option creates a view when you enter a scale factor number. The drawing is then displayed relative to the drawing's limits. The number given can be any positive number. If the number is less than one, the objects within the display are smaller in the new view. If the number is followed by an X, as in 4X, the created view is scaled relative to the current display. If you want to create a scaled view relative to paper space units, type **XP** after the number, as in **5XP**. If the paper space is to be plotted at 1=1 scale, the view shown in this case is scaled to .2 (five times the scale of the paper space units).

TIP

Here is an easy way to figure the proper scaling factor relative to paper space. Use the reciprocal of the desired plotted scale factor. For example, the scale factor of a viewport to be plotted at 1/8"=1'-0" is 96 calculated as follows:

```
1/8"    = 1'-0"
1/8"    = 12"
1/8 * 8 = 12 * 8
1       = 96
```

The Zoom XP scale factor would then be 1/96. If units are set to architectural or fractional, you can type in **1/96** without having to calculate the decimal fraction.

Example

The following example demonstrates the ZOOM command's Window option (see fig. Z.1).

'ZOOM

Choose the ZOOM Window *tool*.	Issues the ZOOM command with the Window option
Command: '_zoom	ZOOM command issued by AutoCAD
All/Center/Dynamic/Extents/Left/ Previous/Vmax/Window/<Scale (X/XP)>: _w	Window option issued by AutoCAD
First corner: *Pick point* ① (see fig. Z.1)	Specifies the first corner of the ZOOM Window
Other corner: *Pick point* ②	Specifies the second corner of the ZOOM Window

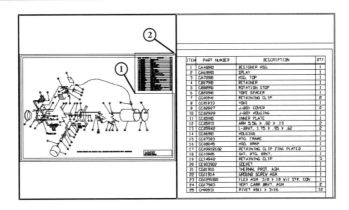

Figure Z.1. *The ZOOM Window in progress.*

Related Commands

| LIMITS | PAN | REGEN | REGENAUTO |
| VIEW | VIEWRES | | |

Related System Variables

| ENTMAX | EXTMIN | LIMMAX | LIMMIN |
| VIEWCTR | VIEWSIZE | VSMAX | VSMIN |

GET CONNECTED
to the ultimate source of computer information!

The MCP Forum on CompuServe

Go online with the world's leading computer book publisher! Macmillan Computer Publishing offers everything you need for computer success!

Find the books that are right for you!
A complete online catalog, plus sample chapters and tables of contents give you an in-depth look at all our books. The best way to shop or browse!

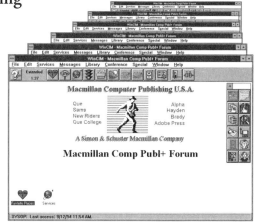

➤ Get fast answers and technical support for MCP books and software

➤ Join discussion groups on major computer subjects

➤ Interact with our expert authors via e-mail and conferences

➤ Download software from our immense library:
  ▷ Source code from books
  ▷ Demos of hot software
  ▷ The best shareware and freeware
  ▷ Graphics files

Join now and get a free CompuServe Starter Kit!

To receive your free CompuServe Introductory Membership, call **1-800-848-8199** and ask for representative #597.

The Starter Kit includes:
➤ Personal ID number and password
➤ $15 credit on the system
➤ Subscription to *CompuServe Magazine*

Once on the CompuServe System, type:

GO MACMILLAN

for the most computer information anywhere!

MACMILLAN COMPUTER PUBLISHING

CompuServe

PLUG YOURSELF INTO...

THE MACMILLAN INFORMATION SUPERLIBRARY™

Free information and vast computer resources from the world's leading computer book publisher—online!

FIND THE BOOKS THAT ARE RIGHT FOR YOU!
A complete online catalog, plus sample chapters and tables of contents give you an in-depth look at *all* of our books, including hard-to-find titles. It's the best way to find the books you need!

- **STAY INFORMED** with the latest computer industry news through our online newsletter, press releases, and customized Information SuperLibrary Reports.
- **GET FAST ANSWERS** to your questions about MCP books and software.
- **VISIT** our online bookstore for the latest information and editions!
- **COMMUNICATE** with our expert authors through e-mail and conferences.
- **DOWNLOAD SOFTWARE** from the immense MCP library:
    - Source code and files from MCP books
    - The best shareware, freeware, and demos
- **DISCOVER HOT SPOTS** on other parts of the Internet.
- **WIN BOOKS** in ongoing contests and giveaways!

TO PLUG INTO MCP:

GOPHER: gopher.mcp.com
FTP: ftp.mcp.com

WORLD WIDE WEB: http://www.mcp.com

INFORMATION?

CHECK OUT THESE RELATED TOPICS OR SEE YOUR LOCAL BOOKSTORE

CAD and 3D Studio | As the number one CAD publisher in the world, and as a Registered Publisher of Autodesk, New Riders Publishing provides unequaled content on this complex topic. Industry-leading products include AutoCAD and 3D Studio.

Networking | As the leading Novell NetWare publisher, New Riders Publishing delivers cutting-edge products for network professionals. We publish books for all levels of users, from those wanting to gain NetWare Certification, to those administering or installing a network. Leading books in this category include *Inside NetWare 3.12*, *CNE Training Guide: Managing NetWare Systems*, *Inside TCP/IP*, and *NetWare: The Professional Reference*.

Graphics | New Riders provides readers with the most comprehensive product tutorials and references available for the graphics market. Best-sellers include *Inside CorelDRAW! 5*, *Inside Photoshop 3*, and *Adobe Photoshop NOW!*

Internet and Communications | As one of the fastest growing publishers in the communications market, New Riders provides unparalleled information and detail on this ever-changing topic area. We publish international best-sellers such as *New Riders' Official Internet Yellow Pages, 2nd Edition*, a directory of over 10,000 listings of Internet sites and resources from around the world, and *Riding the Internet Highway, Deluxe Edition*.

Operating Systems | Expanding off our expertise in technical markets, and driven by the needs of the computing and business professional, New Riders offers comprehensive references for experienced and advanced users of today's most popular operating systems, including *Understanding Windows 95*, *Inside Unix*, *Inside Windows 3.11 Platinum Edition*, *Inside OS/2 Warp Version 3*, and *Inside MS-DOS 6.22*.

Other Markets | Professionals looking to increase productivity and maxmize the potential of their software and hardware should spend time discovering our line of products for Word, Excel, and Lotus 1-2-3. These titles include *Inside Word 6 for Windows*, *Inside Excel 5 for Windows*, *Inside 1-2-3 Release 5*, and *Inside WordPerfect for Windows*.

Orders/Customer Service **1-800-653-6156**   Source Code **NRP95**

New Riders Publishing   201 West 103rd Street ♦ Indianapolis, Indiana 46290 USA

REGISTRATION CARD

New Riders' Reference Guide to AutoCAD Release 13

Name _____ Title _____

Company _____ Type of business _____

Address _____

City/State/ZIP _____

Have you used these types of books before?   ☐ yes   ☐ no

If yes, which ones? _____

_____

How many computer books do you purchase each year?   ☐ 1–5   ☐ 6 or more

How did you learn about this book? _____

Where did you purchase this book? _____

Which applications do you currently use? _____

_____

Which computer magazines do you subscribe to? _____

_____

What trade shows do you attend? _____

_____

Comments: _____

_____

_____

Would you like to be placed on our preferred mailing list?   ☐ yes   ☐ no

☐ **I would like to see my name in print!** You may use my name and quote me in future New Riders products and promotions. My daytime phone number is: _____

New Riders Publishing   201 West 103rd Street ♦ Indianapolis, Indiana 46290 USA

Fax to **317-581-4670**   Orders/Customer Service **1-800-653-6156**   Source Code **NRP95**

Fold Here

NO POSTAGE
NECESSARY
IF MAILED
IN THE
UNITED STATES

BUSINESS REPLY MAIL
FIRST-CLASS MAIL PERMIT NO. 9918 INDIANAPOLIS IN

POSTAGE WILL BE PAID BY THE ADDRESSEE

NEW RIDERS PUBLISHING
201 W 103RD ST
INDIANAPOLIS IN 46290-9058

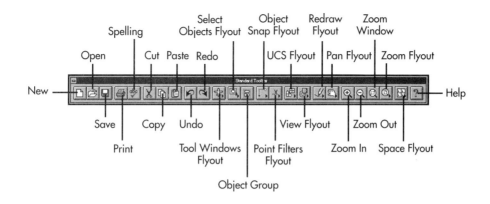
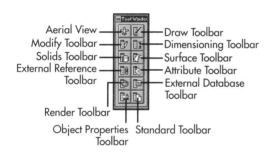
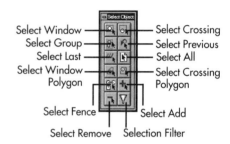
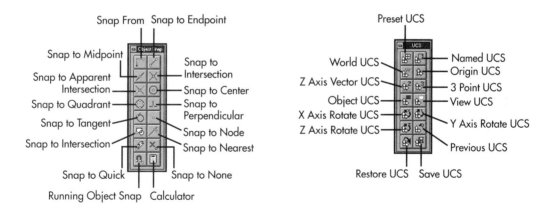
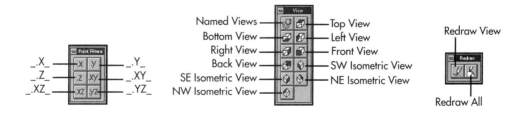

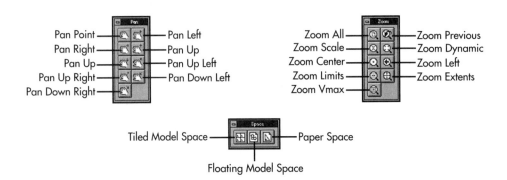
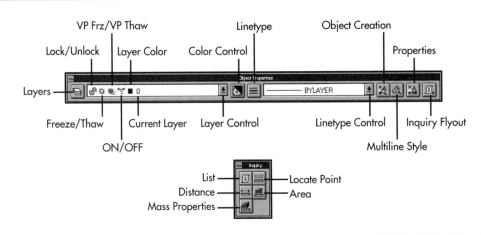
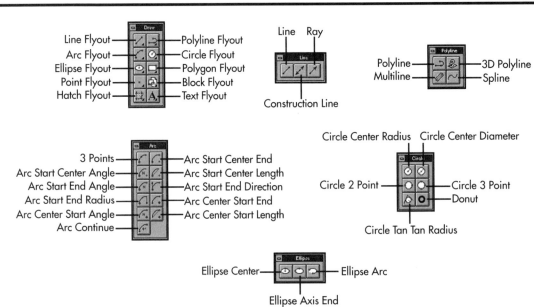

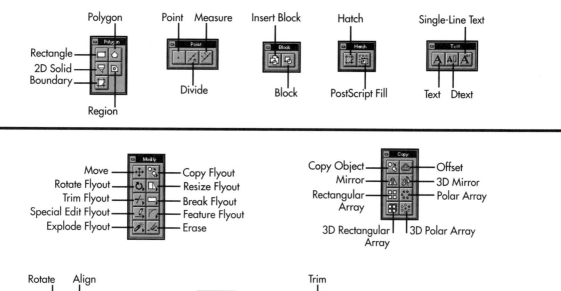
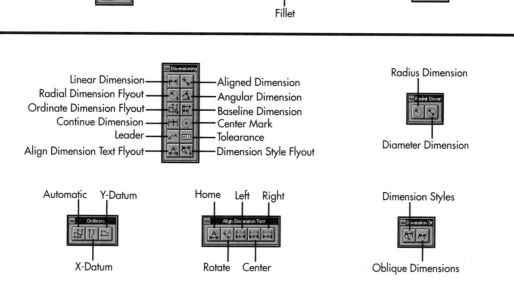

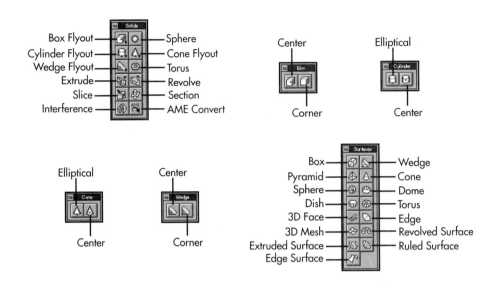
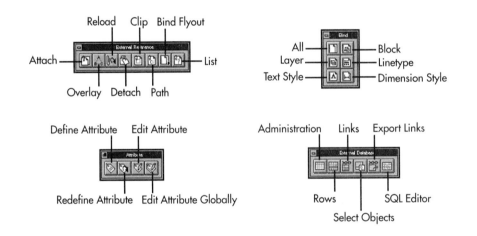
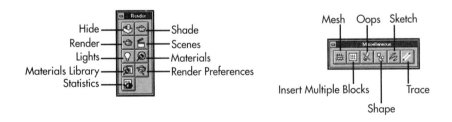

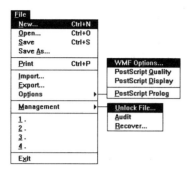

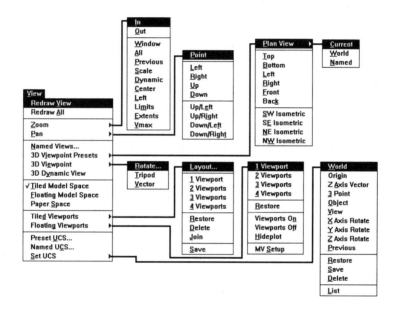

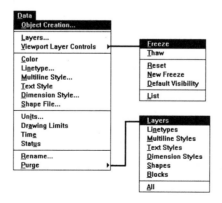

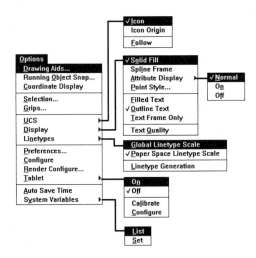

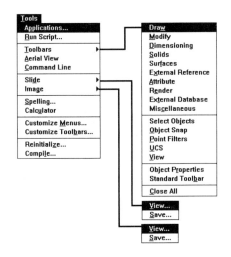